Lecture Notes in Computer Scien

Commenced Publication in 1973
Founding and Former Series Editors:
Gerhard Goos, Juris Hartmanis, and Jan van Leeuwen

Roberto De Prisco   Moti Yung (Eds.)

Security
and Cryptography
for Networks

5th International Conference, SCN 2006
Maiori, Italy, September 6-8, 2006
Proceedings

 Springer

Volume Editors

Roberto De Prisco
Università di Salerno
Dipartimento di Informatica ed Applicazioni
via Ponte don Melillo, 84084 Fisciano (SA), Italy
E-mail: robdep@dia.unisa.it

Moti Yung
RSA Laboratories and Columbia University
Department of Computer Science
Room 464, S.W. Mudd Building, New York, NY 10027, USA
E-mail: moti@cs.columbia.edu

Library of Congress Control Number: 2006931475

CR Subject Classification (1998): E.3, C.2, D.4.6, K.4.1, K.4.4, K.6.5, F.2

LNCS Sublibrary: SL 4 – Security and Cryptology

ISSN   0302-9743
ISBN-10   3-540-38080-9 Springer Berlin Heidelberg New York
ISBN-13   978-3-540-38080-1 Springer Berlin Heidelberg New York

Springer is a part of Springer Science+Business Media

springer.com

© Springer-Verlag Berlin Heidelberg 2006
Printed in Germany

Typesetting: Camera-ready by author, data conversion by Scientific Publishing Services, Chennai, India
Printed on acid-free paper   SPIN: 11832072   06/3142   5 4 3 2 1 0

Preface

The Conference on Security and Cryptography for Networks 2006 (SCN 2006) was held in Maiori, Italy, on September 6-8, 2006. The conference was the fifth in the SCN series, and this year marked a change in its name (the former name was Security in Communication Networks). The name change meant to better describe the scope of the conference while preserving the SCN acronym. This year for the first time we had the proceedings volume ready at the conference. We feel that the SCN conference has matured and that it has become a tradition to hold it regularly in the beautiful setting of the Amalfitan coast as a biennial event.

The conference brought together researchers in the fields of cryptography and security in order to foster the extension of cooperation and exchange of ideas among them, aiming at assuring safety and trustworthiness of communication networks. The topics covered by the conference this year included: foundations of distributed systems security, signatures schemes, block ciphers, anonymity, e-commerce, public key encryption and key exchange, secret sharing, symmetric and public key cryptanalysis, randomness, authentication.

The international Program Committee consisted of 24 members who are top experts in the conference fields. We received 81 submissions amongst which 24 papers were selected for presentation at the conference. These proceedings include the extended abstract versions of the 24 accepted papers and the short abstract of the invited talk by Ivan Damgård.

The Program Committee selected papers on the basis of originality, quality and relevance to the conference scope. Due to the high number of submissions, paper selection was a difficult task and many good papers had to be rejected. Each paper was refereed by three or four reviewers. We thank the members of the Program Committee for their great efforts invested in the selection process. We also gratefully acknowledge the help of the external reviewers who evaluated submissions in their area of expertise. The names of these reviewers are listed on page VII, and we apologize for any inadvertent omissions or mistakes.

We also wish to thank the local organizing committee for their support in running the conference. Finally, we would like to thank the conference participants and the authors of all the submitted papers. It is the authors of all the submitted papers that allow the program committee to choose papers and to ultimately make this conference possible.

September 2006

R. De Prisco
M. Yung

SCN 2006
September 6-8, 2006, Maiori, Italy

Program Chair

Moti Yung   RSA Lab. and Columbia U., USA

General Chair

Roberto De Prisco   Università di Salerno, Italy

Program Committee

Giuseppe Ateniese	JHU, USA
Carlo Blundo	Università di Salerno, Italy
Dario Catalano	ENS, France
Alfredo De Santis	Università di Salerno, Italy
Rosario Gennaro	IBM, USA
Stuart Haber	HP, USA
Amir Herzberg	Bar-Ilan University, Israel
Nick Hopper	University of Minnesota, USA
Markus Jakobsson	Indiana University, USA
Stas Jarecki	UC Irvine, USA
Jonathan Katz	University of Maryland, USA
John Kelsey	NIST, USA
Aggelos Kiayias	University of Connecticut, USA
Eike Kiltz	CWI, Netherlands
Eyal Kushilevitz	Technion, Israel
Anna Lysyanskaya	Brown University, USA
Atsuko Miyaji	JAIST, Japan
David Naccache	ENS, France
Giuseppe Persiano	Università di Salerno, Italy
Carles Padro	Universitat Politècnica de Catalunya, Spain
Nigel Smart	University of Bristol, UK
Gene Tsudik	USC, USA
Shouhuai Xu	UTSA, USA
Moti Yung	RSA Lab. and Columbia U., USA (Chair)

Local Organization

Aniello Castiglione	Università di Salerno, Italy
Luigi Catuogno	Università di Salerno, Italy

External Referees

Michel Abdalla
Amos Beimel
Caroline Belrose
Ran Canetti
Rafi Chen
Liqun Chen
Reza Curtmola
Xuhua Ding
Orr Dunkelman
Karim Edefrawy
Jaume Martí-Farré
Serge Fehr
Amparo Fúster-Sabater
Clemente Galdi
Aline Gouget
Ignacio Gracia
Vanessa Gratzer
Tim Gneysu
Shai Halevi

Helena Handschuh
Javier Herranz
Shoichi Hirose
Dennis Hofheinz
Vishal Kher
Costas Kattirtzis
Hugo Krawczyk
Di Ma
Mitsuru Matsui
Takashi Matsunaka
Chris Mitchell
Anton Mityagin
Sean Murphy
Einar Mykletun
Svetla Nikova
Ivan Osipkov
Dan Page
Gilles Piret
Axel Poschmann

Jordi Pujolàs
S. Raj Rajagopalan
Prasad Rao
Leo Reyzin
Kouichi Sakurai
Nitesh Saxena
Taizo Shirai
Toshio Tokita
Jorge Luis Villar
Ivan Visconti
XiaoFeng Wang
Dai Watanabe
Hoeteck Wee
Stephen Weis
Christopher Wolf
Hong-Sheng Zhou

Sponsoring Institutions

Dipartimento di Informatica ed Applicazioni, Università di Salerno, Italy
Lanfredi Fund, France

Table of Contents

Public Key Encryption and Key Exchange

Secret Sharing

Symmetric Key Cryptanalysis and Randomness

Applied Authentication

Public Key Related Cryptanalysis

Invited Talk

Edge Eavesdropping Games

Amos Beimel[1],[*] and Matthew Franklin[2],[**]

[1] Department of Computer Science, Ben-Gurion University
[2] Department of Computer Science, University of California, Davis

Abstract. Motivated by the proactive security problem, we study the question of maintaining secrecy against a mobile eavesdropper that can eavesdrop to a bounded number of *communication channels* in each round of the protocol. We characterize the networks in which secrecy can be maintained against an adversary that can eavesdrop to t channels in each round. Using this characterization, we analyze the number of eavesdropped channels that complete graphs can withhold while maintaining secrecy.

Keywords: unconditional security, passive adversary, mobile adversary, graph search games.

1 Introduction

Many cryptographic protocols are secure if an unknown *fixed* set of processors of bounded size is dishonest. Proactive security [13,9] considers a more realistic scenario, where a mobile adversary can control a different set of processors of bounded size in each period. Protocols in the proactive model have to cope with a stronger adversary, which, for example, might have controlled every processor by some point during the protocol execution. In protocols secure in the proactive model, each processor has to "spread" the secret information it holds.

Franklin, Galil, and Yung [6] studied maintaining secrecy against a mobile eavesdropper which can eavesdrop to a bounded number of processors in each round of the protocol. Unfortunately, we discovered that the main characterization given in [6] of maintaining secrecy against a mobile eavesdropper is incorrect. We describe the flaw in their proof and the correct characterization, see Section 1.2. The main focus of this paper is a similar question, where a mobile eavesdropper can eavesdrop to a bounded number of *communication channels* in each round of the protocol. As eavesdropping to communication channels is easier than eavesdropping to processors, this is a natural question. Although the two problems are similar, there are differences between the two problems, for example in the number of rounds that an adversary can learn the secret information in a complete graph while eavesdropping to minimal number of vertices or edges respectively.

---

[*] On sabbatical at the University of California, Davis, partially supported by the Packard Foundation.
[**] Partially supported by NSF and the Packard Foundation.

R. De Prisco and M. Yung (Eds.): SCN 2006, LNCS 4116, pp. 1–17, 2006.

To model the question of maintaining the secrecy of a system against a mobile adversary that can eavesdrop to communication channels, we consider the following abstract game, similar to [6], called the distributed database maintenance game. There is a protocol trying to maintain the secrecy of one bit b in the system. The first stage in the game is an initialization stage in which each edge gets an initial value. (This abstracts an intermediate state of a more complex protocol.) In Round i, each vertex receives messages, and sends messages generated based on the messages it received in the previous round and a "fresh" random string. The secret bit b can be reconstructed in each round of the protocol from the messages sent in the system in that round. The mobile adversary eavesdrops to t channels of its choice in each round. We require that an unbounded adversary cannot learn the secret from the messages it heard. The adversary can only eavesdrop to channels; it cannot change, insert, or delete messages.

Following [6], because of the close connection with "graph search games [14,11]," we refer to the eavesdropping to a channel as placing a "guard" on this edge, and we say that a graph is "cleared" at the end of a "search" (finite sequence of subsets of edges the adversary eavesdrops) if the adversary has collected enough information to infer the secret bit b. A protocol maintaining privacy should prevent the adversary from clearing the graph.

We consider two variants of the edge eavesdropping game, depending on whether the underlying communication network is modeled as a directed or an undirected graph. When the network is modeled as an undirected graph, each edge is a full-duplex channel, and a single eavesdropper can monitor the message flow in both directions. When the network is modeled as a directed graph, each edge allows communication in one direction only, and a single eavesdropper can monitor the message flow in that direction only. Note that a full-duplex channel can be represented as a pair of directed edges, but then two eavesdroppers are required to monitor the message flow in both directions.

To see some of the subtleties of edge eavesdropping games, consider the three graphs described in Fig. 1. A single guard can clear these graphs, and thus the distributed database maintenance game on these networks is defeated by an adversary controlling a single mobile eavesdropper. An explanation of these examples can be found in Example 1 in Section 3.1 and in Section 4.3.

1.1   Our Results

Our first result (Theorem 1) is a characterization of when a search clears a graph. Given a directed or undirected graph G and given a search of length ℓ, we construct an undirected layered version of the graph where the number of layers is the length of the search. In the layered graph there are $\ell + 1$ copies of each vertex, and there is an edge between the ith copy of u to the $(i + 1)$th copy of w iff there is an edge between u and v in G. We prove that a search clears a graph iff it cuts the first layer from the last layer in the layered graph. That is, we prove that:

- If there is a search that cuts the first layer from the last layer in the layered graph, then no protocol can maintain privacy against this search. This is proved by a reduction to the impossibility of unconditional key exchange.

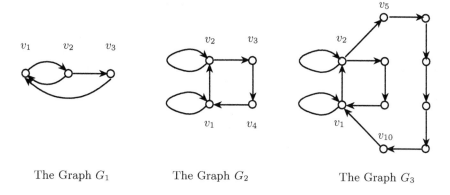

The Graph G_1 The Graph G_2 The Graph G_3

Fig. 1. Three graphs that can be cleared with one guard

- If there is no search with t guards that cuts the first layer from the last layer, then there is a simple protocol that can maintain privacy against any adversary that can eavesdrop to t channels in each round.

Inspired by this characterization, we say that an undirected path in the layered graph is contaminated if all edges in the path are unguarded; a vertex is contaminated after i rounds of the search if there is a contaminated path (through any layers) from the first layer to the copy of the vertex in layer i. That is, contamination "flows" both forwards and backwards in time.

We give a second characterization (Theorem 2) of when a search clears a graph based on the sets of contaminated vertices in each round of the protocol. This characterization is more useful for analyzing the possibility and impossibility of clearing graphs. Based on this second characterization, we prove an upper bound on the length of the search (Theorem 3): If an adversary can clear a graph while eavesdropping to at most t edges in each round, then it can clear the graph in at most 2^n rounds while eavesdropping to at most t edges in each round. We do not know if super-polynomial search length is sometimes necessary.

A search is "monotonic" if once a vertex is cleared, it will remain clear for the entire search. We explore the usefulness and limitations of a generic monotonic searches. On the positive side, we show that monotonic search is essentially optimal for directed and undirected complete graphs. A complete *directed* graph with n vertices can be cleared by $n^2/2$ guards in two rounds when n is even (by monotonic search). We prove that $n^2/2$ guards are required to clear this graph no matter how many rounds the adversary is allowed (by any search). For a complete *undirected* graph with n vertices, we show that it can be cleared by $n^2/4 + n/2$ guards in $O(\sqrt{n})$ rounds (by monotonic search). Furthermore, we prove that $n^2/4 + n/2$ guards are required to clear this graph no matter how many rounds the adversary is allowed (by any search), and $\Omega(\sqrt{n})$ rounds are required to clear the graph even if the adversary uses $n^2/4 + O(n)$ guards (by any search). In contrast, with $3n^2/8 + n/4$ guards, the complete undirected graph can be cleared in two rounds (by monotonic search).

1.2   Comparison to the Vertex Eavesdropping Game

The problem we consider is similar to the vertex eavesdropping games considered in [6]. In the vertex eavesdropping game, a mobile adversary eavesdrops to processors – it monitors their internal state, the computations they perform, and the messages they send and receive. A search is a finite sequence of subsets of vertices; a search succeeds ("clears the graph") if the adversary learns enough information to infer the secret bit b in the distributed database maintenance game. Unfortunately, the main characterization given in [6] of successful searches is incorrect. The correct characterization is similar to the edge eavesdropping games: Given a directed or undirected graph, and given a search, construct the *undirected* layered version of the graph where the number of layers is the length of the search (and with all self-loops added, i.e., an edge from each node in each non-final layer to the same node in the next layer). A search clears a graph iff it cuts the first layer from the last layer in the *undirected* layered graph.

The mistake in [6] is that they considered the *directed* layered version of the graph instead of the undirected case. In particular, the flaw is in the proof of Lemma 4 of [6], i.e., Alice cannot simulate the behavior of every node in V_s by herself. A graph demonstrating this problem is described in Appendix A. The characterization of [6] is correct if we require that each vertex is *deterministic* during the execution of the protocol.

Although, the vertex eavesdropping game and the edge eavesdropping game seem similar, there are differences between them. For example, the search of complete graphs is simple in the vertex eavesdropping game: the complete graph with n vertices can be cleared with n guards in one round, and cannot be cleared by fewer guards in any number of rounds. By contrast, the search of undirected complete graphs in the edge eavesdropping game is more complicated as it requires $\Omega(\sqrt{n})$ rounds even if near optimal number of guards are used. See Sections 4 and 5 for a detailed treatment.

In [6] it was shown that for *directed* layered graphs, super-polynomial search length is sometimes necessary: There exists a family of graphs $\{G_n\}$ such that each G_n has $O(n^2)$ vertices, however, clearing the directed layered graph of G_n requires $\Omega(2^n)$ rounds using the optimal number of guards. This should be contrasted with classic search games, in which linear number of rounds are sufficient to clear a graph with optimal number of guards [12,2] (for background on search games on graphs [14,11]). However, due to the problem in the characterization of [6], the above sequence of graphs *does not* imply that in vertex eavesdropping games super-polynomial search length is sometimes necessary. It is not known if super-polynomial search length is ever necessary for the vertex eavesdropping game or for the edge eavesdropping game.

1.3   Historical Background

Ostrovsky and Yung [13] considered mobile faults under the control of a Byzantine adversary to achieve general secure distributed computation against virus-like waves of attack. Defense against mobile Byzantine faults was subsequently called "proactive" security [9], and was considered in numerous papers. The classic problem of Byzantine Agreement was studied in the mobile Byzantine fault setting by Garay [7] and Buhrman et al. [3]. The distributed database game was analyzed for the vertex eavesdropping game by Franklin et al. [6]. A more elaborate and fully functional distributed storage, with all operations secure against a mobile Byzantine adversary, was treated by Garay et al. [8].

All the above works consider faults of processors, while we consider eavesdropping to communication channels. In [4,10,5], the problem of using a multicast network coding to transmit information securely in the presence of an adversary which can eavesdrop to a *fixed* set of edges of bounded size was studied.

2 Preliminaries

We consider a network described either by an undirected graph or by a directed graph. In the directed case we assume, for technical reasons, that the out-degree, $|\text{OUT}(v)|$, and in-degree, $|\text{IN}(v)|$, of each node v is at least 1. The network is synchronous, and protocols in the network proceed in rounds. In Round i, each vertex v does the following: (1) receives the messages sent by neighboring vertices in Round $i-1$, (2) chooses a random string r_v^i for Round i, (3) computes new messages based on the messages sent to it in Round $i-1$ and the random string r_v^i, and (4) sends the messages it computes in Round i.

We consider the distributed *database maintenance game* (*database game* for short). There is a protocol trying to maintain the secrecy of one bit b. The first stage in the game is an initialization stage in which each edge gets an initial value; there is a initialization function $I(b) = \langle m_{u,v}^0 \rangle_{\langle u,v \rangle \in E}$ that generates initial messages for the edges as a randomized function of the secret bit b. In Round i, where $i \geq 1$, the state of each vertex v is $\langle m_{u,v}^{i-1} \rangle_{u \in \text{IN}(v)}, r_v^i$, that is, the messages it received in the previous round and a random string for the current round. Vertex v computes messages $\mathbf{m_v^i} = \langle m_{v,w}^i \rangle_{w \in \text{OUT}(v)}$, where $\mathbf{m_v^i}$ is a function of the vertex state,[1] and sends $m_{v,w}^i$ to w. The secret can be reconstructed in each round of the protocol; there is a reconstruction function ϕ such that $\phi(\langle m_{u,v}^i \rangle_{\langle u,v \rangle \in E}, i) = b$.

In the model we define, the messages that a vertex sends in Round i depend only on the messages sent to it in Round $i-1$, and on a "fresh" random string for the round, thus, effectively each vertex forgets all information from previous rounds. The reason for this requirement is that otherwise the secrecy in the database game can be maintained in the local memory of some vertex. If we want to allow local memory, that is, remembering the history, then the adversary must be able to read it. Technically, this is done by adding self-loops in the graph. Thus, depending on the graph, we allow or disallow each vertex to remember its history. However, the adversary cannot eavesdrop to the local memory of a vertex during the momentary period of receiving the messages, computing the new messages, and sending them.

---

[1] In the undirected case, $\langle u, v \rangle$ and $\langle v, u \rangle$ are the same edge. However, $m_{u,v}$ and $m_{v,u}$ denote different messages.

A mobile adversary is trying to learn the bit b. The adversary eavesdrops to a possibly different subset of *edges* in each round. In a directed graph, an adversary that eavesdrops to an edge $\langle u, v \rangle$ in Round i, learns the message sent by u to v in Round i. In an undirected graph, an adversary that eavesdrops to an edge $\langle u, v \rangle$ in Round i, learns two messages sent in Round i: the message sent by u to v and the message sent by v to u. The adversary cannot change, insert, or delete messages. A *search* – a behavior of an adversary – is a sequence of subsets of edges $W_1, W_2, \ldots, W_\ell$, where in Round i the adversary eavesdrops to the edges in W_i and learns no additional information on the messages exchanged on other edges. Similarly to other search games, if the adversary eavesdrops to an edge in Round i, then we say that it *guards* the edge in Round i.

The adversary is adaptive, it decides on W_i – the communication channels it eavesdrops in Round i – based on the messages it heard on $W_1, W_2, \ldots, W_{i-1}$ in previous rounds and on its random string r. The *view* of the adversary, after an execution, is its random input, the search $W_1, \ldots, W_\ell$ it chose to eavesdrop, and the messages it heard in this search. An unbounded adversary has not gained information on the secret bit b, if its view is equally distributed when the bit is 0 and when the bit is 1.

Definition 1. *The adversary does not gain information on the secret bit b in Protocol $\mathcal{P}$ if for every possible view h:*

Pr[The view of the adversary is h | The secret bit is 0]

= Pr[The view of the adversary is h | The secret bit is 1],

where the probability is taken over $\{r_v^i : v \in V, 1 \le i \le \ell\}$, the random strings of the vertices, and over the random string used by the initialization function $I(b)$.

An adversary uses t guards if, for every search $W_1, W_2, \ldots, W_\ell$ that it can use, $|W_i| \le t$ for every $1 \le i \le \ell$.

Definition 2. *A system can* maintain its secrecy *in a graph G against t guards if there is a protocol $\mathcal{P}$ for the vertices in G such that every adversary that uses t guards does not gain information on the secret bit. Otherwise, we say that t guards can clear G.*

We next describe a simple protocol, considered in [6], for the database game. In each round of the protocol we maintain the following property

$$b = \bigoplus_{\langle u,v \rangle \in E} m_{u,v}^i. \tag{1}$$

This describes the reconstruction function of the protocol. The basic step in the protocol is the simple sharing of a bit b, generating k bits $b_1, \ldots, b_k$ by randomly choosing the first $k - 1$ bits independently such that each bit is uniformly distributed, and setting $b_k \leftarrow b \oplus \bigoplus_{1 \le i \le k-1} b_i$. In the initialization stage, Protocol $\mathcal{P}_{\text{xor}}$ generates the messages $\langle m_{u,v}^0 \rangle_{\langle u,v \rangle \in E}$ as the sharing of the secret bit b. In

Round i of Protocol $\mathcal{P}_{\text{xor}}$, each vertex computes the bit $b_v^i \leftarrow \bigoplus_{u \in \text{IN}(v)} m_{u,v}^{i-1}$, and shares b_v^i generating the bits $\langle m_{v,w}^i \rangle_{w \in \text{OUT}(v)}$, that is,

$$\bigoplus_{u \in \text{IN}(v)} m_{u,v}^{i-1} = b_v^i = \bigoplus_{w \in \text{OUT}(v)} m_{v,w}^i. \tag{2}$$

As we assume that each vertex has at least one in-going edge and at least one out-going edge, this process is possible. Clearly, the reconstruction described in (1) is correct in the initialization stage. A simple calculation shows, using induction, that the reconstruction described in (1) is correct in each round of the protocol. In the next section we show that this simple protocol is "universal": if there exists a protocol that can maintain secrecy against t guards, then Protocol $\mathcal{P}_{\text{xor}}$ can maintain secrecy against t guards.

3   Characterization Theorems for Clearing Graphs

We give two theorems that characterize graphs that can be cleared with t guards. To understand the evolution of the clearing process throughout the rounds of the protocol, we define a layered graph version of the communication graph. In this graph there are two vertices SOURCE and TARGET that are added for technical reasons.

Definition 3. *Given a directed or an undirected graph $G = \langle V, E \rangle$ and an index ℓ, we construct an undirected layered graph $L(G, \ell) = \langle V^\ell, E^\ell \rangle$ as follows. The vertices of $L(G, \ell)$ are $V^\ell \overset{\text{def}}{=} (V \times \{1, \ldots, \ell + 1\}) \cup \{\text{SOURCE}, \text{TARGET}\}$. The edges of $L(G, \ell)$ are*

$$E^\ell \overset{\text{def}}{=} \{\langle (u, i), (v, i+1) \rangle : \langle u, v \rangle \in E, 1 \leq i \leq \ell\}$$
$$\cup \{\langle \text{SOURCE}, (v, 1) \rangle : v \in V\} \cup \{\langle (v, \ell+1), \text{TARGET} \rangle : v \in V\}.$$

Given a search $W_1, W_2, \ldots, W_\ell$, we say that an edge $\langle (u, i), (v, i+1) \rangle$ in $L(G, \ell)$ is guarded when G is a directed graph if $\langle u, v \rangle \in W_i$. We say that an edge $\langle (u, i), (v, i+1) \rangle$ in $L(G, \ell)$ is guarded when G is an undirected graph if $\langle u, v \rangle \in W_i$ or $\langle v, u \rangle \in W_i$. If an edge is not guarded, then we say that the edge is unguarded. An undirected path in $L(G, \ell)$ is *contaminated* if all edges in the path are unguarded. Note that this path can go forwards and backwards in the layers. A search $W_1, W_2, \ldots, W_\ell$ of length ℓ *cuts* the undirected layered graph $L(G, \ell)$ if there is no contaminated path in $L(G, \ell)$ from SOURCE to TARGET.

3.1   First Characterization Theorem

Theorem 1 (First Characterization Theorem). *Let G be a graph. A system can maintain its secrecy in the graph G against t guards iff for every $\ell \in \mathbb{N}$, every search $W_1, W_2, \ldots, W_\ell$ with t guards does not cut $L(G, \ell)$.*

In light of Theorem 1, if a search cuts the undirected layered graph $L(G, \ell)$, we may say that the search *clears* G. The theorem is implied by the following two lemmas.

Lemma 1. *Let G be a graph, and $W_1, W_2, \ldots, W_\ell$ be a search that cuts $L(G, \ell)$. Then, for every protocol $\mathcal{P}$, the adversary that eavesdrops to W_i in Round i, for $1 \le i \le \ell$, learns the secret after at most ℓ rounds.*

Proof. Fix any protocol $\mathcal{P}$. We assume, for sake of contradiction, that the adversary that eavesdrops to W_i in Round i, for $1 \le i \le \ell$, does not learn the secret in the first ℓ rounds, and construct an information-theoretic secure protocol in which two parties, Alice and Bob, can exchange a secret key on a public channel (without any prior secret information), which is impossible by the fundamental result of Shannon [15].

We next define two sets with respect to $W_1, W_2, \ldots, W_\ell$.

$$R \stackrel{\text{def}}{=} \{\text{SOURCE}\} \cup \{(v, i) : \text{there is a contaminated path from SOURCE to } (v, i)\},$$

and $B \stackrel{\text{def}}{=} V^\ell \setminus R$. Notice that the only edges that connect vertices from R to B are guarded edges.

Informally, to exchange a key Alice and Bob execute $\mathcal{P}$, where Alice simulates the vertices in R and Bob simulates the vertices in B, and the messages that should be sent on guarded edges, that is, the messages the adversary hears, are broadcasted on the public channel. Formally, to transmit a bit b, Alice uses the initialization function $I(b)$ to generate messages $\langle m^0_{u,v} \rangle_{\langle u,v \rangle \in E}$. Now, Alice and Bob simulate $\mathcal{P}$ round by round. In the ith round, Alice simulates the vertices in $R_i \stackrel{\text{def}}{=} \{v \in V : (v, i) \in R\}$ and Bob simulates all other vertices, namely $B_i \stackrel{\text{def}}{=} V \setminus R_i$. We will show that the simulation maintains the following property:

Property 1. Each party knows all messages sent in Round $i - 1$ to the vertices that it simulates in Round i.

Now, Alice (respectively, Bob) chooses random strings r^i_v for every $v \in R_i$ (respectively, $v \in B_i$), computes the messages v sends in $\mathcal{P}$, broadcasts on the public channel all the message that are sent on guarded edges, and remembers all other messages.

Property 1 is maintained for Alice (respectively, for Bob), as all edges from B_{i-1} to R_i (respectively, all edges from R_{i-1} to B_i) are guarded, and, therefore, the messages sent on them are broadcasted on the public channel. This implies that the key-exchange protocol can proceed. On one hand, there is no contaminated path in $L(G, \ell)$, and after the ℓth round of the simulation all vertices in G are in $B_{\ell+1}$. So, Bob can compute the reconstruction function $\phi(\langle m^\ell_{u,v} \rangle_{\langle u,v \rangle \in E}, \ell)$ and learn the message sent by Alice. On the other hand, the view of Eve after the key exchange protocol is exactly the view of the adversary that eavesdrops to $W_1, W_2, \ldots, W_\ell$ in $\mathcal{P}$, so Eve learns nothing about b. This is a contradiction to the fundamental result of Shannon [15] that there no unconditionally secure key exchange protocol that only uses a public channel. Thus, in the original protocol $\mathcal{P}$, the adversary can learn the secret. $\qquad\square$

Notice that in Lemma 1 the adversary is deterministic and non-adaptive as it deterministically chooses the search it uses before the execution of the protocol.

Lemma 2. *Let $\mathcal{P}_{\mathrm{xor}}$ be the XOR protocol, and assume that for some ℓ there is no search with t guards that cuts $L(G, \ell)$. Then, any adversary that uses t guards does not gain information on the secret in the first ℓ rounds of $\mathcal{P}_{\mathrm{xor}}$.*

Proof. To understand the idea of the proof, first consider a deterministic adversary which chooses a search $W_1, W_2, \ldots, W_\ell$ with t guards before the execution of the protocol (that is, its choice of W_i does not depend on the messages it heard in previous rounds). Since the search does not clear the graph, there is a contaminated path in the layered graph from SOURCE to TARGET. This adversary cannot learn the secret bit b, since the value of the secret bit b can be flipped by flipping the values of the messages sent on a contaminated path. This is a valid execution of the protocol in which the adversary sees the same view.

To consider a randomized, adaptive adversary, fix any view h for the adversary, that is, fix a random string r of the adversary, a search $W_1, W_2, \ldots, W_\ell$ with t guards, and the messages sent on the edges of the search. To prove the lemma, we show that there is a one-to-one and onto function from possible executions of $\mathcal{P}_{\mathrm{xor}}$ when the view is h and the secret bit is 0 to possible executions of $\mathcal{P}_{\mathrm{xor}}$ when the view is h and the secret bit is 1. Thus, the number of these executions is the same for both values of the secret, and, as every possible execution of protocol $\mathcal{P}_{\mathrm{xor}}$ has the same probability, the probability of the view is the same for both values of the secret.

Consider any execution of $\mathcal{P}_{\mathrm{xor}}$ when the view is h and the secret bit is 0. There must be a contaminated path from SOURCE to TARGET in $L(G, \ell)$ with respect to $W_1, W_2, \ldots, W_\ell$. Consider the lexicographically first simple contaminated path in $L(G, \ell)$. We map the execution with secret 0 to the following execution of the protocol $\mathcal{P}_{\mathrm{xor}}$ with the secret 1: We flip the values sent of the path as follows.

- For $\langle \text{SOURCE}, (v, 1) \rangle$, the first edge in the path, flip the initial value $m_{u,v}^0$ for the first $u \in \mathrm{IN}(v)$.
- For every "forward" edge $\langle (u, i), (v, i+1) \rangle$ in the path, flip the message sent by u to v in Round i.
- For every "backward" edge $\langle (u, i), (v, i-1) \rangle$ in the path, flip the message sent by v to u in Round $i - 1$.

We claim that this is a legal execution of $\mathcal{P}_{\mathrm{xor}}$, that is, for every v and every i, Equation (2) holds – the exclusive-or of the messages v receives in Round $i-1$ is equal to the exclusive-or of the messages v sends in Round i. This is true since the path is simple, and, therefore, the mapping flipped the values of two edges for every vertex in the path (and changed no messages sent on edges not in the path). Since the mapping flipped the value of exactly one initial message, the value of the secret in the new execution has changed to 1, thus, this is indeed an execution with secret 1.

As the mapping flipped the values only on unguarded edges, in each round of the protocol, the adversary sees the same messages, thus, it cannot notice this change, and it continues to eavesdrop to the same search. Finally, this transformation is one-to-one and onto since if we apply this transformation twice, then the result is the original execution.   □

Example 1. Consider Graph G_1 described in Fig. 1 in the Introduction. The search that guards the edge $\langle v_1, v_2 \rangle$ for three rounds does not clear the graph as SOURCE, $(v_2, 1)$, $(v_3, 2)$, $(v_1, 3)$, $(v_2, 2)$, $(v_3, 3)$, $(v_1, 4)$, TARGET is a contaminated path from SOURCE to TARGET in $L(G_1, 3)$. Notice that this path goes forwards and backwards in the layer graph. There is no contaminated path in $L(G_1, 3)$ that only goes forward; this search illustrates the importance of "backward" edges in the layered graph. Nevertheless, this graph can be cleared with one guard in 4 rounds as follows: In Round 1 guard $\langle v_2, v_3 \rangle$, in Round 2 guard $\langle v_2, v_1 \rangle$, in Round 3 guard $\langle v_2, v_3 \rangle$, and in Round 4 guard $\langle v_1, v_2 \rangle$.

3.2   Second Characterization Theorem

Recall that a *cut* in an undirected graph $H = \langle V, E \rangle$ is a set of edges defined by a set $R \subset V$ containing all edges between R and $\overline{R}$. Theorem 1 implies that a search clears a graph G iff it induces a cut in $L(G, \ell)$ such that all edges in the cut are guarded. That is, there is a search that clears a graph iff there is a cut in the graph $L(G, \ell)$ that, for every i, contains at most t edges between layer i and layer $i + 1$. This is formalized in the next theorem, and illustrated in Fig. 2.

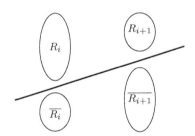

Fig. 2. A description of the ith layer of the cut in $L(G, \ell)$ for a search. The sets R_i and R_{i+1} are the sets of the vertices reachable by an unguarded paths in layers i and $i + 1$, respectively. The edges in the cut are the edges between R_i and $\overline{R_{i+1}}$ and the edges between $\overline{R_i}$ and R_{i+1}.

Theorem 2 (Second Characterization Theorem). *Let G be a graph. The graph G can by cleared by t guards iff there is some $\ell \in \mathbb{N}$ and a sequence of subsets of vertices $R_1, \ldots, R_{\ell+1}$ (that is, $R_i \subseteq V$ for $1 \leq i \leq \ell + 1$) such that*

1. *$R_1 = V$, $R_{\ell+1} = \emptyset$, and*
2. *for every $1 \leq i \leq \ell$ the set $\left(R_i \times \overline{R_{i+1}} \right) \bigcup \left(\overline{R_i} \times R_{i+1} \right)$ contains at most t edges of G.*

Proof. By Theorem 1 it suffices to prove that such sequence of sets $R_1, \ldots, R_{\ell+1}$ exists iff there exists a search with t guards that cuts $L(G, \ell)$.

First, we assume that such sequence of sets $R_1, \ldots, R_{\ell+1}$ exists. We define the search $W_1, \ldots, W_\ell$ with t guards, where W_i contains the edges in E that are in $\left(R_i \times \overline{R_{i+1}}\right) \bigcup \left(\overline{R_i} \times R_{i+1}\right)$. We claim that this search cuts $L(G, \ell)$, that is, every path from SOURCE to TARGET in $L(G, \ell)$ contains a guarded edge. Define

$$R \stackrel{\text{def}}{=} \{\text{SOURCE}\} \cup \{(v, i) : 1 \leq i \leq \ell, v \in R_i\}.$$

The edges in the cut between R and $V^\ell \setminus R$ in $L(G, \ell)$ are exactly the edges guarded by our search. Every path from SOURCE to TARGET in $L(G, \ell)$ passes through this cut, thus, the path contains a guarded edge and is not contaminated.

Now assume that there is a search $W_1, \ldots, W_\ell$ with t guards that cuts $L(G, \ell)$. For every i, where $1 \leq i \leq \ell + 1$, define

$$R_i \stackrel{\text{def}}{=} \{v : \text{ there exists a contaminated path from SOURCE to } (v, i) \text{ in } L(G, \ell)\}.$$

We say that R_i is the set of contaminated vertices in Round i. First, $R_1 = V$, since all edges from SOURCE to the first layer are unguarded. Second, $R_{\ell+1} = \emptyset$, since all edges from the last layer to TARGET are unguarded and there is no contaminated path from SOURCE to TARGET. We need to prove that, for every i, the set $\left(R_i \times \overline{R_{i+1}}\right) \bigcup \left(\overline{R_i} \times R_{i+1}\right)$ contains at most t edges of G. Recall that in each round of the protocol, at most t edges are guarded, thus, it suffices to prove that the edges of E in $\left(R_i \times \overline{R_{i+1}}\right) \bigcup \left(\overline{R_i} \times R_{i+1}\right)$ must be guarded in Round i:

- For every $v \in R_i$ and $w \in \overline{R_{i+1}}$, the edge $\langle v, w \rangle$ (if exists) must be guarded in Round i, otherwise the contaminated path ending at (v, i) together with $\langle (v, i), (w, i+1) \rangle$ is a contaminated path ending at $(w, i+1)$.
- For every $v \in \overline{R_i}$ and $w \in R_{i+1}$, the edge $\langle v, w \rangle$ (if exists) must be guarded in Round i, otherwise the contaminated path ending at $(w, i+1)$ together with $\langle (w, i+1), (v, i) \rangle$ is a contaminated path ending at (v, i).

To conclude the second direction, given a search with t guards that cuts $L(G, \ell)$, we showed that the sets of contaminated vertices satisfy the condition of the theorem. $\square$

Example 2. Consider a directed cycle with n vertices, i.e., the graph $G = \langle V, E \rangle$ where $V = \{v_0, \ldots, v_{n-1}\}$ and $E = \{\langle v_i, v_{(i+1) \bmod n} \rangle : 0 \leq i \leq n-1\}$. This graph can be cleared by one guard sitting on the same edge for $n - 1$ rounds. For concreteness, assume that $W_i = \{\langle v_{n-1}, v_0 \rangle\}$ for $i = 1, \ldots, n$. Define $R_i = \{v_{i-1}, \ldots, v_{n-1}\}$, for $1 \leq i \leq n + 1$. Clearly, $R_1 = V$ and $R_{n+1} = \emptyset$. For $1 \leq i \leq n - 1$, the only edge from the set $R_i = \{v_{i-1}, \ldots, v_{n-1}\}$ to the set $\overline{R_{i+1}} = \{v_0, \ldots, v_{i-1}\}$ is $\langle v_{n-1}, v_0 \rangle$ and there are no edges from $\overline{R_i} = \{v_0, \ldots, v_{i-2}\}$ to $R_{i+1} = \{v_i, \ldots, v_{n-1}\}$. Furthermore, $\langle v_{n-1}, v_0 \rangle$ is the only edge in $\left(R_n \times \overline{R_{n+1}}\right) \bigcup \left(\overline{R_n} \times R_{n+1}\right)$. It can be checked that the sets $R_1, \ldots, R_{n+1}$ are exactly the sets of contaminated vertices in the above search.

As a consequence, we prove that 2^n rounds are sufficient to clear a graph with minimal number of guards.

Theorem 3. *If a graph G can be cleared with t guards, then it can be cleared with t guards in at most 2^n rounds.*

Proof. By Theorem 2, there is a sequence of subsets $R_1, \ldots, R_{\ell+1}$ such that $R_1 = V$, $R_{\ell+1} = \emptyset$, and $\left(R_i \times \overline{R_{i+1}}\right) \bigcup \left(\overline{R_i} \times R_{i+1}\right)$ contains at most t edges from E. Consider a shortest sequence satisfying these conditions. We claim that there are no indices $i_1 < i_2$ such that $R_{i_1} = R_{i_2}$, otherwise, $R_{i_1-1} \times \overline{R_{i_2}} = R_{i_1-1} \times \overline{R_{i_1}}$ and $\overline{R_{i_1-1}} \times R_{i_2} = \overline{R_{i_1-1}} \times R_{i_1}$, and thus their union contains at most t edges in E and $R_1, \ldots, R_{i_1-1}, R_{i_2}, \ldots, R_{\ell+1}$ is a shorter sequence which satisfies the above conditions. Therefore, each set R_i can appear at most once in the search, and the length of the search is at most 2^n. $\square$

4   A Monotonic Search Strategy for Clearing Graphs

In this section we consider a special case of searches that clear a graph. By Theorem 2, to specify a strategy for the adversary, we can specify the contaminated vertices in each round. We say that a search is *monotonic* if $R_\ell \subset R_{\ell-1} \subset \cdots \subset R_2 \subset R_1$, that is, once a vertex is cleared, it will not become contaminated later. In Fig. 3, we formally describe monotonic searches. The advantage of monotonic searches is that they are short; there can be at most n rounds until the adversary clears the graph. However, they are not necessarily optimal, as they can require more guards than general searches (see Section 4.3). In this section we present examples of a monotonic searches that clear directed and undirected complete graphs. As complete graphs are symmetric, it suffices to specify the size of the each set R_i without specifying the exact set of vertices.

A Monotonic Search

$R_1 \leftarrow V;\ i \leftarrow 1$
While $R_i \neq \emptyset$ do:
    Choose a set $A_i \subseteq R_i$ and set $R_{i+1} \leftarrow R_i \setminus A_i$
    Guard the following set of edges W_i:
        $W_i = \left\{ \langle u, v \rangle : u \in R_i, v \in \overline{R_{i+1}} \right\} \cup \left\{ \langle u, v \rangle : u \in \overline{R_i}, v \in R_{i+1} \right\}$
    $i \leftarrow i + 1.$

Fig. 3. A monotonic search strategy for clearing a graph.

4.1   Monotonic Search in Complete Directed Graphs

A complete directed graph, denoted C_n, is a graph with all the possible n^2 edges (including self loops). We show that, when n is even, $n^2/2$ guards can clear C_n in two rounds. To clear the graph, partition the n vertices in C_n to two disjoint sets V_1 and V_2 of size $n/2$ each. In the first round, guard all the $n^2/2$ edges from V to V_1. In the second round, guard all the $n^2/2$ edges from V_2 to V. In this case, $R_1 = V$, $R_2 = V_2$, and $R_3 = \emptyset$.

When n is odd, $(n^2 + 1)/2$ guards can clear C_n in three rounds. To clear the graph, partition the n vertices in C_n to three disjoint sets: V_1 and V_2 of size $(n-1)/2$ each, and a single vertex v. In the first round, guard all the edges from

V to V_1. There are $n|V_1| = n(n-1)/2 < (n^2+1)/2$ such edges. In the second round, guard all edges from V_1 to V_2 and all edges from $V_2 \cup \{v\}$ to $V_1 \cup \{v\}$. There are $(n-1)^2/4 + (n+1)^2/4 = (n^2+1)/2$ such edges. In the third round, guard all the edges from V_2 to V. There are $n|V_2| = n(n-1)/2 < (n^2+1)/2$ such edges. In this case, $R_1 = V$, $R_2 = V_2 \cup \{v\}$, $R_3 = V_2$, and $R_4 = \emptyset$.

4.2 Monotonic Search in Complete Undirected Graphs

A complete undirected graph, denoted U_n, is a graph with all the possible $\binom{n+1}{2}$ edges (including self loops). To simplify calculations, in this section n is even. We first show that $3n^2/8 + n/4$ guards can clear U_n in two rounds. To clear the graph, partition the n vertices in U_n to two disjoint sets V_1 and V_2 of size $n/2$ each. In the first round, guard all the edges with at least one endpoint in V_1. There are $\binom{n/2+1}{2} + n^2/4 = 3n^2/8 + n/4$ such edges. In the second round, guard all the edges with at least one endpoint in V_2. Again, there are $3n^2/8 + n/4$ such edges.

We next describe a search of length n in U_n using $n^2/4 + n/2$ guards. Let $V = \{v_1, \ldots, v_n\}$ be the vertices of the graph. In the ith round of the search we choose $R_i \setminus R_{i+1} \overset{\text{def}}{=} A_i = \{v_i\}$ and $R_i = \{v_i, \ldots, v_n\}$. The guarded edges are

$$\{\langle v_i, v_j \rangle : 1 \leq j \leq n\} \cup \{\langle v_j, v_k \rangle : 1 \leq j \leq i-1, i+1 \leq k \leq n\}.$$

The number of guarded edges in Round i is, thus, $n + (i-1)(n-i) = i(n-i+1)$. The expression is maximized when $i = n/2$, and is $n^2/4 + n/2$. Thus, $n^2/4 + n/2$ guards are sufficient to clear a complete undirected graph in n rounds. In Section 5, we show that this is optimal by showing a matching lower bound.

We next show that, with the same number of guards as in the previous search, the adversary can clear the complete undirected graph in $O(\sqrt{n})$ rounds. (In the full version of this paper [1], we show that if the adversary uses $n^2/4 + O(n)$ guards, then $\Omega(\sqrt{n})$ rounds are necessary to clear the graph.) The idea to reduce the number of rounds is that when $|R_i|$ is small or big, the adversary can take bigger sets A_i than the singletons considered in the previous search.

Let $R_1, \ldots, R_{\ell+1}$ be sets defining a monotonic search of U_n, let $A_i \overset{\text{def}}{=} R_i \setminus R_{i+1}$, and $S_i \overset{\text{def}}{=} \overline{R_i}$. Notice that $R_i = R_{i+1} \cup A_i$, $S_{i+1} = S_i \cup A_i$, and $S_i \cup A_i \cup R_{i+1} = V$. The edges guarded in Round i of the monotonic search are

$$\{\langle u, v \rangle : u \in R_i, v \in S_{i+1}\} \cup \{\langle u, v \rangle : u \in S_i, v \in R_{i+1}\}$$
$$= \{\langle u, v \rangle : u \in (R_{i+1} \cup A_i), v \in (S_i \cup A_i)\} \cup \{\langle u, v \rangle : v \in S_i, u \in R_{i+1}\}$$
$$= \{\langle u, v \rangle : u \in A_i, v \in V\} \cup \{\langle u, v \rangle : v \in S_i, u \in R_{i+1}\}.$$

Thus, the number of edges guarded in Round i is bounded by

$$|A_i||V| + |S_i||R_{i+1}| = |A_i|n + |S_i|(n - |S_i| - |A_i|). \tag{3}$$

In each round, we want to choose the largest set A_i such that the number of guards, as bounded in (3), does not exceed $n^2/4 + n/2$. In the first round, $|S_1| = 0$, thus, the requirement is $|A_1|n \leq n^2/4 + n/2$, that is, we can take $|A_1| \approx n/4$. In the second round $|S_1| \approx n/4$, thus, the requirement is $|A_2|n + \frac{n}{4}(\frac{3n}{4} - |A_2|) \leq n^2/4 + n/2$, that is, we can take $|A_2| \approx \frac{n}{12}$. Similar calculations show that in the ith round we can take $|A_i| \approx \frac{n}{2i(i+1)}$, and, in this case, $|R_i| \approx \frac{n}{2}(1 + \frac{1}{i})$. After $O(\sqrt{n})$ rounds, $|R_i| \approx \frac{n}{2} - \sqrt{n}$. Then, with choosing A_i as a singleton for $O(\sqrt{n})$ additional rounds, the adversary gets $|R_i| = n/2$. Finally, by (3), with additional $O(\sqrt{n})$ rounds the adversary can get $|R_i| = 0$, by using a "reverse" search strategy. That is, if the adversary used sets A_i of size $a_1, a_2, \ldots, a_{O(\sqrt{n})}$ to clear the first $n/2$ vertices, then by using sets A_i of size $a_{O(\sqrt{n})}, \ldots, a_2, a_1$ the adversary clears the last $n/2$ vertices. As $|A_i|$ has to be an integer, there are some technical details to consider. The exact details are omitted for lack of space.

4.3   Monotonic Searches are Not Optimal

We show that monotonic searches can require more guards than non-monotonic searches. This phenomenon is also true for the vertex eavesdropping game [6], but not for the classic search games on graphs [12,2].

In Fig. 4 we describe an example of a simple directed graph, Graph $G_0 = \langle V_0, E_0 \rangle$ where $V_0 = \{v_1, v_2\}$ and $E_0 = \{\langle v_1, v_2 \rangle, \langle v_2, v_1 \rangle, \langle v_2, v_2 \rangle\}$, that can be cleared with one guard using a non monotonic search:

- Guard $\langle v_2, v_1 \rangle$ in the first round,
- Guard $\langle v_2, v_2 \rangle$ in the second round,
- Guard $\langle v_1, v_2 \rangle$ in the third round.

In Fig. 4 we describe the layered graph $L(G_0, 3)$ and the above search. This is a non-monotonic search since v_1 is cleared in the first round and becomes contaminated in the second round.

We next claim that every monotonic search that clears G_0 uses at least two guards. In every search that clears G_0 with one guard, the first vertex that must be cleared is v_1. The only way to keep v_1 clear with one guard is to keep the guard on the edge $\langle v_2, v_1 \rangle$, thus, not clearing the vertex v_2 and not clearing G_0.

We next describe how to clear Graphs G_2 and G_3, described in Fig. 1 in the Introduction, with one guard using non-monotonic searches. To clear Graph G_2, guard $\langle v_2, v_3 \rangle$ for two rounds, guard $\langle v_1, v_1 \rangle$ in the 3rd round, guard $\langle v_2, v_2 \rangle$ in the 4th round, and guard $\langle v_4, v_1 \rangle$ for the last two rounds.

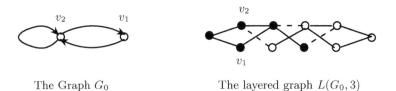

The Graph G_0 The layered graph $L(G_0, 3)$

Fig. 4. The graph G_0 and its layer graph. The guarded edges in the layer graph are the dashed edges, and the contaminated vertices are the black vertices in the layered graph.

Notice that G_3 contains the graph G_2 and, in addition, a path with seven edges. To clear Graph G_3, guard $\langle v_2, v_5 \rangle$ for six rounds (this clears the path), then, in six rounds, clear the G_2 part of G_3 using the search described in the previous paragraph. In these rounds the path becomes contaminated, so we clear it again by guarding $\langle v_{10}, v_1 \rangle$ for 6 rounds. It can be checked that this search clears G_3.

5 Lower Bounds on Clearing a Complete graph

We show that $\lceil n^2/2 \rceil$ guards are necessary to clear C_n (no matter how many rounds the adversary uses to clear the graph). Furthermore, we show that $n^2/4 + n/2$ guards are necessary to clear a complete undirected graph and $\Omega(\sqrt{n})$ rounds are necessary to clear this graph with $n^2/4 + O(n)$ guards.

Theorem 4. *An adversary needs at least $\lceil n^2/2 \rceil$ guards to clear a complete directed graph.*

Proof. Assume that there is a search that clears the graph C_n with t guards. We claim that $t \geq n^2/2$. Let $R_1, \ldots, R_{\ell+1}$ be a sequence satisfying the conditions of Theorem 2. In particular, $|R_1| = n$ and $|R_{\ell+1}| = 0$. Let i be the minimal index such that $|R_{i+1}| < n/2$. Thus, $|R_i| \geq n/2$. We claim that the number of edges guarded in Round i is at least $n^2/2$. In C_n, all edges in $\left(R_i \times \overline{R_{i+1}} \right) \bigcup \left(\overline{R_i} \times R_{i+1} \right)$ exist, and the sets $R_i \times \overline{R_{i+1}}$ and $\overline{R_i} \times R_{i+1}$ are disjoint. Thus, the number of edges is exactly

$$|R_i||\overline{R_{i+1}}| + |\overline{R_i}||R_{i+1}| = |R_i|(n - |R_{i+1}|) + |R_{i+1}|(n - |R_i|) \qquad (4)$$

Since $|R_{i+1}| < n/2$, this expression is an increasing function of $|R_i|$, thus, since $|R_i| \geq n/2$, it is at least $n/2(n - 2|R_{i+1}|) + |R_{i+1}|n = n^2/2$. As the number of guards is an integer, the theorem follows. $\qquad \square$

The following theorems provide lower bounds on the number of guards and rounds needed to clear complete undirected graphs; their proofs appear in the full version of this paper [1].

Theorem 5. *An adversary needs at least $n^2/4 + n/2$ guards to clear a complete undirected graph.*

Theorem 6. *Every search clearing a complete undirected graph using at most $n^2/4 + \gamma n$ guards, for some $\gamma \geq 1/2$, must use at least $\Omega(\sqrt{n/\gamma})$ rounds.*

References

1. A. Beimel and M. Franklin. Edge eavesdropping games.
   www.cs.bgu.ac.il/~beimel/Papers/, 2006.
2. D. Bienstock and P. Seymour. Monotonicity in graph searching. *J. of Algorithms*, 12(2):239–245, 1991.

3. H. Buhrman, J. A. Garay, and J. H. Hoepman. Optimal resiliency against mobile faults. In *25th International Symp. on Fault-Tolerant Computing*, pages 83–88, 1995.

4. N. Cai and R. W. Yeung. Secure network coding. In *International Symposium on Information Theory*, 2002.

5. J. Feldman, T. Malkin, C. Stein, and R. A. Servedio. On the capacity of secure network coding. In *Proc. 42nd Annual Allerton Conference on Communication, Control, and Computing*, 2004.

6. M. Franklin, Z. Galil, and M. Yung. Eavesdropping games: a graph-theoretic approach to privacy in distributed systems. *J. of the ACM*, 47(2):225–243, 2000.

7. J. A. Garay. Reaching (and maintaining) agreement in the presence of mobile faults. In *8th International Workshop on Distributed Algorithms*, volume 857 of *LNCS*, pages 253–264. Springer Verlag, 1994.

8. J. A. Garay, R. Gennaro, C. S. Jutla, and T. Rabin. Secure distributed storage and retrieval. *Theoretical Computer Science*, 243(1-2):363–389, 2000.

9. A. Herzberg, S. Jarecki, H. Krawczyk, and M. Yung. Proactive secret sharing, or: how to cope with perpetual leakage. In *Advances in Cryptology – CRYPTO '95*, volume 963 of *LNCS*, pages 339–352. Springer-Verlag, 1995.

10. K. Jain. Security based on network topology against the wiretapping attack. *IEEE Magazine, Special issue on Topics in Wireless Security*, 2004.

11. L. M. Kirousis and C. H. Papadimitriou. Searching and pebbling. *Theoretical Computer Science*, 47:205–218, 1986.

12. A. LaPaugh. Recontamination does not help to search a graph. *J. of the ACM*, 40(2):224–245, 1993.

13. R. Ostrovsky and M. Yung. How to withstand mobile virus attacks. In *Proc. of the 10th ACM Symp. on Principles of Distributed Computing*, pages 51–59, 1991.

14. T. D. Parsons. Pursuit evasion in a graph. In *Theory and Application of Graphs*, pages 426–441. Springer-Verlag, 1976.

15. C. E. Shannon. Communication theory of secrecy systems. *Bell System Technical Journal*, 28(4):656–715, 1949.

A   An Example of the Problem in the Proof of [6]

We next describe an example in which the characterization in [6] is incorrect. Consider the graph G_4, described in Fig. 5, from the family of graphs $\{G_n\}$ used

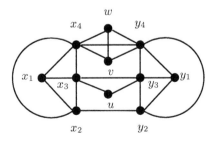

Fig. 5. The graph G_4

in the proof of Theorem 3 in [6]. The graph G_4 consists of a left clique (complete graph) with vertices $\{x_1, x_2, x_3, x_4\}$, a right clique with vertices $\{y_1, y_2, y_3, y_4\}$, a middle clique (M_2) consisting of vertices $\{x_2, y_2\}$, a middle clique (M_3) consisting of vertices $\{x_3, y_3, u\}$, and a middle clique (M_4) consisting of vertices $\{x_4, y_4, v, w\}$.

The following vertex search (suggested by the proof of Theorem 3 in [6]) cuts the directed layered graph, but fails to cut the undirected layered graph:

Round	Guarded set
1	$\{x_1, x_2, x_3, x_4\}$
2	$\{y_2, x_2, x_3, x_4\}$
3	$\{u, y_3, x_3, x_4\}$
4	$\{y_2, x_2, y_3, x_4\}$
5	$\{v, w, y_4, x_4\}$

Round	Guarded set
6	$\{y_2, x_2, y_3, y_4\}$
7	$\{u, y_3, x_3, y_4\}$
8	$\{y_2, x_2, y_3, y_4\}$
9	$\{y_1, y_2, y_3, y_4\}$

One unguarded path in the undirected layered graph goes from y_4 in the first layer, to y_1 in the second layer, to y_4 in the third layer, to y_1 in the fourth layer, to y_3 in the fifth layer, *back* to u in the fourth layer, to x_3 in the fifth layer, to x_1 in the sixth layer, to x_2 in the seventh layer, to x_1 in the eight layer, to x_2 in the ninth layer. With respect to Lemma 4 in [6], note that Alice is unable to simulate the behavior of y_3 in the fifth layer, even though this node is in the set V_s, since the set V_r includes u in the fourth layer.

In fact, the proof of Theorem 3 in [6] implies that the only search that clears the directed layered graph with 4 guards is basically the search described above. Since every search that clears the undirected layered graph clears the directed layered graph, and the above search does not clear the undirected layered graph, every search that cuts the undirected layered graph, uses at least 5 guards.

Universally Composable Simultaneous Broadcast

Alejandro Hevia*

Department of Computer Science, Universidad de Chile
Blanco Encalada 2120, Santiago, Chile
ahevia@dcc.uchile.cl

Abstract. Simultaneous Broadcast protocols allow different parties to broadcast values in parallel while guaranteeing mutual independence of the broadcast values. The problem of simultaneous broadcast was suggested by Chor et al. (FOCS 1985) who proposed a linear-round solution, and later improved by Chor and Rabin (PODC 1987) and Gennaro (IEEE Trans. on Parallel and Distributed Systems 2000). The most efficient solution, in terms of round complexity, is the one due to Gennaro, which is in the common random string model. This construction has constant round complexity but is not very practical, as it requires generic zero-knowledge proofs, non-interactive zero-knowledge proofs of knowledge, and commitment schemes. All the mentioned solutions were proven secure under security definitions with weak or no composition guarantees – only sequential composition for the initial construction by Chor et al.

In this work, we explore the problem of Simultaneous Broadcast under Universally Composable (UC) security (Canetti 2001). We give a definition of Simultaneous Broadcast in this framework, which is shown to imply all past definitions. We also show this notion can be achieved by a computationally efficient, constant-round construction (building on the verifiable secret sharing scheme of Cramer et al. at Eurocrypt 1999), which is secure under an honest majority. Our results rely on (and benefit from) capturing synchronous communication as a functionality within the UC model, as suggested by Canetti (IACR eprint 2005). Indeed, we show that this approach of modeling synchronous communication can lead to better understanding of where synchronicity is needed, and also simpler constructions and proofs.

1 Introduction

Broadcast channels allow one or more senders to efficiently transmit messages to be received by all parties connected to a (physical or virtual) communication network. As a communication primitive, broadcast is fundamental both in the design of network communication protocols, and in the area of secure multiparty computation. The main security property characterizing broadcast communication is consistency: the messages received by all players as a result of a broadcast

---

* Work done while the author was at the Computer Sc. Dept., U.C. San Diego, USA. Supported in part by NSF grant 0313241. Any opinions, findings, and conclusions or recommendations expressed in this material are those of the author(s) and do not necessarily reflect the views of the National Science Foundation.

R. De Prisco and M. Yung (Eds.): SCN 2006, LNCS 4116, pp. 18–33, 2006.

transmission operation are guaranteed to be the same. The problem of achieving consistency when implementing broadcast on top of a point-to-point network (commonly known as Byzantine agreement) is central not only in cryptography, but also to the area of fault-tolerant distributed computation. It has received enormous attention (e.g., [25,18,11,7] among many others).

In secure multiparty computation, it is often desirable that the broadcast channel satisfies some additional properties, besides consistency. For example, in applications where multiple senders must broadcast messages at the same time[1] (e.g., when running in parallel many copies of a broadcast protocol with different senders), it is often important to enforce the *simultaneous* transmission of the messages. The goal is that no sender can decide its broadcast message based on the values broadcast by the other players. Achieving this property, also called *independence*, is not as straightforward as it may seem. In general, naive parallel execution of broadcast protocols does not suffice, nor the more sophisticated round efficient approaches presented in [4,27]. Indeed, a common conservative assumption in settings where (multisender) broadcast channels are provided is to assume *rushing* adversaries – adversaries that, at each round, may see the messages sent by the honest parties before sending out the messages for the corrupted parties for the same round [5]. Nonetheless, this independence property does play a fundamental role in the secure multiparty computation protocol of [12] as well as in many important applications (like contract bidding, coin flipping, and electronic voting schemes, as exemplified in [13,17,19]) where this type of broadcast enormously simplifies the design of protocols.

The concept of *simultaneous broadcast* was introduced by Chor et al. in [12], along with a simulated-based definition. In [12], Chor et al. presented protocols that securely implement simultaneous broadcast on top of a network which allows regular broadcast transmission operations, not necessarily satisfying the simultaneity property. For each simultaneous broadcast operation, their protocols require a number of rounds that is linear in the number of parties. Subsequent works [13,19] focused on reducing the round complexity, obtaining simultaneous broadcast protocols with logarithmic [13] or even constant [19] number of rounds (the latter result achieved in the common random string model.) Even as the round-efficiency of the solutions increased, the definitions of security did not remain the same, and they actually became increasingly restricted, as it was pointed out by Hevia and Micciancio [22]. In particular, there it was shown that the protocol of [19], the most round efficient protocol so far, is secure under a definition of security strictly weaker than the original simulation-based definition [12].[2] Nonetheless, the round efficiency of Gennaro's protocol made attractive

---

[1] Also called *interactive consistency* in [31,4] and *parallel broadcast* in [22]. To avoid confusions, we adopt the term *multisender broadcast* to refer to the operation of multiple senders broadcasting messages at the same time.

[2] Indeed, the definition of simultaneous broadcast proposed in [19] may not exclude protocols that fail to achieve the intuitive notion of independence captured by the simulation-based definition of [12].

the search for either a proof that such protocol achieves a stronger notion of simultaneous broadcast (e.g. [12]), or for a variant of that protocol that does it.

CONCURRENT EXECUTION AND UNIVERSAL COMPOSABILITY: The development of increasingly complex computing environments brought the concern that previously secure protocols (proven as stand-alone primitives) might not remain secure under stronger adversarial conditions, like parallel or concurrent execution with many (possibly different) other protocols [17], or if invoked by other (possibly unknown) protocols. It was in such context that several security frameworks were developed (see [32,8] for a good survey). In [8], Canetti presented the *Universally Composable (UC) Security* framework, which allows modular description and analysis of protocols under concurrent execution and provides strong composability guarantees. Indeed, the security of UC secure protocols is maintained under general composition with an unbounded number of instances of arbitrary protocols running concurrently. Thus, given the benefits of the UC framework, the security of many cryptographic primitives has been revisited to explore whether these stronger UC guarantees can be achieved, and if so, at what cost (in terms of efficiency or assumptions). As we will see in the next section, simultaneous broadcast can be achieved under UC security not only at no cost, but also with *gains* in terms of efficiency.

1.1 Our Contributions

In this work, we present an communication and round efficient solution for the simultaneous broadcast problem. Our solution is based on verifiable secret sharing (VSS) [12] and does not uses zero-knowledge proofs, zero-knowledge proofs of knowledge, not commitments schemes as previous constructions [13,19]. Moreover, our construction is provably secure in the Universally Composable framework against computationally-unbounded adaptive adversaries assuming an honest majority and private channels, with some negligible error probability.[3] To achieve this, we introduce a natural definition of Simultaneous Broadcast in the UC framework which implies all previous definitions. Our simultaneous broadcast construction is very efficient: we run one VSS per party in parallel. While the construction is technically simple, proving UC security present some subtleties, like dealing with rushing adversaries or parties simply "copying" someone else's sharing. We overcome some of the problems by defining a synchronous variant of verifiable secret sharing, which we call *Terminating VSS* (TVSS), and building our simultaneous broadcast protocol invoking such TVSS functionality. We then show that, when formalized as UC functionality, TVSS is intrinsically synchronous. A benefit of this approach is that our simultaneous broadcast protocol does not explicitly requires global synchronous communication since all the synchronicity is provided by the Terminating VSS functionality. Our construction and proof exemplifies the approach, first suggested by Canetti

---

[3] Most of the properties of our solution – namely communication and round complexity, reliability and negligible error probability – are inherited from the VSS used as building block [14].

in [8], of abstracting synchronous communication as a functionality rather than embedding it in the execution model [30,24]. We believe this approach leads to modular analysis, simple protocol design and simpler proofs.

1.2   Related Work

SIMULTANEOUS BROADCAST: As mentioned above, the simultaneous broadcast problem was put forward by Chor et al. [12] who proposed a simulation-based definition and a linear-round protocol. This protocol essentially executed n sequential VSS protocols, where n is the number of communicating parties. The sequential execution was needed to prevent corrupted parties from broadcasting the same value as an honest party, for instance by reusing (copying) the VSS data sent out by the honest party. Then, Chor and Rabin in [13] showed how to reduce the round complexity to $\mathcal{O}(log(n))$ rounds. Their protocol requires, among other things, that each party first broadcast a commitment of her input and then proves knowledge of the broadcasted value. The reduction in rounds comes from using a clever scheduling technique for doing the proofs – for any two players, there is a step in the protocol where one player acts as prover and the other one acts as verifier of the proof of knowledge. Such a scheduling prevents "copying" the proofs. Finally, Gennaro in [19], working in the common random string model, put forward a protocol that greatly simplifies the one in [13] by showing how to run the proofs of knowledge in parallel, essentially employing non-interactive proofs of knowledge [34].

In terms of the previous definitional work for simultaneous broadcast problem, it turns out that each result in [12,13,19] presents a different definition. Hevia and Micciancio [22] show that these definitions form a strict hierarchy when considered in terms of input distributions. They point out that the strongest definition (in a well-defined sense, see [22]) is the simulation-based notion of [12], which preserves security under sequential composition. The notions in [13,19] targeted stand-alone execution and thus provide no composition guarantees.

VERIFIABLE SECRET SHARING: The notion of Verifiable Secret Sharing (VSS) was first proposed by Chor et al. [12] inspired by the need of adding robustness to standard secret sharing (eg. Shamir's [35]) The problem has been extensively studied both in the synchronous setting (e.g. [18,5,20,33,14,1]) and in the asynchronous setting [3,6,11,7]. In the information-theoretic model with adaptive adversaries, Rabin and Ben-Or [33] proposed a VSS secure under an honest majority, by allowing negligible failure probability. Subsequently, in the same model, Cramer et al. [14] improved the information checking protocols of [33] and presented a very efficient constant-round VSS protocol. By instantiating the Terminating VSS required in our construction with the scheme in [14] we obtain our constant-round solution.

RELATED PROTOCOLS AND GENERIC SOLUTIONS: The simultaneous broadcast problem is related to the idea of *common-coin* protocols [18,29], where several parties want to generate one or more unbiased coins in a distributed way. Indeed, the constructions proposed in [18,29] involve executing VSS protocols in parallel, in a similar approach to ours. We remark, however, that the goals are different: while for common-coin generation it suffices that the broadcast value of a single (uncorrupted) value is not correlated to the output of corrupted parties,[4] in the simultaneous broadcast problem we seek to guarantee that every single component of the output vector of the broadcast values remains "uninfluenced" by the other values in the same vector. In addition, our construction must guarantee security under general (UC) composition.

A related, although orthogonal issue, is the problem of *simultaneous termination*, which has been studied by Lindell et al. [27]. The problem arises in the context of parallel composition of multiparty protocols in synchronous networks, where certain protocols (including broadcast protocols) may not terminate in the same round when composed in parallel, thus complicating their sequential composition with other protocols. (We note that, in [27], the term *simultaneous broadcast* is used but with a different meaning than ours, as they refer to what we call multisender broadcast.) The methods in [27] do not attempt to achieve independence (in fact, they do not) since their concern is not adding new functional properties to the resulting parallel protocol, but ensuring that it can be safely composed sequentially with other protocols while preserving round efficiency. Also in the context of composition of broadcast protocols, Lindell et al. discussed some pitfalls in the composition of Authenticated Byzantine Agreement [26]. They show that, unless session identifiers are available, no parallel or concurrent composition of Authenticated Byzantine Agreement is secure if more than one third of the parties are faulty. In our work, we do assume the availability of broadcast channels (in the form of the broadcast functionality $\mathcal{F}_{BC}$) but we put no restrictions on how they are implemented. For example, session identifiers for the broadcast protocols could be initialized using the techniques of Barak et al. [2], or by standard techniques under setup assumptions [10].

Lastly, there are powerful UC constructions for secure multiparty computation of generic protocols (e.g. [10,15]) which could certainly be used to provide a solution to the simultaneous broadcast problem. Indeed, techniques of [10] do provide such a solution tolerating any number of corrupted parties in the common random string model. However, as done in many other examples of multiparty secure computation (eg. threshold signatures, key-exchange, voting), our goal is to look for more specialized, and therefore more efficient, solutions for the simultaneous broadcast problem.

COMPARISON WITH PREVIOUS SOLUTIONS: In terms of efficiency, the number of rounds required in our construction is equal to the number of rounds of the terminating VSS construction we use, which is the one proposed by Cramer et al. [14]. Similarly, the computational complexity of our construction is n times that of the terminating VSS in [14]. Concretely, our solution requires $\mathcal{O}((k + \log n)n^4)$ bits of communication, and only 14 rounds (or 12 if no faults occur). If the model is extended so parties can use digital signatures, the protocol takes only 7 rounds, although security holds only against computationally-bounded

---

[4] In all fairness, in general the mentioned protocols do achieve more than that.

adversaries. In comparison, the previous constant round solution [19] uses at comparable number of rounds (seven for the VSS protocol [5], plus six for the computational zero-knowledge proof [20], plus three rounds) but requires the communication of a large number of bits (n copies of a non-interactive zero-knowledge proof of knowledge for a generic NP statement [34], plus n times the communication complexity of the VSS protocol of [20], a total that in most implementations is often orders of magnitude larger than $\mathcal{O}((k + \log n)n^4)$).

In terms of the adversary tolerated our solution is similar to Gennaro's. The construction of [19] works over public channels under computationally-bounded static adversaries and can be made secure under adaptive adversaries using the compiler of [9]. In comparison, assuming secure channels, our solution tolerates computationally unbounded adaptive adversaries, and security in the public channels (and computationally-bounded adversaries) setting can be obtained by standard techniques, like non-committing encryption [9,16]. In terms of resilience, our construction tolerates at most $t < n/2$ corrupted parties as Gennaro's solution. The constructions of Chor et al. [12] and Chor and Rabin [13] tolerate $t < n/4$ and $t < n/2$ respectively.

ORGANIZATION OF THE PAPER: In the next section, we briefly describe the UC framework. Then, in Sect. 3, we describe and justify our formalization of the notion of Terminating VSS (denoted UC-TVSS), our synchronous variant of VSS, and we mention how it can be efficiently implemented. Sect. 4.1 presents our notion of security for simultaneous broadcast (denoted UC-SB), and shows how to implement it from UC-TVSS. We conclude in Sect. 5 by discussing how to extend our results to the public channel model, and how to model simultaneous broadcast under purely asynchronous communication.

2 Preliminaries

MODEL: Our results are in the Universally Composable framework of Canetti as described in [8]. We briefly and informally outline it here. In the UC framework, the desired properties of cryptographic protocols are defined in terms of tasks or *functionalities*. A functionality is a "trusted third party" that first obtains inputs directly from the parties, performs certain instructions on these inputs, and provides the parties with the appropriate outputs. A protocol securely implements a given cryptographic task, if executing the protocol against a realistic (i.e. real-life) adversary "emulates" the execution of an *ideal process*. In the ideal process, the task is computed by the functionality directly interacting with the parties against a very limited adversary (called the *ideal-adversary*). The notion of "emulation" involves a distinguisher $\mathcal{Z}$ which, by providing the parties with inputs and seeing their outputs, and by interacting with the adversary, attempts to tell whether it is interacting with a real protocol and the real-life adversary, or with the functionality and the ideal-adversary. Good emulation means no such environment is successful. See details and proofs in [8].

In this paper, we consider a network of n parties, $P_1, \ldots, P_n$, connected by perfectly private authenticated channels and a broadcast channel. In the UC terminology, this translates to working in the $(\mathcal{F}_{SMT}, \mathcal{F}_{BC})$-hybrid model, where $\mathcal{F}_{SMT}$ is the *secure message transmission* functionality [8] and $\mathcal{F}_{BC}$ is the *broadcast channel* functionality, which does not satisfy any "fairness" property (i.e. it allows *rushing*). There is a computationally unbounded adversary that can actively corrupt up to $t < n/2$ parties. We consider adaptive corruptions, where the decision to corrupt a party is made during the execution of the protocol, depending on the data gathered so far. Our protocols allow an error probability negligible in the security parameter k. In terms of notation, we let $[n]$ denote the set $\{1, \ldots, n\}$ and $P_{[n]}$ denote the set of all parties $\{P_1, \ldots, P_n\}$.

3   Terminating VSS

MOTIVATION: One inconvenience of the definition of standard VSS schemes (as in [18] or even the UC variant of [1,8]) for our purposes is that it does not guarantee the protocol terminates if the dealer is corrupted. Nonetheless, all synchronous VSS protocols in the literature (e.g. [5,20,33,18,14,1]) seem to satisfy some form of *terminating* condition: there is a round in the execution in which all parties agree that the sharing phase has "time-out" and the secret is fixed. To capture this property while preserving the possibility that the VSS protocol being used *from* higher-level asynchronous protocols, we define the notion of *Terminating VSS* (TVSS).

TVSS protocols are guaranteed to conclude independently of the dealer's actions. We characterize TVSS as a functionality in the UC framework, $\mathcal{F}_{TVSS}$, which is shown in Fig. 1. Intuitively, $\mathcal{F}_{TVSS}$ extends the VSS functionality so that even if a corrupted dealer D fails to call the functionality, a fixed value is eventually associated to D. In fact, honest parties can "force" the functionality to fix a value for D by sending EndSharing messages. Our formulation of $\mathcal{F}_{TVSS}$, is inspired on the UC VSS variant of Abe and Fehr [1], which includes the concept of "spooling" the secret, a syntactic technique that allows the dealer to announce to the adversary – via a Spool message – that a new functionality is being called. The adversary is thus able to adaptively corrupt the dealer before the dealer commits to a value.[5] We say a protocol π achieves UC-TVSS if π UC-realizes functionality $\mathcal{F}_{TVSS}$.

The name *Terminating* VSS reflects that a protocol that UC-realizes $\mathcal{F}_{TVSS}$ concludes (terminates) as long as the adversary delivers all sent messages. The adversary can still delay or block some messages forever – but nothing more. In particular, the protocol does not stall even if the corrupted dealer is irresponsive. This adversarial behavior is a concern in protocols that depend on the termination of a VSS subprotocol, even in the authenticated transmission model, as the parties waiting for a successful completion of the VSS functionality may not

---

[5] A similar technique appears in the formalization of VSS in [8], albeit implicitly in the way the functionality reacts to the corruption messages from the adversary. Another purely syntactic choice is allowing the adversary to trigger the end of the sharing phase – alternative but equivalent formulations are possible (see [21]).

Functionality $\mathcal{F}_{TVSS}$

$\mathcal{F}_{TVSS}$ expects its SID to be of the form $sid = (sid', D, \mathcal{P})$, where $\mathcal{P}$ is a list of parties among which sharing is to be performed. It proceeds as follows.

(1) At first activation, initialize $\mathbf{s}$ as $\bot$.

(2) Upon receiving input $(\texttt{Spool}, sid, s)$ from party $D \in \mathcal{P}$, set $\mathbf{s} \leftarrow s$ and send $(\texttt{SpoolRcvd}, sid, D)$ to adversary A. (Any subsequent input $\texttt{Spool}$ is ignored.)

(3) Upon receiving input $(\texttt{Share}, sid, s')$ from party $D \in \mathcal{P}$, set $\mathbf{s} \leftarrow s'$ and send $(\texttt{ShareRcvd}, sid, D)$ to adversary A. (Any subsequent input $\texttt{Share}$ is ignored.)

(4) Upon receiving input $(\texttt{EndSharing}, sid)$ from uncorrupted party $P \in \mathcal{P}$, record $(\texttt{EndSharing}, P)$ and send $(\texttt{EndSharingRcvd}, sid, P)$ to adversary A.

(5) Upon receiving message $(\texttt{Corrupt}, sid, P)$ from the adversary, do: If $P = D$ then send $\mathbf{s}$ to the adversary. Otherwise, delete record $(\texttt{EndSharing}, P)$, if exists. In both cases, send $(\texttt{Corrupt}, sid)$ message to P.

(6) Upon receiving message $(\texttt{DoEndSharing}, sid)$ from the adversary do: If there is at least one record of the form $(\texttt{EndSharing}, sid, P)$, and
   - D is honest and a message $(\texttt{Share}, sid, u)$ from D has been received, or
   - D is corrupted,

   then send $(\texttt{Shared}, sid)$ to each party in $\mathcal{P}$ and A. (Any subsequent input $\texttt{Share}$ or message $\texttt{DoEndSharing}$ is ignored.) Otherwise, ignore the message.

(7) Upon receiving input $(\texttt{Open}, sid)$ from uncorrupted party P, output $(\texttt{Opened}, sid, \mathbf{s})$ to P and the adversary A.

Fig. 1. The Terminating VSS (with Spooling) functionality, $\mathcal{F}_{TVSS}$

have access to synchronous communication or any "time-out" mechanism.[6] In this context, *termination* means that, once honest parties are instructed to start executing the TVSS protocol, then no matter the actions of the dealer, π concludes with some output (possibly empty) if the adversary delivers all messages. DISCUSSION: One may argue that termination issue seems to disappear if one considers a synchronous version of the UC model (as done in [30,24]). While synchronous communication among all parties certainly allows to implements time-outs (and thus have default sharings if the dealer does not participate), we believe that "encapsulating" synchronicity *inside* the primitive that requires it is useful as higher-level protocols do not need to be aware of it. Concretely, TVSS not only captures a form of synchronous VSS but also keeps the dependence on synchronous communication modularized, as any reliance on it is explicitly and independently handled inside the TVSS functionality. In particular, even though it is possible to show that any implementation of TVSS requires synchronous communication (at least twice) among the parties running it,[7] a higher-level protocol ρ using the TVSS functionality can run in an asynchronous way. In practice, this means that ρ could be implemented in an asynchronous network

---

[6] We remark that, in some applications, the parties "waiting" for the completion of a VSS subprotocol may not be the same as the ones executing the VSS protocol.

[7] This is implied by Claim 4.1 where TVSS is shown to be equivalent to functionality $\mathcal{F}_{SYN}$, synchronous communication with guaranteed delivery [8].

where only limited synchronicity is available (say only within certain subsets of the parties, or when synchronous communication can only be provided very infrequently) as long as the subprotocol that realizes the TVSS functionality has "enough" access to the synchronization capability. For example, applications in cluster networks [36] may exploit the advantage of implementing TVSS locally in each cluster (where synchronization is easier) while the inter-cluster protocol ρ can run asynchronously. Even our concrete application of TVSS, building simultaneous broadcast, where each TVSS involves *all* the parties, may benefit from this modular approach: dealers in different TVSS subprotocols could start the execution at different rounds (because of lack of network connectivity, for example) and still be able to achieve simultaneous broadcast. Furthermore, the simplicity of our construction for simultaneous broadcast shows that this approach may also simplify protocol design and security proofs.

3.1   Instantiating TVSS

In this section, we revisit the very efficient VSS protocol presented by Cramer et al. in [14] in a synchronous model of computation with some negligible error probability. The scheme is based on the bivariate solution of Feldman [18,5] and builds on the information checking techniques of Rabin and Ben-Or [33]. The construction is very efficient: the sharing phase takes fourteen rounds and reconstruction takes two rounds, while the total communication cost is $\mathcal{O}((k + \log n)n^3)$ bits for an error probability of $2^{-k+\mathcal{O}(\log n)}$. This construction π_{TVSS} is detailed in [14,21].

In [14], Cramer et al. prove their construction information-theoretically secure against adaptive corruptions under the classical definition of security [18]. The next proposition shows that their protocol can be proven a secure Terminating VSS in the UC hybrid model we consider here if the model includes the synchronous communication (with guaranteed delivery) functionality $\mathcal{F}_{SYN}$ proposed in [8]. Due to space constraints, the proof is omitted (see [21]).

Proposition 1. *Protocol π_{TVSS} UC-securely realizes functionality $\mathcal{F}_{TVSS}$ in the $(\mathcal{F}_{BC}, \mathcal{F}_{SMT}, \mathcal{F}_{SYN})$-hybrid model for $n > 2t$.*

4   UC Simultaneous Broadcast (UC-SB)

In this section, we generalize the simulation-based definition of Simultaneous Broadcast put forward by Chor et al. [12] to the UC framework. We achieve this by providing a *simultaneous broadcast* functionality $\mathcal{F}_{SB}$ (Fig. 2) which is a variant of the synchronous communication functionality [8] that provides "fairness", in the sense that the adversary is not allowed rushing. We say a protocol π achieves UC-SB if π UC-securely implements functionality $\mathcal{F}_{SB}$.

Intuitively, the definition of $\mathcal{F}_{SB}$ guarantees independence as the adversary cannot access any honest party's input until the broadcast is authorized to proceed, when it is "too late". Notice also that the functionality guarantees output delivery. In some applications, it may be useful to relax this condition.

Functionality $\mathcal{F}_{SB}$

$\mathcal{F}_{SB}$ expects its SID to be of the form $sid = (sid', \mathcal{P})$, where $\mathcal{P}$ is a list of parties among which broadcast is to be performed. It proceeds as follows.

(1) Upon receiving input (Broadcast, sid, m) from party $P \in \mathcal{P}$, record (P, m) and output (sid, P) to the adversary. (If P later becomes corrupted then the record (P, m) is deleted.)

(2) Upon receiving message (Proceed, sid, N) from the adversary, do: If there exist uncorrupted parties $P \in \mathcal{P}$ for which no record (P, m) exists then ignore the message. Else:

    1. Interpret N as the list of messages sent by corrupted parties. That is, $N = \{(S_i, m_i)\}$ where each $S_i \in \mathcal{P}$ is corrupted, and m_i is a message.

    2. Prepare a vector $\mathbf{m} = (m_i)_{i \in \mathcal{P}}$ of messages sent by all parties in $\mathcal{P}$, both corrupted and honest.

(3) Send (Broadcast, sid, $\mathbf{m}$) to the adversary.

(4) Upon receiving input (Receive, sid) from a party $P \in \mathcal{P}$, output (Received, sid, $\mathbf{m}$) to P.

Fig. 2. The simultaneous broadcast functionality, $\mathcal{F}_{SB}$

UC-SB AND PREVIOUS SIMULTANEOUS BROADCAST DEFINITIONS: It is not hard to see that UC-SB implies the (stand-alone) simulation-based definition of simultaneous broadcast in [12]. This is immediate since UC security implies stand-alone security [8]. Then, by the results of [22], it holds that UC-SB implies all the other notions of Simultaneous Broadcast [13,19].

4.1   A Generic Construction of UC-SB from UC-TVSS

In this section, we present our main construction. We show how to implement simultaneous broadcast (UC-SB) using Terminating VSS (UC-TVSS). The construction is simple: each party first runs the share phase of the TVSS in parallel; once all sharings have concluded (terminated), each party starts the reconstruction phase, gather all other parties' secrets and output the vector of values. (see Fig. 3). Moreover, the construction works for any t; the final condition of honest majority comes from instantiating $\mathcal{F}_{TVSS}$ with π_{TVSS} (Prop. 1).

Theorem 1. *Protocol π_{SB} UC-securely realizes $\mathcal{F}_{SB}$ in the $\mathcal{F}_{TVSS}$-hybrid model.*

Proof. Let A be a real-life adversary for π_{SB}. Note that A expects to interact with n parties running π_{SB} with access to n copies of functionality $\mathcal{F}_{TVSS}$. Given A, the ideal adversary S simulates the execution of protocol π_{SB} for adversary A by simulating the parties and functionalities as follows. Let $P_1, \ldots, P_n$ denote the simulated parties, $\tilde{P}_1, \ldots, \tilde{P}_n$ the ideal-world parties. Let sid^* be the session identifier under which each (simulated) party is first invoked (by the environment $\mathcal{Z}$), and $\mathcal{F}_{TVSS}^1, \ldots, \mathcal{F}_{TVSS}^n$ be the (simulated) n copies of functionality $\mathcal{F}_{TVSS}$, where $\mathcal{F}_{TVSS}^k$ denotes the functionality invoked by P_k with session identifier

---

Protocol π_{SB}

Private Inputs: Each P_i holds $x_i \in X$
Public Input: session identifier sid^*
Private Outputs: a vector $\mathbf{y}_i \in (X \cup \{\bot\})^n$ for each P_i
Each party $P_i \in \mathcal{P}$ runs sequentially the following steps:

(1) For each $j \in P_{[n]}$, set $sid_j \leftarrow (sid^*, P_j, P_{[n]})$.
(2) Send ($\mathtt{Spool}, sid_i, x_i$) to $\mathcal{F}_{TVSS}$.
(3) Send ($\mathtt{Share}, sid_i, x_i$) to $\mathcal{F}_{TVSS}$.
(4) For each $j \in P_{[n]}$, send ($\mathtt{EndSharing}, sid_j$) to $\mathcal{F}_{TVSS}$.
(5) Upon receiving ($\mathtt{Shared}, sid_j$) from $\mathcal{F}_{TVSS}$, record ($\mathtt{Shared}, sid_j$). Repeat this step until there is a record ($\mathtt{Shared}, sid_j$) for each $j \in [n]$
(6) For each $j \in P_{[n]}$, send ($\mathtt{Open}, sid_j$) to $\mathcal{F}_{TVSS}$.
(7) Upon receiving ($\mathtt{Opened}, sid_j, v_j$) from $\mathcal{F}_{TVSS}$, record (sid_j, y_j). Once a record (sid_j, y_j) for each $j \in [n]$ exists, output vector $\mathbf{y}_i = (y_j)_{j \in [n]}$ and halt.

Fig. 3. Simultaneous Broadcast protocol in the $\mathcal{F}_{TVSS}$-hybrid model

$sid_k = (sid^*, P_k, P_{[n]})$.[8] Adversary S maintains a set N with the corrupted parties and their inputs, initially $N \leftarrow \emptyset$, and proceeds as follows. If A corrupts any party P_i before the party has submitted a $\mathtt{Share}$ message to $\mathcal{F}^i_{TVSS}$ then S corrupts ideal-world party $\tilde{P}_i$, obtains its input x_i, and pass it to A. If A instructs corrupted party P_i to submit ($\mathtt{Share}, x'_i$) to $\mathcal{F}^i_{TVSS}$, then S simulates the operation, and adds $(\tilde{P}_i, x'_i)$ to N. For all uncorrupted parties P_k, S sets P_k's input to an arbitrary value (eg. $x'_k \leftarrow \bot$) and simulates P_k's interaction with $\mathcal{F}^k_{TVSS}$ by simulating both, party and functionality. Notice that S can do such simulation without the real P_k's input because adversary A's view of the interaction between P_k and $\mathcal{F}^k_{TVSS}$ during the *share* phase of TVSS (steps (1)-(6) of Fig. 1) is independent of P_k's input. Indeed, consider the event E_k defined as "$\mathcal{F}^k_{TVSS}$ has at least one record ($\mathtt{EndSharing}, P$) *and then* it receives a message $\mathtt{DoEndSharing}$ from A". As long as P_k is corrupted anytime before E_k is true, S can proceed as before, that is, S obtains x_k from corrupting $\tilde{P}_k$ and pass it to A. Notice, however, that adversary A must corrupt a party P_i before P_i sends out message $\mathtt{Share}$ to $\mathcal{F}^i_{TVSS}$ if A wants to change the value submitted by P_i.

At some point in the simulation, A may send a $\mathtt{DoEndSharing}$ message to some TVSS functionality. Then, S partitions the simulated parties in four sets. These sets are dynamic in the sense that S may *move* parties from one set to another depending on the subsequent instructions of A. The corrupted parties are partitioned into B_{Sh} and its complement, where B_{Sh} is the set of parties which have submitted a message $\mathtt{Share}$ to $\mathcal{F}_{TVSS}$. (Notice that for all $P_i \in B_{Sh}$, N contains an entry $(\tilde{P}_i, x'_i)$.) Similarly, any honest party P_i is either in G_{Sh} or its complement, where G_{Sh} is the set of parties that have submitted a message $\mathtt{Shared}$ to its $\mathcal{F}^i_{TVSS}$. Notice that if $P_i \in G_{Sh}$, then P_i has sent

---

[8] Notice that, such functionality may also be invoked (and instantiated) by some other party P_j on message $\mathtt{EndSharing}$ if P_k is not activated by $\mathcal{Z}$.

or is about to send a EndSharing message. Let B_{end} (resp. G_{end}) be the set of corrupted (resp. uncorrupted) parties whose corresponding TVSS functionalities have at least one record of the form $(\text{EndSharing}, P_j)$. Assume A sends a message DoEndSharing to functionality $\mathcal{F}^k_{TVSS}$. Then,

(1) If $P_k \notin B_{\text{end}} \cup G_{\text{end}}$, that is, $\mathcal{F}^k_{TVSS}$ has no EndSharing records, then S does nothing (since those messages are ignored by the TVSS functionality).

(2) If $P_k \in G_{\text{end}}$ but $P_k \notin G_{Sh}$, that is, $\mathcal{F}^k_{TVSS}$ has one or more EndSharing records but P_k has yet to submit a Share request to $\mathcal{F}^k_{TVSS}$, then S does nothing (since those messages are ignored by the TVSS functionality).

(3) If $P_k \in B_{\text{end}} \cap B_{Sh}$ or if $P_k \in G_{\text{end}} \cap G_{Sh}$, then S simulates $\mathcal{F}^k_{TVSS}$'s execution by having the functionality send messages (Shared, sid_k) to all parties P_i and the adversary A. If $P_k \in B_{\text{end}} \cap \overline{B_{Sh}}$, then S does the same but also adds $(P_k, \bot)$ into set N.

(4) If A instructs a corrupted party P_i to send a message Open to some $\mathcal{F}^k_{TVSS}$, then S honestly simulates the functionality.

We also let $J \subseteq (G_{\text{end}} \cap G_{Sh}) \cup B_{\text{end}}$ be the set of parties to whose functionality A has sent a message DoEndSharing. S continues the simulation following the above rules (possibly moving parties into G_{Sh}, B_{Sh}, G_{end}, B_{end}, and J as new messages are delivered by A) until $J = [n]$. Assume this happens when A sends a message DoEndSharing to $\mathcal{F}^k_{TVSS}$. *Before* applying rule 3 from above, S sends $(\text{Proceed}, sid^*, N)$ to ideal functionality $\mathcal{F}_{SB}$, and obtains $(\text{Broadcast}, sid^*, \mathbf{m})$. S uses $\mathbf{m}$ to set the secret in each simulated (uncorrupted) $\mathcal{F}^i_{TVSS}$ to $s_i = m_i$, where $\mathbf{m} = (m_1, \ldots, m_n)$. Only then S applies rule 3 from above for party P_k. ¿From then on, S honestly simulates the execution of π_{SB} for A.

We claim that the simulation is perfect. Indeed, observe that adversary A's view before set J becomes equal to $[n]$ is independent of the input of the simulated parties, as it consists of the corrupted parties' inputs, and messages $(\text{SpoolRcvd}, sid_i, P_i)$, $(\text{ShareRcvd}, sid_i, P_i)$, $(\text{EndSharingRcvd}, sid_i, P_i)$, and $(\text{Shared}, sid_j, P_i)$ for one or more party $P_i \in (G_{\text{end}} \cap G_{Sh}) \cup B_{\text{end}}$. The crucial observation is that no uncorrupted party P_k issues an Open message unless P_k has received Shared messages for all parties. This only happens if DoEndSharing messages have been received by each functionality $\mathcal{F}^j_{TVSS}$, $P_j \in J$, which only happens *after* J is set to $[n]$. At that point, the ideal adversary S has obtained the inputs for all parties, so the adversary's view from then on is identical to the real-world experiment. Notice also that once adversary A sends DoEndSharing messages to each functionality $\mathcal{F}^j_{TVSS}$, $P_j \in J = [n]$, A cannot issue a Share message for any (corrupted) party P_i. This is because P_i must also be in $J \subseteq (G_{\text{end}} \cap G_{Sh}) \cup B_{\text{end}}$ which implies P_i is either in $G_{\text{end}} \cup B_{\text{end}}$, and therefore functionality $\mathcal{F}^i_{TVSS}$ has successfully executed step (6) where (Shared, sid_i) was sent out to all parties; after this step, no new Share orDoEndSharinginput is accepted by $\mathcal{F}^i_{TVSS}$. This concludes the proof.

ON THE SYNCHRONICITY OF SIMULTANEOUS BROADCAST AND TVSS: We conclude this section showing that Simultaneous Broadcast is essentially as strong as synchronous communication, namely $\mathcal{F}_{SYN}$. One direction is provided by the reduction to UC-TVSS described above, which says that any solution for UC-TVSS can be used to achieve UC-SB. Notice also that $\mathcal{F}_{SYN}$ implies UC-TVSS by Prop. 1. The other direction holds because UC-SB can be used to implement $\mathcal{F}_{SYN}$ as follows: first parties (non-simultaneously) broadcast their values, and then use simultaneous broadcast to transmit the same values (i.e. those broadcasted non-simultaneously before). Thus, the following claim holds.

Claim. Let π be a protocol that UC-securely realizes $\mathcal{F}_{SB}$ in the $\mathcal{F}_{SMT}$-hybrid model. Then, there exists a protocol that UC-securely realizes $\mathcal{F}_{SYN}$ in the $(\mathcal{F}_{SB}, \mathcal{F}_{SMT})$-hybrid model.

5 Extensions

REMOVING SECURE CHANNELS: Our protocol for simultaneous broadcast is only secure in the secure channel model. To obtain a protocol secure in the public channel model (i.e. authenticated channels), we can use known techniques, like those proposed by Lysyanskaya [28] which require secure erasures, or non-committing encryption [9,16]. For the case of static corruption is much simpler, as encrypting the messages with a semantic secure encryption scheme suffices.

Functionality $\mathcal{F}_{ASB}$

$\mathcal{F}_{SB}$ expects its SID to be of the form $sid = (sid', \mathcal{P}, t)$, where $\mathcal{P}$ is a list of parties among which broadcast may potentially be performed, and $t < n$ is an integer, where $n \stackrel{\text{def}}{=} |\mathcal{P}|$. It proceeds as follows.

(1) Upon receiving input (Broadcast, sid, m) from party $P \in \mathcal{P}$, record (P, m) and output (sid, P) to the adversary. (If P later becomes corrupted then the record (P, m) is deleted.)

(2) Upon receiving a message (Proceed, sid, N, W) from the adversary, do: If W is a subset of parties in $\mathcal{P}$ of size at least $n - t$, and there exist honest parties $P \in W$ for which no record (P, m) exists then ignore the message. Else:
   1. Interpret N as the list of messages sent by corrupted parties. That is, $N = \{(S_i, m_i)\}$ where $S_i \in W$ and S_i is corrupted, and m_i is a message.
   2. Prepare a vector $\mathbf{m} = (m_i)_{i \in W}$ of messages sent by all parties in W, both corrupted and honest.

(3) Send (Broadcast, $sid, \mathbf{m}$) to the adversary.

(4) Upon receiving input (Receive, sid) from a party $P \in \mathcal{P}$, send (Received, $sid, \mathbf{m}$) as delayed output to P.

Fig. 4. The asynchronous simultaneous broadcast functionality, $\mathcal{F}_{ASB}$

ASYNCHRONOUS SIMULTANEOUS BROADCAST (UC-ASB): It is well known that in an asynchronous network, no functionality that depends on all the inputs can be computed [31]. This is because it is impossible to distinguish between failed processes (those instructed to not send messages) and very slow processes. Therefore, no process can afford to wait for messages coming from more than $n - t$

distinct other processes. In this section, we adapt the functionality of Simultaneous Broadcast to comply with this restriction, at the cost of weakening the guarantee that all players can participate in the broadcast (which is unavoidable). We remark that, nonetheless, the modified functionality $\mathcal{F}_{ASB}$ (Fig. 4) still preserves the intuitive notion of *independence*, as long as parties that do not participate in the broadcast are not allowed to contribute later with their inputs. We say a protocol π achieves UC-ASB if π UC-securely realizes $\mathcal{F}_{ASB}$.

We claim (without proof) that there exists a simple construction that achieves UC-ASB for the case $n > 3t$. It suffices to run first the initial phase of the secure multiparty computation of Ben-Or et al. [6]. Spelled out, first, parties run n parallel copies of the *ultimate secret sharing* protocol; then the protocol for *agreement on a common subset* is run. (Both protocols are described in [6].) In this way, all parties agree on the set W of parties that have properly shared their input. The reconstruction protocol is executed next, where the secrets of all parties in W is reconstructed. For computationally bounded adversaries, a similar approach can be obtained using the initialization phase of the computationally efficient construction of [23]. It is an open problem whether more communication efficient solutions exist.

References

1. M. Abe and S. Fehr. Adaptively secure feldman VSS and applications to universally-composable threshold cryptography. In *Advances in Cryptology – CRYPTO*, LNCS 3152, pages 317–334. Springer-Verlag, 2004.
2. B. Barak, Y. Lindell, and T. Rabin. Protocol initialization for the framework of universal composability. Cryptology ePrint Archive, Report 2004/006, 2004. http://eprint.iacr.org/.
3. M. Ben-Or, R. Canetti, and O. Goldreich. Asynchronous secure computation. In *ACM STOC'93*, pages 52–61. ACM Press, 1993.
4. M. Ben-Or and R. El-Yaniv. Resilient-optimal interactive consistency in constant time. *Distributed Computing*, 16(4):249–262, 2003.
5. M. Ben-Or, S. Goldwasser, and A. Wigderson. Completeness theorems for non-cryptographic fault-tolerant distributed computations. In *ACM STOC'88*, pages 1–10. ACM Press, 1988.
6. M. Ben-Or, B. Kelmer, and T. Rabin. Asynchronous secure computations with optimal resilience (extended abstract). In *ACM PODC'94*, pages 183–192, 1994.
7. C. Cachin, K. Kursawe, F. Petzold, and V. Shoup. Secure and efficient asynchronous broadcast protocols. In *Advances in Cryptology – CRYPTO*, LNCS 2139, pages 524–541. Springer-Verlag, 2001.
8. R. Canetti. Universally composable security: A new paradigm for cryptographic protocols. Report 2000/067, Cryptology ePrint Archive, January 2005. Full version of that in IEEE Symposium on Foundations of Computer Science (FOCS'01).
9. R. Canetti, U. Feige, O. Goldreich, and M. Naor. Adaptively secure multi-party computation. In *ACM STOC'96*. ACM Press, 1996.
10. R. Canetti, Y. Lindell, R. Ostrovsky, and A. Sahai. Universally composable two-party and multi-party secure computation. In *ACM STOC'02*, 2002.
11. R. Canetti and T. Rabin. Fast asynchronous Byzantine agreement with optimal resilience (extended abstract). In *ACM STOC'93*, pages 42–51. ACM Press, 1993.

12. B. Chor, S. Goldwasser, S. Micali, and B. Awerbuch. Verifiable secret sharing and achieving simultaneity in the presence of faults. In *IEEE Symposium on Foundations of Computer Science (FOCS'85)*, pages 383–395. IEEE CS, 1985.
13. B. Chor and M. O. Rabin. Achieving independence in logarithmic number of rounds. In *ACM Symposium on Principles of Distributed Computing (PODC'87)*, pages 260–268. ACM Press, 1987.
14. R. Cramer, I. Damgård, S. Dziembowski, M. Hirt, and T. Rabin. Efficient multiparty computations secure against an adaptive adversary. In *Advances in Cryptology – EUROCRYPT'99*, pages 311–326. Springer-Verlag, 1999.
15. I. Damgård and J. B. Nielsen. Universally composable efficient multiparty computation from threshold homomorphic encryption. In *Advances in Cryptology – CRYPTO*, LNCS 2729, pages 247–264. Springer-Verlag, 2003.
16. I. Damgård and J.B. Nielsen. Improved non-committing encryption schemes based on a general complexity assumption. In *Advances in Cryptology – CRYPTO*, LNCS 1880, pages 432–450. Springer-Verlag, 2000.
17. D. Dolev, C. Dwork, and M. Naor. Nonmalleable cryptography. *SIAM Journal on Computing*, 30(2):391–437, April 2001.
18. P. Feldman and S. Micali. An optimal probabilistic protocol for synchronous byzantine agreement. *SIAM Journal on Computing*, 26(4):873–933, 1997.
19. R. Gennaro. A protocol to achieve independence in constant rounds. *IEEE Transactions on Parallel and Distributed Systems*, 11(7):636–647, July 2000.
20. O. Goldreich, S. Micali, and A. Wigderson. Proofs that yield nothing but their validity or all languages in NP have zero-knowledge proof systems. *Journal of the ACM*, 38(3):691–729, July 1991.
21. A. Hevia. Universally composable simultaneous broadcast. Available from http://www.dcc.uchile.cl/~ahevia/pubs/, 2006. Full version of this paper.
22. A. Hevia and D. Micciancio. Simultaneous broadcast revisited. In *ACM PODC'05*, pages 324–333. ACM Press, 2005.
23. M. Hirt, J. B. Nielsen, and B. Przydatek. Cryptographic asynchronous multiparty computation with optimal resilience (extended abstract). In *Advances in Cryptology - EUROCRYPT'05*, LNCS 3494, pages 322–340. Springer-Verlag, 2005.
24. D. Hofheinz and J. Muller-quade. A synchronous model for multi-party computation and the incompleteness of oblivious transfer. Available from http://eprint.iacr.org/2004/016, 2004.
25. L. Lamport, R. Shostak, and M. Pease. The Byzantine generals problem. *ACM Transactions on Programming Languages and Systems*, 4(3):382–401, July 1982.
26. Y. Lindell, A. Lysyanskaya, and T. Rabin. On the composition of authenticated byzantine agreement. In *ACM STOC'02*, pages 514–523. ACM Press, 2002.
27. Y. Lindell, A. Lysyanskaya, and T. Rabin. Sequential composition of protocols without simultaneous termination. In *ACM PODC'02*, pages 203–212, 2002.
28. A. Lysyanskaya. Threshold cryptography secure against the adaptive adversary, concurrently. Report 2000/019, Cryptology ePrint Archive, 2000.
29. S. Micali and T. Rabin. Collective coin tossing without assumptions nor broadcasting. In *Advances in Cryptology – CRYPTO*, LNCS 537, pages 253–266, 1990.
30. J. B. Nielsen. *On Protocol Security in the Cryptographic Model*. Ph.D. thesis, Aarhus University, 2003.
31. M. Pease, R. Shostak, and L. Lamport. Reaching agreements in the presence of faults. *Journal of the ACM*, 27(2):228–234, April 1980.
32. B. Pfitzmann and M. Waidner. A model for asynchronous reactive systems and its application to secure message transmission. In *IEEE Symposium on Security and Privacy (S&P-01)*, pages 184–201. IEEE CS, 2001.

33. T. Rabin and M. Ben-Or. Verifiable secret sharing and multiparty protocols with honest majority. In *ACM STOC'89*, pages 73–85. ACM Press, 1989.
34. A. De Santis and G. Persiano. Zero-knowledge proofs of knowledge without interaction (extended abstract). In *IEEE Symposium on Foundations of Computer Science (FOCS'92)*, pages 427–436. IEEE CS, 1992.
35. A. Shamir. How to share a secret. *Communications of the ACM*, 22(11), 1979.
36. L. von Ahn, A. Bortz, and N.J. Hopper. k-Anonymous message transmission. In *ACM Conference on Computer and Communication Security – CCS'03*, pages 122–130. ACM Press, 2003.

Relations Among Security Notions for Undeniable Signature Schemes

Kaoru Kurosawa[1] and Swee-Huay Heng[2]

[1] Department of Computer and Information Sciences,
Ibaraki University,
4-12-1 Nakanarusawa, Hitachi, Ibaraki 316-8511, Japan
kurosawa@mx.ibaraki.ac.jp
[2] Centre for Cryptography and Information Security,
Faculty of Information Science and Technology,
Multimedia University,
Jalan Ayer Keroh Lama, 75450 Melaka, Malaysia
shheng@mmu.edu.my

Abstract. In this paper, we conduct a thorough study among various notions of security of undeniable signature schemes and establish some relationships among them. We focus on two adversarial goals which are unforgeability and invisibility and two attacks which are chosen message attack and full attack. In particular, we show that unforgeability against chosen message attack is equivalent to unforgeability against full attack, and invisibility against chosen message attack is equivalent to invisibility against full attack. We also present an undeniable signature scheme whose unforgeability is based on the factoring assumption and whose invisibility is based on the composite decision Diffie-Hellman assumption.

Keywords: Undeniable signature, security notions, factoring assumption, composite decision Diffie-Hellman assumption.

1 Introduction

The concept of undeniable signatures was introduced by Chaum and van Antwerpen in 1989 [10]. As opposed to the ordinary digital signatures which are universally verifiable, the validity and invalidity of undeniable signatures can be verified only by executing with the signer or the designated confirmer through a confirmation protocol and a disavowal protocol respectively. Various variants of undeniable signature schemes which possess variable degrees of security and additional features have emerged in the literature over the past 16 years. While it is impossible to list them all, we note some important papers such as [7,5,11,9,8,20,12,16,6,15,14,23,24,25,26,21]. Most of these schemes are discrete logarithm based, with the exception of a few RSA-based schemes [16,15,14], a pairing-based (identity-based) scheme [23] and some other schemes [24,25].

Meanwhile, Bellare et al. showed relations among security notions for public-key encryption schemes [2]. Due to the importance of the above studies, recently we can see an increasing effort in the studying of relations among various security

R. De Prisco and M. Yung (Eds.): SCN 2006, LNCS 4116, pp. 34–48, 2006.
© Springer-Verlag Berlin Heidelberg 2006

notions of cryptographic schemes [3,1,13]. Indeed, by knowing the relationships between the various security notions, one can save much effort to prove the individual security notion since it is sufficient to prove the simpler security notion if it also implies that the scheme fulfills other more complicated notions of security.

In this paper, we conduct a thorough study among various notions of undeniable signature schemes and show some relationships among them. We focus on the notions of *unforgeability* and *invisibility*. The first security notion is similar to the one for ordinary digital signatures, which is the notion of existential unforgeability against adaptive chosen message attack [19]. However, for undeniable signatures, the approach to adapt the previous security by allowing the confirmation/disavowal oracle access has been first considered in [12]. The second security notion is essentially the inability to determine whether a given message-signature pair is valid or not. This notion was first introduced by Chaum, van Heijst and Pfitzmann [11] and further enhanced in [6] and [14].

For each of unforgeability (UF) and invisibility (IV), we consider two different attacks, chosen message attack (CMA) and full attack (FULL). By chosen message attack, we mean that the adversary is only allowed to access to the signing oracle, which is similar to the basic chosen message attack considered in [19]. By full attack, we mean that besides the signing oracle access, the adversary is also allowed to access to the confirmation/disavowal oracle. No effort has been put in previously to study the above notions of security and we note that the results we obtain are somewhat surprising.

By combining the above two adversarial goals and two attacks, we can classify them under four notions of security, namely UF-CMA, UF-FULL, IV-CMA and IV-FULL. The rigorous definitions of the respective notions will be provided in Section 3. In particular, we establish an equivalent result between UF-CMA and UF-FULL, and an equivalence between IV-CMA and IV-FULL if the underlying signature scheme is UF-CMA. We also show that IV-CMA implies UF-CMA if the signing algorithm is deterministic. (We assume that the confirmation protocol and the disavowal protocol are perfect auxiliary-input zero-knowledge.)

More precisely, the relationships among various notions of security that we obtain can be shown as follows:

$$\text{UF-CMA} \Longleftrightarrow \text{UF-FULL}$$

$$\Uparrow$$

$$\text{IV-CMA} \Longleftrightarrow \text{IV-FULL}$$

We remark that the related study on the relationships between two notions of unforgeability of message authentication has been recently conducted by Bellare, Goldreich and Mityagin [3], i.e. they explored the unforgeability of message authentication by considering a single verification attempt and multiple verification attempts respectively by the adversary. They also commented that the multiple verification version of the definition of ordinary digital signatures is clearly equivalent to the standard definition in [19] since verification takes place under a key that is public and which is available to the adversary. However, obviously this is not the case for undeniable signatures since without the consent of the signer or designated confirmer, it is impossible that the adversary can verify the validity or invalidity of a message-signature pair.

The first RSA-based undeniable signature scheme was proposed by Gennaro, Krawczyk and Rabin [16] where they employed the RSA moduli which is a product of safe primes. An extension of the above scheme to allow the use of general RSA moduli was made possible by Galbraith, Mao and Paterson [15]. However, both the above schemes do not have invisibility. Galbraith and Mao [14] showed an improved version which possesses the property of unforgeability and invisibility in the case of RSA moduli which is a product of safe primes.

In this paper, we also present an undeniable signature scheme such that its unforgeability is based on the factoring assumption and its invisibility is based on the composite decision Diffie-Hellman (CDDH) assumption. In the proposed scheme, the size of the signatures is much shorter than the scheme by Galbraith and Mao [14]. Its security can be easily proven by using the relationships we described earlier.

1.1   Organization

The remainder of this paper is organized as follows. In Section 2, we recall the definition of undeniable signatures. In Section 3, we provide the rigorous definitions for the four notions of security: UF-CMA, UF-FULL, IV-CMA and IV-FULL. In Section 4, we conduct a thorough study on the various notions of security of undeniable signatures and establish some important relationships among them. All the related security analyses are given accordingly. In Section 5, we present a new undeniable signature scheme whose unforgeability is based on the factoring assumption and whose invisibility is based on the composite decision Diffie-Hellman assumption. Finally, we conclude this paper in Section 6.

2   Undeniable Signatures

Throughout this paper, k denotes the security parameter and a PPT algorithm denotes a probabilistic polynomial-time algorithm.

An undeniable signature scheme consists of a key generation algorithm G_{sign}, a signing algorithm Sign, a confirmation protocol and a disavowal protocol. We consider undeniable signature schemes such that the confirmation protocol and the disavowal protocol are perfect zero-knowledge in the auxiliary-input model. Hence, we denote an undeniable signature scheme by $\Sigma = (\mathsf{G}_{sign}, \mathsf{Sign})$. G_{sign} is a PPT algorithm which generates (vk, sk), where vk is a verification key and sk is the signing key. Sign is a PPT algorithm which generates a signature σ on input a message m and the signing key sk. We say that (m, σ) is valid if σ is an output of $\mathsf{Sign}(sk, m)$.

An undeniable signature scheme must satisfy unforgeability and invisibility. Invisibility means that for a message m, the receiver cannot tell if σ is a valid signature or a random string. This implies that the receiver cannot verify the validity of (m, σ) by himself. Instead, the cooperation of the signer is needed to prove the validity and invalidity of (m, σ) by running a confirmation protocol and a disavowal protocol with the receiver respectively.

Zero-knowledgeness means that the verifier can generate the communication transcript of the protocol by himself. Hence he cannot prove to the third party that (m, σ) is valid by showing the transcript of the ZK confirmation protocol. This is the central requirement for undeniable signature schemes.

We describe the formal definition of perfect auxiliary-input zero-knowledge below:

Definition 1. *[18,17] A proof system (P, V) is perfect auxiliary-input zero-knowledge on a language L if, for every PPT verifier V^* and every polynomial p, there exists a PPT algorithm M^* such that*

$$\{(P, V^*(y))(x)\}_{x \in L, y \in \{0,1\}^{p(|x|)}} \equiv \{M^*(x, y)\}_{x \in L, y \in \{0,1\}^{p(|x|)}}$$

where the first distribution ensemble denotes the output of V^* when having auxiliary-input y and interacting with prover P on common input $x \in L$; and the second distribution ensemble denotes the output of M^* on inputs $x \in L$ and $y \in \{0,1\}^{p(|x|)}$.

An alternative definition is to require M^* to simulate the *history* of V^*'s interaction with P [17, Remark 3.2].

As shown in [17], auxiliary-input zero-knowledge is preserved under sequential composition. Almost all known zero-knowledge proofs are in fact auxiliary-input zero-knowledge.

3 Definitions of Security

For each of unforgeability (UF) and invisibility (IV), we consider two different attacks, chosen message attack (CMA) and full attack (FULL). By combining two adversarial goals and two attacks, we have the following four notions of security, namely, UF-CMA, UF-FULL, IV-CMA and IV-FULL.

In each attack game, we say that a message-signature pair (m, σ) is unfresh if the adversary A has already queried m to the signing oracle and received σ. Otherwise, we say that (m, σ) is fresh.

3.1 Unforgeability

The unforgeability against CMA (UF-CMA) is defined as follows. Consider the following game between a challenger and an adversary A.

1. The challenger generates a key pair (vk, sk) randomly, and gives the verification key vk to A.
2. For $i = 1, \ldots, q$, A queries a message m_i to the signing oracle adaptively and receives a signature σ_i.
3. Eventually, A outputs a forgery (m^*, σ^*).

   A wins the game if (m^*, σ^*) is valid and fresh.

Definition 2. *We say that Σ is unforgeable against CMA (UF-CMA) if $\Pr(A \text{ wins})$ is negligible for any PPT adversary A in the above game.*

To define the unforgeability against the full attack (UF-FULL), we modify the game against CMA as follows. We allow the adversary A to query (m, σ) to the confirmation/disavowal oracle adaptively at step 2. The confirmation/disavowal oracle responds as follows.

- If (m, σ) is a valid pair, then the oracle returns a bit $\mu = 1$ and proceeds with the execution of the confirmation protocol with A.
- Otherwise, the oracle returns a bit $\mu = 0$ and executes the disavowal protocol with A accordingly.

A wins the game if A outputs a valid and fresh pair (m^*, σ^*) or it queries a valid and fresh pair (m^*, σ^*) to the confirmation/disavowal oracle.

Definition 3. *We say that Σ is unforgeable against the full attack (UF-FULL) if $\Pr[A \text{ wins}]$ is negligible for any PPT adversary A in the above game.*

Remark 1. If the signing algorithm is probabilistic, there are many signatures σ for a fixed message m. In this case, we can consider weak forgery and strong forgery. In the weak forgery, an adversary wins if she can forge (m^*, σ^*) such that m^* has never been queried to the signing oracle by the adversary. In the strong forgery, an adversary wins if she can forge (m^*, σ^*) such that σ^* has never been returned by the signing oracle for a query m^*.

In the above definitions, we consider strong forgery. Note that strongly unforgeable undeniable signature schemes are more secure than weakly unforgeable ones.

If the signing algorithm is deterministic, the two types of forgery coincide.

3.2 Invisibility

The invisibility against CMA (IV-CMA) is defined by using the following game between a challenger and an adversary A.

1. The challenger generates a key pair (vk, sk) randomly, and gives the verification key vk to A.
2. A is permitted to issue a series of signing queries to the signing oracle adaptively and receives a signature σ_i.
3. At some point, A chooses a message m^* and sends it to the challenger.
4. The challenger chooses a random bit b. If $b = 1$, then he computes a signature σ^* on m^*. Otherwise, he chooses σ^* randomly from the signature space S. He then returns σ^* to A.
5. A performs some signing queries again[1].
6. At the end of this attack game, A outputs a guess b'.

---

[1] If the signing algorithm is deterministic, then A is not allowed to query m^* to the signing oracle.

Definition 4. *We say that Σ is invisible against CMA (IV-CMA) if $|\Pr[b = b'] - 1/2|$ is negligible for any PPT adversary A in the above game.*

Finally, to define the invisibility against full attack (IV-FULL), we modify the previous game (IV-CMA) as follows. We allow the adversary A to query (m, σ) to the confirmation/disavowal oracle adaptively at step 2 and at step 5, where A is not allowed to query the challenge (m^*, σ^*) to the confirmation/disavowal oracle at step 5. The confirmation/disavowal oracle responds as follows.

- If (m, σ) is a valid pair, then the oracle returns a bit $\mu = 1$ and proceeds with the execution of the confirmation protocol with A.
- Otherwise, the oracle returns a bit $\mu = 0$ and executes the disavowal protocol with A accordingly.

Definition 5. *We say that Σ is invisible against the full attack (IV-FULL) if $|\Pr[b = b'] - 1/2|$ is negligible for any PPT adversary A in the above game.*

We now say that

- Σ is CMA-secure if it is unforgeable against CMA attack (UF-CMA) and invisible against CMA attack (IV-CMA).
- Σ is fully secure if it is unforgeable against the full attack (UF-FULL) and invisible against the full attack (IV-FULL).

4   Relations Among Security Notions

We use the following notation.

- $X \Longrightarrow Y$: Any undeniable signature scheme Σ meets the security notion of Y if it meets the security notion of X. In this case, we say that X implies Y.
- $X \Longleftrightarrow Y$: Any undeniable signature scheme Σ meets the security notion of Y if and only if it meets the security notion of X. In this case, we say that X and Y are equivalent.

We first show that UF-CMA and UF-FULL are equivalent. That is,

$$\text{UF-CMA} \Longleftrightarrow \text{UF-FULL}.$$

Theorem 1. *UF-CMA and UF-FULL are equivalent if the confirmation protocol and the disavowal protocol are perfect auxiliary-input zero-knowledge.*[2]

Proof. It is clear that UF-FULL $\Longrightarrow$ UF-CMA. Therefore, we will show that UF-CMA $\Longrightarrow$ UF-FULL. Suppose that there exists an adversary A which breaks UF-FULL. We will construct an adversary A' which breaks UF-CMA by using A as a subroutine.

---

[2] We consider strong unforgeability as mentioned in Remark 1 of Section 3.1.

On input a verification key vk, A' starts running A by feeding A with vk. If A makes a signing query for a message m_i, then A' queries m_i to her signing oracle. A' receives a signature σ_i from the signing oracle, and returns σ_i to A.

Next, we consider the case when A makes a confirmation/disavowal query. Let q_v be the number of queries that A issues to the confirmation/disavowal oracle. For convenience, we consider that the final output of A is the $(q_v + 1)$-th query. We say that (m_i, σ_i') is special if it is a valid and fresh message-signature pair queried by A to the confirmation/disavowal oracle. A' guesses the first special query. More precisely, A' guesses the first i such that the i-th query (m_i, σ_i') is special. So, at the beginning, A' chooses $Guess \in \{1, 2, \cdots, q_v + 1\}$ randomly. There are two cases to be considered here, namely, $i < Guess$ and $i = Guess$. First suppose that $i < Guess$.

- If A has never made a signing query for m_i, then A' returns $\mu = 0$ and runs the disavowal protocol with A.
- Otherwise, A has already made a signing query for m_i, and A' answered with a valid signature σ_i. If $\sigma_i = \sigma_i'$ then A' returns $\mu = 1$ and runs the confirmation protocol with A. Otherwise, A' returns $\mu = 0$ and runs the disavowal protocol with A.

Notice that since the confirmation protocol and the disavowal protocol are perfect auxiliary-input zero-knowledge from our assumption, A' can simulate the confirmation/disavowal oracle perfectly (by using the proof technique of [17, Theorem 3.3]).

Now suppose that $i = Guess$. Let (m^*, σ^*) be the i-th query. If A has queried m^* to the signing oracle, then A' aborts. Otherwise, A outputs (m^*, σ^*) as a forgery.

A' guesses the first special query with probability $1/(q_v + 1)$. Therefore, if A wins the game of UF-FULL with non-negligible probability, then A' wins the game of UF-CMA with non-negligible probability too because q_v is polynomially bounded. This completes our proof. $\qquad\qquad\square$

We next show that IV-CMA and IV-FULL are equivalent if Σ is UF-CMA. That is,

$$\text{IV-CMA} \Longleftrightarrow \text{IV-FULL}$$

as long as Σ is UF-CMA.

Theorem 2. *Suppose that an undeniable signature scheme Σ is UF-CMA. Then IV-CMA and IV-FULL are equivalent if the confirmation protocol and the disavowal protocol are perfect auxiliary-input zero-knowledge.*

Proof. It is clear that IV-FULL $\Longrightarrow$ IV-CMA. Therefore, we will show that IV-CMA $\Longrightarrow$ IV-FULL. Suppose that there exists an adversary A which breaks IV-FULL. We will construct an adversary A' which breaks IV-CMA by using A as a subroutine.

On input a verification key vk, A' starts running A by feeding A with the vk. If A makes a signing query for a message m_i, then A' queries m_i to her signing oracle. A' receives a signature σ_i from the signing oracle, and returns σ_i to A.

Next, we consider the case when A makes a confirmation/disavowal query (m_i, σ'_i). We say that (m_i, σ'_i) is *special* if it is a valid and fresh message-signature pair queried by A to the confirmation/disavowal oracle.

Suppose that A makes a *special* confirmation/disavowal query (m_i, σ'_i). with non-negligible probability. Then A wins the game of UF-FULL. However, this is against our assumption because UF-FULL and UF-CMA are equivalent from Theorem 1.

Therefore, A makes a *special* confirmation/disavowal query (m_i, σ'_i) only with negligible probability. Hence A' behaves as follows.

- If A has never made a signing query for m_i, then A' returns $\mu = 0$ and runs the disavowal protocol with A.
- Otherwise, A has already made a signing query for m_i, and A' answered with a valid signature σ_i. If $\sigma_i = \sigma'_i$ then A' returns $\mu = 1$ and runs the confirmation protocol with A. Otherwise, A' returns $\mu = 0$ and runs the disavowal protocol with A.

Notice that since the confirmation protocol and the disavowal protocol are perfect auxiliary-input zero-knowledge from our assumption, A' can simulate the confirmation/disavowal oracle (by using the proof technique of [17, Theorem 3.3]).

At some point, A chooses a message m^* which has never been queried, and sends it to A'. A' queries m^* to its challenger, and receives σ^* from the challenger. A' then returns σ^* to A.

At the end of the attack game, A outputs a guess b'. Then A' outputs $b'' = b'$. Now it is clear that $|\Pr[b = b'] - \Pr[b = b'']|$ is negligible, where b is the hidden bit chosen by the challenger. Hence M can break IV-CMA. $\square$

We finally show that IV-CMA implies UF-CMA if the signing algorithm is deterministic. Note that UF-CMA does not imply IV-CMA: A digital signature scheme which is UF-CMA is not IV-CMA. Hence we cannot prove more than the following figure.

$$\text{UF-CMA} \Longleftrightarrow \text{UF-FULL}$$

$$\Uparrow$$

$$\text{IV-CMA} \Longleftrightarrow \text{IV-FULL}$$

Theorem 3. *IV-CMA implies UF-CMA if the signing algorithm is deterministic.*

Proof. Suppose that there exists an adversary A which breaks UF-CMA. We will construct an adversary A' which breaks IV-CMA by using A as a subroutine.

On input a verification key vk, A' starts running A by feeding A with vk. If A makes a signing query for a message m_i, then A queries m_i to her signing oracle. A' receives a signature σ_i from the signing oracle, and returns σ_i to A.

Eventually, A outputs a forgery (m^*, σ^*). Then A' sends m^* to her challenger. The challenger chooses a random bit b. If $b = 1$, then he computes a signature σ' on m^*. Otherwise, he chooses σ' randomly from the signature space S. The challenger returns σ'.

Finally, if $\sigma' = \sigma^*$, then A' outputs $b' = 1$. Otherwise, A' outputs a random bit b'. Suppose that (m^*, σ^*) is valid with probability ϵ. Then

$$\Pr[b = b'] = \epsilon + (1/2)(1 - \epsilon) = (1/2) + \epsilon/2$$

because the signing algorithm is deterministic. Hence if A outputs a valid forgery with non-negligible probability, then A' wins the game of IV-CMA with non-negligible probability too.   □

Remark 2. The above proof shows that weak IV-CMA implies UF-CMA, where weak IV-CMA is exactly the IV-CMA except the step 5 in Section 3.2. Now we have IV-CMA → weak IV-CMA → IV-FULL.

5 Application to Factoring-Based Undeniable Signatures

Galbraith and Mao showed a factoring-based undeniable signature scheme [14] and proved its security for non-interactive, designated verifier version of confirmation/disavowal protocols [14, page 89, line -7].

Now by using our results, we can prove its security for the 4-move version of confirmation/disavowal protocols due to Chaum [7]. In this section, we present a better factoring-based undeniable signature scheme and prove its security by using our results.

5.1 Proposed Scheme

Galbraith and Mao used PSS-Rabin signature scheme [4]. Instead, we use a Rabin-type signature scheme presented in [22] which has much shorter signature size. Hence the size of our undeniable signatures is much shorter than that of [14].

The details of this new undeniable signature scheme are described as follows.

Definition 6. *Let $N = pq$, where p and q are primes. For $x \in Z_N^*$, let*

$$u = \left(\frac{x}{p}\right), \quad v = \left(\frac{x}{q}\right).$$

Define

$$type(x) \overset{\triangle}{=} \begin{cases} 0 & \text{if } u = v = 1 \\ 1 & \text{if } u = 1, v = -1 \\ 2 & \text{if } u = -1, v = 1 \\ 3 & \text{if } u = v = -1 \end{cases} \tag{1}$$

It is easy to see that $xy \in QR_N$ if and only if $type(x) = type(y)$.

Key Generation. On input 1^k, the system is set up by the signer as follows. Choose two k-bit safe primes p and q such that $p' = (p - 1)/2$ and $q' = (q - 1)/2$ are also primes. Then set $N = pq$ and select an element $e \in Z_{p'q'}^*$ such that $e > 1$.

Choose $g \in Z_N^*$ to be a generator of Z_p^* and Z_q^*, and compute $\beta = g^2 \bmod N$ and $w = \beta^e \bmod N$.

Next, choose α_1 and α_2 such that $type(\alpha_1) = 1$ and $type(\alpha_2) = 2$. Also, let $\alpha_0 \stackrel{\triangle}{=} 1$ and $\alpha_3 \stackrel{\triangle}{=} \alpha_1 \alpha_2 \bmod N$. Note that $type(\alpha_i) = i$ for $i = 0, 1, 2, 3$.

Let $H : \{0,1\}^* \to Z_N^*$ be a hash function.

Finally, set the verification key as $(N, \beta, w, H, \alpha_0, \alpha_1, \alpha_2, \alpha_3)$ and the signing key as (p, q).

Notice that β is a generator of QR_N because $ord_p(\beta) = (p-1)/2 = p'$ and $ord_q(\beta) = (q-1)/2 = q'$, thus $ord_N(\beta) = lcm(p', q') = p'q' = |QR_N|$.

Signing. On input the verification key $(N, \beta, w, H, \alpha_0, \alpha_1, \alpha_2, \alpha_3)$, the signing key (p, q) and a message m , the signer executes the following steps.

Step 1: Compute i such that $type(H(m)) = i$.

Step 2: For this i, compute σ such that $0 < \sigma < N/2$ and

$$\alpha_i H(m) = \sigma^{2e} \bmod N \tag{2}$$

The signature is σ.

We say that (m, σ) is valid if $0 < \sigma < N/2$ and equation (2) is satisfied.

Definition 7. *We say that $(\beta, \beta^x, \beta^y, \beta^{xy}) \in (QR_N)^4$ is a composite Diffie-Hellman (CDH) tuple, where $(x, y) \in Z_{p'q'}^2$.*

In each of the confirmation/disavowal protocols, given a message-signature pair (m, σ), the verifier checks if $0 < \sigma < N/2$. If not, he rejects immediately. if so, he runs the following protocols with the signer.

Confirmation Protocol. The signer first sends i such that $type(H(m)) = i$. The signer next proves that $(\beta, w, \sigma^2, \alpha_i H(m))$ is a CDH-tuple in zero-knowledge.

Disavowal Protocol. The signer first sends i such that $type(H(m)) = i$. Next the signer proves that $(\beta, w, \sigma^2, \alpha_i H(m))$ is not a CDH-tuple in zero-knowledge.

For the confirmation and disavowal protocols, we can use the 4-move protocol due to Chaum [7]. Alternatively, we can use designated verifier proofs which are non-interactive zero-knowledge [20]. They are perfect zero-knowledge in the auxiliary-input model.

Remark 3. 1. It is not necessarily the case that $H(m) \in QR_N$. Therefore, we use the technique of [22]. That is, we have to include $(\alpha_0, \alpha_1, \alpha_2, \alpha_3)$ in the verification key so that $\alpha_i H(m)$ in QR_N for some i.

2. Since the order of β is $p'q'$, Chaum's ZKIP protocols works well on the CDH-tuples and the non CDH-tuples in the group QR_N.

5.2 Security Analysis

Theorem 4. *The above undeniable signature scheme satisfies UF-CMA under the factoring assumption in the random oracle model.*

Proof. Let A be an adversary which breaks UF-CMA with non-negligible probability ϵ. Then we will construct the factoring algorithm M which factors N with non-negligible probability ϵ' by running A as a subroutine. The input of M is $N(= pq)$, where $p = 2p' + 1$ and $q = 2q' + 1$ are safe primes.

M constructs the verification key for A as follows. M chooses a random integer $e \in \{2, \cdots, \lfloor N/4 \rfloor\}$. Next, M chooses a random $g \in Z_N^*$ and defines $\beta = g^2 \bmod N$ and $w = \beta^e \bmod N$. It is easy to see that e is co-prime to $p'q'$ and β is a generator of QR_N with overwhelming probability because N is a product of two safe primes. M also chooses α_1, α_2 randomly in such a way that

$$\left(\frac{\alpha_1}{N}\right) = \left(\frac{\alpha_2}{N}\right) = -1.$$

With probability $1/4$, it holds that $type(\alpha_1) = 1$ and $type(\alpha_2) = 2$. M sets $\alpha_0 = 1$ and $\alpha_3 = \alpha_1 \alpha_2 \bmod N$

M then feeds A with the verification key $(N, \beta, w, H, \alpha_0, \alpha_1, \alpha_2, \alpha_3)$ where H is a random oracle that will be simulated by M. We assume that when A requests a signature on a message m_j, it has already made the corresponding H-query on m_j.

The factoring algorithm M must answer all the queries by itself. When A makes a H-query for a message m_j, A chooses $r_j \in Z_N^*$ and $i \in \{0, 1, 2, 3\}$ randomly, and returns $H(m_j) = r_j^{2e}/\alpha_i \bmod N$. M will maintain a H-query list (m_j, r_j, i).

Suppose that A makes a signing query for a message m_j. Since we have assumed that A has already made the corresponding H-query on m_j, then the H-query list includes (m_j, r_j, i) for some (r_j, i). M then returns $\sigma_j = r_j \bmod N$ as the corresponding signature. Notice that σ_j is a valid signature since

$$\alpha_i H(m_j) = r_j^{2e} \bmod N.$$

Now suppose that A forges (m^*, σ^*). Then

$$\alpha_i H(m^*) = (\sigma^*)^{2e} \bmod N. \tag{3}$$

Since we assumed that A has made the H-query on m^*, so $m^* = m_j$ for some j in the H-query list. Therefore, M can find the triple (m^*, r^*, i) from the H-query list where

$$\alpha_i H(m^*) = (r^*)^{2e} \bmod N. \tag{4}$$

From equation (3) and equation (4),

$$((r^*)^2)^e = ((\sigma^*)^2)^e \bmod N.$$

Since $\gcd(e, p'q')) = 1$ with overwhelming probability, it holds that

$$(r^*)^2 = (\sigma^*)^2 \bmod N$$

with overwhelming probability.

Case 1. Suppose that m^* has never been queried to the signing oracle. In this case, $\gcd(r^* - \sigma^*, N) = p$ or q with probability $1/2$ because r^* is randomly chosen. Hence M can factor N with probability almost $1/2 \times 1/4 = 1/8$.

Case 2. Suppose that m^* has been queried to the signing oracle which returned $\tilde{\sigma}$. In this case, we can see that $\gcd(\sigma^* - \tilde{\sigma}, N) = p$ or q because $0 < \sigma < N/2$. Hence M can factor N with probability almost $1/4$.

In any case, M can factor N with significant probability.   □

Corollary 1. *The above undeniable signature scheme satisfies UF-FULL under the factoring assumption in the random oracle model.*

Proof. From Theorem 4 and Theorem 1.   □

Next we prove the invisibility. It relies on the composite decision Diffie-Hellman (CDDH) assumption which is defined as follows.

We denote $\langle g_1, \ldots, g_m \rangle$ for the subgroup generated by $g_1, \ldots, g_m$. Let N be a product of two safe primes p and q such that $p' = (p-1)/2$ and $q' = (q-1)/2$ are also primes. Consider the two sets

$$\mathcal{T} = \{(N, g, w, u, v, \alpha_1, \alpha_2) : type(\alpha_1) = 1, type(\alpha_2) = 2,$$

$$ord_N(g) = ord_N(u) = 2p'q', \langle g, u \rangle = Z_N^*, (w, v) \in (QR_N)^2\}$$

and

$$\mathcal{T}_{CDDH} = \{(N, g, w, u, v, \alpha_1, \alpha_2) \in \mathcal{T} : w = g^{2e} \bmod N,$$

$$v = u^{2e} \bmod N \text{ for some } e \in Z_{p'q'}\}$$

with the uniform distribution on each. The CDDH problem is to distinguish these two distributions.

Theorem 5. *The above undeniable signature scheme satisfies IV-CMA under the CDDH assumption in the random oracle model.*

Proof. Let A be an adversary which breaks IV-CMA with non-negligible probability ϵ. Then we will construct a composite decision Diffie-Hellman algorithm M with non-negligible probability ϵ' by running A as a subroutine.

Let $(N, g, w, u, v, \alpha_1, \alpha_2)$ be the challenge CDDH problem input to M. M first computes $\beta = g^2 \bmod N$. Let $\alpha_0 = 1$ and $\alpha_3 = \alpha_1 \alpha_2 \bmod N$. M runs A by feeding A with the verification key $(N, \beta, w, H, \alpha_0, \alpha_1, \alpha_2, \alpha_3)$ where H is a random oracle that will be simulated by M. We assume that when A requests a signature on a message m_j, it has already made the corresponding H-query on m_j.

When A makes a H-query for a message m_j, M chooses $x_j, y_j \in \{1, 2, \cdots, \lfloor N/2 \rfloor\}$ randomly and $i \in \{0, 1, 2, 3\}$ randomly, and returns $H(m_j) = (w^{x_j} v^{y_j})^2 / \alpha_i \bmod N$. M will maintain a H-query list (m_j, x_j, y_j, i).

When A makes a signing query for a message m_j, since we have assumed that A has already made the corresponding H-query on m_j, then $H(m_j) = (w^{x_j} u^{y_j})^2 / \alpha_i \bmod N$. M then computes $\sigma_j = g^{x_j} u^{y_j} \bmod N$ and returns σ_j as the corresponding signature.

Eventually, A outputs a message m^*. M then chooses a hidden bit b. If $b = 1$, M generates σ^* using the above signing process and returns σ^* as the signature. If $b = 0$, M chooses $\sigma^* \in Z_N^*$ randomly and returns σ^* as the signature.

Next, A performs some H queries and signing queries again with the restriction that no signing queries on m^* is allowed. Finally, A outputs a bit b' which it thinks is equal to the hidden bit b. If $b' = b$ then M outputs 1 as the answer and if $b' \neq b$ then M outputs 0 as the answer.

Notice that if $(N, g, w, u, v, \alpha_1, \alpha_2) \in \mathcal{T}_{CDDH}$, then the signing oracle behaves perfectly and the simulation is identical to a real attack. Thus we have

$$\Pr[M \text{ outputs } 1] = \Pr[b' = b] = \frac{1}{2} + \epsilon,$$

where ϵ is the advantage of algorithm A.

On the other hand, when the input is a random tuple of $\mathcal{T}$, the signatures generated by the signing oracle are with high probability invalid. The simulation is therefore not indistinguishable from a real attack. However, we can show as in [14, Appendix B] that the hidden bit b is independent of the simulation. That is,

$$\Pr[M \text{ outputs } 1] = \Pr[b' = b] = \frac{1}{2}.$$

It follows that the advantage of algorithm M

$$\epsilon' = \frac{1}{2} + \epsilon - \frac{1}{2} = \epsilon$$

which is non-negligible. □

Corollary 2. *The above undeniable signature scheme satisfies IV-FULL.*

Proof. From Theorem 5, Theorem 4 and Theorem 2 □

6   Conclusion

We have studied on the relationships among various notions of security of undeniable signature schemes, namely, UF-CMA, UF-FULL, IV-CMA and IV-FULL and shown some important relationships among them. We also proposed an undeniable signature scheme where its unforgeability is based on the factoring assumption and its invisibility is based on the CDDH assumption.

References

1. N. Attrapadung,Y. Cui, G. Hanaoka, H. Imai, K. Matsuura, P. Yang and R. Zhang. Relations among notions of security for identity based encryption schemes. *Cryptology ePrint Archive Report 2005/258*. Available from http://eprint.iacr.org/2005/258.
2. M. Bellare, A. Desai, D. Pointcheval and P. Rogaway. Relations among notions of security for public-key encryption schemes. *Advances in Cryptology — CRYPTO '98*, LNCS 1462, pp. 26–45, Springer-Verlag, 1998.

3. M. Bellare, O. Goldreich and A. Mityagin. The power of verification queries in message authentication and authenticated encryption. *Cryptology ePrint Archive Report 2004/309.* Available from http://eprint.iacr.org/2004/309.
4. M. Bellare and P. Rogaway. The exact security of digital signatures – how to sign with RSA and Rabin. *Advances in Cryptology — EUROCRYPT '96*, LNCS 1070, pp. 399–416, Springer-Verlag, 1996.
5. J. Boyar, D. Chaum, I. Damgård and T. Pedersen. Convertible undeniable signatures. *Advances in Cryptology — CRYPTO '90*, LNCS 537, pp. 189–208, Springer-Verlag, 1990.
6. J. Camenisch and M. Michels. Confirmer signature schemes secure against adaptive adversaries. *Advances in Cryptology — EUROCRYPT '00*, LNCS 1870, pp. 243–258, Springer-Verlag, 2000.
7. D. Chaum. Zero-knowledge undeniable signatures. *Advances in Cryptology — EUROCRYPT '90*, LNCS 473, pp. 458–464, Springer-Verlag, 1990.
8. D. Chaum. Designated confirmer signatures. *Advances in Cryptology — EUROCRYPT '94*, LNCS 950, pp. 86–91, Springer-Verlag, 1995.
9. T. Chaum and T. P. Pedersen. Wallet databases with observers. *Advances in Cryptology — CRYPTO '92*, LNCS 740, pp. 89–105, Springer-Verlag, 1993.
10. D. Chaum and H. van Antwerpen. Undeniable signatures. *Advances in Cryptology — CRYPTO '89*, LNCS 435, pp. 212–216, Springer-Verlag, 1989.
11. D. Chaum, E. van Heijst and B. Pfitzmann. Cryptographically strong undeniable signatures, unconditionally secure for the signer. *Advances in Cryptology — CRYPTO '91*, LNCS 576, pp. 470–484, Springer-Verlag, 1991.
12. I. Damgård and T. Pedersen. New convertible undeniable signature schemes. *Advances in Cryptology — EUROCRYPT '96*, LNCS 1070, pp. 372–386, Springer-Verlag, 1996.
13. A. Datta, R. Küsters, J.C. Mitchell and A. Ramanathan. On the relationships between notions of simulation-based security. *Theory of Cryptography Conference — TCC '05*, LNCS 3378, pp. 476–494, Springer-Verlag, 2005.
14. S. Galbraith and W. Mao. Invisibility and anonymity of undeniable and confirmer signatures. *Topics in Cryptology — CT-RSA '03*, LNCS 2612, pp. 80–97, Springer Verlag, 2003.
15. S. Galbraith, W. Mao and K. G. Paterson. RSA-based undeniable signatures for general moduli. *Topics in Cryptology — CT-RSA '02*, LNCS 2271, pp. 200–217, Springer Verlag, 2002.
16. R. Gennaro, H. Krawczyk and T. Rabin. RSA-based undeniable signatures. *Advances in Cryptology — CRYPTO '97*, LNCS 1294, pp. 132–149, Springer-Verlag, 1997.
17. O. Goldreich and Y. Oren. Definitions and properties of zero-knowledge proof systems. *Journal of Cryptology*, vol. 7, no. 1, pp. 1–32, Springer-Verlag, 1994.
18. S. Goldwasser, S. Micali and C. Rackoff. The knowledge complexity of interactive proof systems. *SIAM Journal on Computing*, vol. 18, pp. 186–208, 1989 (Preliminary version in 17th STOC, 1985).
19. S. Goldwasser, S. Micali and R. Rivest. A digital signature scheme secure against adaptive chosen-message attacks. *SIAM Journal on Computing*, vol. 17, no. 2, pp. 281–308, 1988.
20. M. Jakobsson, K. Sako and R. Impagliazzo. Designated verifier proofs and their applications. *Advances in Cryptology — EUROCRYPT '96*, LNCS 1070, pp. 143–154, Springer-Verlag, 1996.
21. K. Kurosawa and S.-H. Heng. 3-Move undeniable signature scheme. *Advances in Cryptology — EUROCRYPT '05*, LNCS 3494, pp. 181–197, Springer-Verlag, 2005.

22. K. Kurosawa and W. Ogata. Efficient Rabin-type digital signature scheme. *Design, Codes and Cryptography*, vol. 16, no. 1, pp. 53–64, 1999.
23. B. Libert and J.-J Quisquater. Identity based undeniable signatures. *Topics in Cryptology — CT-RSA '04*, LNCS 2964, pp. 112–125, Springer-Verlag, 2004.
24. J. Monnerat and S. Vaudenay. Undeniable signatures based on characters: how to sign with one bit. *Public Key Cryptography — PKC '04*, LNCS 2947, pp. 361–396, Springer-Verlag, 2004.
25. J. Monnerat and S. Vaudenay. Generic homomorphic undeniable signatures. *Advances in Cryptology — Asiacrypt '04*, LNCS 3329, pp. 354–371, Springer-Verlag, 2004.
26. W. Ogata, K. Kurosawa and S.-H. Heng. The security of the FDH variant of Chaum's undeniable scheme. *Public Key Cryptography — PKC '05*, LNCS 3386, pp. 328–345, Springer-Verlag, 2005.

Concurrent Blind Signatures Without Random Oracles

Aggelos Kiayias* and Hong-Sheng Zhou*

Computer Science and Engineering
University of Connecticut
Storrs, CT, USA
{aggelos, hszhou}@cse.uconn.edu

Abstract. We present a blind signature scheme that is efficient and provably secure without random oracles under concurrent attacks utilizing only four moves of short communication. The scheme is based on elliptic curve groups for which a bilinear map exists and on extractable and equivocal commitments. The unforgeability of the employed signature scheme is guaranteed by the LRSW assumption while the blindness property of our scheme is guaranteed by the Decisional Linear Diffie-Hellman assumption. We prove our construction secure under the above assumptions as well as Paillier's DCR assumption in the concurrent attack model of Juels, Luby and Ostrovsky from Crypto '97 using a common reference string. Our construction is the first efficient construction for blind signatures in such a concurrent model without random oracles. We present two variants of our basic protocol: first, a blind signature scheme where blindness still holds even if the public-key generation is maliciously controlled; second, a blind signature scheme that incorporates a "public-tagging" mechanism. This latter variant of our scheme gives rise to a partially blind signature with essentially the same efficiency and security properties as our basic scheme.

1   Introduction

Blind signatures were introduced by Chaum in [11] and proved to be a most useful cryptographic scheme that has been the basis of many complex cryptographic constructions including e-cash systems and e-voting schemes. Informally, a blind signature is a signature scheme that incorporates a signing protocol that allows the signer to sign a document submitted by a user blindly, i.e., without obtaining any information about the document itself.

It was observed early on (at least as early as [13], see also [27]) that blind signatures contain an instance of a secure function evaluation protocol in the following sense: the user possesses a private input m and a public-input pk which is the verification key of a digital signature algorithm, and the signer possesses a private input sk which is the signing-key; with this setup the user and the signer should execute a probabilistic secure function evaluation protocol that will allow

---

* Research partly supported by NSF CAREER Award CNS-0447808.

R. De Prisco and M. Yung (Eds.): SCN 2006, LNCS 4116, pp. 49–62, 2006.
© Springer-Verlag Berlin Heidelberg 2006

the user to compute σ, a signature on m under pk, without revealing m to the signer and without the signer revealing sk to the user. Given the complexity of general secure function evaluation though, [31,16], in early work on blind signatures this paradigm was not very motivating. A more motivating paradigm was found in divertible zero-knowledge proofs [24,22,12] and many blind signatures were subsequently designed in this line of reasoning [29,30,28,4,3,1] as well as the first attempt to give provably secure constructions (in the random oracle model) was due to [29], where blind signatures with three moves were proven secure in the random oracle model under the discrete-logarithm assumption assuming only logarithmically many messages were transmitted by the user. This result was later improved to polynomially many messages but five moves [28] and the round complexity was finally decreased to three moves and polynomially many messages in [3,1]. A two move protocol was presented in [5] assuming the RSA inversion oracle assumption. We stress that all these results were proven secure in the random oracle model.

Concurrency in the context of blind signatures was put forth by Juels, Luby and Ostrovsky [17] who presented the first security model for blind signatures that takes into account that the adversary may launch many concurrent sessions of the blind signing protocol (operating as either the user or the signer). Concurrency is particularly important since in implementations of blind signatures in e-voting and e-cash schemes, see e.g., [11,15,19], the signer is a multi-threaded server that accepts many concurrent sessions of users that are executing the signing protocol. Thus, it is of crucial importance to consider the security of blind signatures, when *(1)* a malicious signer attempts to defeat the blindness of many concurrently joining users, and *(2)* a coalition of malicious users attempts to extract information about the signing key of the multi-threaded signer server. Still, the design of schemes that satisfied such stronger models proved elusive. In fact, Lindell [20] showed that unbounded concurrent security for blind signatures modelled using black-box simulation is unattainable in the plain model (i.e., without any setup assumption). On the other hand, in the CRS model, Canetti et al. [10] gave a generic construction for multi-party secure function evaluation that achieves an even stronger notion of security than concurrency (universal composition) and can be used to solve (generically) the blind signature problem using a CRS. Note that this construction would not result in a practical scheme. Recently, Camenisch et al. [8] using a weaker model than that of [17] that only allowed sequential attacks presented a blind signature scheme based on the Strong-RSA assumption leaving as open problem the possibility of achieving concurrent security in an efficient scheme. Okamoto [23] presented an efficient blind signature scheme using a stronger variant of the SDH assumption [6]; based on the techniques we put forth in our work (which appeared originally in [18]) he also extended his blind signature scheme to handle concurrent attacks as well.

Our Contribution. In this paper, we give the first efficient construction for blind signatures to achieve concurrent security in the sense of [17] assuming a common reference string. The four-move interactions between the user and the signer in the signing protocol requires overall communication not exceeding 2 Kbytes (about 10.2 Kbits to be precise) for a full signature generation. Achieving this level of efficiency while simultaneously maintaining provability in a concurrency model required the careful composition of a number of cryptographic primitives. As our underlying digital signature scheme (i.e., the type of signature that is obtained by users) we use the elliptic curve based signature scheme of Camenisch and Lysyanskaya [9] (henceforth called a CL signature). We also employ a variant of Linear Encryption, an encryption scheme that was originally introduced in the context of group signatures by Boneh, Boyen and Shacham [7]. Here we find a novel use of this primitive in the context of blind signatures. In addition to these primitives, our construction makes essential use of discrete-logarithm equivocal commitments based on Pedersen commitments [26] and extractable commitments based on Paillier encryption [25].

The central idea of our construction is to use a variant of Linear Encryption to produce a very efficient secure function evaluation protocol for CL signatures that proceeds roughly as follows: the user selects on the fly a key for the encryption scheme and encrypts her message with it. The signer upon receiving this encryption takes advantage of the homomorphic properties of the encryption to blindly transform the ciphertext into a randomized encryption of a CL signature and then transmits the resulting rerandomized ciphertext back to the user. We make an essential use of the homomorphic properties of the underlying encryption in the efficient generation of non-adversarial randomness between the mutually distrustful players. In order to prove security under concurrent attacks a number of provisions have to be taken in the blind signature protocol design. Most importantly, in our signing protocol, both sides will be required to prove statements about their local computations. As a result, performing the whole protocol in four moves is one of the most delicate parts of our construction. The homomorphic encryption based interaction that is used for the secure signature computation needs to be paired with an extractable commitment. Moreover, an equivocal commitment is used for ensuring that no information leakage occurs from the user to the signer or vice versa. Finally, the signer, proves to the user that he is following the protocol specifications and is applying his signing key to the user's ciphertext whereas the user has to prove that he is consistent across his commitments. The construction is proven to satisfy the two properties of the [17] model as follows: the blindness property is ensured under the Decisional Composite Residuosity assumption of [25] and the Decision Linear Diffie-Hellman assumption of [7]. The unforgeability property is proven under the LRSW assumption of [21]. Note that the resulting signature from the signing protocol is about half the size of an RSA based Chaum blind signature.

We also present two variants of our basic protocol. (i) We consider a stronger adversarial model for blindness where the public-key is adversarially controlled; we show how it is possible to modify our basic protocol in a straightforward way to achieve this stronger blindness property. (ii) We provide an extension of our scheme that allows the public-tagging of blindly signed messages, i.e., all messages that are obtained by the users also contain a publicly known tag that is decided prior to the signing protocol execution. This extension is essentially equivalent to a partially blind signature construction, a notion that was formalized in [2]. Due to lack of space these protocols are omitted; please refer to the full version [18] for more details.

2   Preliminaries

Bilinear Groups. Let $\mathbb{G} = \langle g \rangle$ be a cyclic group of prime order p such that $e : \mathbb{G} \times \mathbb{G} \to \mathbb{G}_T$ is a bilinear map, i.e., for all $t, v \in \mathbb{G}$ and $a, b \in \mathbb{Z}$, it holds that $e(t^a, v^b) = e(t, v)^{ab}$ and e is non-trivial, i.e., $e(g, g) \neq 1$.

Camenisch-Lysyanskaya Signature. Camenisch and Lysyanskaya [9] proposed a digital signature scheme (we call it CL-signature for short) that was adaptively chosen message secure in the standard model. Our blind signature will be based on this signature scheme: *(1)* key generation algorithm $\texttt{gen}^{CL}$: generate the bilinear group parameter $(p, \mathbb{G}, \mathbb{G}_T, g, e)$; then choose $x, y \xleftarrow{r} \mathbb{Z}_p^*$, and compute $X = g^x$ and $Y = g^y$; set secret key as $sk = (x, y)$ and public key as $pk = (p, \mathbb{G}, \mathbb{G}_T, g, e; X, Y)$.   *(2)* signing algorithm $\texttt{sign}^{CL}$: on input message m, secret key $sk = (x, y)$, and public key $pk = (p, \mathbb{G}, \mathbb{G}_T, g, e; X, Y)$, choose a random $a \in \mathbb{G}$, and output the signature $\sigma = (a, a^y, a^{x+mxy})$.   *(3)* verification algorithm $\texttt{verify}^{CL}$: on input public key $pk = (p, \mathbb{G}, \mathbb{G}_T, g, e; X, Y)$, message m, and signature $\sigma = (a, b, c)$, check whether the verification equations $e(a, Y) = e(g, b)$ and $e(X, a)e(X, b)^m = e(g, c)$ hold.

The underlying assumption of CL-signatures is called the LRSW assumption, which was introduced by Lysyanskaya et al. [21].

Assumption 1 (LRSW Assumption). *Given the bilinear group parameters $(p, g, \mathbb{G}, \mathbb{G}_T, e)$. Let $X, Y \in \mathbb{G}, X = g^x, Y = g^y$ and define $O_{X,Y}()$ to be an oracle that, on input a value $m \in \mathbb{Z}_p$, it outputs a triple (a, b, c) such that $b = a^y$, and $c = a^{x+mxy}$ where $a \xleftarrow{r} \mathbb{G}$. Then, for all probabilistic polynomial time adversaries $\mathcal{A}$,*

$$\Pr \left[\begin{array}{c} x, y \in \mathbb{Z}_p; X = g^x; Y = g^y; (m, a, b, c) \leftarrow \mathcal{A}^{O_{X,Y}} : \\ m \notin \mathsf{Q} \wedge m \in \mathbb{Z}_p \wedge m \neq 0 \wedge a \in \mathbb{G} \wedge b = a^y \wedge c = a^{x+mxy} \end{array} \right] \leq \epsilon$$

where ϵ is a negligible function in security parameter λ, and Q is the set of queries that $\mathcal{A}$ made to $O_{X,Y}()$.

Linear Encryption. We give a description of Linear Encryption [7]. We call it LE for short. *(1)* $\texttt{gen}^{LE}$: the public key pk is a triple of generators $t, v, w \in \mathbb{G}$ and the secret key sk is the exponents $x, y \in \mathbb{Z}_p^*$ such that $t^x = v^y = w$.   *(2)* $\texttt{enc}^{LE}$: to encrypt a message $m \in \mathbb{G}$, choose random $a, b \in \mathbb{Z}_p$, and output the triple $(t^a, v^b, m \cdot w^{a+b})$.   *(3)* $\texttt{dec}^{LE}$: given an encryption (T, V, W), we recover the plaintext m as follows $m = \texttt{dec}^{LE}(T, V, W) = \frac{W}{T^x \cdot V^y}$.

The Linear encryption is based on the Decision Linear Diffie-Hellman assumption, which was introduced by Boneh et al. [7]. With $g \in \mathbb{G}$, along with arbitrary generators $t, v, w \in G$, consider the following problem:

Definition 1 (Decision Linear Diffie-Hellman Problem in $\mathbb{G}$). *Given* $t, v, w, t^\alpha, v^\beta, w^\gamma \in \mathbb{G}$ *as input, output* 1 *if* $\alpha + \beta = \gamma$ *and* 0 *otherwise.*

Now we define the advantage of an algorithm $\mathcal{A}$ in deciding the DLDH problem in $\mathbb{G}$ as

$$\mathsf{Adv}_{\mathsf{DLDH}}^{\mathcal{A}} = \left| \begin{array}{l} \Pr[1 \leftarrow \mathcal{A}(t, v, w, t^\alpha, v^\beta, w^{\alpha+\beta}) : t, v, w \in \mathbb{G}, \alpha, \beta \in \mathbb{Z}_p] \\ - \Pr[1 \leftarrow \mathcal{A}(t, v, w, t^\alpha, v^\beta, \chi) : t, v, w, \chi, \in \mathbb{G}, \alpha, \beta \in \mathbb{Z}_p] \end{array} \right|$$

Assumption 2 (Decision Linear Diffie-Hellman Assumption). *We say that the Decision Linear Diffie-Hellman assumption holds in $\mathbb{G}$ if for all PPT algorithms $\mathcal{A}$ it holds that $\mathsf{Adv}_{\mathsf{DLDH}}^{\mathcal{A}}$ is negligible in the security parameter λ.*

Paillier-Encryption. Here we describe Paillier encryption [25]: *(1)* gen^{Pai}: let p and q be random primes, $\mathsf{p} \neq \mathsf{q}$, $|\mathsf{p}| = |\mathsf{q}|$ and $\gcd(\mathsf{pq}, (\mathsf{p}-1)(\mathsf{q}-1)) = 1$; let $\mathsf{n} = \mathsf{pq}$, $\pi = \mathrm{lcm}(\mathsf{p}-1, \mathsf{q}-1)$, and $\mathsf{g} = (1+\mathsf{n})$; the key pair are $pk = (\mathsf{n}, \mathsf{g})$ and $sk = (\mathsf{p}, \mathsf{q})$. *(2)* enc^{Pai}: the plaintext set is $\mathbb{Z}_\mathsf{n}$; given a plaintext m, choose a random $\zeta \in \mathbb{Z}_\mathsf{n}^*$, and let the ciphertext be $E_m = \mathsf{enc}^{Pai}(m, \zeta) = \mathsf{g}^m \zeta^\mathsf{n} \bmod \mathsf{n}^2$. *(3)* dec^{Pai}: given a ciphertext E_m, let $K = \pi^{-1} \bmod \mathsf{n}$, then $m = \frac{((E_m)^{\pi K} \bmod \mathsf{n}^2) - 1}{\mathsf{n}} \bmod \mathsf{n}$.

The cryptosystem above has been proven semantically secure if and only if the Decisional Composite Residuosity (DCR) assumption [25] is true. The advantage of an algorithm $\mathcal{A}$ in deciding the DCR problem is defined as follows:

$$\mathsf{Adv}_{\mathsf{DCR}}^{\mathcal{A}} = \left| \Pr[1 \leftarrow \mathcal{A}(z) : z \in \mathbb{Z}_{\mathsf{n}^2}^*] - \Pr[1 \leftarrow \mathcal{A}(z) : z \in HR_{\mathsf{n}^2}^\mathsf{n}] \right|$$

where $HR_{\mathsf{n}^2}^\mathsf{n}$ is the subgroup of n-th residues modulo n^2.

Assumption 3 (Decisional Composite Residuosity Assumption). *We say that the DCR assumption holds in $\mathbb{G}$ if for all PPT algorithms $\mathcal{A}$ it holds that $\mathsf{Adv}_{\mathsf{DCR}}^{\mathcal{A}}$ is negligible in the security parameter λ.*

Commitment Schemes. A commitment scheme is a protocol with two stages, the commit stage and the decommit stage, between two parties, the committer and the receiver. A commitment scheme consists of a key generation algorithm gen which can be used to produce a public key pk, a commitment algorithm com which is used by the committer to produce a commitment to the message m and the decommitment information ζ, i.e., $(c, \zeta) \leftarrow \mathsf{com}_{pk}(m)$, and a decommitment verification algorithm dec which can be used by the receiver to verify the decommitment information ζ and the message m with respect to the commitment c, i.e., $\mathsf{dec}(c, m, \zeta) \in \{0, 1\}$. Frequently the decommitment information ζ is the random coins used by the commitment algorithm and we will write $c \leftarrow \mathsf{com}_{pk}(m, \zeta)$.

A commitment scheme satisfies two properties: *hiding*, the receiver can not obtain any information about m given $\mathsf{com}_{pk}(m, \zeta)$; and *binding*, the committer cannot change his mind about m later. In an *extractable* commitment, there is a trapdoor information xk associated to each public key pk that allows the trapdoor owner to compute m from any $\mathsf{com}_{pk}(m, \zeta)$. In an *equivocal* commitment on the other hand, there is a trapdoor information ek associated to each public key pk that allows a trapdoor owner to open c into any m.

Common Reference String Model. In the common reference string (CRS) model, we assume that each player can access a common string that is guaranteed to come from a prescribed distribution. Furthermore, no players (including the adversaries) will know the trapdoor information related to the procedure of choosing the string. The trapdoor will be known to the simulator in the proof of security. In practice, a trusted third party can generate the CRS by running the CRS generator K, i.e. $(\mathtt{crs}, \tau) \leftarrow \mathtt{K}(1^\lambda)$, and discarding the trapdoor τ. The string $\mathtt{crs}$ is published, and all parties receive it as additional input.

3   Formal Model for Blind Signatures

We revisit the formal model for blind signatures as introduced in [17] and we reformulate it to use a common reference string (CRS).

Definition 2 (Blind Signature Scheme). *A blind digital signature scheme consists of two interactive Turing machines (S, U) and two algorithms (gen,verify). Here S denotes the signer, and U the user.*

- *$\mathtt{gen}(1^\lambda)$ is a PPT key-generation algorithm which takes as an input a security parameter 1^λ and outputs a pair (pk, sk) of public and secret keys.*
- *$\mathsf{S}(pk, sk)$ and $\mathsf{U}(pk, m)$ is a pair of PPT interactive Turing machines, where both machines have the following tapes: read-only input tape, write-only output tape, a read/write work tape, a read-only random tape, and two communication tapes, a read-only and a write-only tape. They are both given on their input tapes as a common input a pk produced by the key generation algorithm. Additionally S is given on his input tape the corresponding secret key sk and U is given on his input tape a message m, where the length of all inputs must be polynomial in the security parameter 1^λ. Both U and S engage in an interactive protocol for some polynomial in λ number of moves. At the end of this protocol S outputs either completed or not-completed and U outputs either σ or $\bot$.*
- *$\mathtt{verify}(m, \sigma, pk)$ is a deterministic polynomial time algorithm, which outputs 1 or 0.*

The correctness requirement for the above is that for any message m, and for all random choices of the key generation algorithm, if both S and U follow the protocol then S always outputs completed, and if the output of the user is σ then $\mathtt{verify}(m, \sigma, pk) = 1$.

Note that in the CRS model, both S, U receive as additional input the $\mathtt{crs}$ string. The security properties for blind signatures defined in [17] are **blindness** and **unforgeability**. Below we revisit their modelling and we give detailed definitions for these properties in the CRS model.

Definition 3 (Blindness). *Assume $(\mathtt{crs}, \tau) \leftarrow \mathtt{K}(1^\lambda)$, $(pk, sk) \leftarrow \mathtt{gen}(1^\lambda)$. We define an oracle $\mathcal{I}^\phi$ with public input $(1^\lambda, \mathtt{crs}, pk)$ which simulates two user in-*

stantiations U^L *and* U^R, *where* $\phi \in \{0, 1\}$. *The adversary* $\mathcal{A}$ *will be communicating with this oracle trying to predict* ϕ *given input* $(1^\lambda, \text{crs}, pk, sk)$. *The oracle* $\mathcal{I}^\phi$ *operates as follows:*

- *Given* $\langle \text{challenge}, m_0, m_1 \rangle$, *the oracle* $\mathcal{I}^\phi$ *simulates two user instantiations* U^L *and* U^R *with input* pk *and the messages* m_ϕ *and* $m_{1-\phi}$ *respectively. The oracle* $\mathcal{I}^\phi$ *keeps a database with the state of each user instantiation; the state includes all coin tosses of the user instantiation and the contents of all tapes. The oracle uses* st^L *(resp.* st^R) *to record the state of* U^L *(resp.* U^R).

- *Given* $\langle \text{advance}, \rho, msg \rangle$, *where* $\rho \in \{L, R\}$, *the oracle* $\mathcal{I}^\phi$ *recovers the state of* st^ρ, *and simulates the user instantiation* U^ρ *with* msg *till* U^ρ *either terminates or returns a response to the signer. If* U^ρ *returns a response, then* $\mathcal{I}^\phi$ *returns this to* $\mathcal{A}$. *The oracle will record the current state* st, *i.e.* $st^\rho = st^\rho \| st$. *Note that this kind of query can be executed several times depending on the number of moves of the blind signature protocol.*

- *Given* $\langle \text{terminate}, msg^L, msg^R \rangle$, *the oracle* $\mathcal{I}^\phi$ *recovers the state* st^L *(resp.* st^R), *and simulates the user instantiation* U^L *(resp.* U^R) *with* msg^L *(resp.* msg^R) *till* U^L *(resp.* U^R) *terminates or fails. If both user instantiations terminate successfully and output two signatures, then the oracle returns these signatures to* $\mathcal{A}$, *otherwise returns* $(\perp, \perp)$.

Given any PPT $\mathcal{A}$, *we define its advantage against blindness as:*

$$\text{Adv}_{\text{blind}}^{\mathcal{A}}(\lambda) = \left| \Pr \left[\begin{array}{c} \phi \leftarrow \mathcal{A}^{\mathcal{I}^\phi(1^\lambda, \text{crs}, pk)}(1^\lambda, \text{crs}, pk, sk) : \\ \phi \xleftarrow{\text{r}} \{0,1\}, (\text{crs}, \tau) \leftarrow \text{K}(1^\lambda), (pk, sk) \leftarrow \text{gen}(1^\lambda) \end{array} \right] - \frac{1}{2} \right|$$

and say that the scheme satisfies the blindness property if $\text{Adv}_{\text{blind}}^{\mathcal{A}}(\lambda)$ *is negligible in* λ.

Definition 4 (Unforgeability). *We define an oracle* $\mathcal{I}$ *that is simulating concurrently an arbitrary number of signer instantiations. The oracle accepts two types of queries defined as follows:*

- $\langle \text{start}, msg \rangle$. *The oracle* $\mathcal{I}$ *selects a session identifier* sid, *and simulates the signer instantiation* S *with* msg *till* S *either terminates or returns a response. If the signer instance returns a response to the user,* $\mathcal{I}$ *returns this with the* sid *as an answer to the oracle query.* $\mathcal{I}$ *keeps a database with the state of* S *for the* sid; *the state includes all coin tosses of* S, *and the contents of all tapes.*

- $\langle \text{advance}, sid, msg \rangle$. *The oracle* $\mathcal{I}$ *looks up the table of sessions and recovers the state of* S *for the session with* sid *(if* sid *exists). Subsequently,* $\mathcal{I}$ *writes* msg *in the communication tape of* S *and simulates it till it either terminates or returns a response to the user. If it returns a message to the user,* $\mathcal{I}$ *returns this as an answer to the oracle query. If no session* sid *exists the oracle returns "fail."*

The oracle $\mathcal{I}$ *maintains a counter* ℓ *that counts the number of times that the oracle has successfully terminated a signer session. Each time that* $\mathcal{I}$ *successfully*

terminates a signer session it increases the counter ℓ by 1. A "one-more forgery"
adversary against the blind signature is a PPT machine $\mathcal{A}$ that is given as in-
put $(1^\lambda, \text{crs}, pk)$ where $(\text{crs}, \tau) \leftarrow \mathsf{K}(1^\lambda)$ and $(pk, sk) \leftarrow \text{gen}(1^\lambda)$. The adver-
sary $\mathcal{A}$ interacts with $\mathcal{I}(\text{crs}, pk, sk)$ and terminates by returning a sequence of
$(m_1, \sigma_1), ..., (m_{\ell'}, \sigma_{\ell'})$ where $m_i \neq m_j$ for all $i, j : 1 \leq i \neq j \leq \ell'$. We define
the advantage of $\mathcal{A}$ in the above attack by

$$\mathsf{Adv}_{\text{unforge}}^{\mathcal{A}}(\lambda) = \Pr[\wedge_{i=1}^{\ell'}(1 \leftarrow \text{verify}(pk, m_i, \sigma_i)) \wedge (\ell' > \ell)]$$

and say that the scheme is unforgeable if $\mathsf{Adv}_{\text{unforge}}^{\mathcal{A}}(\lambda)$ is negligible in λ.

4   The Proposed Scheme

We start the description of our construction by describing the setup definition
as well as the way that the involved parties, the user and the signer generate
their keys.

Public Parameters. The public parameter pub contains general information
about all protocol executions as well as a specific bilinear group parameter
$(p, \mathbb{G}, \mathbb{G}_T, g, e)$ appropriately selected.

Common Reference String. The common reference string crs includes two
parts, crs_1 and crs_2. First, we generate parameters for a Pedersen-like [26]
commitment scheme over an elliptic curve group: let $\mathbf{G} = \langle \mathbf{g} \rangle$ be a cyclic elliptic
curve group of prime order Q; select $r \xleftarrow{\text{r}} \mathbb{Z}_Q^*$ and compute $\mathbf{h} = \mathbf{g}^r$; set $\text{crs}_1 = \langle Q, \mathbf{g}, \mathbf{h}, \mathbf{G}, \mathcal{H} \rangle$, where $\mathcal{H} : \{0,1\}^* \to \mathbb{Z}_Q$ is a collision resistant hash function
and set the trapdoor to be $\tau_1 = r$. Then we generate parameters for the Paillier
encryption: let p and q be random primes, $\mathsf{p} \neq \mathsf{q}$, $|\mathsf{p}| = |\mathsf{q}|$ and $\gcd(\mathsf{pq}, (\mathsf{p} - 1)(\mathsf{q} - 1)) = 1$; let $\mathsf{n} = \mathsf{pq}$, and $\mathsf{g} = (1 + \mathsf{n})$; set $\text{crs}_2 = \langle \mathsf{n}, \mathsf{g} \rangle$ and the trapdoor
$\tau_2 = \langle \mathsf{p}, \mathsf{q} \rangle$. Now we have $\text{crs} = (\text{crs}_1, \text{crs}_2)$; the two trapdoors τ_1, τ_2 as well as
any random coins used for the generation of crs are discarded.

Signer Parameters. The signer S uses gen to generate his public and secret
parameters based on pub: select $x, y \xleftarrow{\text{r}} \mathbb{Z}_p^*$ and compute $X = g^x$, $Y = g^y$; set
$PK_\mathsf{S} = \langle X, Y \rangle$ and $SK_\mathsf{S} = \langle x, y \rangle$ as his key pair. We note that the parameters
selected above will be used for many executions of the signing protocol, while
the user has no such long-lived parameters. Still, as part of each signing protocol
the user will select some public and secret key that will have the lifetime of one
signing protocol execution. We stress that this is not a necessity and each user
may also keep his public-key parameters the same across signing protocol executions; in fact these parameters can be part of a PKI that all users are members
of. This will make the protocol's time-complexity somewhat more efficient on
the side of the user (but will have the cost of maintaining a user PKI).

User Parameters. Each user U generates his key pair on the fly: select $w \xleftarrow{\text{r}} \mathbb{G}\backslash\{1\}$, $\delta, \xi \xleftarrow{\text{r}} \mathbb{Z}_p^*$, and set $t, v \in \mathbb{G}$ such that $t^\delta = v^\xi = w$; set $PK_\mathsf{U} = \langle t, v, w \rangle$
and $SK_\mathsf{U} = \langle \delta, \xi \rangle$ as his key-pair.

Choice of Parameter Lengths. The length of each parameter p, n, Q is ν_p, ν_{n}, ν_Q respectively and should be selected so that the following are satisfied: (i) The DLDH assumption holds over the bilinear group parameter $(p, \mathbb{G}, \mathbb{G}_T, g, e)$, (ii) The LSRW assumption holds over the bilinear group parameter $(p, \mathbb{G}, \mathbb{G}_T, g, e)$, (iii) The discrete-logarithm (DLOG) assumption holds over the elliptic curve cyclic group $\mathbf{G}$, (iv) The DCR assumption holds over $\mathbb{Z}^*_{\mathsf{n}^2}$. Based on the present state of the art with respect to the solvability of the above problems, a possible choice of the parameters is for example $\nu_p = 171$ bits, $\nu_{\mathsf{n}} = 1024$ bits, $\nu_Q = 171$ bits.

Signing Protocol. We give a high-level description of our protocol before presenting it in detail. (1) First, both the user and the signer obtain the public inputs pub, crs, and PK_S, the signer gets the private input SK_S, and the user gets the private input message m. (2) Then the user generates his key pair $(PK_\mathsf{U}, SK_\mathsf{U})$ for Linear Encryption, and keeps SK_U secret; the user generates a Paillier ciphertext for message m which is used as an extractable commitment; the user generates a special Linear Encryption ciphertext for m which will be signed by the signer. (3) To guarantee that the Linear Encryption ciphertext and the Paillier ciphertext are consistent, the user interleaves within the protocol execution a 3-move Σ-protocol that shows the consistency of the commitment and the encryption. This protocol employs an equivocal Pedersen commitment scheme to allow zero-knowledge in the concurrent setting (cf. [14]). When the signer successfully verifies the 3-move protocol which was initialized by the user, he will transform the Linear Encryption ciphertext by using his signing key SK_S and appropriately rerandomize it. This will result in the encryption of a CL-signature which will be recovered by the user using his secret key SK_U. (4) To guarantee that the signer follows the protocol specifications, the signer is required to interleave a 3-move Σ-protocol as well in order to show that he is applying his secret-key appropriately on the Linear Encryption ciphertext that is provided by the user. Again we employ an equivocal Pedersen commitment to allow for concurrent zero-knowledge. (5) When the user verifies successfully the final step of the signing protocol computation, he decrypts the CL-signature from the signer's ciphertext using his secret-key SK_U and obtains a CL-signature for the message m. Then he refreshes the randomness of the signature taking advantage of the homomorphic property of CL-signatures.

Σ-protocols and Round-complexity. In our signing protocol we employ two Σ-protocols from both sides of the interaction. Both these protocols have the form $\langle commitment; challenge; response, decommitment \rangle$. A subtle difficulty in the design of our protocol is that if the two Σ-protocols are executed sequentially they will result in an overall round complexity of six moves. In order to maintain the four-move protocol complexity we want to "start" the Σ-protocol for the signer side before the user side Σ-protocol terminates. Nevertheless this will violate the security property of our scheme. So, in order to allow an early start of the signer side Σ-protocol we have the signer commit to the value he will prove a statement about and open the commitment *only in case* the user's side Σ-protocol verifies.

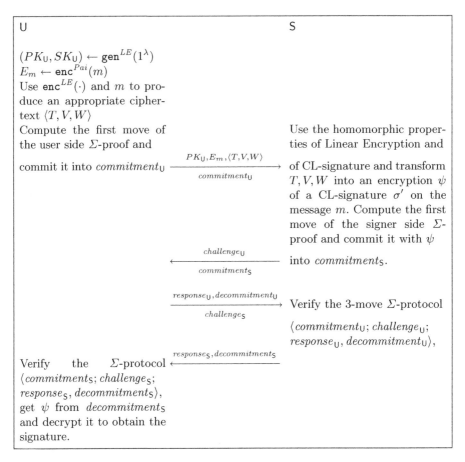

Fig. 1. Overview of our blind signature generation protocol

We outline the high-level description of our signing protocol in figure 1. In the first step, the user U prepares two different encryptions of his private input m, called E_m and $\langle T, V, W \rangle$. Moreover, it computes the first move of a Σ-protocol that shows the consistency of the two encryptions and commits to it into $commitment_U$. In the second step, the signer prepares an encryption ψ that can be decrypted by the user into a CL-signature but does not transmit yet this value to the user. Instead, it prepares the first move of a Σ-protocol that shows that he computed ψ correctly and commits to ψ as well as the first move into $commitment_S$. In the third step, the user, given the challenge of the signer, completes the Σ-protocol that shows he computed the two encryptions E_m and $\langle T, V, W \rangle$ in a consistent way and transmits to the signer the decommitment information necessary to verify the consistency of the ciphertexts. In the fourth step, the signer verifies the Σ-protocol of the user and if it is accepted, the signer completes his Σ-protocol and transmits to the user the encryption ψ as well as the decommitment information necessary to verify the claim that ψ

$$\mathtt{crs} = \langle Q, \mathbf{g}, \mathbf{h}, \mathbf{G}, \mathcal{H}; \mathsf{n}, g \rangle; \mathtt{pub} = \langle p, g, \mathbb{G}, \mathbb{G}_T, e \rangle; PK_S = \langle X, Y \rangle$$

$\boxed{\mathsf{U}}$	$\boxed{\mathsf{S}}$
$MSG = \langle m \rangle,\ m \in [0, 2^{\nu_p}]$	$SK_S = \langle x, y \rangle$

$(PK_U, SK_U) \leftarrow \mathbf{gen}^{LE}(1^\lambda)$
$PK_U = \langle t, v, w \rangle,\ SK_U = \langle \delta, \xi \rangle$
$\widehat{m} \xleftarrow{\mathit{r}} \pm[0, 2^{\lambda_0 + \lambda_1 + \nu_p}],$
$A_m, B_m \xleftarrow{\mathit{r}} \mathbb{Z}_{\mathsf{n}}^*,\ \mu_1 \xleftarrow{\mathit{r}} \mathbb{Z}_Q$
$\alpha, k, l, \widehat{k}, \widehat{l} \xleftarrow{\mathit{r}} \mathbb{Z}_p,\ \theta \xleftarrow{\mathit{r}} \mathbb{G} \backslash \{1\}$
$E_m = \mathbf{g}^m (A_m)^{\mathsf{n}} \bmod \mathsf{n}^2$
$\widehat{E}_m = \mathbf{g}^{\widehat{m}} (B_m)^{\mathsf{n}} \bmod \mathsf{n}^2$

$\quad\quad d_1 \xleftarrow{\mathit{r}} \{0,1\}^{\lambda_1}, \mu_2 \xleftarrow{\mathit{r}} \mathbb{Z}_Q$
$\quad\quad a', k', l', \widehat{x}, \widehat{k}', \widehat{l}' \xleftarrow{\mathit{r}} \mathbb{Z}_p$

$T = t^k,\ V = v^l,\ W = \theta^m w^{k+l}$ $\xrightarrow{\ PK_U, E_m\ }$ $a' = \theta^{\alpha'},\ b' = \theta^{y\alpha'}$
$\xleftarrow{\langle \theta, T, V, W \rangle, C_1}$

$\widehat{T} = t^{\widehat{k}},\ \widehat{V} = v^{\widehat{l}},\ \widehat{W} = \theta^{\widehat{m}} w^{\widehat{k}+\widehat{l}}$ $\quad T' = T^{xy\alpha'} t^{k'\alpha'},$
$\omega_1 = \mathcal{H}(\widehat{E}_m, \widehat{T}, \widehat{V}, \widehat{W}),$ $\quad V' = V^{xy\alpha'} v^{l'\alpha'},$
$C_1 = \mathbf{g}^{\omega_1} \mathbf{h}^{\mu_1}$ $\quad W' = W^{xy\alpha'} \theta^{x\alpha'} w^{k'\alpha'+l'\alpha'}$
$\quad L_T = e(T, b')^{\widehat{x}} e(t, a')^{\widehat{k}'}$
$\quad L_V = e(V, b')^{\widehat{x}} e(v, a')^{\widehat{l}'}$
$\quad L_W = (e(W, b') e(\theta, a'))^{\widehat{x}} \cdot$
$\quad\quad\quad e(w, a')^{\widehat{k}'+\widehat{l}'}$
$\quad \omega_2 = \mathcal{H}(a', b', T', V', W',$
$\quad\quad\quad L_T, L_V, L_W)$

$d_2 \xleftarrow{\mathit{r}} \{0,1\}^{\lambda_2}$ $\xleftarrow{\quad d_1, C_2 \quad}$ $C_2 = \mathbf{g}^{\omega_2} \mathbf{h}^{\mu_2}$

$s_m = \widehat{m} - d_1 m \quad (\text{in } \mathbb{Z})$
$s_k = \widehat{k} - d_1 k,\ s_l = \widehat{l} - d_1 l$
$F_m = B_m (A_m)^{-d_1} \bmod \mathsf{n}$ $\xrightarrow{d_2, \langle s_m, s_k, s_l, F_m \rangle}$ $E_m \in^? \mathbb{Z}_{\mathsf{n}^2}^*,$
$\xleftarrow{\langle \widehat{E}_m, \widehat{T}, \widehat{V}, \widehat{W}, \mu_1 \rangle}$

$\quad s_m \in^? \pm[0, 2^{\lambda_0 + \lambda_1 + \nu_p + 1}]$
$\quad \omega_1 = \mathcal{H}(\widehat{E}_m, \widehat{T}, \widehat{V}, \widehat{W}),$
$\quad C_1 =^? \mathbf{g}^{\omega_1} \mathbf{h}^{\mu_1}$
$\quad \widehat{E}_m =^? \mathbf{g}^{s_m} F_m^{\mathsf{n}} E_m^{d_1} \bmod \mathsf{n}^2$
$\quad \widehat{T} =^? t^{s_k} T^{d_1},\ \widehat{V} =^? v^{s_l} V^{d_1}$

$\omega_2 = \mathcal{H}(a', b', T', V', W',$ $\quad \widehat{W} =^? \theta^{s_m} w^{s_k + s_l} W^{d_1}$
$\quad\quad L_T, L_V, L_W)$ $\quad s_x = \widehat{x} - d_2 x,$

$C_2 =^? \mathbf{g}^{\omega_2} \mathbf{h}^{\mu_2}$ $\xleftarrow[\ V', W', L_T, L_V, L_W, \mu_2 \rangle\ ]{\langle s_x, s_{k'}, s_{l'} \rangle, \langle a', b', T',}$ $s_{k'} = \widehat{k}' - d_2 k',\ s_{l'} = \widehat{l}' - d_2 l'$

$e(a', Y) =^? e(b', g)$
$L_T =^? e(T, b')^{s_x} e(t, a')^{s_{k'}} \cdot$
$\quad\quad\quad e(T', \theta)^{d_2}$
$L_V =^? e(V, b')^{s_x} e(v, a')^{s_{l'}} \cdot$
$\quad\quad\quad e(V', \theta)^{d_2}$
$L_W =^? (e(W, b') e(\theta, a'))^{s_x} \cdot$
$\quad e(w, a')^{s_{k'} + s_{l'}} e(W', \theta)^{d_2}$
$a = (a')^\alpha,\ b = (b')^\alpha,$
$c = \left(\frac{W'}{T'^\delta V'^\xi} \right)^\alpha,\ \sigma = \langle a, b, c \rangle$
output $(m; \sigma)$

Fig. 2. Blind signature generation protocol

is correctly computed based on the signer's public-key. Finally the user verifies the Σ-protocol and if accepted it outputs the computed blind signature. The detailed description of the protocol is shown in figure 2. Note that $d_1 < p$, $d_2 < p$, i.e. $\lambda_1 < \nu_p$, $\lambda_2 < \nu_p$. For example $\lambda_0 = \lambda_1 = \lambda_2 = 80$ bits.

Signature Verification. Given a message-signature pair $(m; \sigma)$, where $\sigma = \langle a, b, c \rangle$, the verification algorithm is based on the two verification equations below: $e(a, Y) = e(g, b)$ and $e(X, a)e(X, b)^m = e(g, c)$.

Correctness and Security. The correctness and security of our scheme is captured by Theorem 4 (refer to the full version [18] for proof details).

Theorem 4. *If both the signer and the user follow the signing protocol, the resulting signature satisfies the verification with probability 1; under the LRSW assumption, the proposed scheme is unforgeable; under the DLDH assumption, the proposed scheme is blind.*

References

1. M. Abe. A secure three-move blind signature scheme for polynomially many signatures. In B. Pfitzmann, editor, *EUROCRYPT 2001*, volume 2045 of *Lecture Notes in Computer Science*, pages 136–151. Springer, 2001.
2. M. Abe and E. Fujisaki. How to date blind signatures. In K. Kim and T. Matsumoto, editors, *ASIACRYPT 1996*, volume 1163 of *Lecture Notes in Computer Science*, pages 244–251. Springer, 1996.
3. M. Abe and M. Ohkubo. Provably secure fair blind signatures with tight revocation. In C. Boyd, editor, *ASIACRYPT 2001*, volume 2248 of *Lecture Notes in Computer Science*, pages 583–602. Springer, 2001.
4. M. Abe and T. Okamoto. Provably secure partially blind signatures. In M. Bellare, editor, *CRYPTO 2000*, volume 1880 of *Lecture Notes in Computer Science*, pages 271–286. Springer, 2000.
5. M. Bellare, C. Namprempre, D. Pointcheval, and M. Semanko. The power of RSA inversion oracles and the security of Chaum's RSA-based blind signature scheme. In P. F. Syverson, editor, *Financial Cryptography 2001*, volume 2339 of *Lecture Notes in Computer Science*, pages 319–338. Springer, 2001.
6. D. Boneh and X. Boyen. Short signatures without random oracles. In C. Cachin and J. Camenisch, editors, *EUROCRYPT 2004*, volume 3027 of *Lecture Notes in Computer Science*, pages 56–73. Springer, 2004.
7. D. Boneh, X. Boyen, and H. Shacham. Short group signatures. In M. K. Franklin, editor, *CRYPTO 2004*, volume 3152 of *Lecture Notes in Computer Science*, pages 41–55. Springer, 2004.
8. J. Camenisch, M. Koprowski, and B. Warinschi. Efficient blind signatures without random oracles. In C. Blundo and S. Cimato, editors, *SCN 2004*, volume 3352 of *Lecture Notes in Computer Science*, pages 134–148. Springer, 2004.
9. J. Camenisch and A. Lysyanskaya. Signature schemes and anonymous credentials from bilinear maps. In M. K. Franklin, editor, *CRYPTO 2004*, volume 3152 of *Lecture Notes in Computer Science*, pages 56–72. Springer, 2004.
10. R. Canetti, Y. Lindell, R. Ostrovsky, and A. Sahai. Universally composable two-party and multi-party secure computation. In *STOC 2002*, pages 494–503, 2002. Full version at `http://www.cs.biu.ac.il/~lindell/PAPERS/uc-comp.ps`.

11. D. Chaum. Blind signatures for untraceable payments. In D. Chaum, R. L. Rivest, and A. T. Sherman, editors, *CRYPTO 1982*, pages 199–203. Plemum Press, 1982.

12. L. Chen, I. Damgård, and T. P. Pedersen. Parallel divertibility of proofs of knowledge (extended abstract). In A. De Santis, editor, *EUROCRYPT 1994*, volume 950 of *Lecture Notes in Computer Science*, pages 140–155. Springer, 1994.

13. I. Damgård. Payment systems and credential mechanisms with provable security against abuse by individuals. In S. Goldwasser, editor, *CRYPTO 1988*, volume 403 of *Lecture Notes in Computer Science*, pages 328–335. Springer, 1988.

14. I. Damgård. Efficient concurrent zero-knowledge in the auxiliary string model. In B. Preneel, editor, *EUROCRYPT 2000*, volume 1807 of *Lecture Notes in Computer Science*, pages 418–430. Springer, 2000.

15. A. Fujioka, T. Okamoto, and K. Ohta. A practical secret voting scheme for large scale elections. In J. Seberry and Y. Zheng, editors, *ASIACRYPT 1992*, volume 718 of *Lecture Notes in Computer Science*, pages 244–251. Springer, 1992.

16. O. Goldreich, S. Micali, and A. Wigderson. How to play any mental game or A completeness theorem for protocols with honest majority. In *STOC 1987*, pages 218–229. ACM, 1987.

17. A. Juels, M. Luby, and R. Ostrovsky. Security of blind digital signatures (extended abstract). In B. S. Kaliski Jr., editor, *CRYPTO 1997*, volume 1294 of *Lecture Notes in Computer Science*, pages 150–164. Springer, 1997.

18. A. Kiayias and H.-S. Zhou. Concurrent blind signatures without random oracles. In *Cryptology ePrint Archive: Report 2005/435*, 2005. http://eprint.iacr.org/2005/435/.

19. K. Kim. Lessons from Internet voting during 2002 FIFA WorldCup Korea/Japan(TM). In *DIMACS Workshop on Electronic Voting – Theory and Practice*, 2004.

20. Y. Lindell. Bounded-concurrent secure two-party computation without setup assumptions. In *STOC 2003*, pages 683–692. ACM, 2003. Full version at http://www.cs.biu.ac.il/~lindell/PAPERS/conc2party-upper.ps.

21. A. Lysyanskaya, R. L. Rivest, A. Sahai, and S. Wolf. Pseudonym systems. In H. M. Heys and C. M. Adams, editors, *Selected Areas in Cryptography 1999*, volume 1758 of *Lecture Notes in Computer Science*, pages 184–199. Springer, 1999.

22. T. Okamoto. Provably secure and practical identification schemes and corresponding signature schemes. In E. F. Brickell, editor, *CRYPTO 1992*, volume 740 of *Lecture Notes in Computer Science*, pages 31–53. Springer, 1992.

23. T. Okamoto. Efficient blind and partially blind signatures without random oracles. In S. Halevi and T. Rabin, editors, *TCC 2006*, volume 3876 of *Lecture Notes in Computer Science*, pages 80–99. Springer, 2006. An extended version at http://eprint.iacr.org/2006/102/.

24. T. Okamoto and K. Ohta. Divertible zero knowledge interactive proofs and commutative random self-reducibility. In J.-J. Quisquater and J. Vandewalle, editors, *EUROCRYPT 1989*, volume 434 of *Lecture Notes in Computer Science*, pages 134–148. Springer, 1989.

25. P. Paillier. Public-key cryptosystems based on composite degree residuosity classes. In J. Stern, editor, *EUROCRYPT 1999*, volume 1592 of *Lecture Notes in Computer Science*, pages 223–238. Springer, 1999.

26. T. P. Pedersen. Non-interactive and information-theoretic secure verifiable secret sharing. In J. Feigenbaum, editor, *CRYPTO 1991*, volume 576 of *Lecture Notes in Computer Science*, pages 129–140. Springer, 1991.

27. B. Pfitzmann and M. Waidner. How to break and repair a "provably secure" untraceable payment system. In J. Feigenbaum, editor, *CRYPTO 1991*, volume 576 of *Lecture Notes in Computer Science*, pages 338–350. Springer, 1991.

28. D. Pointcheval. Strengthened security for blind signatures. In K. Nyberg, editor, *EUROCRYPT 1998*, volume 1403 of *Lecture Notes in Computer Science*, pages 391–405. Springer, 1998.

29. D. Pointcheval and J. Stern. Provably secure blind signature schemes. In K. Kim and T. Matsumoto, editors, *ASIACRYPT 1996*, volume 1163 of *Lecture Notes in Computer Science*, pages 252–265. Springer, 1996.

30. D. Pointcheval and J. Stern. New blind signatures equivalent to factorization (extended abstract). In *CCS 1997*, pages 92–99. ACM, 1997.

31. A. C. Yao. How to generate and exchange secrets (extended abstract). In *FOCS 1986*, pages 162–167. IEEE Computer Society, 1986.

Universal Designated Verifier Signatures Without Random Oracles or Non-black Box Assumptions

Fabien Laguillaumie[1], Benoît Libert[2], and Jean-Jacques Quisquater[2]

[1] Projet TANC - INRIA Futurs
Laboratoire d'informatique (LIX)
École polytechnique, 91128 Palaiseau cedex, France
[2] UCL Crypto Group
Place du Levant, 3. B-1348 Louvain-La-Neuve, Belgium

Abstract. Universal designated verifier signatures (UDVS) were introduced in 2003 by Steinfeld *et al.* to allow signature holders to monitor the verification of a given signature in the sense that any plain signature can be publicly turned into a signature which is only verifiable by some specific designated verifier. Privacy issues, like non-dissemination of digital certificates, are the main motivations to study such primitives. In this paper, we propose two fairly efficient UDVS schemes which are secure (in terms of unforgeability and anonymity) in the *standard model* (i.e. without random oracles). Their security relies on algorithmic assumptions which are much more *classical* than assumptions involved in the two only known UDVS schemes in standard model to date. The latter schemes, put forth by Zhang *et al.* in 2005 and Vergnaud in 2006, rely on the Strong Diffie-Hellman assumption and the strange-looking *knowledge of exponent assumption* (KEA). Our schemes are obtained from Waters's signature and they do not need the KEA assumption. They are also the first random oracle-free constructions with the anonymity property.

1 Introduction

Many electronic applications have a crucial need for privacy which has been of central interest in the cryptographic community since the early eighties with the introduction of "special-purpose signatures". In 2003, Steinfeld *et al.* [31] suggested the idea of transforming a digital signature into a certain special signature (designated verifier). This notion is very useful in the design of sensitive e-applications with privacy issues. In this paper, we make a step forward in this area by designing efficient schemes which are secure without random oracles under more classical assumptions than the previous secure schemes that are secure in a standard model of computation.

Designated Verifier Signatures. Designated verifier proofs were introduced in 1996 by Jakobsson, Sako and Impagliazzo [19] in order to serve during confirmation and denial procedures of undeniable signatures [11] with the motivation to face *blackmailing* or *mafia* attacks. Designated verifier signatures (DVS) were

R. De Prisco and M. Yung (Eds.): SCN 2006, LNCS 4116, pp. 63–77, 2006.
© Springer-Verlag Berlin Heidelberg 2006

built using designated verifier proofs to convince a unique verifier chosen by the signer so that the verifier cannot transfer his conviction regarding the correctness of the signature. Roughly speaking, DVS schemes were obtained from Jakobsson *et al.*'s designated verifier proofs via the Fiat-Shamir heuristic [15].

Several years after the seminal paper of Jakobsson *et al.* [19], many new schemes appeared in the literature, but not always with a precise formalization of security requirements. The first "modern" scheme, proposed by Saeednia *et al.* in 2003 [28], was based on Schnorr's signature [30] but it still was not supported by a formal security model. At Asiacrypt'03, Steinfeld, Bull, Wang and Pieprzyk [31] gave a new proper definition of unforgeability. Laguillaumie and Vergnaud [22] subsequently adapted the notion of anonymity for undeniable signatures to the context of DVS schemes: they defined the *privacy signer's identity*, which protects the anonymity of the signer and captures the notion of *strong* DVS introduced in [19]. The notion of DVS schemes was then extended in [23] to allow the designation of several verifiers. More recently, Bender, Katz and Morselli [6] described 2-user ring signatures that immediately give rise to designated verifier signatures in the standard model.

Universal Designated Verifier Signature. Along with a formal security model for DVS schemes, Steinfeld *et al.* [31] defined a new useful property for traditional signatures. Basically, anyone holding a valid digital signature should be able to transform it so that only a specific user is able to ascertain the correctness of the signature. This transformation removes the self-authenticating property of signatures, and the resulting process was called *universal designated verifier signatures* (UDVS). At PKC'04, Steinfeld, Wang and Pierpzyk [32] proposed UDVS extensions of Schnorr and RSA signatures. A further extension termed "universal multi-designated verifier signatures" was considered in [26].

Except [6], all aforementioned works conduct security analyzes in the random oracle model [5] where hash functions are viewed as idealized random functions. As security in this model does *not* [10] imply the security in the real world, an important effort is currently achieved to avoid it and obtain security results in the standard model. A pairing-based random oracle-free signature algorithm due to Boneh and Boyen [7] is often used in the design of special-purpose signatures such as UDVS schemes put forth by Zhang *et al.* [35] and Vergnaud [33]. Nonetheless, the computational assumption (called Strong Diffie-Hellman assumption or SDH for short) underlying the Boneh-Boyen scheme is ad-hoc and non-standard. Besides, security proofs of schemes in [35, 33] additionally need an even stronger and odd assumption known as the *knowledge-of-exponent assumption*[1] (KEA) [13, 18, 4] which is *non-black box* in that security reductions from this assumption entail some kind of access to the internal state of the adversary.

---

[1] Intuitively, this assumption states that, given $(g, h = g^a)$ in a cyclic group $\mathbb{G} = \langle g \rangle$, the only way to generate pairs $(y_1, y_2) \in \mathbb{G} \times \mathbb{G}$ s.t. $y_2 = y_1^a$ without knowing a is to set $y_1 = g^r$ and $y_2 = h^r$ for a randomly chosen r. Any adversary $\mathcal{A}$ producing such a pair (y_1, y_2) necessarily "knows" the exponent r that could be extracted by accessing $\mathcal{A}$'s memory.

Our contributions. Avoiding random oracles in security proofs often leads to use strong and ad-hoc assumptions. Hence, actual security benefits of this break-through are not always clear. The only secure UDVS schemes in the standard model [35, 33] rely on the combined SDH and KEA assumptions. The former was recently reconsidered [12] and the latter is non-black box and so odd that it is generally disliked and avoided whenever possible although it holds in generic groups [14]. It was shown in [33] that the KEA may be avoided in [35, 33], but both constructions then have a security resting on a very exotic assumption.

In this work, we aim at obtaining UDVS schemes satisfying strong security notions in the standard model and under more classical assumptions. We start from Waters's signature [34] which is (not strongly) existentially unforgeable under the Diffie-Hellman assumption in groups equipped with bilinear maps. We turn it into a UDVS scheme which is unforgeable under an alleviated version of the Gap Bilinear Diffie-Hellman assumption and protects the anonymity of signers under the Decisional Bilinear Diffie-Hellman assumption.

In a second step, we use a technique due to Boneh, Shen and Waters [9] to make our scheme *strongly* unforgeable. The main motivation to consider such an enhanced unforgeability is two-fold. First, it allows for a security resting on the weaker Bilinear Diffie-Hellman assumption (in other words, we bypass the use of a fancy decision oracle in the proof) at the expense of a loss of "tightness" in the reduction. Yet, the security of this variant relies on an assumption whose strength is totally independent of the number of adversarial queries (unlike [35, 33]). Underlying assumptions aside, our second scheme features a provable anonymity in a stronger sense (i.e. in a game where verification queries are allowed to adversaries). Our constructions turn out to be the *only* random oracle-free UDVS that meet an anonymity property in the "find-then-guess" sense following [22]. Indeed, solutions given in [35, 33] are provably not anonymous in this sense.

2   Ingredients

2.1   Universal Designated Verifier Signatures

Definition 1 (UDVS schemes). *A* universal designated verifier signature *scheme* UDVS *is a 5-tuple* UDVS = (Σ, Register, VKeyGen, Designate, DVerify) *of algorithms parameterized by a security parameter* k.

- Σ = (Setup, KeyGen, Sign, Verify) *is a traditional digital signature scheme;*
- UDVS.Register *is a protocol between a "key registration authority" (KRA) and a user, both taking as input public parameters and the verifier's public key* pk_v. *The outcome is a notification decision from the KRA[2];*
- UDVS.VKeyGen *is a probabilistic algorithm which takes public parameters as input, and produces a pair of keys* (sk_V, pk_V) *for the designated verifier;*

---

[2] The protocol typically consists in having the KRA check that users know their private key.

- *UDVS.Designate is a (possibly probabilistic) algorithm which takes as inputs public parameters, a public key pk_S, a message m, a putative signature σ on m with respect to the public key pk_S, and the public key of a designated verifier pk_V, and produces a designated verifier signature $\tilde{\sigma}$;*
- *UDVS.DVerify is a deterministic algorithm which takes as inputs public parameters, a message m, a putative designated verifier signature $\tilde{\sigma}$, a public key pk_S, a pair of keys (sk_V, pk_V). The output is 1 if the signature $\tilde{\sigma}$ is accepted and 0 otherwise.*

The usual correctness requirement imposes that correctly formed plain or designated signatures are always accepted by the relevant verification algorithm.

In terms of security, an UDVS scheme must fit a natural variant of the standard notion of *existential unforgeability under chosen-message attacks* [17]. It should also achieve two anonymity properties: (1) the notion of (unconditional) *source hiding* which is the ambiguity about whom among the signer and the designated verifier a signature emanates from; (2) the *signer's privacy*, which is analogous to the notion of anonymity for undeniable signatures.

Source hiding. An UDVS scheme is *source hiding* if there exists an algorithm that takes as input only the secret key of the designated verifier and which produces bit strings which are perfectly indistinguishable (even knowing all secret keys) from the distribution of actual designated verifier signatures.

Unforgeability. We consider the notion of unforgeability introduced in [32] which is an extension of the *chosen-message* security introduced in [17]. Informally speaking, an attacker is given a signer's public key pk_S, a designated verifier's public key pk_V and access to a signing oracle and a verification oracle. He should be unable to produce a signature on a new message.

Definition 2. *An UDVS scheme is said (not strongly) existentially unforgeable if no PPT adversary $\mathcal{F}$ has a non-negligible advantage in the following game.*

1. *The challenger $\mathcal{C}$ takes as input a security parameter k and executes* params $\leftarrow$ *UDVS.Σ.Setup(k), $(sk_S^\star, pk_S^\star) \leftarrow$ UDVS.Σ.KeyGen$(k,$ params$)$, $(sk_V^\star, pk_V^\star) \leftarrow$ UDVS.VKeyGen$(k,$ params$)$. It gives $pk_S^\star$ and $pk_V^\star$ to the forger $\mathcal{F}$ and keeps $sk_S^\star$ and $sk_V^\star$ to itself.*
2. *The forger $\mathcal{F}$ can issue the following queries:*
   i) a registration query for a public key pk; the attacker engages in the registration protocol with the KRA;
   ii) a signing query for some message m; the challenger $\mathcal{C}$ executes $\sigma \leftarrow$ UDVS.Σ.Sign$(k,$ params$, m, sk_S^\star)$ and hands σ to $\mathcal{F}$;
   iii) a verification query for pairs $(m, \tilde{\sigma})$ of his choice; $\mathcal{C}$ returns to $\mathcal{F}$ the value UDVS.DVerify$(k,$ params$, m, \tilde{\sigma}, pk, (sk_V^\star, pk_V^\star))$;
3. *$\mathcal{F}$ outputs a V-designated verifier signature $\tilde{\sigma}^\star$ for a new message $m^\star$.*

The adversary $\mathcal{F}$ succeeds if UDVS.DVerify$\big(k,$ params$, pk_S^\star, (sk_V^\star, pk_V^\star)\big) = 1$ and $m^\star$ has not been asked by $\mathcal{F}$ in a signing query in step 2 of the game. An attacker $\mathcal{F}$ is said to $(\tau, q_s, q_v, \varepsilon)$-break the unforgeability of the UDVS scheme if he *succeeds in the game within running time τ and with probability ε after having made q_s signing queries and q_v verification queries.*

Strong Unforgeability. Definition 2 only captures the standard level of unforgeability. In the strengthened notion of *strong* unforgeability [1], the forger is allowed to output a fake designated signature $\tilde{\sigma}$ on a previously signed message $m^\star$. Here, we impose that $\tilde{\sigma}$ must differ from designated signatures obtained by applying the (deterministic) designation algorithm to all outputs of signing queries with input $m^\star$ during the game. We emphasize that this model only makes sense for schemes using a deterministic designation algorithm[3].

Privacy of signer's identity/Anonymity. Privacy of signer's identity was formally defined for designated verifier signatures by Laguillaumie and Vergnaud [22]. It captures the *strong anonymity* property introduced by Jakobsson *et al.* in [19]. Although designated verifier signatures are *signer ambiguous* regarding the signer and the designated verifier, it might remain possible to distinguish the actual issuer of a given signature between two potential signers. The next definition captures that it should be (computationally) infeasible. It is analogous to the notion of anonymity for undeniable signatures [16].

Definition 3. *An UDVS has the signer-privacy property if no PPT distinguisher $\mathcal{D}$ has a non-negligible advantage in the next game.*

1. *The challenger $\mathcal{C}$ takes as input a security parameter k and executes params $\leftarrow$ UDVSΣ.Setup(k), $(sk_{S,0}^\star, pk_{S,0}^\star), (sk_{S,1}^\star, pk_{S,1}^\star) \leftarrow$ UDVS.Σ.KeyGen$(k, params)$, $(sk_V^\star, pk_V^\star) \leftarrow$ UDVS.VKeyGen$(k, params)$. It hands public keys $pk_{S,0}^\star, pk_{S,1}^\star$ and $pk_V^\star$ to $\mathcal{D}$ and keeps $sk_{S,0}^\star, sk_{S,1}^\star, sk_V^\star$ to itself.*
2. *The distinguisher $\mathcal{D}$ issues a number of queries exactly as in the game modeling the unforgeability property. Those queries may pertain to both of the challenge public keys $pk_{S,0}^\star, pk_{S,1}^\star$.*
3. *$\mathcal{D}$ produces a message $m^\star$ of her choosing. The challenger $\mathcal{C}$ then flips a fair coin $b^\star \xleftarrow{R} \{0, 1\}$, generates a signature in the name of one of the signers $\sigma \leftarrow$ UDVS.Σ.Sign$(k, params, m^\star, sk_{S,b^\star}^\star)$ and designates it into $\tilde{\sigma}^\star \leftarrow$ UDVS.Designate$(k, params, pk_{S,b^\star}^\star, m, \sigma, pk_V^\star)$ which is sent to $\mathcal{D}$.*
4. *$\mathcal{D}$ issues new queries with the restriction of not querying $\tilde{\sigma}^\star$ for verification.*
5. *Eventually, $\mathcal{D}$ outputs a bit b and wins if $b = b^\star$.*

---

[3] Defining strong unforgeability for schemes with probabilistic designation is more subtle. A reasonable option is the following. We still forbid *plain* signature queries for the message $m^\star$. Instead, $\mathcal{F}$ is equipped with a designated signing oracle taking as input a message m and some registered verifier's public key pk_B. The latter may differ from the target verifier's public key $pk_V^\star$ as long as it was registered and $\mathcal{F}$ proved her knowledge of the matching secret sk_B. The designated signing oracle first generates a plain signature $\sigma \leftarrow$ UDVS.Σ.Sign$(k, params, m, sk_S^\star)$ and designates it into $\tilde{\sigma} \leftarrow$ UDVS.Designate$(k, params, pk, m, \sigma, pk_B)$ which is given to $\mathcal{F}$. The latter has to come up with a pair $(m^\star, \tilde{\sigma}^\star)$ designated to the target verifier $pk_V^\star$ and $(m^\star, \tilde{\sigma}^\star)$ may not result from a designated signing query with $pk_V^\star$ as a verifier's public key.

If $\mathcal{D}$ has advantage $\varepsilon = |Pr[b = b^\star] - 1/2|$ when making at most q_s and q_v signing and verification queries within running time τ, then we say that he $(\tau, q_s, q_v, \varepsilon)$- breaks the anonymity of the UDVS scheme.

2.2 Bilinear Maps

We now recall basics about bilinear maps which are the main algebraic tool to design our new UDVS construction.

Definition 4. *Let $(\mathbb{G}, +)$ and $(\mathbb{H}, \cdot)$ be groups of prime order q and $P \in \mathbb{G}$. A symmetric admissible bilinear map $e : \mathbb{G} \times \mathbb{G} \to \mathbb{H}$ has the following properties:*

1. *bilinearity: $e(aP, bQ) = e(P, Q)^{ab}$ for any $(P, Q) \in \mathbb{G} \times \mathbb{G}$ and $a, b \in \mathbb{Z}$;*
2. *efficient computability for any possible input pair;*
3. *non-degeneracy: $e(P, P)$ generates $\mathbb{H}$ whenever P generates $\mathbb{G}$.*

Definition 5. *A BDH-parameter-generator is a probabilistic algorithm that takes a security parameter λ as input and outputs a 5-tuple $(q, P, \mathbb{G}, \mathbb{H}, e)$ where q is a λ-bit prime number, $(\mathbb{G}, +)$ and $(\mathbb{H}, \cdot)$ are groups of order q, $P \in \mathbb{G}$ is a generator, and $e : \mathbb{G} \times \mathbb{G} \to \mathbb{H}$ is an admissible bilinear map.*

Complexity assumptions. Let $(q, P, \mathbb{G}, \mathbb{H}, e)$ be the output of a prime-order-BDH-parameter-generator for a security parameter k. Basically,

1. the (computational) **Bilinear Diffie-Hellman Problem** (BDH) [20, 8] is to compute $e(P, P)^{abc} \in \mathbb{H}$ given $(P, aP, bP, cP) \in \mathbb{G}^4$;
2. the **Decisional Bilinear Diffie-Hellman Problem** (DBDH) is to distinguish the distribution of BDH tuples $(aP, bP, cP, e(P, P)^{abc})$ from the distribution of random tuples $(aP, bP, cP, e(P, P)^z)$. We say that an algorithm $\mathcal{B}$ solving the DBDH problem has advantage ε if

$$\left| \Pr[\mathcal{B}(P, aP, bP, cP, e(P, P)^{abc}) = 1 | a, b, c \xleftarrow{R} \mathbb{Z}_q^*] \right.$$
$$\left. - \Pr[\mathcal{B}(P, aP, bP, cP, e(P, P)^z) = 1 | a, b, c, z \xleftarrow{R} \mathbb{Z}_q^*] \right| \geq \varepsilon;$$

3. the **Gap Bilinear Diffie-Hellman Problem** (GBDH) consists in solving the BDH problem (P, aP, bP, cP) with the help of an oracle deciding whether tuples $(P, xP, yP, zP, h) \in \mathbb{G}^4 \times \mathbb{H}$ satisfy $h = e(P, P)^{xyz}$;
4. the **weak Gap Bilinear Diffie-Hellman Problem** (wGDBH) is to solve a BDH instance $(P, aP, bP, cP) \in \mathbb{G}^4$ using a *restricted* decision oracle deciding whether pairs $(zP, h) \in \mathbb{G} \times \mathbb{H}$ satisfy $h = e(P, P)^{abz}$.

The last problem is not easier than the GBDH problem in that fewer degrees of freedom are allowed when using the decision oracle. We call *weak* Gap Bilinear Diffie-Hellman assumption its intractability for any PPT algorithm.

The security of our scheme relies on the wGBDH assumption which, although non-standard, is a black box assumption (see [27] for the historical definition of a *gap problem*). In section 5, we shall explain how to get rid of interactive assumptions and modify our scheme to end up with a security resting on the softer Bilinear Diffie-Hellman assumption.

3   Our UDVS Scheme

We present in this section the design of our new universal designated verifier signatures. It is based on Waters' signature scheme [34].

In our notation, hashed messages **m** are always represented as n-bit vectors $(m_1, \ldots, m_n)$ with $m_i \in \{0, 1\}$ for all $i \in \{1, \ldots, n\}$.

- UDVS.Σ.Setup: public parameters include the output $(q, P, \mathbb{G}, \mathbb{H}, e)$ of a BDH-parameter-generator as well as an integer n, a collision-resistant hash function $h : \{0, 1\}^* \to \{0, 1\}^n$, random elements $P', U' \in \mathbb{G}$ and a random n-tuple $(U_1, \ldots, U_n) \in \mathbb{G}^n$. We call $F : \{0, 1\}^n \to \mathbb{G}$ the application mapping strings **m** onto $F(\mathbf{m}) = U' + \sum_{i=1}^n m_i U_i$.
  $$\mathsf{params} := \{n, q, \mathbb{G}, \mathbb{H}, e, P, P', U', U_1, \ldots, U_n, F, h\}.$$
- UDVS.Σ.KeyGen: a signer's private key is a randomly chosen $\alpha_S \xleftarrow{R} \mathbb{Z}_q^*$; his public key consists of a group element $P_S = \alpha_S P$.
- UDVS.Σ.Sign: given a message $M \in \{0, 1\}^*$, the signer computes $\mathbf{m} = h(M)$ and picks $r \xleftarrow{R} \mathbb{Z}_q^*$. The signature is $\sigma = (\sigma_1, \sigma_2) = (\alpha_S P' + r F(\mathbf{m}), rP)$.
- UDVS.Register: a public key is registered by letting the user prove the knowledge of its secret key to the KRA.
- UDVS.Σ.Verify: a plain signature $\sigma = (\sigma_1, \sigma_2)$ on M is accepted if $e(\sigma_1, P) = e(P_S, P')e(\sigma_2, F(\mathbf{m}))$ where $\mathbf{m} = h(M)$.
- UDVS.VKeyGen : a designated verifier's private key is a random element $\alpha_V \xleftarrow{R} \mathbb{Z}_q^*$; the matching public key is $P_V = \alpha_V P \in \mathbb{G}$.
- UDVS.Designate: the holder of a signature $\sigma = (\sigma_1, \sigma_2)$, who chooses V as designated verifier produces the designated verifier signature $\tilde{\sigma} = (\tilde{\sigma}_1, \sigma_2)$ with $\tilde{\sigma}_1 = e(\sigma_1, P_V)$.
- UDVS.DVerify: given a purported signature $(\tilde{\sigma}_1, \sigma_2)$, the designated verifier checks whether $\tilde{\sigma}_1 = e(P_S, P')^{\alpha_V} e(\sigma_2, F(\mathbf{m}))^{\alpha_V}$ where $\mathbf{m} = h(M)$.

4   Security

Correctness and unconditional source hiding are straightforward.

4.1   Unforgeability

The proof of the next theorem follows the same strategy as the security proof of Waters's identity based encryption scheme [34].

Theorem 1. *Assuming that a forger $\mathcal{F}$ is able to $(t, q_s, q_v, \varepsilon)$-break the scheme, there is an algorithm $\mathcal{B}$ that (t', ε')-breaks the wGBDH assumption where*

$$\varepsilon' \geq \frac{\varepsilon}{4q_s(n+1)} \qquad t' \leq t + O((q_s + q_v)\tau_m + q_v \tau_p)$$

and τ_m, τ_p respectively denote the cost of a scalar multiplication in $\mathbb{G}$ and the time complexity of a pairing calculation.

Proof. Algorithm $\mathcal{B}$ is given a group $\mathbb{G}$ together with a generator P, elements $(aP, bP, cP) \in \mathbb{G}^3$ and an oracle $\mathcal{O}_{DBDH}(., bP, cP, .)$ deciding whether tuples of the shape $(aP, bP, cP, h) \in \mathbb{G}^3 \times H$ satisfy $h = e(P, P)^{abc}$. It uses $\mathcal{F}$ to extract $e(P, P)^{abc}$. The attack environment is simulated as follows.

Setup and key generation: $\mathcal{B}$ randomly chooses $k \in \{0, \ldots, n\}$ and defines $\ell = 2q_s$. We assume[4] that $\ell(n + 1) < q$ which implies $0 \leq k\ell < q$. The simulator $\mathcal{B}$ randomly selects $x' \xleftarrow{R} \mathbb{Z}_\ell$ and a vector $(x_1, \ldots, x_n)$ of elements with $x_i \in \mathbb{Z}_\ell$ for all i. It also chooses at random an integer $y' \xleftarrow{R} \mathbb{Z}_q$ and a vector $(y_1, \ldots, y_n)$ with $y_j \in \mathbb{Z}_q$ for all j. For ease of explanation, we shall consider two functions

$$J(\mathbf{m}) = x' + \sum_{i=1}^{n} m_i x_i - k\ell \quad \text{and} \quad K(\mathbf{m}) = y' + \sum_{i=1}^{n} m_i y_i.$$

System-wide parameters are then chosen as $P' = cP$ and

$$U' = (x' - k\ell)P' + y'P \qquad U_i = x_i P' + y_i P \text{ for } 1 \leq i \leq n$$

which means that, for any string $\mathbf{m} \in \{0, 1\}^n$, we have

$$F(\mathbf{m}) = U' + \sum_{i=1}^{n} m_i U_i = J(\mathbf{m})P' + K(\mathbf{m})P.$$

Besides, signer and verifier's public keys are set to $P_S = aP$ and $P_V = bP$.

Queries: once $\mathcal{F}$ is started with public parameters and public keys P_S, P_V as input, two kinds of queries may occur.

Signing queries: let $\mathbf{m} = h(M)$ be a message for which $\mathcal{F}$ requests a signature. If $J(\mathbf{m}) = 0 \bmod q$, $\mathcal{B}$ aborts. Otherwise, it can construct a signature by picking $r \xleftarrow{R} \mathbb{Z}_q$ and computing

$$\sigma = (\sigma_1, \sigma_2) = \left(-\frac{K(\mathbf{m})}{J(\mathbf{m})} P_S + rF(\mathbf{m}), -\frac{1}{J(\mathbf{m})} P_S + rP \right).$$

If we define $\tilde{r} = r - a/J(\mathbf{m})$, σ is a valid signature as

$$\sigma_1 = -\frac{K(\mathbf{m})}{J(\mathbf{m})} P_S + rF(\mathbf{m})$$

$$= -\frac{K(\mathbf{m})}{J(\mathbf{m})} P_S + \tilde{r}F(\mathbf{m}) + \frac{a}{J(\mathbf{m})}(J(\mathbf{m})P' + K(\mathbf{m})P)$$

$$= aP' + \tilde{r}F(\mathbf{m})$$

and $\sigma_2 = (r - a/J(\mathbf{m}))P = \tilde{r}P$. The plain signature σ is then transformed using the public designation algorithm.

---

[4] This is a realistic requirement as parameters should be chosen s.t. $n \geq 160$, $q > 2^{160}$ and it is common to suppose $q_s < 2^{30}$.

Verification queries: at any time, $\mathcal{F}$ may enquire for the (in)validity of a designated signature $\tilde{\sigma} = (\tilde{\sigma}_1, \sigma_2)$ on a message $\mathbf{m} = h(M)$ and expects $\mathcal{B}$ to (in)validate it using the (unknown) private key $\alpha_V = b$. To answer such a query, $\mathcal{B}$ evaluates $J(\mathbf{m})$ and $K(\mathbf{m})$, invokes the decision oracle on the tuple $(P_S + J(\mathbf{m})\sigma_2, P_V, P', \tilde{\sigma}_1/e(K(\mathbf{m})\sigma_2, P_V))$ and returns 1 (meaning that $\tilde{\sigma}$ is a valid designated signature) if $\mathcal{O}_{DBDH}(.)$ deems it as a valid tuple. Otherwise, it returns 0 and declares $\tilde{\sigma}$ as invalid. We observe that, whenever $\tilde{\sigma}$ is correct, we have $\sigma_2 = rP$ and

$$
\begin{aligned}
\tilde{\sigma}_1 &= e\left(aP' + r(J(\mathbf{m})P' + K(\mathbf{m})P), bP\right) \\
&= e\left(aP' + rJ(\mathbf{m})P', bP\right) e\left(K(\mathbf{m})rP, bP\right) \\
&= e\left(acP + J(\mathbf{m})rcP, bP\right) e\left(K(\mathbf{m})rP, bP\right) \\
&= e(P, P)^{(a+J(\mathbf{m})r)bc} e\left(K(\mathbf{m})\sigma_2, bP\right)
\end{aligned}
$$

for some $r \in \mathbb{Z}_q^*$ and $\tilde{\sigma}_1/e(K(\mathbf{m})\sigma_2, P_V)$ is the solution of the bilinear Diffie-Hellman instance

$$
((a + rJ(\mathbf{m}))P, bP, cP) = (P_S + J(\mathbf{m})\sigma_2, P_V, P').
$$

If $\mathcal{F}$ ever issues such a verification query where $J(\mathbf{m}) = 0$ and $\mathcal{O}_{DBDH}(.)$ returns 1, $\mathcal{B}$ immediately halts and outputs $\tilde{\sigma}_1/e(K(\mathbf{m})\sigma_2, P_V)$.

Forgery: if $\mathcal{B}$ did not abort, $\mathcal{F}$ is expected to come with a fake designated signature $\tilde{\sigma}^\star = (\tilde{\sigma}_1^\star, \sigma_2)$ on some new message $\mathbf{m}^\star = h(M^\star)$. At that point, $\mathcal{B}$ reports "failure" if $J(\mathbf{m}^\star) \neq 0 \bmod q$. Otherwise, $F(\mathbf{m}^\star) = K(\mathbf{m}^\star)P$ and, given that $\tilde{\sigma}^\star$ is a valid designated signature, we have

$$
\tilde{\sigma}_1^\star = e(aP' + rK(\mathbf{m}^\star)P, bP) = e(P, P)^{abc} e(K(\mathbf{m}^\star)\sigma_2^\star, bP)
$$

and $\sigma_2^\star = rP$ for some $r \in \mathbb{Z}_q^*$, wherefrom $e(P, P)^{abc} = \tilde{\sigma}_1^\star/e(K(\mathbf{m}^\star)\sigma_2^\star, bP)$ is extractable by $\mathcal{B}$.

The simulator $\mathcal{B}$'s probability of success remains to be assessed. We remark that it terminates without aborting if, $J(\mathbf{m}) \neq 0 \bmod q$ for all messages m submitted in a signing query. As $0 \leq k\ell < q$ and $x' + \sum_{i=1}^n m_i x_i < \ell(n + 1) < q$, we note that $J(\mathbf{m}) = 0 \bmod q$ implies $J(\mathbf{m}) = 0 \bmod \ell$ (and thus $J(\mathbf{m}) \neq 0 \bmod \ell$ implies $J(\mathbf{m}) \neq 0 \bmod q$). Hence, to simplify the analysis, we may force $\mathcal{B}$ to abort whenever $J(\mathbf{m}) = 0 \bmod \ell$ in a signing query. Besides, $\mathcal{B}$ is successful if the target message happens to satisfy $J(\mathbf{m}^\star) = 0 \bmod q$.

More formally, if $\mathbf{m}_1, \ldots, \mathbf{m}_{q_s}$ are messages appearing in some signing query and if we define the events $A_i : J(\mathbf{m}_i) \neq 0 \bmod \ell$ and $A^\star : J(\mathbf{m}^\star) = 0 \bmod q$, the probability that $\mathcal{B}$ does not fail is $\Pr[\neg \text{abort}] \geq \Pr[\bigwedge_{i=1}^{q_s} A_i \wedge A^\star]$. Given that $J(\mathbf{m}^\star) = 0 \bmod q$ implies $J(\mathbf{m}^\star) = 0 \bmod \ell$ and that, if $J(\mathbf{m}^\star) = 0 \bmod \ell$, there is a unique value $k \in \{0, \ldots, n\}$ that yields $J(\mathbf{m}^\star) = 0 \bmod q$, we have $\Pr[A^\star] = \Pr[J(\mathbf{m}^\star) = 0 \bmod \ell]\Pr[J(\mathbf{m}^\star) \bmod q | J(\mathbf{m}^\star) = 0 \bmod \ell] = \dfrac{1}{\ell}\dfrac{1}{n+1}$.

Moreover, $\Pr[\bigwedge_{i=1}^{q_s} A_i | A^\star] = 1 - \sum_{i=1}^{q_s} \Pr[\neg A_i | A^\star] = 1 - \frac{q_s}{\ell}$, where the rightmost equality stems from the fact that A_i is independent of $A^\star$ for any i (hence $\Pr[\neg A_i | A^\star] = 1/\ell$). Putting the above together, we find that

$$\Pr[\neg\text{abort}] = \Pr[A^\star]\Pr[\bigwedge_{i=1}^{q_s} A_i | A^\star] = \frac{1}{\ell(n+1)}\left(1 - \frac{q_s}{\ell}\right) = \frac{1}{4q_s(n+1)}$$

thanks to the choice of $\ell = 2q_s$.   □

4.2   Anonymity

The following theorem states the signer's privacy in a weaker sense than definition 3: verification queries are indeed disallowed throughout the game. The proof follows ideas from [34] and is detailed in the full version of the paper.

Theorem 2. *If an attacker $\mathcal{D}$ is able to $(t, q_s, 0, \varepsilon)$-break the anonymity, there is an algorithm $\mathcal{B}$ that (t', ε')-breaks the DBDH assumption where*

$$\varepsilon' \geq \frac{\varepsilon}{32q_s(n+1)} \qquad t' \leq t + O(q_s\tau_m + \varepsilon^{-2}\ln(\varepsilon^{-1})\mu^{-1}\ln(\mu^{-1}))$$

where τ_m denotes the cost of a scalar multiplication in $\mathbb{G}$.

The next section shows a variant of our scheme where the anonymity property holds in the strong sense of definition 3.

Remark 1. In [24], Lipmaa, Wang and Bao identified a new security requirement for designated verifier signatures: the *non-delegability*. This means that neither the signer nor the designated verifier should be able to produce a "meta-key" which allows to generate new signatures without revealing their secret. Even if this requirement is debatable, our scheme is delegatable (for instance the verifier can publish $\alpha_V P'$). As suggested in [33], delegability is inherent to all UDVS.

5   Strong Unforgeability Under the BDH assumption

In this section, we modify our scheme to obtain a variant which is strongly unforgeable under a weaker assumption. This version is obtained using the generic construction of Boneh, Shen and Waters [9] that makes strongly unforgeable any weakly unforgeable signature of some particular kind.

As in [9], we assume that group elements have unique encoding as the scheme would not be strongly unforgeable otherwise.

- UDVS.Σ.Setup is as in section 3 except that it additionally selects a generator $Q \xleftarrow{R} \mathbb{G}$. Hash function h is also replaced by a collision-resistant family $[H]_\kappa$ of hash functions $H_\kappa : \{0,1\}^* \to \{0,1\}^n$ indexed by keys $\kappa \in \mathcal{K}$. Public parameters consist of params $:= \{n, q, \mathbb{G}, \mathbb{H}, e, P, P', Q, U', U_1, \ldots, U_n, F, [H]_\kappa, \mathcal{K}\}$.

- UDVS.Σ.KeyGen: a signer's private key is a random $\alpha_S \xleftarrow{R} \mathbb{Z}_q^*$; his public key is made of a group element $P_S = \alpha_S P$ and a key $\kappa \in \mathcal{K}$.
- UDVS.Σ.Sign: given a message $M \in \{0,1\}^*$,
  1. Pick at random $r, s \xleftarrow{R} \mathbb{Z}_q^*$ and set $\sigma_2 = rP \in \mathbb{G}$.
  2. Compute $t = H_\kappa(M\|\sigma_2) \in \{0,1\}^n$ and view it as an element of $\mathbb{Z}_q$.
  3. Compute $\mathbf{m} = H_\kappa(tP + sQ) \in \{0,1\}^n$.
  4. Compute $\sigma_1 = \alpha_S P' + rF(\mathbf{m}) \in \mathbb{G}$.

  The signature is $\sigma = (\sigma_1, \sigma_2, s) = (\alpha_S P' + rF(\mathbf{m}), rP, s)$
- UDVS.Register is as in section 3.
- UDVS.Σ.Verify: given an ordinary signature $\sigma = (\sigma_1, \sigma_2, s)$ on M,
  1. Set $t = H_\kappa(M\|\sigma_2) \in \{0,1\}^n$ and view it as an element of $\mathbb{Z}_q$.
  2. Compute $\mathbf{m} = H_\kappa(tP + sQ) \in \{0,1\}^n$ and accept if and only if

$$e(\sigma_1, P) = e(P_S, P')e(\sigma_2, F(\mathbf{m}))$$

- UDVS.VKeyGen is as in section 3.
- UDVS.Designate: to designate a signature $\sigma = (\sigma_1, \sigma_2, s)$ for a verifier V, a signature holder turns it into $\tilde{\sigma} = (\tilde{\sigma}_1, \sigma_2, s)$ with $\tilde{\sigma}_1 = e(\sigma_1, P_V)$.
- UDVS.DVerify: given a purported signature $(\tilde{\sigma}_1, \sigma_2, s)$ on M, the verifier computes $t = H_\kappa(M\|\sigma_2)$ (which is viewed as an element of $\mathbb{Z}_q$), $\mathbf{m} = H_\kappa(tP + sQ) \in \{0,1\}^n$ and checks whether $\tilde{\sigma}_1 = e(P_S, P')^{\alpha_V} e(\sigma_2, F(\mathbf{m}))^{\alpha_V}$

5.1 Security

The present construction has a security proof under the Bilinear Diffie-Hellman assumption which is deemed reasonable by now. However, its strength does not depend on how many signing or verification requests are allowed to adversaries whatsoever. This is a noticeable improvement over [35, 33] and the scheme of section 3. The proof uses a technique which goes back to Ogata *et al.* [21] who showed how to avoid gap assumptions in the security proof [27] of a variant of the Chaum-van Antwerpen undeniable signature [11].

Theorem 3. *If a forger $\mathcal{F}$ can $(t, q_s, q_v, \varepsilon)$-break the strong unforgeability, there exits an algorithm $\mathcal{B}$ that (t', ε')-breaks the BDH assumption where*

$$\varepsilon' \geq \frac{\varepsilon}{12(q_s + q_{ds})(n+1)(q_v+1)} \qquad t' \leq t + O((q_s + q_{ds} + q_v)\tau_m + q_v\tau_p)$$

and τ_m, τ_p stand for the same quantity as in theorem 1.

The key idea is that, unless the scheme is not strongly existentially unforgeable, all verification queries necessarily involve signatures that were obtained from signing oracles or that are invalid. The simulator's strategy is to guess which verification query involves a forged signature and reject signatures involved in all other queries. Such a proof strategy does not apply to our first UDVS scheme where signatures obtained from a signing oracle may be publicly turned into other signatures on the same messages.

Proof. Algorithm $\mathcal{B}$ combines the technique of [9] with a strategy introduced in [21] to prove the security of a variant of the Chaum-van Antwerpen [11] undeniable signature under the CDH assumption. In the simulation, $\mathcal{B}$ maintains a history L_S of all signing queries and their outputs. Whenever $\mathcal{F}$ asks for a plain signature, $\mathcal{B}$ also computes and stores in L_S the unique (recall that designation is deterministic) matching designated signature for the target verifier P_{V^*}.

As in theorem 1 of [9], the forger makes her signing queries on messages $M_1, \ldots, M_{q_s}$ that result in a list of triples $(\tilde{\sigma_{i,1}}, \sigma_{i,2}, s_i)$ for $i = 1, \ldots, n$. Let $t_i = H_\kappa(M_i || \sigma_{2,i})$ and $w_i = t_i P + s_i Q$. Let also $\langle M^*, (\tilde{\sigma}_1{}^*, \sigma_2^*, s^*) \rangle$ be the fake designated signature produced by $\mathcal{F}$ and $t^* = H_\kappa(M^* || \sigma_2^*)$, $w^* = t^* P + s^* Q$. Just like the proof of theorem 1 in [9], we distinguish three kinds of forgeries:

Type I: a forgery with $w^* = w_i$ and $t^* = t_i$ for some $i \in \{1, \ldots, q_s + q_{ds}\}$.
Type II: a forgery with $w^* = w_i$ and $t^* \neq t_i$ for some $i \in \{1, \ldots, q_s + q_{ds}\}$.
Type III: a forgery for a new element $w^* \neq w_i$ for any $i \in \{1, \ldots, q_s + q_{ds}\}$.

A successful forger comes with a forgery of Type I, Type II or Type III and $\mathcal{B}$ has to guess which kind of forger $\mathcal{F}$ will be at the outset of the simulation.

In all cases, $\mathcal{F}$ is allowed making up to q_v verification queries on triples $\tilde{\sigma}_j = (\tilde{\sigma_{j,1}}, \sigma_{j,2}, s)$ which are likely to be designated signatures intended to the target verifier V^* and bearing the name of the target signer S^*. The main difficulty for $\mathcal{B}$ is to deal with those queries without resorting to a decision oracle. For convenience, $\mathcal{F}$'s forgery is viewed as her $q_v + 1^{th}$ query to the verification oracle. A verification request $(M_j, \tilde{\sigma}_j)$, with $j \in \{1, \ldots, q_v + 1\}$, is called *special* if $\tilde{\sigma}_j$ is a valid signature on M_j for signer S^* and designated verifier V^* and if it does not appear in $\mathcal{B}$'s history L_S of signing queries. Clearly, a *special* verification query is a breach (which is assumed to occur at least once in a real attack) in the strong unforgeability property. Before the simulation starts, $\mathcal{B}$ has to guess the index $j^* \in \{1, \ldots, q_v + 1\}$ of the first special query.

Upon reception of a verification query $(M_j, \tilde{\sigma}_j)$, $\mathcal{B}$ distinguishes two cases

- if $j < j^*$, $\mathcal{B}$ declares the signature as 'invalid' if $(M_j, \tilde{\sigma}_j)$ does not appear in the history L_S. Otherwise, it returns 'valid'.
- if $j = j^*$, $\mathcal{B}$ aborts if $(M_{j^*}, \tilde{\sigma}_{j^*})$ appears in L_S (which means that $\mathcal{B}$ failed to guess the index of the first special query). Otherwise, $\mathcal{B}$ halts and bets that $(M_{j^*}, \tilde{\sigma}_{j^*})$ is indeed an existential forgery of either Type I, Type II or Type III . In this desired event, the BDH solution is extracted as explained below.

If signing queries are correctly answered, a sufficient condition for $\mathcal{B}$ to perfectly simulate the verification oracle is to correctly guess the index j^* of the first special verification request. This obviously happens with probability $1/(q_v + 1)$.

We now explain how $\mathcal{B}$ solves a BDH instance (aP, bP, cP) using $\mathcal{F}$. It first chooses $c_{mode} \in \{1, 2, 3\}$ in an attempt to foresee which kind of forger $\mathcal{F}$ will be.

- If $c_{mode} = 1$, $\mathcal{B}$ bets on a Type I forgery which is easily seen to break the collision-resistance of $[H]_\kappa$. A random key $k \in \mathcal{K}$ is chosen by $\mathcal{B}$ that generates the remaining public key components following the specification of the protocol. All queries are dealt with using the relevant private elements. When $\mathcal{F}$ outputs a forgery $\langle M^{\star}, \tilde{\sigma}^{\star} = (\tilde{\sigma}_1^{\star}, \sigma_2^{\star}, s^{\star})\rangle$, we have $t^{\star} = H_\kappa(M^{\star}\|\sigma_2^{\star}) = H_\kappa(M_i\|\sigma_{i,2}) = t_i$ and $w^{\star} = t^{\star}P + s^{\star}Q = t_iP + s_iQ = w_i$ for some $i \in \{1, \ldots, q_s + q_{ds}\}$. Hence, we must also have $s^{\star} = s_i$. Assuming that $M^{\star}\|\sigma_2^{\star} = M_i\|\sigma_{i,2}$, we should have $\tilde{\sigma}_1^{\star} \neq \sigma_{i,1}^{\star}$ (as $\tilde{\sigma}^{\star}$ would not be a forgery otherwise) which is impossible as $\tilde{\sigma}_1^{\star}$ is uniquely determined by $t^{\star}$, $\sigma_2^{\star}$ and $s^{\star}$ if $\tilde{\sigma}^{\star}$ is valid. Therefore, we have a collision $H_\kappa(M^{\star}\|\sigma_2^{\star}) = H_\kappa(M_i\|\sigma_{i,2})$ with $M^{\star}\|\sigma_2^{\star} \neq M_i\|\sigma_{i,2}$.

- If $c_{mode} = 2$, $\mathcal{B}$ expects a Type II forgery and prepares public parameters with $Q = aP$ being part of the input of its BDH instance. The other public parameters and public key components are generated following the protocol. All adversarial queries are answered using the relevant private keys. As $\mathcal{F}$ comes with her forgery $\langle M^{\star}, \tilde{\sigma}^{\star} = (\tilde{\sigma}_1^{\star}, \sigma_2^{\star}, s^{\star})\rangle$, we have $w^{\star} = t^{\star}P + s^{\star}Q = t_iP + s_iQ = w_i$ with $t^{\star} = H_\kappa(M^{\star}\|\sigma_2^{\star}) \neq H_\kappa(M_i\|\sigma_{i,2}) = t_i$. This allows $\mathcal{B}$ to extract $a = (t_i - t^{\star})/(s^{\star} - s_i)$ and thereby solve the BDH problem by computing $e(bP, cP)^a$.

- If $c_{mode} = 3$, $\mathcal{B}$ expects a forgery on a new "message" $w^{\star}$ and proceeds in the same way as the simulator of theorem 1.

When assessing $\mathcal{B}$'s advantage, we already observed that it correctly guesses the index of the first special verification query with probability $1/(q_v + 1)$. As it succeeds in foresee the right kind of forgery with probability $1/3$, the lower bound on its advantage easily follows from theorem 1.   □

Strong unforgeability also implies a provable anonymity in the strict sense of definition 3. The proof of the following theorem is very similar to the one of theorem 2. By virtue of strong unforgeability, all verification queries pertain to designated signatures that are either invalid or that result from a signing query. Hence, for each verification query, the simulator just has to compare the candidate signature to those it returned when dealing with signing queries.

Theorem 4. *If an attacker $\mathcal{D}$ can $(t, q_s, q_v, \varepsilon)$-break the anonymity, there is an algorithm $\mathcal{B}$ that (t', ε')-breaks the DBDH assumption where*

$$\varepsilon' \geq \frac{\varepsilon}{32q_s(n+1)} \qquad t' \leq t + O((q_s + q_{ds})\tau_m + q_{ds}\tau_p + \varepsilon^{-2}\ln(\varepsilon^{-1})\mu^{-1}\ln(\mu^{-1}))$$

where τ_m, τ_p denote the same quantity as in theorem 1.

6   Conclusion

We proposed the first UDVS schemes which are secure under reasonable complexity assumptions in the standard model where our constructions are also the only ones to achieve anonymity in the sense of [22].

The next table compares various existing systems. Our new scheme appears to be competitive with other constructions in the standard model. Its main drawback remains the size of public parameters. We leave open the problem of finding

UDVS schemes that are secure under mild assumptions in the standard model without using large public parameters. A trick independently suggested in [25] and [29] allows for a step towards this purpose.

Scheme	DVSBMH [22]	ZFI [35]	UDVS-BB [33]	ours
Model	ROM	standard	standard	standard
Assumptions	GBDH	q-SDH + KEA	q-SDH + KEA	GBDH
Sign	1 exp$_{\mathbb{G}}$	1 exp$_{\mathbb{G}}$	1 exp$_{\mathbb{G}}$	1 multi-exp$_{\mathbb{G}}$
Verify	2 P.	1 P. + 2 exp$_{\mathbb{G}}$	1 P. + 2 exp$_{\mathbb{G}}$	2 P.†
Designate	1 P.	1 P. + 2 exp$_{\mathbb{G}}$	3 exp$_{\mathbb{G}}$	1 P.
DVerify	1 P.	2 P. + 2 exp$_{\mathbb{G}}$	4 P. + 2 exp$_{\mathbb{G}}$	1 P. + 1 exp$_{\mathbb{G}}$ †
Designated size	160	1366*	684	342*

($\dagger$) In both of our schemes, we assume that $e(P_S, P')$ is stored as part of the signer's public key.

($\star$) These sizes can be obtained using asymmetric pairings and curves of [3] with compression [2].

References

1. J.-H. An, Y. Dodis, T. Rabin. On the security of joint signature and encryption. Proc. of Eurocrypt'02, Springer LNCS vol. 2332, 83–107 (2002).
2. P. S. L. M. Barreto, M. Scott. Compressed Pairings. Proc. of Crypto'04, Springer LNCS vol. 3152, 140–156 (2004).
3. P. S. L. M. Barreto, M. Naehrig. Pairing-Friendly Elliptic Curves of Prime Order. Proc. of SAC'05, Springer LNCS vol. 3897, 319–331 (2005).
4. M. Bellare, A. Palacio. The Knowledge-of-Exponent Assumptions and 3-Round Zero-Knowledge Protocols. Proc. of Crypto'04, Springer LNCS vol. 3152, 273-289 (2004)
5. M. Bellare, P. Rogaway. Random oracles are practical: A paradigm for designing efficient protocols. Proc. of ACM CCS'93, ACM Press, 62–73 (1993)
6. A. Bender, J. Katz, R. Morselli. Ring Signatures: Stronger Definitions, and Constructions without Random Oracles. Proc. of TCC'06. Springer LNCS vol. 3876, 60–79 (2006)
7. D. Boneh, X. Boyen. Short Signatures Without Random Oracles. Proc. of Eurocrypt'04, Springer LNCS vol. 3027, 56–73 (2004)
8. D. Boneh, M. Franklin. Identity-based encryption from the Weil pairing. Proc. of Crypto'01, Springer LNCS vol. 2139, 213–229 (2001)
9. D. Boneh, E. Shen, B. Waters, Strongly Unforgeable Signatures Based on Computational Diffie-Hellman. Proc. of PKC'05, Springer LNCS vol. 3958, 229–240 (2005).
10. R. Canetti, O. Goldreich, S. Halevi. The random oracle methodology, revisited. Journal of the ACM 51(4), 557–594 (2004)
11. D. Chaum, H. van Antwerpen. Undeniable Signatures, Proc. of Crypto'89, Springer LNCS vol. 435, 212–216 (1989).
12. J. H. Cheon. Security Analysis of the Strong Diffie-Hellman Problem. Proc. of Eurocrypt'06, Springer LNCS vol. 4004, 1–11 (2006)
13. I. Damgård. Towards practical public-key cryptosystems provably-secure against chosen-ciphertext attacks. Proc. of Crypto'91, Springer LNCS vol. 576, 445–456 (1991)

14. A. Dent. The Hardness of the DHK Problem in the Generic Group Model. Cryptology ePrint Archive: report 2006/156 (2006)
15. A. Fiat, A. Shamir. How to prove yourself: Practical solutions to identification and signature problems. Proc. of Crypto'86. Springer LNCS vol. 263, 186–194 (1986)
16. S. Galbraith, W. Mao: Invisibility and Anonymity of Undeniable and Confirmer Signatures. Proc. of CT-RSA 2003, Springer LNCS vol. 2612, 80–97 (2003)
17. S. Goldwasser, S. Micali, R. L. Rivest. A Digital Signature Scheme Secure Against Adaptive Chosen-Message Attacks. SIAM J. Comput. 17(2), 281–308 (1988)
18. S. Hada, T. Tanaka. On the Existence of 3-Round Zero-Knowledge Protocols. Proc. of Crypto'98. Springer LNCS vol. 1462, 408–42 (1998)
19. M. Jakobsson, K. Sako, R. Impagliazzo: Designated Verifier Proofs and their Applications. Proc. of Eurocrypt'96, Springer LNCS vol. 1070, 142–154 (1996)
20. A. Joux. A one round protocol for tripartite Diffie-Hellman. Proc. of ANTS-IV, Springer LNCS vol. 1838, 385–394 (2000)
21. W. Ogata, K. Kurosawa, S.-H. Heng. The Security of the FDH Variant of Chaum's Undeniable Signature Scheme. Proc of PKC'05, Springer LNCS vol. 3386, 328–345 (2005)
22. F. Laguillaumie, D. Vergnaud. Designated Verifiers Signature: Anonymity and Efficient Construction from *any* Bilinear Map. Proc. of SCN'04, Springer LNCS vol. 3352, 107–121 (2005)
23. F. Laguillaumie, D. Vergnaud. Multi-Designated Verifiers Signature Schemes. Proc. of ICICS'04, Springer LNCS vol. 3269, 495–507 (2004)
24. H. Lipmaa, G. Wang, F. Bao. Designated Verifier Signature Schemes: Attacks, New Security Notions and A New Construction. Proc. of ICALP 2005, Springer LNCS vol. 3580, 459–471 (2005)
25. D. Naccache. Secure and *Practical* Identity-Based Encryption. Cryptology ePrint Archive : report 2005/369 (2005)
26. C. Y. Ng, W. Susilo, Y. Mu. Universal Designated Multi Verifier Signature Schemes. Proc. of SNDS 2005, IEEE Press, 305–309 (2005)
27. T. Okamoto, D. Pointcheval: The Gap-Problems: a New Class of Problems for the Security of Cryptographic Schemes. Proc. of PKC'01 Springer LNCS vol. 1992, 104–118 (2001)
28. S. Saeednia, S. Kremer, O. Markowitch. An Efficient Strong Designated Verifier Signature Scheme. Proc. of ICISC 2003, Springer LNCS vol. 2836, 40–54 (2003)
29. P. Sarkar, S. Chatterjee. Trading time for space: Towards an efficient IBE scheme with short(er) public parameters in the standard model. To appear in Proc. of ICISC'05 (2006)
30. C. P. Schnorr. Efficient identification and signatures for smart cards. Proc. of Crypto'89, Springer LNCS vol. 435, 239–252 (1989)
31. R. Steinfeld, L. Bull, H. Wang, J. Pieprzyk. Universal Designated Verifier Signatures. Proc. of Asiacrypt'03, Springer LNCS vol. 2894, 523–542 (2003)
32. R. Steinfeld, H. Wang, J. Pieprzyk. Efficient Extension of Standard Schnorr/RSA signatures into Universal Designated-Verifier Signatures. Proc. of PKC'04, Springer LNCS vol. 2947, 86–100 (2004)
33. D. Vergnaud. New extensions of Pairing-based Signatures into Universal Designated Verifier Signatures. To appear in Proc. of ICALP 2006.
34. B. Waters. Efficient Identity-Based Encryption Without Random Oracles. Proc. of Eurocrypt'05. Springer LNCS vol. 3494, 114–127 (2005)
35. R. Zhang, J. Furukawa, H. Imai. Short signature and Universal Designated Verifier Signature without Random Oracles. Proc. of ACNS'05, Springer LNCS vol. 3531, 483–498 (2005)

Understanding Two-Round Differentials in AES[*]

Joan Daemen[1] and Vincent Rijmen[2,3]

[1] STMicroelectronics Belgium
joan.daemen@st.com
[2] IAIK, Graz University of Technology
vincent.rijmen@iaik.tugraz.at
[3] Cryptomathic A/S

Abstract. In this paper we study the probability of differentials and characteristics over 2 rounds of the AES with the objective to understand how the components of the AES round transformation interact in this respect. We extend and correct the analysis of the differential properties of the multiplicative inverse in $GF(2^n)$ given in [9]. We study the number of characteristics with EDP > 0 whose probability adds up to the probability of a differential and derive formulas that allow to produce a close estimate of this number for any differential. We use the properties discovered in our study to explain the differentials with the maximum EDP values and describe the impact of the linear transformation in the AES S-box in this respect.

1 Introduction

In this paper we study the probability of differentials and characteristics [1,6] over 2 rounds of the AES where the difference is the bitwise XOR. Bounds on the expected differential probability (EDP) of characteristics were proven in the design documentation of Rijndael [2]. Bounds on the EDP of differentials have been investigated in [3,10,11].

We investigated differential propagation in AES, with the objective to understand how the components of the AES interact. We explain observed EDP values, including the maximum over 2 rounds. The EDP value of differentials is important in the resistance against differential cryptanalysis. In general, the EDP of differentials over multiple rounds of AES is difficult to compute. In this paper we have thoroughly investigated the distribution of the EDP of differentials over two rounds of AES, rather than focusing on upper bounds. As far as we know, this is the first paper that studies the distribution of EDP values in AES. We believe the results of this paper can be used to obtain tighter bounds for the EDP over 4 rounds of AES and generally a better understanding of its distribution.

---

[*] The work described in this paper has been partly supported by the European Commission under contract IST-2002-507932 (ECRYPT). The information in this paper is provided as is, and no warranty is given or implied that the information is fit for any particular purpose. The user thereof uses the information at its sole risk and liability.

R. De Prisco and M. Yung (Eds.): SCN 2006, LNCS 4116, pp. 78–94, 2006.

In Section 3, we extend and correct the analysis of the differential properties of the multiplicative inverse in $GF(2^n)$ given in [9]. In Section 4 we introduce the concept of bundles, which are classes of related characteristics contributing to the same differential. In Section 5 we study the conditions characteristics must satisfy to have a non-zero EDP. In Section 6 and Section 7 we study the EDP of bundles, which leads in Section 8 to results on the EDP of differentials. We discuss the maximum EDP value of [4] in the light of our results in Section 9 and conclude in Section 10. But first we briefly introduce some new terminology and define notations.

2   AES and Differential Cryptanalysis Basics

2.1   Differentials, Characteristics and Trails

We denote a differential over an arbitrary map by (a, b) and assume that it is clear from the context which map we mean. We call a the input difference and b the output difference. The probability of a differential is denoted by $DP(a, b)$. We define the expected differential probability (EDP) of a differential over a keyed map as the average of the differential probability $DP(a, b)$ over all keys. Let $B[k]$ denote a keyed function consisting of a sequence of R transformations $\rho^i[k]$:

$$B[k](x) = (\rho^R[k] \circ \cdots \circ \rho^2[k] \circ \rho^1[k])(x), \tag{1}$$

Then we define a differential trail as follows:

Definition 1. A differential trail *through B is a sequence of differences a, b, c, ..., z such that there are pairs $\{x, x \oplus a\}$ and keys such that*

$$\rho^1[k](x) + \rho^1[k](x + a) = b$$
$$(\rho^2[k] \circ \rho^1[k])(x) + (\rho^2[k] \circ \rho^1[k])(x + a) = c$$
$$\cdots$$
$$B[k](x) + B[k](x + a) = z.$$

Hence, a differential trail Q is a characteristic with non-zero expected differential probability: $EDP(Q) > 0$. For Markov ciphers, the EDP of a trail Q is the product of the DP of its S-boxes [6]. A trail $Q = (a, b, \ldots, e)$ is *in* a differential (f, g) if $a = f$ and $e = g$. We denote the number of trails in a differential (a, e) by $N_t(a, e)$. The EDP of a differential is the sum of the the EDP values of all the trails in that differential

$$EDP(a, e) = \sum_{Q \text{ in } (a,e)} EDP(Q) . \tag{2}$$

2.2   The AES Super Box

The AES S-box operates on $GF(2^8)$ and can be described as

$$S[x] = L^{-1}(x^{-1}) + q, \tag{3}$$

Here x^{-1} denotes the multiplicative inverse of x in $\mathrm{GF}(2^8)$, extended with 0 being mapped to 0. L is a linear transformation over $\mathrm{GF}(2)$ and q a constant. Note that L is not linear over $\mathrm{GF}(2^8)$ and can be expressed as a so-called *linearized polynomial* [7]. The additive group of the finite field $\mathrm{GF}(2^8)$ forms a vector space. In the remainder of this paper, we will sometimes tacitly switch from one representation to another.

For reasons of clarity, we introduce the structure of the (*AES*) *super box* (our notation). The differential probabilities over this structure are equivalent to those over 2 AES rounds. The AES super box maps a 4-byte array $a = [a_0, a_1, a_2, a_3]$ to a 4-byte array e and takes a 4-byte key k. It consists of the sequence of four transformations:

SubBytes $b_i = S[a_i]$ with S the AES S-box
MixColumns $c = \mathrm{M_c} b$ with $\mathrm{M_c}$ a 4×4 matrix
AddRoundKey $d = c \oplus k$ with k the round key
SubBytes $e_i = S[d_i]$

If we consider two AES rounds, swap the steps ShiftRows and SubBytes in the first round, and remove the linear transformations before the first SubBytes transformation and after the second SubBytes transformation, then we obtain a map that can also be described as 4 parallel instances of the AES super box.

We can partition the set of 4-byte vectors by considering *truncated* differences [5]. All vectors in a given equivalence class have zeroes in the same byte positions and non-zero values in the other byte positions. An equivalence class is characterized by an *activity pattern*. The activity pattern has a single bit for each byte position indicating whether its value must be 0 (passive) or not (active). The activity pattern of a differential (a, e) is the couple of the activity patterns of a and e. We say that two differences are *compatible* if they have the same activity pattern. Due to the diffusion properties of $\mathrm{M_c}$, activity patterns of differentials must have a minimum of 5 active positions. In total there are 93 such activity patterns.

A characteristic through the AES super box consists of a sequence of 5 differences: a, b, c, d and e. Since the AES S-box is invertible, $\mathrm{EDP}(a, b)$ over SubBytes can be non-zero only if a and b are compatible. Other necessary conditions to have $\mathrm{EDP} > 0$ are $c = d$, $d = \mathrm{M_c} b$, and d has to be compatible with e. In the remaining of this paper we only consider characteristics that satisfy these conditions (and we will omit c from the notation). Such a characteristic is fully determined by the differential (a, e) it is in and the intermediate difference b. We call b_i and d_i corresponding with active S-boxes the *inner differences* of a characteristic. We make the distinction between trails and characteristics because the number of trails in a differential is closely related to its EDP.

3   The Multiplicative Inverse in $\mathrm{GF}(2^n)$

In this section we discuss the differential properties of the single component in AES that is non-linear over $\mathrm{GF}(2)$: the multiplicative inverse in $\mathrm{GF}(2^n)$, extended with 0 being mapped to 0. In fact this is the operation of raising to the power $2^n - 2$. For readability we use the notation x^{-1} rather than x^{2^n-2}. Hence we adopt the convention that $0^{-1} = 0$. Differential properties of this map were previously already studied in [9]. In the following, a and b denote arbitrary non-zero differences. We need the *trace map* defined over a finite field $GF(p^n)$ with respect to $GF(p)$, denoted by $Tr(x)$:

$$Tr(x) = \sum_{i=0}^{n-1} x^{p^i} \tag{4}$$

Note that the trace map is linear over $GF(p)$ and that $Tr(x^{p^i}) = Tr(x)$ for any value of i. The differential (a, b) over the multiplicative inverse map has $DP(a, b) > 0$ if and only if the equation

$$(x + a)^{-1} + x^{-1} = b \tag{5}$$

has solutions. If $x = a$ or $x = 0$ is a solution of (5), we have $b = a^{-1}$ and both are solutions. Otherwise, $x = a$ or $x = 0$ is not a solution, we can transform (5) by multiplying with $b^{-1}x(x + a)$ yielding:

$$x^2 + ax + ab^{-1} = 0,$$

if we substitute x by $a^{-1}y$, this becomes:

$$y^2 + y + (ab)^{-1} = 0, \tag{6}$$

To investigate the condition for this equation to have solutions we have the following lemma:

Lemma 1 ([7, Theorem 2.25]). $Tr(t) = 0$ *iff* $t = z^p - z$ *for some* $z \in GF(p^n)$.

If we take $p = 2$, from this follows easily that:

Lemma 2. *For* $b \neq a^{-1}$, *equation (5) has 2 solutions if* $Tr((ab)^{-1}) = 0$, *and zero solutions otherwise.*

Consider now the case $b = a^{-1}$. Let ν and ν^2 denote the elements of $GF(2^n)$ of order 3. Then $\nu^2 + \nu = 1$ and $GF(2^2) = \{0, 1, \nu, \nu^2\}$. We present now the following new result:

Lemma 3. *For even* n, *the solutions of*

$$(x + a)^{-1} + x^{-1} = a^{-1} \tag{7}$$

form the set $T_a = \{0, a, \nu a, \nu^2 a\}$.

Proof. $x = a$ and $x = 0$ are solutions of (7). Assume there are other solutions. We can write such a solution as a product of a with an element z different from 0 or 1. We have

$$(za + a)^{-1} + (za)^{-1} = a^{-1} . \tag{8}$$

Or, equivalently,

$$(z+1)^{-1} + z^{-1} = 1 . \tag{9}$$

Multiplication with $z(z+1)$ yields:

$$z^2 + z + 1 = 0 . \tag{10}$$

According to Lemma 1, Equation (10) has two solutions iff $\mathrm{Tr}(1) = 0$ and none otherwise. $\mathrm{Tr}(1) = 0$ iff n is even. Since a solution of (10) satisfies $z^3 = 1$, its solutions are the two elements of $\mathrm{GF}(2^n)$ of order three.   □

Note that the description of the solutions given in [9]: $T_a = \{0, a, a^{1+d}, a^{1+2d}\}$ with $d = (2^n - 1)/3$ is only correct if $a^d \neq 1$, i.e. if the order of a does not divide $(2^n - 1)/3$. From these lemmas follow several corollaries.

Corollary 1 ([9]). *For odd n,*

$$(x + a)^{-1} + x^{-1} = a^{-1}$$

has two solutions: 0 and a.

Corollary 2. *For even n, the possible output differences b for a given input difference a are those with $\mathrm{Tr}((ab)^{-1}) = 0$ except $b = 0$. For odd n, the possible output differences b for a given input difference a are those with $\mathrm{Tr}((ab)^{-1}) = 0$ except $b = 0$ and extended with $b = a^{-1}$.*

Together with the fact that (5) has 4 solutions only if $b = a^{-1}$, this leads to the following corollary:

Corollary 3. *For all non-zero $c \in \mathrm{GF}(2^n)$ and for all positive integers t:*

$$DP(a, b) = DP(b, a) = DP(ca, bc^{-1}) = DP(a^{2^t}, b^{2^t}),$$

4   Bundles

For the EDP of a differential over the AES super box, we have:

$$\mathrm{EDP}(a, e) = \sum \mathrm{EDP}(a, b, \mathrm{M}_c e) = \sum_b \mathrm{EDP}_S(a, b)\mathrm{EDP}_S(\mathrm{M}_c b, e) . \tag{11}$$

with $\mathrm{EDP}_S(x, y)$ the EDP of a differential (x, y) over SubBytes. In order to compute the EDP of a differential, we first determine the number of trails in the differential. The number of trails is determined by means of *bundles*, which we define below. We start with an example.

Example 1. Consider the characteristics in a differential (a, e) with $a = [a_0, 0, 0, 0]$. Then clearly we must have $b = [b_0, 0, 0, 0]$ and thanks to MixColumns we have $d_0 = 2b_0$, $d_1 = b_0$, $d_2 = b_0$ and $d_3 = 3b_0$, or equivalently $d = b_0[2, 1, 1, 3]$, where $b_0[2, 1, 1, 3]$ denotes the scalar multiplication of the vector $[2, 1, 1, 3]$ with the (non-zero) scalar b_0. There are 255 characteristics in the differential, one for each nonzero value of b_0.

This can be generalized to any AES super box differential with 5 active S-boxes. If $Q = (a, b, d, e)$ and $Q' = (a, b', d', e)$ are two trails of the same differential with 5 active S-boxes, then there exists a γ such that $b_i = \gamma b_i'$, and $d_i = \gamma d_i'$, and b, b'.

We define a *bundle* as follows.

Definition 2. *The bundle $B(u^b)$ associated with the vector u^b, is the set of 255 vectors defined as follows:*

$$B(u^b) = \{\gamma u^b | \gamma \in GF(2^8) \text{ and } \gamma \neq 0\} \ .$$

Scalar multiplication doesn't change the activity pattern of a vector. Furthermore, the linearity of MixColumns over $GF(2^8)$ implies that $M_c(\gamma b) = \gamma(M_c b)$. Hence also the activity pattern of $u^d = M_c u^b$ is the same for all vectors u^b of a bundle. If (a, u^b, u^d, e) is a characteristic through the AES super box, then $(a, b, M_c b, e)$ is a characteristic through the AES super box $\forall b \in B(u^b)$. Hence, the set of characteristics in (a, e) can be partitioned into a number of classes. Each class contains the 255 characteristics $(a, b, M_c b, e)$ defined by keeping a, e constant and varying b over all the values of a bundle $B(u^b)$. In the following, we use 'bundle' also to refer to such a class of characteristics. A characteristic in the bundle $B(u^b)$ of the differential (a, e) is uniquely identified by the value of γ.

We can count the number of trails in (a, e) by counting the number of trails in each bundle and adding the results. In the following, we will explain how the number of trails in a bundle can be counted. As explained in Example 1, a differential with 5 active S-boxes only has a single bundle of characteristics. Table 1 lists the activity patterns with 5 active S-boxes and the corresponding

Table 1. Activity patterns with 5 active S-boxes and the corresponding values of (u^b, u^d) (in hexadecimal notation)

Activity Pattern	u^b	u^d
(1000;1111)	[1,0,0,0]	[2,1,1,3]
(1100;1110)	[1,3,0,0]	[7,7,2,0]
(1100;1101)	[1,1,0,0]	[1,3,0,2]
(1100;1011)	[2,1,0,0]	[7,0,3,7]
(1100;0111)	[3,2,0,0]	[0,7,1,7]
(1010;1110)	[1,0,3,0]	[1,4,7,0]
(1010;0111)	[1,0,2,0]	[0,7,5,1]
(1110;1010)	[1,4,7,0]	[9,0,B,0]
(0111;1010)	[0,7,5,1]	[D,0,E,0]
(1110;1100)	[3,7,2,0]	[D,B,0,0]
(1101;1100)	[1,7,0,2]	[9,D,0,0]
(1011;1100)	[1,0,1,1]	[2,3,0,0]
(0111;1100)	[0,7,1,3]	[B,E,0,0]
(1111;1000)	[E,9,D,B]	[1,0,0,0]

values of (u^b, u^d). In total there are 56 patterns. They can be derived by rotation of the 14 patterns listed.

For the bundles of a differential with 6 active positions, the u^b values can be found by taking (almost) all possible combinations of two u^b values of bundles with 5 active positions. For example, for activity pattern $(1110; 1110)$ we combine the bundles for $(1010; 1110)$ and $(0110; 1110)$ as given by Table 1. This gives $u^b = [1, 0, 3, 0] + z[0, 1, 1, 0] = [1, z, 3 + z, 0]$ and $u^d = [1, 4, 7, 0] + z[2, 1, 3, 0] = [1 + 2z, 4 + z, 7 + 3z, 0]$.

This results in 255 different bundles, one for each nonzero value of z. However, for u^b, u^d to have activity pattern $(1110; 1110)$ the value of z must be different from 3, 1/2, 4 and 7/3, where x/y denotes $x.y^{-1}$ in $\mathrm{GF}(2^8)$. Hence, a differential with 6 active S-boxes has 251 bundles. We derive the number of bundles for differentials with 7 or 8 active S-boxes in Appendix A.

5 Differentials over SubBytes with EDP > 0

A characteristic $(a, b, \mathrm{M_c}b, e)$ is a trail if both differentials (a, b) and $(\mathrm{M_c}b, e)$ are differentials with EDP > 0. We will now study the conditions this imposes on the trails within a bundle.

5.1 Sharp Conditions

Consider differentials over four parallel applications of the multiplicative inverse in $\mathrm{GF}(2^8)$. We have from Corollary 2:

$$\mathrm{EDP}(x, y) > 0 \Leftrightarrow \begin{cases} \mathrm{Tr}((x_i y_i)^{-1}) = 0 \\ x_i \neq 0 \text{ iff } y_i \neq 0 \end{cases}, \quad 0 \leq i < 4, \qquad (12)$$

Since the trace map is linear over $\mathrm{GF}(2)$, the solution space of $\mathrm{Tr}(y_0^{-1}v) = 0$ is a vector space of dimension 7 over $\mathrm{GF}(2)$. The intersection of $\mathrm{Tr}(y_0^{-1}v) = 0$ and $\mathrm{Tr}(y_1^{-1}v) = 0$ is a vector space of dimension 6 or 7. If the dimension is 7, this implies $y_0 = y_1$. In general, the dimension of the intersection of a system of equations $\mathrm{Tr}(y_j^{-1}v) = 0$ is equal to 8 minus the dimension of the vector space generated by the elements y_j^{-1}. For example, the solution space of $\mathrm{Tr}(y_0^{-1}v) = \mathrm{Tr}(y_1^{-1}v) = \mathrm{Tr}(y_2^{-1}v) = 0$ with $y_0 \neq y_1 \neq y_2 \neq y_0$ has dimension 6 if $y_2 = y_0 + y_1$ and dimension 5 otherwise.

Consider now a bundle $B(u)$ with u compatible with y. The number of vectors x in B with $\mathrm{EDP}(x, y) > 0$ equals the number of non-zero values γ for which

$$\mathrm{Tr}((\gamma u_i y_i)^{-1}) = 0, \quad 0 \leq i < 4. \qquad (13)$$

This can also be written as:

$$\mathrm{Tr}((u_i y_i)^{-1} \gamma^{-1}) = 0, \quad 0 \leq i < 4. \qquad (14)$$

The γ^{-1} values satisfying these four conditions form the vector space orthogonal to the vector space generated by the set

$$V_i = \{(u_0 y_0)^{-1}, (u_1 y_1)^{-1}, (u_2 y_2)^{-1}, (u_3 y_3)^{-1}\}. \qquad (15)$$

The number of non-zero solutions equals $2^{8-\alpha} - 1$, where α is the dimension of V_i. Hence, in one bundle, there can be 127, 63, 31 or 15 vectors x with $EDP(x, y) > 0$. Exactly the same analysis can be performed when x is fixed and we want to determine the number of y values in a bundle with $EDP(x, y) > 0$. We call (14) the *sharp* conditions on trails.

5.2 Blurred Conditions

If we consider differentials over SubBytes then we have to take into account the effect of the linear transformation L in the AES S-box. In order to determine the number of input differences x compatible to a fixed output difference y, it suffices to replace V_i by

$$V_a = \{(u_0 L(y_0))^{-1}, (u_1 L(y_1))^{-1}, (u_2 L(y_2))^{-1}, (u_3 L(y_3))^{-1}\} \ . \tag{16}$$

However, when determining the number of output differences y compatible with a fixed input difference x, (13) becomes:

$$\mathrm{Tr}((x_i L(\gamma u_i))^{-1}) = 0 \ , \ 0 \leq i < 4 \ , \tag{17}$$

which can't be easily reworked and are harder to analyse. Therefore we call these conditions the *blurred* conditions.

6   Number of Trails in a Bundle

The number of trails in a bundle $B(u^b)$ for a given differential (a, e) is now the number of γ values that satisfy the sharp conditions due to $(\gamma u^d, e)$ over SubBytes and the blurred conditions due to $(a, \gamma u^b)$ over SubBytes. In this section we first derive formulas to estimate the number of trails in $B(u^b)$ for the special case of a differential with one active S-box in the first round followed by formulas and a discussion for the general case.

6.1 Bundles with One Active S-Box in the First Round

Consider a differential (a, e) with activity pattern $(1000; 1111)$. There is a single bundle $B(u^b)$ with $u^b = [1, 0, 0, 0]$ and $u^d = [2, 1, 1, 3]$. The sharp conditions become:

$$\mathrm{Tr}((2L(e_0))^{-1}\gamma^{-1}) = 0$$
$$\mathrm{Tr}((L(e_1))^{-1}\gamma^{-1}) = 0$$
$$\mathrm{Tr}((L(e_2))^{-1}\gamma^{-1}) = 0$$
$$\mathrm{Tr}((3L(e_3))^{-1}\gamma^{-1}) = 0 \ .$$

If $e = [L^{-1}(z/2), L^{-1}(z), L^{-1}(z), L^{-1}(z/3)]$ for any nonzero value z, then $V_a = \{z^{-1}\}$ resulting in $\alpha = 1$ and hence there are 127 trails satisfying the sharp conditions.

The effect of the blurred condition can be modeled as a sampling process. The space sampled are the 255 vectors of $B(u)$. 127 out of the 255 vectors may satisfy the blurred condition. These are called the good ones, the 128 others the bad ones. The joint sharp conditions take a sample with size $2^{8-\alpha} - 1$. This gives rise to a hypergeometric distribution $H(N_t; n, m, N)$ [8] with the following parameters:

- Number of ways for a good selection $n = 127$.
- Number of ways for a bad selection $m = 255 - 127 = 128$.
- Sample size N: $2^{8-\alpha} - 1$.

Denoting the event that one vector is compatible (the outcome of a single sampling) by x_i, we obtain $E[x_i] = n/(m+n)$. Since $N_t = \sum_i x_i$,

$$E[N_t] = \frac{n}{m+n} N = \frac{127}{255}(2^{8-\alpha} - 1).$$

This gives formula (18). For the variance, we obtain:

$$\sigma^2(N_t) = \frac{mnN(m+n-N)}{(m+n)^2(m+n-1)} = \frac{128 \times 127(2^{8-\alpha}-1)(256-2^{8-\alpha})}{255^2 254},$$

which corresponds to (19). The exact distributions of the number of trails per differential for all four values of α are given in Appendix C.

6.2   Any Bundle

Every differential (a, e) imposes on γ a number of sharp conditions, determined by e and u^d, and a number of blurred conditions, determined by a and u^b. Following (16), the sharp conditions state that γ^{-1} has to be orthogonal to

$$V_a = \{v_0, v_1, v_2, v_3\},$$

with $v_i^{-1} = u^d{}_i L(e_i)$. The parameter α is defined as the dimension of V_a. Hence γ^{-1} is in a vector space of dimension $8 - \alpha$ ranging from 4 to 7.

The number of blurred conditions is denoted by β, and given by the number of different non-zero elements in the following set of couples:

$$\{(a_0, u^b{}_0), (a_1, u^b{}_1), (a_2, u^b{}_2), (a_3, u^b{}_3)\}.$$

For the vast majority of differentials, β equals the number of active S-boxes in a. β is smaller only when two a_i values are the same and the corresponding u_i in the bundle are also equal. Hence a reduction of β occurs much less often than a reduction of α. Both α and β range from 1 to 4 limited by $\alpha + \beta \le 5$.

The number of trails in the bundle $B(u^b)$ can be described as a stochastic variable with the expected value and variance given by:

$$E[N_t] = \left(\frac{127}{255}\right)^{\beta}(2^{8-\alpha} - 1), \tag{18}$$

$$\sigma^2(N_t) = E[N_t] \times \left[1 - \left(\frac{127}{255}\right)^\beta + (2^{8-\alpha} - 2)\left(\left(\frac{63}{127}\right)^\beta - \left(\frac{127}{255}\right)^\beta\right)\right]. \quad (19)$$

We give a derivation for (18) and (19) in Appendix B. The numerical values computed with these formulae are given in Table 2. We have conducted a large number of experiments that confirm the mean and variance predicted by (18) and (19) for any combination of α and β.

Table 2. Mean (left) and variance (right) of the number of trails for a differential given α and β

α, β	1	2	3	4
1	63.25	31.50	15.69	7.81
2	31.38	15.63	7.78	3.88
3	15.44	7.69	3.83	1.91
4	7.47	3.72	1.85	0.92

α, β	1	2	3	4
1	16.00	15.89	10.86	6.38
2	11.91	9.85	6.11	3.40
3	6.83	5.33	3.19	1.73
4	3.54	2.70	1.59	0.85

7   EDP of a Bundle

The distributions for the number of trails in a bundle can be converted to distributions of the EDP of a bundle by taking into account the EDP of the trails. The EDP of a trail is the product of the DP values of its active S-box differentials. If we apply Section 3 to the AES S-box, we see that for an S-box differential with given input (output) difference, there are 126 output (input) differences with DP $= 2^{-7}$ and a single output (input) difference with DP $= 2^{-6} = 2 \times 2^{-7}$. We call the latter double differentials. It follows that the EDP of a trail is $2^i 2^{-7\nu}$ with ν the number of active S-boxes and i the number of double S-box differentials. One could say that the presence of i double S-box differentials multiplies the EDP of the trail by a factor 2^i.

Let (a, b, d, e) be a characteristic in a bundle $B(u^b)$ of a differential (a, b), determined by γ. A characteristic has a double S-box differential in the i-th S-box of the first round if and only if

$$b_i = L^{-1}(a_i^{-1}) \Leftrightarrow \gamma = (u^b{}_i)^{-1} L^{-1}(a_i^{-1}). \quad (20)$$

The condition for a double S-box differential in the second round is:

$$d_j = L(e_j)^{-1} \Leftrightarrow \gamma = (u^d{}_j L(e_j))^{-1}. \quad (21)$$

Hence each double S-box differential occurs in exactly one characteristic of the bundle. Two observations can be made here.

Multiple solutions: If a solution of the equations in (20) and (21) is a multiple solution, then the corresponding characteristic (potentially) has a higher EDP. Consider for example a differential with 5 active S-boxes. There are seven different cases, of which the two extremes are:

'Poker': the double differentials are all in the same characteristic,
'No Pair': the double differentials occur in 5 different characteristics,

The other five cases are 'One Pair', 'Two Pairs', 'Three of a Kind', 'Full House' and 'Four of a Kind'. The occurrence of these cases is related to the values of α and β. The number of different solutions for (21) equals the number of different elements in V_a. If α is 1 or 4, this number is equal to α. If α is 2 or 3 and the number of active S-boxes in e is higher than α, the number of solutions can also be $\alpha + 1$. The number of solutions for (21) usually equals β, but it can also be smaller. For a given input difference a there can be at most one output difference e for which all double S-box differentials are in the same trail.

Occurrence in trails: The solutions of (20) and (21) still have to satisfy the remaining sharp conditions and blurred conditions in order to have an EDP > 0. Clearly, the expected number of characteristics satisfying the remaining conditions decreases when there are more conditions, i.e. when α and β increase. A 'Poker' characteristic, i.e. one in which the S-box differentials of all active S-boxes are double differentials, is always a trail.

7.1 How L Can Make a Difference

If we remove L from the S-box, the set of blurred conditions is replaced by a second set of sharp conditions. The number of trails in a bundle is then given by $2^{8-\alpha} - 1$, with $1 \leq \alpha < 8$. The maximum EDP occurs for differentials with 5 active S-boxes and $\alpha = 1$. There are 56×255 such differentials in the super box. For these, the double S-box differentials are in the same trail and hence the EDP is equal to $2^5 \times 2^{-35} + 126 \times 2^{-35} = 19.75 \times 2^{-32}$, where for AES this is 13.25×2^{-32} [4].

8 N_t and EDP of a Differential

Differentials with 5 active S-boxes contain only a single bundle, hence they are covered by the previous sections. For differentials with more active S-boxes, there are more bundles. Given a differential (a, e), we can compute for each of its bundles the value of (α, β). With α and β we can compute the mean number of trails in the bundle and the variance. The mean number of trails in a differential is the sum of the mean number of trails in these bundles. For the variance of the number of trails, the sum of the variances in the bundles gives a good idea.

The value of the differences a and e determine the distribution of α and β over the different bundles in the differential (a, e). As the number of active S-boxes grows, the analysis becomes more and more involved. Therefore we start with an example.

8.1 Differentials with Activity Pattern $(1110; 1110)$

There are in total 251 bundles with activity pattern $(1110; 1110)$. The distribution of α over the 251 bundles in (a, e) is completely determined by e, or more

Table 3. Distribution of α for differentials with activity pattern $(1110; 1110)$

α distribution			# couples	mean	standard deviation	
$\alpha = 3$	$\alpha = 2$	$\alpha = 1$	$(L(e_1)/L(e_0), L(e_2)/L(e_0))$		theory	exp.
250	1	0	21	965.2	28.42	25.65
249	2	0	1501	969.1	28.47	25.14
248	3	0	31170	973.1	28.53	25.15
247	4	0	2175	977.0	28.58	25.16
246	5	0	29907	981.0	28.63	25.23
250	0	1	3	973.1	28.42	23.28
249	1	1	248	977.0	28.47	25.01

specifically, by the couple $(L(e_1)/L(e_0), L(e_2)/L(e_0))$. Table 3 lists the seven distributions that are possible and gives for each of them the number of output differences e for which they occur.

The distribution of β depends on the values of a_0, a_1 and a_2. If they are three different values, then β is always equal to 3. For this case, Table 3 gives the theoretical mean and standard deviation of the number of trails (assuming independence between the bundles). If two of the values a_0, a_1 and a_2 are equal, then β will be 2 for at most one bundle and 3 for all other bundles. If they are all three equal, then either β will be 2 for at most three bundles, or β will be 1 for at most one bundle and 3 for all the other bundles.

In principle, the distributions for α and β combine to a two-dimensional distribution. In the worst case, the small values of β occur in bundles with a small value of α. All in all, there are only few bundles where β is smaller than 3, hence we can approximate by working with $\beta = 3$ for all bundles.

We have experimentally verified this theory by computing the number of trails for a large set of differentials with 6, 7 and 8 active S-boxes. The measured mean values coincide with the theoretically predicted values. The measured standard deviations, also listed in Table 3 are systematically smaller than the theoretical ones, implying that the number of trails in the bundles of a differential are not independent.

8.2   A Bound on the Multiplicity

In Section 4 we have shown that the bundles with activity pattern $(1110; 1110)$ can be enumerated by $u^{\mathrm{b}} = [1, z, 3 + z, 0]$ and $u^{\mathrm{d}} = [1 + 2z, 4 + z, 7 + 3z, 0]$ with z different from 0, 3, 1/2, 4 and 7/3.

Lemma 4. *If two double S-box differentials occur in the same characteristic of one bundle with activity pattern $(1110; 1110)$, then they occur in different characteristics for the 250 other bundles with the same activity pattern.*

Proof. Assume we have a bundle where the double differential in the first and the second S-box of the second round occur in the same characteristic. Then we have from (21):

$$((1 + 2z)L(e_1))^{-1} = ((4 + 7z)L(e_2))^{-1} .$$

This equation is linear in z and has at most one solution. Hence the double differentials can't be in the same characteristic for any other bundle. The same holds for any other pair of active S-box positions.   □

The expected contribution of the double S-box differentials to the EDP of a differential is maximum when there is a bundle in which they are all 6 in the same trail. This trail contributes 64×2^{-42} to the EDP of the differential. Lemma 4 implies that in the remaining 250 bundles, there can be no trails with more than one double S-box differential. Hence each of these bundles will contribute at most $(N_t + \min(6, N_t))2^{-42}$ to the EDP of the differential. On the average the presence of the double S-box differentials makes the contribution of these trails only rise from $N_t 2^{-42}$ for the hypothetical case where no double S-box differentials exist to $(132/127)N_t 2^{-42}$.

We conclude that for this type of differential, the distribution of the EDP values is much more centered around its mean value than is the case for differentials with 5 active S-boxes. This is mainly due to the fact that the distribution of the EDP of the differential is the convolution of the distributions of many bundles. Moreover, Lemma 4 implies that the different bundles compensate for one another.

The same phenomena can be observed for the other types of differentials with 6 active S-boxes. For differentials with 7 or 8 active S-boxes the average numbers of trails are even much higher and the EDP values much smaller. Furthermore, the individual trails have all very small EDP values. This all makes that the EDP values of differentials with 6 or more active S-boxes have a very narrow distribution.

9   Differentials with the Maximum EDP Value

The maximum EDP value obtained in [4] occurs for exactly 12 differentials over the AES super box. Due to the rotational symmetry of the AES super box, they come in 3 sets, where the differentials in a set are just rotated versions of each other. It is no surprise that they are differentials with 5 active S-boxes, where the deviations from the average value 2^{-32} are largest. Moreover, they have $\alpha = 1$ and $\beta = 1$ for which the expected number of trails is the highest over all differentials with 5 active S-boxes, as is clear from Figure 1 in Appendix C. The differentials are the following:

$$\left([x,0,0,0], [L^{-1}(y/2), L^{-1}(y), L^{-1}(y), L^{-1}(y/3)]\right),$$
$$\left([x,x,0,0], [L^{-1}(y), L^{-1}(y/3), 0, L^{-1}(y/2)]\right),$$
$$\left([x,x,x,0], [0, 0, L^{-1}(y/2), L^{-1}(y/3)]\right),$$

with $x = 75_x$ and $y = 41_x$. For these differentials, the number of trails is 75: 74 trails with EDP 2^{-35} and one with EDP 2^{-30}, resulting in EDP value $2^{-30} + 74 \times 2^{-35} = 13.25 \times 2^{-32}$. Clearly all five double S-box differentials are in the same trail. Note that there are differentials with 5 active S-boxes that have 82 trails (see Appendix C) but these have a lower EDP value due to the fact that the double S-box differentials are not in the same trail.

To prove the correctness of the maximum EDP value, [4] uses so-called 5-lists, a concept similar to, but different from, the bundles defined in this paper. Both bundles and 5-lists group sets of 255 b-differences. Bundles with 5 active S-boxes correspond with the 5-lists of type 1. In bundles with more than 5 active S-boxes the ratios between the inner differences are fixed, while in 5-lists of type 2, a number of inner differences are fixed. Their goal is also different: the concept of 5-lists helps in efficiently finding bounds, while bundles help to gain insight in the distribution of trails in differentials.

10   Conclusions and Future Work

The AES super box can be compared with an idealized keyed 32-bit map which is constructed as a family of 2^{32} randomly selected permutations (one permutation for each value of the key). In this idealized model, the distribution of the EDP over all differentials (a, b) with both a and b different from zero has a normal distribution with expected value 2^{-32} and standard deviation $2^{-47.5}$.

The AES super box differentials deviate from the idealized model: differentials with 4 or less active S-boxes have EDP = 0, and differentials with 5 active S-boxes can have EDP values as large as 13.25×2^{-32} [4]. Our results on differentials with 6 active S-boxes indicate that for differentials with 6 or more active S-boxes the distribution of the EDP is very narrowly centered around 2^{-32}. Further analysis can lead to strict bounds.

It is a well known fact that the linear transformation L in the AES S-box doesn't influence the EDP of S-box differentials and the bounds on the EDP of trails as proven in [2]. Our results explain how the presence of L influences the EDP of two-round differentials.

Bounds on the EDP of two-round differentials can be used to derive bounds on the EDP of four-round differentials [3]. The results of our paper allow to describe the full distribution of the EDP of two-round differentials. We expect that this information can be used to derive sharper bounds on the EDP of four-round differentials.

References

1. E. Biham and A. Shamir, "Differential Cryptanalysis of DES-like Cryptosystems," *Journal of Cryptology*, Vol. 4, No. 1, 1991, pp. 3–72.
2. J. Daemen, V. Rijmen, *The design of Rijndael — AES, The Advanced Encryption Standard*, Springer-Verlag, 2002.
3. L. Keliher, "Refined analysis of bounds related to linear and differential cryptanalysis for the AES," *Advanced Encryption Standard – AES, 4th international conference (AES 2004), LNCS 3373*, Springer-Verlag, 2005, pp. 42–57.
4. L. Keliher and J. Sui, "Exact maximum expected differential and linear probability for 2-round advanced encryption standard (AES)," Cryptology ePrint archive, Report 2005/321, 2005, http://eprint.iacr.org.
5. L.R. Knudsen, "Truncated and higher order differentials," *Fast Software Encryption '94, LNCS 1008*, B. Preneel, Ed., Springer-Verlag, 1995, pp. 196–211.

6. X. Lai, J.L. Massey and S. Murphy, "Markov Ciphers and Differential Cryptanalysis," *Advances in Cryptology, Proc. Eurocrypt'91, LNCS 547,* D.W. Davies, Ed., Springer-Verlag, 1991, pp. 17–38.
7. R. Lidl, H. Niederreiter, *Introduction to finite fields and their applications,* Cambridge University Press, 1986 (Reprinted 1988).
8. Mathworld, `http://mathworld.wolfram.com/`.
9. K. Nyberg, "Differentially uniform mappings for cryptography," *Advances in Cryptology, Proc. Eurocrypt'93, LNCS 765,* T. Helleseth, Ed., Springer-Verlag, 1994, pp. 55–64.
10. S. Park, S.H. Sung, S. Chee, E-J. Yoon and J. Lim, "On the security of Rijndael-like structures against differential and linear cryptanalysis," *Advances in Cryptology, Proceedings of Asiacrypt '02, LNCS 2501,* Y. Zheng, Ed., Springer-Verlag, 2002, pp. 176–191.
11. S. Park, S.H. Sung, S. Lee and J. Lim, "Improving the upper bound on the maximum differential and the maximum linear hull probability for SPN structures and AES," *Fast Software Encryption '03, LNCS 2887,* T. Johansson, Ed., Springer-Verlag, 2003, pp. 247–260.

A   Number of Bundles per Differential

The total number of nonzero vectors of 4 bytes is $2^{32} - 1$. Each bundle groups 255 such vectors, so the total number of bundles is

$$\frac{2^{32} - 1}{2^8 - 1} = 2^{24} + 2^{16} + 2^8 + 1 \; .$$

The number of bundles with a given activity pattern is determined by the number of active S-boxes in the activity pattern. If we denote the number of bundles for an activity pattern with x active S-boxes by $\mathrm{BN}(x)$, we have:

$$
\begin{aligned}
\mathrm{BN}(5) &&=& 1 \\
\mathrm{BN}(6) = 255 - 4\mathrm{BN}(5) &&=& 251 \\
\mathrm{BN}(7) = 255^2 - 4\mathrm{BN}(6) - 6\mathrm{BN}(5) &&=& 64015 \\
\mathrm{BN}(8) = 255^3 - 4\mathrm{BN}(7) - 6\mathrm{BN}(6) - 4\mathrm{BN}(5) &&=& 16323805
\end{aligned}
$$

The number of trails with i active S-boxes is

$$\binom{8}{i} 255 \mathrm{BN}(i) 127^i \; .$$

The total number of trails is 2.8×10^{26}.

B   Derivation of (18) and (19)

Assuming that the blurred conditions are independent, we can generalize the sampling model introduced in Section 6.1. The space sampled is now the set of β-component vectors where each of the components can take any nonzero value in $\mathrm{GF}(2^8)$. There are 255^β such vectors. A good selection is one in which the first component satisfies the first condition, the second component satisfies the second condition and so on. There are 127^β such vectors. Denoting by x_{it} the event that characteristic i satisfies condition t, we obtain:

$$E\left[N_t\right] = \sum_{i=1}^{N} E\left[x_i\right] = \sum_{i=1}^{N} E\left[x_{i1}\right] E\left[x_{i2}\right] \cdots E\left[x_{i\beta}\right] = N\left(\frac{n}{n+m}\right)^\beta$$

The variance satisfies

$$\sigma^2(N_t) = \sum_{i=1}^{N} \sigma^2(x_i) + \sum_{i=1}^{N}\sum_{\substack{j=1\\j\neq i}}^{N} \text{Cov}(x_i, x_j).$$

Since x_i takes only the values 0, 1, it is a Bernoulli variable, and

$$\sigma^2(x_i) = E\left[x_i\right]\left(1 - E\left[x_i\right]\right) \tag{22}$$

$$\text{Cov}(x_i, x_j) = E\left[x_i x_j\right] - E\left[x_i\right] E\left[x_j\right] \tag{23}$$

$$E\left[x_i\right] = \left(\frac{n}{n+m}\right)^\beta. \tag{24}$$

Since two trails of the same bundle differ in the value of each of their components, we have:

$$E\left[x_i x_j\right] = \left(\frac{n(n-1)}{(n+m)(n+m-1)}\right)^\beta. \tag{25}$$

Putting everything together results in (19).

C   Distributions of the Number of Trails per Differential

We have experimentally verified the distributions of the number of trails per differential for all 16 combinations of α and β. For the combination of (α, β) equal to $(1, 1)$, $(2, 1)$, $(3, 1)$, $(4, 1)$ and $(1, 2)$ we were able to do this exhaustively, covering all possible cases. As a side result we found for these values of (α, β) the minimum and maximum values for the number of trails per differential, listed in Table 4.

Table 4. Minimum and maximum number of trails in differentials with 5 active S-boxes given (α, β)

(α, β)	minimum	maximum
$(1, 1)$	48	82
$(2, 1)$	14	48
$(3, 1)$	3	29
$(4, 1)$	0	15
$(1, 2)$	10	56

For the other values of (α, β), the number of combinations becomes too large to compute exhaustively. Still, our sampling experiments confirm the shape predicted by formulas (18) and (19). As α and β grow, the mean and variance of the distributions shrink. Clearly, the majority of differentials with 5 active S-boxes and $\alpha = 1$ and $\beta = 1$ have more trails than any differential with 5 active S-boxes where $\alpha + \beta$ has a higher value. Figure 1 depicts the four distributions for $\beta = 1$ on a logarithmic scale. The distributions appear as slightly skewed parabolas, which is the typical shape of hypergeometric distributions.

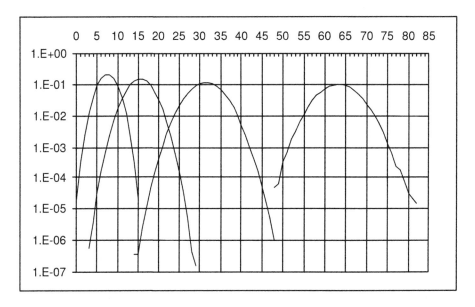

Fig. 1. Distributions of the number of trails per differential for $\beta = 1$ and for α ranging from 4 (leftmost) to 1 (rightmost)

Related-Key Attacks on the Full-Round Cobra-F64a and Cobra-F64b

Jiqiang Lu[1,*], Changhoon Lee[2,**], and Jongsung Kim[3,***]

[1] Information Security Group, Royal Holloway, University of London
Egham, Surrey TW20 0EX, UK
Jiqiang.Lu@rhul.ac.uk
[2] Center for Information Security Technologies(CIST), Korea University
Anam Dong, Sungbuk Gu, Seoul, Korea
crypto77@cist.korea.ac.kr
[3] Katholieke Universiteit Leuven, ESAT/SCD-COSIC
Kasteelpark Arenberg 10, B-3001 Leuven-Heverlee, Belgium
Kim.Jongsung@esat.kuleuven.be

Abstract. Cobra-F64a and Cobra-F64b, designed for firmware-oriented applications, are 64-bit Data-dependent Permutation based block ciphers with 128 key bits, which consist of 16 and 20 rounds, respectively. In this paper, we investigate their security against related-key attacks. Our investigation shows that the full 16-round Cobra-F64a can be broken by our related-key rectangle attack and that the full 20-round Cobra-F64b can be broken by our related-key differential attack.

Keywords: Block cipher, Cobra-F64a, Cobra-F64b, Data-dependent permutation, Differential cryptanalysis, Related-key attacks.

1 Introduction

Recently, many Data-dependant Permutation (DDP) based block ciphers, namely SPECTR-H64 [5], the CIKS family — CIKS-1 [18], CIKS-128 [6] and CIKS-128H [19], and the Cobra family — Cobra-128, Cobra-F64a and Cobra-F64b [8], Cobra-H64 and Cobra-H128 [20], have been proposed for encryption

---

* This author as well as his work was supported by a Royal Holloway Scholarship and the European Commission under contract IST-2002-507932 (ECRYPT).
** This author was supported by the Korea Research Foundation Grant funded by the Korean Government(MOEHRD)(KRF-2005-908-C00007) and by the MIC(Ministry of Information and Communication), Korea, under the ITRC(Information Technology Research Center) support program supervised by the IITA(Institute of Information Technology Assessment).
*** This author was financed by a Ph.D. grant of the Katholieke Universiteit Leuven and by the Korea Research Foundation Grant funded by the Korean Government(MOEHRD) (KRF-2005-213-D00077) and supported by the Concerted Research Action (GOA) Ambiorics 2005/11 of the Flemish Government and by the European Commission through the IST Programme under Contract IST2002507932 ECRYPT.

R. De Prisco and M. Yung (Eds.): SCN 2006, LNCS 4116, pp. 95–110, 2006.
© Springer-Verlag Berlin Heidelberg 2006

applications that require a small amount of data to be encrypted with frequently changed user keys, such as IPsec. To achieve high network speeds in such applications, these ciphers usually use agile key schedules as well as simple data transformation structures. As a result, although the proposers have considered their security against conventional cryptanalysis such as differential cryptanalysis [1] and linear cryptanalysis [17], most of them have been shown vulnerable to related-key [2] based cryptanalytic attacks [13,14,15,16]; however, Cobra-F64a and Cobra-F64b [8] are two exceptions. Although their names are similar, they are quite different ciphers.

The existing cryptanalytic results on Cobra-F64a and Cobra-F64b are due to Lee *et al.* [15], who mounted a related-key differential attack on the first 11 rounds of Cobra-F64a after exploiting a 11-round related-key differential with probability 2^{-48}, and mounted a related-key differential attack on the first 18 rounds of Cobra-F64b after exploiting a 18-round related-key differential with probability 2^{-56}.

In this paper, we find that there exist some shorter related-key differentials with much higher probabilities in Cobra-F64a. We construct a 15-round related-key rectangle distinguisher with probability $2^{-123.62}$ in Cobra-F64a, which can be used to mount a related-key rectangle attack on the full-round Cobra-F64a. For Cobra-F64b, we exploit a 19.5-round related-key differential with probability 2^{-57}, which can be used to mount a related-key differential attack on the full-round Cobra-F64b.

Like the amplified boomerang attack [11] and the rectangle attack [3], the related-key rectangle attack [4,9,12] is a variant of the boomerang attack [21]. Thus, it shares the same basic idea of using two short differentials with larger probabilities instead of a long differential with a smaller probability, but requires an additional assumption that the attacker knows the specific differences between two pairs of unknown keys. This additional assumption makes it difficult or even infeasible to conduct in many cryptographic applications; however, as demonstrated in [10], certain current real-world applications may allow for practical related-key attacks, including key-exchange protocols and hash functions.

The rest of this paper is organised as follows. In the next section, we briefly describe the DDP-Boxes, the Cobra-F64a and Cobra-F64b ciphers and related-key rectangle attacks. In Section 3, we introduce several properties of Cobra-F64a and Cobra-F64b. In Sections 4 and 5, we present our related-key attacks on the full-round Cobra-F64a and Cobra-F64b, respectively. Section 6 concludes this paper.

2   Preliminaries

2.1   DDP-Boxes

Definition 1. *The two-variable function $F : \{0,1\}^n \times \{0,1\}^m \rightarrow \{0,1\}^n$ is called a DDP-Box if, for each fixed m-bit control vector V, $F(\cdot, V)$ is a bijective mapping.*

The $n \times m$ DDP-Box F, denoted by $P_{n/m}$ below, uses the 2×1 DDP-Box $P_{2/1}$ as its elementary components. See Figure 2 in Appendix A. If $x = (x_1, x_2)$, then $P_{2/1}(x, v) = (x_{1+v}, x_{2-v})$. That is, it swaps the two input bits if $v = 1$; otherwise, doesn't.

Figure 3 in Appendix A depicts the DDP-Boxes $P_{32/96}$ and $P_{32/96}^{-1}$ used in Cobra-F64a and Cobra-F64b. Because of their symmetric structure, the mutual inverses of $P_{32/96}$ and $P_{32/96}^{-1}$ differ only in the distribution of the controlling bits over the DDP-boxes $P_{2/1}$; specifically, $P_{32/96}(\cdot, V)$ and $P_{32/96}^{-1}(\cdot, V')$ are mutually inverse when $V = (V_1, V_2, \cdots, V_6)$ and $V' = (V_6, V_5, \cdots, V_1)$.

2.2   The Cobra-F64a and Cobra-F64b Ciphers

The N-round encryption procedure of Cobra-F64a (N=16) or Cobra-F64b (N=20) can be described as follows.

1. The 64-bit plaintext P is divided into two 32-bit words (A_0, B_0).
2. For $i = 1$ to N:
   if $i \leq N - 1$,
   $$(A_i, B_i) := Crypt^{(e)}(A_{i-1}, B_{i-1}, Q_i^{(1,e)}, Q_i^{(2,e)}),$$
   $$(A_i, B_i) := (B_i, A_i).$$
   else
   $$(A_i, B_i) := Crypt^{(e)}(A_{i-1}, B_{i-1}, Q_i^{(1,e)}, Q_i^{(2,e)}).$$
3. Perform final transformation:
   - For Cobra-F64a: the ciphertext $(C_l, C_r) := (A_N \boxminus Q_{N+1}^{(1,e)}, B_N \boxplus Q_{N+1}^{(2,e)})$.
   - For Cobra-F64b: the ciphertext $(C_l, C_r) := (A_N \oplus Q_{N+1}^{(1,e)}, B_N \oplus Q_{N+1}^{(2,e)})$.
4. The 64-bit ciphertext C is (C_l, C_r),

where $Crypt^{(e)}$ is the round function, $(Q_i^{(1,e)}, Q_i^{(2,e)})$ is the 64-bit i-th round subkey, $(Q_{N+1}^{(1,e)}, Q_{N+1}^{(2,e)})$ is the 64-bit subkey used in the final transformation, $\boxplus/\boxminus$ denote addition/subtraction modulo 2^{32}, respectively, $\oplus$ denotes the bit-wise logical exclusive OR (XOR) operation, and $e \in \{0, 1\}$, with 0/1 denoting encryption/decryption, respectively. Figure 4 in Appendix A depicts $Crypt^{(e)}$, where $>>> i$ denotes right cyclic rotation by i bit positions. In addition, we assume that in an n-bit word $P = (p_1, p_2, \cdots, p_n)$, p_1 is the most significant bit and p_n is the least significant bit.

As shown in Figure 5(b), $Crypt^{(e)}$ is composed of an extension transformation E, a simple transposition $P_{96/1}^{(e)}$ and the DDP-Box $P_{32/96}$. Given an input $L = (l_1, \cdots, l_{32})$, the extension E outputs $V = (V_1, V_2, V_3, V_4, V_5, V_6) = (L_l, L_l^{>>>6}, L_l^{>>>12}, L_r, L_r^{>>>6}, L_r^{>>>12})$, where $L_l = (l_1, \cdots, l_{16})$ and $L_r = (l_{17}, \cdots, l_{32})$. As shown in Figure 5(a), the transposition $P_{96/1}^{(e)}$ consists of a series of DDPs $P_{2/1}^{(e)}$ controlled with the same bit e.

Both Cobra-F64a and Cobra-F64b use a 128-bit user key K that is divided into four 32-bit words $K = (K_1, K_2, K_3, K_4)$. The round subkeys $(Q_i^{(1,e)}, Q_i^{(2,e)})$, as well as the final subkey $(Q_{N+1}^{(1,e)}, Q_{N+1}^{(2,e)})$, are generated as shown in Table 1.

Table 1. The key schedules of Cobra-F64a and Cobra-F64b

i	1	2	3	4	5	6	7	8	9	10	11	12	13	14	15	16	17	18	19	20	21
$Q_i^{(1,0)}$	K_1	K_2	K_3	K_4	K_2	K_1	K_4	K_3	K_1	K_2	K_4	K_3	K_1	K_4	K_2	K_3	K_2	K_4	K_3	K_1	K_2
$Q_i^{(2,0)}$	K_4	K_3	K_1	K_2	K_3	K_2	K_1	K_4	K_2	K_3	K_1	K_2	K_3	K_1	K_3	K_4	K_3	K_1	K_4	K_2	K_3

2.3   Related-Key Rectangle Attacks

Related-key rectangle attacks treat a block cipher $E : \{0,1\}^n \times \{0,1\}^k \to \{0,1\}^n$ as a cascade of two sub-ciphers $E = E^1 \circ E^0$. They assume that there exist a related-key differential $\alpha \to \beta$ with probability p_β for E^0 (i.e. $Pr_{K,X}[E_K^0(X) \oplus E_{K \oplus \Delta K_0}^0(X') = \beta | X \oplus X' = \alpha] = p_\beta$), and a related-key differential $\gamma \to \delta$ with probability q_γ for E^1 (i.e. $Pr_{K,X}[E_K^1(X) \oplus E_{K \oplus \Delta K_1}^1(X') = \delta | X \oplus X' = \gamma] = q_\gamma$), where ΔK_0 and ΔK_1 are two known key differences.

Two pairs of plaintexts $(P_1, P_2 = P_1 \oplus \alpha)$ and $(P_3, P_4 = P_3 \oplus \alpha)$ are called a right quartet if the following three conditions hold:

C1: $E_{K_A}^0(P_1) \oplus E_{K_B}^0(P_2) = E_{K_C}^0(P_3) \oplus E_{K_D}^0(P_4) = \beta$,
C2: $E_{K_A}^0(P_1) \oplus E_{K_C}^0(P_3) = E_{K_B}^0(P_2) \oplus E_{K_D}^0(P_4) = \gamma$,
C3: $E_{K_A}^1(E_{K_A}^0(P_1)) \oplus E_{K_C}^1(E_{K_C}^0(P_3)) = E_{K_B}^1(E_{K_B}^0(P_2)) \oplus E_{K_D}^1(E_{K_D}^0(P_4)) = \delta$,

where the four unknown keys K_A, K_B, K_C and K_D satisfy $K_B = K_A \oplus \Delta K_0$, $K_C = K_A \oplus \Delta K_1$ and $K_D = K_C \oplus \Delta K_0$. Assuming that the intermediate values after E^0 distribute uniformly over all possible values, we get $E_{K_A}^0(P_1) \oplus E_{K_C}^0(P_3) = \gamma$ with probability 2^{-n}. Once this occurs, by C1 we know that $E_{K_B}^0(P_2) \oplus E_{K_D}^0(P_4) = \gamma$ holds with probability 1, for $E_{K_B}^0(P_2) \oplus E_{K_D}^0(P_4) = (E_{K_A}^0(P_1) \oplus E_{K_B}^0(P_2)) \oplus (E_{K_C}^0(P_3) \oplus E_{K_D}^0(P_4)) \oplus (E_{K_A}^0(P_1) \oplus E_{K_C}^0(P_3)) = \beta \oplus \beta \oplus \gamma = \gamma$. As a result, the probability of satisfying C3 is approximately $\sum_{\beta, \gamma} (p_\beta)^2 \cdot 2^{-n} \cdot (q_\gamma)^2 = 2^{-n} \cdot (\widehat{p} \cdot \widehat{q})^2$, where $\widehat{p} = \sqrt{\sum_\beta Pr^2(\alpha \to \beta)}$ and $\widehat{q} = \sqrt{\sum_\gamma Pr^2(\gamma \to \delta)}$.

On the other hand, for a random cipher, this probability is about 2^{-2n}. Therefore, if $\widehat{p} \cdot \widehat{q} > 2^{-n/2}$, the related-key rectangle distinguisher can distinguish between E and a random cipher. Please refer to [4,9,12] for illustrations.

Note that when one of the three cases $\Delta K_1 \neq \Delta K_0 = 0$, $\Delta K_0 \neq \Delta K_1 = 0$ and $\Delta K_0 = \Delta K_1 \neq 0$ occurs, the number of required related keys will decrease from 4 to 2. In our attacks, we use the third case $\Delta K_0 = \Delta K_1 \neq 0$ in which two keys K_A and $K_B = K_A \oplus \Delta K_0$ are used (note $K_C = K_B$ and $K_D = K_A$). If we use N pairs of plaintexts $(P_i, P_i' = P_i \oplus \alpha)$, where all P_i and P_i' are encrypted under the key K_A and the key K_B, respectively, then about $N^2/2$ quartets are considered for the above rectangle test. Thus, the expected number of right quartets is about $N^2 \cdot 2^{-n-1} \cdot (\widehat{p} \cdot \widehat{q})^2$.

3   Properties of Cobra-F64a and Cobra-F64b

In [13,14], Ko *et al.* showed the following three properties of the DDP-Boxes $P_{2/1}$, $P_{8/12}$ and $P_{n/m}$, respectively:

Property 1. *Let Δx be the difference between two inputs x and x' of $P_{2/1}$, Δv be the difference between two control vectors v and v' of $P_{2/1}$, and Δy be the difference between the two outputs $P_{2/1}(x,v)$ and $P_{2/1}(x',v')$, respectively. Then,*

a) *$P_{2/1}(x, v = 0) = P_{2/1}(x, v = 1)$ holds if and only if the two bits of the input x are equal, i.e. it holds with probability 2^{-1}.*
b) *$Prob.\{\Delta y = 10|\Delta x = 10/01, \Delta v = 0\} = Prob.\{\Delta y = 01|\Delta x = 10/01, \Delta v = 0\} = \frac{1}{2}$.*
c) *$Prob.\{\Delta y = 10|\Delta x = 10/01, \Delta v = 1\} = Prob.\{\Delta y = 01|\Delta x = 10/01, \Delta v = 1\} = \frac{1}{2}$.*
d) *$Prob.\{\Delta y = 11|\Delta x = 00, \Delta v = 1\} = Prob.\{\Delta y = 00|\Delta x = 00, \Delta v = 1\} = \frac{1}{2}$.*

Property 2. *Let $X \oplus X' = e_i$, then $P_{8/12}(X,V) \oplus P_{8/12}(X',V) = e_j$, for some j, where e_i denotes a n-bit word with zeros in all positions but bit i ($1 \le i, j \le n$). Besides, if i and j are fixed, then the trace (i.e. path) from i to j is also fixed.*

Property 3. *Let X and X' be two inputs of $P_{n/m}$, and V and $V'(= V \oplus e_i)$ ($1 \le i \le m$) be two control vectors of $P_{n/m}$. Then,*

a) *$P_{n/m}(X, V) = P_{n/m}(X, V')$ holds with probability 2^{-1}.*
b) *$Hw(X \oplus X') = Hw(P_{n/m}(X,V) \oplus P_{n/m}(X',V))$, where $Hw(\cdot)$ denotes the hamming weight function.*

In [15], Lee *et al.* showed two properties of the DDP-Boxes $P_{32/96}$ and $P_{32/32}$ in Cobra-F64a and Cobra-F64b; we now describe these two properties, correcting some errors in the versions described in [15]:

Property 4. *Let ΔX and ΔV be the input difference and the control vector difference of $P_{32/96}$, respectively. Then,*

a) *$P_{32/96}(\Delta V = 0)(\Delta X = 0) = 0$ holds with probability 1.*
b) *$P_{32/96}(\Delta V = e_1)(\Delta X = 0) = 0$ holds with probability 2^{-1}.*
c) *$P_{32/96}(\Delta V = 0)(\Delta X = e_1) = e_1$ holds with probability 2^{-5}.*
d) *$P_{32/96}(\Delta V = e_1)(\Delta X = e_1) = e_1$ holds with probability 2^{-5}.*

Property 5. *Let ΔX and ΔL be input difference and control vector difference of $P_{32/32}$, respectively. Then,*

a) *$P_{32/32}(\Delta L = 0)(\Delta X = 0) = 0$ holds with probability 1.*
b) *$P_{32/32}(\Delta L = e_1)(\Delta X = 0) = 0$ holds with probability 2^{-3}.*
c) *$P_{32/32}(\Delta L = 0)(\Delta X = e_1) = e_1$ holds with probability 2^{-5}.*
d) *$P_{32/32}(\Delta L = e_1)(\Delta X = e_1) = e_1$ holds with probability 2^{-7}.*
e) *$P_{32/32}(\Delta L = e_9)(\Delta X = e_1) = e_1$ holds with probability 2^{-8}.*
f) *$P_{32/32}(\Delta L = e_{1,9})(\Delta X = e_1) = e_1$ holds with probability 2^{-10}.*

4   Related-Key Rectangle Attack on Cobra-F64a

Let $E^f \circ E^0 \circ E^1$ be the full-round Cobra-F64a, where E^f denotes Round 1, E^0 denotes Rounds 2 to 9, and E^1 denotes Rounds 10 to 16 including the final transformation. Note that our full-round attack presented in this section works through the decryption process of Cobra-F64a, but for clarification, we describe our 15-round related-key rectangle distinguisher in terms of the encryption process.

4.1   A 15-Round Related-Key Rectangle Distinguisher

As shown in Table 2, the first related-key differential we exploit for this 15-round distinguisher is the 8-round related-key differential $\alpha \to \beta$ with probability $p = 2^{-18}$ for Rounds 2 to 9 (E^0): $(e_1, 0) \to (0, e_1)$, where the key difference is $K_A \oplus K_B = K_C \oplus K_D = (e_1, 0, 0, 0)$, and the second related-key differential is the 7-round related-key differential $\gamma \to \delta$ with probability $q = 2^{-12}$ for Rounds 10 to 16, and the final transformation (E^1): $(e_1, 0) \to (0, 0)$, where the key difference is $K_A \oplus K_C = K_B \oplus K_D = (e_1, 0, 0, 0)$. Note that $\Delta K_0 = \Delta K_1 = (e_1, 0, 0, 0)$ in this distinguisher, so $K_C = K_B$ and $K_D = K_A$.

Table 2. The two related-key differentials in the 15-round distinguisher in Cobra-F64a

Round(i)	$(\Delta A_i, \Delta B_i)$	$(\Delta Q_i^{(1,0)}, \Delta Q_i^{(2,0)})$	Probability
2	$(e_1, 0)$	$(0, 0)$	2^{-6}
3	$(0, e_1)$	$(0, e_1)$	1
4	$(0, 0)$	$(0, 0)$	1
5	$(0, 0)$	$(0, 0)$	1
6	$(0, 0)$	$(e_1, 0)$	2^{-6}
7	$(0, e_1)$	$(0, e_1)$	1
8	$(0, 0)$	$(0, 0)$	1
9	$(0, 0)$	$(e_1, 0)$	2^{-6}
output	$(0, e_1)$	/	/
10	$(e_1, 0)$	$(0, 0)$	2^{-6}
11	$(0, e_1)$	$(0, e_1)$	1
12	$(0, 0)$	$(0, 0)$	1
13	$(0, 0)$	$(e_1, 0)$	2^{-6}
14	$(0, e_1)$	$(0, e_1)$	1
15	$(0, 0)$	$(0, 0)$	1
16	$(0, 0)$	$(0, 0)$	1
FT	$(0, 0)$	$(0, 0)$	1
output	$(0, 0)$		/	/

To compute $\hat{p}$ (defined in Section 2.3) in our attack, we need to sum the square of the probability of all differentials $\alpha \to \beta^*$ with the same input difference α through E^0, which is computationally infeasible. Instead, we just count those 8-round related-key differentials $\alpha \to \beta^*$ in each of which only the difference propagation of the second $P_{32/32}^{A,e}$ in Round 9 is different from the 8-round related-key differential $\alpha \to \beta$ in Table 2, that is, the input difference and the controlling vector difference of the second $P_{32/32}^{A,e}$ in Round 9 is 0 and e_1, respectively, and its 32-bit output difference t has a hamming weight of 2 with one bit difference in the first byte and the other bit in the second byte (Case A) or one bit difference in the first two bytes and the other bit in the last two bytes (Case B). The contributions of the remaining 8-round related-key differentials are negligible. We now analyze the probabilities corresponding to these two cases. Consider the

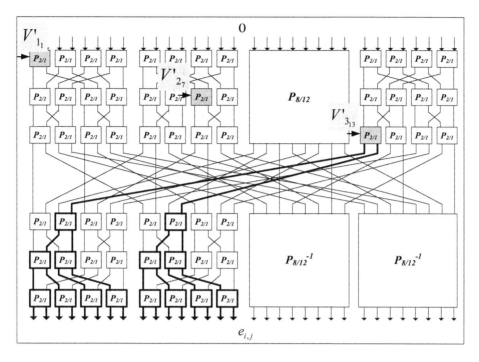

Fig. 1. The $P_{32/96}$ in $P_{32/32}(\Delta X = 0, \Delta V = e_1)$

second $P_{32/32}^{(A,e)}$ in Round 9, where the controlling vector difference is e_1 and the input difference is 0. The controlling vector difference e_1 is propagated to V'_{1_1}, V'_{2_7} and $V'_{3_{13}}$ after the extension E and the transposition $P_{96/1}^{(e)}$ in this $P_{32/32}^{(A,e)}$. See Figure 1.

- For Case A, there exist only the following two possible sources:
  1. The DDP-Box $P_{2/1}$ corresponding to $V'_{3_{13}}$ produces a difference 11, and the other two DDP-Boxes $P_{2/1}$ corresponding to V'_{1_1} and V'_{2_7} produce a difference 00. From Property 1-d, this holds with a probability of $2^{-1} \cdot 2^{-1} \cdot 2^{-1} = 2^{-3}$. Then, to get any specific difference in Case A, we have a probability of $2^{-3} \cdot 2^{-3} = 2^{-6}$, as there are three layers of DDP-Boxes to reach each one-bit difference. As a result, the probability of getting any specific difference in Case A from this source is $2^{-3} \cdot 2^{-6} = 2^{-9}$.
  2. The DDP-Box $P_{2/1}$ corresponding to V'_{1_1} produces a difference 11, and the other two DDP-Boxes $P_{2/1}$ corresponding to V'_{2_7} and $V'_{3_{13}}$ produce a difference 00. Again, we can learn from Property 1-d that this holds with a probability of 2^{-3}. Then, since there are two traces to reach any specific difference in Case A and there are five layers of DDP-Boxes to reach each one-bit difference, we have a probability of $2 \cdot 2^{-5} \cdot 2^{-5} = 2^{-9}$. As a result, the probability of getting any specific difference in Case A from this source is $2^{-3} \cdot 2^{-9} = 2^{-12}$.

Finally, we can conclude from the above analysis that the probability of getting any specific difference in Case A is $2^{-9} + 2^{-12}$.

– For Case B, there also exist only the following two possible sources:

1. The DDP-Box $P_{2/1}$ corresponding to V'_{2_7} produces a difference 11, and the other two DDP-Boxes $P_{2/1}$ corresponding to V'_{1_1} and $V'_{3_{13}}$ produce a difference 00, which holds with a probability of $2^{-1} \cdot 2^{-1} \cdot 2^{-1} = 2^{-3}$. Then, as there are four layers of DDP-Boxes to reach each one-bit difference of any specific difference in Case B, we have a probability of $2^{-4} \cdot 2^{-4} = 2^{-8}$. As a result, the probability of getting any specific difference in Case B from this source is $2^{-3} \cdot 2^{-8} = 2^{-11}$.

2. The DDP-Box $P_{2/1}$ corresponding to V'_{1_1} produces a difference 11, and the other two DDP-Boxes $P_{2/1}$ corresponding to V'_{2_7} and $V'_{3_{13}}$ produce a difference 00, which holds with a probability of 2^{-3}. Then, since there are two traces to reach any specific difference in Case B and there are five layers of DDP-Boxes to reach each one-bit difference, we have a probability of $2 \cdot 2^{-5} \cdot 2^{-5} = 2^{-9}$. As a result, the probability of getting any specific difference in Case B from this source is $2^{-3} \cdot 2^{-9} = 2^{-12}$.

Finally, we can conclude from the above analysis that the probability of getting any specific difference in Case B is $2^{-11} + 2^{-12}$.

Therefore, after considering the probability 2^{-3} incurred in the first $P_{32/32}^{(A,e)}$ in Round 9, we can compute a lower bound $\widehat{p} = \{1 \cdot (2^{-18})^2 + \binom{8}{1} \cdot \binom{8}{1} \cdot [2^{-12} \cdot 2^{-3} \cdot (2^{-9} + 2^{-12})]^2 + \binom{16}{1} \cdot \binom{16}{1} \cdot [2^{-12} \cdot 2^{-3}(2^{-11} + 2^{-12})]^2\}^{\frac{1}{2}} \approx 2^{-17.98}$ for the 321 possible 8-round related-key differentials $(e_1, 0) \rightarrow (t, e_1)$, where $t \in \{0,$ Case A, Case B$\}$.

To compute $\widehat{q}$ (defined in Section 2.3), we need to sum the square of the probability of all differentials $\gamma^* \rightarrow \delta$ with the same output difference δ through E^1, which is also computationally infeasible. Alternatively, we just count those 7-round related-key differentials $\gamma^* \rightarrow \delta$ in each of which only the difference propagation of the first $P_{32/32}^{A,e}$ in Round 10 is different from the 7-round related-key differential $\gamma \rightarrow \delta$ in Table 2, that is, the output difference and the controlling vector difference of the first $P_{32/32}^{A,e}$ in Round 10 (through the encryption direction) is 0 and e_1, respectively, and its 32-bit input difference s has a hamming weight of 2. After noting that the two one-bit differences of such a differential can only distribute in the input to one of the three DDP-Boxes $P_{2/1}$ corresponding to V'_{1_1}, V'_{2_7} and $V'_{3_{13}}$, we can similarly compute a loose lower bound $\widehat{q} = [1 \cdot (2^{-12})^2 + 1 \cdot (2^{-13})^2 + \binom{2}{1} \cdot \binom{2}{1} \cdot (2^{-16})^2 + \binom{4}{1} \cdot \binom{4}{1} \cdot (2^{-18})^2]^{\frac{1}{2}} \approx 2^{-11.83}$ for the 22 possible 7-round related-key differentials $\gamma^* \rightarrow \delta$. As a result, the distinguisher holds probability $2^{-123.62} (= 2^{-64} \cdot (2^{-17.98} \cdot 2^{-11.83})^2)$ for a right pair, while it holds probability 2^{-128} for a wrong pair.

Consequently, we can apply this distinguisher to a chosen ciphertext related-key rectangle attack on the full-round Cobra-F64a. Our attack procedure is as follows.

4.2   Attack Procedure

1. Choose $2^{63.81}$ ciphertext pairs (C_i, C_i^*), $i = 1, \cdots, 2^{63.81}$ such that $C_i = C_i^*$. Then, with a chosen ciphertext related-key attack, decrypt all C_i and C_i^* with the user keys K_A and K_B to get the corresponding plaintexts P_i and P_i^*, respectively, where $K_A \oplus K_B = (e_1, 0, 0, 0)$.

2. Guess two 32-bit subkeys (K_1, K_4) for Round 1 in E^f, do the following:

   2.1 Partially encrypt all the plaintexts P_i with (K_1, K_4) to get their inter-mediate values just after Round 1: we denote these encrypted values by T_i. Again, partially encrypt all the plaintexts P_i^* with $(K_1 \oplus e_1, K_4)$ to get their intermediate values just after Round 1: we denote these encrypted values by T_i^*. Then, store all the values T_i and T_i^* into a hash table. Finally, check if $T_{i_1} \oplus T_{i_2}^* = T_{i_1}^* \oplus T_{i_2} = (e_1, 0)$, for $1 \le i_1 < i_2 \le 2^{63.81}$.

   2.2 If the number of the quartets passing Step 2.1 is greater than or equal to 6, then record (K_1, K_4) and all the qualified $(T_{i_1}, T_{i_1}^*, T_{i_2}, T_{i_2}^*)$; otherwise, repeat Step 2 with another 64-bit key (K_1, K_4).

   2.3 Guess two 32-bit subkeys (K_2, K_3) for Round 2 in E^0, do the following:

      (a) Partially encrypt all remaining quartets $(T_{i_1}, T_{i_1}^*, T_{i_2}, T_{i_2}^*)$ with (K_2, K_3) to get their intermediate values just after Round 2: we de-note these encrypted values by $(\overline{T}_{i_1}, \overline{T}_{i_1}^*, \overline{T}_{i_2}, \overline{T}_{i_2}^*)$. Finally, check if $\overline{T}_{i_1} \oplus \overline{T}_{i_2}^* = \overline{T}_{i_1}^* \oplus \overline{T}_{i_2} = (0, e_1)$ for each quartet.

      (b) If the number of the quartets passing Step 2.3-(a) is greater than or equal to 6, then record (K_1, K_2, K_3, K_4); otherwise, repeat Step 2.3 with other two 32-bit subkeys (K_2, K_3) (if all the 2^{64} possible (K_2, K_3) are tested, repeat Step 2 with other two 32-bit subkeys (K_1, K_4)).

3. For a suggested (K_1, K_2, K_3, K_4), do a trial encryption with one known plaintext/ciphertext pair. If one is suggested, output it as the user key of Cobra-F64a; otherwise, go to Step 2.

The data complexity of this attack is $2^{64.81}$ related-key chosen ciphertexts. The required memory for this attack is dominated by the encrypted plaintext pairs (Step 2.1), which is approximately $2^{64.81} \cdot 8 = 2^{67.81}$ memory bytes.

The time complexity of Step 1 is $2^{64.81}$ encryptions. The time complexity of Step 2.1 is about $2^{64} \cdot 2^{64.81} \cdot \frac{1}{2} \cdot \frac{1}{16} \approx 2^{123.81}$ encryptions, where $\frac{1}{2}$ means the average fraction of 64-bit key pairs that are tested in Step 2.1. In Step 2.2, the probability that the number of the quartets for a wrong subkey is no less than 6 is approximately $\sum_{i=6}^{t} \binom{t}{i} \cdot (2^{-64 \times 2})^i \cdot (1 - 2^{-64 \times 2})^{t-i} \approx 2^{-17.77}$, where $t = 2^{126.62}$ representing the number of the possible quartets. Thus, about $2^{64} \cdot 2^{-17.77} \cdot \frac{1}{2} \approx 2^{45.23}$ subkeys on average pass through Step 2.2, resulting in about $2^{108.65}(= 2^{45.23} \cdot 2^{64} \cdot 6 \cdot 4 \cdot \frac{1}{16})$ full-round encryptions in Step 2.3-(a). In Step 2.3-(b), probability 2^{-6} is required to satisfy the one-round differential characteristic for Round 2, and the number of the quartets to be tested in this step is at least 6, therefore, the probability that a wrong subkey pair (K_2, K_3) passes Step 2.3-(b) is about $2^{-96}(= (2^{-6})^{6 \times 2})$. As a result, the expected number of the suggested 128-bit subkeys (K_1, K_2, K_3, K_4) in Step 2.3-(b) is $2^{13.23}(= 2^{45.23} \cdot 2^{64} \cdot 2^{-96})$. The time complexity for Step 3 is $2^{13.23}$. Therefore, this attack requires a total time complexity of $2^{123.81}(\approx 2^{64.81} + 2^{123.81} + 2^{108.65} + 2^{13.23})$ encryptions.

Since the probability that a wrong 128-bit key is suggested in Step 3 is approximately 2^{-64}, the expected number of suggested wrong 128-bit keys is about $2^{-64} \cdot 2^{13.23} \approx 2^{-50.77}$, which is quite low. Due to the probability $\widehat{p} \cdot \widehat{q} = 2^{-29.81}$ in our attack, the expected number of quartets for the right key pair is 8 $(\approx 2^{126.62} \cdot 2^{-64} \cdot (2^{-29.81})^2)$ and the probability that the number of the quartets for the right subkey is no less than 6 is approximately $\sum_{i=6}^{t}(\binom{t}{i} \cdot (2^{-64} \cdot 2^{-29.81 \times 2})^i \cdot (1 - 2^{-64} \cdot 2^{-29.81 \times 2})^{t-i}) \approx 0.8$. Therefore, with a success probability of 0.8, our related-key rectangle attack can break Cobra-F64a.

5   Related-Key Differential Attack on Cobra-F64b

5.1   A 19.5-Round Related-Key Differential Characteristic

As shown in Table 3, we exploit a 19.5-round related-key differential characteristic $(0, e_1) \rightarrow (e_1, 0)$ with probability 2^{-57}, where the key difference is (e_1, e_1, e_1, e_1). It is derived from the full-round related-key differential characteristic presented in [15].

Table 3. The 19.5-round related-key differential characteristic in Cobra-F64b

Round(i)	$(\Delta A_i, \Delta B_i)$	$(\Delta Q_i^{(1,0)}, \Delta Q_i^{(2,0)})$	Probability
1	$(0, e_1)$	(e_1, e_1)	2^{-3}
2	$(0, e_1)$	(e_1, e_1)	2^{-3}
3	$(0, e_1)$	(e_1, e_1)	2^{-3}
$\vdots$	$\vdots$	$\vdots$	$\vdots$
18	$(0, e_1)$	(e_1, e_1)	2^{-3}
19	$(0, e_1)$	(e_1, e_1)	2^{-3}
20($half$)	$(0, e_1)$	(e_1, e_1)	$1^{\dagger}$
$output$	$(e_1, 0)$	/	/

$\dagger$: This probability is just for the difference between the intermediate values XORed with the 20-th round subkey

In order to reduce the time complexity of our attack, we use the following filtering property: some possible differences between a pair of ciphertexts can be partially determined from the output difference $(e_1, 0)$ of the 19.5-round related-key differential, for those ciphertext pairs that do not meet these differences can be discarded immediately. More precisely, as the input difference and the controlling vector difference of the DDP-Box $P_{32/32}^{(A,e)}$ in Round 20 are 0 and e_1, respectively, the output difference of this $P_{32/32}^{(A,e)}$ should have a hamming weight of 0, 2, 4 or 6, which is caused by the three inherent DDP-Boxes $P_{2/1}$

corresponding to V'_{1_1}, V'_{2_7} and $V'_{3_{13}}$. After an analysis on the $P^{(A,e)}_{32/32}$, we conclude that there are at most $\binom{32}{2} \cdot \binom{16}{1} \cdot \binom{16}{1} \cdot \binom{8}{1} \cdot \binom{8}{1} = 31 \cdot 2^{18}$ possible values for those that have a hamming weight of 6, at most $\binom{32}{2} \cdot \binom{16}{1} \cdot \binom{16}{1} + \binom{32}{2} \cdot \binom{8}{1} \cdot \binom{8}{1} + \binom{16}{1} \cdot \binom{16}{1} \cdot \binom{8}{1} \cdot \binom{8}{1} = 31 \cdot 2^{12} + 31 \cdot 2^{10} + 2^{14}$ possible values for those that have a hamming weight of 4, at most $\binom{32}{2} = 31 \cdot 2^4$ possible values for those that have a hamming weight of 2, and only 1 with a hamming weight of 0. Therefore, the number of possible output differences of the $P^{(A,e)}_{32/32}$ is totally $31 \cdot 2^{18} + 31 \cdot 2^{12} + 31 \cdot 2^{10} + 2^{14} + 31 \cdot 2^4 + 1 = 8302065$. After XORed with the subkey difference $\Delta K_3 = e_1$ in the final transformation, these 8302065 possible output differences of the $P^{(A,e)}_{32/32}$ incur 8302065 possible output differences between the right halve of the pair of ciphertexts. We denote the resultant 8302065 possible output differences by the set $\mathcal{S}$. We will not count the possible number for the left halve, for it seems infeasible due to the right rotation and addition modulo 2^{32} operations in Round 20.

Consequently, we can conduct the following related-key differential attack to break the full-round Cobra-F64b.

5.2   Attack Procedure

1. Choose 2^{60} pairs of plaintexts (P_i, P^*_i) with $P_i \oplus P^*_i = (0, e_1)$, $i = 1, \cdots, 2^{60}$. Then, with a related-key chosen plaintext attack, encrypt all P_i with the user key K_A to get the respective ciphertexts C_i, and encrypt P^*_i with the related user key K_B to get the respective ciphertexts C^*_i, where $K_A \oplus K_B = (e_1, e_1, e_1, e_1)$. Finally, check if the right halve of the difference $C_i \oplus C^*_i$ belongs to the set $\mathcal{S}$ defined above. If not, discard (C_i, C^*_i).

2. Guess two 32-bit keys K_2 and K_3 for the final transformation, do the following:

   2.1 Partially decrypt all the remaining ciphertexts C_i with (K_2, K_3) to get their respective intermediate values just after the data (A_{19}, B_{19}) XORed with the 20-th round subkey $(Q^{(1,0)}_{20}, Q^{(2,0)}_{20})$ in Round 20 (i.e., just after the last 0.5 round in Round 20 through the backward direction): we denote the decrypted values by T_i. Again, partially decrypt all the remaining ciphertexts C^*_i with $(K_2 \oplus e_1, K_3 \oplus e_1)$ to get their respective intermediate values just after the last 0.5 round in Round 20 through the backward direction: we denote the decrypted values by T^*_i. Then, check if $T_i \oplus T^*_i = (e_1, 0)$.

   2.2 If the number of the pairs (T_i, T^*_i) passing Step 2.1 is greater than or equal to 6, then record K_2, K_3 and all the qualified (T_i, T^*_i); otherwise, repeat Step 2 with other two 32-bit subkeys K_2 and K_3.

   2.3 Guess a 32-bit key K_1, do the following:

     (a) For each remaining pair (T_i, T^*_i), partially decrypt T_i with (K_1, K_2) to get its intermediate value just after the data (A_{18}, B_{18}) XORed with the 19-th round subkey $(Q^{(1,0)}_{19}, Q^{(2,0)}_{19})$ in Round 19 (i.e., just after the last 1.5 round in Rounds 20 and 19 through the backward direction): we denote the decrypted values by $\overline{T}_i$. Again, partially decrypt T_i^* with $(K_1 \oplus e_1, K_2 \oplus e_1)$ to get its intermediate value just after the last 1.5 round in Rounds 20 and 19 through the backward direction: we denote the decrypted values by $\overline{T}_i^*$. Then, check if $\overline{T}_i \oplus \overline{T}_i^* = (e_1, 0)$.

(b) If the number of the pairs passing Step 2.3-(a) is greater than or equal to 6, then output K_1, K_2 and K_3; otherwise, repeat Step 2.3 with another 32-bit subkey K_1 (if all the 2^{32} possible K_1 are tested, repeat Step 2 with other two 32-bit subkeys K_2 and K_3).

3. For a suggested K_1, K_2 and K_3, do an exhaustive search for the remaining 32-bit subkey K_4 using trial encryption. Two known plaintext/ciphertext pairs are enough for this trial process. If a 128-bit key is suggested, output it as the user key of the full-round Cobra-F64b; otherwise, go to Step 2.

This attack requires 2^{61} related-key chosen plaintexts. The required memory for this attack is dominated by the ciphertext pairs, which is approximately $2^{61} \cdot 8 = 2^{64}$ memory bytes.

The time complexity of Step 1 is 2^{61} full-round Cobra-F64b encryptions. Due to the filtering condition in Step 1, there are only $2^{60} \cdot \frac{8302065}{2^{32}} \approx 2^{50.99}$ remaining pairs. So the time complexity of Step 2.1 is about $2^{64} \cdot 2^{51.99} \cdot \frac{1}{2} \cdot \frac{1}{20} \approx 2^{110.67}$ full-round Cobra-F64b encryptions, where $\frac{1}{2}$ means the average fraction of 64-bit key pairs that are tested in Step 2.1. In Step 2.2, the expected number of pairs recorded for each guessed key is about $2^{-41.01} \cdot 2^{50.99} = 2^{9.98}$, for the probability that each decrypted pair passes the test of Step 2.1 is about $2^{-64} \cdot 8302065 = 2^{-41.01}$, which is due to the fact that the filtering step holds $8302065 = 2^{22.99}$ ciphertext differences. It follows that Step 2.3-(a) requires about $2^{9.98} \cdot 2 \cdot 2^{96} \frac{1}{2} \cdot \frac{1}{20} \approx 2^{101.66}$ full-round Cobra-F64b encryptions on average. Moreover, in Step 2.3-(a), probability 2^{-3} is required to satisfy the one-round differential characteristic for Round 19 (refer to Table 3), and the probability that a wrong subkey (K_1, K_2, K_3) passes Step 2.3-(b) is about $\sum_{i=6}^{t} (\binom{t}{i} \cdot (2^{-3})^i \cdot (1 - 2^{-3})^{t-i}) \approx 2^{-53}$, where $t = 2^{9.98}$ representing the expected number of the remaining pairs. The time complexity for Step 3 is $2^{74} (= 2^{32} \cdot 2^{96} \cdot 2^{-53} \cdot \frac{1}{2})$. Therefore, this attack requires a total time complexity of $2^{110.67} (\approx 2^{61} + 2^{110.67} + 2^{101.66} + 2^{74})$ encryptions.

Since the probability that a wrong 128-bit key is suggested in Step 3 is approximately 2^{-128}, the expected number of suggested wrong 128-bit keys is about $2^{-128} \cdot 2^{74} \approx 2^{-54}$, which is extremely low. One the other hand, the expected number of text pairs for the right key pair is 8 $(\approx 2^{60} \cdot 2^{-57})$ and the probability that the number of the pairs for the right subkey is no less than 6 is approximately $\sum_{i=6}^{2^{60}} (\binom{2^{60}}{i} \cdot (2^{-57})^i \cdot (1 - 2^{-57})^{2^{60}-i}) \approx 0.8$. Therefore, with a success probability of 0.8, our related-key differential attack can break the full-round Cobra-F64b.

6   Conclusions

In this paper, we mount related-key attacks on the two DDP-based block ciphers Cobra-F64a and Cobra-F64b. The related-key rectangle attack on the full-round

Cobra-F64a requires $2^{64.81}$ related-key chosen ciphertexts and a time complexity of $2^{123.81}$ Cobra-F64a encryptions, while the related-key differential attack on the full-round Cobra-F64b requires 2^{61} related-key chosen plaintexts and a time complexity of $2^{110.67}$ Cobra-F64b encryptions.

Acknowledgments

The authors are very grateful to Jiqiang Lu's supervisor Prof. Chris Mitchell for his editorial comments and to the anonymous referees for their helpful technical and editorial comments.

References

1. E. Biham and A. Shamir, Differential cryptanalysis of the Data Encryption Standard, Springer-Verlag, 1993.
2. E. Biham, New types of cryptanalytic attacks using related keys, Advances in Cryptology — EUROCRYPT'93, T. Helleseth (ed.), Volume 765 of Lecture Notes in Computer Science, pp. 398–409, Springer-Verlag, 1993.
3. E. Biham, O. Dunkelman, and N. Keller, The rectangle attack — rectangling the Serpent, Proceedings of EUROCRYPT'01, B. Pfitzmann (ed.), Volume 2045 of Lecture Notes in Computer Science, pp. 340–357, Springer-Verlag, 2001.
4. E. Biham, O. Dunkelman, and N. Keller, Related-key boomerang and rectangle attacks, Advances in Cryptology — EUROCRYPT'05, R. Cramer (ed.), Volume 3494 of Lecture Notes in Computer Science, pp. 507–525, Springer-Verlag, 2005.
5. N. D. Goots, A. A. Moldovyan, and N. A. Moldovyan, Fast encryption algorithm SPECTR-H64, Proceedings of MMM-ACNS'01, V. I. Gorodetski et al. (eds.), Volume 2052 of Lecture Notes in Computer Science, pp. 275–286, Springer-Verlag, 2001.
6. N. D. Goots, B. V. Izotov, A. A. Moldovyan, and N. A. Moldovyan, Modern cryptography: protect your data with fast block ciphers, A-LIST Publishing, Wayne, 2003.
7. N. D. Goots, B. V. Izotov, A. A. Moldovyan, and N. A. Moldovyan, Fast ciphers for cheap hardware: differential analysis of SPECTR-H64, Proceedings of MMM-ACNS'03, V. Gorodetsky et al. (eds.), Volume 2776 of Lecture Notes in Computer Science, pp. 449–452, Springer-Verlag, 2003.
8. N. D. Goots, N. A. Moldovyan, P. A. Moldovyanu and D. H. Summerville, Fast DDP-based ciphers: from hardware to software, Proceedings of The 46th IEEE Midwest International Symposium on Circuits and Systems, pp. 770–773, 2003.
9. S. Hong, J. Kim, S. Lee, and B. Preneel, Related-key rectangle attacks on reduced versions of SHACAL-1 and AES-192, Proceedings of FSE'05, H. Gilbert and H. Handschuh (eds.), Volume 3557 of Lecture Notes in Computer Science, pp. 368–383, Springer-Verlag, 2005.
10. J. Kelsey, B. Schneier, and D. Wagner, Key-schedule cryptanalysis of IDEA, G-DES,GOST, SAFER, and Triple-DES, Advances in Cryptology — CRYPTO'96, N. Koblitz (ed.), Volume 1109 of Lecture Notes in Computer Science, pp. 237–251, Springer-Verlag, 1996.
11. J. Kelsey, T. Kohno, and B. Schneier, Amplified boomerang attacks against reduced-round MARS and Serpent, Proceedings of FSE'00, B. Schneier (ed.), Volume 1978 of Lecture Notes in Computer Science, pp. 75–93, Springer-Verlag, 2001

12. J. Kim, G. Kim, S. Hong, S. Lee, and D. Hong, The related-key rectangle attack
    — application to SHACAL-1, Proceedings of ACISP'04, H. Wang, J. Pieprzyk,
    and V. Varadharajan (eds.), Volume 3108 of Lecture Notes in Computer Science,
    pp. 123–136, Springer-Verlag, 2004.
13. Y. Ko, C. Lee, S. Hong, and S. Lee, Related key differential cryptanalysis of full-
    round SPECTR-H64 and CIKS-1, Proceedings of ACISP'04, H. Wang, J. Pieprzyk,
    and V. Varadharajan (eds.), Volume 3108 of Lecture Notes in Computer Science,
    pp. 137–148, Springer-Verlag, 2004.
14. Y. Ko, C. Lee, S. Hong, J. Sung, and S. Lee, Related-key attacks on DDP based
    ciphers: CIKS-128 and CIKS-128H, Proceedings of INDOCRYPT'04, A. Canteaut
    and K. Viswanathan (eds.), Volume 3348 of Lecture Notes in Computer Science,
    pp. 191–205, Springer-Verlag, 2004.
15. C. Lee, J. Kim, S. Hong, J. Sung, and S. Lee, Related-key differential attacks on
    Cobra-S128, Cobra-F64a and Cobra-F64b, Proceedings of Mycrypt'05, E. Daw-
    son and S. Vaudenay (eds.), Volume 3715 of Lecture Notes in Computer Science,
    pp. 244–262, Springer-Verlag, 2005.
16. C. Lee, J. Kim, J. Sung, S. Hong, S. Lee, and D. Moon, Related-key differential
    attacks on Cobra-H64 and Cobra-H128, Proceedings of Cryptography and Cod-
    ing'05, N. P. Smart (ed.), Volume 3796 of Lecture Notes in Computer Science,
    pp. 201–219, Springer-Verlag, 2005.
17. M. Matsui, Linear cryptanalysis method for DES cipher, Advances in Cryptology
    — EUROCRYPT'93, T. Helleseth (ed.), Volume 765 of Lecture Notes in Computer
    Science, pp. 386–397, Springer-Verlag, 1994.
18. A. A. Moldovyan and N. A. Moldovyan, A cipher based on Data-dependent Per-
    mutations, Journal of Cryptology, Vol. 15(1), pp. 61–72, 2002.
19. N. Sklavos, N. A. Moldovyan, and O. Koufopavlou, A new DDP-based cipher
    CIKS-128H: architecture, design and VLSI implementation optimization of CBC-
    encryption and hashing over 1 GBPS, Proceedings of The 46th IEEE Midwest
    International Symposium on Circuits and Systems, pp. 463–466, 2003.
20. N. Sklavos, N. A. Moldovyan, and O. Koufopavlou, High speed networking security:
    design and implementation of two new DDP-based ciphers, Mobile Networks and
    Applications, Kluwer Academic Publishers, Vol. 10, Issue 1-2, pp. 219–231, 2005.
21. D. Wagner, The boomerang attack, Proceedings of FSE'99, L. Knudsen (ed.), Vol-
    ume 1636 of Lecture Notes in Computer Science, pp. 156–170, Springer-Verlag,
    1999.

A   Components of Cobra-F64a and Cobra-F64b

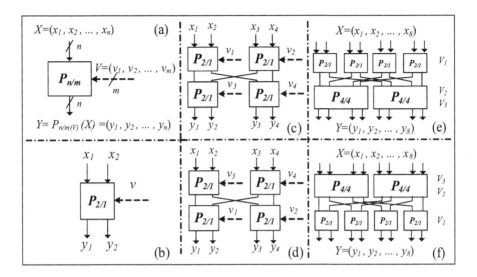

Fig. 2. (a) $P_{n/m}$; (b) $P_{2/1}$; (c) $P_{4/4}$; (d) $P_{4/4}^{-1}$; (e) $P_{8/12}$; (f) $P_{8/12}^{-1}$

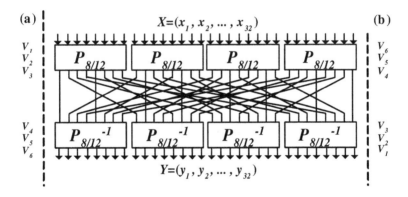

Fig. 3. (a) $P_{32/96}$; (b) $P_{32/96}^{-1}$

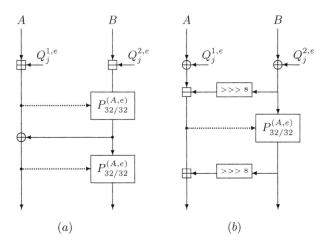

Fig. 4. (a)$Crypt^{(e)}$ of Cobra-F64a; (b) $Crypt^{(e)}$ of Cobra-F64b

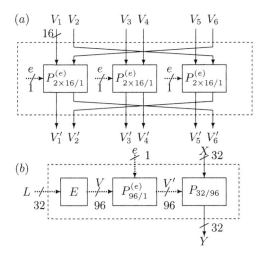

Fig. 5. (a) $P^e_{96/1}$; (b) $P^e_{32/32}$

Constant-Size Dynamic k-TAA*

Man Ho Au, Willy Susilo, and Yi Mu

Center for Information Security Research
School of Information Technology and Computer Science
University of Wollongong, Wollongong 2522, Australia
{mhaa456, wsusilo, ymu}@uow.edu.au

Abstract. k-times anonymous authentication (k-TAA) schemes allow members of a group to be authenticated anonymously by application providers for a bounded number of times. Dynamic k-TAA allows application providers to independently grant or revoke users from their own access group so as to provide better control over their clients. In terms of time and space complexity, existing dynamic k-TAA schemes are of complexities $O(k)$, where k is the allowed number of authentication. In this paper, we construct a dynamic k-TAA scheme with space and time complexities of $O(\log(k))$. We also outline how to construct dynamic k-TAA scheme with a constant proving effort. Public key size of this variant, however, is $O(k)$.

We then construct an ordinary k-TAA scheme from the dynamic scheme. We also describe a trade-off between efficiency and setup freeness of AP, in which AP does not need to hold any secret while maintaining control over their clients.

To build our system, we modify the short group signature scheme into a signature scheme and provide efficient protocols that allow one to prove in zero-knowledge the knowledge of a signature and to obtain a signature on a committed block of messages. We prove that the signature scheme is secure in the standard model under the q-SDH assumption.

Finally, we show that our dynamic k-TAA scheme, constructed from bilinear pairing, is secure in the random oracle model.

Keywords: k-TAA, dynamic k-TAA.

1 Introduction

Teranisi *et al.* [18] proposed k-times anonymous authentication (k-TAA) so that users of a group can access applications anonymously while application providers (AP) can decide the number of times users can access their applications. In k-TAA, there are three entities, namely, group manager (GM), application providers (AP) and users. Users first register to GM and each AP announce independently the allowable number of access to its application. A registered user can then authenticate himself to the AP's anonymously, up to the allowed number of times. Anyone can trace a dishonest user who tries to access an application for more than the allowable number of times.

* This work is partially supported by ARC Linkage Project Grant LP0667899.

R. De Prisco and M. Yung (Eds.): SCN 2006, LNCS 4116, pp. 111–125, 2006.
© Springer-Verlag Berlin Heidelberg 2006

In k-TAA, AP's have no control over the group of users accessing their applications. In actual scenarios, AP's may wish to select their own group of users. Dynamic k-TAA, proposed by Nguyen *et al.* [15], has added this flexibility over ordinary k-TAA systems. In a dynamic k-TAA, the role of AP's is more active and they can select their user groups, granting and revoking access of registered users independently.

Many existing k-TAA schemes (and dynamic k-TAA schemes) [18,15] are quite efficient, with time and space complexities independent of the total number of users. However, size of the public key of AP's, together with the communication cost between users and AP's, are both of order $O(k)$. The computational cost of the user for an authentication protocol is also of order $O(k)$. In this paper, we construct k-TAA and dynamic k-TAA scheme with complexity of $O(\log(k))$. We also outline how to reduce the proving cost to $O(1)$ at the cost of public key size of AP.

In constructing our scheme, we modify the short group signature from Boneh *et al.* [2] into a signature scheme, which we shall referred to as BBS+ signature, with two protocols, similar to [8,10] (referred to as CL, CL+ respectively hereafter). We do not claim originality of this modification as it has been outlined in [10]. However, we supply the details of the modification, together with the protocols and analyze its security. In particular, the protocol of showing possession of a signature is different from [2] in which the modified protocol achieve perfect zero-knowledge while the original protocol is computational. We prove that BBS+ signature is secure in the standard model under the q-SDH assumption. This BBS+ signature could be used as building blocks for other cryptographic systems. It has similar properties to CL (based on Strong RSA) and CL+ signatures (based on LRSW). To sign a block of messages, the signature scheme outperforms the existings schemes in the literature (signature size of CL+ is linear to number of messages in the block to be signed, CL is 1346 bits while BBS+ is only 511 bits).

The recently proposed group signature from [5] can also be modified into signature scheme with efficient protocol secured in the stand model. However, the signing of a message have to be done in a bit-by-bit manner.

1.1   Related Works

Very recently, Teranishi and Sako [19] proposed an ordinary k-TAA scheme with constant proving cost. We shall refer to it as TS06 hereafter. Our ordinary k-TAA scheme, constructed from the dynamic one following the outline of [15], is very similar to TS06. Our construction can be thought of as an extension of TS06 to dynamic k-TAA to give AP more control over their clients. This is achieved by the use of dynamic accumulator and the idea of using dynamic accumulator for access control was introduced in [9]. Finally, as pointed out in [19], k-TAA shares certain similarities with compact e-cash schemes, introduced in [7]. The main difference being in k-TAA schemes, each provider may chooses its only k and a user could authenticated himself k_1 times to provider-1, k_2 times to provider-2, etc., while in a compact e-cash scheme, the user can only spend his wallet a total of k times to all the shops combined. Nevertheless, the techniques used in our scheme is very similar to the compact e-cash scheme [7]. The main difference being we show how to incorporate the provider's name into the pseudo-random function such that authentication to different providers cannot be linked together.

Finally, the BBS+ signature we analyzed can be regarded as an extension of a digital signature scheme very recently proposed by [16] to support signing of block of committed messages.

Our Contributions

- we construct efficient dynamic k-TAA, k-TAA scheme.
- we reduce the security of our scheme to well-known intractable assumptions in the random oracle model.
- we analyze an modification of the BBS group signature, provide efficient protocols, and show its security in the standard model.

Organization. The rest of the paper is as follows. Preliminaries are presented in Section 2. We then briefly review the security notions in section 3. Our construction is shown in Section 4, followed by its variants in Section 5. Complexity and security analysis are given in Section 6. Finally, we conclude in Section 7.

2   Preliminaries

2.1   Notations

Let e be a bilinear map such that $e : \mathbb{G}_1 \times \mathbb{G}_2 \to \mathbb{G}_T$.

- $\mathbb{G}_1$ and $\mathbb{G}_2$ are cyclic multiplicative groups of prime order p.
- each element of $\mathbb{G}_1$, $\mathbb{G}_2$ and $\mathbb{G}_T$ has unique binary representation.
- g_0, h_0 are generators of $\mathbb{G}_1$ and $\mathbb{G}_2$ respectively.
- $\psi : \mathbb{G}_2 \to \mathbb{G}_1$ is a computable isomorphism from $\mathbb{G}_2$ to $\mathbb{G}_1$, with $\psi(h_0) = g_0$.
- (Bilinear) $\forall x \in \mathbb{G}_1$, $y \in \mathbb{G}_2$ and $a, b \in \mathbb{Z}_p$, $e(x^a, y^b) = e(x, y)^{ab}$.
- (Non-degenerate)$e(g_0, h_0) \neq 1$.

$\mathbb{G}_1$ and $\mathbb{G}_2$ can be same or different groups. We say that two groups ($\mathbb{G}_1$, $\mathbb{G}_2$) are a bilinear group pair if the group action in $\mathbb{G}_1$, $\mathbb{G}_2$, the isomorphism ψ and the bilinear mapping e are all efficiently computable.

2.2   Mathematical Assumptions

Definition 1 (Decisional Diffie-Hellman). *The Decisional Diffie-Hellman (DDH) problem in $\mathbb{G}$ is defined as follow: On input a quadruple $(g, g^a, g^b, g^c) \in \mathbb{G}^4$, output 1 if $c = ab$ and 0 otherwise. We say that the (t, ϵ)-DDH assumption holds in $\mathbb{G}$ if no t-time algorithm has advantage at least ϵ over random guessing in solving the DDH problem in $\mathbb{G}$.*

Definition 2 (q-Strong Diffie-Hellman). *The q-Strong Diffie-Hellman (q-SDH) problem in $(\mathbb{G}_1, \mathbb{G}_2)$ is defined as follow: On input a $(q+2)$-tuple $(g_0, h_0, h_0^x, h_0^{x^2}, \cdots, h_0^{x^q}) \in \mathbb{G}_1 \times \mathbb{G}_2^{q+1}$, output a pair (A, c) such that $A^{(x+c)} = g_0$ where $c \in \mathbb{Z}_p^*$. We say that the (q, t, ϵ)-SDH assumption holds in $(\mathbb{G}_1, \mathbb{G}_2)$ if no t-time algorithm has advantage at least ϵ in solving the q-SDH problem in $(\mathbb{G}_1, \mathbb{G}_2)$.*

The q-SDH assumption is shown to be true in the generic group model [1].

Definition 3 (y-Decisional Diffie-Hellman Inversion Assumption). *The y-Decisional Diffie-Hellman Inversion problem (y-DDHI) in prime order group $\mathbb{G}$ is defined as follow: On input a $(y+2)$-tuple $g, g^x, g^{x^2}, \cdots, g^{x^y}, g^c \in \mathbb{G}^{y+2}$, output 1 if $c = 1/x$ and 0 otherwise. We say that the (y, t, ϵ)-DDHI assumption holds in $\mathbb{G}$ if no t-time algorithm has advantage at least ϵ over random guessing in solving the y-DDHI problem in $\mathbb{G}$.*

2.3   Building Blocks

Verifiable Random Function. Our constant-size dynamic k-TAA make use of verifiable random function (VRF), introduced in [13]. Informally speaking, a VRF is a pseudo-random function with non-interactive proof of correctness of its output. The VRF used in our paper is due to Dodis *et al.* [11] and is described as follows. The pseudo-random function f is defined by a tuple $(\mathbb{G}_p, p, g, s)$, where $\mathbb{G}_T$ is a cyclic group of prime order p, g a generator of $\mathbb{G}_p$ and s is a seed in $\mathbb{Z}_p$. On input x, $f_{\mathbb{G}_p, p, g, s}(x) = g^{\frac{1}{s+x+1}}$. Efficient proof such that the output is correctly formed (with respect to s and x in some commitment scheme such as Pedersen Commitment [17]) exists and the output of f is indistinguishable from random elements in $\mathbb{G}_p$ if the y-DDHI assumption in $\mathbb{G}_p$ holds. The verifiable random function in [11] uses a stronger bilinear version of the y-DDHI assumption, see [7] for details.

Accumulator. Our construction is built based on the accumulator with one-way domain due to [14]. Rougly speaking, an accumulator is an algorithm to combine a large set of values $(\{x_i\})$ into a short value v. For each value $x_j \in \{x_i\}$, a witness w_j exists and with w_j, it can be proved that x is indeed accumulated into v. An accumulator is dynamic if it allows values to be added or deleted dynamically.

Signature Scheme with Efficient Protocols. In this paper, a signature scheme with efficient protocols refers to signature scheme with two protocols: (1) a protocol between a user and a signer with keys (pk, sk). Both user and signer agreed on a commitment scheme such as Pedersen commitment. The user input is a block of messages $(m_1, \cdots, m_L)$ and a random value r such that C=PedersenCommit$(m_1, \cdots, m_L, r)$. After executing the protocol, user obtains a signature on $(m_1, \cdots, m_L)$ from the signer while the signer learns nothing about the block of messages. (2) a protocol to proof the knowledge of a signature. This allows the user to prove to a verifier that he is in possession of a signature. Examples include CL signature, CL+ signature [8,10]. In this paper, we analyze another signature scheme with efficient protocols which is a modification of the short group signature from Boneh *et al.*[2], that we referred to as BBS+ signature.

3   Security Model

3.1   Syntax

We follow the model of dynamic k-TAA in [15] and briefly review them. A dynamic k-times anonymous authentication is a tuple (GMSetup, Join, APSetup, GrantingAccess, RevokeingAccess, Authentication, PublicTracing) of six polynomial time algorithms between three entities GM, APs, users. The following enumerates the syntax.

- GMSetup. On input a unary string 1^λ, where λ is a security parameter, the algorithm outputs GM secret key gsk and group public key gpk. All algorithms below have implicitly gpk as one of their inputs.
- Join Protocol. This protocol allows a user to join the group and obtain a member public/secret key pair (mpk, msk) from GM. The GM also add the user's identification and member public key to an identification list.
- APSetup. An AP publishes its identity ID and announces the number of times k a group member can access its application. It may also generate certain public and private key for the AP.
- GrantingAccess. Each AP manages its own access group AG which is initially empty. This procedure allows the AP to give selected group members the permission to access his application.
- RevokingAccess. It allows the AP to remove a member from his access group and stop a member from accessing his application.
- Authentication Protocol. The user authenticated himself to an AP under this protocol. The user is authenticated only if it is in the access group of the AP and the number of accesses have not exceeded the allowed number k. AP records the transcripts of authentication in an authentication log.
- PublicTracing. Anyone can execute this procedure using public information and the authentication log. The outputs are user i's identity, GM or NO-ONE which indicates "user i tries to access more than k times", "the GM cheated" and "there is no malicious entity in this authentication log" respectively.

A dynamic k-times anonymous authentication must possess *Correctness* which means that an honest member who is in the access group of an honest AP, and has not authenticate himself for more than the allowed number of times, must be authenticated by the AP.

3.2   Security Notions

We briefly recall security requirements, for formal definition please refer to [15,18].

- *D-Detectability.* Roughly speaking, it means that a subset of colluded users cannot perform the authentication procedure with the same honest AP for more than the allowed number of times, or they must be detected by the PublicTracing algorithm.
- *D-Anonymity.* It is required that no collusion of AP, users and GM can distinguish between authentication executions of two honest group members who are in the access group of the AP.
- *D-Exculpability.* It is required that an honest user cannot be accused of having performed the authentication procedure with the same honest AP for more than the allowed number of time. It is also required that the Public-Tracing algorithm shall not output GM if the GM is honest even though the AP and the users colludes.

4   Our Construction

Our dynamic k-TAA is built from the q-SDH based accumulator due to Nguyen [14] and a modification of the BBS group signature [2], that we call BBS+ signature, which is a signature scheme with efficient protocols. BBS+ signature is unforgeable against adaptive chosen message attack in the standard model under the q-SDH assumption and we also propose two protocols:(1) for issuing a signature on a committed value (so the signer has no information about the signed value), and (2) for proving knowledge of a signature on a committed value. We first describe the global common parameters, followed by descriptions of BBS+ signature and finally our dynamic k-TAA scheme.

4.1   Global Common Parameters

Let λ be the security parameter. Let $(\mathbb{G}_1, \mathbb{G}_2)$ be a bilinear group pair with computable isomorphism ψ as discussed such that $|\mathbb{G}_1| = |\mathbb{G}_2| = p$ for some prime p of λ bits. Assume $\mathbb{G}_p$ be a group of order p where DDH is intractable. Let $H : \{0,1\}^* \to \mathbb{Z}_p$, $H_{evt}\{0,1\}^* \to \mathbb{G}_p$ be cryptographic hash functions. Let g_0, g_1, g_2, g_3 be generators of $\mathbb{G}_1$, h_0, h_1, h_2, h_3 be generators of group $\mathbb{G}_2$ such that $\psi(h_i) = g_i$ and u_0, u_1, u_2, u_3 be generators of $\mathbb{G}_p$ such that relative discrete logarithm of the generators are unknown. One possible way is to make use of some hash functions $f : \{0,1\}^* \to \mathbb{G}_1$, $g : \{0,1\}^* \to \mathbb{G}_p$ and set $h_i = f(seed, i)$, $g_i = \psi(h_i)$, $u_i = g(seed, i)$ for some publicly known $seed$.

Remarks: the generation of this common parameters can be done by GM or some trusted third parties.

4.2   BBS+ Signature

The idea of modifying the BBS group signature into a signature with efficient protocols is stated in [10]. We supply the details, provide efficient protocols and prove its security.

KenGen. Randomly choose $\gamma \in_R \mathbb{Z}_p^*$ and compute $w = h_0{}^\gamma$. The secret key is γ and the public key is w.

Signing block of messages. On input $(m_1, \cdots, m_L) \in \mathbb{Z}_p^L$, choose e and a random number s, compute $A = [g_0 g_1^s g_2^{m_1} g_3^{m_2} \cdots g_{L+1}^{m_L}]^{\frac{1}{e+\gamma}}$. Signature on $(m_1, \cdots, m_L)$ is (A, e, s).

Signature Verification. To verify a signature (A, e, s) on $(m_1, \cdots, m_L)$, check if $e(A, wh_0^e) = e(g_0 g_1^s g_2^{m_1} g_3^{m_2} \cdots g_{L+1}^{m_L}, h_0)$.

Regarding security of BBS+ signature whose proof shall appear in the full version of the paper.

Theorem 1. *BBS+ signature is unforgeable against adaptively chosen message attack under the q-SDH assumption.*

Protocol for Signing Committed Block of Messages. The user computes a Pedersen Commitment on the block of messages to be signed by $C_m = g_1^{s'} g_2^{m_1} g_3^{m_2} \cdots g_{L+1}^{m_L}$. The user also needs to prove to the signer that C_m is correctly formed by the following PK: $PK\{(s', m_1, \cdots, m_L) : C_m = g_1^{s'} g_2^{m_1} g_3^{m_2} \cdots g_{L+1}^{m_L}\}$. The signer then chooses s'', e, computes $A = [g_0 g_1^{s''} C_m]^{\frac{1}{e+\gamma}}$ and sends back (A, e, s'') back to the user. The user computes $s = s' + s''$ and the signature on the block of messages is (A, e, s). For whatever block of messages $(m_1, \cdots, m_L)$, there exists an s' such that $C_m = g_1^{s'} g_2^{m_1} g_3^{m_2} \cdots g_{L+1}^{m_L}$ and s' completely hides the information about the block of messages. Thus, the signer learns nothing about the block of messages to be signed.

Proof of Knowledge of A Signature. We give a zero-knowledge proof of knowledge protocol for showing possession of a signature. Using any protocol for proving relations among components of a discrete-logarithm representations of a group element [6], it can be used to demonstrate relations among components of a signed block of messages. A user possessing a signature (A, e, s) on the block of message $(m_1, \cdots, m_L)$ can compute $SPK\{(A, e, s, m_1, \cdots, m_L) : A^{e+\gamma} = g_0 g_1^s g_2^{m_1} g_3^{m_2} \cdots g_{L+1}^{m_L}\}(M)$ by first computing the following quantities: $A_1 = g_1^{r_1} g_2^{r_2}$, $A_2 = A g_2^{r_1}$ for some randomly generated $r_1, r_2 \in_R \mathbb{Z}_p^*$. Then it computes the following SPK Π_5.

$$\Pi_5 : SPK\Big\{(r_1, r_2, e, \delta_1, \delta_2, e, s, m_1, \cdots, m_L) :$$
$$A_1 = g_1^{r_1} g_2^{r_2} \wedge A_1^e = g_1^{\delta_1} g_2^{\delta_2} \wedge \frac{e(A_2, w)}{e(g_0, h_0)} =$$
$$e(A_2, h_0)^{-e} e(g_2, w)^{r_1} e(g_2, h_0)^{\delta_1} e(g_1, h_0)^s e(g_2, h_0)^{m_1} \cdots e(g_{L+1}, h_0)^{m_L}\Big\}(M)$$
where $\delta_1 = r_1 e$ and $\delta_2 = r_2 e$.

Regarding SPK Π_5, we have the following theorem which is straight forward and the proof is thus omitted.

Theorem 2. *Π_5 is an non-interactive honest-verifier zero-knowledge proof-of-knowledge protocol with special soundness.*

Remarks: this protocol is a different from the protocol in [2], where the HVZK is computational (under the DLDH assumption) while Π_5 is perfect. One possible reason is that the SDH protocol in [2] is used for group signature scheme where certain user information in 'verifiably encrypted' within the protocol for GM to revoke identity of the signer.

4.3   Overview of Our Construction

Join. The GM is in possession of the public/secret key pair of BBS+ signature. User randomly generates $x \in \mathbb{Z}_p^*$ and u_0^x is the identity of the user. A membership certificate of a user is a BBS+ signature (of the form (A, e)) on the set of values (s, t, x), where s and t are also random elements in $\mathbb{Z}_p*$. Finally, (u_0^x, e) are placed on an identification list.

GrantingAccess/RevokeAccess. Each AP generates its own accumulator due to Nguyen [14]. It accumulates the value e into the accumulator and gives the witness w_{AP} to the user. To revoke access, the AP removes the value e from the accumulator.

   In the variant of our scheme (to be shown in the next section), AP only publishes the access group and let the users work with the accumulator itself. This makes it possible to remove the interactive granting access/revoke access protocol. The cost is that user has to perform $O(|AccessGroup|)$ operations to obtain his own witness.

Authentication. The idea is to have the users prove to the AP that it is in possession of a BBS+ signature (A, e, s) from the GM on the values (t, x), and that e is inside the accumulator of the AP. To restrict the user from authenticating himself for more than k times, pseudo-random function(PRF) due to Dodis and Yampolskiy [11] is used as follow. Let u_{AP} be a random element in a cyclic group equal to hash of identity of the AP. The user computes $S = u_{AP}^{\frac{1}{s+J_{AP}+1}}$ and proves that S is correctly formed with respect to the BBS+ signature component s. Also, user needs to prove that $1 \leq J_{AP} \leq k$. In this way, for a particular AP, the user can only generate k valid S, which we called serial number. If he attempts to authenticate himself for more than k times, duplicated serial number has to be used and can thus be detected.

   Finally, to allow revocation of identity of user attempting to authenticate himself for more than k times, another component $T = u_0^x u_{AP}^{\frac{R}{t+J_{AP}+1}}$ is added, where R is a random nonce chosen by the AP during each authentication attempt. User needs to prove that T is correctly formed. In case the user attempts to use the same serial number to authenticate twice, due to R being different, the two T's shall be different. With different T's, identity of the cheater, u_0^x, can be computed.

Remarks: it is obvious that other signature schemes with efficient protocol such as CL, CL+ could also be used for our scheme. However, in our case, BBS+ is most suitable for two reasons: (1) it is most efficient in our context and (2) the accumulator we used is based on the q-SDH assumption for which security of BBS+ signature also relies on.

4.4   Details of Our Construction

GMSetup. The GM randomly selects $\gamma \in_R \mathbb{Z}_p^*$ and computes $w = h_0^\gamma$. The GM also manages an identification list which is a tuple (i, U_i, e_i) where i refers to user i and U_i is an entry for identification of user and e_i is called the membership public key of user i. See Join for a more detailed description of this item.

APSetup. Each AP publishes his identity ID and a number k, much smaller than 2^λ. In addition, each AP selects $h_{AP} \in \mathbb{G}_2$, $q_{AP} \in \mathbb{Z}_p^*$. The public and secret keys for the AP are $h_{AP}, p_{AP} = h_{AP}^{q_{AP}}$ and q_{AP} respectively. The AP maintains an authentication log, an accumulated value, which is published and updated after granting or revoking access of a member, and a public archive ARC which is describe as follows. The ARC is a 3-tuple (arc_1, arc_2, arc_3) where arc_1 is a component of the membership public key of a user, arc_2 is a single bit $0/1$ indicating if the member was granted (1) or revoked (0). Finally, arc_3 is the accumulated value after granting or revoking the member. Initially, the authentication log and ARC are empty while the accumulated value is set to h_{AP}.

Join. User i obtains his membership secret key from GM through the following interactive protocol.

1. User i randomly selects $s', t, x \in_R \mathbb{Z}_p^*$ and sends $C' = g_1^{s'} g_2^t g_3^x$, along with the proof $\Pi_0 = PK\{(s', t, x) : C' = g_1^{s'} g_2^t g_3^x\}$ to GM.
2. GM verifies that Π_0 is valid and randomly selects $s'' \in_R \mathbb{Z}_p^*$. It sends s'' to the user.
3. User computes $s = s' + s''$ and add an entry $(i, U_i) = (i, u_0^x)$ to the identification list and send a proof $\Pi_1 = PK\{(s, t, x) : U_i = u_0^x \wedge C = g_1^s g_2^t g_3^x \wedge C = C' g_1^{s''}\}$.
4. GM computes $C = C' g_1^{s''}$, check that Π_1 is valid , and selects $e \in_R \mathbb{Z}_p^*$. It then computes $A = (g_0 C)^{\frac{1}{e+\gamma}}$ and sends (A, e, s'') to the user. GM also appends e to the entry (i, U_i) to make it (i, U_i, e)
5. User checks if $e(A, wh_0^e) = e(g_0 g_1^s g_2^t g_3^x, h_0)$. It then stores (A, e, s, t, x). User's membership public key is e and membership secret key is (A, s, t, x).

GrantingAccess. An AP grants access to user i with membership public key e and secret key (A, s, t, x) as follows. Suppose there are j tuples in the AP's ARC and the current accumulated value is v_j. The AP computes a new accumulated value $v_{j+1} = v_j^{e+q_{AP}}$. Then the AP adds $(e, 1, v_{j+1})$ to the ARC. The user keeps $w = v_j$ as his witness that his public key has been accumulated in the accumulated value. Existing members in the access group update their own witness by the information of ARC as follows. User with membership key e_k and witness w_e such that $w_e^{e_k+q_{AP}} = v_j$ computes $w_{new} = v_j w_e^{e-e_k}$. In this case $w_{new}^{e_k+q_{AP}} = v_{j+1}$ and w_{new} serves as a new witness for user e_k.

RevokingAccess. An AP revokes access from user i with membership public key e, such that $(e, 1, v)$ is a tuple in the ARC, as follows. Suppose there are j tuples in the AP's ARC and the current accumulated value is v_j. The AP computes $v_{j+1} = v_j^{\frac{1}{e+q_{AP}}}$. It then adds $(e, 0, v_{j+1})$ to ARC. Similar to the case of GrantingAccess, existing members in the access group update their own witness by the information of ARC, which is shown as follows. Suppose user e_k possesses witness such that $w_e^{e_k+q_{AP}} = v_j$, it computes $w_{new} = (w_e/v_{j+1})^{\frac{1}{e-e_k}}$ such that

$$w_{new}^{e_k+q_{AP}} = [\frac{v_j}{v_{j+1}^{q_{AP}+e_k}}]^{\frac{1}{e-e_k}} = [\frac{v_{j+1}^{q_{AP}+e}}{v_{j+1}^{q_{AP}+e_k}}]^{\frac{1}{e-e_k}} = v_{j+1}.$$

Authentication. The user manages a set of counters, one for each AP , J_{AP}, such that it did not attempt to sign more than k times for each AP. User with membership public key e and secret key (A, s, t, x), having granted access from the AP and thus possesses a witness w_{AP} such that $w_{AP}^{e+q_{AP}} = v_{AP}$ where v_{AP} is the current accumulated value of the AP authenticates himself by the following interactive protocol. For simplicity we drop the subscript AP for q_{AP} and v_{AP}.

- AP sends a random $seed \in \{0,1\}^*$ to user. In practice, $seed$ can be some random number or information about the current session. Both parties compute $R = H(seed)$ locally.
- User computes $u_{AP} = H_{evt}(ID_{AP})$ where ID_{AD} is the identity of the AP. User then computes $S = u_{AP}^{\frac{1}{J_{AP}+s+1}}$, $T = u_0^x u_{AP}^{\frac{R}{J_{AP}+t+1}}$ and proves in zero-knowledge manner (1) - (5):
  1. $A^{e+\gamma} = g_0 g_1^s g_2^t g_3^x$.
  2. $w_{AP}^{e+q} = v$.
  3. $S = u_{AP}^{\frac{1}{J_{AP}+s+1}}$.
  4. $T = u_0^x u_{AP}^{\frac{R}{J_{AP}+t+1}}$.
  5. $1 \le J_{AP} \le k$
- The above can be abstracted as

$$\Pi_2 : SPK\left\{ (A, e, s, t, x, w, J_{AP}) : \right.$$
$$A^{e+\gamma} = g_0 g_1^s g_2^t g_3^x \ \wedge \ w^{e+q} = v \ \wedge \ S = u_{AP}^{\frac{1}{J_{AP}+s+1}} \ \wedge$$
$$\left. T = u_0^x u_{AP}^{\frac{R}{J_{AP}+t+1}} \ \wedge \ 1 \le J_{AP} \le k \right\}(M)$$

- AP then verifies that the SPK is correct. If yes, then accept and saves S, T, R into database.
- User then increases its counter, J_{AP}, by one.

Instantiation of Π_2. Upon receiving $seed$, the user computes the following quantities: $A_1 = g_1^{r_1} g_2^{r_2} g_3^{r_3}$, $A_2 = A g_2^{r_2}$, $A_3 = w_{AP} g_3^{r_2}$, $A_4 = g_1^{J_{AP}} g_2^t g_3^{r_4}$, $S = u_{AP}^{\frac{1}{J_{AP}+s+1}}$, $T = u_0^x u_{AP}^{\frac{R}{J_{AP}+t+1}}$, $R = H(seed)$ and computes the following SPK Π_3.

$$\Pi_3 : SPK\left\{ (r_1, r_2, r_3, r_4, \delta_1, \delta_2, \delta_3, \delta_4, \delta_J, \delta_t, e, s, t, x, J_{AP}) : \right.$$
$$A_1 = g_1^{r_1} g_2^{r_2} g_3^{r_3} \ \wedge \ A_1^e = g_1^{\delta_1} g_2^{\delta_2} g_3^{\delta_3} \ \wedge$$
$$\frac{e(A_3, P_{AP})}{e(v, h_{AP})} = e(g_3, h_{AP})^{\delta_2} e(g_3, p_{AP})^{r_2} e(A_3, h_{AP})^{-e} \ \wedge$$
$$\frac{e(A_2, w)}{e(g_0, h_0)} = e(g_1, h_0)^s e(g_2, h_0)^t e(g_3, h_0)^x e(g_3, h_0)^{\delta_1} e(g_3, w)^{r_1} e(A_2, h_0)^{-e} \ \wedge$$
$$\frac{u_{AP}}{S} = S^{J_{AP}} S^s \ \wedge \ A_4 = g_1^{J_{AP}} g_2^t g_3^{r_4} \ \wedge \ A_4^x = g_1^{\delta_J} g_2^{\delta_t} g_3^{\delta_4} \ \wedge$$
$$\left. \frac{u_{AP}^R}{T} = T^{J_{AP}} T^t u_0^{-\delta_J} u_0^{-\delta_t} u_0^x \ \wedge \ 1 \le J_{AP} \le k \right\}(M)$$

where $\delta_1 = r_1 e, \delta_2 = r_2 e, \delta_3 = r_3 e, \delta_J = J_{AP} x, \delta_t = t x, \delta_4 = r_4 x$.

For a more detail protocol for the range check of J_{AP}, please refer to the appendix A.

PublicTracing. For two entries (SPK, S, T, R) and (SPK', S', T', R'), if $S \neq S'$, then the underlying user of both authentications has not exceeded its prescribed usage k or they are from different user.

If $S = S'$, then everyone can compute $u_0^x = (\frac{T^{R'}}{T'^R})^{((R'-R)^{-1})}$. From u_0^x and the identification list, output i as the cheating user. Now if u_0^x does exist, it can be concluded that GM has deleted some data from the identification list and output GM.

5 Variants of Our Scheme

5.1 Trading Computation Efficiency for Setup-Freeness

We propose a variant of our scheme where the AP enjoys a high degree of setup-freeness. That is, the AP only needs to publish its access group, identity ID and bound k. In this new scheme, interactive GrantingAccess and RevokingAccess are no longer needed and there is no need for the AP to keep the ARC, too. The price is that user will have to compute the witness for the AP by himself with a procedure of $O(n)$ steps, where n is the size of the access group. Moreover, each time the access group changes, user need to perform this $O(n)$ steps to compute a new witness again.

We highlight the changes as follow. In the init phase, a common accumulator is initialized for all AP's by randomly selecting $q \in_R \mathbb{Z}_p^*$ and computing $q_i = h_0^{q^i}$ for $i = 1, \cdots, t_{max}$, where t_{max} is the maximum number of users in an access group. This procedure can be done by the GM or a trusted third party.

In APSetup, the AP only needs to publish is identity and bound k. It also needs to maintain a list of users allowed to access its application. Interactive grating access and revoking access are removed. The AP simply needs to change the content of the list of users in its access group.

Finally, users in the access group have to compute their own witness as follow. Retrieve the list of membership public key $\{e_j\}$ of the AP's access group. User with membership public key $e_i \in \{e_j\}$ first accumulates the set $\{e_j\}$ into a value v by computing $v = h_0^{\prod_{k=1}^{k=|\{e_j\}|} (e_k+q)}$. This quantity could be computed without knowledge of q using the q_i. Note that both user and AP can compute v locally. The user also computes the witness w by $h_0^{\prod_{k=1, k \neq i}^{k=|\{e_j\}|} (e_k+q)}$ such that $v_w^{(q+e_i)} = v$.

The rest of the protocol follows the original scheme, and same SPK Π_3 is used.

5.2 Trading Key-Size for Constant Proving Effort

Motivated by [19], we outline how to a construct dynamic k-TAA with constant proving effort. Each AP has to publish k signatures $Sig(1), \cdots, Sig(k)$. In the proof, instead of proving $1 \leq J_{AP} \leq k$ (which has complexity $O(\log(k))$), the user proves possession of signature on J_{AP} (which has complexity $O(1)$). This indirectly proves that J_{AP} is within the range. The price to pay is that, the public key size of the AP is now linear in k, and user colluding with AP can be untraceable (since the malicious AP can issue several $Sig(J_{AP})$ for the user. BBS+ signature is a natural candidate for the signature scheme used by the AP.

5.3   A New k-TAA Scheme

Our scheme can be further modified into an ordinary k-TAA scheme following the outline in [15]. It should be noted that the scheme constructed this way is very similar to the TS06 scheme. The modification is shown in appendix B.

6   Security and Efficiency Analysis

6.1   Efficiency Analysis

Following the parameters suggested by Boneh *et al.*[3,2], we can take $p = 170$ bits and each group element in $\mathbb{G}_1$, $\mathbb{G}_2$ can be represented by 171 bits. The authentication protocol will then consists of AP sending a 160-bit *seed* to the prover, while SPK Π_3 consists of 16 elements in $\mathbb{Z}_p^*$, 4 elements in $\mathbb{G}_1$ and 2 elements in $\mathbb{G}_p$. Assume elements in $\mathbb{G}_p$ is represented by 171 bits (using another elliptic curve group where pairing is not available[12]). Range proof of J_{AP} could be efficiently done if we set $k = 2^\kappa$ for some integer κ, using the protocol in appendix A, bits transmitted is $((5 + 3\kappa) * 170 + 171\kappa)$.

Then Π_3 consists of $574.5 + 85\log(k)$ bytes. On the other hand, if we implement the tradeoff described in Section 5, the range proof is replaced by the possession of a BBS+ signature, which is of size 213 bytes. The following table summarizes the communication cost of most (dynamic) k-TAA schemes in the literature. Security parameters of all schemes are set such that they have comparable security with standard 1024-bit RSA signature (though it should be noted that, the parameters are in slight favor towards NS05 [15], since they use group of orders of a 160-bit prime which result in a slightly weaker security than the 1024-bit RSA signature). The first 3 entries of the table are taken from [15]. Note that k is the allowable number of authentication.

	Bytes sent by AP	Bytes sent by User	Dynamic
TFS04 scheme	40	$60k + 1617$	No
NS05 ordinary	20	$60k + 224$	No
NS05 dynamic	20	$60k + 304$	Yes
Our dynamic scheme	20	700 or $574 + 85\log(k)$	Yes
TS06 scheme	20	500 or $300 + 85\log(k)$	No

In TS06[19], full details of the proof of knowledge protocol is not given and thus the figure is just an estimation. We assume same proof of knowledge on range is used. TS06 makes use of a group signature scheme [12](referred to as FI scheme hereafter) as we use the BBS+ signature scheme for the join protocol. Assume TS06 uses the signature protocol of the FI scheme for proving knowledge of a membership certificate, which is 1711 bits(very similar to BBS+). A point to note is that if used this way, the zero-knowledge of the protocol is computational (under the DDH assumption).

6.2 Security Analysis

Regarding the security of our dynamic k-TAA, we have the following theorem whose proof shall appear in the full version of the paper.

Theorem 3. *Our scheme possesses D-Detectability, D-Anonymity and D-Exculpability under the y-DDHI assumptions in the random oracle model.*

7 Conclusion

We constructed a constant-size dynamic k-TAA scheme, modified it to an ordinary k-TAA scheme, and proved its security. We also analyzed the efficiency of our system and compare it with existing (dynamic) k-TAA schemes. Our scheme outperforms any existing dynamic k-TAA schemes in the literature. Finally, the BBS+ signature we analyze could be useful for other cryptographic systems.

References

1. D. Boneh and X. Boyen. Short Signatures Without Random Oracles. In *Eurocrypt 2004*, pages 56-73, 2004.
2. D. Boneh, X. Boyen, and H. Shacham. Short Group Signatures. In *Crypto 2004*, pages 41-55, 2004.
3. D. Boneh, B. Lynn, and H. Shacham. Short Signatures from the Weil Pairing. In *Asiacrypt 2001*, pages 514-532, 2001.
4. F. Boudot. Efficient Proofs that a Committed Number Lies in an Interval. In *Eurocrypt 2000*, pages 431-444, 2000.
5. X. Boyen and B. Waters. Compact Group Signatures Without Random Oracles. In *Eurocrypt 2006*, also available at http://www.cs.stanford.edu/~xb/eurocrypt06/.
6. J. Camenisch. Group Signature Schemes and Payment Systems Based on the Discrete Logarithm Problem. PhD Thesis, ETH ZAurich, 1998. Diss. ETH No. 12520, Hartung Gorre Verlag, Konstanz., 1998.
7. J. Camenisch, S. Hohenberger, and A. Lysyanskaya. Compact E-Cash. In *Eurocrypt 2005*, pages 302-321, 2005.
8. J. Camenisch and A. Lysyanskaya. A Signature Scheme with Efficient Protocols. In *SCN 2002*, pages 268-289, 2002.
9. J. Camenisch and A. Lysyanskaya. Dynamic Accumulators and Application to Efficient Revocation of Anonymous Credentials. In *Crypto 2002*, pages 61-76, 2002.
10. J. Camenisch and A. Lysyanskaya. Signature Schemes and Anonymous Credentials from Bilinear Maps. In *Crypto 2004*, pages 56-72, 2004.
11. Y. Dodis and A. Yampolskiy. A Verifiable Random Function with Short Proofs and Keys. In *PKC 2005*, pages 416-431, 2005.
12. J. Furukawa and H. Imai. An Efficient Group Signature Scheme from Bilinear Maps. In *ACISP 2005*, pages 455-467, 2005.

13. S. Micali, M. O. Rabin, and S. P. Vadhan. Verifiable Random Functions. In *FOCS 1999*, pages 120-130, 1999.
14. L. Nguyen. Accumulators from Bilinear Pairings and Applications. In *CTRSA 2005*, pages 275-292, 2005.
15. L. Nguyen and R. Safavi-Naini. Dynamic k-times Anonymous Authentication. In *ACNS 2005*, pages 318-333, 2005.
16. T. Okamoto. Efficient Blind and Partially Blind Signatures Without Random Oracles. In *TCC 2006*, pages 80-99, 2006.
17. T. P. Pedersen. Non-Interactive and Information-Theoretic Secure Verifiable Secret Sharing. In *Crypto 1991*, pages 129-140, 1991.
18. I. Teranishi, J. Furukawa, and K. Sako. k-Times Anonymous Authentication (Extended Abstract). In *Asiacrypt 2004*, pages 308-322, 2004.
19. I. Teranishi and K. Sako. k-Times Anonymous Authentication With a Constant Proving Cost. In *PKC 2006*, pages 525-542, 2006.

A   Range Proof for J_{AP}

Secure and efficient exact proof of range is possible in groups of unknown order under factorization assumption [4]. Here, we make use of the fact that if we set $k = 2^t$ for some integer t, efficient range check for J_{AP} could be achieved as follows.

Let g, h be two generators of a cyclic group $\mathbb{G}$ of order p whose relative discrete logarithm is unknown. To prove knowledge of a number J such that $0 < J \leq k$ in a commitment $C_J = g^J h^r$, let J_i be the i-th bit of J for $i = 1, \cdots t$. Compute $C_i = g^{J_i} h^{r_i}$ for some $r_i \in_R \mathbb{Z}_p^*$ for $i = 1, \cdots, t$. Compute the following SPK.

$$\Pi_{range} : SPK\Big\{(J, a, b, r, r_i) :$$
$$C_J = g^J h^r \ \wedge \ C_J/g = g^a h^r \ \wedge \ \prod_{j=1}^{t} (C_j)^{2^j} = g^J h^b \ \wedge$$
$$[C_i = h^{r_i} \vee C_i/g = h^{r_i}]_{i=1}^{i=t} \Big\}(M)$$

where $a = J - 1$, $b = \prod_{j=1}^{t} r_j 2^j$.

The total protocol consists of $4+t$ elements in $\mathbb{Z}_p$, $2t+1$ challenges also in $\mathbb{Z}_p$ and t C_i's in $\mathbb{G}$. In our protocol, total size of the range proof is $(5 + 3t) * 170 + t * 171$ bits.

B   A New k-TAA Scheme

We show how to modify our dynamic k-TAA scheme to an ordinary k-TAA scheme. It turns out to be very similar to TS06. As mentioned in [15], a user in dynamic k-TAA needs to prove to an AP three conditions:

1. he has been registered as a group member;
2. he is in the access group of the AP;
3. he has not accessed the AP for more than the allowable number of times.

For ordinary k-TAA, a user just need to prove condition (1) and (3). The modification is outline as follow. The setup of the accumulator is removed and there are no GrantingAccess and RevokingAccess. In the authentication procedure, the following SPK is carried out.

$$SPK\left\{(A, e, s, t, x, J_{AP}) : \right.$$

$$A^{e+\gamma} = g_0 g_1^s g_2^t g_3^x \ \wedge \ S = u_{AP}^{\frac{1}{J_{AP}+s+1}} \ \wedge$$

$$T = u_0^s u_{AP}^{\frac{R}{J_{AP}+t+1}} \ \wedge \ 1 \le J_{AP} \le k \left.\right\}(M)$$

The above can be instantiated as the following SPK Π_4. Upon receiving $seed$, the user compute the following quantities: $A_1 = g_1^{r_1} g_2^{r_2}$, $A_2 = A g_2^{r_1}$, $A_3 = g_1^{J_{AP}} g_2^t g_3^{r_3}$, $S = u_{AP}^{\frac{1}{J_{AP}+s+1}}$, $T = u_0^x u_{AP}^{\frac{R}{J_{AP}+t+1}}$, $R = H(seed)$ and compute the following SPK.

$$\Pi_4 : SPK\left\{(r_1, r_2, r_3, \delta_1, \delta_2, \delta_3, \delta_J, \delta_t, e, s, t, x, J_{AP}) : \right.$$

$$A_1 = g_1^{r_1} g_2^{r_2} \ \wedge \ A_1^e = g_1^{\delta_1} g_2^{\delta_2} \ \wedge$$

$$\frac{e(A_2, w)}{e(g_0, h_0)} = e(g_1, h_0)^s e(g_2, h_0)^t e(g_3, h_0)^x e(g_2, h_0)^{\delta_1} e(g_2, w)^{r_1} e(A_2, h_0)^{-e} \ \wedge$$

$$\frac{u_{AP}}{S} = S^{J_{AP}} S^s \ \wedge \ A_3 = g_1^{J_{AP}} g_2^t g_3^{r_3} \ \wedge \ A_3^x = g_1^{\delta_J} g_2^{\delta_t} g_3^{\delta_3} \ \wedge$$

$$\frac{u_{AP}^R}{T} = T^{J_{AP}} T^t u_0^{-\delta_J} u_0^{-\delta_t} u_0^x \ \wedge \ 0 \le J_{AP} \le k \left.\right\}(M)$$

where $\delta_1 = r_1 e, \delta_2 = r_2 e, \delta_J = J_{AP} x, \delta_t = tx, \delta_3 = r_3 x$.

On Secure Orders in the Presence of Faults

Amir Herzberg and Igal Yoffe

Computer Science Department, Bar Ilan University,
Ramat Gan, 52900, Israel
{herzbea, ioffei}@cs.biu.ac.il

Abstract. We present specifications and provably-secure protocol, for fully automated resolution of disputes between a provider of digital goods and services, and its customers. Disputes may involve the timely receipt of orders and goods, due to communication failures and malicious faults, as well as disputes on the fitness of the goods to the order. Our design is a part of a layered architecture for secure e-commerce applications [1], with precise yet general-purpose interfaces, agreements and validation functions (e.g. automatically resolving disputes on quality or fitness of goods). The modular design of the protocol and specifications, allows usage as an underlying service to different e-commerce, e-banking and other distributed systems. Our protocol operates efficiently, reliably and securely under realistic failure and delay conditions.

1   Introduction

Modern commerce allows clients to securely place orders at providers, and receive goods or services in timely manner. Clients and providers can use different mechanisms to resolve disputes on the delivery of the orders and of the goods, and on the quality or fitness of the goods (for the given order).

Obviously, the efficiency and security of the dispute resolution process are critical - and especially for digital transactions (electronic commerce). Indeed, there are many works on avoiding disputes and/or on enabling dispute resolution for secure e-commerce; specifically, this is of the main applications of digital signatures.

However, surprisingly, existing works do not provide fully automated resolution of disputes on the timely provision of appropriate goods/services, to satisfy a given order. There are many works on *avoiding* specific disputes, e.g. ensuring atomic contract-signing or fair exchange; however these apply only to specific interactions, and not to general orders. Other works deal with dispute resolution via evidences ('non-repudiation'), however without rigor specifications and proofs, and without clear interfaces allowing modular design. As a result, existing electronic commerce lack appropriate automated dispute-resolution processes, and depend on manual resolution - or simply on customers accepting the records of the service providers (e.g., broker). Considering that communication systems are subject to failures, and that computer systems are subject to attacks by third parties, we find the current situation of e-commerce (e.g. e-banking) rather disturbing.

R. De Prisco and M. Yung (Eds.): SCN 2006, LNCS 4116, pp. 126–140, 2006.

In this work, we present specifications and provably-secure protocol, for fully automated resolution of disputes between a provider of digital goods and services, and its customers. The protocol is extremely efficient and quite simple; however, the definition of appropriate, flexible, extensible yet well-defined *specifications* is non-trivial. The specifications allow resolving of disputes involving the timely receipt of orders and goods, due to communication failures and malicious faults, as well as disputes on the fitness of the goods to the order.

The design we present is flexible, and supports any type of e-commerce orders or transactions, allowing its use as underlying layer for many secure commerce protocols. In our layered architecture design [1] each network principal employs secure e-commerce application layers, including *payment* layers, the *order* layer (in this paper) and an *attestation* layer, as a bottom layer; see Figure 1.

One aspect of the flexibility of our design, unlike typical fair-exchange or contract signing protocols, is the support for arbitrary *trade validation function* for orders, provided as a 'black box' function to e-commerce protocols. The trade function is defined as part of an *agreement* between the order client and order server. Additional aspect in the architecture [1] is that each layer provides its own *evidences* for upper layers. For instance, the attestation layer, which is used by our protocol, issues to the sender evidences of message delivery (EOD) or of failure to submit message (EOFS) (see 1); these become part of the evidences (e.g. of goods delivery) produced by the order layer.

We present concrete specifications of liveness and correctness for our protocol. For example, we specify a formal experiment of failed goods delivery, where for a non adversarial client and notary, connected by non-faulty channel, a server cannot obtain an evidence of failed delivery of goods, if no such delivery was actually made (see Section 4, Experiment 4). We provide the mechanisms to build protocols with concrete security proofs, on top of our protocol.

Related Work. Many payment models and schemes have been developed over the years. Many of these protocols focused on aspects of the payment process, where the widely-used credit card system is not satisfactory. The two main directions here are micropayments [2,3,4] and digital (anonymous) cash [5]. An important exception is *iKP*, the i-Key-Protocol [6], a family of protocols for secure credit-card payments, which was adopted by MasterCard and Visa for the SET standard (which seems to have been abandoned). Another important exception is the *NetBill* [7] protocol, which is a distributed transactional payment protocol featuring atomic delivery, where payment proceeds only if the customer had received the goods. Additional, notable layered architecture, though lacking automated resolution process, is SEMPER [8], which aimed to create a global, decentralized and secure marketplace. The literature also includes vast research regarding non-repudiation and fair exchange [9,10,11] along with dispute resolution [12] for different levels of a trusted third party involvement [13]; for survey see [14]. The mentioned works lack the proofs to match between orders and issued goods, or don't handle failed submission of orders, payments or payment option deposits, which makes them unsuitable as underlying infrastructure for secure e-commerce services.

Contribution of this work. Our main contribution is the specifications for e-commerce order layer as a fully-automated service, underlying secure e-commerce protocols and applications. Another contribution is in presenting an efficient, practical e-commerce protocol, along with solid, reduction-based proof of security; this is the first application of the framework of [15]. A final contribution is our validation constructions, where every e-commerce layer defines its validation functions for automated dispute resolution, which is efficient and fair to all parties.

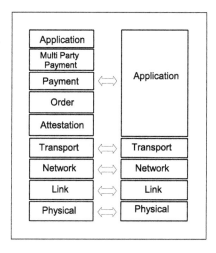

Fig. 1. Secure E-commerce layers vs. Internet layers

Table 1. Attestation evidence structure

Evidence Field	Description
type	Evidences of origin, delivery and failed submission, *EOO, EOD, EOFS*, respectively.
agr	Attestation agreement.
msg	The message sent.
ci	Creation time interval.
σ	Signature over evidence fields.

Organization. The rest of the paper is as follows. In the next section we describe the lower layers (model) assumed by our specifications and protocol; specifically, attestation layer, as well as basic communication and digital signatures. In Section 3 we describe the *order* layer and protocol implementation. We present the formal specifications only in Section 4, and then, in Section 5, we present analysis of the protocol and prove that it meets the specifications. The last section concludes.

Table 2. Attestation agreement

Agreement Field	Description
Δ_{att}	Bound on attestation layer answer, for message delivery.
Client, Server, Notary	The identities of the principals participating in the agreement. Principal's identity is an $(addr, vk)$ tuple, of principal's address and public validation key, respectively.

2 Lower Layers: Attestation, Communication and Signatures

2.1 Attestation Layer

The *Attestation* layer is the lowest secure e-commerce layer. Attestation layer is based on top of a transport layer, such as, for example, TCP/IP, TLS/SSL, working on top of socket or SSL API, respectively, and provides additional certification services. Attestation layer has three parties: client, server, and a notary (trusted third party), which acts as time-stamping and certification (attestation) provider. For specification and analysis see [16].

An *attestation evidence* (Table 1) is a time-stamped and signed statement, regarding the delivery of messages. Attestation layer provides three evidences:

Evidence of delivery (EOD) , is a proof for the message sender, that the intended message receipient received the message (during given time interval). EOD is signed by the recipient (and used by the sender).

Evidence of origin (EOO) , is proof that that the message originated from the claimed sender (during given time interval). EOO is signed by the sender (and used by the recipient).

Evidence of failure and submission (EOFS) , allows the sender to prove sending the message in question (during given time interval), even if the message wasn't received due to communication faults, or if the recipient failed to acknowledge receiving it. The attestation layer doesn't try to re-deliver a message; reliability service should be provided by layers below attestation, e.g., TCP. EOD is signed by the notary (and used by the sender).

Attestation Agreement. An attestation channel requires the parties to agree on an attestation agreement, specified in Table 2. The agreement specifies identities (by address and public key), for sender, recipient and notary. The agreement also includes Δ_{att}, a bound on the time required for the attestation service to return an evidence, EOD or EOFS, for a sent message.

Validation. The validation functionality is not related to any particular instance of attestation module, and could be invoked by any third party, which had obtained the attested communication agreement and the evidence in question. *Validate(e)* is an efficient predicate that returns whether the evidence e is valid.

Attestation interface. The interface between payment and attestation layers is described in Table 3, and consists of initialization interface and an interface to send and receive message along with their respective evidences.

Table 3. Attestation layer interface

Method	Direction	Description
$Init(1^k)$	in	Initializes layer, with a security parameter.
$InitResult(vk,addr)$	out	Returns generated validation key vk of the initializer, and the principal's address $addr$ in the payment network.
$OpenChannel(AttAgr,\rho)$	in	Establishes an attested channel for the role $\rho \in \{C, S, N\}$, client, server and notary, respectively.
$OpenChannelResult(success)$	out	Notifies the principal on attestation channel establishment.
$CloseChannel()$	in	Closes an attested communication channel.
$Send(AttAgr,m)$	in	Sends a message m on an open channel.
$SendResult(e)$	out	Returns an attestation evidence, Table 1, for the sent message.
$Receive(e)$	out	Delivery of evidence of origin, Table 1, which also includes the message, $e.msg$.

Initialization. Attestation initialization is two phased, where in $Init$, the attestation layer generates secret and validation key pair, keeps the secret key and in $InitResult$ returns the validation key, along with the (communication) address of the attested instance. These values, address and validation key, compose principal's identity, for the above layer, e.g., payment or application layers, and would be used to sign evidences, as specified in Table 1.

2.2   Communication Layer and Signature Scheme

Communication Layer. We can use any basic communication mechanism for direct communication between the notary and the client/server. We only need two methods: $Comm.Send(\rho,m)$, $Comm.Receive(\rho,m)$, for sending or respectively receiving a message m to or from a party ρ. We assume communication delay is bounded by $\Delta < \Delta_{att}$. For brevity, when we present the protocol in Section 3 we assume ρ is mapped to the address of the ρ party in the context of attestation agreement used to open an attestation channel.

Signature Scheme. We also assume typical signature scheme construction of $PKS=(PKS.KG,PKS.Sign,PKS.ValidateSig)$ for key generation, signing and signature validation services, respectively. Where $vk=PKS.KG(1^k)$ receives an unary security parameter, returns a validation key, and keeps the signing key. The $Sign(m)$ algorithm digitally signs a message m, and returns (m,σ) tuple, where σ is the signature, and $ValidateSig(m,\sigma,vk)$ validates signature σ for the message m, using supplied validation key vk.

3   Order Layer

The order layer encapsulates operations ("orders") related to goods and services. The layer provides the service for placing an order for goods or services by a client, and validating that the server returned order result adhere to an order agreement between the principals.

Order Agreement. We define an order agreement between trading parties as specified in Table 4. An order agreement is used to generate attestation agreements between order client and server, and a trade validation function, *Validate-Trade(order,goods)*. Abandoning generality in sake of brevity, we would assume that the order layer notary is the the the same notary as for attestation. Therefore, we only use attestation layer between client and server, and ordinary communication between notary and client/server.

The *ValidateTrade* function provides versatility of trade by allowing the client and the server to agree on arbitrary goods and services similarly to traditional trade agreements. The function should should have *BadOrder, BadGoods, OrderOk, GoodsOk* return values. The *BadOrder* return value is issued for an order which is invalid under the agreement, regardless of the value of goods. The second, *BadGoods* return value, is issued for goods which do not match the order (which should also include the amount), the *OrderOk* returned for valid order, without goods; and the *GoodsOk* status is returned when the corresponding goods match the order, in the context of the agreement.

Table 4. Order agreement

Agreement Field	Description
Δ_{order}	Bound on order layer answer for an order request.
ValidateTrade(order,goods) returns *status*;	Trade validation function. Validates that issued goods match the order.
C,S,N	Order layer participating principals. A (C)lient, (S)erver and a (N)otary, $(addr, vk)$ identities.
$N.vk$	Order layer notary validation key, for signing order evidences.
$AttAgr^{\{C,S\}}, AttAgr^{\{S,C\}}$	Encapsulated attestation agreements, see Table 2.

Order interface. The interface between the application and order layer, Table 5, defines the initialization, ordering goods or services, and validation of order results. In the first, *Init* phase, each order layer machine establishes its own identity, as returned by attestation layer. Using this information a principal may establish order agreements with other network principals.

When an order channel is established, order transaction are invoked with *Order* event, supplying client specified order information which defines the deposited option or type of goods to acquire, the payment amount, and possibly other relevant information (e.g., original merchant offer). We then expect an

Table 5. Order layer interface

Method	Direction	Description
Init(k)	in	Initializes the order layer, with security parameter k.
InitResult(vk,addr)	out	Returns initializer's address *addr*, and validation key(s) *vk*.
OpenChannel(OrderAgr,ρ)	in	Opens an order channel with the principals specified by *OrderAgr* agreement using role ρ.
OpenChannelResult(status)	out	Notifies the application of the order channel establishment success.
CloseChannel()	in	Closes an order channel.
OrderResult(e)	out	Returns *CommFail* or order evidence *e* result.
Client		
Order(order)	in	Instructs the order layer to issue an order, described by *order*, over an established order channel.
Server		
VendRequest(order)	out	Instructs the application layer to issue goods, described by *order*, and implicitly by the order agreement, in the order context.
VendRequestResult(goods)	in	Returns goods vended by upper layer.

OrderResult event within finite time, as governed by Δ_{att}, specified in the order agreement.

On the server side, we assume an application (or upper) level functionality to issue goods or services, using *VendRequest* interface. The goods and services are issued in the context of the order agreement specified for the open order channel, and are verifiable by order agreement's *ValidateTrade*.

Table 6. Order layer evidences structure

Order Evidence Field	Description
type	Evidences of placed order, failed order, goods delivery, or failed goods delivery, *EOGR*, *EOFO*, *EOGD*, *EOFGD*, respectively.
OrderAgr	Order layer agreement.
order	The order specified by the evidence.
goods	The corresponding goods.
σ	Order layer proof, for the above evidence.

Order Evidences. The structure of order layer evidences is shown in Table 6. The evidences include various trade related evidences, as specified below, and evidence's *e* proof *e.σ* consists of lower, attestation layer evidences.

- **EOGR.** The order layer *Evidence of Goods and Receipt*, is client's (buyer) proof that the corresponding order had reached the server (seller), and that goods had been obtained for the order.

- **EOGD.** The order layer *Evidence of Goods Delivery*, is server's (seller) proof that the goods issued for client's order had reached the client.

- **EOFO.** The order layer *Evidence of Failed Order*, is client's proof that the order process had failed. It could either be the case that the order message itself wasn't acknowledged by the server, or if it was acknowledged but the server didn't issue goods.

- **EOFGD.** The order layer *Evidence of Failed Goods Delivery*, is server's proof that the goods delivry process had failed, since the goods message wasn't acknowledged by the client.

Notation. We use the dot notation to refer to elements of records or tuples, e.g., for an attestation evidence e, $e.type$ denotes the evidence type, as specified in Table 1.

1	$Order.Init(1^k, \rho)$	$: (vk, addr) = Att.Init(1^k)$
2		$: \text{if } \rho = N$
3		$: \quad N.vk = PKS.KG(1^k)$
4		$: \quad Order.InitResult((vk, N.vk), addr)$
5		$: \text{else } Order.InitResult(vk, addr)$
6	$Order.OpenChannel($	$: OrderAgr = OrderAgr'$
7	$OrderAgr', \rho)$	$: AttAgr^{\{C,S\}} = OrderAgr.AttAgr^{\{C,S\}}$
8		$: AttAgr^{\{S,C\}} = OrderAgr.AttAgr^{\{S,C\}}$
9		$: \text{if } \rho \in \{C, S\}$
10		$: \quad success = Att.OpenChannel(AttAgr^{\{C,S\}}, C) \land$
11		$: \quad Att.OpenChannel(AttAgr^{\{S,C\}}, S)$
12		$: Order.OpenChannelResult(success)$

Fig. 2. Initialization protocol for order layer parties, $\rho \in \{C, S, N\}$, saves $OrderAgr$ and included agreements as principal's state

1	$on\ Receive(e = \{EOO, AttAgr^{\{C,S\}}, order, ci, \sigma\}) :$
2	$: \text{if } ValidateTrade(order, \bot) = OrderOk$
3	$: \quad goods = VendRequest(order)$
4	$: \quad se = Send(AttAgr^{\{S,C\}}, goods)$
5	$: \quad \text{if } (se.type = EOD)\ OrderResult(\{EOGD, OrderAgr, order, goods, \{e, se\}\})$
6	$: \quad \text{if } (se.type = EOFS)\ OrderResult(\{EOFGD, OrderAgr, order, goods, \{e, se\}\})$
7	$: \quad \text{if } (se = CommFail)\ OrderResult(CommFail)$
8	$on\ Comm.Receive(N, e = \{EOD, AttAgr^{\{C,S\}}, order, ci, \sigma\}) :$
9	$: \text{if } Att.Validate(e)$
10	$: \quad Comm.Send(N, se)$

Fig. 3. Order layer protocol for the Server. For conciseness the protocol is for a single, unique, *order*; extension for multiple orders is trivial.

---

1 *on Comm.Receive(C,e={EOD,AttAgr$^{\{C,S\}}$,order,ci,σ}) :*
2 : if *Att.Validate(e)* ∧ *ValidateTrade(order,⊥) = OrderOk*
3 :   set *timer* for *AttAgr$^{\{S,C\}}$.Δ$_{att}$*
4 :   *Comm.Send(S,e)*

---

5 *on Comm.Receive(S,e={EOFS∥EOD,AttAgr$^{\{S,C\}}$,goods,ci,σ}) :*
6 : if *timer* set ∧ *Att.Validate(e)*
7 :   cancel *timer*
8 :   if *ValidateTrade(order,goods) = GoodsOk*
9 :   if *e.type = EOD* return *//client is cheating, server did deliver*
10 :   else *Comm.Send(C,e)*
11 :   else goto 13

---

12 *on timer :*
13 : *Comm.Send(C,PKS.Sign({EOFO,OrderAgr,order,⊥}))*

Fig. 4. Order layer protocol for the Notary. For conciseness the protocol is for a single, unique, *order*; extension for multiple orders is trivial.

---

1 *on Order(order) :*
2   : *se = Send(AttAgr$^{\{C,S\}}$,order)*
3   : if *(se = EOFS) OrderResult({EOFO,OrderAgr,order,⊥,{se}})*
4   : if *(se = EOD)* set *timer$_1$* for *AttAgr$^{\{S,C\}}$.Δ$_{att}$*

---

5 *on timer$_1$:* set *timer$_2$* for *AttAgr$^{\{C,S\}}$.Δ$_{att}$ + AttAgr$^{\{S,C\}}$.Δ$_{att}$*
6   : *Comm.Send(N,se)*

---

7 *on Comm.Receive(N,e={EOFO,OrderAgr,order,⊥,σ,σ^e}) :*
8   : if *PKS.ValidateSig(e,N.vk)*
9   :   *OrderResult(e)*

---

10 *on Comm.Receive(N,e={EOFS,AttAgr$^{\{S,C\}}$,goods,ci,σ}) :*
11   : if *Att.Validate(e) =* **true** goto 13
12 *on Receive(e={EOO,AttAgr$^{\{S,C\}}$,goods,ci,σ}) :*
13   : if *ValidateTrade(order,goods) = GoodsOk*
14   :   *OrderResult({EOGR,OrderAgr,order,goods,{e,se}})*

---

15 *on timer$_2$: OrderResult(CommFail)*

Fig. 5. Order layer protocol for the Client. For conciseness the protocol is for a single, unique, *order*; extension for multiple orders is trivial. The protocol terminates for the *order* and cancels timers after *OrderResult*.

Order Layer Protocol. We show the order layer protocol in Figures 2, 3, 4, 5, for common initialization, server-side, notary-side and client-side, respectively. In initialization, the attested channels are opened between each pair of roles specified in the order agreement (Table 4), namely, client, server and notary. The protocol implementation describes how each party acts upon receiving a messages, both attested and non-attested. The presented protocol is optimistic. The client tries first to send the order over an attested channel to the server. When the client obtains evidence of delivery for the order, it sets a timer for delivery of goods. If the optimistic approach fails, and the goods haven't been delivered, the client forwards the order EOD to the notary. The notary, validates the EOD and in turn, forwards the EOD to the server. If the goods aren't received the notary issues an EOFO to the client. Upon receiving order EOD, the server already aware of the order (the client did obtain EOD) should send the notary the corresponding goods EOD or EOFS.

Validation. The validation functionality, *Validate(e)*, Figure 6, is common to all parties. That is, an automatic dispute resolution system, or an arbiter, upon dispute, would instantiate the order layer, and supply the relevant order agreement along with the the protocol-specific order evidence *e*. The aforementioned evidences typically composed of pairs of relevant attestation evidences.

Non-Notarized Communication Failures. Recovery from non-notarized communication failures is possible for honest parties. Consider the case where a client (or similarly a server) issuing an order request, receives in return a communication failure (instead of an EOD). The client could not possibly know whether the channel had failed, before the request had been delivered (and server had obtained an EOO), or afterwards, and the failure had prevented the client from receiving an EOD (or EOFS). For recovery from the former, honest parties could include with the next order or goods response the received EOOs, or indication of such. Thus, the state of order which had experience communication failure would be unknown only until the next successful one.

$Order.Validate(e)$:
1   if $PKS.ValidateSig(e,e.OrderAgr.N.vk) \wedge e.type{=}EOFO$ **return** true
2   $e_0^{\mathrm{att}} = e.\sigma[0],\ e_1^{\mathrm{att}} = e.\sigma[1]$
3   if $e.type{=}EOFO$
4   **return** $Att.Validate(e_0^{\mathrm{att}}) \wedge e.order = e_0^{\mathrm{att}}.msg$
5     $\wedge\ ValidateTrade(e.order,\bot){=}OrderOk \wedge e_0^{\mathrm{att}}.type = EOFS$
6   if $e.type{=}EOGR$
7   **return** $Att.Validate(e_0^{\mathrm{att}}) \wedge Att.Validate(e_1^{\mathrm{att}}) \wedge$
8     $\wedge\ ValidateTrade(e.order,e.goods){=}GoodsOk \wedge e_0^{\mathrm{att}}.type = EOO\|EOFS \wedge$
9     $\wedge\ e_1^{\mathrm{att}}.type = EOD \wedge e_0^{\mathrm{att}}.msg = e.goods \wedge e_1^{\mathrm{att}}.msg = e.order$
10 if $e.type{=}EOFGD$
11   **return** $Att.Validate(e_0^{\mathrm{att}}) \wedge Att.Validate(e_1^{\mathrm{att}}) \wedge$
12     $\wedge\ ValidateTrade(e.order,e.goods){=}GoodsOk \wedge e_0^{\mathrm{att}}.type = EOO \wedge$
13     $\wedge\ e_1^{\mathrm{att}}.type = EOFS \wedge e_0^{\mathrm{att}}.msg = e.order \wedge e_1^{\mathrm{att}}.msg = e.goods$
14 if $e.type{=}EOGD$
15   **return** $Att.Validate(e_0^{\mathrm{att}}) \wedge Att.Validate(e_1^{\mathrm{att}}) \wedge$
16     $\wedge\ ValidateTrade(e.order,e.goods){=}GoodsOk \wedge e_0^{\mathrm{att}}.type = EOO \wedge$
17     $\wedge\ e_1^{\mathrm{att}}.type = EOD \wedge e_0^{\mathrm{att}}.msg = e.order \wedge e_1^{\mathrm{att}}.msg = e.goods$

Fig. 6. Implementation of order layer *Validate* efficient algorithm for order evidence validation. In the algorithm, for brevity and simplicity, we assume that the notary N, is also the notary of the order agreement attestation channels.

4   Specifications

For the protocol analysis we adapt a new layered adversarial specifications framework method. While full details may be obtained in [15], intuitively, having concrete and well-defined specifications for both the layer below the analyzed layer and the analyzed layer itself, we would like to relate the two specifications and show that given an adversary which 'breaks' the analyzed layer specifications, we could use this adversary to 'break' the lower-layer specifications.

In our simplified model the protocol flow is 'single threaded', with a single thread (or queue) of instantaneous events for each machine. For simplicity we assume reliable clock services, though we believe the model could be easily extended to support bounded clock drifts.

We define execution as a deterministic function of the protocol machines initial states and random tapes (which could be supplied to the protocol machines during initialization).

Definition 1. *An execution,* $\mathbb{X}$*, is a set of protocol machine events, ordered by time. Given an execution* $\mathbb{X}$*, let* $\mathbb{X}.time$ *be the execution running time and let* $view(\mathbb{X}, u)$*, the* u*-view of* $\mathbb{X}$*, be the sequence of events, subset of* $\mathbb{X}$*, applied to protocol machine* u *only.*

We now define a $VR : \{\mathbb{X}\} \times \{OrderAgr\} \times \{\rho\} \rightarrow \{\mathtt{true}, \mathtt{false}\}$ predicate, to specify parties which were properly initialized in executions. For simplicity, we don't specify special inputs for adversarial takeover in the middle of execution, therefore we consider as adversarial, parties which weren't properly initialized.

Notation. We use $<u,Method,params>$ to denote an event, an interface method *Method* invocation of a protocol role (or machine) u, invoked with arguments *params*. To shorthand, we write $retval = <u,Method,params>$ to denote the output of a subsequent event $<u,MethodResult,retval>$.

Definition 2. *A role* ρ *of agreement OrderAgr, in execution* $\mathbb{X}$ *is properly initialized,* $VR(\mathbb{X}, OrderAgr, \rho)$ *if* $view(\mathbb{X}, \rho)$ *contains one and only one* $(addr, vk)$ $=<\rho, 'Init', 1^k>$ *and* $\mathtt{true} =<\rho, 'OpenChannel', OrderAgr>$.

Experiment 1. Forging Evidence of Goods and Receipt. An execution $\mathbb{X}$ is won, i.e., $\mathbb{X}.win^{EOGR} = \mathtt{true}$, if adversary outputs $e = \{EOGR, OrderAgr, order, goods, \sigma\}$, s.t.,

1. $Validate(e) = \mathtt{true}$, and
2. $VR(\mathbb{X}, e.OrderAgr, N) = \mathtt{true}$, and
3. $VR(\mathbb{X}, e.OrderAgr, S) = \mathtt{true}$, and
4. $\mathbb{X}$ doesn't contain $<S, 'VendRequestResult', e.goods>$

Experiment 2. Forging Evidence of Goods Delivery. An execution $\mathbb{X}$ is won, i.e., $\mathbb{X}.win^{EOGD} = \mathtt{true}$, if adversary outputs $e = \{EOGD, OrderAgr, order, goods, \sigma\}$, s.t.,

1. $Validate(e) = \text{true}$, and
2. $VR(\mathbb{X}, e.OrderAgr, C) = \text{true}$, and
3. either,
   (a) $\mathbb{X}$ doesn't contain $<C, \text{'Order'}, e.order>$.
   (b) $\mathbb{X}$ doesn't contain $<C, \text{'OrderResult'}, \{EOGR, OrderAgr, order, e.goods, \sigma\}>$.

Experiment 3. Forging Evidence of Failed Order. An execution $\mathbb{X}$ is won, i.e., $\mathbb{X}.win^{EOFO} = \text{true}$, if adversary outputs $e = \{EOFO, OrderAgr, order, \bot, \sigma\}$, s.t.,

1. $Validate(e) = \text{true}$, and
2. $VR(\mathbb{X}, e.OrderAgr, N) = \text{true}$, and
3. $VR(\mathbb{X}, e.OrderAgr, S) = \text{true}$, and
4. adversary returns $goods = <S, \text{'VendRequest'}, order>$, s.t., $ValidateTrade(order, goods) = GoodsOk$, whenever $ValidateTrade(order, \bot) = OrderOk$.
5. no faults specified by adversary for communication between N and S.

Experiment 4. Forging Evidence of Failed Goods Delivery. An execution $\mathbb{X}$ is won, i.e., $\mathbb{X}.win^{EOFGD} = \text{true}$, if adversary outputs $e = \{EOFGD, OrderAgr, order, \bot, \sigma\}$, s.t.,

1. $Validate(e) = \text{true}$, and
2. $VR(\mathbb{X}, e.OrderAgr, N) = \text{true}$, and
3. $VR(\mathbb{X}, e.OrderAgr, C) = \text{true}$, and
4. no faults specified by adversary for communication between N and C.

We now define additional specifications [15], for the attestation and order e-commerce layers.

Definition 3. *Let $EX(\mathbb{A}, \pi, r)$ be execution of protocol π with adversary $\mathbb{A}$ and random tapes r. Attestation implementation π_{ATT} is $\epsilon(t, n)$-secure if for sufficiently large n and adversary $\mathbb{A}$ running up to time t, it holds that:*

$$Pr_{\mathbb{X}=EX(\mathbb{A},\pi_{ATT},r)}[(\mathbb{X}.win^{EOO} \vee \mathbb{X}.win^{EOD}$$
$$\vee \mathbb{X}.win^{EOFS}) \wedge \quad \wedge |\mathbb{X}| < n \wedge \mathbb{X}.time < t] < \epsilon(t, n)$$

Definition 4. *Let $EX(\mathbb{A}, \pi_{HIGH}, \pi_{LOW}, r)$ be execution of protocol π_{HIGH} on top of protocol π_{LOW} with adversary $\mathbb{A}$ and random tapes r. Order protocol implementation π_{ORDER} is $\epsilon(t, n)$-secure, if for sufficiently large n and adversary $\mathbb{A}$ running up to time t, it holds that:*

$$Pr_{\mathbb{X}=EX(\mathbb{A},\pi_{ORDER},\pi_{\mathbb{A}-ATT},r)}[(\mathbb{X}.win^{EOGR} \vee \mathbb{X}.win^{EOFO} \vee \mathbb{X}.win^{EOGD}$$
$$\vee \mathbb{X}.win^{EOFGD}) \wedge |\mathbb{X}| < n \wedge \mathbb{X}.time < t] < \epsilon(t, n)$$

Liveness 1. Δ-CN-Liveness for honest Client, Notary and non-faulty communication. For an $o_1 =< C, \text{'Order'}, order >$ event, in the interval $[t - \Delta, t]$, the protocol ensures $o_2 =< C, \text{'OrderResult'}, e >$, in the interval $[t, t + \Delta]$, where $e.order=order$, $e.type=EOGR$ or $e.type=EOFO$ and $Validate(e)=\text{true}$ whenever:

1. $VR(\mathbb{X}, e.OrderAgr, N) = $ **true**, and
2. $VR(\mathbb{X}, e.OrderAgr, C) = $ **true**, and
3. no faults specified by adversary for communication between N and C.

Liveness 2. Δ-SN-Liveness for honest Server, Notary and non-faulty communication. For an $o_1 = < S, 'VendRequestResult', goods >$ event, in the interval $[t - \Delta, t]$, the protocol ensures $o_2 = < S, 'OrderResult', e >$, in the interval $[t, t + \Delta]$, where $e.goods=goods$, $e.type=EOGD$ or $e.type=EOFGD$ and $Validate(e)=$**true** whenever:

1. $VR(\mathbb{X}, e.OrderAgr, N) = $ **true**, and
2. $VR(\mathbb{X}, e.OrderAgr, S) = $ **true**, and
3. no faults specified by adversary for communication between N and S.

5   Analysis

In this section we present a short analysis for our protocol implementation provided the specifications in previous Section 4.

Theorem 1. *If adversarial attestation layer protocol $\pi_{\mathbb{A}-ATT}$ is $\epsilon(t, n)$-secure (Definition 3), then order protocol implementation π_{ORDER} is $\epsilon(t, n)$-secure (Definition 4).*

Due to space considerations we show only a sketch of proof for EOGD forgery experiment part (Experiment 2).

Proof. Suppose some adversary, $\mathbb{A}$, breaks π_{order} by having $\mathbb{X}.win^{EOGR} = $ **true**, with probability $\epsilon' > \epsilon(t, n)$. We use π_{order} and $\mathbb{A}$ to show that the execution is $\mathbb{X}.win^{EOO} = $ **true**, i.e., a $\pi_{\mathbb{A}-ATT}$ forgery of EOO. In π_{order}, the server, S, party will never invoke $Send(AttAgr^{\{S,C\}}, goods)$, Figure 3 line 4, since Figure 3 line 3 didn't happen, and server is properly initialized (not controlled by adversary); however, $\mathbb{A}$ was able to output a valid EOGR evidence e, which contains an attestation EOD for the order, and, w.l.o.g, attestation EOO for the origin of $goods$. Therefore $\mathbb{X}.win^{EOO} = $ **true**, because $Order.Validate(e)=$**true** implies $Att.Validate(e.\sigma[0])=$**true**, where $e.\sigma[0]$ is EOO for the goods.

Theorem 2. *The protocol π_{ORDER} upholds*
$2 \cdot max\{OrderAgr.AttAgr^{\{\{\rho,\rho'\}| \rho,\rho' \in \{C,S\}\}}.\Delta_{att}\}$-*CN/SN-liveness.*

Due to space considerations we show only a sketch of proof for Δ-CN-Liveness property.

Proof. Let $\Delta = 2 \cdot max\{OrderAgr.AttAgr^{\{\{\rho,\rho'\}| \rho,\rho' \in \{C,S\}\}}.\Delta_{att}\}$. By the protocol, Figure 5 line 2, client immediately invokes $Send(AttAgr^{\{C,S\}}, order)$ and upon EOD for the order, sets a timer for the answer. Consider the more complex case where no goods had been received from the server. On timer wakeup, Figure 5 line 5, the order EOD is sent to the notary, and since the communication doesn't fail during $[t - \Delta, t + \Delta]$, the notary would proceed by forwarding the order EOD to the server, Figure 4 line 4, setting a timer to bound server's response time. In the case of goods delivery by the server, verified with *ValidateTrade*, the goods EOFS would be forwarded back to the client on the channel, formerly guaranteed to be non-faulty, causing an EOGR, or upon notary's timer expiration, the client will receive an explicit EOFO, since the server didn't provide the required evidence of sent goods, in time.

6   Conclusions

We have introduced a simple yet versatile trade protocol, with arbitrable transactions and concrete, well-defined specifications, which allow provable security and resolution of disputes with arbitrary validation of goods to order fitness in presence of malicious faults or communication failures. An interested reader may refer to [1] regarding how to use the protocol for further construction of final and conditional final payments between principals, or how to conduct trade when a PSP is a trusted party. Our design is practical, layered, and attains automatic dispute resolution, based on precise agreements and relatively simple cryptographic constructions assumed.

References

1. Herzberg, A., Yoffe, I.: Layered Architecture for Secure E-Commerce Applications. In: SECRYPT'06 - International Conference on Security and Cryptography (*to appear*), INSTICC Press (2006)
2. Rivest, R., Shamir, A.: PayWord and MicroMint: Two Simple Micropayment Schemes. In: Proceedings of the International Workshop on Security Protocols. (1996) 69–87
3. Micali, S., Rivest, R.: Micropayments revisited. In: Progress in Cryptology — CT-RSA 2002. Volume 2271 of LNCS., In Bart Preneel, editor, Springer-Verlag (2002)
4. Herzberg, A.: *Payment technologies for E-commerce*, Chapter 13, Micropayments. Springer-Verlag (2003)
5. Chaum, D.: Blind Signatures for Untraceable Payments. In: Advances in Cryptology - Proceedings of CRYPTO '82, D. Chaum, R. L. Rivest, and A. T. Sherman, Eds., Plenum, NY (1983) 199–203
6. Bellare, M., Garay, J., Hauser, R., Herzberg, A., Krawczyk, H., Steiner, M., Herrenweghen, E.V., Waidner, M.: Design, Implementation and Deployment of the iKP Secure Electronic Payment System. In: Journal on Selected Areas in Communication, special issue on Network Security. Volume 18. (2000) 611–627
7. Cox, B., Tygar, J.D., Sirbu, M.: NetBill security and Transaction Protocol. In: The First USENIX Workshop on Electronic Commerce. (1995) 77–88
8. Lacoste, G., Pfitzmann, B., Steiner, M., Waidner, M., eds.: SEMPER - Secure Electronic Marketplace for Europe. Volume 1854 of Lecture Notes in Computer Science. Springer-Verlag (2000)
9. Nenadic, A., Zhang, N.: Non-repudiation and Fairness in Electronic Data Exchange. In: Proceedings of 5th International Conference on Enterprise Information Systems (ICEIS), Angers, France (2003) 55–62

10. Pfitzmann, B., Schunter, M., Waidner, M.: Provably Secure Certified Mail. In: IBM Research Report RZ 3207 (#93253), IBM Research Division, Zurich (2000)
11. Ray, I., Ray, I.: Fair exchange in E-commerce. SIGecom Exch. **3**(2) (2002) 9–17
12. Kremer, S., Markowitch, O.: Fair Multi-Party Non-Repudiation Protocols. International Journal on Information Security **1**(4) (2003) 223–235
13. Zhou, J., Deng, R.H., Bao, F.: Evolution of Fair Non-repudiation with TTP. In: ACISP '99: Proceedings of the 4th Australasian Conference on Information Security and Privacy, London, UK, Springer-Verlag (1999) 258–269
14. Kremer, S., Markowitch, O., Zhou, J.: An Intensive Survey of Non-repudiation Protocols. Computer Communications **25**(17) (2002) 1606–1621
15. Herzberg, A.: The Layered Adversarial Specifications Framework (*in progress*). (2006)
16. Herzberg, A.: Towards Provably-Secure Timed E-Commerce: The Trusted Delivery Layer. In: Cryptology ePrint Archive, Report 2002/084. (2004)

Balancing Accountability and Privacy
Using E-Cash
(Extended Abstract)

Jan Camenisch[1] and Susan Hohenberger[1,*] and Anna Lysyanskaya[2]

[1] IBM Research, Zurich Research Laboratory, CH-8803 Rüschlikon
[2] Computer Science Department, Brown University, Providence, RI 02912, USA

Abstract. In an electronic cash (e-cash) system, a user can withdraw coins from the bank, and then spend each coin anonymously and unlinkably. For some applications, it is desirable to set a limit on the dollar amounts of anonymous transactions. For example, governments require that large transactions be reported for tax purposes. In this work, we present the first e-cash system that makes this possible without a trusted party. In our system, a user's anonymity is guaranteed so long as she does not: (1) double-spend a coin, or (2) exceed the publicly-known spending limit with any merchant. The spending limit may vary with the merchant. Violation of either condition can be detected, and can (optionally) lead to identification of the user and discovery of her other activities. While it is possible to balance accountability and privacy this way using e-cash, this is impossible to do using regular cash.

Our scheme is based on our recent compact e-cash system. It is secure under the same complexity assumptions in the random-oracle model. We inherit its efficiency: 2^ℓ coins can be stored in $O(\ell + k)$ bits and the complexity of the withdrawal and spend protocols is $O(\ell + k)$, where k is the security parameter.

1 Introduction

Electronic cash (e-cash) was invented by David Chaum [18,19]. Its main goal is to match the untraceability properties of physical coins: the same bank is responsible for dispensing e-cash to users, and for later accepting it for deposit from merchants, and yet it cannot trace how users spent their money.

An important difference between electronic cash and physical cash, is that electronic cash is represented by data. Data is easy to duplicate, while physical coins may be made of precious metals so the cost to minting them is high. Therefore, an e-cash scheme must incorporate a way to ensure that an electronic coin (e-coin) cannot be spent more than once (double-spent). Typically [20] this is done by ensuring that, even though spending a coin once does not leak any information about a user's identity, spending it twice leaks information that leads to identification. An e-cash scheme with such a mechanism is a good illustration of how one can balance anonymity with accountability: a user can remain

---

* Part of work performed at the Massachusetts Institute of Technology.

R. De Prisco and M. Yung (Eds.): SCN 2006, LNCS 4116, pp. 141–155, 2006.

anonymous unless she performs a forbidden action. The system is designed in a way that prevents this type of anonymity abuse.

In this paper we consider what other actions may be forbidden, and how to realize e-cash schemes that would hold users accountable should they perform such actions. At the same time, we protect the anonymity of those users who obey the rules.

We introduce the *bounded-anonymity business model*. In this model, associated with each merchant there is a publicly-known limit to the number of e-coins that a user may anonymously give to this merchant. This limit cannot be exceeded even if the user and the merchant collude. Should any user attempt to exceed the limit with any merchant, and should this merchant attempt to submit the resulting e-coins for deposit to the bank, the user's identity will be discovered, and further penalties may be imposed.

In the real world, this corresponds to restrictions that governments set on unreported transactions. For example, in the U.S., banks are required by law to log and report all transactions over $10,000. These restrictions are set up to ensure proper taxation and to prevent money laundering and other monetary frauds. Another example application is an anonymous pass with usage limitations. For example, consider the following amusement park pass: "This pass is good to enter any Disney park up to four times, with the restriction that the Magic Kingdom can be entered at most twice." Until now, it was not known how to realize such passes anonymously.

Interestingly, in the real world it is impossible to set such restrictions on cash transactions. A merchant may be required by law to report that he received a lot of money in cash, but he may choose not to obey the law! In contrast, we show that with e-cash, it is possible to enforce the bounded-anonymity business model. The cost for achieving this is roughly double the cost of achieving regular anonymous e-cash.

There have been several previous attempts to solve this problem, but until now it remained an elusive open problem in electronic cash, as well as one of the arguments why the financial community resisted any serious deployment of e-cash, due money laundering regulations.

Some of the past efforts suggested using a trusted third party to mitigate this problem [40,9,31]. This TTP could trace transactions to particular users. The TTP approach is undesirable. First of all, the whole idea of electronic cash is to ensure that no one can trace e-cash transactions. Secondly, in these past solutions, the only way that a TTP can discover money laundering or other violations of the bounded-anonymity model is by tracing each transaction, which is very expensive. In a variant that reduces the trust assumption about the TTP, Kügler and Vogt [30] propose an e-cash scheme where the bank has the ability to trace coins by specially marking them during the withdrawal protocol. This tracing is auditable, i.e., a user can later find out whether or not his coins were traced (this involves an additional trusted judge). Still, this system does not allow to discover money laundering, unless it involves the marked coins, and the user must still trust the judge and bank for her anonymity. Another variant [35,29] prevents money laundering by offering users only a limited form of anonymity. Users' coins are anonymous, but linkable, i.e., coins from the same user can be identified as such. Here it is easy to detect if a user exceeds the spending limit with some merchant. However, this weak form of anonymity is not suitable for all applications, and goes against the principle of e-cash.

Another set of papers [41,34] addressed a related problem of allowing a user to show a credential anonymously and unlinkably to any given verifier up to k times. They give a nice solution, but it is not clear how it can be applied to *off-line* electronic cash as opposed to on-line anonymous authentication. I.e., showing an anonymous credential in their scheme more than k times allows a verifier to link the $k + 1$ *st* show to a previous transaction, but does not lead to the identification of the misbehaving user. In contrast, in our scheme, any such violation leads to identification of the user even if the verifier (merchant) colludes with the user.

Finally, Sander and Ta-Shma [37] propose to limit money laundering by dividing time into short time periods and issuing at most k coins to a user per time period (a user can deposit his unspent coins back into his account). This way, a user cannot spend more than k coins in a single transactions because he has at most k coins at any given time.

Our contribution. We present the first e-cash scheme in the bounded-anonymity business model. A user may withdraw, and anonymously and unlinkably spend an unlimited number of coins, so long as she does not: (1) double-spend a coin, or (2) exceed the spending limit with any merchant. Our scheme allows to efficiently detect either of these violations. We also show how to augment it so as to allow to reveal the identity of the misbehaving user. Finally, in addition to identifying a misbehaving user, one is also able to trace all of the user's previous e-coins.

Our construction takes as a starting point the e-cash system of Camenisch, Hohenberger, and Lysyanskaya (CHL) [11], which is the most efficient known. The cost of our resulting withdrawal and spend protocols is roughly double that of CHL. The size of the coin storage remains the same, but we also require the user to store a counter for each merchant with whom the user does business, which appears to be optimal. Thus we maintain CHL's asymptotic complexity: 2^ℓ coins can be stored in $O(\ell + k)$ bits and the complexity of the withdrawal and spend protocols is $O(\ell + k)$, where k is the security parameter.

2   Definition of Security

We now generalize the definition of CHL [11] to handle violations beyond double-spending. Our offline e-cash scenario consists of the three usual players: the user, the bank, and the merchant; together with the algorithms BKeygen, UKeygen, Withdraw, Spend, Deposit, {DetectViolation$^{(i)}$, IdentifyViolator$^{(i)}$, VerifyViolation$^{(i)}$}, Trace, and VerifyOwnership. Informally, the key generation algorithms BKeygen and UKeygen are for the bank and the user, respectively. A user interacts with the bank during Withdraw to obtain a wallet of 2^ℓ coins;

the bank stores optional tracing information in database D. In Spend, a user spends one coin from his wallet with a merchant; as a result the merchant obtains the serial number S of the coin, the merchant record locator V of the coin, and a proof of validity π. In Deposit, whenever an honest merchant accepted a coin $C = (S, V, \pi)$ from a user, there is a guarantee that the bank will accept this coin for deposit. The bank stores $C = (S, V, \pi)$ in database L. At this point, however, the bank needs to determine if C violates any of the system conditions.

For each violation i, a tuple of algorithms {DetectViolation$^{(i)}$, IdentifyViolator$^{(i)}$, VerifyViolation$^{(i)}$} is defined. Here, we have two violations.

Violation 1: Double-spending. In DetectViolation$^{(1)}$, the bank tests if two coins, $C_1 = (S_1, V_1, \pi_1)$ and $C_2 = (S_2, V_2, \pi_2)$, in L have the same *serial number* $S_1 = S_2$. If so, the bank runs the IdentifyViolator$^{(1)}$ algorithm on (C_1, C_2) and obtains the public key pk of the violator and a proof of guilt Π. Anyone can run VerifyViolation$^{(1)}$ on (pk, S_1, V_1, Π) to be convinced that the user with public key pk double-spent the coin with serial number S_1.

Violation 2: Money-laundering. In DetectViolation$^{(2)}$, the bank tests if two coins, $C_1 = (S_1, V_1, \pi_1)$ and $C_2 = (S_2, V_2, \pi_2)$, in L have the same *merchant record locator* $V_1 = V_2$. If so, the bank runs the IdentifyViolator$^{(2)}$ algorithm on (C_1, C_2) and obtains the public key pk of the violator and a proof of guilt Π. Anyone can run VerifyViolation$^{(2)}$ on (pk, S_1, V_1, Π) to be convinced that the user with public key pk exceeded the bounded-anonymity business limit with the coin with merchant record locator V_1.

Optionally, after any violation, the bank may also run the Trace algorithm on a valid proof of guilt Π to obtain a list of all serial numbers S_i ever spent by the cheating user, with public key pk, along with a proof of ownership Γ. Anyone can run VerifyOwnership on (pk, S_i, Γ) to be convinced that the user with public key pk was the owner of the coin with serial number S_i.

Security. We generalize the security definition of CHL for e-cash [11]. Their formalizations of correctness, balance, and anonymity of users remain unchanged. Roughly, *balance* guarantees that an honest bank will never have to accept for deposit more coins than users withdrew, while *anonymity of users* assures users that they remain completely anonymous unless they violate one of the known system conditions. We now informally describe three additional properties. These properties are generalizations of CHL's identification and tracing of double-spenders, and their exculpability, to apply to any specified violation, in particular those above. Let *params* be the global parameters, including the number of coins per wallet, 2^ℓ, and a (possibly unique) spending limit for each merchant. (Recall that each merchant may have a different spending limit, but that a merchant's limit will apply uniformly for all of its customers.)

Identification of violators. Suppose two coins $C_1 = (S_1, V_1, \pi_1)$ and $C_2 = (S_2, V_2, \pi_2)$ are the output of an honest merchant (or possibly merchants) running two Spend protocols with the adversary or they are two coins that an honest bank accepted for deposit. This property guarantees that, with high probability, if, for some i, the algorithm DetectViolation$^{(i)}$(params, C_1, C_2) accepts, then IdentifyViolator$^{(i)}$(params, C_1, C_2) outputs a key pk and a proof Π such that VerifyViolation$^{(i)}$(params, pk, S_1, V_1, Π) accepts.

Tracing of violators. Suppose VerifyViolation$^{(i)}$(params, pk, S, V, Π) accepts for some violation i derived from coins C_1, C_2. This property guarantees that, with high probability, Trace(params, pk, C_1, C_2, Π, D) outputs the serial numbers $S_1, \ldots, S_m$ of all coins belonging to the user of pk along with proofs of ownership $\Gamma_1, \ldots, \Gamma_m$ such that for all j, we have that VerifyOwnership(params, pk, S_j, Γ_j) accepts.

Exculpability. Suppose an adversary participates any number of times in the Withdraw protocol with an honest user with key pk, and subsequently to that, in any number of *non-violation* Spend protocols with the same user. The adversary then outputs an integer i, a coin serial number S, and a purported proof Γ that the user with key pk committed violation i and owns coin S. The *weak* exculpability property states that, for all adversaries, the probability that VerifyOwnership(params, pk, S, Γ) accepts is negligible.

Furthermore, the adversary may continue to engage the user in Spend protocols, forcing her to violate the system conditions. The adversary then outputs (i, S, V, Π). The *strong* exculpability property states that, for all adversaries: (1) when S is a coin serial number *not* belonging to the user of pk, weak exculpability holds, and (2) when the user of pk did *not* commit violation i, the probability that VerifyViolation$^{(i)}$(params, pk, S, V, Π) accepts is negligible.

The formal definitions follow in a straight-forward manner by applying the above intuition to the CHL definitions [11].

3   Technical Preliminaries

Our e-cash system use a variety of known protocols as building blocks, which we now briefly review. Many of these protocols can be shown secure under several different complexity assumptions, a flexibility that will extend to our e-cash systems. **Notation:** we write $G = \langle g \rangle$ to denote that g generates the group G.

3.1   Bilinear Maps

Let Bilinear_Setup be an algorithm that, on input the security parameter 1^k, outputs the parameters for a bilinear mapping as $\gamma = (q, g_1, h_1, \mathbb{G}_1, g_2, h_2, \mathbb{G}_2, \mathbb{G}_T, e)$ [6]. Each group $\mathbb{G}_1 = \langle g_1 \rangle = \langle h_1 \rangle$, $\mathbb{G}_2 = \langle g_2 \rangle = \langle h_2 \rangle$, and $\mathbb{G}_T$ are of prime order $q = \Theta(2^k)$. The efficiently computable mapping $e : \mathbb{G}_1 \times \mathbb{G}_2 \to \mathbb{G}_T$ is both: (*Bilinear*) for all $g_1 \in \mathbb{G}_1$, $g_2 \in \mathbb{G}_2$, and $a, b \in \mathbb{Z}_q$, $e(g_1^a, g_2^b) = e(g_1, g_2)^{ab}$; and (*Non-degenerate*) if g_1 is a generator of $\mathbb{G}_1$ and g_2 is a generator of $\mathbb{G}_2$, then $e(g_1, g_2)$ generates $\mathbb{G}_T$.

3.2   Complexity Assumptions

The security of our scheme relies on the same assumptions as CHL, which are:

Strong RSA Assumption [3,27]: Given an RSA modulus n and a random element $g \in \mathbb{Z}_n^*$, it is hard to compute $h \in \mathbb{Z}_n^*$ and integer $e > 1$ such that $h^e \equiv g$ mod n. The modulus n is of a special form pq, where $p = 2p' + 1$ and $q = 2q' + 1$ are safe primes.

y-Decisional Diffie-Hellman Inversion Assumption (y-DDHI) [4,25]: Given a random generator $g \in G$, where G has prime order q, the values $(g, g^x, \ldots, g^{(x^y)})$ for a random $x \in \mathbb{Z}_q$, and a value $R \in G$, it is hard to decide if $R = g^{1/x}$ or not.

External Diffie-Hellman Assumption (XDH) [28,39,32,5,2]: Suppose Bilinear_Setup(1^k) produces the parameters for a bilinear mapping $e : \mathbb{G}_1 \times \mathbb{G}_2 \to \mathbb{G}_T$. The XDH assumption states that the Decisional Diffie-Hellman (DDH) problem is hard in $\mathbb{G}_1$. This implies that there does *not* exist an efficiently computable isomorphism $\psi' : \mathbb{G}_1 \to \mathbb{G}_2$.

Sum-Free Decisional Diffie-Hellman Assumption (SF-DDH) [24]: Suppose that $g \in G$ is a random generator of order q. Let L be any polynomial function of $|q|$. Let $O_a(\cdot)$ be an oracle that, on input a subset $I \subseteq \{1, \ldots, L\}$, outputs the value $g_1^{\beta_I}$ where $\beta_I = \prod_{i \in I} a_i$ for some $\boldsymbol{a} = (a_1, \ldots, a_L) \in \mathbb{Z}_q^L$. Further, let R be a predicate such that $R(J, I_1, \ldots, I_t) = 1$ if and only if $J \subseteq \{1, \ldots, L\}$ is DDH-independent from the I_i's; that is, when $v(I_i)$ is the L-length vector with a one in position j if and only if $j \in I_i$ and zero otherwise, then there are no three sets I_a, I_b, I_c such that $v(J) + v(I_a) = v(I_b) + v(I_c)$ (where addition is bitwise over the integers). Then, for all probabilistic polynomial time adversaries $\mathcal{A}^{(\cdot)}$,

$$Pr[\boldsymbol{a} = (a_1, \ldots, a_L) \leftarrow \mathbb{Z}_q^L; (J, \alpha) \leftarrow \mathcal{A}^{O_a}(1^{|q|}); y_0 = g^{\prod_{i \in J} a_i}; y_1 \leftarrow G;$$

$$b \leftarrow \{0,1\}; b' \leftarrow \mathcal{A}^{O_a}(1^{|q|}, y_b, \alpha) \ : \ b = b' \wedge R(J, Q) = 1] < 1/2 + 1/\text{poly}(|q|),$$

where Q is the set of queries that $\mathcal{A}$ made to $O_a(\cdot)$.

3.3   Key Building Blocks

Known Discrete-Logarithm-Based, Zero-Knowledge Proofs. In the common parameters model, we use several previously known results for proving statements about discrete logarithms, such as (1) proof of knowledge of a discrete logarithm modulo a prime [38] or a composite [27,23], (2) proof of knowledge of equality of representation modulo two (possibly different) prime [21] or composite [15] moduli, (3) proof that a commitment opens to the product of two other committed values [14,16,8], (4) proof that a committed value lies in a given integer interval [17,14,7], and also (5) proof of the disjunction or conjunction of any two of the previous [22]. These protocols modulo a composite are secure under the strong RSA assumption and modulo a prime under the discrete logarithm assumption. We can apply the Fiat-Shamir heuristic [26] to turn such proofs of knowledge into *signature proofs of knowledge* on some message m.

DY Pseudorandom Function (PRF). Let $G = \langle g \rangle$ be a group of prime order q. Let s be a random element of $\mathbb{Z}_q$. Dodis and Yampolskiy [25] recently proposed a pseudorandom function $f_{g,s}^{DY}(x) = g^{1/(s+x)}$ for inputs $x \in \mathbb{Z}_q^*$. This construction is secure under the y-DDHI. [1]

Pedersen Commitments. Pedersen proposed a perfectly-hiding, computationally-binding commitment scheme [36] based on the discrete logarithm assumption, in which the public parameters are a group of prime order q, and generators $(g_0, \dots, g_m)$. In order to commit to the values $(v_1, \dots, v_m) \in \mathbb{Z}_q^m$, pick a random $r \in \mathbb{Z}_q$ and set $C = \text{PedCom}(v_1, \dots, v_m; r) = g_0^r \prod_{i=1}^m g_i^{v_i}$. Fujisaki and Okamoto [27] showed how to expand this scheme to composite order groups.

CL Signatures. Camenisch and Lysyanskaya [12] came up with a secure signature scheme based on the Strong RSA assumption with two protocols: (1) An efficient protocol between a user and a signer with keys (pk_S, sk_S). The common input consists of pk_S and C, a Pedersen commitment. The user's secret input is the set of values $(v_1, \dots, v_\ell, r)$ such that $C = \text{PedCom}(v_1, \dots, v_\ell; r)$. As a result of the protocol, the user obtains a signature $\sigma_{pk_S}(v_1, \dots, v_\ell)$ on his committed values, while the signer does not learn anything about them. The signature has size $O(\ell \cdot \log q)$. (2) An efficient proof of knowledge of a signature protocol between a user and a verifier. The common inputs are pk_S and a commitment C. The user's private inputs are the values $(v_1, \dots, v_\ell, r)$, and $\sigma_{pk_S}(v_1, \dots, v_\ell)$ such that $C = \text{PedCom}(v_1, \dots, v_\ell; r)$. These signatures are secure under the strong RSA assumption. For our current purposes, it does not matter *how* CL signatures actually work, all that matters are the facts stated above.

Verifiable Encryption. We use a technique by Camenisch and Damgård [10] for turning any semantically-secure encryption scheme into a verifiable encryption scheme. A verifiable encryption scheme is a two-party protocol between a prover and encryptor $\mathcal{P}$ and a verifier and receiver $\mathcal{V}$. Roughly, their common inputs are a public encryption key pk and a commitment A. As a result of the protocol, $\mathcal{V}$ either rejects or obtains the encryption c of the opening of A. The protocol ensures that $\mathcal{V}$ accepts an incorrect encryption only with negligible probability and that $\mathcal{V}$ learns nothing meaningful about the opening of A. Together with the corresponding secret key sk, transcript c contains enough information to recover the opening of A efficiently. We hide some details here and refer to Camenisch and Damgård [10] for the full discussion.

Bilinear Elgamal Encryption. In particular, we apply the verifiable encryption techniques above to a bilinear variant of the Elgamal cryptosystem [6,1], which is semantically secure under an assumption implied by either y-DDHI or Sum-Free DDH. What we will need is a cryptosystem where g^x is sufficient for decryption and then the public key is $f(g^x)$ for some function f.

---

[1] It is possible to eliminate the y-DDHI assumption from our e-cash system by replacing the DY PRF with a DDH-based PRF such as the one due to Naor and Reingold [33]. However, this approach would enlarge our wallets from $\mathcal{O}(\ell + k)$ bits to $\mathcal{O}(\ell \cdot k)$ bits. Thus, we present only the most optimal building blocks.

Assume we run Bilinear_Setup on 1^k to obtain $\gamma = (q, g_1, h_1, \mathbb{G}_1, g_2, h_2, \mathbb{G}_2,$ $\mathbb{G}_T, e)$, where we have bilinear map $e : \mathbb{G}_1 \times \mathbb{G}_2 \to \mathbb{G}_T$. In bilinear Elgamal [1], a public-secret keypair is of the form $(e(g_1^u, g_2), g_1^u)$ for a random $u \in \mathbb{Z}_q$. Thus, we can think of $f(\cdot) := e(\cdot, g_2)$ where the value g_1^u is enough to decrypt.

4   Compact E-Cash in the Bounded-Anonymity Model

Overview of our construction. As in the CHL compact e-cash scheme, a user withdraws a wallet of 2^ℓ coins from the bank and spends them one by one. Also, as in the CHL scheme, we use a pseudorandom function $F_{(\cdot)}(\cdot)$ whose range is some group G of large prime order q.

At a high level, a user forms a wallet of $2^\ell = N$ coins by picking five values, (x, s, t, v, w) from an appropriate domain to be explained later, and running an appropriate secure protocol with the Bank to obtain the Bank's signature σ on these values.

Suppose that the user wants to spend coin number i by buying goods from merchant M. Suppose that only up to K transactions with this merchant may be anonymous. Let's say that this is the user's j-th transaction with M, $j \leq K$. Associated with the i-th coin in the wallet is its serial number $S = F_s(i)$. Associated with the j-th transaction with the merchant M is the merchant's record locator $V = F_v(M, j)$.

The first idea is that in the Spend protocol, the user should give to the merchant the values (S, V), together with a (non-interactive zero-knowledge) proof that these values are computed as a function of (s, i, v, M, j), where $1 \leq i \leq N$, $1 \leq j \leq K$, and (s, v) correspond to a wallet signed by the Bank. Note that S and V are pseudorandom, and therefore computationally leak no information; and the proof leaks no information because it is zero-knowledge.

Suppose that a user spends more than N coins. Then he must have used some serial number more than once, since there are only N possible values S of the form $F_s(i)$ where $1 \leq i \leq N$. (This is the CHL observation.) Similarly, suppose that a user made more than K transactions with M. Then he must have used some merchant record locator more than once, since for a fixed M, there are only K different values $V = F_v(M, j)$, $1 \leq j \leq K$. Therefore it is easy to see that double-spending and violations of the bounded-anonymity business model can be detected.

Now we need to explain how to make sure that using any S or V more than once leads to identification. Remember that besides s and v, the wallet also contains x, t and w. The value $x \in \mathbb{Z}_q$ is such that g^x is a value that can be publicly linked to the user's identity. (Where g is a generator of the group G.) For example, for some computable function f, $f(g^x)$ can be the user's public key. Suppose that as part of the transaction the merchant contributes a random value $r \neq 0$, and the user reveals $T = g^x F_t(i)^r$ and $W = g^x F_w(M, j)^r$, together with a proof that T and W are computed appropriately as a function of (r, x, t, i, w, M, j) corresponding to the very same wallet and the same i and j. Again, T and W are pseudorandom and therefore do not leak any information.

If a user uses the same serial number $S = F_s(i)$ twice, and q is appropriately large, then with high probability in two different transactions she will receive different r's, call them r_1 and r_2, and so will have to respond with $T_1 = g^x F_t(i)^{r_1}$, $T_2 = g^x F_t(i)^{r_2}$. It is easy to see that the value g^x can then be computed as follows: $g^x = T_1/(T_1/T_2)^{r_1/(r_1-r_2)}$. This was discovered by CHL building on the original ideas of offline e-cash [20].

We show that it is also the case that if the user uses the same merchant's record locator number V twice, then g^x can be found in exactly the same fashion. Suppose that in the two transactions the merchant used the same r. In that case, the Bank can simply refuse to deposit this e-coin (since it is the same merchant, he is responsible for his own lack of appropriate randomization). So suppose that the merchant used two different r's, r_1 and r_2, giving rise to W_1 and W_2. It is easy to see that $g^x = W_1/(W_1/W_2)^{r_1/(r_1-r_2)}$.

Thus, a double-spending or a violation of the bounded-business model leads to identification. The only remaining question is how this can be adapted to trace other transactions of the same user. Note that g^x is not necessarily a public value, it may also be the case that only $f(g^x)$ is public, while knowledge of g^x gives one the ability to decrypt a ciphertext which was formed by verifiably encrypting s (for example, Boneh and Franklin's cryptosystem [6] has the property that g^x is sufficient for decryption). When withdrawing a wallet, the user must give such a ciphertext to the bank. In turn, knowledge of s allows to discover serial numbers of all coins from this wallet and see how they were spent.

Finally, note that the values (x, v, w) should be tied to a user's identity and not to a particular wallet. This way, even if a user tries to spend too much money with a particular merchant from different wallets, it will still lead to detection and identification.

4.1 Our Protocols

Recall our building blocks from Section 3: the Dodis-Yampolskiy pseudo-random function [25], i.e., $f_{(g,s)}^{DY}(x) = g^{1/(s+x)}$, where g is the generator of a suitable group; CL-signatures [12] and the related protocols to issue signatures and prove knowledge of signatures; and the Bilinear Elgamal cryptosystem [6,1] used with the Camenisch-Damgård [10] verifiable encryption techniques.

Notation: Let $F_{(g,s)}(x) = f_{(g,s)}^{DY}(x)$, and when H is a hash function whose range is an appropriate group, let $G_s^H(M, x) = f_{(H(M),s)}^{DY}(x)$.

We are now describing the protocols of our system: Setup, Withdraw, Spend, and Deposit (including the protocols in response to violations).

Setup: Let k be the security parameter. The common system parameters are the bilinear map parameters Bilinear_Setup$(1^k) \rightarrow (q, g_1, \mathbb{G}_1, g_2, h_2, \mathbb{G}_2, \mathbb{G}_T, e)$, a wallet size ℓ, and two hash functions $H_1 : \{0,1\}^* \rightarrow \mathbb{G}_T$ and $H_2 : \{0,1\}^* \rightarrow \mathbb{G}_1$. The bank generates CL signing keys $(pk_\mathcal{B}, sk_\mathcal{B})$ as before.

Each user generates a key pair of the form $sk_\mathcal{U} = (x, v, w)$ and $pk_\mathcal{U} = (e(g_1, h_2)^x, e(g_1, h_2)^v, e(g_1, h_2)^w)$, where x, v, and w are chosen randomly from $\mathbb{Z}_q$. Each user also generates a signing keypair for any secure signature scheme.

Each merchant publishes a unique identity string $id_\mathcal{M}$. Also, an upper-bound $N_\mathcal{M}$ for the number of coins each user can spend with merchant $id_\mathcal{M}$ is fixed.

Withdraw: A user $\mathcal{U}$ withdraws 2^ℓ coins from the bank $\mathcal{B}$ as follows. The user and the bank engage in an interactive protocol, and if neither report an error, then at the end:

1. $\mathcal{U}$ obtains (s, t, σ), where s, t are random values in $\mathbb{Z}_q$, and σ is the bank's signature on $(sk_\mathcal{U}, s, t)$, i.e., (x, v, w, s, t).
2. $\mathcal{B}$ obtains a verifiable encryption of s under $e(g_1, h_2)^x$, i.e., the first element from the user's public key $pk_\mathcal{U}$, together with the user's signature on this encryption.
3. $\mathcal{B}$ does not learn anything about $sk_\mathcal{U}$, s, or t.

Step one can be efficiently realized using the Camenisch-Lysyanskaya signatures and the related protocols [13]. Step two can be realized by applying the Camenisch-Damgård [10] verifiable encryption techniques to the Bilinear Elgamal cryptosystem [6,1]. Step three follows from the other two. All these steps are essentially the same as in the CHL e-cash scheme, the exception being the secret key signed which now also includes v and w besides x.

Spend: A user $\mathcal{U}$ spends one coin with a merchant $\mathcal{M}$ with a spending limit of $N_\mathcal{M}$ coins as follows. As in CHL, the user keeps a private counter i from 1 to 2^ℓ for the number of coins spent in her wallet. Additionally, the user now also keeps a counter $j_\mathcal{M}$ for each merchant $\mathcal{M}$ representing the number of coins she has spent with that merchant.

1. $\mathcal{U}$ checks that she is under her spending limit with merchant $\mathcal{M}$; that is, that $j_\mathcal{M} < N_\mathcal{M}$. If not, she aborts.
2. $\mathcal{M}$ sends random $r_1, r_2 \in \mathbb{Z}_q^*$ to $\mathcal{U}$.
3. $\mathcal{U}$ sends $\mathcal{M}$ the i-th coin in her wallet on her $j_\mathcal{M}$-th transaction with $\mathcal{M}$. Recall that $sk_\mathcal{U} = (x, v, w)$. This coin consists of a serial number S and a wallet check T, where

$$S = F_{(e(g_1, h_2), s)}(i) = e(g_1, h_2)^{1/(s+i)} \,,\, T = g_1^x (F_{(g_1, t)}(i))^{r_1} = g_1^{x + r_1/(t+i)}$$

and two money laundering check values V and W, where

$$V = G_v^{H_1}(id_\mathcal{M}, j_\mathcal{M}) = H_1(id_\mathcal{M})^{1/(v + j_\mathcal{M})} \,,$$
$$W = g_1^x (G_w^{H_2}(id_\mathcal{M}, j_\mathcal{M}))^{r_2} = g_1^x H_2(id_\mathcal{M})^{r_2/(w + j_\mathcal{M})}$$

and a zero-knowledge, proof of knowledge (ZKPOK) π of $(i, j_\mathcal{M}, sk_\mathcal{U} = (x, v, w), s, t, \sigma)$ such that
(a) $1 \leq i \leq 2^\ell$;
(b) $1 \leq j_\mathcal{M} \leq N_\mathcal{M}$;
(c) $S = F_{(e(g_1, h_2), s)}(i)$, i.e., $S = e(g_1, h_2)^{1/(s+i)}$;
(d) $T = g_1^x (F_{(g_1, t)}(i))^{r_1}$, i.e., $T = g_1^{x + r_1/(t+i)}$;

(e) $V = G_v^{H_1}(id_\mathcal{M}, j_\mathcal{M})$, i.e., $V = H_1(id_\mathcal{M})^{1/(v+j_\mathcal{M})}$;

(f) $W = g_1^x(G_w^{H_2}(id_\mathcal{M}, j_\mathcal{M}))^{r_2}$, i.e., $W = g_1^x H_2(id_\mathcal{M})^{r_2/(w+j_\mathcal{M})}$; and

(g) VerifySig$(pk_\mathcal{B}, (sk_\mathcal{U} = (x, v, w), s, t), \sigma)$=true.

The proof π can be made non-interactive using the Fiat-Shamir heuristic [26].

4. If π verifies and the value V_j was never seen by $\mathcal{M}$ before, then $\mathcal{M}$ accepts and saves the coin $(r_1, r_2, S, T, V, W, \pi)$. If the value V_j was previously seen before in a coin $(r_1', r_2', S', T', V, W', \pi')$, then $\mathcal{M}$ runs $Open(W', W, r_2', r_2)$. Let us define the $Open(\cdot, \cdot, \cdot, \cdot)$ algorithm as:

$$Open(A, B, C, D) := \frac{A}{(A/B)^{C/(C-D)}} \ .$$

If $\mathcal{M}$ executed the Spend protocols honestly (i.e., chose fresh random values at the start of each protocol), then with high probability $r_2 \neq r_2'$, and $Open(W', W, r_2', r_2) = g_1^x$. Thus, the merchant can identify the user by computing $e(g_1^x, h_2)$, which is part of $\mathcal{U}$'s public key. This allows an honest merchant to protect itself from customers who try to overspend with it. (If the merchant is dishonest, the bank will catch the overspending at deposit time.)

Steps 3(a,c,d) are the same as in the CHL scheme whereas Steps 3(b,e,f) are new, and Step 3(g) needs to be adapted properly. Consequently, Steps 3(a) and 3(b) can be done efficiently using standard techniques [17,14,7]. Steps 3(c) to 3(f) can be done efficiently using techniques of Camenisch, Hohenberger, and Lysyanskaya [11]. Step 3(g) can be done efficiently using the Camenisch and Lysyanskaya signatures [13].

Deposit: A merchant $\mathcal{M}$ deposits a coin with bank $\mathcal{B}$ by submitting the coin $(r_1, r_2, S, T, V, W, \pi)$. The bank checks the proof π; it if does not verify, the bank rejects immediately. Now, the bank must make two additional checks.

First, $\mathcal{B}$ checks that the spender of the coin has not overspent her wallet; that is, the bank searches for any previously accepted coin with the same serial number S. Suppose such a coin $(r_1', r_2', S, T', V', W', \pi')$ is found. If $r_1 = r_1'$, $\mathcal{B}$ refuses to accept the coin. Otherwise, $\mathcal{B}$ accepts the coin from the merchant, but now must punish the user who double spent.

1. $\mathcal{B}$ executes $Open(T', T, r_1', r_1) = g_1^x$.
2. $\mathcal{B}$ identifies user as person with public key containing $e(g_1^x, h_2)$.
3. $\mathcal{B}$ uses g_1^x to decrypt the encryption of s left with the bank during the withdraw protocol. Next, $\mathcal{B}$ uses s to compute the serial numbers $S_j = F_{(e(g_1, h_2), s)}(j)$ for each coin $j = 1$ to 2^ℓ of all coins in the user's wallet. (In fact, the bank can use g_1^x to decrypt the secret of all the user's wallets and trace those transactions in the same way.)

Second, $\mathcal{B}$ checks that the spender of the coin has not exceeded her spending limit with merchant $\mathcal{M}$. That is, the bank searches for any previously accepted coin with the same money-laundering check value V_j. Suppose such a coin $(r_1', r_2', S', T', V, W', \pi')$ is found. The bank immediately refuses to accept the deposit and punishes the merchant. The bank now must also determine if the spender is to blame. If $r_2 = r_2'$, $\mathcal{B}$ punishes the merchant alone. Otherwise, $\mathcal{B}$ must also punish the user who attempted to money launder.

1. $\mathcal{B}$ executes $Open(W', W, r_2', r_2) = g_1^x$.
2. $\mathcal{B}$ identifies user as person with public key containing $e(g_1^x, h_2)$.
3. $\mathcal{B}$ uses g_1^x to decrypt the encryption of s left with the bank during the withdraw protocol. Next, $\mathcal{B}$ uses s to compute the serial numbers $S_j = F_{(e(g_1, h_2), s)}(j)$ for each coin $j = 1$ to 2^ℓ of all coins in the user's wallet. (In fact, the bank can use g_1^x to decrypt the secret of all the user's wallets and trace those transactions in the same way.)

If all checks pass, $\mathcal{B}$ accepts the coin for deposit in $\mathcal{M}$'s account.

The deposit protocol is again very similar to the deposit protocol of the CHL scheme, i.e., instead of only checking for double spending, the bank now also checks for money laundery. Thus, if the user was honest, the bank needs now to perform two database lookup's instead of one before.

For completeness, we point out explicitly how the violation-related protocols work. Let $C_1 = (r_1, r_2, S, T, V, W, \pi)$ and $C_2 = (r_1', r_2', S', T', V', W', \pi')$ be one existing and one newly deposited coin. Detecting double-spending or money-laundering involves checking $S_1 = S_2$ or $V_1 = V_2$, respectively. The identification algorithm runs $Open$ on the appropriate inputs, and the resulting proof of guilt is $\Pi = (C_1, C_2)$. Verifying the violation entails successfully checking the validity of the coins, detecting the claimed violation, running $Open$ to obtain g_1^x, and checking its relation to pk. (Recall that knowledge of x, not just g_1^x, is required to create a valid coin. Thus the leakage of one violation cannot be used to spend the user's coins or fake another violation.) The trace algorithm involves recovering s, from the encryption E signed by the user during Withdraw, and computing all serial numbers. The proof of ownership $\Gamma = (E, \sigma, g_1^x)$, where σ is the user's signature on E. Verifying ownership for some serial number S involves verifying the signature σ, checking that $e(g_1^x, h_2) = pk$, decrypting E to recover s, computing all serial numbers S_i, and testing if, for any i, $S = S_i$.

Theorem 1. *In the bounded-anonymity business model, our scheme achieves correctness, balance, anonymity of users, identification of violators, tracing of violators, and strong exculpability under the Strong RSA, y-DDHI, and either the XDH or Sum-Free DDH assumptions in the random oracle model.*

Due to space limitations, we refer to the full version of this paper for the proof of Theorem 1. We briefly provide some informal intuition.

Balance. For each wallet, s deterministically defines exactly 2^ℓ values that can be valid serial numbers for coins. To overspend a wallet, a user must either use one serial number twice, in which case she is identifiable, or she must forge a CL signature or fake a proof of validity.

Anonymity of users. A coin is comprised of four values (S, T, V, W), which are pseudorandom and thus leak no information about the user, together with a non-interactive, zero-knowledge proof of validity, which since it is zero-knowledge also leaks nothing. The only abnormality here is that, when computing V and W, the base used for the PRF is the hash of the merchant's identity (as opposed to the fixed bases used to compute S and T). Treating hash H as a random oracle, we see that given $G_v^H(id_{\mathcal{M}}, j)$, the output of $G_v^H(\cdot, \cdot)$ on any other input, in particular $G_v^H(id'_{\mathcal{M}}, j)$ for $id_{\mathcal{M}} \neq id'_{\mathcal{M}}$, is indistinguishable from random. Specifically, if an adversary given $G_v^H(id_{\mathcal{M}}, j) = f_{(H(id_{\mathcal{M}}), v)}^{DY}(j) = H(id_{\mathcal{M}})^{1/(v+j)}$ can distinguish $H(id'_{\mathcal{M}})^{1/(v+j)}$ from random for some random, fixed $H(id_{\mathcal{M}})$ and $H(id'_{\mathcal{M}})$, then it is solving DDH.

Exculpability. First, an honest user cannot be proven guilty of a crime he didn't commit, because the proof of guilt includes the user's *secret* value g_1^x. If a user is honest, only he knows this value. Second, even a cheating user cannot be proven guilty of a crime he didn't commit— e.g., double-spending one coin does not enable a false proof of money-laundering twenty coins —because: (1) guilt is publicly verifiable from the coins themselves, and (2) knowledge of x is required to create coins. The value g_1^x, which is leaked by a violation, is not enough to spend a coin from that user's wallet.

4.2   Scaling Back the Punishment for System Violators

When tracing is deemed too harsh a punishment or simply to make the system more efficient when tracing is not needed, two other options are available:

Option (1): violation is detected and user's identity is revealed. This system operates as the above except that during the Withdraw protocol the user does not give the bank verifiable encryptions of her wallet secret s. Then later during the Deposit protocol, the bank may still detect the violation and identify the user, but will not be able to compute the serial numbers of other transactions involving this user.

Option (2): violation is detected. This system operates as the Option (1) system, except that during Spend, the user does not provide the merchant with either values T or W. Then later during the Deposit protocol, the bank may still detect a violation, but will not be able to run *Open* and identify the user.

4.3   Efficiency Considerations

We give the detailed protocols in the full version of the paper (they are rather similar to the detailed ones of the CHL scheme [11] and require slightly less than double the work of the participants). As indication of the protocols efficiency let us state some numbers here. One can construct Spend such that a user must compute fourteen multi-base exponentiations to build the commitments and twenty more for the proof. The merchant and bank need to do twenty multi-base exponentiations to check that the coin is valid. The protocols require two rounds of communication between the user and the merchant and one round between the bank and the merchant. If one takes Option (2) above, then it is thirteen multi-base exponentiations to build the commitments and eighteen more for the proof. Verification by bank and merchant takes eighteen multi-base exponentiations.

Acknowledgments

Part of Jan Camenisch's work reported in this paper is supported by the European Commission through the IST Programme under Contract IST-2002-507932 ECRYPT and by the IST Project PRIME. The PRIME projects receives research funding from the European Community's Sixth Framework Programme and the Swiss Federal Office for Education and Science. The information in this document reflects only the author's views, is provided as is and no guarantee or warranty is given that the information is fit for any particular purpose. The user thereof uses the information at its sole risk and liability.

Part of Susan Hohenberger's work is supported by an NDSEG Fellowship. Anna Lysyanskaya is supported by NSF Career grant CNS 0347661.

References

1. G. Ateniese, K. Fu, M. Green, and S. Hohenberger. Improved Proxy Re-encryption Schemes with Applications to Secure Distributed Storage. In *NDSS*, p. 29–43, 2005.
2. L. Ballard, M. Green, B. de Medeiros, and F. Monrose. Correlation-Resistant Storage. Johns Hopkins University, CS Technical Report # TR-SP-BGMM-050705. http://spar.isi.jhu.edu/~mgreen/correlation.pdf, 2005.
3. N. Barić and B. Pfitzmann. Collision-free accumulators and fail-stop signature schemes without trees. In *EUROCRYPT '97*, volume 1233, p. 480–494, 1997.
4. D. Boneh and X. Boyen. Short signatures without random oracles. In *EUROCRYPT 2004*, volume 3027 of *LNCS*, p. 54–73, 2004.
5. D. Boneh, X. Boyen, and H. Shacham. Short group signatures using strong Diffie-Hellman. In *CRYPTO*, volume 3152 of LNCS, p. 41–55, 2004.
6. D. Boneh and M. Franklin. Identity-based encryption from the Weil pairing. In J. Kilian, editor, *CRYPTO 2001*, volume 2139 of *LNCS*, p. 213–229, 2001.
7. F. Boudot. Efficient proofs that a committed number lies in an interval. In *EUROCRYPT '00*, volume 1807 of *LNCS*, p. 431–444, 2000.
8. S. Brands. Rapid demonstration of linear relations connected by boolean operators. In *EUROCRYPT '97*, volume 1233 of *LNCS*, p. 318–333, 1997.
9. E. Brickell, P. Gemmel, and D. Kravitz. Trustee-based tracing extensions to anonymous cash and the making of anonymous change. In *SIAM*, p. 457–466, 1995.
10. J. Camenisch and I. Damgård. Verifiable encryption, group encryption, and their applications to group signatures and signature sharing schemes. In T. Okamoto, editor, *ASIACRYPT '00*, volume 1976 of *LNCS*, p. 331–345, 2000.
11. J. Camenisch, S. Hohenberger, and A. Lysyanskaya. Compact E-Cash. In *EUROCRYPT*, volume 3494 of LNCS, p. 302–321, 2005.
12. J. Camenisch and A. Lysyanskaya. A signature scheme with efficient protocols. In *SCN 2002*, volume 2576 of *LNCS*, p. 268–289, 2002.
13. J. Camenisch and A. Lysyanskaya. Signature schemes and anonymous credentials from bilinear maps. In *CRYPTO 2004*, volume 3152 of *LNCS*, p. 56–72, 2004.
14. J. Camenisch and M. Michels. Proving in zero-knowledge that a number n is the product of two safe primes. In *EUROCRYPT '99*, volume 1592, p. 107–122, 1999.
15. J. Camenisch and M. Michels. Separability and efficiency for generic group signature schemes. In *CRYPTO '99*, volume 1666 of *LNCS*, p. 413–430, 1999.
16. J. L. Camenisch. *Group Signature Schemes and Payment Systems Based on the Discrete Logarithm Problem*. PhD thesis, ETH Zürich, 1998.

17. A. Chan, Y. Frankel, and Y. Tsiounis. Easy come – easy go divisible cash. In *EUROCRYPT '98*, volume 1403 of *LNCS*, p. 561–575, 1998.
18. D. Chaum. Blind signatures for untraceable payments. In *CRYPTO '82*, p. 199–203. Plenum Press, 1982.
19. D. Chaum. Blind signature systems. In *CRYPTO '83*, p. 153–156. Plenum, 1983.
20. D. Chaum, A. Fiat, and M. Naor. Untraceable electronic cash. In *CRYPTO '90*, volume 403 of *LNCS*, p. 319–327, 1990.
21. D. Chaum and T. P. Pedersen. Wallet databases with observers. In *CRYPTO '92*, volume 740 of *LNCS*, p. 89–105, 1993.
22. R. Cramer, I. Damgård, and B. Schoenmakers. Proofs of partial knowledge and simplified design of witness hiding protocols. In *CRYPTO '94*, p. 174–187, 1994.
23. I. Damgård and E. Fujisaki. An integer commitment scheme based on groups with hidden order. In *ASIACRYPT 2002*, volume 2501 of *LNCS*, 2002.
24. Y. Dodis. Efficient construction of (distributed) verifiable random functions. In *Public Key Cryptography*, volume 2567 of *LNCS*, p. 1–17, 2003.
25. Y. Dodis and A. Yampolsky. A Verifiable Random Function with Short Proofs an Keys. In *Public Key Cryptography*, volume 3386 of LNCS, p. 416–431, 2005.
26. A. Fiat and A. Shamir. How to prove yourself: Practical solutions to identification and signature problems. In *CRYPTO*, volume 263 of LNCS, p. 186–194, 1986.
27. E. Fujisaki and T. Okamoto. Statistical zero knowledge protocols to prove modular polynomial relations. In *CRYPTO '97*, volume 1294 of *LNCS*, p. 16–30, 1997.
28. S. D. Galbraith. Supersingular curves in cryptography. In C. Boyd, editor, *ASIACRYPT*, volume 2248 of LNCS, p. 495–513, 2001.
29. S. Jarecki and V. Shmatikov. Handcuffing big brother: an abuse-resilient transaction escrow scheme. In *EUROCRYPT*, volume 3027 of *LNCS*, p. 590–608, 2004.
30. D. Kügler and H. Vogt. Fair tracing without trustees. In *Financial Cryptography '01*, volume 2339 of LNCS, p. 136–148, 2001.
31. A. Kiayias, Y. Tsiounis, and M. Yung. Traceable signatures. In *EUROCRYPT*, volume 3027 of LNCS, p. 571–589, 2004.
32. N. McCullagh and P. S. L. M. Barreto. A new two-party identity-based authenticated key agreement. In *CT-RSA*, volume 3376 of LNCS, p. 262–274, 2004.
33. M. Naor and O. Reingold. Number-theoretic constructions of efficient pseudorandom functions. *Journal of the ACM*, 51, Number 2:231–262, 2004.
34. L. Nguyen and R. Safavi-Naini. Dynamic k-times anonymous authentication. In *ACNS 2005*, number 3531 in LNCS, p. 318–333. Springer Verlag, 2005.
35. T. Okamoto and K. Ohta. Disposable zero-knowledge authentications and their applications to untraceable elec. cash. In *CRYPTO*, volume 435, p. 481–496, 1990.
36. T. P. Pedersen. Non-interactive and information-theoretic secure verifiable secret sharing. In *CRYPTO '92*, volume 576 of *LNCS*, p. 129–140, 1992.
37. T. Sander and A. Ta-Shma. Flow control: a new approach for anonymity control in electronic cash systems. In *FC*, volume 1648 of *LNCS*, p. 46–61, 1999.
38. C. P. Schnorr. Efficient signature generation for smart cards. *Journal of Cryptology*, 4(3):239–252, 1991.
39. M. Scott. Authenticated ID-based key exchange and remote log-in with simple token and PIN number. Available at http://eprint.iacr.org/2002/164, 2002.
40. M. Stadler, J.-M. Piveteau, and J. Camenisch. Fair blind signatures. In *EUROCRYPT '95*, volume 921 of *LNCS*, p. 209–219, 1995.
41. I. Teranishi, J. Furukawa, and K. Sako. k-times anonymous authentication (extended abstract). In *Asiacrypt 2004*, volume 3329 of *LNCS*, p. 308–322, 2004.

About the Security of MTI/C0 and MQV

Sébastien Kunz-Jacques[1,2] and David Pointcheval[1]

[1] École normale supérieure, 45 rue d'Ulm, 75005 Paris, France
David.Pointcheval@ens.fr
[2] DCSSI Crypto Lab, 51 boulevard de La Tour-Maubourg
F-75700 Paris 07 SP, France
kunzjacq@yahoo.fr

Abstract. The main application of cryptography is the establishment of secure channels. The most classical way to achieve this goal is definitely the use of variants of the signed Diffie-Hellman protocol. It applies a signature algorithm on the flows of the basic Diffie-Hellman key exchange, in order to achieve authentication. However, signature-less authenticated key exchange have numerous advantages, and namely from the efficiency point of view. They are thus well-suited for some constrained environments. On the other hand, this efficiency comes at the cost of some uncertainty about the actual security.

This paper focuses on the two most famous signature-less authenticated key exchange protocols, MTI/C0 and MQV. While the formal security of MTI/C0 has never been studied, results for the plain MQV protocol are still debated. We point out algorithmic assumptions on which some security proofs can be built in the random oracle model. The stress is put on implementation aspects that must be properly dealt with in order to obtain the expected security.

Some formalizations about authenticated key exchange, and the generic model, are of independent interest.

Keywords: Key Exchange, MTI, MQV, Diffie-Hellman, Security Proof.

1 Introduction

Since the introduction of the Diffie-Hellman protocol in the seminal paper [13], key exchange has played a prominent role in public-key cryptography. It provides two entities communicating on an insecure channel with a common secret value, which can thereafter be used to setup a secure channel. The plain Diffie-Hellman protocol does not provide entity authentication and is therefore vulnerable to "man-in-the-middle" attacks. A classical way to overcome this weakness is to authenticate the flows with strong authentication mechanisms, such as message authentication codes (MAC) or signature schemes (as for instance in the Station-To-Station protocol [14]).

A few proposals apply weaker authentication techniques, which are specific to the key agreement method. Whereas they are signature-less, they provide both strong authentication (the so-called "mutual authentication") and strong

R. De Prisco and M. Yung (Eds.): SCN 2006, LNCS 4116, pp. 156–172, 2006.

secrecy (the so-called "forward-secrecy"). Furthermore, since no signature computations/verifications are needed, they are quite efficient.

This paper focuses on some of these "signature-less protocols". The most well-known algorithms in that category are the MTI family [19,21] and MQV [20,27]. More specifically, among the MTI family, we focus on MTI/C0, which is the only variant of the MTI family that can be expected to provide the forward-secrecy. MQV was proposed as a solution to overcome some security weaknesses of MTI/C0. However, one can remark that attacks against the "basic MTI/C0" protocol can be easily prevented when proper and classical safeguards (eg. key confirmation rounds) are added.

As a conclusion, we show that when properly set-up, that is, in a suitably chosen group and with a proper key derivation mechanism, both MTI/C0 and MQV are secure authenticated key exchange protocols, and even achieve forward-secrecy. We focus on the 3-pass variants of these protocols because no two-pass protocol achieves mutual authentication: the first message can always be replayed by an active attacker. Some two-pass protocols are analyzed in [15,18].

Related work. Key exchange is closely related to authentication, as illustrated by the "man-in-the-middle attacks". A very general model for these two problems was introduced by Bellare and Rogaway [7]. Bellare, Canetti and Krawczyk [3] followed a different path, by providing a general tool to transform a protocol secure when communications are authenticated into a new protocol secure against an active adversary (able to alter messages). Among other applications, this framework can be applied to the "authenticated key exchange" (AKE) problem.

An extensive comparison of the security properties of some signature-less AKE protocols can be found in [9]; however, no security proof is provided. On the other hand, [8] provides security analyzes of several authenticated variants of the Diffie-Hellman scheme. For such studies, a formal security model is required. We thus review the strongest one, based on the seminal work of Bellare and Rogaway [7], and various extensions from [1,2,8].

The security of MQV was recently analyzed and a "hashed" variant, HMQV, was proved [17]. We focus on the plain MQV protocol, and show that proper key derivation is enough to overcome its security weaknesses, like the Unknown Key Share attack of Kaliski [16]. As for MTI/C0, no formal security result was available to our knowledge.

Security Model. Informally, we want to model resistance of a key exchange protocol against active and adaptive attackers. The required security properties are:

- **Semantic security.** If an execution of the protocol successfully terminates between a user A and its intended correspondent B, no one but A and B should possess any information about the key agreed upon;
- **Mutual authentication.** A user A engaged in a key exchange session accepts (actually gets a session key) with B only if it is indeed speaking to B;

- **Forward secrecy.** The disclosure of some user's private keys does not compromise (the semantic security of) previously negotiated keys.

By "active and adaptive attackers", as in [7], we mean that the attacker E has entire control of the communication network, and thus controls all flows between users. Therefore, there is no canonical definition of the partner of some user that runs the protocol. Partnership is defined with the help of views of the exchanged messages between two users. Since we consider forward-secrecy, E is also allowed to (adaptively) corrupt users, which then provide her with their long-term private keys.

More formally, the attacker plays a real-or-random game with a simulator, in which it succeeds if it distinguishes between true negotiated keys and random values. This game models the semantic security (and even the forward-secrecy, if the corruption of players is allowed). Strictly speaking, not mutual authentication, but only *implicit authentication* is guaranteed: when A negotiates a key with B, only A and B can compute the key, however from the point of view of A, there is no guarantee that B did compute the key or even that B was involved in the exchange at all. Key confirmation rounds are however well-known to enhance semantic security into mutual authentication [5,11].

Note that the classical definition of the semantic security involves a find-then-guess game [7,4]. In this paper, we use a real-or-random game, which is both stronger [2] and simpler to handle.

Contributions. Proofs are performed in the random oracle model [6] and rely on custom variants of the Diffie-Hellman problem: f-RCDH for MQV and 2-3-CDH for MTI/C0. f-RCDH is a rather non-standard problem, and might well be weaker than plain CDH; however we show that the f-RCDH intractability hypothesis is **equivalent** to the semantic security of MQV, which gives a strong motivation to introduce this new algorithmic problem (while the reduction of f-RCDH to MQV is performed in the random oracle model, the reduction of MQV to f-RCDH is in the standard model) . On the other hand, 2-3-CDH is a rather natural extension of CDH, but we only show that 2-3-CDH intractability hypothesis is at least as strong as the semantic security of MTI/C0.

Since new assumptions are always questionable, besides the security analysis, a large part of the paper is devoted to study the two new problems 2-3-CDH and f-RCDH. In particular, we build on generic group results to provide arguments towards the actual hardness of both problems: they are hard in the generic sense. Moreover, f-RCDH is shown to be equivalent to the classical CDH, under the additional assumption that the truncation function f used in MQV can be modeled as a random oracle. This motivates the replacement of this function of MQV by a proper hash function, as performed in [17].

For this analysis, we construct a simple and new tool of independent interest that allows one to check whether a particular variant of the Diffie-Hellman problem is hard in the generic sense or not.

Organization. The paper is organized as follows. Section 2 introduces a common framework for signature-less authenticated key exchange protocols. Many different protocols, among which MTI variants and MQV, can be plugged into that framework. MTI/C0 and MQV are presented in section 3, together with the corresponding algorithmic hypotheses, 2-3-CDH and f-RCDH. A sketch of the security proof is presented in section 4. Next, in section 5, the new algorithmic assumptions are analyzed. Finally, we sum up in section 6 the key design choices that help make a signature-less key exchange protocol secure. The security model, which is the classical one, is reviewed in appendix A.

The proof is omitted from this extended abstract and is available in the full version of the paper.

2   A Framework for Signature-Less Authenticated Key Exchange

We describe a general framework, in order to deal with signature-less authenticated key exchange protocols. Users are assumed to own public/private key pairs, and the public keys are supposed to be authentic and known to any party of the system.

First, we need some description of the view that a user (A or B) has of the messages exchanged during a session, since this will define the partnership relation.

Session Flow, Partners. We denote by $\mathsf{Flow}(\mathsf{U}, i)$ the bit-string encoding the messages seen by user $\mathsf{U} \in \{\mathsf{A}, \mathsf{B}\}$ during session i, *up to the key material agreement*. It is assumed that

$$\mathsf{Flow}(\mathsf{A}, i) = \mathsf{Flow}(\mathsf{B}, i) \quad \Longleftrightarrow \quad \left\{ \begin{array}{l} \text{no message between A and B was} \\ \text{altered in any way during session } i \end{array} \right\}$$

A and B are said to be *partners* in a session i if $\mathsf{Flow}(\mathsf{A}, i) = \mathsf{Flow}(\mathsf{B}, i)$. Informally, if A and B are partners in session i, they share the same key at the end of the session, and the converse should hold except with negligible probability.

Key Material Agreement. Let us now describe a key agreement between two users A and B. In a preliminary phase, one of the users asks the other party to initiate a key negotiation. From the cryptographic standpoint, the only interest of this phase is that the messages exchanged ends up in the session flow like the rest of the exchange: as a consequence, we can assume that the identities of A and B are contained in the session flows.

This phase of the protocol allows A and B to agree on common secret key material from which both the session key and key confirmations are derived:

- A chooses at random an element r_A in some space $\mathcal{R}$. Some function φ of r_A is sent to B. The function φ might additionally take as input A's private/public key, and B's public key. We name M_A all this long term key material available to A.

- B performs the same operation towards A.
- A and B both derive some *key material* KM through another operation ψ satisfying[1] a kind of commutativity property

$$\mathsf{KM} = \psi(\varphi(r_\mathsf{A}, M_\mathsf{A}), r_\mathsf{B}, M_\mathsf{B}) = \psi(\varphi(r_\mathsf{B}, M_\mathsf{B}), r_\mathsf{A}, M_\mathsf{A}).$$

Key Confirmation. When a user $\mathsf{U} \in \{\mathsf{A}, \mathsf{B}\}$ has computed KM, it can compute the common key $K \in \mathcal{K}$ and the *key confirmations* KC(U') for any partners U' (and himself) by

$$K = H(\mathsf{KM}\|0\|\mathsf{Flow}(\mathsf{U})) \quad \mathsf{KC}(\mathsf{U}') = H(\mathsf{KM}\|1\|\mathsf{ID}_{\mathsf{U}'}\|\mathsf{Flow}(\mathsf{U}))).$$

In this relation, the flows consist of the messages up to and including the exchange of random elements, H is a h-bit hash function (assumed to behave like a random oracle). Both A and B can compute the two key confirmations KC(A) and KC(B). But A sends KC(A) to B, while B sends KC(B) to A. Each user checks the value sent by the other and rejects the key if this value is incorrect.

3   Formalization of MTI/C0 and MQV

For both MTI/C0 and MQV, G is a cyclic group of prime order p, and g is a generator of G. All random elements are drawn uniformly in the sets mentioned.

3.1   MTI/C0

The private key s_u of a user U is a random element in $\mathbb{Z}_p^\star$ and the corresponding public key equals $K_u = g^{s_u}$.

Key Material Agreement. A (resp. B) draws a random element r_a (resp. r_b) in $\mathbb{Z}_p^\star$. A then computes $R_a = K_b{}^{r_a}$ and sends it to B, while A computes $R_b = K_a{}^{r_b}$ and sends it to A. The key material KM is then computed by each user according to the relation

$$\mathsf{KM} = g^{r_a r_b} = R_a{}^{r_b/s_b} = R_b{}^{r_a/s_a}$$

Note that if one of the received values (R_a or R_b) is equal to 1, the recipient aborts the protocol. Thus, using the framework of section 2, we have

$$\varphi(r_a, M_a = (s_a, K_a, K_b)) = R_a = K_b^{r_a}$$

and
$$\psi(R_a, r_b, M_b = (s_b, K_a, K_b)) = \begin{cases} \texttt{abort} & \text{if } R_a = 1 \\ R_a^{r_b/s_b} & \text{otherwise} \end{cases}$$

---

[1] ψ might reject some values of its first input: the relation holds only when neither $\varphi(r_\mathsf{A}, M_\mathsf{A})$ nor $\varphi(r_\mathsf{B}, M_\mathsf{B})$ is rejected.

2-out-of-3 Computational Diffie-Hellman Problem. In order to prove the security of MTI/C0, we clearly need to make the assumption that the Computational Diffie-Hellman problem is intractable: given g^x and g^y, it is hard to compute g^{xy} for random elements $x, y \in \mathbb{Z}_p$. In order to deal with active attacks, we also need another computational hardness hypothesis that is an extension of the above CDH:

2-out-of-3 Computational Diffie-Hellman.

Given $X = g^x$ and $Y = g^y$, for random $x, y \in \mathbb{Z}_p$, compute a pair (Z, T) of elements in G, where $Z \neq 1$ and T is the CDH value of X, Y and Z: $T = Z^{xy}$.

First, it is clear that 2-3-CDH is at most as difficult as CDH. Indeed, if an adversary manages to compute $h = g^{xy}$, (g^z, h^z) is a correct 2-3-CDH answer for any choice of $z \in \mathbb{Z}_p^\star$. Moreover, it is not more difficult than the inverse-DH because by setting $Z = g^{1/y}$ where $Y = g^y$, (Z, X) is a correct answer. As a consequence, a tight reduction from 2-3-CDH to CDH would imply a tight reduction from Inv-CDH to CDH.

In a cyclic group of composite order, the probability in breaking 2-3-CDH is not smaller than $1/\omega$, where ω is the size of the smallest non-trivial subgroup of G. Indeed, an attacker can always choose at random two elements (Z, T) of order ω and then, since the order of $T' = \text{CDH}(X, Y, Z)$ divides ω, and since there is only one subgroup of order ω in the cyclic group G, $T = T'$ with probability $1/\omega$.

In groups of prime order where the discrete logarithm is hard, which our analysis focuses on, it seems reasonable to expect that no adversary can break 2-3-CDH in polynomial time and with a non-negligible probability. Let us denote by $\text{Succ}_{\text{CDH}}(t)$ and $\text{Succ}_{\text{2-3-CDH}}(t)$, for the maximum winning probability of an attacker running in time t against CDH and 2-out-of-3 Computational Diffie-Hellman in G, respectively. The probability is averaged over all possible challenges (X, Y) and over the randomness of the attacker.

2-3-CDH and Active Attacks. In the next section, we show that the intractability of 2-3-CDH is enough to guarantee the security of MTI/C0. Conversely, solving 2-3-CDH does not seem to be enough for an attacker to impersonate a user in a MTI/C0 session.

3.2   MQV

In the specification of MQV, we have a function f from $G \to \mathbb{Z}_p$. In the actual description of MQV [20,27], G is a prime order subgroup of an elliptic curve group over a finite field $\mathbb{F}_q$, where q is a n-bit prime; for $P = (x, y) \in G$, $x, y \in [0, q-1]$, $f(P) = x \bmod 2^{\lceil n/2 \rceil} + 2^{\lceil n/2 \rceil}$.

In the following, we use the multiplicative notation for the group G.

The private key s_u of a user U is a random element in $\mathbb{Z}_p$ and the corresponding public key equals $K_u = g^{s_u}$.

Key Material Agreement. A (resp. B) draws a random element r_a (resp. r_b) in $\mathbb{Z}_p$. Then A computes $R_a = g^{r_a}$ and sends it to B. Similarly, B computes $R_b = g^{r_b}$ and sends it to A. The key material KM is then computed by each person according to the relation

$$\mathsf{KM} = g^{(r_a + f(g^{r_a})s_a)(r_b + f(g^{r_b})s_b)} = \left(R_a \times K_a{}^{f(R_a)} \right)^{(r_b + f(R_b)s_b)}$$

$$= \left(R_b \times K_b{}^{f(R_b)} \right)^{(r_a + f(R_a)s_a)}.$$

Therefore
$$\varphi(r_a, M_A = (s_a, K_a, K_b)) = g^{r_a} = R_a$$

and
$$\psi(R_a, r_b, M_B = (s_b, K_a, K_b)) = \left(R_a \times K_a{}^{f(R_a)} \right)^{(r_b + f(g^{r_b})s_b)}.$$

f-Randomized Computational Diffie-Hellman Problem. As for MTI/C0, we need a new assumption, derived from CDH, for proving the security of MQV. It depends on the function f, hence the notation f-RCDH. As shown below, f-RCDH must be hard for MQV to withstand active attacks. We also show in section 5.1 that the intractability of RCDH can be reduced to the one of CDH under some additional assumptions on f.

---

f-RCDH

Given $X = g^x$ and $Y = g^y$, for randomly chosen $x, y \in \mathbb{Z}_p$, find $R, Z \in G$ such that $Z = R^x \times g^{f(R)\,x\,y}$.

With $r = \log_g R$ (which the attacker does not need to know), the above relation rewrites $Z = g^{x(r + f(R)y)}$.

As for any computational problem, $\mathsf{Succ}_{f\text{-RCDH}}(t)$ is the maximum winning probability of an adversary running in time t against f-RCDH in G, averaged over X, Y and the random tape of the adversary.

Note that f-RCDH is not more difficult than CDH, because knowing $h = g^{xy} = \mathsf{CDH}(X, Y)$, one can answer a valid pair (Z, R), by choosing $R = g^r$ and $Z = X^r h^{f(R)}$.

f-RCDH and Active Attacks. Solving f-RCDH allows to impersonate the responder (denoted by B in our description) in a MQV session: given the public keys K_A, K_B of A and B and the random value R_A sent by A, B can be impersonated to A using a correct f-RCDH answer (R_B, KM) to the challenge $(X = R_A \times K_A^{f(R_A)}, Y = K_B)$. Indeed, if R_B is used as the random value sent to A, then the resulting key material is KM. Note that no random oracle hypothesis is used here.

4   Sketch of Proof

As explained in the introduction, we follow the real-or-random model, as described in appendix A. In this scenario, the attacker E plays against a simulator S and has complete control of the exchanges between user instances. The simulator S draws a random bit b at the beginning of the game and E's goal is to guess this bit b. The attacker E can perform Test and Corrupt queries to obtain respectively session keys and long-term private keys of users. Before any Corrupt query occurs, the answers of Test queries depend on b: they are either the real keys (if $b = 1$) or random values (if $b = 0$). In both cases, the answers to two queries asked to partners in a session are the same. After a Corrupt query occurs, Test queries are answered by the real keys only. After getting long-term private keys, the adversary is indeed able to compute the session keys itself. Furthermore, forward-secrecy only considers the semantic security of keys agreed before any corruption.

Note that Test queries can only be asked to users who actually hold a session key, and thus after reception of a correct key confirmation at the end of the protocol run, so that they are "convinced" that they actually share a session key with their intended partner.

The proof is performed with the now classical game technique [25,26]. The first game is the real game in which we want to upper bound the success probability of E.

First, session flow collisions are ruled out. This is easy, because not all the randomness of the exchanged values in a protocol run is controlled by the attacker: at least one of the two values exchanged at the beginning of a run is properly drawn in G by S, and the collision probability between two sessions is therefore upper-bounded by $1/p$. Informally, in the remaining game executions, session keys are uncorrelated because of the random oracle hypothesis and the inclusion of the session flow in key derivations.

Next, the attacker key confirmations that are correct "by chance", i.e. although the right query was not made to the random oracle, are refused. There are not too many of them if the output size of H, h, is large enough.

Active attacks before Corrupt queries are then artificially blocked. This is performed by refusing key confirmations not originating from the simulator.

Because correct key confirmations produced with incorrect oracle inputs are already forbidden, E sees the difference between this new game and the previous one only if it manages to produce a correct oracle input for a key confirmation. To show that this happens with negligible probability, an instance of a custom problem is introduced in the public keys of two users, such that the oracle input corresponding to a key confirmation is the answer to this challenge.

After this crucial step, we are in a game where no active attack can be performed in sessions before Corrupt queries. A CDH challenge is finally introduced in one of these sessions; key confirmations and the final key are simulated by random values. Again because of the random oracle hypothesis, E has to solve the CDH problem to be able to ask a relevant question to the oracle, in order to gain some advantage in guessing b or observing inconsistencies in key confirmations.

We could use the Diffie-Hellman random self-reducibility to introduce a CDH challenge in *all* sessions before a Corrupt query, thereby gaining a factor q_s in the security reduction. However, in a concurrent model, many sessions can be "pending" when the first Corrupt query occurs; these sessions require a special simulation. The simulator would therefore have to guess correctly the set of pending sessions, leading to a loss factor 2^{q_s}. This is why the challenge is only introduced in one session.

For simplicity, we limited the scope of the model (appendices A) to a two-user setting. However, since the identities of both parties are included in the session flows and in all key derivations, the generalization of the proof to a n-user setting is straightforward.

Finally, we prove that E's advantage in distinguishing real keys from random ones within time t in a prime-order group G having p elements is bounded by

$$2q_H \times (\mathsf{Succ}_{\mathsf{P}}(t, G) + q_s \mathsf{Succ}_{\mathsf{CDH}}(t, G)) + \frac{q_s^2}{p} + q_s 2^{-h}.$$

where $\mathsf{Succ}_{\mathsf{P}} = \mathsf{Succ}_{\mathsf{2\text{-}3\text{-}CDH}}$ for MTI/C0 and $\mathsf{Succ}_{\mathsf{P}} = \mathsf{Succ}_{f\text{-}\mathsf{RCDH}}$ for MQV.

5   Intractability Results

5.1 f-RCDH and CDH are Equivalent for a Random Oracle f

In this section, we prove that if the function f of f-RCDH can be modeled by a random oracle, f-RCDH is equivalent to CDH. We already know that f-RCDH reduces to CDH without any special assumption (see section 3.2). For the converse implication, we suppose E is an attacker against f-RCDH that has advantage $\mathsf{Adv}(t, q_f)$, where q_f is the number of E's f-queries. Given a CDH challenge (X, Y), we get it as a f-RCDH challenge and assume that E returns (R, Z) such that

$$Z = \mathsf{CDH}(X, R \times Y^{f(R)}) = \mathsf{CDH}(X, Y)^{f(R)} \times \mathsf{CDH}(X, R).$$

Then we can replay part of that successful run and change the function f at the crucial query R to induce the attacker into producing another correct answer (Z', R) to the challenge, with a different value $f'(R)$. Then $Z'/Z = \mathsf{CDH}(X, Y)^{f'(R)-f(R)}$, which easily leads to $\mathsf{CDH}(X, Y)$.

To compute a lower-bound for the success probability of this technique, we need the following splitting lemma [22]:

Lemma 1 (Splitting Lemma). *Let P a probability on a product space $X \times Y$ and $Q \subset X \times Y$.*

Define $Q' = \left\{ (x, y) \in Q \,\middle|\, \Pr_{y' \in Y}[(x, y') \in A] \geq P[Q]/2 \right\}$

Then $P[Q'|Q] \geq 1/2$

Let p_c be the collision probability of f and p_{max} be the guessing probability of $f \bmod p$, i.e. the maximum probability of any output value of $f \bmod p$, with $\#G = p$. If the output of f is a random uniform h-bit string with $2^h < p$, $p_c = p_{max} = 2^{-h}$.

We suppose without loss of generality that each query is submitted at most once by the attacker. With probability less than $2/p$, X or Y is equal to 1. In the other cases, $\mathsf{CDH}(X, Y)$ is a generator of G. Then, if R is not among the f-queries submitted by the attacker, its probability of success is bounded by p_{max} because of the term $\mathsf{CDH}(X, Y)^{f(R)}$ in the f-RCDH relation. Overall, with probability $\mathsf{Adv}' \geq \mathsf{Adv} - 2/p - p_{max}$, the attacker produces a correct output (R, Z) and makes the query $f(R)$. Now, let Q_i be the event "E produces a correct output (Z, R), the i-th f-query of E being $f(R)$". Let Adv'_i be the probability of Q_i. Then

$$\sum_{i \leq q_f} \mathsf{Adv}'_i = \mathsf{Adv}'.$$

Let us fix i. The whole behavior of the attacker only depends on its random tape and on the oracle answers. Let us split these inputs into the ones occurring before the ith oracle answer ($x \in X$) and the ones after and including that answer ($y \in Y$). Let us now apply the splitting lemma 1 with $Q = Q_i$. It states that, given $u = (x, y) \in_R Q_i$, with probability $1/2$, we have

$$P[Q_{i,x}] \geq \mathsf{Adv}'_i/2 \quad \text{with} \quad Q_{i,x} = \{y' \in Y | (x, y') \in Q_i\}.$$

Therefore, we can perform two executions of E as follows. The first execution is random. With probability greater than Adv', it yields a correct answer (R, Z), and $f(R)$ is queried on some query of index i. Let x (resp. y) the inputs of E before (resp. after) the ith query. We run again the same execution with inputs x before query i, but y' after query i. With probability $1/2$, inputs x of the attacker before query i are such that $P[Q_{i,x}] \geq \mathsf{Adv}'_i/2$. In that case, with probability $\mathsf{Adv}'_i/2$, E produces again a correct output (Z', R') and $f(R')$ is queried on query i. Since inputs before query i are equal in both executions, $R = R'$. Finally, except with probability $1 - p_c$, answers f_1 and f_2 for $f(R)$ are different in both executions. If all these conditions are met, $\mathsf{CDH}(X, Y)$ can be easily extracted. Overall, since the probability to be in case i is $q_i = \mathsf{Adv}'_i/\mathsf{Adv}'$, the attacker breaks CDH with probability

$$\mathsf{Succ}_{\mathsf{CDH}} \geq \mathsf{Adv}'/2 \sum_i \left[q_i \, \mathsf{Adv}'_i/2 \right] - p_c = 1/4 \sum_i \left[\mathsf{Adv}'^2_i \right] - p_c \geq \frac{\mathsf{Adv}'^2}{4q_f} - p_c$$

because of the Cauchy-Schwarz inequality. Finally, if E runs in time t the attacker against CDH runs in time $2t$ and succeeds with probability not less than

$$\mathsf{Succ}_{\mathsf{CDH}}(2t) \geq \frac{[\mathsf{Succ}_{f\text{-RCDH}}(t, q_f) - 2/p - p_{max}]^2}{4q_f} - p_c.$$

This proof of equivalence between f-RCDH and CDH shows that replacing the function f of MQV by a cryptographic hash function can improve the security of

MQV, while not much impairing its performance. This is a case for HMQV [12], where each term $f(R)s_A + R$ in the key material is replaced by $H(R||B)s_A + R$ with H a hash function modeled by a random oracle.

5.2   Generic Group Model

Generic groups were introduced in [24]: a *generic group* is a group $(G, +)$ whose elements are represented randomly. Thus an algorithm E working in a generic group G does not perform group computations itself, but rather makes queries to oracles that answer with representations, in some set I, of the results. Two representations are equal if and only if the corresponding elements are equal. In the sequel, $G = \mathbb{Z}_p$ and $I = [0, p-1]$. Through the group oracle, E can multiply existing elements, and introduce new random elements.

Elements of G represent logarithms, and the representation of some x corresponds to g^x. In a generic group, nothing can be learned from g^x, except log equality: if $g^x = g^y$, $x = y$.

We define a *Generic group problem* that enables to study variants of the computational Diffie-Hellman problem in that model. An adversary E plays against a generic group. Some multivariate polynomial $\varphi(X_1, \ldots, X_k, Y_1, \ldots, Y_\ell)$ is fixed. Some coefficients of φ might depend in an arbitrary way of E's behavior. For values of $x_1, \ldots, x_k$ chosen by the simulator, and knowing $g^{x_1}, \ldots, g^{x_k}$, the goal of E is to compute $Y_1 = g^{y_1}, \ldots, Y_\ell = g^{y_\ell}$ such that $\varphi(x_1, \ldots, x_k, y_1, \ldots, y_\ell) = 0$.

All elements manipulated by E are linear polynomials in $x_1, \ldots, x_k$ and some new random elements $x_{k+1}, \ldots$ introduced through the group oracle. Let us call P_i the polynomial corresponding to y_i. P_i is a random variable. Then we have the following

Theorem 1. *Let $d = \deg(\varphi)$ and P_m be an upper bound for the probability*

$$P_m = P[\varphi(X_1, \ldots, X_k, P_1(X_1, \ldots, X_k), \ldots, P_\ell(X_1, \ldots, X_k)) = 0]$$

Then the probability that E wins after q_G queries satisfies

$$\mathsf{Succ}\,(q_G) \leq P_m + \frac{(3q_G + k + 2)^2}{2p} + \frac{d}{p}$$

For example, the plain CDH problem corresponds to $\varphi(x_1, x_2, y_1) = x_1 x_2 - y_1$; in that case, $P_m = 0$ because for any linear expression y_1 in x_1 and x_2, and possibly other variables, $\varphi \neq 0$.

Proof. We define a game corresponding to the challenge of E.

Generic Group Game 0. A simulator S chooses $x_1, \ldots, x_k$ randomly in G^k, outputs the corresponding representations $r_1, \ldots, r_k$ to E. E has access to an oracle σ that, on input $(a, b, r, r') \in \mathbb{Z}^2 \times I^2$, answers with the representation of $ax + bx'$, where r is the representation of x and r' the representation of x'. The connection between representations and elements of G is managed by the simulator through a list $\mathcal{L}$ of pairs (x, r) associating an element with its representation. A representation r in a σ-query input does not need to correspond to an element of G in $\mathcal{L}$; if it does, the corresponding element is used, otherwise a random element x is drawn by the simulator in G and bound to r, that is, (x, r) is added to $\mathcal{L}$. The same rule applies for the answer to the query: if $ax + bx' = x''$ with $(x'', r'') \in \mathcal{L}$, r'' is answered. Otherwise, a random representation r'', not yet bound to any element of G, is chosen in G, (x'', r'') is added to $\mathcal{L}$, and the answer to the σ query is r''. Overall, each σ-query adds at most 3 pairs to $\mathcal{L}$.

Initially, $\mathcal{L} = \{(0, r_z), (1, r_e), (x_1, r_1), \ldots, (x_k, r_k)\}$; E is given $r_z, r_e, r_1, \ldots, r_k$. E's goal is to output $r'_1, \ldots, r'_\ell$ corresponding to $y_1, \ldots, y_\ell$ in G that, together with the x_i's, cancel φ. The last ℓ queries of E are assumed to be of the form $\sigma(1, 0, r'_i, \_)$. E has won if $\varphi(x_1, \ldots, x_k, y_1, \ldots, y_\ell) = 0$ where $(y_i, r'_i) \in \mathcal{L}$.

Generic Group Game 1. In Game 1, random values in G are replaced by unknowns X_i. Representations of elements correspond to linear combinations of these unknowns with coefficients in $\mathbb{Z}_p$, or polynomials in $\mathbb{Z}_p[X_1, \ldots, X_n, \ldots]$, as follows.

Initially, $\mathcal{L} = \{(0, r_z), (1, r_e), (X_1, r_1), \ldots, (X_k, r_k)\}$; E is given $r_z, r_e, r_1, \ldots, r_k$. When E performs a σ-query using a representation r not yet bound to any element of G, instead of choosing a new random element in G, the simulator introduces a new unknown X_i. In a query (a, b, r, r'), if r represents a polynomial F and r' represents F' (F and F' are either new unknowns or polynomials coming from $\mathcal{L}$), the simulator first computes $F'' = aF + bF'$. As before, if (F'', r'') is in $\mathcal{L}$, r'' is answered, and otherwise a random representation is chosen among the ones not yet appearing in $\mathcal{L}$. All polynomials in $\mathcal{L}$ are affine.

Before stopping the game, E outputs $r'_1, \ldots, r'_\ell$ through σ-queries as in game 0. E wins if $\varphi(X_1, \ldots, X_k, P_1, \ldots, P_\ell) = 0$ where $(P_i, r'_i) \in \mathcal{L}$.

Difference between E's success probabilities in game 0 and game 1. In game 1, representations of different polynomials P_1, P_2 always differ, while in game 0 they differ if and only if $P_1(x_1, \ldots, x_k) \neq P_2(x_1, \ldots, x_k)$.

Let $F_1 = 0, F_2 = 1, F_3 = X_1, \ldots, F_n$ be the polynomials of $\mathcal{L}$ at the end of the game: n is bounded by $3q_G + k + 2$. Note that $\Delta_{i,j} = F_i - F_j \neq 0$ for $i \neq j$. We need the following lemma from [23]:

Lemma 2. *Let p be a prime and F a m-variable polynomial with coefficients in $\mathbb{Z}_p$, of total degree d. Then the probability that a random value of $\mathbb{Z}_p^m$ is a root of R is at most d/p.*

The probability that one of the $\Delta_{i,j}$ cancels at some specific value $\mathbf{x} = (x_1, \ldots, x_k)$ is therefore bounded by $n^2/2p$.

Assuming no $\Delta_{i,j}$ cancels in $\mathbf{x}$, game 2 perfectly simulates game 1. However, the success criterion in game 2 is stricter than in game 1. The probability that $\psi(X_1, \ldots, X_k) = \varphi(X_1, \ldots, X_k, P_1, \ldots, P_\ell) \neq 0$ but $\psi(\mathbf{x}) = 0$ for the polynomials $P_1 = F_{i_1} \ldots, P_\ell = F_{i_\ell}$ chosen by E among $\mathcal{L}$ is bounded by d/p. Indeed, if $\psi \neq 0$, it is of degree $\leq d$ because the P_i are linear, and vanishes in $\mathbf{x}$ with probability $\leq d/p$.

Overall,

$$|\mathsf{Succ}_1 - \mathsf{Succ}_0| \leq \frac{(3q_G + k + 2)^2}{2p} + \frac{d}{p}.$$

Finally, in game 1, E wins if and only if $\varphi(X_1, \ldots, X_k, P_1, \ldots, P_\ell) = 0$. This happens with probability $\mathsf{P_m}$. □

5.3 2-3-CDH and the Generic Group Model

Our 2-3-CDH problem corresponds to the polynomial $\varphi(x_1, x_2, y_1, y_2) = x_1 x_2 y_1 - y_2$. Indeed, the answer (Z, T) to the 2-3-CDH challenge $(X = g^x, Y = g^y)$ is supposed to satisfy $T = Z^{xy}$. This is equivalent to the above equation provided $X = g^{x_1}$, $Y = g^{x_2}$, $Z = g^{y_1}$ and $T = g^{y_2}$. Since $Z \neq 1$, a valid answer of the adversary is such that y_1 is a non-zero affine polynomial and $\varphi \neq 0$, therefore $\mathsf{P_m} = 0$. Therefore, using $k = 2$ and $d = 2$, theorem 1 yields

$$\mathsf{Succ}_{\text{2-3-CDH}}(q_G) \leq \frac{(3q_G + 4)^2}{2p} + \frac{2}{p} = 9 \times \frac{q_G^2}{2p} + 12 \times \frac{q_G}{p} + \frac{10}{p}.$$

5.4 f-RCDH and the Generic Group Model

For our f-RCDH problem, $\varphi(x_1, x_2, y_1, y_2) = x_1(f(r)x_2 + y_1) - y_2$, where r is the representation of y_1. This case is a little bit more complicated than for 2-3-CDH, because φ depends on E's answers through the term $f(r)$.

Let $\psi(X_1, X_2, \ldots) = X_1(f(r)X_2 + P_1(X_1, X_2, \ldots)) - P_2(X_1, X_2, \ldots)$ where the P_i are the polynomial representations of the Y_i. Unknowns X_i for $i > 2$ represent random values in the group introduced by E. We want an upper bound on $\mathsf{P}[\psi = 0]$ at the end of the game.

We know that $\deg(\psi) \geq 2$ as soon as $f(r)X_2 + P_1$ is not constant. Either r was chosen by the adversary and $P_1 = X_i$ with $i > 2$, or P_1 is an affine polynomial chosen by the adversary through some sequence of computations and r is random. In the first case $f(r)X_2 + P_1$ is not constant. In the second case, r is a random uniform value in $I \backslash I'$, where $I' = \{r_1, \ldots, r_n\}$ and the r_i are the other representations already in $\mathcal{L}$ at the time of the query producing r. The best E can do is to set P_1 to $-u X_2$ where u is the most likely output of f for a random input x in $I \backslash I'$.

Let $p_{max}(I') = \max_{i \in I \backslash I'} \mathsf{P}[f(x) = i | f(x) \notin I']$: $f(r)X_2 + P_1$ is constant with probability less than $p_{max}(I')$. Overall if $p_{max}(n)$ is a uniform bound over I' of $p_{max}(I')$ for $\#I' \leq n$, $\mathsf{P_m} \leq n p_{max}(n)$ and theorem 1 yields with $n = 3q_G + 4$

$$\mathsf{Succ}_{f\text{-RCDH}}(q_G) \leq n\, p_{max}(n) + \frac{n^2}{2p} + \frac{2}{p}$$

Discussions about the Maximum Probability p_{max}. In the specification of MQV [27], f is the truncation of the $\ell = \lfloor \log_2(p)/2 \rfloor + 1$ LSBs of its input. Let $\alpha = \lceil p/2^\ell \rceil$. Then every element in $[0, 2^{\ell-1}]$ is the image of at most α elements in

I, therefore $p_{max}(0) \leq \alpha/p$. If n elements are removed in I, $p_{max}(n) \leq \alpha/(p-n)$, and therefore if $n \leq p/2$,

$$p_{max}(n) \leq \frac{p/2^\ell + 1}{p - n} \leq 2\,\frac{p/2^\ell + 1}{p} = 2\left(2^{-\ell} + \frac{1}{p}\right) \leq 2\left(\frac{1}{\sqrt{p}} + \frac{1}{p}\right).$$

Overall, with MQV, the winning probability of E against f-RCDH satisfies

$$\mathsf{Succ}_{f\text{-RCDH}}(q_G) \leq \frac{9\,q_G^2}{2p} + \frac{18\,q_G}{p} + \frac{18}{p} + \frac{6\,q_G}{\sqrt{p}} + \frac{8}{\sqrt{p}}$$

As long as $n = 3\,q_G + 4 \leq p/2$, this last hypothesis being perfectly sensible for cryptographic purposes.

6   Key Exchange Implementation Choices

Our security proof highlights the importance of several implementation choices when working with Diffie-Hellman-like key exchange algorithms:

- **Work in a prime order group** G. In our case, the computational problem related to MTI/C0, 2-3-CDH, has a security that depends on the size of the smallest non-trivial subgroup of G. As for f-RCDH, if G has non-trivial subgroups, trade-offs can be devised to force the common key to belong to some subgroup of G; the proof of hardness of f-RCDH in a composite-order generic group would yield a bound depending on the size of the largest prime order subgroup of G.
- **Use the session flow, including parties identities, to derive keys.** This "freezes" active attacks by de-correlating keys between users and sessions. Note that this is not specific to the signature-less case: an unknown key-share attack can be devised against STS because it does not follow this principle [10]. Including the user identities is of course crucial in a setting with more than two users.
- **Confirm the keys.** Without key confirmations, an adversary against a signature-less protocols can impersonate a user during the key negotiation, and then wait for a long-term key leakage to compute the session key. On the contrary, a key confirmation prevents the other party to output material enciphered with the session key before it is sure that its partner actually knows the key.

References

1. M. Abdalla, O. Chevassut, and D. Pointcheval. One-time Verifier-based Encrypted Key Exchange. In S. Vaudenay, editor, *Public Key Cryptography*, volume 3386 of *LNCS*, pages 47–74. Springer-Verlag, 2005.
2. M. Abdalla, P.-A. Fouque, and D. Pointcheval. Password-Based Authenticated Key Exchange in the Three-Party Setting. In S. Vaudenay, editor, *Public Key Cryptography*, volume 3386 of *LNCS*, pages 65–84. Springer-Verlag, 2005.

3. M. Bellare, R. Canetti, and H. Krawczyk. A modular Approach to the design and Analysis of Authentication and Key Exchange Protocols (extended abstract). In *STOC '98*, pages 419–428. ACM Press, 1998.
4. M. Bellare, A. Desai, E. Jokipii, and P. Rogaway. A Concrete Security Treatment of Symmetric Encryption: Analysis of the DES Modes of operation. In *Proceedings of the 38th Symposium of Foundations of Computer Science*, pages 394 – 403. IEEE Computer Security Press, 1997.
5. M. Bellare, D. Pointcheval, and P. Rogaway. Authenticated Key Exchange Secure Against Dictionary Attacks. In B. Preneel, editor, *Advances in Cryptology – Eurocrypt 2000*, volume 1807 of *LNCS*, pages 470–484. Springer-Verlag, 2000.
6. M. Bellare and P. Rogaway. Random Oracles are Practical: A Paradigm for Designing Efficient Protocols. In *Proceedings of the 1st ACM Conference on Computer and Communications Security*, pages 62 – 73. ACM Press, 1993.
7. M. Bellare and P. Rogaway. Entity Authentication and Key Distribution. In *Advances in Cryptology – Crypto '93*, volume 773 of *LNCS*, pages 232–249. Springer-Verlag, 1994.
8. S. Blake-Wilson, D. Johnson, and A. Menezes. Key Agreement Protocols and their Security Analysis. In *Cryptography and Coding*, volume 1355 of *LNCS*, pages 30–45. Springer Verlag, 1997.
9. S. Blake-Wilson and A. Menezes. Authenticated Diffie-Hellman Key Agreement Protocols. In *Selected Areas in Cryptography*, pages 339–361, 1998.
10. S. Blake-Wilson and A. Menezes. Unknown Key-Share Attacks on the Station-to-Station (STS) Protocol. In *Public Key Cryptography*, pages 154–170, 1999.
11. E. Bresson, O. Chevassut, D. Pointcheval, and J.-J. Quisquater. Provably Authenticated Group Diffie-Hellman Key Exchange. In *ACM Conference on Computer and Communications Security*, pages 255–264. ACM Press, 2001.
12. R. Canetti and H. Krawczyk. Analysis of Key-Exchange Protocols and Their Use for Building Secure Channels. In *Advances in Cryptology – Eurocrypt'01*, volume 2045 of *LNCS*, pages 453–474, London, UK, 2001. Springer-Verlag.
13. W. Diffie and M. E. Hellman. New Directions in Cryptography. *IEEE Transactions on Information Theory*, 1976.
14. W. Diffie, P. van Oorschot, and M. Wiener. Authentication and Authenticated Key Exchanges. *Design, Codes and Cryptography*, 2(2):107–125, 1992.
15. I. R. Jeong, J. Katz, and D. H. Lee. One-Round Protocols for Two-Party Authenticated Key Exchange. In *Applied Cryptography and Network Security 2004 Proceedings*, volume 3089 of *Lecture Notes in Computer Science*, pages 220–232. Springer, 2004.
16. B. S. Kaliski Jr. An Unknown Key-share Attack on the MQV Key Agreement Protocol. *ACM Trans. Inf. Syst. Secur.*, 4(3):275–288, 2001.
17. H. Krawczyk. HMQV: A High-Performance Diffie-Hellman Protocol. In Victor Shoup, editor, *Proceedings of CRYPTO 2005*, volume 3621 of *LNCS*, pages 546–566. Springer-Verlag, August 2005.
18. K. Lauter and A. Mityagin. Security Analysis of KEA Authenticated Key Exchange. Cryptology ePrint archive, Report 2005/265, available at `http://eprint.iacr.org`.
19. T. Matsumoto, Y. Takashima, and H. Imai. On Seeking Smart Public-key Distribution Systems. *Transactions of the IECE of Japan*, E69:99–106, 1986.
20. A. Menezes, M. Qu, and S. Vanstone. Some New Key Agreement Protocols Providing Mutual Implicit Authentication. *Workshop on Selected Areas in Cryptography (SAC '95)*, pages 22–32, 1995.

21. A. Menezes, P. van Oorschot, and S. Vanstone. *Handbook of Applied Cryptography*. CRC Press, 1996.
22. D. Pointcheval and J. Stern. Security Arguments for Digital Signatures and Blind Signatures. *Journal of Cryptology*, 13(3):361–396, 2000.
23. J. T. Schwartz. Fast Probabilistic Algorithms for Verification of Polynomial Identities. *J. ACM*, 27(4):701–717, 1980.
24. V. Shoup. Lower Bounds for Discrete Logarithms and Related Problems. In W. Fumy, editor, *Advances in Cryptology – Eurocrypt 2000*, volume 1233 of *LNCS*, pages 256–266. Springer Verlag, 1997.
25. V. Shoup. OAEP reconsidered (Extended Abstract). In J. Kilian, editor, *Advances in Cryptology – Crypto'01*, volume 2139 of *LNCS*, pages 239 – 259. Springer-Verlag, 2001.
26. V. Shoup. A proposal for an iso standard for public key encryption, 2001. Cryptology ePrint report 2001/112.
27. Standard for Efficient Cryptography Website. `http://www.secg.org/`.

A   Security Model

The security requirements are formalized in a Real-or-Random game between an attacker E and a simulator S simulating two users A and B. H is modeled by a random oracle. However, we *do not use the random oracle programmability*; therefore it is only assumed that H is "black-box". H can be seen as a random oracle that is outside the attacker *but also outside the simulator*. Each time E "presses the button" to get a hash value of some message, S gets the input message together with the hash value chosen by the oracle. The image space of H is $\mathcal{K}$, the key space.

At the beginning of the game between S and E, S draws a random bit b uniformly; b decides whether random values or actual keys will be shown to E. The goal of E is to correctly guess the value of b.

Simulation and Attacker's Queries. E can issue the following queries to S to control sessions and messages exchanged by A and B:

- $j = $ `Initiate` : initiate a new session. The attacker receives a string that is a session ID used in `Test` and `Send` queries.
- `Send`(U, M, j): send message M to user U for session j.

Messages that are supposed to be sent by A or B in the real protocol are actually given by S to the attacker E, along with the index of the session which the messages belong to.

Additionally, E can perform the following queries:

- `Test`(U, j): obtain the session key negotiated after session j from user U (U = A or B);
- `Corrupt`(U): obtain the long-term private key of U = A or B.

Each of the `Send`, `Test`, and `Corrupt` queries models a different attack: `Send` queries allow E to perform Man-in-the-Middle attacks by altering, deleting or inserting messages between A and B, Test queries model session key material leakage, while Corrupt queries model long-term key material leakage.

A Test(U, j) query is answered as follows: if U did not accept the key negotiation of session j (see "Accepted keys" below), an error is returned. Otherwise, U has computed a key k and E gets the following answer:

- if a Corrupt query was issued before the Test query, the key k is returned;
- if no Corrupt query has been issued so far, the answer depends on b: if $b = 1$, k is returned; if $b = 0$, a random value $H'(\mathsf{Flow}(U, i)) \in \mathcal{K}$ is returned, for some private random oracle H' simulated by the simulator.

Notice that the answer to Corrupt queries in the random case $(b = 0)$ does not depend on the user on which the query was performed if A and B are partners for the session, as in the real case.

E wins the game if at some point it outputs its answer b' with $b' = b$. E's *advantage* is then

$$\mathsf{Adv} = |\mathsf{P}_{b=1}[b' = 1] - \mathsf{P}_{b=0}[b' = 1]|.$$

We are looking for an upper bound for Adv, depending on its running time t, its number of H-queries q_H and its number of Initiate queries q_s.

Accepted keys. Suppose A and B negotiate a key. If the agreement succeeds, at some point, A will start using the key, which might then leak (this is modeled by Test queries). A should not use the key before it is convinced that it actually shares the key with B and B only. To capture this notion, we say that A (or B) *accepts* (the key negotiation) when it is convinced of the authenticity of the computed key, and authorize Test query only on accepted keys.

Chosen-Ciphertext Secure Threshold Identity-Based Key Encapsulation Without Random Oracles

David Galindo[1] and Eike Kiltz[2]

[1] Radboud University Nijmegen
The Netherlands
d.galindo@cs.ru.nl
[2] CWI Amsterdam
The Netherlands
kiltz@cwi.nl

Abstract. We describe the first identity-based key encapsulation mechanism with threshold key delegation and decapsulation that is secure in the standard model against chosen-ciphertext (CCA2) attacks. Our scheme is unconditionally consistent and proved secure under the Bilinear Decisional Diffie-Hellman assumption.

1 Introduction

IDENTITY-BASED ENCRYPTION AND KEY ENCAPSULATION. An Identity-Based Encryption (IBE) scheme is a public-key encryption scheme where any string is a valid public key. In particular, email addresses and dates can be public keys. The ability to use identities as public keys avoids the need to distribute public key certificates. IBE encryption is performed in such a way that only the owner of an identity (the receiver) can decrypt ciphertexts encrypted with respect to his identity. In order to perform decryption the receiver gets a "user secret key" associated to his identity. Creating this user secret is called key-delegation and it is usually done by a master knowing a master secret key.

After Shamir proposed the concept of IBE in 1984 [19] it remained an open problem for almost two decades to come up with a satisfying construction for it. In 2001, Boneh and Franklin [8] proposed formal security notions for IBE systems and designed a fully functional secure IBE scheme using bilinear maps. Independently, in 2000, Sakai, Ohgishi, and Kasahara [18] already gave an informal description of an IBE scheme. These schemes and the tools developed in their design have been successfully applied in numerous cryptographic settings, transcending by far the identity based cryptography framework.

Instead of providing the full functionality of an IBE scheme, in many applications it is sufficient to let sender and receiver agree on a common random session key. This can be accomplished with an *identity-based key encapsulation mechanism* (IB-KEM) as formalized in [5]. Here an encapsulation algorithm creates a random session key and encapsulates it into a ciphertext with respect to the receiver's identity. Given the ciphertext and the user secret key associated to his

R. De Prisco and M. Yung (Eds.): SCN 2006, LNCS 4116, pp. 173–185, 2006.

identity, the receiver can successfully decapsulate the ciphertext to recover the encapsulated session key.

This common random session key may now be fed into any symmetric primitive, for instance into a symmetric encryption scheme.

THRESHOLD IDENTITY-BASED KEY ENCAPSULATION. Threshold techniques are applied to cryptographic protocols whenever one wants to decentralize crucial cryptographic operations that need some additional secret input. The idea is to share this secret input among a number of independent players and only if a sufficiently large fraction of players (determined by a threshold bound) interact (in an honest way), the cryptographic operation can be successfully accomplished. No useful information should be leaked otherwise.

In Identity-Based Key Encapsulation there are many operations to which one can possibly apply threshold techniques. Here we consider making key decapsulation and key delegation threshold. We will call such schemes threshold identity-based key encapsulation mechanisms, or threshold IB-KEM for short.

Threshold key delegation means that the user secret key (with respect to some identity) is shared among many players. Sufficiently many players are needed to reconstruct the full user secret key that enables to decapsulate any ciphertext received by the identity.

Threshold decapsulation means that a ciphertext is shared among many players into ciphertext shares. Again, sufficiently many ciphertext shares are needed to combine the shares into the original encapsulated session key. Note that no (shares of the) user secret key is needed to perform the reconstruction of the encapsulated key from its shares. Threshold decapsulation in the context of IBE was first introduced in [2], whereas threshold key delegation was first informally introduced in [9].

For several reasons, the notion of chosen-ciphertext security has emerged as the "right" notion of security for standard public-key encryption/key encapsulation [3]. In this work we also consider this form of attacks against the security of our threshold scheme. In such a chosen-ciphertext attack, the adversary is given access to an oracle that allows him to obtain partial decapsulation shares of ciphertexts and partial user secret key shares of identities of his choosing. Intuitively, security in this setting means that an adversary obtains (effectively) no information about an encapsulated session key, provided he did not receive sufficiently many partial decapsulation/user secret key shares.

Additionally every threshold IB-KEM has to fulfill some "consistency requirements". That is, roughly, it should be impossibly to "abuse" a set of valid shares (i.e. shares that pass their respective consistency tests) to make the scheme inconsistent, which means (for instance) that the same ciphertext is decapsulated into distinct session keys.

1.1   Our Contributions

Our two main contributions can be summarized as follows.

A RIGOROUS SECURITY MODEL FOR THRESHOLD IB-KEM. Extending [20,2,7] we introduce the concept *identity-based key encapsulation with threshold key-*

delegation and decapsulation (or short "threshold IB-KEM") and provide full security definitions to model chosen-ciphertext attacks and consistency requirements. To the best of our knowledge we are the first to define a rigorous model for threshold IB-KEM – all previously proposed models either did not consider consistency requirements [2] or were only defined for a weaker threshold functionality (i.e., [12,7] only consider threshold key-delegation and not threshold decryption).[1]

A THRESHOLD IB-KEM. We give a new construction of a threshold IB-KEM in the above sense. Our scheme is unconditionally consistent and can be proved chosen-ciphertext secure under the BDDH assumption in the standard model. To the best of our knowledge, it is the first threshold IB-KEM proved secure in the standard model.

1.2   Related Work

Baek and Zheng [2] give an IBE scheme with threshold decryption. The drawback of this scheme is that generic proofs of knowledge (POK) of the equality of two discrete logarithms are used and therefore it inherently relies on *random oracles* to make the POK non-interactive. The random oracle model [4] is an idealized world where all parties magically get black-box access to a truly random function. Unfortunately a proof in the random oracle model can only serve as a heuristic argument and has proved to possibly lead to insecure schemes when the random oracles are implemented in the standard model (see, e.g., [11]).

Our threshold IB-KEM is the first such scheme that is provably secure in the standard model. Our construction is direct and avoids any form of generic POK. We remark that an existing "threshold IBE" in the standard model [12] is based on a much weaker security model that in particular avoids all difficulties encountered in [2] that would made POK necessary. More concretely, the scheme in [12] does not deal with chosen ciphertext attacks. In [7] it was shown how to transform any IBE scheme with threshold key delegation into a threshold (standard) encryption scheme. A special instance of that transformation was already worked out in [10]. We stress that, however, in order to obtain a full threshold IB-KEM, different techniques than used in [7,10] seem to be necessary to make the decapsulation algorithm threshold (and at the same time secure against chosen-ciphertext attacks).

Our threshold IB-KEM construction is based on our recent IB-KEM from [14] (which itself is a chosen-ciphertext variant of Waters' original chosen-plaintext secure IBE scheme [21]). The proof of security of our scheme is inspired by the original proof from Waters [21] and the game-based proof of the IB-KEM from [14]. However, there are important differences reflecting the nature of the threshold scheme that have to be taken care off. A full version of this paper including all proofs is available on eprint [17].

---

[1] Here we don't claim that the scheme from [2] does not fulfill the necessary consistency requirements. We further remark that the security model from [7] is sufficient for their purpose.

2   Definitions

2.1   Notation

If x is a string, then $|x|$ denotes its length, while if S is a set then $|S|$ denotes its size. If $k \in \mathbb{N}$ then 1^k denotes the string of k ones. If S is a set then $s \xleftarrow{\$} S$ denotes the operation of picking an element s of S uniformly at random. We write $\mathcal{A}(x, y, \ldots)$ to indicate that $\mathcal{A}$ is an algorithm with inputs $x, y, \ldots$ and by $z \xleftarrow{\$} \mathcal{A}(x, y, \ldots)$ we denote the operation of running $\mathcal{A}$ with inputs $(x, y, \ldots)$ and letting z be the output. We write $\mathcal{A}^{\mathcal{O}_1, \mathcal{O}_2, \cdots}(x, y, \ldots)$ to indicate that $\mathcal{A}$ is an algorithm with inputs $x, y, \ldots$ and access to oracles $\mathcal{O}_1, \mathcal{O}_2, \ldots$ and by $z \xleftarrow{\$} \mathcal{A}^{\mathcal{O}_1, \mathcal{O}_2, \cdots}(x, y, \ldots)$ we denote the operation of running $\mathcal{A}$ with inputs $(x, y, \ldots)$ and access to oracles $\mathcal{O}_1, \mathcal{O}_2, \ldots$, and letting z be the output.

2.2   Parameter Generation Algorithms for Bilinear Groups

All pairing based schemes will be parameterized by a *pairing parameter generator*. This is a PTA (probabilistic polynomial-time algorithm) $\mathcal{G}$ that on input 1^k returns the description of an multiplicative cyclic group $\mathbb{G}_1$ of prime order p, where $2^k < p < 2^{k+1}$, the description of a multiplicative cyclic group $\mathbb{G}_T$ of the same order, and a non-degenerate bilinear pairing $\hat{e} \colon \mathbb{G}_1 \times \mathbb{G}_1 \to \mathbb{G}_T$. See [9] for a description of the properties of such pairings. We use $\mathbb{G}_1^*$ to denote $\mathbb{G}_1 \setminus \{0\}$, i.e. the set of all group elements except the neutral element. Throughout the paper we use $\mathcal{PG} = (\mathbb{G}_1, \mathbb{G}_T, p, \hat{e})$ as shorthand for the description of bilinear groups.

2.3   The BDDH Assumption

Let $\mathcal{PG}$ be the description of pairing groups. Consider the following problem first considered by Joux [16] and later formalized by Boneh and Franklin [9]: Given $(g, g^a, g^b, g^c, W) \in \mathbb{G}_1^4 \times \mathbb{G}_T$ as input, output yes if $W = \hat{e}(g, g)^{abc}$ and no otherwise. More formally, to a parameter generation algorithm for pairing-groups $\mathcal{G}$ and an adversary $\mathcal{B}$ we associate the following experiment.

> **Experiment $\mathbf{Exp}_{\mathcal{G}, \mathcal{B}}^{\mathrm{bddh}}(k)$**
> $\mathcal{PG} \xleftarrow{\$} \mathcal{G}(1^k)$
> $a, b, c, w \xleftarrow{\$} \mathbb{Z}_p^*$
> $\beta \xleftarrow{\$} \{0, 1\}$
> If $\beta = 1$ then $W \leftarrow \hat{e}(g, g)^{abc}$ else $W \leftarrow \hat{e}(g, g)^w$
> $\beta' \xleftarrow{\$} \mathcal{B}(1^k, \mathcal{PG}, g, g^a, g^b, g^c, W)$
> If $\beta \neq \beta'$ then return 0 else return 1

We define the advantage of $\mathcal{B}$ in the above experiment as

$$\mathbf{Adv}_{\mathcal{G}, \mathcal{B}}^{\mathrm{bddh}}(k) = \left| \Pr\left[\mathbf{Exp}_{\mathcal{G}, \mathcal{B}}^{\mathrm{bddh}}(k) = 1 \right] - \frac{1}{2} \right|.$$

We say that the *Bilinear Decision Diffie-Hellman (BDDH) assumption relative to generator* $\mathcal{G}$ holds if $\mathbf{Adv}_{\mathcal{G},\mathcal{B}}^{\text{bddh}}$ is a negligible function in k for all PTAs $\mathcal{B}$. The BDDH assumption was shown to hold in the generic group model in [6].

3   Definitions for IB-KEM with Threshold Key-Delegation and Decapsulation

We start with some history and motivation. Threshold key-delegation for IBE was introduced in [8,7]. The idea is that the master key msk is distributed among different secret key generation players. Given a master-key share sk_i, each player can compute a partial secret key $sk[id]_i$ for the user with identity id. Finally, a sufficiently large fraction of partial user secret keys is needed to reconstruct the user secret key $sk[id]$.

In contrast, in the model given in [2] the master key is not shared but only the user secret key $sk[id]$. Then partial user secret key shares $sk[id]_i$ are distributed among a number of decryption players. Given the share $sk[id]_i$, the i-th decryption player can compute a partial decryption share C_i of a given an ciphertext C. A sufficiently large fraction of correctly generated ciphertext shares is needed to finally reconstruct the message. No information about the message should be leaked otherwise.

Our model of threshold IB-KEM is aimed at capturing the functionalities of both threshold key-delegation IBE and threshold decryption IBE. That is, in a threshold IB-KEM the players can act at the same time as private key generation players and decapsulation players, so that they can choose which role they want to assume depending on the application. Therefore, an encapsulation C sent to user id can be decapsulated either by reconstructing the user secret key $sk[id]$, or by joining together a large enough fraction of decapsulation shares C_i.

We now give a formal definition of the functionality of a threshold IB-KEM. A threshold IB-KEM $\mathcal{TIBKEM}$ = (Tkg, Tkey.Share, Tkey.Vfy, Tkey.Comb, Tenc, Tdec, Tdec.Share, Tdec.Vfy, Tdec.Comb) with participating players $1, \ldots, m$ consists of nine polynomial-time algorithms. Via $(pk, vk, sk) \xleftarrow{\$} \mathsf{Tkg}(1^k, l, m)$ the randomized key-generation algorithm produces a public key pk, a public verification key vk, and the m master-key shares $sk = (sk_i)_{1 \leq i \leq m}$ for security parameter $k \in \mathbb{N}$ and threshold parameter l; via $(C, K) \xleftarrow{\$} \mathsf{Tenc}(pk, id)$ a sender creates a random session key K and a corresponding ciphertext C with respect to identity id; via $sk[id]_i \xleftarrow{\$} \mathsf{Tkey.Share}(pk, i, id, sk_i)$ the ith share $sk[id]_i$ of the user secret key $sk[id]$ is generated; via $\{\texttt{accept}, \texttt{fail}\} \leftarrow \mathsf{Tkey.Vfy}(vk, i, id, sk[id]_i)$ the validity of the ith user secret key share $sk[id]_i$ is verified; via $\{sk[id], \texttt{fail}\} \leftarrow \mathsf{Tkey.Comb}(pk, vk, id, (sk[id]_i)_{i \in I_r})$ sufficiently many valid user secret key shares $\{(sk[id]_i)_{i \in I_r}$ are combined to reconstruct the user secret key $sk[id]$. The set of players I_r is called the *user secret key reconstruction set*. Via $\{K, \texttt{fail}\} \leftarrow \mathsf{Tdec}(pk, sk[id], C)$ the possessor of the user secret key $sk[id]$ decapsulates the ciphertext C; via $\{(i, C_i), \texttt{fail}\} \leftarrow \mathsf{Tdec.Share}(pk, vk, id, i, sk[id]_i, C)$ the possessor of the ith user secret key share $sk[id]_i$ partially decapsulates the ciphertext C encrypted with respect to id to get back the ith decapsulation share C_i; via $\{\texttt{accept}, \texttt{fail}\} \leftarrow \textsf{Tdec.Vfy}(i, pk, vk, id, C_i, C)$ it can be publicly verified if the ith decapsulation share C_i is valid; via $\{M, \texttt{fail}\} \leftarrow \textsf{Tdec.Comb}(pk, vk, id, (C_i)_{i \in I'_r}, C)$ sufficiently many valid decapsulation shares $\{C_i\}_{i \in I'_r}$ are combined to reconstruct the session key K. The set of players I'_r is called the *session key reconstruction set* (and may be distinct from I_r).

Roughly speaking, for correctness we require that all correctly generated shares pass their respective verification tests. Furthermore, any set of at least l honest players holding shares of a common identity id should be able to correctly operate the threshold IB-KEM, i.e. they should be able to reconstruct the user secret key $sk[id]$, or alternatively to decapsulate any correctly generated encapsulation sent to id. We say that a user secret key or decapsulation share is *correctly generated* if it has been obtained by following the protocol specification. Moreover, a user secret key or decapsulation share is said to be *valid* if it passes the corresponding verification test.

Each threshold IB-KEM naturally has to fulfull security and consistency requirements. In terms of security we have to extend the security models in [2,7] to our setting, meaning that an adversary, in addition to the master-key shares for corrupted players, gets access to oracles for user secret key and decapsulation shares. Regarding consistency, we must recall that often one wants threshold key-delegation (resp. threshold decryption) to be robust, namely if the reconstruction of $sk[id]$ (resp. threshold decapsulation of a valid encapsulation C) fails, it is useful to detect the players that supplied invalid partial user secret keys (resp. invalid partial decapsulation shares). This also means that it should be impossibly to "abuse" shares that passed their respective consistency tests (i.e. shares that are valid) to make the scheme inconsistent, for instance by decapsulating the same encapsulation into distinct session keys. We will call this property consistency of the threshold IB-KEM.

3.1   Security Requirements

Formally, we associate to a threshold IB-KEM $\mathcal{TIBKEM}$ and an adversary $\mathcal{A}$ the experiment $\textbf{Exp}^{tibkem\text{-}cca}_{\mathcal{TIBKEM}, \mathcal{A}}$ as follows:

> **Experiment $\textbf{Exp}^{tibkem\text{-}cca}_{\mathcal{TIBKEM}, \mathcal{A}}(k)$**
>
> $(I_c, st_0) \xleftarrow{\$} \mathcal{A}(1^k, \texttt{init})$ //adversary outputs the set of corrupted users
> $(pk, sk, vk) \xleftarrow{\$} \textsf{Tkg}(1^k, l, m)$
> $(id^*, st) \xleftarrow{\$} \mathcal{A}^{\textsc{KeyShare}(\cdot, \cdot), \textsc{DecShare}(\cdot, \cdot, \cdot)}(\texttt{find}, pk, vk, \{sk_i\}_{i \in I_c}, st_0)$
> $K_0^* \xleftarrow{\$} \textsf{KeySp}\,;\ (C^*, K_1^*) \xleftarrow{\$} \textsf{Tenc}(pk, id)$
> $\delta \xleftarrow{\$} \{0,1\}\,;\ K^* \leftarrow K_\delta^*$
> $\delta' \xleftarrow{\$} \mathcal{A}^{\textsc{KeyShare}(\cdot, \cdot), \textsc{DecShare}(\cdot, \cdot, \cdot)}(\texttt{guess}, K^*, C^*, st)$
> If $\delta \neq \delta'$ then return 0 else return 1

The set $I_c \subset \{1, \ldots, m\}$ is called the *set of corrupted players* and its cardinality, $|I_c|$ must be upper bounded by $l - 1$. The oracle $\textsc{KeyShare}(i, id)$ returns $sk_i \xleftarrow{\$} \textsf{Tkey.Share}(pk, i, id, sk_i)$ with the restriction that $\mathcal{A}$ is not allowed to query for $id \neq id^*$ for non-corrupted players $i \notin I_c$. The oracle $\mathrm{DECSHARE}(i, id, C)$ returns $C_i \overset{\$}{\leftarrow} \mathsf{Tdec.Share}(pk, vk, i, id, sk_i, C)$ (where the user secret key $sk[id]_i$ was generated using $sk[id]_i \overset{\$}{\leftarrow} \mathsf{Tkey.Share}(pk, i, id, sk_i)$) with the restriction that $\mathcal{A}$ is not allowed to query for (i, id^*, C^*) for non-corrupted players $i \notin I_c$. We define the advantage of $\mathcal{A}$ in the experiment as

$$\mathbf{Adv}_{\mathcal{TIBKEM},\mathcal{A}}^{tibkem\text{-}cca}(k) \;=\; \left| \Pr\left[\mathbf{Exp}_{\mathcal{TIBKEM},\mathcal{A}}^{tibkem\text{-}cca}(k) = 1 \right] - \frac{1}{2} \right| .$$

Definition 1. *A threshold IB-KEM $\mathcal{TIBKEM}$ is said to be secure against chosen-ciphertext attacks if for any l, m with $0 < l \leq m$, the advantage function $\mathbf{Adv}_{\mathcal{TIBKEM},\mathcal{A}}^{tibkem\text{-}cca}(k)$ is a negligible function in k for all polynomial-time adversaries $\mathcal{A}$.*

3.2 Consistency Requirements

Any threshold IB-KEM $\mathcal{TIBKEM}$ should satisfy two consistency requirements. On the one hand, *user secret key consistency* requires that for any reconstructed user secret key $sk[id]$ (obtained from a set of l valid user secret key shares) the same session key is obtained when decapsulating (via Tdec) a valid ciphertext under the corresponding id. Secondly, *decapsulation consistency* requires that reconstructing the session key via $\mathsf{Tdec.Comb}$ for the same ciphertext C and identity id but for several different sets of l valid decapsulation shares results in the same session key.

Following [20,7] we will formalize both consistency requirements using an adversary "attacking" the consistency of the schemes. Here we refer to reader to [1] for a general discussion on defining adveraries attacking consistency of a cryptographic scheme. As usual, "adversary" refers to a PTA but we stress that the consistency of our particular scheme can be proven with respect to unbounded adversaries.

For secret key consistency, we associate to an adversary $\mathcal{A}$ the experiment

Experiment $\mathbf{Exp}_{\mathcal{TIBKEM},\mathcal{A}}^{tibkem\text{-}key\text{-}consist}(k)$

> $(I_c, st_0) \overset{\$}{\leftarrow} \mathcal{A}(1^k, \texttt{init})$ //adversary outputs the set of corrupted users
> $(pk, sk, vk) \overset{\$}{\leftarrow} \mathsf{Tkg}(1^k, l, m)$
> $(id, D, D', C) \overset{\$}{\leftarrow} \mathcal{A}^{\mathrm{KEYSHARE}(\cdot,\cdot),\mathrm{DECSHARE}(\cdot,\cdot,\cdot)}(\texttt{find}, pk, vk, \{sk_i\}_{i \in I_c}, st_0)$
> $sk[id] \leftarrow \mathsf{Tkey.Comb}(pk, vk, id, D)$; $K \leftarrow \mathsf{Tdec}(pk, sk[id], C)$
> $sk[id]' \leftarrow \mathsf{Tkey.Comb}(pk, vk, id, D')$; $K' \leftarrow \mathsf{Tdec}(pk, sk[id]', C)$
> If $\texttt{fail} \neq sk[id] \neq sk[id]' \neq \texttt{fail}$ and $K \neq K'$ then output 1 else output 0

The set I_c and the oracles $\mathrm{KEYSHARE}(i, id)$ and $\mathrm{DECSHARE}(i, id, C)$ are as defined in the experiment $\mathbf{Exp}_{\mathcal{TIBKEM},\mathcal{A}}^{tibkem\text{-}cca}$. The sets $D = \{D_1, \ldots, D_l\}$ and $D' = \{D'_1, \ldots, D'_l\}$ are two sets of valid key shares with respect to identity id. We define the advantage of $\mathcal{A}$ in the experiment as

$$\mathbf{Adv}_{\mathcal{TIBKEM},\mathcal{A}}^{tibkem\text{-}key\text{-}consist}(k) \;=\; \Pr\left[\mathbf{Exp}_{\mathcal{TIBKEM},\mathcal{A}}^{tibkem\text{-}key\text{-}consist}(k) = 1 \right] .$$

For decapsulation consistency we associate to an adversary $\mathcal{A}$ the following experiment:

Experiment $\mathbf{Exp}_{\mathcal{TIBKEM},\mathcal{A}}^{tibkem\text{-}dec\text{-}consist}(k)$

$(I_c, st_0) \xleftarrow{\$} \mathcal{A}(1^k, \mathtt{init})$ //adversary outputs the set of corrupted users

$(pk, sk, vk) \xleftarrow{\$} \mathsf{Tkg}(1^k, l, m)$

$(id, S, S', C) \xleftarrow{\$} \mathcal{A}^{\mathrm{KEYSHARE}(\cdot,\cdot),\mathrm{DECSHARE}(\cdot,\cdot,\cdot)}(\mathtt{find}, pk, vk, \{sk_i\}_{i \in I_c}, st_0)$

$K \leftarrow \mathsf{Tdec}.\mathsf{Comb}(pk, vk, id, S, C)$

$K' \leftarrow \mathsf{Tdec}.\mathsf{Comb}(pk, vk, id, S', C)$

If $\mathtt{fail} \neq K \neq K' \neq \mathtt{fail}$ then return 1 else return 0

The set I_c and the oracles $\mathrm{KEYSHARE}(i, id)$ and $\mathrm{DECSHARE}(i, id, C)$ are as defined in the experiment $\mathbf{Exp}_{\mathcal{TIBKEM},\mathcal{A}}^{tibkem\text{-}cca}$. The sets $S = \{C_1, \ldots, C_l\}$ and $S' = \{C_1', \ldots, C_l'\}$ are two sets of valid decapsulation shares with respect to (id, C). We define the advantage of $\mathcal{A}$ in the experiment as

$$\mathbf{Adv}_{\mathcal{TIBKEM},\mathcal{A}}^{tibkem\text{-}dec\text{-}consist}(k) = \Pr\left[\mathbf{Exp}_{\mathcal{TIBKEM},\mathcal{A}}^{tibkem\text{-}dec\text{-}consist}(k) = 1\right].$$

The experiment $\mathbf{Exp}_{\mathcal{TIBKEM},\mathcal{A}}^{tibkem\text{-}key\text{-}consist}$ has already been considered in [7], while the experiment $\mathbf{Exp}_{\mathcal{TIBKEM},\mathcal{A}}^{tibkem\text{-}dec\text{-}consist}$ is considered here for the first time. In particular, previous papers [2,12] did not consider decapsulation consistency.

Definition 2. *A threshold IB-KEM $\mathcal{TIBKEM}$ is said to be consistent if for any l, m with $0 < l \leq m$, and for any PTA adversaries $\mathcal{A}_1$ and $\mathcal{A}_2$ the two functions $\mathbf{Adv}_{\mathcal{TIBKEM},\mathcal{A}_1}^{tibkem\text{-}key\text{-}consist}(k)$ and $\mathbf{Adv}_{\mathcal{TIBKEM},\mathcal{A}_2}^{tibkem\text{-}dec\text{-}consist}(k)$ are negligible.*

3.3 Discussion and Difficulties

It is already known how to make the key derivation threshold [7]. The crucial trick is to use bilinear pairings to explicitly check if a shared secret key $sk[id]_i$ was correctly generated. If not it can be rejected *before* the secret is reconstructed.

The difficulty for a full fledged threshold IB-KEM lies in the decapsulation shares. A similar method as above for generating decapsulation shares does not work since the session key K in an element from the target group $\mathbb{G}_T$ and we are not given a bilinear pairing from the group $\mathbb{G}_T$ (which does not exist since DDH in $\mathbb{G}_T$ and hence BDDH would be easy otherwise). In existing solutions [2] (based on the Boneh-Franklin IBE [9]) generic proofs of knowledge (POK) are used instead to prove ciphertext consistency and random oracles are essential to make the proofs non-interactive.

We propose a different technique that completely avoids generic POK. The key idea is to make the decapsulation shares elements from $\mathbb{G}_1$. That makes possible to use pairings to check for consistency of the decapsulation shares. Our technique is reminiscent to the one proposed in [13] based on the 2-level hierarchical IBE from Gentry and Silverberg [15]. However, chosen-ciphertext security was not considered in [13]. In contrast to [13] our scheme does not add any further information to the ciphertext, i.e. we basically get "threshold for free" from chosen-ciphertext properties of the original IB-KEM [14]. A crucial property of the scheme from [14] we exploit in our threshold IB-KEM is the "public verifiability" of ciphertexts which makes it possible to check if a given ciphertext is valid without knowing the master/user secret key.

4   A New Threshold IB-KEM

In this section we present our new chosen-ciphertext secure threshold IB-KEM. We will use the recent chosen-ciphertext secure IB-KEM from [14] as a basic building block for the threshold IB-KEM. Indeed encapsulation and decapsulation are exactly the same as in [14]. Hereby we benefit of the public-verifiability property of the ciphertexts of this IB-KEM to check for consistency of a ciphertext. In the context of a threshold IB-KEM that means that we can identify a given encapsulation as malicious without having to decapsulate it. This particular feature is a key point to protect the scheme against chosen-ciphertext attacks.

From now on let $\mathcal{PG} = (\mathbb{G}_1, \mathbb{G}_T, p, \hat{e}, g)$ be public system parameters obtained by running the group parameter algorithm $\mathcal{G}(1^k)$.

4.1   Waters' Hash

We review the hash function $\mathsf{H} : \{0,1\}^n \rightarrow \mathbb{G}_1$ used in Waters' identity based encryption schemes [21]. On input of an integer n, the randomized hash key generator $\mathsf{HGen}(\mathbb{G}_1)$ chooses $n+1$ random groups elements $h_0, \ldots, h_n \in \mathbb{G}_1$ and returns $h = (h_0, h_1, \ldots, h_n)$ as the public description of the hash function. The hash function $\mathsf{H} : \{0,1\}^n \rightarrow \mathbb{G}_1^*$ is evaluated on a string $id = (id_1, \ldots, id_n) \in \{0,1\}^n$ as the product

$$\mathsf{H}(id) = h_0 \prod_{i=1}^{n} h_i^{id_i}.$$

4.2   The Scheme

For the user secret key reconstruction set $I_r \subseteq \{1, \ldots, m\}$ we define the *Lagrange Coefficients* λ_i $(i \in I_r)$ as $\lambda_i = \prod_{j \in I_r \setminus \{i\}} \frac{j}{j-i} \in \mathbb{Z}_p^*$. For any polynomial $F \in \mathbb{Z}_p[X]$ of degree at most $|I_r| - 1$ this entails $\sum_{i \in I_r} F(i)\lambda_i = F(0)$. The coefficients $\lambda_i' = \prod_{j \in I_r' \setminus \{i\}} \frac{j}{j-i} \in \mathbb{Z}_p^*$ are defined analogously for the session key reconstruction set $I_r' \subseteq \{1, \ldots, m\}$. We call a (user secret key/ciphertext) share valid if it passes the respective consistency check. Let $\mathsf{TCR} : \mathbb{G}_1 \rightarrow \mathbb{Z}_p$ be a *target collision restant hash function* (i.e. given $\mathsf{TCR}(x)$ for a random and external x it should be infeasible to find $y \in \mathbb{G}_1 \setminus \{x\}$ such that $\mathsf{TCR}(x) = \mathsf{TCR}(y)$; we refer to [17] for a formal definition). Our threshold IB-KEM for identity space $\{0,1\}^n$ and threshold parameters m and l (l-out-of-m threshold scheme – at least l honest players are needed to perform threshold operations) is described by the following algorithms:

Key generation $\mathsf{Tkg}(1^k, l, m)$

Choose $u_1, u_2 \xleftarrow{\$} \mathbb{G}_1^*$ and $b \xleftarrow{\$} \mathbb{Z}_p$, and compute $\alpha = u_1^b$ and $z \leftarrow \hat{e}(g, \alpha)$. Choose a random hash function $\mathsf{H} \xleftarrow{\$} \mathsf{HGen}(\mathbb{G}_1)$ and a parameters the the target collision resistant hash function TCR. The public key is defined as $pk = (u_1, u_2, z, \mathsf{TCR}, \mathsf{H})$.

Generate shared keys using l-out-of-m secret sharing by choosing $F_i \xleftarrow{\$} \mathbb{Z}_p$ for $i = 1, \ldots, l-1$ and defining $F(X) = b + \sum_{i=1}^{l-1} F_i \cdot X^i$. The verification key is defined as $vk = (vk_1, \ldots, vk_m)$, where $vk_i = g^{F(i)}$. The shared secret key is defined as $sk = (sk_1, \ldots, sk_m)$, where $sk_i = u_1^{F(i)}$.

Shared user secret key delegation $\mathsf{Tkey.Share}(pk, i, id, sk_i)$

Choose $s_i \xleftarrow{\$} \mathbb{Z}_p$ and compute $d_{i,1} \leftarrow sk_i \cdot \mathsf{H}(id)^{s_i}$ and $d_{i,2} \leftarrow g^{s_i}$. The shared user secret key for player i is defined as $sk[id]_i = (d_{i,1}, d_{i,2})$.

Shared user secret key verification $\mathsf{Tkey.Vfy}(pk, vk, i, id, sk[id]_i)$

Parse $sk[id]_i = (d_{i,1}, d_{i,2})$ and check if $\hat{e}(d_{i,1}, g) = \hat{e}(vk_i, u_1) \cdot \hat{e}(d_{i,2}, \mathsf{H}(id))$

Shared user secret key combine $\mathsf{Tkey.Comb}(pk, vk, id, (sk[id]_i)_{i \in I_r})$

If $|I_r| < l$ or if one of the shares user secret keys $sk[id]_i$ ($i \in I_r$) is not valid return $\mathtt{fail}$. Otherwise parse $sk[id]_i = (d_{i,1}, d_{i,2})$ and return $sk[id] = (d_1, d_2) = (\prod_{i \in I_r} d_{i,1}^{\lambda_i}, \prod_{i \in I_r} d_{i,2}^{\lambda_i})$.

Encapsulation $\mathsf{Tenc}(pk, id)$

Choose $r \xleftarrow{\$} \mathbb{Z}_p^*$ and compute the encapsulation $C = (c_1, c_2, c_3) \in \mathbb{G}_1^3$ as

$$(c_1 = g^r, \quad c_2 = \mathsf{H}(id)^r, \quad c_3 = (u_1^t u_2)^r),$$

where $t = \mathsf{TCR}(c_1)$. The corresponding session key is $K = z^r \in \mathbb{G}_T$.

Decapsulation $\mathsf{Tdec}(pk, sk[id], C)$

Parse C as (c_1, c_2, c_3) and $sk[id]$ as (d_1, d_2). Compute $t = \mathsf{TCR}(c_1)$. We call a encapsulation C consistent iff $(g, c_1, u_1^t u_2, c_3)$ and $(g, c_1, \mathsf{H}(id), c_2)$ are DH tuples[2]. (Checking for a DH tuple can be done by computing the ration of two pairings, i.e. $(g, c_1, u_1^t u_2, c_3)$ is a DH tuple if $\hat{e}(g, c_1) = \hat{e}(u_1^t u_2, c_3)$.) If C is not consistent then return $\mathtt{fail}$. Otherwise reconstruct the session key as

$$K = \hat{e}(c_1, d_1) / \hat{e}(c_2, d_2) .$$

Shared decapsulation $\mathsf{Tdec.Share}(pk, vk, i, id, sk[id]_i, C)$

Parse C as (c_1, c_2, c_3) and compute $t = \mathsf{TCR}(c_1)$. If C is not consistent the return $\mathtt{fail}$. Otherwise choose $r_i \xleftarrow{\$} \mathbb{Z}_p$ and return the shared decapsulation for player i, $C_i = (C_{i,1}, C_{i,2}, C_{i,3})$ as

$$(C_{i,1} = g^{r_i}, \quad C_{i,2} = d_{i,1} \cdot (u_1^t u_2)^{r_i}, \quad C_{i,3} = d_{i,2}) .$$

Decapsulation share verification $\mathsf{Tdec.Vfy}(pk, vk, i, id, C_i, C)$

If C is not consistent or if

$$\hat{e}(g, C_{i,2}) \neq \hat{e}(vk_i, u_1) \cdot \hat{e}(C_{i,3}, \mathsf{H}(id)) \cdot \hat{e}(C_{i,1}, u_1^t u_2)$$

then return $\mathtt{fail}$.

---

[2] A tuple $(g, g^a, g^b, g^c) \in \mathbb{G}_1^4$ is said to be a *Diffie-Hellman tuple* (DH tuple) if $ab = c \bmod p$.

Combine decapsulation shares $\mathsf{Tdec.Comb}(pk, vk, id, (C_i)_{i \in I'_r}, C)$
Parse C as (c_1, c_2, c_3) and compute $t = \mathsf{TCR}(c_1)$. If $|I'_r| < l$ or if one of the shares C_i is not valid then return $\mathtt{fail}$. Otherwise compute the values $B_1 = \prod_{i \in I'_r} C_{i,1}^{\lambda'_i}$, $B_2 = \prod_{i \in I'_r} C_{i,2}^{\lambda'_i}$, and $B_3 = \prod_{i \in I'_r} C_{i,3}^{\lambda'_i}$. Reconstruct the session key as

$$K = \frac{\hat{e}(c_1, B_2)}{\hat{e}(c_2, B_3) \cdot \hat{e}(u_1^t u_2, B_1)}.$$

CORRECTNESS AND SECURITY. It is easy to verify that all verification checks are passed for correctly generated keys/encapsulations.

We now show correctness of the reconstructed private key. Let I_r a set of cardinality at least l. Assume the shares $sk[id]_i$ are all correct, that is $d_{i,1} = sk_i \cdot \mathsf{H}(id)^{s_i}$ and $d_{i,2} = g^{s_i}$. Let us define $s = \sum_{i \in I_r} s_i \lambda_i$. Then $d'_2 = \prod_{i \in I_r} d_{i,2}^{\lambda_i} = g^s$ and

$$d'_1 = \prod_{i \in I_r} d_{i,1}^{\lambda_i} = \prod_{i \in I_r} sk[id]_i \cdot \mathsf{H}(id)^{s_i \lambda_i} = \mathsf{H}(id)^s \prod_{i \in I_r} u_1^{F(i)} = u_1^b \mathsf{H}(id)^s,$$

as in key derivation.

We now show correctness of the reconstructed session key. Let I'_r be a set of cardinality at least l. Assume the shares C_i are all correct, i.e. $C_{i,1} = g^{r'_i}$, $C_{i,2} = d_{i,1} \cdot (u_1^t u_2)^{r'_i} = sk_i \cdot \mathsf{H}(id)^{s_i} \cdot (u_1^t u_2)^{r'_i}$, and $C_{i,3} = d_{i,2} = g^{s_i}$. We define $r' = \sum_{i \in I'_r} r'_i \lambda'_i$ and $s = \sum_{i \in I'_r} s_i \lambda'_i$. Then $B_1 = \prod_{i \in I'_r} C_{i,1}^{\lambda'_i} = g^{r'}$ and $B_3 = \prod_{i \in I'_r} C_{i,3}^{\lambda'_i} = g^s$. Furthermore,

$$B_2 = \prod_{i \in I'_r} C_{i,2}^{\lambda'_i} = \prod_{i \in I'_r} g^{F(i) \cdot \lambda'_i} \cdot \mathsf{H}(id)^{s_i \cdot \lambda'_i} \cdot (u_1^t u_2)^{r'_i \cdot \lambda'_i}$$

$$= g^{\sum_{i \in I'_r} F(i) \lambda'_i} \cdot \mathsf{H}(id)^s \cdot (u_1^t u_2)^{r'}$$

$$= \alpha \cdot \mathsf{H}(id)^s \cdot (u_1^t u_2)^{r'}$$

The key is computed as

$$K = \hat{e}(c_1, C'_2) / (\hat{e}(c_2, C'_3) \cdot \hat{e}(c_3, C'_1))$$

$$= \hat{e}(g^r, \alpha \cdot \mathsf{H}(id)^s \cdot (u_1^t u_2)^{r'}) / (\hat{e}(\mathsf{H}(id)^r, g^s) \cdot \hat{e}(u_1^{rt} u_2^r, g^{r'}))$$

$$= \hat{e}(g^r, \alpha) \cdot \hat{e}(g^r, \mathsf{H}(id)^s) / \hat{e}(\mathsf{H}(id)^r, g^s) \cdot \hat{e}(g^r, (u_1^t u_2)^{r'}) / \hat{e}(u_1^{rt} u_2^r, g^{r'}))$$

$$= z^r,$$

as in encapsulation.

Theorem 3. *Assume* TCR *is a target collision resistant hash function. Under the Bilinear Decisional Diffie-Hellman (BDDH) assumption relative to generator* $\mathcal{G}$, *our threshold IB-KEM is secure against chosen-ciphertext attacks. In particular, we have*

$$\mathbf{Adv}^{tibkem\text{-}cca}_{\mathcal{TIBKEM}, \mathcal{A}} = \mathcal{O}\big(nq \cdot (\epsilon + q/p) + \mathbf{Adv}^{hash\text{-}tcr}_{\mathsf{TCR}, \mathcal{H}}(k) \big) ,$$

for any adversary $\mathcal{A}$ running for time $\mathbf{Time}_{\mathcal{A}}(k) = \mathbf{Time}_{\mathcal{B}} - \Omega\big(\epsilon^{-2}\cdot\ln(\epsilon^{-1})+q\big)$, *where* $\epsilon = \mathbf{Adv}^{\mathrm{bddh}}_{\mathcal{G},\mathcal{B}}(k)$ *and q is an upper bound on the number of key derivation/decapsulation share queries made by adversary $\mathcal{A}$.*

Theorem 4. *Our threshold IB-KEM is consistent. In particular, we have*

$$\mathbf{Adv}^{tibkem\text{-}key\text{-}consist}_{\mathcal{TBKEM},\mathcal{A}_1}(k) = \mathbf{Adv}^{tibkem\text{-}dec\text{-}consist}_{\mathcal{TBKEM},\mathcal{A}_2}(k) = 0 \ .$$

The above statement even holds for unbounded adversaries $\mathcal{A}_1$ and $\mathcal{A}_2$, i.e. we have perfect consistency.

The proofs of the two theorems are given in the full version of this paper [17]. The proof of Theorem 4 is relatively straightforward given the correctness of Shamir secret sharing.

Acknowledgements

We thank the anonymous SCN referees for their useful comments. This research was partially supported by the research program Sentinels (http://www.sentinels.nl).) Sentinels is being financed by Technology Foundation STW, the Netherlands Organization for Scientific Research (NWO), and the Dutch Ministry of Economic Affairs.

References

1. M. Abdalla, M. Bellare, D. Catalano, E. Kiltz, T. Kohno, T. Lange, J. Malone-Lee, G. Neven, P. Paillier, and H. Shi. Searchable encryption revisited: Consistency properties, relation to anonymous IBE, and extensions. In V. Shoup, editor, *CRYPTO 2005*, LNCS. Springer-Verlag, Aug. 2005.
2. J. Baek and Y. Zheng. Identity-based threshold decryption. In F. Bao, R. Deng, and J. Zhou, editors, *PKC 2004*, volume 2947 of *LNCS*, pages 262–276. Springer-Verlag, Mar. 2004.
3. M. Bellare, A. Desai, D. Pointcheval, and P. Rogaway. Relations among notions of security for public-key encryption schemes. In H. Krawczyk, editor, *CRYPTO'98*, volume 1462 of *LNCS*, pages 26–45. Springer-Verlag, Aug. 1998.
4. M. Bellare and P. Rogaway. Random oracles are practical: A paradigm for designing efficient protocols. In *ACM CCS 93*, pages 62–73. ACM Press, Nov. 1993.
5. K. Bentahar, P. Farshim, J. Malone-Lee, and N. Smart. Generic constructions of identity-based and certificateless KEMs. Cryptology ePrint Archive, Report 2005/058, 2005. http://eprint.iacr.org/.
6. D. Boneh, X. Boyen, and E.-J. Goh. Hierarchical identity based encryption with constant size ciphertext. In R. Cramer, editor, *EUROCRYPT 2005*, volume 3494 of *LNCS*, pages 440–456. Springer-Verlag, May 2005.
7. D. Boneh, X. Boyen, and S. Halevi. Chosen ciphertext secure public key threshold encryption without random oracles. In *Topics in Cryptology—CT-RSA 2006*, volume 3860 of *Lecture Notes in Computer Science*, pages 226–243. Berlin: Springer-Verlag, 2006.

8. D. Boneh and M. K. Franklin. Identity-based encryption from the Weil pairing. In J. Kilian, editor, *CRYPTO 2001*, volume 2139 of *LNCS*, pages 213–229. Springer-Verlag, Aug. 2001.

9. D. Boneh and M. K. Franklin. Identity based encryption from the Weil pairing. *SIAM Journal on Computing*, 32(3):586–615, 2003.

10. X. Boyen, Q. Mei, and B. Waters. Simple and efficient CCA2 security from IBE techniques. In *ACM Conference on Computer and Communications Security—CCS 2005*, pages 320–329. New-York: ACM Press, 2005. Available at http://eprint.iacr.org/2005/288/, August 2005.

11. R. Canetti, O. Goldreich, and S. Halevi. The random oracle methodology, revisited. In *30th ACM STOC*, pages 209–218. ACM Press, May 1998.

12. Z. Chai, Z. Cao, and R. Lu. ID-based threshold decryption without random oracles and its application in key escrow. Proceedings of ICISC, 2004.

13. Y. Dodis and M. Yung. Exposure-resilience for free: The hierarchical id-based encryption case. In *Proceedings of IEEE Security in Storage Workshop 2002*, pages 45–52, 2002.

14. D. Galindo and E. Kiltz. Direct chosen-ciphertext secure identity-based key encapsulation without random oracles. In *ACISP 2006*, volume 4058 of *LNCS*. Springer-Verlag, 2006.

15. C. Gentry and A. Silverberg. Hierarchical ID-based cryptography. In Y. Zheng, editor, *ASIACRYPT 2002*, volume 2501 of *LNCS*, pages 548–566. Springer-Verlag, Dec. 2002.

16. A. Joux. A one round protocol for tripartite diffie-hellman. In *Algorithmic Number Theory – ANTS IV*, volume 1838 of *LNCS*, pages 385–394. Springer-Verlag, 2000.

17. E. Kiltz and D. Galindo. Direct chosen-ciphertext secure identity-based key encapsulation without random oracles, Jan. 2006. Available at http://eprint.iacr.org/2006/034/.

18. K. O. R. Sakai and M. Kasahara. Cryptosystems based on pairings. In *Proceedings of the Symposium on Cryptography and Information Security — SCIS 2000*, pages 26–28, jan 2000.

19. A. Shamir. Identity-based cryptosystems and signature schemes. In G. R. Blakley and D. Chaum, editors, *CRYPTO'84*, volume 196 of *LNCS*, pages 47–53. Springer-Verlag, Aug. 1985.

20. V. Shoup and R. Gennaro. Securing threshold cryptosystems against chosen ciphertext attack. In K. Nyberg, editor, *EUROCRYPT'98*, volume 1403 of *LNCS*, pages 1–16. Springer-Verlag, May 1998.

21. B. R. Waters. Efficient identity-based encryption without random oracles. In R. Cramer, editor, *EUROCRYPT 2005*, volume 3494 of *LNCS*, pages 114–127. Springer-Verlag, May 2005.

A New Key Exchange Protocol Based on MQV Assuming Public Computations

Sébastien Kunz-Jacques[1,2] and David Pointcheval[1]

[1] École normale supérieure, 45 rue d'Ulm, 75005 Paris, France
David.Pointcheval@ens.fr
[2] DCSSI Crypto Lab, 51 boulevard de La Tour-Maubourg
F-75700 Paris 07 SP, France
kunzjacq@yahoo.fr

Abstract. Designing authenticated key exchange algorithms is a problem well understood in cryptography: there are established security models, and proposals proved secure in these models. However, models currently used assume that a honest entity involved in a key exchange is trusted as a whole. In many practical contexts, the entity is divided in an *authentication device* storing a private key and having low computing power, and a *computing device*, that performs part of the computations required by protocol runs. The computing device might be a PC connected to the Internet, and the authenticating device a smart card. In that case as well in many others, a compromise of the computing device is to be expected. We therefore propose a variant of the MQV and HMQV key exchange protocols secure in that context, unlike the original protocols. The security claim is supported by a proof in a model derived from the Canetti-Krawczyk one, which takes into account more general rogue behaviours of the computing device.

1 Introduction

Key exchange, together with other basic primitives like encryption and signature, constitutes a building block of modern cryptography. Key exchange algorithms enable two parties communicating on an insecure channel to agree on a common secret value. The Diffie-Hellman algorithm [7] was the first key-exchange algorithm not requiring a pre-shared static secret between the parties. It does not however enforce parties authentication, and is therefore vulnerable to man-in-the-middle attacks. After that seminal paper, many authenticated key-exchange (AKE) protocols were proposed, some of them with security proofs.

Current security models for key exchange [4,3,5,6] take into account active attackers, and model the secrecy of session keys together with the mutual authentication property, that is, the assurance for each participant of a protocol run that it talks to whom it *thinks* it is talking to.

Our purpose is to motivate a new attack scenario that arises naturally when implementing an AKE protocol. We thus define a security model including this attack capability and then build a protocol secure given this new constraint. We namely focus on situations where it is convenient to split an entity performing a

R. De Prisco and M. Yung (Eds.): SCN 2006, LNCS 4116, pp. 186–200, 2006.

run of a key exchange protocol into an *authentication device* and an untrusted *computing device*. The authenticating device enforces the confidentiality of the authentication data while some computing operations required by the protocol are carried out by the computing device. This allows to use an authentication device with little computing power, and to make computing devices independent from users.

In such a framework, an AKE protocol is expected to mitigate the consequences of a computing device compromise. Specifically, an attacker that had the opportunity to interact offline with some authentication devices should not be able to authenticate itself in subsequent protocol runs.

Several applications might benefit from an AKE protocol able to cope with a computing device. Mobile phones include smart cards which store the user authentication data; the handsets themselves are the computing devices. PCs equipped with a crypto token have a lot more computing power than the token itself, but may be plagued by spyware or viruses. New designs can also be devised. For example, using an AKE protocol secure in our model, one could build authenticated and escrowable end-to-end encrypted communications in mobile phone networks: the handsets act as the authentication devices and the mobile phone base stations as the computing devices. Session keys are negotiated between two handsets when a communication is initiated. With such a setup, the network operator knows session keys and can therefore decipher calls as required by the law, but *is still unable to fake the users authentication*.

The security model we define takes into account the capacity for an attacker to compromise a computing device, in the following strong sense: the attacker performs itself the operations normally assumed by the computing device, and therefore interacts with the authenticating device as a computing device would do. In that situation, the attacker can compute session keys, but the the model requires that after an arbitrary number of such interactions, the attacker is unable to fake the identity of the authenticating device it interacted with. The model is named the *public computation model*, because the attacker has both passive and active access to the computation devices.

MQV, a well-known signature-less AKE protocol, is a good candidate to build a protocol that is secure in the public computation model, although it was not designed to take into account such threats. We show that MQV itself [15,23], or its variant HMQV [11], are not secure if scalar multiplications are moved into the computing device; however, only slight changes are required to make MQV secure in that setting. We present a 4-pass variant of MQV that is provably secure in our model. The security proof assumes the difficulty of the CDH problem and lies in the random oracle model.

Related Work. The public computation model is analogous to the Canetti-Krawczyk model [5]. In the latter, access to the computing device would have been granted through "Session State Queries". We chose what seemed a simpler path to remove the computing device altogether and allow the attacker to interact freely with authentication devices. Instead of performing Session State queries, the attacker therefore assumes the role the computing device itself. This allows not only access to values in an honest computing device, but also arbitrary man-in-the-middle scenarios where the computing device behaves abnormally to gain information about long-term secrets.

In [11], all variants of HMQV including the 3-pass variant HMQV-C are proved secure in the CK model, *assuming intermediate scalar values are stored in protected memory*, that is, out of reach of Session State queries. This is not very satisfactory as these values are inherently ephemeral. The protocol we propose is designed to overcome this drawback. Our security proof result can therefore be seen as an extension of what is proved in [11].

Contrary to [11], it is assumed that the protocol uses a *prime-order* group. We do not pretend to eliminate the need for subgroup membership tests when a non prime-order group is used. As shown in [14], these membership issues can cause subtle errors in security proofs.

The access of the attacker to the authentication device is very much like the Access queries of [22], which addresses a problem similar to ours for the Needham and Shroeder protocol.

Overall, the model introduced is a very classical Real-or-Random one. It is built around two natural notions for key exchange protocols, real partnership and intended partnership: they designate respectively the relationship between users really exchanging messages and intending to exchange messages. Real partners are "peers" while intended partners are "assumed peers" in the CK model; the "real partnership" relation comes from the "session IDs" of [4]. To slice proofs into more palatable parts, properties relevant to un-authenticated key exchange and authenticated key exchange are covered by two separate security games. As a side effect, it is very simple to specialize the model to un-authenticated protocols.

The introduction of a "computing device" in key exchange is analogous to some works on "server-aided computations" aimed at improving the efficiency of RSA signatures [12,2]. While the resulting protocols were proved insecure [21,18,19], our protocol proposal uses a mix of external help (the computing device) and use-and-throw coupons to avoid computing scalar multiplications. Coupons are a well-known trick to improve the efficiency of discrete log based signature schemes [17], which MQV is related to. We do not provide a general solution for relying on an external device to compute scalar multiplications like in [8], but rather provide an ad-hoc solution tailored to MQV. [8] could be used to eliminate completely the need for coupons in our variant of MQV, however it requires to independent computing units in the computing device, an hypothesis which cannot be easily verified by the authenticating device.

Paper Outline. The paper is structured as follows. First, we review some general concepts related to the security of key exchange protocols in section 2. In section 3, we introduce the public computation model. We then review MQV in section 4.1 and explain why its natural implementation with both an authentication device and a computing device cannot be secure in that model. The variant of MQV in the public computation model, MQV-p, is presented in paragraph 4.2. The algorithmic problems used in the proof and the proof results are summarized in section 5. A sketch of proof outlining the motivations of some choices of proof techniques is then provided section 6. The proof itself is omitted due to lack of space in this extended abstract. It is available in the full version of the paper.

2 Security Goals and Related Concepts

We build the security notions for key exchange around the concepts of intended partner and real partner. The real partner of a user U is the user who receives (resp. sends) the messages sent (resp. received) by U; it is not necessarily known by U. On the other hand, the intended partner of U, which is defined only in the authenticated case, is the user U thinks it is talking to. The security of an unauthenticated key exchange protocol is then expressed as follows: the key resulting from a key exchange must be secret for anybody except U and its real partner. This is the *semantic security* property. An AKE protocol must further satisfy the *mutual authentication* (MA) requirement: a protocol run should complete successfully for some user U only if the *intended partner* of U matches its real partner. In an AKE protocol, the combination of semantic security and mutual authentication yields the property that a key computed after a protocol run completed successfully is shared with the intended partner, and with it only. To define rigorously these security goals, we need to take a closer look at some general concepts related to authenticated key exchange.

2.1 Session Identifiers

Throughout the paper, we need to put labels on protocol runs. Formally, we could use a "global" naming scheme, where each run is uniquely identified throughout all runs performed by all users. This would not have a concrete meaning however, since users only know about the protocol runs they perform themselves. Therefore we identify protocol runs by user - session index pairs. This way, we can assume that each user U engaged in a session (U, s) knows about s.

2.2 Key Material, Session View, Real Partners

For any KE protocol, the moment when a user has enough information to compute the session key can be defined. In the protocols we consider, we represent this by a flag, KeyMaterialReceived, that is set to true when the session key can be computed. The data exchanged required to compute the session key are called the *key material*.

For some session (U, s), we denote by $View(U, s)$ all the messages sent and received by U during session s before KeyMaterialReceived = true, described in a user-independent way. $View(U, s)$ is only defined when U has set KeyMaterialReceived to true in session s. The session key is computed by U as a function of its View and its private key. When $View(U, s) = View(U', s')$, we say that sessions (U, s) and (U', s') *match*, and that U and U' are *real* partners for sessions s and s'.

2.3   Intended Partners, Key Acceptance and Mutual Authentication

In an honest protocol run of an authenticated key exchange algorithm, each user has an intended partner. The intended partner is defined in a protocol-dependent way but it must be possible to express it as a function of the messages exchanged during a session and of the public key of the user. This function might not be easily computable; this happens for example in the case of a protocol including some identity hiding functionality, like -I and -R variants of SIGMA [10]. When the way to derive the intended partner identity is not obvious, it should be clearly stated in a protocol description. Except in these special cases, it is usually straightforward to define the identity of the intended partner in terms of the messages exchanged during a protocol run.

During an AKE protocol run, a user acknowledges at some point that it is talking to its intended partner. In the protocols we describe, this is again materialized by a flag, KeyAccepted. Therefore a user state in an AKE protocol is defined by the Boolean values KeyMaterialReceived and KeyAccepted. The mutual authentication property of an AKE protocol can now be easily defined: a protocol has the MA property if whenever a session (U, s) completes successfully (KeyAccepted = true), user U has a real partner U' for session s, and it is equal to its intended partner. Note that for U' to be U's real partner for some session s', View(U', s') must be defined, which implies that KeyMaterialReceived = true for session (U', s').

3   Security Model

We define in this section our AKE security model. The security goals are formalized into games between an attacker E and a simulator S running instances of an AKE protocol between several users. In these games, E directs the users actions regarding executions of the protocol, and has total control over the messages exchanged between the users.

E's capabilities correspond to *queries* that it can make to S. Queries are listed in section 3.1. In particular, E can get the long-term private keys corresponding to legitimate identities in two ways: it can obtain keys of existing users controlled by S through Corrupt queries, or register its own users through Register queries. The public computation model therefore allows the presence of users controlled by the attacker alongside the ones controlled by S. In particular, attacks requiring to dynamically register a public key, like the one of Kaliski on MQV [9], are within the scope of the model.

S *does not* stop simulating a corrupted user. A user that was targeted by a Corrupt query can therefore be simulated by S *and* impersonated by E. Therefore a corrupted user might still be involved in honest protocol runs, managed by S. We name them *honest* sessions and session views.

The new attack scenario that we take into account translates into two new queries available to E, IniAuth and SendAuth, enabling it to interact freely with the authentication device of any user.

The model is composed of two games: a real-or-random game G_{ror} modeling the secrecy of the negotiated key, as explained in section 3.3; and a game G_{ma} where the goal of the attacker is to break mutual authentication, defined in section 3.4.

Differences between the public computation model and the Canetti-Krawczyk model [5] are as follows:

- Each user is split in two parts: an authentication device and a computing device. This corresponds somewhat to the "protected" and "unprotected" memory in the CK model, but is more flexible because the attacker can impersonate a computing device in an arbitrary way instead of only be granted access to the memory of honest computing devices.
- Security notions for un-authenticated and authenticated key exchange protocols are modelled by two separate security games.
- Key secrecy is modeled by a real-or-random game instead of the find-then-guess game of [5,4]. The two corresponding security properties are equivalent, but there is a loss factor linear in the number of sessions from the find-then-guess game to the real-or-random game [1] in the security bounds obtained.

3.1 Simulation and Attacker's Queries

E can issue different queries to S to control sessions and messages exchanged by users. It is also given complete control over messages between users: messages that are supposed to be sent by users in the real protocol are actually handed over by S to E, along with the corresponding session identifier. E can send messages to users through Send queries: $Send(U, s, M)$ sends message M to user U as part of session s.

New sessions are opened through Initiate queries: $s = Initiate(ID_U, ID_{U'})$ tells user U to initiate a new session with user U'. U is therefore the initiating user of the session. The attacker is answered a session identifier s that is later used in Send queries. ID_U and $ID_{U'}$ must match registered identities of users either simulated by S or created by E through Register queries as described below.

When some user U' controlled by the simulator receives a message that does not belong to an existing session, and that can be interpreted as the first message of a new session, it creates a new session identifier s' that is handed over to E.

E's attack capabilities are modeled by the following queries:

- $Corrupt(U)$: obtain the long-term private key of U.
- $Register(k, ID_V)$: register public key k for identity ID_V. The public key may have already been assigned to some user, however ID_V must not match the identity of an existing user. ID_V is the identity of a new legitimate user V controlled by the attacker. Remark that the model *does not require* the CA to ask for proofs of knowledge of the private keys during identity registration.
- $t = IniAuth(U)$ and $SendAuth(t, M)$: these two queries mimic Initiate and Send queries and model E's access to authentication devices. An "authentication session index" t is used to allow and to keep track of concurrent authentication sessions.

In a signed Diffie-Hellman protocol for instance, $\mathsf{SendAuth}(\mathsf{t}, M)$ would simply return the signature of message M by user U if the authentication session t has been opened for user U.

Corrupt queries model long-term key material leakage; Register queries model users that are created by E, for example when E chooses a public key depending on some observed data. IniAuth and SendAuth queries model the access to the authentication device.

3.2   Common Framework for Security Games

In the two games G_{ma} and G_{ror}, S simulates real protocol sessions according to the queries made by E as in section 3.1. The simulations used in these games differ only by the value handed over to E when a session completes successfully ($\mathsf{KeyAccepted} \leftarrow \mathsf{true}$): in game G_{ma}, nothing is given to E whereas in game G_{ror}, a "real-or-random" value is revealed.

3.3   Semantic Security Game G_{ror}

The real-or-random game G_{ror} models the key secrecy in front of passive attacks. E wins that game if it manages to distinguish real session keys from random values.

In that game, S first draws a global random bit b. This bit decides whether real session keys or random values are to be revealed to E, whose goal is to guess b correctly. If $b = 1$, a simulation $\mathcal{S}^{\mathsf{Real}}$ is used: the real session key is revealed to E after a session completes successfully. If $b = 0$, the simulation $\mathcal{S}^{\mathsf{Random}}$ is performed as follows: first, S sets up a private random oracle H_0. Next, S simulates protocol runs as in $\mathcal{S}^{\mathsf{Real}}$. When a session (U, s) completes successfully with at least one honest matching session $(\mathsf{U}', \mathsf{s}')$, the value revealed to E is equal to $\mathsf{H}_0(\mathsf{View}(\mathsf{U}, \mathsf{s}))$ (remember that a honest session is a session simulated by S, irrespectively of whether the corresponding user was corrupted or not.) If the session completes successfully without a honest matching session, the real key is revealed, as E might be in a position to compute it, for example because it impersonated U's real partner for session s.

Let b' be E's answer. E's *advantage* in game G_{ror} is

$$\mathsf{Adv}_{\mathsf{ror}} = |\mathsf{P}_{b=1}[b' = 1] - \mathsf{P}_{b=0}[b' = 1]| .$$

3.4   Mutual Authentication Game G_{ma}

Game G_{ma} models the mutual authentication property of the protocol which, together with the key secrecy property from game G_{ror}, guarantees the resistance to active attacks of an AKE protocol. In game G_{ma}, E's goal is to get some user U to end successfully some session s ($\mathsf{KeyAccepted}(\mathsf{U}, \mathsf{s}) = \mathsf{true}$) while its real partner differs from its intended partner U' (including while U has no real partner for that session.) The targeted session is called the attacked session.

To succeed, E must additionally not perform

- a SendAuth query targeted at the authenticating device of U' (that is, a SendAuth query on an authentication session t opened with IniAuth(U'))
- a Corrupt query on U or U'

between the beginning of the attacked session and the moment when U set KeyAccepted to true in the attacked session.

Since Corrupt queries on the user involved in the attacked session and its intended partner are banned, the model does not take into account key-compromise impersonation attacks.

3.5 The Public Computation Model in the Un-authenticated Setting

Our model can be adapted very simply to the un-authenticated setting. In that context, only key secrecy can be expected. In an un-authenticated protocol a key is accepted as soon as it can be computed; in our formalism, KeyAccepted is by definition equal to KeyMaterialReceived. Key secrecy is then modelled by game G_{ror} alone.

4 MQV Revisited with Public Computations in Sight: MQV-p

The MQV protocol with key confirmation is a well-known authenticated key-exchange algorithm that is forward-secure and that does not use signatures. It can be compared with some variants of the MTI protocols [13,16]. One of the distinctive features of MQV is however to allow for an efficient split of its implementation between an authentication device and a computing device, as described in the introduction.

Key Confirmation. We consider the MQV variant that includes a key confirmation round: a key is used only if a value proving that the other party has managed to compute the session key, the *confirmation key*, has been received from the other party. With the conventions of paragraph 2.3, KeyAccepted is set to true only when the correct key confirmation has been received.

Key Derivation Function. In our protocol descriptions, KDF is a key derivation function: $KDF(i, S)$ derives a key k_i from some secret s. It can classically be constructed from PRFs and universal hash functions (this is folklore; see for example [20].) In the proofs, KDF is modeled as a random oracle H_1: $KDF(i, s) = H_1(i||s)$.

4.1 The MQV Protocol

Let G be a large subgroup of an elliptic curve group over a finite field. G is assumed to be of prime order p, and P is a generator of G. The private key sk_U of a user U is an element of $\mathbb{Z}_p$ and the corresponding public key pk_U is $sk_U P$. For $Q \in G$, $T(Q)$ is the lower half of the x-coordinate of Q. The MQV protocol is depicted on figure 1.

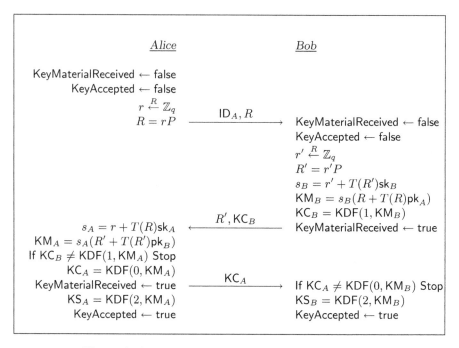

Fig. 1. An honest execution of the plain MQV protocol

Intended Partner Definition. The initiator of a session, Alice, knows who it intends to talk to before starting a protocol run; therefore the intended partner of Alice is fixed before the session starts. The intended partner of the responder Bob is set to the identity received in the first message.

MQV with Public Computations. The natural way to split authentication data storage and computations in MQV is as follows (see figure 2):

- The authentication device for user U computes pairs $(rP, r + T(rP)s_\mathsf{U})$ for random $r \in \mathbb{Z}_p$;
- For each protocol run, the computing device requests such a pair (R, s), sends R to the other party, receives R', and computes the key material $\mathsf{KM} = s(R' + T(R')P_{\mathsf{U}'})$.

In this description, it seems that the authentication device has to perform the scalar multiplication $r \to rP$ which is a costly operation. However, this can be practically avoided by pre-computing and storing in the authentication device pairs (r, rP) or even the authentication pairs $(rP, r + T(rP)s_\mathsf{U})$ themselves.

This approach however has one major security shortcoming: if a corrupted computing device stores a valid authentication pair $(rP, r + T(rP)s_\mathsf{U})$, it can authenticate as user U indefinitely without interacting with the authentication device anymore. This is clearly not desired and is a violation of the mutual authentication property in our security model; see section 3.4.

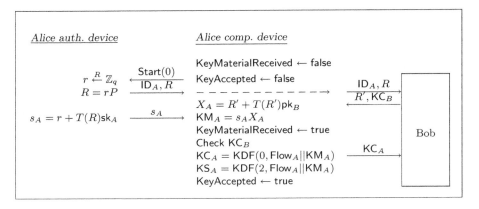

Fig. 2. Plain MQV honest execution with an authentication token, point of view of Alice

HMQV. The same difficulty arises with HMQV which uses $H(R||ID_{U'})$ instead of $T(R)$, where U' is the intended partner of U. In any case, the authentication information is static and can be reused indefinitely.

4.2 MQV-p

The main idea to enhance MQV is to introduce some variability that cannot be controlled by the user in authentication tokens. This is performed by making them depend on the random point of the partner. In MQV-p, the truncation function $T(\cdot)$ is therefore replaced by a hash function H whose input consists in the identities of both users and the two exchanged random points. Unfortunately, applying this simple change to MQV leads to a three-pass protocol whose proof seems difficult even in the random oracle model; indeed, in this three-pass protocol, the adversary has partial control on input values of the oracle whose output we need to program. Because of this, we are unable to simulate sessions correctly when some private keys are replaced by challenges. There are several ways to overcome this issue, either using a random value revealed later in the protocol, or making the responding user commit its random point first. These two techniques lead to a 4-pass protocol. Using a random value, one obtains the scheme described figure 3. In MQV-p, intended partner identities are derived as in the MQV protocol.

5 Algorithmic Hypotheses and Security Results

5.1 CDH Problem

On input $(xP, yP) \in_R G^2$, output xyP in G. $\mathsf{Succ}_{\mathsf{CDH}}(t, G)$ is the maximum success rate of an attacker against CDH running in time t in group G.

Alice   *Bob*

KeyMaterialReceived ← false
KeyAccepted ← false
$z \xleftarrow{R} \{0,1\}^u$
$r \xleftarrow{R} \mathbb{Z}_q$
$R = rP$ $\xrightarrow{\quad \mathsf{ID}_A, R \quad}$ KeyMaterialReceived ← false
                                                       KeyAccepted ← false
                                                       $r' \xleftarrow{R} \mathbb{Z}_q$
$\mathsf{Flow}_A = \{\mathsf{ID}_A, R, \mathsf{ID}_B, R'\}$ $\xleftarrow{\quad R' \quad}$ $R' = r'P$
$s_A = r + \mathsf{H}(0||z||\mathsf{Flow}_A)\mathsf{sk}_A$
$\mathsf{KM}_A = s_A(R' + \mathsf{H}(1||\mathsf{Flow}_A)\mathsf{pk}_B)$
$\mathsf{KC}_A = \mathsf{KDF}(0, \mathsf{Flow}_A||\mathsf{KM}_A)$ $\xrightarrow{\quad z, \mathsf{KC}_A \quad}$ $\mathsf{Flow}_B = \{\mathsf{ID}_A, R, \mathsf{ID}_B, R'\}$
KeyMaterialReceived ← true $s_B = r' + \mathsf{H}(1||\mathsf{Flow}_B)\mathsf{sk}_B$
                                                       $\mathsf{KM}_B = s_B(R + \mathsf{H}(0||z||\mathsf{Flow}_B)\mathsf{pk}_A)$
                                                       If $\mathsf{KC}_A \neq \mathsf{KDF}(0, \mathsf{Flow}_B||\mathsf{KM}_B)$ Stop
                                                       KeyMaterialReceived ← true
                                  $\xleftarrow{\quad \mathsf{KC}_B \quad}$ $\mathsf{KC}_B = \mathsf{KDF}(1, \mathsf{Flow}_B||\mathsf{KM}_B)$
If $\mathsf{KC}_B \neq \mathsf{KDF}(1, \mathsf{Flow}_A||\mathsf{KM}_A)$ Stop $\mathsf{KS}_B = \mathsf{KDF}(2, \mathsf{Flow}_B||\mathsf{KM}_B)$
$\mathsf{KS}_A = \mathsf{KDF}(2, \mathsf{Flow}_A||\mathsf{KM}_A)$ KeyAccepted ← true
KeyAccepted ← true

Fig. 3. An honest execution of 4-pass MQV-p

5.2 HCDH problem

HCDH depends on a random oracle H' having a h-bit output size. On input $(X = xP, Y) \in_R G^2$, an answer to this HCDH instance is a pair

$$(R', x(R' + \mathsf{H}'(R')Y)) \in G^2. \tag{1}$$

$\mathsf{Succ}_{\mathsf{HCDH}}(t, G, q_{\mathsf{H}'})$ is the maximum success rate of an attacker against HCDH running in time t in group G, and making at most $q_{\mathsf{H}'}$ H'- queries.

An adversary against HCDH can be transformed into one against CDH by a classical splitting lemma argument, yielding the following inequality:

$$\frac{[\mathsf{Succ}_{\mathsf{HCDH}}(2t, G, q_{\mathsf{H}'}) - 2/p - 2^{-h}]^2}{4q_{\mathsf{H}'}} - 2^{-h} \leq \mathsf{Succ}_{\mathsf{CDH}}(t, G). \tag{2}$$

Due to lack of space, the proof is omitted from this extended abstract.

5.3 Security Bounds for Game G_{ror} and G_{ma}

In the two next theorems, h is the bit-size of the output of H, k is the one of KDF, u is the bit size of z, n_u is the maximal number of users simulated, p is the (prime) order of G, and $t_{\exp}$ is the scalar multiplication computation time[1].

---

[1] The time to compute a sum of k scalar multiplications, $a_1, P_1, \ldots, a_k, P_k \rightarrow \sum a_i P_i$ is assumed to be equal to $t_{\exp}$ if k is small. This is the case if Shamir's trick is used.

Theorem 1. *If H is modeled as a random oracle, an adversary against the privacy of the session key of MQV-p in a group G, running in time t and making at most q_{KDF} KDF-queries, and q_s Initiate-queries, has advantage at most*

$$Adv_{ror}(t, G, q_{KDF}, q_s) \leq q_{KDF} q_s \left[Succ_{CDH}(t + (2q_s + 1)t_{exp}, G) + \frac{2q_s^2}{p} \right].$$

Theorem 2. *If H is modeled as a random oracle, an adversary against the mutual authentication of MQV-p in a group G, running in time t and making at most q_H H-queries, q_{KDF} KDF queries, and q_s Initiate-queries, has advantage at most*

$$Succ_{ma}(t, G, q_H, q_{KDF}, q_s) - 2^{-k} \leq (2 q_s n_u^2 \beta + q_{KDF}) Succ_{HCDH}(t + 2q_s t_{exp}, G)$$

with $\beta = [(1 - q_{KDF}2^{-k})(1 - q_H/p)(1 - q_H \max\{2^{-u}, 1/p\})]^{-1}$.

6   MQV-p Security: Sketch of Proof

We are looking for an upper bound for E's advantage in game G_{ror} and E's success rate in game G_{ma}. H and KDF are modeled as random oracles.

6.1   Game G_{ror}

We want to bound $|P_{\mathcal{S}^{Real}}[b' = 1] - P_{\mathcal{S}^{Random}}[b' = 1]|$, where b' is E's answer, in the context of a passive attack

The idea is to modify $\mathcal{S}^{Real}$ and $\mathcal{S}^{Random}$ by inserting a CDH challenge in the random points exchanged during some selected sessions.

Suppose some user U successfully completes a session s. Because real keys are revealed both in simulations $\mathcal{S}^{Real}$ and $\mathcal{S}^{Random}$ whenever (U, s) has no honest matching session, E must rely on successful sessions where there is at least one honest matching session to distinguish between the two simulations. Because KDF is modeled by a random oracle,

- either E makes at least one KDF-query containing a correct key material for some pair of honest matching sessions (event QH)
- or it has advantage 0 in distinguishing between simulations $\mathcal{S}^{Real}$ and $\mathcal{S}^{Random}$.

We therefore only need to bound $P(QH)$, in simulation $\mathcal{S}^{Real}$ or $\mathcal{S}^{Random}$. To this end, transform these simulations as follows: S guesses a session index (U, s) for which QH occurs and U is the session initiator, and introduces a CDH challenge in the random points of U for this session, and of one of its honest matching session (U', s'). Because U is the session initiator, it sends its random point first, and any real partner of U receives it before sending its own. Therefore S does not need to guess (U', s') in advance. Key confirmations cannot be properly computed by S; however, random values can be used as placeholders. Once again, because of the random oracle model used for KDF, E does not see the change before it performs the right KDF-query.

To extract a CDH answer, S processes all KDF-queries relevant to the target session, and chooses at random one of the corresponding candidates.

This proof yields a loss factor between $P(QH)$ and the probability of S to break CDH equal to $q_s q_{KDF}$, because S guesses a target session and chooses a CDH answer candidate.

It would be tempting to use the CDH random self-reducibility to introduce the challenge in all simulated sessions and eliminate the factor q_s. The problem with this approach is that it does not allow S to simulate correctly sessions between a user U and a user U' impersonated by E. In such a case, S cannot compute the resulting session key, but E can; in particular, S is not able to decide if a confirmation key output by E is correct or not[2].

6.2 Game G_{ma}

To bound E's success probability in game G_{ma}, we tie it to the probability of the simulator of solving the HCDH problem, which itself reduces to CDH (section 5.)

Introducing the HCDH challenge in the simulation of game G_{ma} requires to guess the first session (U, s) where mutual authentication is defeated, and the intended correspondent U' of U for this session. The HCDH challenge is then introduced in the public keys corresponding to these identities. This translates into the final security bound into a loss factor depending on the number of users simulated and the number of sessions.

The difficulty with this simulation is to deal with sessions involving U or U': since S does not know the private keys of these users, it heavily relies on random oracle programmability to make consistent simulations.

As for game G_{ror}, it seems a better approach would be to try to extract a HCDH answer from *any* session (U, s') with intended correspondent U' instead of focusing on (U, s): this would save the term q_s in the final security reduction. There is however an issue with that idea: in "target" sessions where S tries to extract a HCDH answer, S is unable to emit correct key confirmations or to check key confirmations sent by E. Therefore with several target sessions, E could use some of them to test the behavior of the simulator w.r.t. incorrect key confirmations, thereby distinguishing with arbitrary high probability between unmodified game G_{ma} and the game with the HCDH challenge introduced.

References

1. M. Abdalla, P.-A. Fouque, and D. Pointcheval. Password-Based Authenticated Key Exchange in the Three-Party Setting. In S. Vaudenay, editor, *Public Key Cryptography*, volume 3386 of *LNCS*, pages 65–84. Springer-Verlag, 2005.
2. P. Beguin and J. J. Quisquater. Fast Server-Aided RSA Signatures Secure Against Active Attacks. In *Advances in Cryptology – Crypto'95*, volume 963 of *LNCS*, pages 57–69. Springer-Verlag, 1995.

---

[2] Things would be different in a gap group, where S would have access to a DDH oracle.

3. M. Bellare, R. Canetti, and H. Krawczyk. A modular Approach to the design and Analysis of Authentication and Key Exchange Protocols (extended abstract). In *STOC '98*, pages 419–428. ACM Press, 1998.
4. M. Bellare and P. Rogaway. Entity Authentication and Key Distribution. In *Advances in Cryptology – Crypto '93*, volume 773 of *LNCS*, pages 232–249. Springer-Verlag, 1994.
5. R. Canetti and H. Krawczyk. Analysis of Key-Exchange Protocols and Their Use for Building Secure Channels. In *Advances in Cryptology – Eurocrypt'01*, volume 2045 of *LNCS*, pages 453–474, London, UK, 2001. Springer-Verlag.
6. R. Canetti and H. Krawczyk. A Universally Composable Notions of Key Exchange and Secure Channels. In *Advances in Cryptology – Eurocrypt'02*, volume 2332 of *LNCS*, pages 337–351, London, UK, 2002. Springer-Verlag.
7. W. Diffie and M. E. Hellman. New Directions in Cryptography. *IEEE Transactions on Information Theory*, 1976.
8. S. Hohenberger and A. Lysyanskaya. How to Securely Outsource Cryptographic Computations. In *TCC '05*, volume 3378 of *LNCS*. Springer Verlag, 2005.
9. B. S. Kaliski Jr. An Unknown Key-share Attack on the MQV Key Agreement Protocol. *ACM Trans. Inf. Syst. Secur.*, 4(3):275–288, 2001.
10. H. Krawczyk. SIGMA: The 'SIGn-and-MAc' Approach to Authenticated Diffie-Hellman and Its Use in the IKE-Protocols. In D. Boneh, editor, *Proceedings of CRYPTO 2003*, volume 2729 of *LNCS*, pages 400–425. Springer Verlag, 2003.
11. H. Krawczyk. HMQV: A High-Performance Diffie-Hellman Protocol. In Victor Shoup, editor, *Proceedings of CRYPTO 2005*, volume 3621 of *LNCS*, pages 546–566. Springer-Verlag, August 2005.
12. T. Matsumoto, K. Kato, and H. Imai. Speeding Up Secret Computations with Insecure Auxiliary Devices. In *Advances in Cryptology – Crypto' 88*, volume 403 of *LNCS*, pages 497–506. Springer-Verlag, 1988.
13. T. Matsumoto, Y. Takashima, and H. Imai. On Seeking Smart Public-key Distribution Systems. *Transactions of the IECE of Japan*, E69:99–106, 1986.
14. A. Menezes. Another Look at HMQV. Cryptology ePrint archive, Report 2005/205, available at `http://eprint.iacr.org`.
15. A. Menezes, M. Qu, and S. Vanstone. Some New Key Agreement Protocols Providing Mutual Implicit Authentication. *Workshop on Selected Areas in Cryptography (SAC '95)*, pages 22–32, 1995.
16. A. Menezes, P. van Oorschot, and S. Vanstone. *Handbook of Applied Cryptography*. CRC Press, 1996.
17. D. Naccache, D. M'Raïhi, S. Vaudenay, and D. Raphaeli. Can D.S.A. be Improved? Complexity Trade-Offs with the Digital Signature Standard. In *Advances in Cryptology – Eurocrypt'94*, volume 950 of *LNCS*, pages 77–85. Springer-Verlag, 1994.
18. P. Q. Nguyen and J. Stern. The Bguin-Quisquater Server-Aided RSA Protocol from Crypto '95 is not Secure. In *Advances in Cryptology – Asiacrypt'98*, volume 1514 of *LNCS*, pages 372–379. Springer-Verlag, 1998.
19. P. Q. Nguyen and J. Stern. The Two Faces of Lattices in Cryptography. In J. Silverman, editor, *Proc. of Cryptography and Lattices Conference*, volume 2146 of *LNCS*, pages 146 – 180. Springer-Verlag, 2001.
20. O. Chevassut, P.-A. Fouque, P. Gaudry, and D. Pointcheval. Key Derivation and Randomness Extraction. Cryptology ePrint archive, Report 2005/061, available at `http://eprint.iacr.org`.

21. B. Pfitzmann and M. Waidner. Attacks on Protocols for Server-aided RSA Computation. In *Advances in Cryptology – Eurocrypt'92*, volume 658 of *LNCS*, pages 153–162. Springer-Verlag, 1992.
22. V. Shoup and A. Rubin. Session Key Distribution Using Smart Cards. In *Advances In Cryptology - Eurocrypt'96*, volume 1070 of *LNCS*, pages 321–331. Springer Verlag, 1996.
23. Standard for Efficient Cryptography Website. `http://www.secg.org/`.

Ideal Secret Sharing Schemes Whose Minimal Qualified Subsets Have at Most Three Participants

Jaume Martí-Farré and Carles Padró

Dept. of Applied Maths. IV, Technical University of Catalonia, Barcelona*
{jaumem, cpadro}@ma4.upc.edu

Abstract. One of the main open problems in secret sharing is the characterization of the access structures of ideal secret sharing schemes. As a consequence of the results by Brickell and Davenport, every one of those access structures is related in a certain way to a unique matroid. We study this open problem for access structures with rank three, that is, structures whose minimal qualified subsets have at most three participants. We prove that all access structures with rank three that are related to matroids with rank greater than three are ideal. After the results in this paper, the only open problem in the characterization of the ideal access structures with rank three is to characterize the matroids with rank three that can be represented by an ideal secret sharing scheme.

Keywords: Secret sharing, Ideal secret sharing schemes, Ideal access structures, Secret sharing representable matroids, Information rate.

1 Introduction

1.1 The Characterization of Ideal Access Structures

A *secret sharing scheme* is a method to distribute a *secret value* into *shares* in such a way that only some *qualified subsets* of *participants* are able to recover the secret from their shares. Secret sharing schemes were independently introduced by Shamir [24] and Blakley [3]. Only *unconditionally secure perfect secret sharing schemes* will be considered in this paper. That is, the shares of the participants in a non-qualified subset must not contain any information (in the information-theoretic sense) about the secret value. The family of the qualified subsets is the *access structure* of the scheme, which is supposed to be *monotone increasing*, that is, every subset containing a qualified subset must be qualified. Then, the access structure is determined by its *minimal qualified subsets*.

The complexity of a secret sharing scheme can be measured by the length of the shares. In all secret sharing schemes, the length of every share is greater

---

* This work was partially supported by the Spanish Ministry of Education and Science under project TIC 2003-00866. This work was done while the second author was in a sabbatical stay at CWI, Amsterdam, enjoying a grant from the *Secretaría de Estado de Educación y Universidades* of the Spanish Ministry of Education.

R. De Prisco and M. Yung (Eds.): SCN 2006, LNCS 4116, pp. 201–215, 2006.

than or equal to the length of the secret [11]. A secret sharing scheme is said to be *ideal* if all shares have the same length as the secret.

The characterization of the *ideal access structures*, that is, the access structures of ideal secret sharing schemes, is one of the main open problems in secret sharing. Brickell and Davenport [7] discovered important connections of this problem with Matroid Theory. Specifically, they proved that every ideal secret sharing scheme on a set of participants P defines a unique matroid $\mathcal{M}$ on the set $Q = P \cup \{D\}$, where $D \notin P$ is a special participant, usually called *dealer*. The access structure of the scheme is determined by the matroid $\mathcal{M}$, because $A \subset P$ is a minimal qualified subset if and only if $A \cup \{D\}$ is a circuit of $\mathcal{M}$. In this case, we say that the access structure is *matroid-related*. Actually, if Γ is an ideal access structure, the family of the minimal qualified subsets of Γ is a *matroid port*, a combinatorial object introduced by Lehman [12] in 1964, before the invention of secret sharing.

The matroids that are obtained from ideal secret sharing schemes are generally called *secret sharing matroids*, but we prefer to call them *secret sharing representable matroids* or *ss-representable matroids*. This is due to the fact that the ideal secret sharing scheme can be seen as a representation of its associated matroid. Actually, this is a generalization of the linear representation of matroids, because the *vector space secret sharing schemes* introduced by Brickell [6] correspond exactly to the linear representations and, hence, their associated matroids are precisely the representable ones. The access structures that are related to representable matroids are called *vector space access structures*. Secret sharing representable matroids have been studied under different points of view by Simonis and Ashikhmin [25] and by Matúš [18], and are known under different names: *almost affinely representable matroids* in [25], and *partition representable matroids* in [18].

The results by Brickell and Davenport [7] reduce the open problem of characterizing the access structures of ideal secret sharing schemes to the characterization of matroid-related access structures and secret sharing representable matroids.

A more general open problem is to determine the complexity of the best secret sharing scheme for any given access structure. For instance, we can try to maximize the *information rate* which is the ratio between the length in bits of the secret and the maximum length of the shares. The *optimal information rate* of an access structure Γ, which is denoted by $\rho(\Gamma)$, is defined as the supremum of the information rates of all secret sharing schemes with access structure Γ. Clearly, $0 < \rho(\Gamma) \leq 1$ and $\rho(\Gamma) = 1$ if Γ is ideal.

1.2   Related Work

As a sequel of the results by Brickell and Davenport [7], there is a number of works dealing with the characterization of ss-representable matroids. The Vamos matroid was the first matroid that was proved to be non-ss-representable. This was done by Seymour [23] and a shorter proof was given later by Simonis and Ashikhmin [25]. All representable matroids are ss-representable. The first example of a ss-representable matroid that is not representable, the non-Pappus matroid, was presented in [25]. This matroid can be represented by an ideal *linear* secret sharing scheme. The matroids with this property are said to be *multilinearly representable*, a class that includes the representable matroids. The existence of ss-representable matroids that are not multilinearly representable is an open question.

A number of important results and interesting ideas for future research on the characterization of ss-representable matroids can be found in the works by Simonis and Ashikhmin [25] and Matúš [18]. The first one deals with the geometric structure that lies behind ss-representations of matroids. The second one analyzes the algebraic properties that the matroid induces in all its ss-representations. These properties make it possible to find some restrictions on the ss-representations of a given matroid and, in some cases, to exclude the existence of such representations. By using these tools, Matúš [18] presented an infinite family of non-ss-representable matroids with rank three.

Seymour [22] presented in 1976 a forbidden minor characterization of matroid ports, that improves a previous characterization by Lehman [13]. Of course, this gives a characterization of matroid-related access structures. Nevertheless, the results by Lehman and Seymour have not been noticed until recently by the researchers working on secret sharing. By combining Seymour's characterization with the techniques to find bounds on the optimal information rate from [4,9,20], a new characterization of matroid-related access structures is given in a recent work [17]. As a consequence of the results in [17], a generalization of the result by Brickell and Davenport [7] is obtained. Namely, every access structure with optimal information rate greater than $2/3$ is matroid-related.

Very little is known about the optimal information rate of the matroid-related access structures that are not ideal. Several bounds on the length of the shares in secret sharing schemes for the access structures related to the Vamos and the non-Desargues matroids have been presented recently in [1,17].

Due to the difficulty of finding general results on the characterization of ideal access structures, this problem has been studied in several particular classes of access structures: the ones on sets of four [26] and five [10] participants, those defined by graphs [5,7,8], the bipartite access structures [20], the structures with three or four minimal qualified subsets [15], the ones with intersection number equal to one [16], and the weighted threshold acess structures [2]. Even though this is no stated in all those works, a common procedure is followed in all them. First, the matroid-related access structures in the studied family are characterized and described. Second, the corresponding matroids are proved to be representable and, hence, the matroid-related access structures in every one of those families coincide with the ideal ones. Finally, in most of those works, one proves that the optimal information rate of the non-ideal structures in the corresponding families is at most $2/3$. Therefore, there is no structure Γ in those families with information rate $2/3 < \rho(\Gamma) < 1$. Actually, this last fact is a consequence of a more general result in [17]: the optimal information rate of every non-matroid-related access structure is at most $2/3$.

A natural question that arises at this point is to determine to which extent these results can be generalized to other families. The *rank* of an access structure is the maximum number of participants in a minimal qualified subset. The access structures with rank two are precisely those defined by graphs. The structures with rank three have been previously studied by several authors. Lower bounds on their optimal information rate were given in [21,27]. A particular class of structures with rank three was studied in [14] and it appeared to have the same properties as the aforementioned families. Nevertheless, those properties do not apply to the class of all access structures with rank 3 because, as a consequence of the results in [18,25], there exist in that family ideal access structures that are not vector space, and matroid-related structures that are not ideal.

1.3   Our Results

We present in this paper some new results on the characterization of the ideal access structures with rank three. Namely, we present a characterization of the matroid-related access structures in that family.

We describe in Propositions 14, 15 and 16 the access structures with rank three that are related to matroids with rank greater than three and we prove that they are vector space structures. We present in Proposition 6 a characterization of the structures that are related to matroids with rank three. Some of them are not ideal because there exist matroids with rank three that are not ss-representable [18].

After our results, the only open problem in the characterization of the ideal access structures with rank three is to determine which matroids with rank three are ss-representable. This appears to be a very difficult problem that should be attacked by following the algebraic methods proposed by Matúš [18].

The paper is organized as follows. The basic concepts and results about matroids and secret sharing are recalled in Section 2. A survey of some recent results about the characterization of matroid-related access structures, as well as some facts about different ways to compose matroids and access strcutures are presented in Section 3. Our main results are proved in Section 4.

2   Secret Sharing Schemes and Matroids

2.1   Matroid Theory Definitions

Matroids are combinatorial objects that generalize the properties of linear dependence among a finite set of vectors. There exist many different equivalent definitions of matroid. The one we present here is based on the concept of *rank*. The reader is referred to [19,29] for general references on Matroid Theory. We notate $\mathcal{P}(Q)$ for the power set of the set Q.

A *matroid* $\mathcal{M}$ is a pair (Q, r), where Q is a finite set and r is a mapping $r \colon \mathcal{P}(Q) \to \mathbb{N}$ such that:

1. $0 \le r(X) \le |X|$ for every $X \subset Q$, and
2. if $X \subset Y \subset Q$, then $r(X) \le r(Y)$, and
3. if $X, Y \subset Q$, then $r(X \cup Y) + r(X \cap Y) \le r(X) + r(Y)$.

The set Q and the mapping r are called, respectively, the *set of points* and the *rank function* of the matroid $\mathcal{M}$. The value $r(X)$ is called the *rank* of the subset X while the *rank of the matroid* $\mathcal{M}$ is defined to be $r(\mathcal{M}) = r(Q)$.

A subset $X \subset Q$ is said to be *independent* if $r(X) = |X|$. The *dependent* subsets are those that are not independent. A *circuit* is a minimally dependent subset while a *basis* is a maximally independent subset. All bases have the same number of elements, which coincide with the rank of the matroid.

A matroid $\mathcal{M}$ is said to be *connected* if, for every two different points $p, q \in Q$, there exists a circuit C with $p, q \in C$. We say that $X \subset Q$ is a *flat* of the matroid $\mathcal{M}$ if $r(X \cup \{p\}) > r(X)$ for every $p \notin X$. The flat $\langle X \rangle = \{p \in Q : r(X \cup \{p\}) = r(X)\}$ is called the *flat spanned by* X. If X is a flat, any maximally independent subset $B \subset X$ is called a *basis* of the flat X. The matroid $\mathcal{M} \setminus T$, where $T \subset Q$, is the matroid on the set of points $Q - T$ whose rank function is the restriction of the rank function of $\mathcal{M}$ to $\mathcal{P}(Q - T)$.

Let $\mathbb{K}$ be a finite field and let M be a $r_0 \times n$ matrix with entries in $\mathbb{K}$. If $|Q| = n$ and the points in Q are put in a one-to-one correspondence with the columns of M, then a matroid $\mathcal{M}$ on the set Q is obtained by considering that the rank of a subset $X = \{i_1, \dots, i_\ell\} \subset Q$ is equal to the rank of the corresponding columns of M. In this situation, the matrix M is said to be a $\mathbb{K}$-*representation* of the matroid $\mathcal{M}$. The matroids that can be defined in this way are called *representable*.

2.2   Basics on Secret Sharing Schemes

Let Q be a finite set of *participants* and $D \in Q$ a special participant called *dealer*. Consider a finite set E with a probability distribution on it. For every $i \in Q$, consider a finite set E_i and a surjective mapping $\pi_i \colon E \to E_i$. Those mappings induce random variables on the sets E_i. We notate $H(E_i)$ for the Shannon entropy of those random variables. For a subset $A = \{i_1, \dots, i_r\} \subset Q$, we write $H(A)$ for the joint entropy $H(E_{i_1} \dots E_{i_r})$, and a similar convention is used for conditional entropies: for instance, $H(E_j|A) = H(E_j|E_{i_1} \dots E_{i_r})$.

The mappings π_i define a *secret sharing scheme* Σ on the set of participants $P = Q - \{D\}$ with *access structure* $\Gamma \subset \mathcal{P}(P)$ if $H(E_D) > 0$ and $H(E_D|A) = 0$ if $A \in \Gamma$ while $H(E_D|A) = H(E_D)$ if $A \notin \Gamma$. In that situation, every random choice of an element $\mathbf{x} \in E$, according to the given probability distribution, results in a *distribution of shares* $((s_i)_{i \in P}, s)$, where $s_i = \pi_i(\mathbf{x}) \in E_i$ is the *share* of the participant $i \in P$ and $s = \pi_D(\mathbf{x}) \in E_D$ is the *shared secret value*.

The *rank* of an access structure Γ, denoted by $\operatorname{rank} \Gamma$, is the maximum cardinality of its minimal qualified subsets. From now on, we are going to suppose that every participant in P is at least in a minimal qualified subset, that is, that the access structure is *connected*.

The ratio $\rho(\Sigma) = H(E_D)/(\max_{i \in P} H(E_i))$ is called the *information rate* of the scheme Σ, and the *optimal information rate* $\rho(\Gamma)$ of the access structure

Γ is the supremum of the information rates of all secret sharing schemes with access structure Γ. It is not difficult to check that $H(E_i) \geq H(E_D)$ for every $i \in P$ and, hence, $\rho(\Sigma) \leq 1$. Secret sharing schemes with $\rho(\Sigma) = 1$ are said to be *ideal* and their access structures are called *ideal* as well. Of course, $\rho(\Gamma) = 1$ for every ideal access structure Γ.

If the sets E and E_i are vector spaces over some finite field $\mathbb{K}$, the mappings π_i are linear mappings, and the uniform probability distribution is considered in E, then Σ is said to be a $\mathbb{K}$-*linear secret sharing scheme*. We say that Σ is a $\mathbb{K}$-*vector space secret sharing scheme* if, in addition, $E_i = \mathbb{K}$ for every $i \in Q$. These latter schemes are ideal and their access structures are called $\mathbb{K}$-*vector space access structures*.

2.3   Ideal Secret Sharing Schemes and Matroids

Related to a matroid $\mathcal{M} = (Q, r)$, we consider the access structure on the set $P = Q - \{D\}$ defined by $\Gamma_D(\mathcal{M}) = \{A \subset P : r(A \cup \{D\}) = r(A)\}$. The structures in this form are called *matroid-related*. Observe that $A \subset P$ is a minimal qualified subset of $\Gamma_D(\mathcal{M})$ if and only if $A \cup \{D\}$ is a circuit of $\mathcal{M}$.

Given a secret sharing scheme Σ on a set of participants $P = Q - \{D\}$, we consider the mapping $r \colon \mathcal{P}(Q) \to \mathbb{R}$ defined by $r(A) = H(A)/H(E_D)$. As a consequence of the results in [7], if Σ is ideal, this mapping is the rank function of a matroid $\mathcal{M}(\Sigma) = (Q, r)$. Moreover, the access structure Γ of the ideal scheme Σ is $\Gamma = \Gamma_D(\mathcal{M})$. Therefore, the following result is obtained.

Theorem 1. (Brickell and Davenport, 1991). *If Γ is an ideal access structure, then Γ is matroid-related.*

If Γ is a matroid-related connected access structure, then there exists a unique connected matroid $\mathcal{M}$ with $\Gamma = \Gamma_D(\mathcal{M})$. This is a consequence of the following two facts. First, by [19, Proposition 4.1.2], the matroid $\mathcal{M}$ is connected if and only if the access structure $\Gamma_D(\mathcal{M})$ is connected. Second, a connected matroid is determined by the circuits that contain some given point [19, Theorem 4.3.2].

A matroid $\mathcal{M}$ is said to be *secret sharing representable*, or *ss-representable* for short, if $\mathcal{M} = \mathcal{M}(\Sigma)$ for some ideal secret sharing scheme Σ. Finally, it is interesting to notice that a matroid $\mathcal{M}$ is $\mathbb{K}$-representable if and only if there exists a $\mathbb{K}$-vector space secret sharing scheme Σ with $\mathcal{M} = \mathcal{M}(\Sigma)$. Therefore, all representable matroids are ss-representable. Moreover, vector space access structures are precisely those related to representable matroids.

3   Matroid-Related Access Structures

3.1   Two Characterizations of Matroid-Related Access Structures

The characterization of matroid ports by forbidden minors due to Seymour [22] and the consequences of that result presented in [17] provide two characterizations of matroid-related access structures (Theorems 2 and 3) that are discussed in this section.

The *port of the matroid* $\mathcal{M} = (Q, r)$ *at the point* $D \in Q$ is the family of subsets of $P = Q - \{D\}$ defined by $\Lambda(\mathcal{M}) = \{A \subset P : A \cup \{D\}$ is a circuit of $\mathcal{M}\}$. Observe that neither $A \subset B$ nor $B \subset A$ for every two different subsets $A, B \in \Lambda(\mathcal{M})$, that is, $\Lambda(\mathcal{M})$ is a *clutter* on P. Matroid ports were introduced by Lehman [12] in 1964 to solve a problem in Game Theory: the Shannon switching game. Seymour [22] presented a characterization of matroid ports by excluded minors that is based on a previous characterization by Lehman [13].

Clearly, $\Lambda(\mathcal{M})$ coincides with the family of the minimal qualified subsets of the access structure $\Gamma_D(\mathcal{M})$. Nevertheless, researchers on secret sharing have not been aware of the results by Lehman and Seymour for many years.

The forbidden minor characterization of matroid ports by Seymour [22] is stated in Theorem 2 in our terminology. Several definitions are needed before doing that. Let Γ be an access structure on a set P and let $Z \subset P$. We define the access structures $\Gamma \backslash Z$ and Γ / Z on the set $P - Z$ by $\Gamma \backslash Z = \{A \subset P - Z : A \in \Gamma\}$ and $\Gamma / Z = \{A \subset P - Z : A \cup Z \in \Gamma\}$. Every access structure that can be obtained from Γ by repeatedly applying the operations $\backslash$ and $/$ is called a *minor of the access structure* Γ. The set of participants of the structures Φ, $\widehat{\Phi}$ and $\widehat{\Phi}^*$ is $P = \{p_1, p_2, p_3, p_4\}$. The minimal qualified subsets of Φ are $\{p_1, p_2\}$, $\{p_2, p_3\}$ and $\{p_3, p_4\}$, while the minimal qualified subsets $\widehat{\Phi}$ are $\{p_1, p_2\}$, $\{p_2, p_3\}$, $\{p_2, p_4\}$ and $\{p_3, p_4\}$, whereas the minimal qualified subsets of $\widehat{\Phi}^*$ are $\{p_1, p_3, p_4\}$, $\{p_2, p_3\}$ and $\{p_2, p_4\}$. For every $s \geq 3$, the set of participants of the access structure Ψ_s is $P = \{p_1, \ldots, p_s, p_{s+1}\}$ and its minimal qualified subsets are $\{p_1, \ldots, p_s\}$ and $\{p_i, p_{s+1}\}$ for every $i = 1, \ldots, s$.

Theorem 2. (Seymour, 1976). *An access structure Γ is matroid-related if and only if Γ has no minor isomorphic to Φ, $\widehat{\Phi}$, $\widehat{\Phi}^*$ or Ψ_s with $s \geq 3$.*

In a recent work [17], an interesting generalization of Theorem 1 is obtained by combining Theorem 2 with the techniques from [4,9,20] to find bounds on the optimal information rate. Specifically, we use the *independent sequence method*. Let Γ be an access structure on a set of participants P. Consider $A \subset P$ and an increasing sequence of subsets $B_1 \subset \cdots \subset B_m \subset P$. We say that $(B_1, \ldots, B_m \mid A)$ is an *independent sequence* in Γ with *length* m and *size* s if $|A| = s$ and, for every $i = 1, \ldots, m$, there exists $X_i \subset A$ such that $B_i \cup X_i \in \Gamma$, while $B_m \notin \Gamma$ and, if $i \geq 2$, $B_{i-1} \cup X_i \notin \Gamma$.

Theorem 3. (Martí-Farré and Padró, 2006). *An access structure Γ is matroid-related if and only if there does not exist in Γ any independent sequence with length $m = 3$ and size $s = 2$. As a consequence, every access structure Γ with optimal information rate $\rho(\Gamma) > 2/3$ is matroid-related.*

3.2   Composing Matroids and Matroid-Related Access Structures

The study of the problems we are considering here can be simplified by taking into account that some access structures can be expressed as combinations of smaller ones, that is, by using Proposition 5. The different ways of combining access structures we discuss in the following are related to well-known operations on matroids: the parallel connection and the 2-sum.

Let $\mathcal{M}_1$ and $\mathcal{M}_2$ be connected matroids on the set of points Q_1 and Q_2, respectively. Let $r_i \colon \mathcal{P}(Q_i) \to \mathbb{N}$, where $i = 1, 2$, be their rank functions. Suppose that $Q_1 \cap Q_2 = \{p\}$. The *parallel connection* of the matroids $\mathcal{M}_1$ and $\mathcal{M}_2$ with *basepoint* p is the matroid $\mathcal{M} = \mathcal{M}_1 \oplus_p \mathcal{M}_2$ on the set of points $Q = Q_1 \cup Q_2$ whose rank function $r \colon \mathcal{P}(Q) \to \mathbb{N}$ is defined by $r(A) = r_1(A \cap Q_1) + r_2(A \cap Q_2) - \delta$, where, $\delta = 1$ if $r_i(A \cap Q_i) = r_i((A \cap Q_i) \cup \{p\})$ for every $i = 1, 2$ and $\delta = 0$ otherwise. We define also the *2-sum* of the matroids $\mathcal{M}_1$ and $\mathcal{M}_2$ with *basepoint* p as $\mathcal{M}_1 \widehat{\oplus}_p \mathcal{M}_2 = (\mathcal{M}_1 \oplus_p \mathcal{M}_2) \setminus \{p\}$. Proofs for the properties of those operations that are going to be used in the following can be found in [19, Chapter 7].

Since we are assuming that both $\mathcal{M}_1$ and $\mathcal{M}_2$ are connected, the same holds for the matroids $\mathcal{M}_1 \oplus_p \mathcal{M}_2$ and $\mathcal{M}_1 \widehat{\oplus}_p \mathcal{M}_2$. In addition, the parallel connection and the 2-sum of two $\mathbb{K}$-representable matroids are equally $\mathbb{K}$-representable.

Those operations on matroids are related to two different ways to compose access structures. If Γ is an access structure on a set P and $B \subset P$, we define the access structure $\Gamma(B) = \{A \subset B : A \in \Gamma\}$. We notate $\Gamma \setminus B = \Gamma(P - B)$. The family of the minimal qualified subsets of Γ will be denoted by $\min \Gamma$.

Let Γ_1 and Γ_2 be connected access structures on the sets of participants P_1 and P_2, where $P_1 \cap P_2 = \emptyset$, and let $p \in P_1$. The qualified subsets in the *composed access structure* $\Gamma = \Gamma_1[\Gamma_2; p]$ on the set of participants $P = P_1 \cup P_2$ are the subsets $A \subset P$ with $A \cap P_1 \in \Gamma_1$, or $A \cap P_2 \in \Gamma_2$ and $(A \cap P_1) \cup \{p\} \in \Gamma_1$. We define also $\Gamma_1[\Gamma_2; \widehat{p}] = \Gamma_1[\Gamma_2; p] \setminus \{p\}$.

The *disjoint union* of those access structures, $\Gamma = \Gamma_1 \sqcup \Gamma_2$ is the structure on the set of participants $P_1 \cup P_2$ whose minimal qualified subsets are $\min \Gamma = \min \Gamma_1 \cup \min \Gamma_2$. We say that Γ is *strongly connected* if it is not the disjoint union of two smaller structures. For every connected structure Γ, there exists a unique partition of the set of participants, $P = P_1 \cup \cdots \cup P_r$ such that $\Gamma = \Gamma(P_1) \sqcup \cdots \sqcup \Gamma(P_r)$, being the induced substructures $\Gamma(P_i)$ strongly connected. Those substructures are called the *strongly connected components* of Γ.

The relation between these operations on access structures and the previously defined operations on matroids is given in the next Proposition 4, whose proof is straightforward. As a consequence, in Proposition 5, we see that the properties considered in this paper can be independently analyzed in every component if the access structure is the composition of smaller structures.

Proposition 4. *Let $\mathcal{M}_1$ and $\mathcal{M}_2$ be matroids on the sets Q_1 and Q_2, respectively, where $Q_1 \cap Q_2 = \{p\}$. Consider the access structures $\Gamma_1 = \Gamma_p(\mathcal{M}_1)$ and $\Gamma_2 = \Gamma_p(\mathcal{M}_2)$, and the matroids $\mathcal{M} = \mathcal{M}_1 \oplus_p \mathcal{M}_2$ and $\widehat{\mathcal{M}} = \mathcal{M}_1 \widehat{\oplus}_p \mathcal{M}_2$. The following statements describe the access structures related to those matroids.*

1. *$\Gamma_p(\mathcal{M}) = \Gamma_1 \sqcup \Gamma_2$.*
2. *If $p_1 \in Q_1 - \{p\}$ and $\Gamma_1' = \Gamma_{p_1}(\mathcal{M}_1)$, then $\Gamma_{p_1}(\mathcal{M}) = \Gamma_1'[\Gamma_2; p]$ and $\Gamma_{p_1}(\widehat{\mathcal{M}}) = \Gamma_1'[\Gamma_2; \widehat{p}]$.*

Proposition 5. *Let Γ_1 and Γ_2 be connected access structures on the sets of participants P_1 and P_2, where $P_1 \cap P_2 = \emptyset$. Then $\Gamma_1 \sqcup \Gamma_2$ is matroid-related (or $\mathbb{K}$-vector space) if and only if both Γ_1 and Γ_2 are matroid-related (or $\mathbb{K}$-vector space). The same applies to the structures $\Gamma_1[\Gamma_2; p]$ and $\Gamma_1[\Gamma_2; \widehat{p}]$.*

4 Matroid-Related Access Structures with Rank Three

The aim of this section is to characterize and classify the matroid-related access structures with rank three, that is, whose minimal qualified subsets have at most three participants. First, we provide in Proposition 6 a characterization of the access structures that are related to matroids with rank three. If Γ is a strongly connected access structure such that $\Gamma = \Gamma_D(\mathcal{M})$ for some matroid $\mathcal{M}$ with $r(\mathcal{M}) = 3$, then rank $\Gamma = 3$. Afterwards, we completely describe in Propositions 14, 15 and 16 the structures with rank three that are in the form $\Gamma_D(\mathcal{M})$, where $\mathcal{M}$ is a matroid with $r(\mathcal{M}) \geq 4$. We prove that all them are vector space and, hence, the corresponding matroids are representable.

By using the results is Section 3.2, several assumptions can be made when studying the problems we are considering here. First of all, observe that we can remove the participants $x \in P$ such that $\{x\} \in \Gamma$. In addition, since we are considering only connected access structures, all matroids are supposed to be connected as well. Moreover, we can assume that the access structures are strongly connected. Two participants $a_1, a_2 \in P$ are said to be *equivalent* in Γ if there does not exist any minimal qualified subset $A \in \min \Gamma$ with $a_1, a_2 \in A$ and, if $A \in \min \Gamma$ is such that $a_1 \in A$, then $(A - \{a_1\}) \cup \{a_2\} \in \min \Gamma$. In this situation, $\Gamma \cong \Gamma_1[\Gamma_2; \widehat{a_1}]$, where $\Gamma_1 = \Gamma \setminus \{a_2\}$ amd Γ_2 is the access structure related to the uniform matroid $U_{2,3}$. Then, Γ is matroid-related if and only if Γ_1 is so. Moreover, two equivalent participants can receive the same share in every secret sharing scheme for Γ. If $\Gamma = \Gamma_D(\mathcal{M})$, every pair of equivalent participants in Γ correspond to a circuit of $\mathcal{M}$ with two points. From now on, we are going to suppose that the access structures do not have any pair of equivalent participants and that the circuits in all matroids have at least three points.

The next proposition characterizes the access structures with rank three that are related to a matroid with rank three.

Proposition 6. *Let Γ be an access structure on the set P with rank three and Let $\mathcal{D}_1 = \mathcal{D}_1(\Gamma)$ be the family of the maximally unqualified subsets. Consider the family $\mathcal{D}_2 = \mathcal{D}_2(\Gamma)$ of subsets of $Q = P \cup \{D\}$ such that $G \in \mathcal{D}_2$ if and only if*

- *$D \in G$ and $|G| \geq 3$, and*
- *if $A \subset G \cap P$ and $|A| = 2$, then $A \in \Gamma$, and*
- *if $x \in P$ is such that $\{x, y\} \in \Gamma$ for every $y \in G - \{x, D\}$, then $x \in G$.*

Then, there exists a matroid $\mathcal{M}$ with $r(\mathcal{M}) = 3$ and $\Gamma = \Gamma_D(\mathcal{M})$ if and only if $|G_1 \cap G_2| \leq 1$ for every two different subsets $G_1, G_2 \in \mathcal{D}_1$ and $G_1 \cap G_2 = \{D\}$ for every two different subsets $G_1, G_2 \in \mathcal{D}_2$.

Proof. From the definition of the families $\mathcal{D}_1$ and $\mathcal{D}_2$, it is clear that $|G_1 \cap G_2| \leq 1$ if $G_1 \in \mathcal{D}_1$ and $G_2 \in \mathcal{D}_2$.

If there exists a matroid $\mathcal{M}$ with $r(\mathcal{M}) = 3$ and $\Gamma = \Gamma_D(\mathcal{M})$, then every $G \in \mathcal{D}_1 \cup \mathcal{D}_2$ is a flat with $r(G) = 2$. Since we are assuming that every two points are independent in $\mathcal{M}$, every two of those flats intersect in at most one point.

We prove now the converse. A matroid is determined by its family of circuits [19]. Consider the family of subsets $\mathcal{C} \subset \mathcal{P}(Q)$ such that $C \in \mathcal{C}$ if and only if $|C| = 3$ and $C \subset G$ for some $G \in \mathcal{D}_1 \cup \mathcal{D}_2$ or $|C| = 4$ and $|C \cap G| \leq 2$ for every $G \in \mathcal{D}_1 \cup \mathcal{D}_2$. We are going to prove now that $\mathcal{C}$ is the family of circuits of a matroid $\mathcal{M}$. Clearly, $\emptyset \notin \mathcal{C}$ and $C_1 = C_2$ if $C_1, C_2 \in \mathcal{C}$ and $C_1 \subset C_2$. Then, according to [19, Corollary 1.1.5], we only have to prove that, for every pair of different subsets $C_1, C_2 \in \mathcal{C}$ and for every $x \in C_1 \cap C_2$, there exists $C_3 \in \mathcal{C}$ with $C_3 \subset (C_1 \cup C_2) - \{x\}$. Observe that, for every subset $B \subset Q$ with $|B| \geq 4$, there exists $C \subset B$ with $C \in \mathcal{C}$. Consider two different subsets $C_1, C_2 \in \mathcal{C}$. The existence of C_3 is clear if $|C_1 \cup C_2| \geq 5$. If $|C_1 \cup C_2| \leq 4$, then $|C_1| = |C_2| = 3$ and $|C_1 \cap C_2| = 2$. In this case, there exists $G \in \mathcal{D}_1 \cup \mathcal{D}_2$ such that $C_1, C_2 \subset G$. Therefore, $(C_1 \cup C_2) - \{x\} \in \mathcal{C}$ for every $x \in C_1 \cap C_2$. It is not difficult to check that $r(\mathcal{M}) = 3$ and $\Gamma = \Gamma_D(\mathcal{M})$ if $\mathcal{M}$ is the matroid determined by the family of circuits $\mathcal{C}$. $\qquad\square$

In the following we completely describe the matroids $\mathcal{M}$ with $r(\mathcal{M}) \geq 4$ such that the access structure $\Gamma = \Gamma_D(\mathcal{M})$ has rank 3. We prove that these matroids are representable and, hence, the related access structures are vector space access structures. This is done in Propositions 14, 15 and 16. A number of Lemmas are needed.

Let $\mathcal{M}$ be a matroid on the set Q such that $\Gamma = \Gamma_D(\mathcal{M})$ has rank 3. For every minimal qualified subset A, the flat $\langle A \rangle$, whose rank is equal to $|A|$, contains the point D. Consider the family $\mathcal{F} = \mathcal{F}(\mathcal{M}, D) = \{\langle A \rangle : A \in \min \Gamma, |A| = 3\}$.

Lemma 7. *Let $A_1, A_2 \in \min \Gamma$ be minimal qualified subsets. Consider the flats $F_i = \langle A_i \rangle$, where $i = 1, 2$. Then,*

1. *If $|A_1| = 2$ and $A_1 \cap F_2 \neq \emptyset$, then $F_1 \subset F_2$.*
2. *If $|A_1| = |A_2| = 3$ and $|A_1 \cap F_2| \geq 2$, then $F_1 = F_2$.*
3. *If $|A_1| = 2$ and $|A_2| = 3$, then $|F_1 \cap A_2| \leq 1$.*

Proof. If $A_1 = \{x, y\}$ and $x \in F_2$, then $F_1 = \langle x, D \rangle \subset F_2$. If $|A_1| = |A_2| = 3$ and $x, y \in A_1 \cap F_2$, then $F_1 = F_2 = \langle x, y, D \rangle$. Finally, we prove the third statement. Suppose that there are two different points $x, y \in F_1 \cap A_2$. Since $r(F_1) = 2$, we have $D \in \langle x, y \rangle$ and, hence, $\{x, y\} \in \Gamma$, a contradiction with $A_2 \in \min \Gamma$. $\qquad\square$

Lemma 8. *Let $A \in \min \Gamma$ with $|A| = 2$ and the flat $G = \langle A \rangle$. Then, $G \subset F$ for some $F \in \mathcal{F} = \mathcal{F}(\mathcal{M}, D)$.*

Proof. Suppose that $G \not\subset F$ for every $F \in \mathcal{F} = \mathcal{F}(\mathcal{M}, D)$. If $A' \in \min \Gamma$ is such that $|A'| = 3$ or $|A'| = 2$ and $A' \not\subset G$, then $A' \cap G = \emptyset$. Therefore, Γ is not strongly connected, a contradiction. $\qquad\square$

Observe that $r(\mathcal{M}) = 3$ if and only if $|\mathcal{F}| = 1$. This case has been studied in Proposition 6. From now on, we suppose that $|\mathcal{F}| \geq 2$. We introduce in Proposition 13 an equivalence relation in $\mathcal{F} = \mathcal{F}(\mathcal{M}, D)$. Several lemmas are needed to prove that result. Consider $F_1, F_2 \in \mathcal{F}$ such that $r(F_1 \cup F_2) = 4$. Let $A_1 = \{a_1, b_1, c_1\} \subset P$ and $A_2 = \{a_2, b_2, c_2\} \subset P$ be minimal qualified subsets such that $F_i = \langle A_i \rangle$. From Lemma 7, $|A_1 \cap F_2| \leq 1$ and $|A_2 \cap F_1| \leq 1$. Then, we can suppose that $a_1, b_1 \notin F_2$ and $a_2, b_2 \notin F_1$.

Lemma 9. *In that situation, $\{a_1, b_1, a_2, b_2\} \notin \Gamma$.*

Proof. Suppose that, on the contrary, there exists a minimal qualified subset $A \subset \{a_1, b_1, a_2, b_2\}$. If $|A| = 2$ and, for instance, $A \cap F_1 \neq \emptyset$, then $A \subset F_1$, a contradiction with Lemma 7. If $|A| = 3$ and $|A \cap F_1| = 2$, then $\langle A \rangle = F_1$, a contradiction again. $\square$

Lemma 10. *If there exists a minimal qualified subset $A_3 = \{x, y\} \subset F_1 \cup F_2$, then $A_3 \subset F_1 \cap F_2$.*

Proof. By Lemma 7, $y \in F_1$ if $x \in F_1$. Then, we can suppose that $A_3 \subset F_1$. Suppose that $A_3 \not\subset F_1 \cap F_2$. In that case, $A_3 \cap F_2 = \emptyset$. We notate $F_3 = \langle A_3 \rangle$. Applying Lemma 7 again, $|A_1 \cap F_3| \leq 1$. Therefore, we can suppose that $a_1 \notin F_3 \cup F_2$. Then, neither $\{a_1, x\}$ nor $\{a_1, y\}$ can be qualified. Consider now the sets $B_1 = \{a_1, x, a_2, b_2\}$ and $B_2 = \{a_1, y, a_2, b_2\}$ and the flat $H = \langle a_1, a_2, b_2 \rangle$. Clearly, $r(H) = 3$ and $H \neq F_1$. If $r(B_i) = 4$, then $\langle B_i \rangle = \langle F_1 \cup F_2 \rangle$ and, hence, $B_i \in \Gamma$. Suppose that $B_1, B_2 \notin \Gamma$. In this case, $\langle B_1 \rangle = \langle B_2 \rangle = H$ and $\{a_1, x, y\} \subset H \cap F_1$. But that is impossible because $r(H \cap F_1) \leq 2$ and $a_1 \notin F_3$. Therefore, we can suppose that $B_1 \in \Gamma$. Let $A \subset B_1$ be a minimal qualified subset. Clearly, $|A| = 3$ and, hence, $|A \cap F_1| = 2$ or $|A \cap F_2| = 2$, that is, $\langle A \rangle = F_1$ or $\langle A \rangle = F_2$, a contradiction because $A \not\subset F_1$ and $A \not\subset F_2$. $\square$

Lemma 11. $c_1, c_2 \in F_1 \cap F_2$ *and* $r(F_1 \cap F_2) = 2$.

Proof. Suppose that $c_1 \notin F_2$. Then at least one of the sets $B_1 = \{a_1, c_1, a_2, b_2\}$ and $B_2 = \{b_1, c_1, a_2, b_2\}$ is qualified. Suppose that, on the contrary, $B_1, B_2 \notin \Gamma$. In this case, $r(B_i) = 3$ and, since $c_1 \notin F_2$, we have that $\langle B_1 \rangle = \langle B_2 \rangle = \langle c_1, a_2, b_2 \rangle$. Then $a_1, b_1 \in \langle c_1, a_2, b_2 \rangle$ and $\{c_1, a_2, b_2\}$ is qualified, a contradiction. Therefore, we can suppose that $B_1 \in \Gamma$. Let $A \subset B_1$ be a minimal qualified subset. From Lemma 10, $|A| = 3$ and, hence, $\langle A \rangle = F_1$ or $\langle A \rangle = F_2$, a contradiction that implies $c_1 \in F_2$. Symmetrically, $c_2 \in F_1$. Finally, $F_1 \cap F_2 = \langle c_1, D \rangle$ and, hence, $r(F_1 \cap F_2) = 2$. $\square$

Lemma 12. *Consider* $B = (F_1 \cup F_2) - (F_1 \cap F_2)$. *Then* $r(B) = 3$ *and* $B \notin \Gamma$.

Proof. The result is proved by checking that $\langle B \rangle = \langle a_1, b_1, a_2, b_2 \rangle$. In any other case, there must exist $c \in B$ with $c \notin \langle a_1, b_1, a_2, b_2 \rangle$. We can suppose that $c \in F_1$. Then, $A = \{a_1, b_1, c\}$ is a minimal qualified subset and $\langle A \rangle = F_1$. Observe that Lemma 11 can be applied to the sets A, A_2 and the flats F_1, F_2 and, hence, $c \in F_1 \cap F_2$, a contradiction. $\square$

Proposition 13. *Let $\mathcal{M}$ be a matroid on the set $Q = P \cup \{D\}$ such that the access structure $\Gamma = \Gamma_D(\mathcal{M})$ has rank three. Then, the relation on $\mathcal{F} = \mathcal{F}(\mathcal{M}, D)$ defined by $F_1 \sim F_2$ if and only if $r(F_1 \cup F_2) \leq 4$ is an equivalence relation.*

Proof. We only have to prove the transitivity. Let $F_1, F_2, F_3 \in \mathcal{F}$ be three different flats with $F_1 \sim F_2$ and $F_2 \sim F_3$. Then, $r(F_1 \cap F_2) = r(F_2 \cap F_3) = 2$. For every $i = 1, 2, 3$, we consider a minimal qualified subset $A_i = \{a_i, b_i, c_i\} \subset P$ such that $F_i = \langle A_i \rangle$. Suppose, without loss of generality, that $c_1, c_2 \in F_1 \cap F_2$, and $a_1, b_1 \notin F_2$ and $a_2, b_2 \notin F_1$.

If $F_1 \cap F_2 = F_2 \cap F_3$, then $r(F_1 \cap F_3) = 2$ and, hence, $F_1 \sim F_3$. If $c_1 \neq c_2$, we have that $\{c_1, c_2\}$ is a minimal qualified subset. Applying Lemma 10 to the flats F_2 and F_3, we get $\{c_1, c_2\} \subset F_2 \cap F_3$ and, hence, $F_1 \cap F_2 = F_2 \cap F_3$.

Suppose that $F_1 \cap F_2 \neq F_2 \cap F_3$. In this case, $c_1 = c_2$ and $F_1 \cap F_2 \cap F_3 = \{D\}$. Moreover, $|A| = 3$ for every minimal qualified subset $A \subset F_1 \cup F_2 \cup F_3$. Clearly, $c_1 \notin F_3$. We can suppose that $a_2, a_3 \in F_2 \cap F_3$, and $b_2, c_2 \notin F_3$ and $b_3, c_3 \notin F_2$. That implies $a_2 = a_3$. Consider the set $B = \{a_1, b_1, b_2, b_3, c_3\}$. From Lemma 12, the subsets $\{a_1, b_1, a_2, b_2\}$ and $\{b_2, c_2, b_3, c_3\}$ are not qualified and have rank three. Then, $a_2, c_2 \in \langle B \rangle$ and, hence, $B \in \Gamma$. Let $A_4 \subset B$ be a minimal qualified subset. Clearly, $A_4 \neq \{a_1, b_1, b_2\}, \{b_2, b_2, c_2\}$. If $A_4 = \{a_1, b_1, b_3\}$, then $\langle A_4 \rangle = F_1$ and, hence, $A_4 \cap F_2 \neq \emptyset$, a contradiction. Therefore, $|A_4 \cap A_i| \leq 1$ for every $i = 1, 2, 3$ and we can suppose that $A_4 = \{a_1, b_2, c_3\}$. Consider the flat $F_4 = \langle A_4 \rangle \in \mathcal{F}$. Observe that $\{a_1, b_2, D\} \subset F_4 \cap (F_1 \cup F_2)$ and, hence, $F_4 \subset F_1 \cup F_2$. Therefore, $\{a_3, c_3, D\} \subset F_3 \cap (F_1 \cup F_2)$ and $F_3 \subset F_1 \cup F_2$, which implies $r(F_1 \cup F_3) = 4$.   □

Consider the partition $\mathcal{F} = \mathcal{E}_1 \cup \cdots \cup \mathcal{E}_r$ given by the equivalence classes of the relation defined in Proposition 13. This induces a partition $P = P_1 \cup \cdots \cup P_r$ of the set P, where $P_j = \bigcup_{F \in \mathcal{E}_j} (F \cap P)$. This is due to the fact that $F_1 \cap F_2 = \{D\}$ for every $F_1, F_2 \in \mathcal{F}$ with $F_1 \not\sim F_2$. In addition, $\Gamma = \Gamma(P_1) \sqcup \cdots \sqcup \Gamma(P_r)$. Since we are supposing that the access structure Γ is strongly connected, there is only one equivalence class in $\mathcal{F} = \mathcal{F}(\mathcal{M}, D)$, that is, $r(F_1 \cup F_2) \leq 4$ for every $F_1, F_2 \in \mathcal{F}$.

Proposition 14. *Let $\mathcal{M}$ be a matroid on the set $Q = P \cup \{D\}$ such that the access structure $\Gamma = \Gamma_D(\mathcal{M})$ has rank three. Consider $\mathcal{F} = \mathcal{F}(\mathcal{M}, D) = \{F_1, \ldots, F_\ell\}$. Suppose that there exists a flat G of $\mathcal{M}$ such that $r(G) = 2$ and $G = F_i \cap F_j$ for every two different flats $F_i, F_j \in \mathcal{F}$. Take $n_0 = |G| + 1$ and $n_i = |F_i - G| + 1$, where $i = 1, \ldots, \ell$. Then,*

- $\mathcal{M} \cong U_{2,n_0} \widehat{\oplus}_p (U_{2,n_1} \oplus_p \cdots \oplus_p U_{2,n_\ell})$, or
- $\mathcal{M} \cong U_{2,n_0-1} \oplus_p U_{2,n_1} \oplus_p \cdots \oplus_p U_{2,n_\ell}$.

In particular, $r(\mathcal{M}) = \ell + 2$. Besides, $\mathcal{M}$ and $\Gamma_D(\mathcal{M})$ are, respectively, a $\mathbb{K}$-representable matroid and a $\mathbb{K}$-vector space access structure for every finite field $\mathbb{K}$ with $|\mathbb{K}| \geq \max_{0 \leq i \leq \ell} n_i$.

Proof. Clearly, a subset $A \subset P$ with $|A| = 2$ is qualified if and only if $A \subset G$. Consider now a minimal qualified subset $A \in \min \Gamma$ with $|A| = 3$. Then $\langle A \rangle \in \mathcal{F}(\mathcal{M}, D)$ and, hence, $\langle A \rangle = F_i$ for some $i = 1, \ldots, \ell$. From Lemma 11,

$|A \cap G| = 1$. Therefore, $B = P - G$ is not qualified. Consider the flat $H = \langle B \rangle$. Since $B \notin \Gamma$, we get that $r(H \cap G) \leq 1$ and, hence, $|H \cap G| \leq 1$. Let $G_0 = H \cap G$. The proof is concluded by checking that the minimal qualified subsets of Γ are precisely all subsets $\{x, y\} \subset G$ and all subsets $\{a, b, x\}$, with $a, b \in F_i - G$ and $x \in G - G_0$. As we said before, subset $A \subset P$ with $|A| = 2$ is qualified if and only if $A \subset G$. In addition, if $A \in \min \Gamma$ and $|A| = 3$, then $A = \{a, b, x\}$, with $a, b \in F_i - G$ and $x \in G$. Suppose now that there exist a subset $A = \{a, b, p\} \notin \Gamma$, with $a, b \in F_i - G$ and $p \in G$, and let $H' = \langle A \rangle$. Since $H' \subsetneq F_i$, we get $r(H') = 2$. Then, $H' \subset B$ and $p \in G_0$. $\qquad\square$

Let P be the set of the points of the *Fano Plane*, the projective plane over the finite field $\mathbb{Z}_2$, that is, $P = \mathbb{Z}_2^3 - \{(0, 0, 0)\}$. We can put $P = \{1, 2, \ldots, 7\}$ by considering the points as the binary representations of those integers. Let Υ be the access structure on the set P whose minimal qualified subsets are precisely the lines of the Fano Plane: $A_1 = \{2, 4, 6\}$, $A_2 = \{1, 4, 5\}$, $A_3 = \{3, 4, 7\}$, $A_4 = \{1, 2, 3\}$, $A_5 = \{2, 5, 7\}$, $A_6 = \{1, 6, 7\}$, $A_7 = \{3, 5, 6\}$. Let $\mathbb{K}$ be a finite field with characteristic 2, consider $Q = P \cup \{8\}$, and let $\mathcal{M}_1$ be the matroid on Q that is represented over $\mathbb{K}$ by the matrix

$$\begin{pmatrix} 1 & 1 & 1 & 1 & 1 & 1 & 1 & 1 \\ 0 & 0 & 0 & 1 & 1 & 1 & 1 & 0 \\ 0 & 1 & 1 & 0 & 0 & 1 & 1 & 0 \\ 1 & 0 & 1 & 0 & 1 & 0 & 1 & 0 \end{pmatrix}.$$

Then, $\Upsilon = \Gamma_8(\mathcal{M}_1)$ and, hence, Υ is a $\mathbb{K}$-vector space access structure. Consider the matroid $\mathcal{M}_2 = \mathcal{M}_1 \setminus \{7\}$ and the access structure $\Upsilon' = \Gamma_8(\mathcal{M}_2) = \Upsilon \setminus \{7\}$, which are, respectively, a $\mathbb{K}$-representable matroid and a $\mathbb{K}$-vector space access structure.

Proposition 15. *Let $\mathcal{M}$ be a matroid on the set $Q = P \cup \{D\}$ such that the access structure $\Gamma = \Gamma_D(\mathcal{M})$ has rank three. Consider $\mathcal{F} = \mathcal{F}(\mathcal{M}, D)$ and suppose that $|\mathcal{F}| \geq 3$ and $F_1 \cap F_2 \cap F_3 = \{D\}$ for every three different flats $F_1, F_2, F_3 \in \mathcal{F}$. Then, $\mathcal{M} \cong \mathcal{M}_2$ and $\Gamma \cong \Upsilon'$.*

Proof. Take three different flats $F_1, F_2, F_3 \in \mathcal{F}$. Since $F_1 \cap F_2 \neq F_2 \cap F_3$, this is the same situation as in the last part of the proof of Proposition 13. Therefore, all minimal qualified subsets have three elements. Then, by Lemma 11, if $A, A' \subset P$ are minimal qualified subsets with $\langle A \rangle \neq \langle A' \rangle$, then $A \cap A' \neq \emptyset$.

If we consider minimal qualified subsets $A_i = \{a_i, b_i, c_i\}$ such that $F_i = \langle A_i \rangle$ for $i = 1, 2, 3$, we can suppose that $c_1 = c_2$ and $a_2 = a_3$ and that $A_4 = \{a_1, b_2, c_3\}$ is a minimal qualified subset. Observe that $F_4 = \langle A_4 \rangle \in \mathcal{F}$. Moreover, by taking into account that $A_1 \cap A_3 \neq \emptyset$ and the positions of the other points and flats, we get that $b_3 = b_1$.

We claim that $F_i = A_i \cup \{D\}$ for every $i = 1, \ldots, 4$. If this is not true and, for instance, there exists $a \in F_1 - (A_1 \cup \{D\})$, we can suppose that $A = \{a, b_1, c_1\}$ is a basis of F_1. Then A is a minimal qualified subset and $a \in A \cap A_4$ because $A \cap A_4 \neq \emptyset$ and $b_1, c_1 \notin F_4$. Since $a_1 \in A \cap A_4$, we get that $a, a_1 \in F_1 \cap F_4$ and $a = a_1$, a contradiction.

The proof is concluded by checking that $A_1, \ldots, A_4$ are all the minimal qualified subsets of Γ because this implies $\Gamma \cong \Upsilon'$. If there were another minimal qualified subset A_5, the flat $F_5 = \langle A_5 \rangle$ would be different from the flats $F_1, \ldots, F_4$. Then, $A \cap A_1 \neq \emptyset$. If, for instance, $A \cap A_1 = \{a_1\}$, we get that $F_1 \cap F_5 = \langle a_1, D \rangle = F_1 \cap F_4$ and, hence, $r(F_1 \cap F_4 \cap F_5) = 2$, a contradiction. $\square$

Proposition 16. *Let $\mathcal{M}$ be a matroid on the set $Q = P \cup \{D\}$ such that the access structure $\Gamma = \Gamma_D(\mathcal{M})$ has rank three. Consider $\mathcal{F} = \mathcal{F}(\mathcal{M}, D)$ and suppose that there exist three different flats $F_1, F_2, F_3 \in \mathcal{F}$ such that $F_1 \cap F_2 \cap F_3 = \{D\}$ and there exists a flat $F \in \mathcal{F} - \{F_1, F_2, F_3\}$ such that $F_1 \cap F_2 = F_1 \cap F$. Then, $\mathcal{M} \cong \mathcal{M}_1$ and $\Gamma \cong \Upsilon$.*

Proof. If we consider minimal qualified subsets $A_i = \{a_i, b_i, c_i\}$, where $i = 1, 2, 3$, such that $F_i = \langle A_i \rangle$, we can suppose, as in the proof of Proposition 15, that $c_1 = c_2$, $a_2 = a_3$ and $b_3 = b_1$ and that $A_4 = \{a_1, b_2, c_3\}$ is a minimal qualified subset. Consider $F_4 = \langle A_4 \rangle \in \mathcal{F}$. Observe that $F_i \cap F_j \cap F_4 = \{D\}$ whenever $1 \leq i < j \leq 3$.

Besides, by applying again the arguments in the proof of Proposition 15, all minimal qualified subsets of Γ have three elements and $|A \cap A'| = 1$ if $A, A' \subset P$ are minimal qualified subsets with $\langle A \rangle \neq \langle A' \rangle$. Besides, $F_i = A_i \cup \{D\}$ for every $i = 1, \ldots, 4$.

Let A_5 be a minimal qualified subset such that $F_1 \cap F_5 = F_1 \cap F_2 = \langle c_1, D \rangle$, where $F_5 = \langle A_5 \rangle$. Then, $A_5 \cap A_1 = A_5 \cap A_2 = \{c_1\}$. Observe that both $A_5 \cap A_3$ and $A_5 \cap A_4$ must be equal to $\{c_3\}$. It is easy to check that $A_5 = \{c_1, c_3, d\}$ with $d \notin \{a_1, b_1, c_1, a_2, b_2, c_3\}$.

Since $F_1 \cap F_3 \cap F_5 = \{D\}$, we use the arguments in the proof of Proposition 13 and we get that $A_6 = \{a_1, a_2, d\}$ is a minimal qualified subset. Equally, $A_7 = \{b_1, b_2, d\}$ is also a minimal qualified subset because $F_2 \cap F_3 \cap F_5 = \{D\}$. Besides, in the same way as in the proof of Proposition 15, we can check that $F_i = A_i \cup \{D\}$ for every $i = 5, 6, 7$. Finally, observe that the minimal qualified subsets of Γ must be precisely $A_1, \ldots, A_7$, because it is not possible to find a set with three elements such that $|A \cap A_i| = 1$ for every $i = 1, \ldots, 7$. $\square$

References

1. A. Beimel, N. Livne. On Matroids and Non-ideal Secret Sharing. *Third Theory of Cryptography Conference, TCC 2006. Lecture Notes in Comput. Sci.* **3876** (2006) 482–501.
2. A. Beimel, T. Tassa, E. Weinreb. Characterizing Ideal Weighted Threshold Secret Sharing. *Second Theory of Cryptography Conference, TCC 2005. Lecture Notes in Comput. Sci.* **3378** (2005) 600–619.
3. G.R. Blakley, Safeguarding cryptographic keys. *AFIPS Conference Proceedings.* **48** (1979) 313–317.
4. C. Blundo, A. De Santis, R. De Simone, U. Vaccaro. Tight bounds on the information rate of secret sharing schemes. *Des. Codes Cryptogr.* **11** (1997) 107–122.
5. C. Blundo, A. De Santis, L. Gargano, U. Vaccaro. On the information rate of secret sharing schemes. *Advances in Cryptology - CRYPTO'92, Lecture Notes in Comput. Sci.* **740** 148–167.

6. E.F. Brickell. Some ideal secret sharing schemes. *J. Combin. Math. and Combin. Comput.* **9** (1989) 105–113.

7. E.F. Brickell, D.M. Davenport. On the classification of ideal secret sharing schemes. *J. Cryptology* **4** (1991) 123–134.

8. R.M. Capocelli, A. De Santis, L. Gargano, U. Vaccaro. On the size of shares of secret sharing schemes. *J. Cryptology* **6** (1993) 157–168.

9. L. Csirmaz. The size of a share must be large. *J. Cryptology* **10** (1997) 223–231.

10. W.-A. Jackson, K.M. Martin. Perfect secret sharing schemes on five participants. *Des. Codes Cryptogr.* **9** (1996) 267–286.

11. E.D. Karnin, J.W. Greene, M.E. Hellman. On secret sharing systems. *IEEE Trans. Inform. Theory* **29** (1983) 35–41.

12. A. Lehman. A solution of the Shannon switching game. *J. Soc. Indust. Appl. Math.* **12** (1964) 687–725.

13. A. Lehman. Matroids and Ports. *Notices Amer. Math. Soc.* **12** (1976) 356–360.

14. J. Martí-Farré, C. Padró. Secret sharing schemes on sparse homogeneous access structures with rank three. *Electronic Journal of Combinatorics* **11(1)** (2004) Research Paper 72, 16 pp. (electronic).

15. J. Martí-Farré, C. Padró. Secret sharing schemes with three or four minimal qualified subsets. *Des. Codes Cryptogr.* **34** (2005) 17–34.

16. J. Martí-Farré, C. Padró. Secret sharing schemes on access structures with intersection number equal to one. *Discrete Appl. Math.* **154** (2006) 552-563.

17. J. Martí-Farré, C. Padró. On Secret Sharing Schemes, Matroids and Polymatroids. Preprint. Available at *Cryptology ePrint Archive*, Report **2006/077**, `http://eprint.iacr.org/2006/077`.

18. F. Matúš. Matroid representations by partitions. *Discrete Math.* **203** (1999) 169–194.

19. J.G. Oxley. *Matroid theory.* Oxford Science Publications. The Clarendon Press, Oxford University Press, New York, 1992.

20. C. Padró, G. Sáez. Secret sharing schemes with bipartite access structure. *IEEE Trans. Inform. Theory* **46** (2000) 2596–2604.

21. C. Padró, G. Sáez. Lower bounds on the information rate of secret sharing schemes with homogeneous access structure. *Inform. Process. Lett.* **83** (2002) 345–351.

22. P.D. Seymour. A forbidden minor characterization of matroid ports. *Quart. J. Math. Oxford Ser.* **27** (1976) 407–413.

23. P.D. Seymour, On secret-sharing matroids, *J. Combin. Theory Ser. B*, **56** (1992) pp. 69–73.

24. A. Shamir, How to share a secret, *Commun. of the ACM*, **22** (1979) pp. 612–613.

25. J. Simonis, A. Ashikhmin, Almost affine codes, *Des. Codes Cryptogr.*, **14** (1998) pp. 179–197.

26. D.R. Stinson. An explication of secret sharing schemes. *Des. Codes Cryptogr.* **2** (1992) 357–390.

27. D.R. Stinson. New general lower bounds on the information rate of secret sharing schemes. *Advances in Cryptology - CRYPTO'92, Lecture Notes in Comput. Sci.* **740** (1993) 168-182.

28. D.R. Stinson. Decomposition constructions for secret-sharing schemes. *IEEE Trans. Inform. Theory* **40** (1994) 118–125.

29. D.J.A. Welsh. *Matroid Theory.* Academic Press, London, 1976.

Cheating Immune $(2, n)$-Threshold Visual Secret Sharing

Roberto De Prisco* and Alfredo De Santis

Università di Salerno
Dipartimento di Informatica ed Applicazioni
84081 Baronissi (SA), Italy
{robdep, ads}@dia.unisa.it

Abstract. Cheating in secret sharing has been considered in several papers. Recently cheating in visual cryptography has been considered in [10], where $(2, n)$-threshold visual cryptography schemes are provided. In this paper we provide new $(2, n)$-threshold visual cryptography schemes. Our model is different from the one considered in [10]; in particular we aim at constructing cheating immune schemes without the use of extra information, like additional shares or images as done in [10]. We have provided a formal definition of cheating which requires that a group of cheaters be able to deterministically force a honest participant to reconstruct a wrong secret. The $(2, n)$-threshold schemes that we provide do not allow such cheating, regardless of the number of cheaters.

1 Introduction

A secret sharing scheme is a cryptographic protocol which allows the participants to share a secret in such a way that only certain qualified subset of participants can reconstruct the secret. Visual secret sharing (or visual cryptography) is a particular form of secret sharing where the secret is an image and the shares are printed transparencies allowing the reconstruction of the secret by means of shares superposition. Secret sharing was introduced independently by Blakey [1] and Shamir [15]. Visual secret sharing was introduced by Naor and Shamir [13].

The goal of a secret sharing scheme (visual or not) is that of sharing a secret so that only qualified subsets of participants are able to reconstruct the secret. Other (non-qualified) subsets of participants should not be able to gain any information about the secret. When the qualified sets consist of all the subsets of at least k out of the n participants the secret sharing scheme is called a (k, n)-threshold scheme. In a secret sharing scheme each participant receives a share, that is a piece of information related to the secret. Combining the shares of a qualified subsets of participants the secret is revealed while any other combination of shares gives no information on the secret. However in some cases if some participants misbehave they could be able to gain information about the secret or the secret itself even if they are not qualified. For example in the

---

* This author is also a member of the Akamai Faculty Group, Akamai Technologies, 8 Cambridge Center, Cambridge, MA 02142, USA.

R. De Prisco and M. Yung (Eds.): SCN 2006, LNCS 4116, pp. 216–228, 2006.
© Springer-Verlag Berlin Heidelberg 2006

secret sharing scheme of Shamir [15] (and in all linear secret sharing schemes), a dishonest participant can submit a fake share eliciting a wrong reconstruction of the secret from which the dishonest participant can infer the real secret, while the other participants are left with the wrong secret. Tompa and Woll [18] show how to modify Shamir scheme to avoid such an attack by a dishonest participant. In the above context, dishonest participants, that try to fool other participants, are called cheaters. Constructing schemes that are robust against cheaters is clearly desirable. The robustness against cheaters depends on the model considered. Some papers that have considered such a problem are, for example, [4,5,8,11,12,19].

With visual secret sharing there are inherent constraints on the form of the share and the reconstruction process. Hence the results about cheating for general secret sharing might not hold for visual secret sharing. In a recent paper Horng et al. [10] considered the problem of constructing cheating-immune visual secret sharing schemes. They propose two methods to fight cheating in visual cryptography. The first one uses additional shares and a confidential image for each participant; such additional information is used before the reconstruction process to verify the integrity of the share that will be used to reconstruct the secret. The second one uses a $(2, n+d)$-threshold scheme, for some $d > 0$, and takes only n out of the $n + d$ shares; however such an approach prevents the cheaters from fooling honest participants when the secret is black but the cheaters can fool honest participants when the secret is white. As pointed out in [10], the use of a complementary secret image (where white and black are swapped) solves the problem.

In this paper we aim at constructing cheating immune visual cryptography schemes without the use of additional information, like additional shares or other images. We focus on $(2, n)$-threshold visual cryptography schemes. First we provide a formal definition of cheating, which requires a group of cheaters to be able to deterministically fool a honest participant. Then we provide $(2, n)$-threshold visual cryptography schemes that are immune to cheating, in the sense of the above definition. Compared to [10] our schemes do not suffer of the problem of protecting only black secret pixels and thus they do not require the use of a complementary image; moreover we don't need to produce additional shares.

2   The Model

A secret image, consisting of black and white pixels, has to be shared among a set $\mathcal{P} = \{1, \ldots, n\}$ of *participants*. A trusted party, which is called the *dealer* and is not a participant, knows the secret image. The dealer has to distribute *shares* to the n participants in the form of printed transparencies. The subsets of $\mathcal{P}$ consisting of at least k participants are called *qualified sets*. Participants in a qualified subset have to be able to "visually" recover the secret image, by stacking together their shares (transparencies) and holding the stacked set of transparencies to the light. All other subsets, that is, those which have less than k participants, are called *forbidden sets*. Participants in a forbidden set should not be able to get any information on the secret image from their shares, neither by stacking together the transparencies nor by any other computation. Schemes where the forbidden and qualified sets are defined as above are called (k,n)-threshold schemes.

From now on we concentrate on how to deal with just one pixel of the image. In order to share the entire image it is enough to repeat the sharing process for each pixel of the image.

Each secret pixel is divided into m subpixels. This implies a loss of resolution: the pixels of the reconstructed image will be m times bigger compared to the ones of the original image. A *share* is a "version" of the secret pixel consisting of a particular assignment of black and white to the m subpixels. When superimposing two or more shares the participants need to align the shares so that the (sub)pixels corresponding to a given pixel are superimposed to each other. The resulting image will have a black pixel whenever there is a share with a black pixel and a white pixel only when all the shares have white pixels. In other words the human eye performs, for each subpixel of the overall picture, an or operation among the superimposed pixels

Given a matrix M and a set X of natural numbers, which represent participants, we denote by $M|X$ the matrix consisting of only the rows of M corresponding to the integers in X, if they exists in M. For example, assuming that M has at least 6 rows, if $X = \{2,3,6\}$, then $M|X$ is the submatrix of M consisting of the second, the third and the sixth row of M.

The *weight* of a binary vector is denoted with $w(\cdot)$ and is the number of 1s in the vector.

Next we provide the definition of a visual cryptography scheme.

Definition 1. *Fix k and n, with $2 \leq k \leq n$. Fix ℓ, h and m such that $0 \leq \ell < h \leq m$. A (k,n)-threshold visual cryptography scheme consists of 2 $n \times m$ binary matrices B^0, B^1, satisfying:*

1. *Given a qualified set X, $|X| = k$, it holds that $w(\text{or}(B^1|X)) = h$ and $w(\text{or}(B^0|X)) = \ell$.*
2. *Given a forbidden set X, $|X| < k$, the 2 matrices of dimension $|X| \times m$, $B^i|X$, $i = 0, 1$, are equal up to a permutation of the columns.*

The matrices B^0 and B^1 are called base matrices of the scheme.

White pixels are represented with a "0" and black pixels are represented with a "1". In the rest of the paper we will often use "0" and "white" as synonymous and also "1" and "black" as synonymous. B^0 is the white base matrix and B^1 is the black base matrix.

In order to distribute the shares the dealer chooses a random permutation of the columns of the base matrix corresponding to the secret pixel and gives to each participant a row of the permuted base matrix.

The first property is called the contrast property and requires the correct reconstruction of the secret pixel. In particular if the secret pixel is white then the reconstructed pixel must have exactly ℓ black subpixels and if the secret pixel is black then the reconstructed pixel must have exactly h black subpixels. The second property is called the safety property and requires that any non qualified subset of participants has no information about the secret pixel.

Notice that the above definition requires that a white secret pixel be reconstructed with exactly ℓ black subpixels and a black secret pixel be reconstructed with exactly h black subpixels. This can be used to detect a cheating attempt. Indeed if a reconstruction gives a number of black subpixels that is different from both ℓ and h it means that some shares have been forged.

2.1 Definition of Cheating

A group of $c < n$ participants can cheat by forming a coalition and producing fake shares in order to fool honest participants. In this paper we focus on $(2, n)$-threshold schemes, hence we provide a definition of cheating against a single honest participant.

Given a $(2, n)$-threshold scheme with parameters ℓ and h, a group of $c < n$ participants are called "cheaters" when they get together, construct a fake share and present such a share to a honest participant with the intention of forcing the honest participant to reconstruct a wrong secret.

Since the cheaters have to build a fake share they can potentially choose any possible share (i.e. any possible combination of the m subpixels). However the honest participant can actually perform a validity check on the share that he receives. Such a validity check consists in checking that the share appears in the distribution matrices of the scheme. Hence the cheaters are bound to choose as a fake share only the shares that appear in the rows of the base matrices, or that are permutations of the rows of the base matrices. We call such shares *valid* and we use the word *fake* to indicate a share which has been constructed by the group of cheaters. Hence the goal of the cheaters is to create a fake but valid share that induces the honest participant to reconstruct the wrong color.

For example, consider the following $(2, 3)$ scheme defined by the base matrices

$$B^0 = \begin{bmatrix} 1 & 0 & 0 \\ 1 & 0 & 0 \\ 1 & 0 & 0 \end{bmatrix}$$

$$B^1 = \begin{bmatrix} 1 & 0 & 0 \\ 0 & 1 & 0 \\ 0 & 0 & 1 \end{bmatrix}$$

In this scheme $m = 3$, $\ell = 1$ and $h = 2$ and all and only the binary strings with exactly 1 one and 2 zeroes are valid shares. A white secret pixel is reconstructed with exactly 1 black subpixel out of the 3 subpixels and a black secret pixel is reconstructed with 2 black subpixels. Assume that participants corresponding to the first two rows are cheaters and the participant corresponding to the third row is a honest one.

If the secret pixel is white, when the cheaters collude they can reconstruct the secret and also know the share of the honest participant (it will have a 1 exactly in the same place where the shares of the two cheaters have a 1). With such information the two cheaters can build a forged share having a 1 in any of the position where the honest participant has a 0. When presented with such a share the honest participant will reconstruct a black secret pixel.

Similarly if the secret pixel is black the two cheaters know that the share of the honest participant will have a 1 in the position where both their shares have a 0 and thus to force the honest participant to reconstruct a wrong secret they will forge a share with a 1 in the same position where the share of the honest participant has a 1.

Notice that in the above example the cheaters have been able to cheat with probability 1 because they were able to know exactly the share of the honest participant.

Recall that by the safety property we have that a share of a honest participant is present, up to a permutation of the columns, in both base matrices.

Definition 2. In a $(2, n)$-threshold secret sharing scheme with parameters ℓ and h, a group of $c < n$ cheaters cheats if given a secret pixel of color white (resp. black) the c cheaters are able to construct a valid share of the black (resp. white) base matrix such that the weight of the **or** of such a share and that of the honest participant is h (resp. ℓ).

Notice that the definition of cheating requires that the cheaters be able to construct a fake share which will surely (i.e. with probability 1) induce the honest participant to reconstruct a wrong secret.

3   A $(2, n)$-Threshold Cheating Immune Scheme

In this section we provide the $(2, n)$-threshold cheating immune scheme.

Construction 1 Fix n, $n \geq 3$. The base matrices of the scheme have dimension $n \times (2^n + n + 1)$. The white base matrix W_n has the following columns: all the possible 2^n binary column-vectors of length n, one additional column with all ones and n additional columns with all zeroes. The black base matrix B^n has the following columns: all the possible 2^n binary column-vectors of length n, one additional column with all zeroes the n columns of the identity matrix of dimension $n \times n$.

Example for $n = 3$.

$$W_3 = \begin{bmatrix} 0\,1\,0\,1\,0\,1\,0\,1 & 0 & 1\,0\,0 \\ 0\,0\,1\,1\,0\,0\,1\,1 & 0 & 1\,0\,0 \\ 0\,0\,0\,0\,1\,1\,1\,1 & 0 & 1\,0\,0 \end{bmatrix}$$

$$B_3 = \begin{bmatrix} 0\,1\,0\,1\,0\,1\,0\,1 & 0 & 1\,0\,0 \\ 0\,0\,1\,1\,0\,0\,1\,1 & 0 & 0\,1\,0 \\ 0\,0\,0\,0\,1\,1\,1\,1 & 0 & 0\,0\,1 \end{bmatrix}$$

Example for $n = 4$.

$$W_4 = \begin{bmatrix} 0\,1\,0\,1\,0\,1\,0\,1\,0\,1\,0\,1\,0\,1\,0\,1\,|0|1\,0\,0\,0 \\ 0\,0\,1\,1\,0\,0\,1\,1\,0\,0\,1\,1\,0\,0\,1\,1\,|0|1\,0\,0\,0 \\ 0\,0\,0\,0\,1\,1\,1\,1\,0\,0\,0\,0\,1\,1\,1\,1\,|0|1\,0\,0\,0 \\ 0\,0\,0\,0\,0\,0\,0\,0\,1\,1\,1\,1\,1\,1\,1\,1\,|0|1\,0\,0\,0 \end{bmatrix}$$

$$B_4 = \begin{bmatrix} 0\,1\,0\,1\,0\,1\,0\,1\,0\,1\,0\,1\,0\,1\,0\,1\,|0|1\,0\,0\,0 \\ 0\,0\,1\,1\,0\,0\,1\,1\,0\,0\,1\,1\,0\,0\,1\,1\,|0|0\,1\,0\,0 \\ 0\,0\,0\,0\,1\,1\,1\,1\,0\,0\,0\,0\,1\,1\,1\,1\,|0|0\,0\,1\,0 \\ 0\,0\,0\,0\,0\,0\,0\,0\,1\,1\,1\,1\,1\,1\,1\,1\,|0|0\,0\,0\,1 \end{bmatrix}$$

Each row has exactly $2^{n-1} + 1$ black pixels (ones).

A qualified set of 2 participants reconstructs a white secret pixel with exactly $3 \cdot 2^{n-2} + 1$ black subpixels and a black secret pixels with exactly $3 \cdot 2^{n-2} + 2$ black subpixels.

The pixel expansion is $m = 2^n + n + 1$.

Before proving that Construction 1 gives a scheme that does not allow cheaters to cheat with probability 1, let us consider the $(2, 3)$-threshold scheme and see why the scheme is cheating immune. Assume that participants 1 and 2 are cheaters and participant 3 is honest. Assume also that the secret is white. Then when the cheaters collude they know that the secret is white but do not have an exact knowledge of the share of the honest participant. Indeed using their 2 shares the cheaters can infer the following information:

- in the columns for which the cheaters see 2 zeroes, which are exactly 5 (in general they are $2 + n$ – see below), the honest share has 4 zeroes and 1 one. However since the dealer can choose any permutation of the base matrix, the cheaters cannot tell where the black subpixel will be placed, i.e., the 1 can be placed in correspondence of any of the 5 double-zero columns seen by the cheaters.
- in the columns for which the cheaters see a 0 over a 1, which are exactly 2, the honest share has a 1 and a 0, but the cheaters cannot tell where the 1 and 0 of the honest share are placed
- in the columns for which the cheaters see a 1 over a 0, which are exactly 2, the honest share has a 1 and a 0, but the cheaters cannot tell where the 1 and 0 of the honest share are placed
- in the columns for which the cheaters see 2 ones, which are exactly 3 the honest share has 1 zero and 2 ones. Again they cannot tell where the honest share has the 0 and the 2 ones.

The uncertainty that results from this partial information does not allow the cheaters to deterministically construct a share that will fool the honest participants. As we will argue more formally in the rest of the section, the only cases where the cheaters can compute the number of black supixels of the reconstruction provided by their fake share and the share of the honest participant are cases where the honest participant is not fooled. This means that the cheaters cannot fool the honest participant with probability 1. Formally we have the following theorem.

Theorem 2. *For any $c, c < n$, any group of c participants cannot cheat with probability 1.*

From now on we assume that $c = n - 1$. It is obvious that if a group of $n - 1$ cheaters cannot cheat with probability 1 then also any smaller group of cheaters cannot cheat with probability 1.

Fix the $n - 1$ cheaters and consider their shares, and in particular look at the columns formed by the $n - 1$ shares and partition them into *blocks* of identical columns. There will be one block for each possible binary column-vector of length $n - 1$. The number of identical columns in each block depends on the block and on the secret pixel.

Let us first consider the case when the secret pixel is white. So the shares of the $n - 1$ cheaters are taken from W_n.

A simple combinatorial argument is sufficient to identify the cardinality of each block. The block of columns with $n - 1$ zeroes has cardinality $2 + n$. Indeed 2 columns with all zeroes in the $n - 1$ shares of the cheaters come from the portion of the base matrix that contains all possible binary vectors of length n while n come from the additional n all-zeroes columns.

Similarly the block of columns with $n - 1$ ones has cardinality 3. Any other block has cardinality 2.

Now we classify the blocks into four groups:

A: block of the $(n - 1)$-zero columns (one block)
B: blocks with columns with 1 one and $n - 2$ zeroes (exactly $n - 1$ blocks)
C: blocks with columns with at least 2 ones and at most $n - 2$ ones ($2^{n-1} - n - 1$ blocks)
D: block of the $(n - 1)$-one columns (one block)

Notice that the columns within each block are indistinguishable by the cheaters, in the sense that the cheaters cannot tell whether a 0 or a 1 will appear in the honest share for each of the column, but only the total number of 0s and 1s. In particular the cheaters know that the block of the $(n - 1)$-zero columns (group A) correspond to exactly $n + 1$ zeroes and 1 one in the honest share. However the cheaters cannot tell where the 0s and 1s will appear since the honest participant can have a share for any possible placement of 0s and 1s within the block.

Similarly for each block of columns in group B, a honest share has exactly 1 zero and 1 one, and again they can be placed in any possible position.

For blocks in group C it happens the same: the corresponding portion of the honest share has exactly 1 zero and 1 one that can be placed in any possible position.

Finally, the block with all-one columns correspond to a portion of a honest share having exactly 1 zero and 2 ones, and they can be placed in any possible position.

The following table summarizes what the group of $n - 1$ cheaters knows about the share of the honest participant:

Group of $n-1$ cheaters with a white secret.				
Group:	A	B	C	D
Type:	$\begin{bmatrix} 0 \\ 0 \\ \dots \\ 0 \end{bmatrix}$	$\begin{bmatrix} 1 \\ 0 \\ \dots \\ 0 \end{bmatrix}$	$\begin{bmatrix} 1 \\ 1 \\ \dots \\ 0 \end{bmatrix}$	$\begin{bmatrix} 1 \\ 1 \\ \dots \\ 1 \end{bmatrix}$
Number of blocks:	1	$n-1$	$2^{n-1} - n - 1$	1
Columns in each block:	$2 + n$	2	2	3
0s in remaining share:	$n+1$	1	1	1
1s in remaining share:	1	1	1	2

The group of $n-1$ cheaters needs to make up a share to present to the honest participant. The share must have exactly $2^{n-1} + 1$ ones, otherwise the share can be identified as a fake one. Moreover the cheaters want to have a reconstructed pixel that is black, which means the reconstruction has to yield a pixel with exactly $3 \cdot 2^{n-2} + 2$ black subpixels.

Given that the knowledge about the honest share is only partial, there are many strategies for which the number of black subpixels in the reconstruction is a random variable. There are few strategies that the cheaters can follow in order to obtain a certain number of black subpixels in the reconstructed secret pixel with probability 1. We will call such strategies *exact*. Exact strategies are those for which the made up share places all ones covering exactly all the columns in one or more blocks (with no block covered only partially). Indeed placing the 1s as described above, the number of black subpixels is independent of the honest share and can be computed exactly (with no uncertainty). All other strategies will inevitably lead to some uncertainty on the total number of black subpixels in the reconstructed share and thus any such strategy will not be exact. Recall that in our definition of cheating we require that the cheaters be able to fool the honest participant with probability 1. Hence we want to show that any exact strategy will not allow the cheaters to cheat with probability 1.

In order to analyze all the exact strategies let us denote with α, β, γ and δ be, respectively, the number of blocks from groups A, B, C and D that the cheaters choose to place the ones in the fake share. Such numbers are constrained by $\alpha \leq 1$, $\beta \leq n-1$, $\gamma \leq 2^{n-1} - n - 1$ and $\delta \leq 1$. Since a valid share has exactly $2^{n-1} + 1$ black subpixels the cheaters must choose values for α, β, γ and δ such that

$$(2 + n)\alpha + 2\beta + 2\gamma + 3\delta = 2^{n-1} + 1. \tag{1}$$

We distinguish 4 possible cases and show that in each of them the cheaters cannot cheat with probability 1. Before examining each case we observe that the number of black subpixels in the share reconstructed from the fake share and the honest one is given by

$$(2+n)\alpha+(1-\alpha)+2\beta+(n-1-\beta)+2\gamma+(2^{n-1}-n-1-\gamma)+3\delta+2(1-\delta). \quad (2)$$

Indeed when $\alpha = 1$ the block of group A contributes for $(2+n)$ black subpixels while when $\alpha = 0$ the block of group A contributes only for the 1s in the honest share. Similarly each of the β blocks chosen by the cheaters will contribute to the number of black subpixels with 2 black subpixels while the remaining $(n-1-\beta)$ blocks will contribute each for 1 subpixel. For the blocks of group C we have γ of them that contribute for 2 black subpixels each, while the remaining $2^{n-1}-n-1-\gamma$ contribute with only 1 black subpixels. Finally when $\delta = 1$ the block of group D contributes for 3 black subpixels while when $\delta = 0$ the same block contributes for 2 black subpixels. Equation 2 can be simplified to

$$2^{n-1} + 1 + (n+1)\alpha + \beta + \gamma + \delta. \quad (3)$$

We now consider the four possible cases:

case 1: $\alpha = 0, \delta = 0$. Equation (1) becomes $2\beta + 2\gamma = 2^{n-1} + 1$ which has no solution for β and γ integers.

case 2: $\alpha = 0, \delta = 1$. Equation (1) becomes $2\beta + 2\gamma + 3 = 2^{n-1} + 1$ which is equivalent to $\beta + \gamma = 2^{n-2} - 1$.

Hence, the number of ones in the reconstructed secret pixel, given by Equation (3) is:

$$2^{n-1} + 1 + 2^{n-2} - 1 + 1 = 3 \cdot 2^{n-2} + 1.$$

This means that the reconstructed pixel is a white pixel (the honest participant is not fooled).

case 3: $\alpha = 1, \delta = 0$. Equation (1) becomes $2 + n + 2\beta + 2\gamma = 2^{n-1} + 1$ which is equivalent to $2\beta + 2\gamma = 2^{n-1} - n - 1$. This has no solutions for n even but for n odd the cheaters can choose $\beta + \gamma = 2^{n-2} - \frac{n+1}{2}$. With such a choice the number of black subpixels in the reconstructed secret pixel, given by Equation (3), is:

$$2^{n-1} + 1 + 2^{n-2} - \frac{n}{2} - \frac{1}{2} = 3 \cdot 2^{n-2} + 1/2 + 3n/2.$$

The above number is always strictly greater than $3 \cdot 2^{n-2} + 2$ which is the number of black subpixels in the reconstructed pixel. Hence the honest participant can detect an anomaly in the reconstructed share.

case 4: $\alpha = 1, \delta = 1$. Equation (1) becomes $2 + n + 2\beta + 2\gamma + 3 = 2^{n-1} + 1$ which is equivalent to $2\beta + 2\gamma = 2^{n-1} - n - 4$. This has no solution for n odd but for n even the cheaters can choose $\beta + \gamma = 2^{n-2} - \frac{n}{2} - 2$. With such a choice the number of black subpixels in the reconstructed secret pixels, given by Equation (3), is:

$$2^{n-1} + 1 + 2^{n-2} - \frac{n}{2} - 2 + 1 = 3 \cdot 2^{n-2} + 1 + n/2$$

which is always strictly greater than $3 \cdot 2^{n-2} + 2$ (for all even $n \geq 3$). Hence also in this case the honest participant can detect an anomaly in the reconstructed share.

Thus we can conclude that no exact strategy can fool the honest participant when the secret pixel is white.

With a similar reasoning we can analyze the case when the secret pixel is black.

Again the exact strategies are those for which the cheaters choose α, β, γ and δ blocks from, respectively, blocks from groups A, B, C and D and place ones in such blocks. Such numbers are again constrained by $\alpha = 0, 1$, $\beta \leq n - 1$, $\gamma \leq 2^{n-1} - n - 1$ and $\delta = 0, 1$. The following table summarizes the information that the cheaters have about the remaining share.

Group of $n-1$ cheaters with a black secret.				
Group:	A	B	C	D
Blocks:	1	$n - 1$	$2^{n-1} - n - 1$	1
Columns (each block):	4	3	2	2
Type:	$\begin{bmatrix} 0 \\ 0 \\ \cdots \\ 0 \end{bmatrix}$	$\begin{bmatrix} 1 \\ 0 \\ \cdots \\ 0 \end{bmatrix}$	$\begin{bmatrix} 1 \\ 1 \\ \cdots \\ 0 \end{bmatrix}$	$\begin{bmatrix} 1 \\ 1 \\ \cdots \\ 1 \end{bmatrix}$
0 in remaining share:	2	1	1	1
1 in remaining share:	2	1	1	1

With a black secret pixel the constraint on the total number of ones in the fake share becomes

$$4\alpha + 3\beta + 2\gamma + 2\delta = 2^{n-1} + 1. \tag{4}$$

For a given exact strategy the number of black subpixels in the reconstructed secret pixel is given by:

$$4\alpha + 2(1 - \alpha) + 3\beta + (n - 1 - \beta) + 2\gamma + (2^{n-1} - n - 1 - \gamma) + 2\delta + (1 - \delta). \tag{5}$$

Again the above is due to the fact that the cheaters have filled with 1s α blocks of type A, β blocks of type B, γ blocks of type C and δ blocks of type D. When a block has been filled with 1 by the cheaters its contribution to the total number of black subpixels in the reconstructed pixel is given by the width of the block, while for the other blocks (filled with 0 by the cheaters) the contribution to the total number of black subpixels is given by the number of 1s in the honest share.

Equation (5) can be simplified to

$$2^{n-1} + 1 + 2\alpha + 2\beta + \gamma + \delta. \tag{6}$$

As for the white secret, we distinguish 4 possible cases and for each of them we show that any exact strategy does not allow the cheaters to cheat with probability 1.

case 1: $\alpha = 0, \delta = 0$. Equation (4) becomes $3\beta + 2\gamma = 2^{n-1} + 1$. This is impossible for β even but for β odd the cheaters can get an exact strategy by choosing $\gamma = 2^{n-2} - \frac{3\beta - 1}{2}$. The number of ones in the reconstructed secret pixel, given by Equation (6), is:

$$2^{n-1} + 1 + 2\beta + 2^{n-2} - \frac{3}{2}\beta + \frac{1}{2} = 3 \cdot 2^{n-2} + \frac{3}{2} + \frac{\beta}{2}$$

which is always strictly greater than $3 \cdot 2^{n-2} + 1$ and thus the reconstructed pixel cannot be classified as white (i.e. the honest participant cannot be fooled).

case 2: $\alpha = 0, \delta = 1$. Equation (4) becomes $3\beta + 2\gamma + 2 = 2^{n-1} + 1$ which is equivalent to $3\beta + 2\gamma = 2^{n-1} - 1$. This is impossible for β even but for β odd the cheaters can choose $\gamma = 2^{n-2} - \frac{3\beta + 1}{2}$. The number of ones in the reconstructed secret pixel, given by Equation (6), is:

$$2^{n-1} + 1 + 2\beta + 2^{n-2} - \frac{3}{2}\beta - \frac{1}{2} + 1 = 3 \cdot 2^{n-2} + \frac{3}{2} + \frac{\beta}{2}$$

which is always strictly greater than $3 \cdot 2^{n-2} + 1$ and thus the reconstructed pixel cannot be classified as white (i.e. the honest participant cannot be fooled).

case 3: $\alpha = 1, \delta = 0$. Equation (4) becomes $4 + 3\beta + 2\gamma = 2^{n-1} + 1$ which is equivalent to $3\beta + 2\gamma = 2^{n-1} - 3$. This is impossible for β even but for β odd the cheaters can choose $\gamma = 2^{n-2} - \frac{3\beta + 3}{2}$. The number of ones in the reconstructed secret pixel, given by Equation (6), is:

$$2^{n-1} + 1 + 2 + 2\beta + 2^{n-2} - \frac{3}{2}\beta - \frac{3}{2} = 3 \cdot 2^{n-2} + \frac{3}{2} + \frac{\beta}{2}$$

which is always strictly greater than $3 \cdot 2^{n-2} + 1$ and thus the reconstructed pixel cannot be classified as white (i.e. the honest participant cannot be fooled).

case 4: $\alpha = 1, \delta = 1$. Equation (4) becomes $4 + 3\beta + 2\gamma + 2 = 2^{n-1} + 1$ which is equivalent to $3\beta + 2\gamma = 2^{n-1} - 5$. This is impossible for β even but for β odd the cheaters can choose $\gamma = 2^{n-2} - \frac{3\beta + 5}{2}$. The number of ones in the reconstructed secret pixel, given by Equation (6), is:

$$2^{n-1} + 1 + 2 + 2\beta + 2^{n-2} - \frac{3}{2}\beta - \frac{5}{2} + 1 = 3 \cdot 2^{n-2} + \frac{3}{2} + \frac{\beta}{2}$$

which is always strictly greater than $3 \cdot 2^{n-2} + 1$ and thus the reconstructed pixel cannot be classified as white (i.e. the honest participant cannot be fooled).

Thus we can conclude that no exact strategy can fool the honest participant also when the secret pixel is black.

4   Conclusions

We have considered the problem of cheating in visual cryptography. We have provided a formal definition of cheating and $(2, n)$-threshold schemes which are robust against cheaters. To our knowledge the problem of cheating in visual cryptography has been considered only in this paper and in [10]; many open problems remain. For example one can provide (k, n)-threshold cheating-immune visual cryptography schemes for any k; or one could study the minimal pixel expansion or the best contrast of cheating immune schemes. Another interesting question is the difference between the power of a group of cheaters that is able to reconstruct the secret and the power of a group of cheaters that is not able to reconstruct the secret. In this paper, since we considered $(2, n)$-threshold schemes, any coalition of cheaters is a qualified set and thus is able to reconstruct the secret.

References

1. G. R. Blakley. Safeguarding Cryptographic keys, in *AFIPS Conference Proceedings*, vol. 48, 1979, pp. 313–317.
2. G. R. Blakley and C. Meadows. Security of Ramp Schemes, *Lecture Notes in Computer Science*, n. 196 (1985), 242–268 (CRYPTO '84).
3. M. Ben-Or, S. Goldwasser, and A. Wigderson. Completeness Theorems for Non-Cryptographic Fault-Tolerant Distributed Computation, in *Proceedings of STOC '88*, 1988, pp. 1–10.
4. M. Carpentieri. A perfect threshold secret sharing scheme to identify cheaters, *Designs, Codes, and Cryptography* n. 5 (1995), 183–187.
5. M. Carpentieri, A. De Santis, and U. Vaccaro. Size of shares and probability of cheating in threshold schemes, *Lecture Notes in Computer Science*, n. 765 (1993), 118–125 (EUROCRYPT '93).
6. D. Chaum. C. Crépeau, and I. Damgård. Multiparty Unconditionally Secure Protocols, in *Proceedings of STOC '88*, 1988, pp. 11–19.
7. B. Chor, S. Goldwasser, S. Micali, and B. Awerbach. Verifiable Secret Sharing and Achieving Simultaneity in Presence of Faults, in *Proceedings of FOCS '85*, 1985, pp. 383–395.
8. P. D'Arco, W. Kishimoto, and D. Stinson. Properties and Constraints of Cheating-Immune Secret Sharing Scheme, to appear in *Discrete Applied Mathematics*.
9. P. Feldman. Non-interactive and Information Theoretic Secure Verifiable Secret Sharing, in *Proceedings of FOCS '87*, 1987, pp. 427–437.
10. G. Horng, T. Chen, D.-S. Tsai. Cheating in Visual Cryptography, *Designs, Codes and Cryptography*, n. 38 (2006), 219–236.
11. J. Pieprzyk and X. M. Zhang. Cheating Prevention in Secret Sharing over $GF(P^t)$, *Lecture Notes in Computer Science*, n. 2247 (2001), 79–90 (INDOCRYPT '01).
12. J. Pieprzyk and X. M. Zhang. Constructions of Cheating Immune Secret Sharing, *Lecture Notes in Computer Science*, n. 2288 (2001), 226–243 (ICISC '01).
13. M. Naor and A. Shamir, Visual Cryptography. In *Advances in Cryptology – EUROCRYPT '94*, LNCS 950, pp. 1–12, 1995.
14. T. Rabin and M. Ben-Or. Verifiable Secret Sharing and Multiparty Protocols with Honest Majority, in *Proceedings of STOC '89*, 1989, pp. 73–85.

15. A. Shamir. How to Share a Secret, *Communications of the ACM*, n. 22 (1979), 612–613.
16. D. R. Stinson. An Explication of Secret Sharing Schemes, *Designs, Codes and Cryptography*, n. 2 (1992), 357–390.
17. D. R. Stinson and R. Wei. Unconditionally Secure Proactive Secret Sharing Scheme with Combinatorial Structures. *Lecture Notes in Computer Science*, n. 1758 (2000), 200–214 (SAC '99).
18. M. Tompa and H. Woll. How to Share a Secret with Cheaters, *Journal of Cryptology*, n. 1 (1988), 133–138.
19. X. M. Zhang and J. Pieprzyk. Cheating Immune Secret Sharing, *Lecture Notes in Computer Science*, n. 2229 (2001), 144–149 (ICICS '01).

Rational Secret Sharing, Revisited

S. Dov Gordon and Jonathan Katz[*]

Dept. of Computer Science, University of Maryland, College Park, MD, USA
{gordon, jkatz}@cs.umd.edu

Abstract. We consider the problem of secret sharing among n rational players. This problem was introduced by Halpern and Teague (STOC 2004), who claim that a solution is *impossible* for $n = 2$ but show a solution for the case $n \geq 3$. Contrary to their claim, we show a protocol for rational secret sharing among $n = 2$ players; our protocol extends to the case $n \geq 3$, where it is simpler than the Halpern-Teague solution and also offers a number of other advantages. We also show how to avoid the continual involvement of the dealer, in either our own protocol or that of Halpern and Teague.

Our techniques extend to the case of rational players trying to securely compute an arbitrary function, under certain assumptions on the utilities of the players.

1 Introduction

The classical problem of *t-out-of-n secret sharing* [13,2] involves a "dealer" D who wishes to entrust a secret s to a group of n players $P_1, \ldots, P_n$ so that (1) any group of t or more players can reconstruct the secret without further intervention of the dealer, yet (2) any group of fewer than t players has no information about the secret. As an example, consider the scheme due to Shamir [13]: assume the secret s lies in a finite field $\mathbb{F}$, with $|\mathbb{F}| > n$. The dealer chooses a random polynomial $f(x)$ of degree at most $t - 1$ subject to the constraint $f(0) = s$, and gives the "share" $f(i)$ to player P_i (for $i = 1, \ldots, n$). Any set of t players can recover $f(x)$ (and hence s) by broadcasting their shares and interpolating the polynomial; furthermore, no set of fewer than t players can deduce any information about s.

The implicit assumption above is that at least t players are willing to cooperate and pool their shares[1] when it is time to recover the secret; equivalently, at least t players are *honest* but up to $n - t$ players may be arbitrarily *malicious*. Halpern and Teague [7] consider a scenario in which players are neither completely honest nor arbitrarily malicious, but instead all players are assumed to be *rational* (however, up to $n - t$ players may be unavailable at the time the secret is to be

---

[*] This research was supported by NSF Trusted Computing grants #0310499 and #0310751; NSF CAREER award #0447075; and US-Israel Binational Science Foundation grant #2004240.
[1] We assume adversarial behavior is limited to refusal to cooperate, and ignore the case that a player reports an incorrect share. In the present context, reporting an incorrect share is easily prevented by having the dealer sign the shares.

R. De Prisco and M. Yung (Eds.): SCN 2006, LNCS 4116, pp. 229–241, 2006.
© Springer-Verlag Berlin Heidelberg 2006

recovered). Depending on the utility functions of the players, Shamir's protocol may no longer succeed in this scenario [7]. Specifically, assume that all players prefer to learn the secret above all else, but otherwise prefer that the fewest number of other players learn the secret. (We will treat the utilities of the players more precisely later in the paper.) Given these utility functions, no player has any incentive to reveal their share. Consider P_1: if strictly fewer than $t-1$ other players reveal their shares to the rest of the group, then no one learns the secret regardless of whether P_1 reveals his share or not. If more than $t-1$ players reveal their shares, then everyone learns the secret and P_1's actions again have no effect. On the other hand, if *exactly* $t-1$ other players reveal their shares, then P_1 learns the secret (using his share) but P_1 can prevent other players from learning the secret by *not* publicly revealing his share.

Let t, n be as above, and let $t^* \geq t$ denote the number of players present when the secret is to be reconstructed. Given the above discussion, we can thus conclude the following about the game-theoretic equilibria of "standard" Shamir secret sharing in the above situation (definitions of Nash equilibria and weakly dominating strategies are given in Section 2):

- For any t, n, t^*, it is a Nash equilibrium for no one to reveal their share.
- If $t^* > t$, it is a Nash equilibrium for all t^* participating players to reveal their shares. However, as discussed above, it is a weakly dominating strategy for each player *not* to reveal his share; thus, the Nash equilibrium likely to be reached is the one mentioned earlier in which no one reveals their share.
- If $t^* = t$, then having all t^* participating players reveal their shares is not even a Nash equilibrium, since each player can profitably deviate by not revealing his share.

Thus, Shamir's protocol with the trivial reconstruction procedure does not suffice in the presence of rational players. Does there exist *any* protocol for reconstructing the secret in which it is in rational players' best interests to follow the protocol? Generalizing the argument above, Halpern and Teague rule out any protocol terminating in a *fixed* number of rounds. (Essentially, the above argument is applied to the last round and then backwards induction is used.) This leaves open the possibility of *probabilistic* protocols without a fixed upper bound on their round complexity, and indeed Halpern and Teague show the existence of such protocols for $t, n \geq 3$. In contrast, they claim a solution is *impossible* for $n = 2$ even if probabilistic protocols are allowed.

1.1   Our Results

We revisit the question of rational secret sharing, in the model of Halpern and Teague [7]. As perhaps our most surprising result, we show a simple, probabilistic protocol for $n = 2$ parties to reconstruct a shared secret, thus disproving the claim of Halpern and Teague mentioned earlier. Interestingly, the *proof* given by Halpern and Teague appears to be correct; the problem is that their *assumptions* regarding the types of protocols that might be used are too restrictive (and are not implied by the model). By relaxing their assumptions in a manner consistent with the model of rational secret sharing they introduce, we are able to circumvent their impossibility result.

Our protocol generalizes in a straightforward way to the case of $n \geq 3$ and arbitrary t. Although Halpern and Teague also claim a general solution of this sort, our solution is much simpler. Furthermore, for $n > 3$ our solution has a number of advantages as compared with the solution offered by Halpern and Teague; perhaps most importantly, our solution eliminates a second (undesirable) equilibrium that is present in the Halpern-Teague protocol. Other advantages of our approach are summarized in Section 3.3.

Both the Halpern-Teague protocol and our protocol (as initially described) require the continual, periodic involvement of the dealer. At best, this is inconvenient; at worst, this calls into question the motivation for the problem in the first place. We show in Section 4 an intuitively simple way to avoid the involvement of the dealer (after the initial share distribution phase) that applies in all scenarios considered here.

As in [7], our techniques extend to the more general case of rational players trying to securely compute an arbitrary function of their inputs, under certain assumptions on the utilities of the players. See Section 5 for further details.

1.2   Related Work

There has been much interest of late in bridging cryptography (in which guarantees are provided in the face of worst-case adversarial behavior) and game theory (which concerns itself only with rational deviations). A point to bear in mind is that neither the cryptographic or the game-theoretic model is strictly stronger than the other: typical cryptographic protocols tolerate arbitrary malicious behavior under the assumption that some fraction of the players will follow the protocol exactly as specified; game-theoretic protocols are designed to tolerate "only" rational behavior but do not assume any completely honest players.

Besides the work of Halpern and Teague, the most relevant prior work is the recent sequence of papers by Lepinski, et al. [9,10] and Izmalkov, et al. [8]. Lepinski, Micali, Peikert, and Shelat [9] show a protocol for *completely fair secure function evaluation* (SFE), in which all players receive output if any player receives output, even if up to $n - 1$ players are malicious. In "standard" communication networks this is known to be impossible [3], and therefore Lepinski, et al. rely on the physical assumption of "secure envelopes" (see the discussion in [9] for the exact properties these should satisfy) to achieve their result. They then show how to use any protocol for completely fair SFE to implement *cheap talk* in the presence of malicious coalitions; basically, this enables players to reach a correlated equilibrium without having to rely on any external trusted party.

The work of Lepinski, Micali, and Shelat [10] and Izmalkov, Micali, and Lepinski [8] deals (directly or indirectly) with mechanisms for preventing coalitions in the first place. More specifically, these works are concerned with eliminating covert (e.g., steganographic) channels in the secure computation protocol itself so as to prevent signaling between players. Again, they achieve this by relying on physical assumptions (secure envelopes and, in the case of [8], ballot boxes) in addition to standard communication channels. A consequence of the work of Izmalkov, et al. (indeed, the main motivation for their work) is a protocol Π for securely implementing any mediated game Γ such that (informally) any equilibrium in Γ corresponds to an equilibrium in Π, and vice versa.

Comparison to our work. The work of Lepinski, et al. [9] as well as that of Izmalkov, et al. [8] both offer different solutions to the problems we consider here. Specifically:

- Completely fair SFE [9] guarantees (roughly speaking) that all players learn the output if any player learns the output. This clearly implies a solution for rational secret sharing (even in the presence of collusion), and can also be used to solve the problem of rational SFE[2] under certain assumptions on player utilities.
- Since rational secret sharing can be implemented as a mediated game, the work of [8] gives a solution to the problem (without any mediator). Their work is in fact much more general, as it implies a protocol for rational SFE for arbitrary player utilities and even in the presence of coalitions.

The main difference in our work is that we give intuitively-simple and/or very efficient protocols at the expense of providing weaker guarantees. Specifically, we focus only on single-player deviations (and do not handle collusion), and also make specific assumptions regarding the utilities of the players. Under these assumptions, our protocol for general secure function evaluation in Section 5 can be viewed as either a weak form of rational SFE, or completely fair SFE in the presence of rational (rather than arbitrarily malicious) parties.

An additional important difference between our work and that of [9,10,8] is that we rely on weaker assumptions with respect to the model of communication. Instead of relying on "secure envelopes" and "ballot boxes" as in [9,10,8] — which seem to be difficult primitives to realize unless parties are physically co-located — our solutions rely on standard communication channels with the exception that, as in [7], we assume *simultaneous broadcast* whereby each party broadcasts a message at the same time. (Equivalently, we do not allow "rushing.") Whether one finds the assumption of simultaneous broadcast realistic or not, we note that it is a strictly *weaker* assumption than secure envelopes or ballot boxes since simultaneous broadcast can be constructed from either of the latter but not vice versa.

Concurrent work. Concurrently and independently of our own work, Abraham, et al. [1] and Lysyanskaya and Triandopoulos [11] consider problems related to those considered here. Abraham, et al. define a notion of resistance to *coalitions* of rational players and show a coalition-resistant protocol; we note that our protocols are resistant to coalitions as well. Lysyanskaya and Triandopoulos examine the case of "mixed" security when *both* arbitrarily malicious and rational players might be present. Both papers also show, under certain conditions, how protocols can be designed without exact knowledge of players' utilities (though

---

[2] There are numerous definitions of rational SFE, and so everything we say in this section is somewhat informal.

utilities are still assumed to have a certain form). Interestingly (and somewhat serendipitously!), both those works as well as our own all rely on essentially the same underlying techniques.

2   Definitions for Rational Secret Sharing

We briefly review the model of rational secret sharing we assume in this paper. Our model is intended to match the model used by Halpern and Teague, though there are many details they do not make explicit.

As discussed earlier, we have a dealer D holding a secret s, and n players $P_1, \ldots, P_n$. There is also a threshold $t \leq n$, known to all players, which is fixed at the outset. A protocol proceeds in a sequence of *iterations*, where each iteration may consist of multiple *communication rounds*. At the beginning of each iteration, D distributes some information (privately) to each of the n players; at this point, no subset of fewer than t players should have any information about s. During an iteration, the dealer does not take part in the protocol. Instead, some set of $t^* \geq t$ players, all of whom are assumed to be rational, run the protocol amongst themselves by simultaneously broadcasting messages in a series of rounds. (Halpern and Teague additionally allow private communication between the players but we do not need this.) For simplicity, we assume the same set of t^* players runs the protocol in every iteration. At the end of an iteration, the protocol either terminates or proceeds to the next iteration. We assume the dealer is honest, and follows the protocol as specified. To rule out trivial protocols, we require that if $t^* \geq t$ players follow the protocol in each iteration, then the secret is eventually reconstructed (with probability 1).

We stress that broadcast in a given round is assumed to occur simultaneously for all players; that is, we do not allow "rushing" as in the standard literature on secure multi-party computation. Rational secret sharing is easily seen to be impossible if rushing is allowed: all players will simply wait to see what other players do, and no one will ever broadcast anything.

In the above description, as in [7], the dealer is assumed to be involved at the beginning of each iteration. In Section 4, we show that it is possible for the dealer to be involved only once at the beginning of the protocol.

We let σ_i denote the (possibly randomized) strategy employed by player P_i, and let $\boldsymbol{\sigma} = (\sigma_1, \ldots, \sigma_n)$ denote the vector of players' strategies. Following standard game-theoretic notation, we let $(\sigma_i', \boldsymbol{\sigma}_{-i}) \overset{\text{def}}{=} (\sigma_1, \ldots, \sigma_{i-1}, \sigma_i', \sigma_{i+1}, \ldots, \sigma_n)$; that is, $(\sigma_i', \boldsymbol{\sigma}_{-i})$ denotes the strategy vector $\boldsymbol{\sigma}$ with P_i's strategy changed to σ_i'.

Let $\mu_i(o)$ denote the utility of player P_i for the outcome o. For a particular outcome o of the protocol, we let $\delta_i(o)$ be a bit denoting whether or not P_i learns the secret, and let $\mathsf{num}(o) = \sum_i \delta_i(o)$; i.e., $\mathsf{num}(o)$ is simply the number of players who learn the secret. Following [7], we make the following assumptions about the utility functions of the players:

- $\delta_i(o) > \delta_i(o') \Rightarrow \mu_i(o) > \mu_i(o')$.
- If $\delta_i(o) = \delta_i(o')$, then $\mathsf{num}(o) < \mathsf{num}(o') \Rightarrow \mu_i(o) > \mu_i(o')$.

That is, player P_i first prefers outcomes in which he learns the secret; as long as δ_i remains constant, player P_i prefers strategies in which the fewest number of other players learn the secret. We let $U_i(\boldsymbol{\sigma})$ denote the expected value of the utility of P_i under strategy vector $\boldsymbol{\sigma}$, and assume that rational players wish to maximize this value.

Our notion of a *protocol* corresponds to a *game* along with a prescribed strategy vector $\boldsymbol{\sigma}$. As in [7], we are interested in protocols whose prescribed strategy vector $\boldsymbol{\sigma}$ corresponds to a Nash equilibrium that survives iterated deletion of weakly dominated strategies. We review these definitions briefly, and refer the reader to [12,7] for more extensive discussion.

Definition 1. *A vector of strategies $\boldsymbol{\sigma}$ is a* Nash *equilibrium if the following holds for all i: for any $\sigma_i' \neq \sigma_i$, we have $U_i(\sigma_i', \boldsymbol{\sigma}_{-i}) \leq U_i(\boldsymbol{\sigma})$.*

That is, given that all other players are following $\boldsymbol{\sigma}_{-i}$, there is no incentive for P_i to deviate and follow any strategy other than σ_i.

In general, multiple Nash equilibria may exist. An inherently "unstable" Nash equilibrium (i.e., one unlikely to be reached) is one in which any of the players' strategies are *weakly dominated* by other strategies. Informally, a strategy σ_i of player P_i is weakly dominated by another strategy σ_i' if (1) P_i is sometimes better off playing σ_i' than playing σ_i, and (2) P_i is never worse off playing σ_i' than playing σ_i. Recalling the example from the introduction, say a secret is shared using t-out-of-n secret sharing (with $t < n$) and consider the strategy vector in which all n players reveal their shares. This is a Nash equilibrium: the secret is reconstructed even if any single player deviates. On the other hand, for each player P_i, revealing the share is weakly dominated by *not* revealing the share: if fewer than $t - 1$ other players or more than $t - 1$ other players reveal their shares, then nothing changes; if exactly $t - 1$ other player reveal their shares then P_i learns the secret but no one else does. Formal definitions follow.

Definition 2. *Let S_i denote a set of strategies for P_i, and let $S_{-i} \stackrel{\text{def}}{=} S_1 \times \cdots \times S_{i-1} \times S_{i+1} \cdots \times S_n$. A strategy $\sigma_i \in S_i$ is* weakly dominated by a strategy $\sigma_i' \in S_i$ *with respect to S_{-i} if (1) there exists a $\boldsymbol{\sigma}_{-i} \in S_{-i}$ such that $U_i(\sigma_i, \boldsymbol{\sigma}_{-i}) < U_i(\sigma_i', \boldsymbol{\sigma}_{-i})$ and (2) for all $\boldsymbol{\sigma}_{-i} \in S_{-i}$, it holds that $U_i(\sigma_i, \boldsymbol{\sigma}_{-i}) \leq U_i(\sigma_i', \boldsymbol{\sigma}_{-i})$.*

Strategy σ_i is weakly dominated with respect to S_{-i} *if there exists a $\sigma_i' \in S_i$ such that σ_i is weakly dominated by σ_i' with respect to S_{-i}.*

Definition 3. *Let $\mathsf{DOM}_i(S_1 \times \cdots \times S_n)$ denote the set of strategies in S_i that are weakly dominated with respect to S_{-i}. Let S_i^0 denote the initial set of allowable strategies of P_i. For all $k \geq 1$, define S_i^k inductively as $S_i^k \stackrel{\text{def}}{=} S_i^{k-1} \setminus \mathsf{DOM}_i(S_1^{k-1} \times \cdots \times S_n^{k-1})$. Let $S_i^\infty \stackrel{\text{def}}{=} \cap_k S_i^k$.*

We say σ_i survives iterated deletion of weakly dominated strategies if $\sigma_i \in S_i^\infty$.

3   Protocols for Rational Secret Sharing

We review the Halpern-Teague solution, and then describe our protocol. We conclude with some discussion of the relative merits of our approach.

3.1   The Halpern-Teague Solution

We provide a high-level overview of the solution of Halpern and Teague for 3-out-of-3 secret sharing. We later discuss how they propose to generalize their solution for $n > 3$ and $t \geq 3$.

The Halpern-Teague protocol in the 3-out-of-3 case proceeds as follows: at the beginning of each iteration, the dealer runs a fresh invocation of the Shamir secret-sharing scheme and sends the appropriate shares to each player. (Actually, a simpler additive secret-sharing scheme could also be used.) During an iteration, each player P_i flips a biased coin c_i which is equal to 1 with some probability α. The players then run what is essentially an information-theoretically secure multi-party computation protocol to compute the value $c^* = \bigoplus c_i$. (Here is where Halpern and Teague need to assume the existence of private channels between the players.) In particular, it is impossible for any player to cheat (except for aborting the protocol; see below), or to learn information about the $\{c_i\}$ values of the other parties that is not implied by c^*. If $c^* = c_i = 1$, player P_i broadcasts his share. If all shares are revealed, the secret is reconstructed and the protocol ends. If $c^* = 1$ and either no shares or exactly two shares are revealed, or if the secure computation of c^* was aborted, then all players refuse to run the protocol from then on (and so, effectively, the protocol is terminated). In any other case, players proceed to the next iteration.

Note that the secret is only reconstructed if $c_1 = c_2 = c_3 = 1$. Thus, assuming players act honestly, the expected number of iterations until the protocol terminates is α^{-3}.

To see intuitively why the above gives a Nash equilibrium, assume P_1, P_2 follow the protocol and consider whether P_3 should deviate. First note that there is no incentive for P_3 to bias c_3 to be 0 with higher probability, since when $c_3 = 0$ at least one of P_1, P_2 will not broadcast their shares in that iteration. There is also no incentive for P_3 to bias c_3 to be 1 with higher probability, either: although this may cause the secret to be reconstructed sooner, it will have no effect on P_3's utility. It is also easy to see that, given $c^* = 0$ or $c_3 = 0$, there is no incentive for P_3 to deviate from the protocol. Finally, when $c^* = c_3 = 1$, player P_3 does not know whether $c_1 = c_2 = 1$ (which occurs with probability $\frac{\alpha^2}{\alpha^2+(1-\alpha)^2}$) or $c_1 = c_2 = 0$ (which occurs with the remaining probability). Thus, if P_3 does not broadcast its share it runs the risk of having the protocol terminate without ever learning the secret. If α is set appropriately based on P_3's utility function, it can be shown that it is not in P_3's best interest to deviate.

For $n > 3$ and $t \geq 3$, Halpern and Teague suggest the following: of the $t^* \geq t$ players who are present, t players are designated. Players are split into 3 groups, such that there is at least one designated player in each group. One designated player in each group is chosen as a leader. The designated players send their shares to the leader of their group, and then the leaders run essentially the 3-out-of-3 solution described above. (When the leaders are supposed to broadcast, they broadcast the shares of all the players in their group in such a way that all t^* players can hear.)

Halpern and Teague also describe a solution for 2-out-of-n secret sharing for $n \geq 3$, but in this case they require that the number of participating players t^* is strictly greater than 2 (and so this solution does not satisfy the model as we have described it here).

3.2   Our Solution

Recall that Halpern and Teague claim that rational secret sharing is *impossible* when $n = 2$. In their impossibility proof, however, they implicitly assume that the dealer is limited to sending valid shares of the secret to the players at the beginning of each iteration. They therefore focus only on possible actions of the players *during* an iteration. We see no reason to impose any such restriction on the dealer's actions; note that the model, as described earlier, does not impose any such restriction. As we show in this section, once this assumption is removed a solution is possible even when $n = 2$, and things become simpler in the case of general t, n.

Specifically, consider the following protocol: say the dealer holds a secret s which lies in a *strict subset* S of a finite field $\mathbb{F}$ (if s lies in some field $\mathbb{F}'$, this is easy to achieve by taking a larger field $\mathbb{F}$ containing $\mathbb{F}'$ as a subfield). We assume players know S. At the beginning of each iteration, with probability β the dealer generates a random Shamir sharing of s, and with probability $1 - \beta$ the dealer generates a random Shamir sharing of an arbitrary element $\hat{s} \in \mathbb{F} \setminus S$; we describe how β is chosen below. These shares are distributed to the players. Note that no player can tell from their share whether the players were given a share of $\hat{s}$ or the true secret s.

During an iteration, the players simply broadcast their shares. If in any iteration some player does not broadcast his share, the other players all refuse to participate in all subsequent iterations (and, effectively, the protocol is terminated). Otherwise, all shares were broadcast and the players can reconstruct some value s'. If $s' \in S$ then the players know that this is the true secret, and can terminate the protocol successfully. If $s' \in \mathbb{F} \setminus S$, the players know this is an invalid secret and proceed to the next iteration.

Theorem 1. *For appropriate choice of β, the above protocol constitutes a Nash equilibrium for t-out-of-n secret sharing that survives iterated deletion of weakly dominated strategies.*

Proof. We first consider the case of $t = n = 2$, and then discuss how to generalize the proof for arbitrary t, n. It is not hard to see that the protocol is a Nash equilibrium for appropriate choice of β: Say P_2 acts according to the protocol and consider whether P_1 has any incentive to deviate. Without loss of generality, consider a deviation in the first iteration. The only possible deviation is for P_1 to refuse to broadcast his share. In this case, he learns the secret (while P_2 does not) with probability β, but with probability $1 - \beta$ he will never learn the secret.

Say P_1's utility is U^+ if he learns the secret but P_2 does not; U if both players learn the secret; and U^- if neither player learns the secret, where $U^+ > U > U^-$.

If P_1 follows the protocol, his expected utility is U. If P_1 deviates, his expected utility is $\beta \cdot U^+ + (1-\beta) \cdot U^-$. So as long as

$$U > \beta \cdot U^+ + (1-\beta) \cdot U^- ,$$

it is in P_1's best interest to follow the protocol. For appropriate $\beta \in (0,1)$, then, the strategy profile in which both parties follow the protocol is a Nash equilibrium.

It is immediate that the same analysis holds for general t, n, regardless of the number of participating players t^*.

We next prove that our protocol survives iterated deletion of weakly dominated strategies by showing that *no* strategies are weakly dominated. We again begin with the case $t = n = 2$. We show that for all deterministic strategies σ, σ' of P_1, there exist strategies τ, τ' of P_2 such that $U_1(\sigma, \tau) > U_1(\sigma', \tau)$ but $U_1(\sigma, \tau') < U_1(\sigma', \tau')$. This proves that all deterministic strategies of P_1 are incomparable, and so none are ever deleted (and thus no randomized strategies are deleted either).

Let $h_i(\sigma, \tau)$ denote the history of actions (by both players) through iteration i given the indicated strategies σ and τ, with $h_0(\sigma, \tau)$ denoting the empty (starting) history. Let $A_i(\sigma, \tau)$ denote the action taken by P_1 in iteration i, again for the indicated strategies. We say a player *cooperates* in some iteration if they reveal their share, and *defects* if they do not.

Now take arbitrary deterministic strategies $\sigma \neq \sigma'$ for P_1. Let τ^0 be a strategy of P_2 and $i \geq 1$ be an integer such that

$$h_{i-1}(\sigma, \tau^0) = h_{i-1}(\sigma', \tau^0) \tag{1}$$

but

$$A_i(\sigma, \tau^0) \neq A_i(\sigma', \tau^0); \tag{2}$$

i.e., iteration i is the first iteration in which the actions of P_1 differ. (Note that some such τ^0, i must exist or else $\sigma = \sigma'$.) Without loss of generality, assume $A_i(\sigma, \tau^0)$ is to defect and $A_i(\sigma', \tau^0)$ is to cooperate.

Consider the following strategy τ of P_2: (1) act identically to τ^0 through iteration $i - 1$; (2) in iteration i, defect; (3) in all subsequent iterations: if P_1 defected in iteration i, then cooperate; if P_1 cooperated in iteration i, defect. Since $A_i(\sigma, \tau) = A_i(\sigma, \tau^0) =$ "defect," it is fairly immediate that $U_1(\sigma, \tau) > U_1(\sigma', \tau)$.

Next consider the following strategy τ': (1) act identically to τ^0 through iteration $i - 1$; (2) in iteration i, cooperate; (3) in all subsequent iterations: if P_1 defected in iteration i, then defect; if P_1 cooperated in iteration i, cooperate. Exactly as when we argued earlier that our protocol was a Nash equilibrium, we have $U_1(\sigma, \tau') < U_1(\sigma', \tau')$.

The same argument extends to the case of general t, n, regardless of the number of participating players t^*. We simply replace τ^0 with a strategy profile of $n - 1$ strategies such that Equations (1) and (2) above are still valid, and then define τ and τ' as above, but modifying the strategies of all other players. ∎

We remark that when $t^* = t$ our protocol has no additional Nash equilibrium which is preferred, by any player, to the prescribed equilibrium.

3.3 Discussion

Our approach has a number of advantages as compared to [7]:

- Most obvious, we circumvent their impossibility result for the case $n = 2$. We also show an admissible solution for the 2-out-of-n case.
- Our protocol is (in our opinion) much simpler than the Halpern-Teague protocol. This is true for all settings of t, n, but is especially true for the case of $n > 3, t \geq 3$ where the Halpern-Teague protocol requires players to somehow delegate specific roles and select group leaders.
- Our protocol requires only a broadcast channel, in contrast to the Halpern-Teague protocol which relies on private channels in addition to broadcast.
- At least for the case $t^* = t$ (which is always the case when $t = n$), our protocol has no "undesirable" Nash equilibria. This is in contrast to the Halpern-Teague solution for general n, where there is the undesirable equilibrium in which the three "group leaders" pool the shares they receive from all the designated players and reconstruct the secret only amongst themselves.

4   Removing the Dealer

A drawback of both our protocol (as described in the previous section) as well as that of Halpern and Teague is that the dealer must be involved at the beginning of every iteration. It would be much nicer to have a solution that works exactly like standard secret sharing, where the dealer is involved only once at the beginning of the protocol.

We sketch here a conceptually simple (though inefficient) way to avoid continual involvement of the dealer while still ensuring that parties eventually reconstruct the secret with probability 1. Our idea applies both to our protocol and that of Halpern and Teague, but for simplicity we describe it in the context of our protocol only. The protocol proceeds as follows:

Setup: To share a secret s, the dealer prepares a valid t-out-of-n Shamir sharing $\{s_i\}$ of s. The dealer also generates a signature σ_i on each share s_i with respect to a publicly-known verification key PK (alternately, PK can simply be sent to each player). The dealer sends (s_i, σ_i) to player P_i.

The protocol: At the beginning of each iteration, the players proceed as follows:

1. The t^* participating parties run a secure computation protocol [15,6,5] secure against one malicious player. The protocol computes the following probabilistic functionality:
   - Each party inputs the values (s_i, σ_i) received from the dealer. The functionality checks that each σ_i is a valid signature on s_i (with respect to the dealer's public key PK), and aborts if this is not the case.

- The $t^* \geq t$ input shares define a secret s. With probability β, the functionality generates a fresh t-out-of-n Shamir sharing $\{s_i'\}$ of s, and each player P_i receives output s_i'.
- With probability $1 - \beta$, the functionality generates a fresh t-out-of-n Shamir sharing $\{s_i'\}$ of a bogus secret $\hat{s} \in \mathbb{F} \setminus S$, and each player P_i receives output s_i'.

2. If cheating is detected in the secure computation protocol above (i.e., the secure computation protocol is aborted), then parties terminate the overall protocol without ever reconstructing the secret.

3. Next, parties proceed as in the previous section; specifically, each player P_i broadcasts the output s_i' they received from the secure computation protocol.[3] If this enables reconstruction of a secret $s \in S$, the protocol terminates and the true secret has been reconstructed. If some player refused to broadcast their output share, then parties terminate the protocol without reconstructing the secret. In any other case, players erase the $\{s_i'\}$ and proceed to the next iteration (using (s_i, σ_i) as before).

A subtlety (which applies also in the following section) is the question of whether security of the secure computation protocol used above should hold *information-theoretically* or *computationally*. In the former case, an argument similar to that used in the previous section shows that — under appropriate conditions on β — the above protocol is a Nash equilibrium surviving iterated domination of weakly dominated strategies. To implement such a solution, however, we need the additional assumption of private channels between the players.

If a computationally-secure protocol is used, one way to proceed is to work in a concrete setting: that is, assume all players are limited to running for at most t steps (in some fixed computational model); assume the protocol is secure (defined appropriately) except with some (small) probability ϵ against adversaries running in time t; and then modify the analysis appropriately. Rigorously formalizing this is left for future work. See [11] for a slightly different approach.

5   General Secure Function Evaluation

The techniques outlined above generalize to the case of the secure computation of an arbitrary function f. In this sense, they yield a protocol for a weak notion of completely fair SFE [9] requiring that (1) all players are rational; and (2) players' utility functions are such that they all prefer to learn the output. (In contrast, the work of [9] shows a protocol for completely fair SFE tolerating malicious

---

[3] Actually, to prevent players from broadcasting a modified value for s_i', it is necessary to have the functionality authenticate the $\{s_i'\}$ in some way. There are many ways to do this. Perhaps the conceptually-simplest solution is to have the dealer also distribute shares of his secret signing key in a t-out-of-n manner among the players. Then the functionality can also generate valid dealer signatures on the $\{s_i'\}$ (the iteration number should also be signed to prevent replay of an earlier output value). We omit any further details for simplicity.

players, but under a stronger assumption on the available communication. See Section 1.2.) We also assume (as in [7,1,11]) that players prefer that their own inputs remain private (other than what is leaked by evaluation of f).

To compute the (possibly randomized) single-output function f:

1. Let f' be the following (multi-output, randomized) function: on inputs x_1, $\ldots$, x_n, compute $y \leftarrow f(x_1, \ldots, x_n)$. Then generate a random t-out-of-n Shamir sharing $(s_1, \ldots, s_n)$ of the result y, and give output s_i to player P_i.

2. Players run a secure computation protocol for f', and obtain outputs $s_1, \ldots,$ s_n. If this protocol is aborted, all players terminate the entire protocol and the output is never reconstructed.

3. As in the previous section, players compute a functionality that takes as input[4] $(s_1, \ldots, s_n)$ and, with probability β computes a random Shamir sharing $\{s'_i\}$ of the value y these shares define, and with probability $1 - \beta$ computes a random Shamir sharing $\{s'_i\}$ of some default value not in the range of f. Each player P_i receives output s'_i. If this protocol is aborted, all players terminate the entire protocol and the output is never reconstructed.

4. Players simultaneously broadcast the s'_i and reconstruct the value s' these shares define. If some player did not broadcast a (valid) share, then all players terminate the protocol and do not participate in any future iterations. If s' is in the range of f then $y = s'$ is the desired output and the protocol is done; in any other case, players proceed to the next iteration.

The protocol can be suitably generalized for the case where f outputs a vector of values, one for each player.

We remark that, as in standard formulations of secure multi-party computation, players who choose not to follow the protocol may change their "true" inputs to an arbitrary other value. (I.e., a player P_i with "true" input x_i may cause $f(x_1, \ldots, x'_i, \ldots, x_n)$ to be evaluated for arbitrary x'_i.) For rational players, this may occur if a player would prefer to change his input value even if a completely incorruptible third party were to evaluate f based on inputs given to it by the players. Shoham and Tennenholtz [14] define the class of *NCC functions* and argue that if f is an NCC function then no rational player has any incentive to modify their inputs. It seems to us, however, that there are some subtle problems with the way NCC functions are defined there. We leave further exploration of this issue for future study.

6 Conclusions

We have provided a new approach to rational secret sharing and secure computation that improves, in many respects, on an earlier solution of Halpern and Teague. Our work also offers an alternate approach to the generic (and more powerful) solutions of [9,8]: our protocols are simpler, and rely on weaker assumptions regarding the communication between players.

---

[4] As before, there is the issue of authenticating the shares $s_1, \ldots, s_n$ provided as input to this functionality. This can be handled in a similar manner as before.

Acknowledgments

We thank Silvio Micali for clarifications regarding the relationship between our work and [9,10,8], as well as for prompting us to think about using our techniques to obtain rational SFE.

References

1. I. Abraham, D. Dolev, R. Gonen, and J. Halpern. Distributed Computing Meets Game Theory: Robust Mechanisms for Rational Secret Sharing and Multiparty Computation. *25th ACM Symposium on Principles of Distributed Computing (PODC 2006)*, to appear.
2. G.R. Blakley. Safeguarding Cryptographic Keys. *National Computer Conference*, vol. 48, pp. 313–317, AFIPS Press, 1979.
3. R. Cleve. Limits on the Security of Coin Flips when Half the Processors are Faulty. *18th Annual ACM Symposium on Theory of Computing (STOC 1986)*.
4. D. Fudenberg and J. Tirole. *Game Theory*. MIT Press, 1991.
5. O. Goldreich. *Foundations of Cryptography, vol. 2: Basic Applications*, Cambridge University Press, 2004.
6. O. Goldreich, S. Micali, and A. Wigderson. How to Play any Mental Game or A Completeness Theorem for Protocols with Honest Majority. *19th Annual ACM Symposium on Theory of Computing (STOC 1987)*.
7. J. Halpern and V. Teague. Rational Secret Sharing and Multiparty Computation. *36th Annual ACM Symposium on Theory of Computing (STOC 2004)*.
8. S. Izmalkov, S. Micali, and M. Lepinski. Rational Secure Function Evaluation and Ideal Mechanism Design. *46th Annual IEEE Symposium on Foundations of Computer Science (FOCS 2005)*.
9. M. Lepinski, S. Micali, C, Peikert, and A. Shelat. Completely Fair SFE and Coalition-Safe Cheap Talk. *23rd ACM Symposium on Principles of Distributed Computing (PODC 2004)*.
10. M. Lepinski, S. Micali, and A. Shelat. Collusion-Free Protocols. *37th Annual ACM Symposium on Theory of Computing (STOC 2005)*.
11. A. Lysyanskaya and N. Triandopoulos. Rationality and Adversarial Behavior in Multi-Party Computation. *Advances in Cryptology — Crypto 2006*, to appear.
12. M.J. Osborne and A. Rubinstein. *A Course in Game Theory*. MIT Press, 1994.
13. A. Shamir. How to Share a Secret. *Comm. ACM*, 22(11): 612–613 (1979).
14. Y. Shoham and M. Tennenholtz. Non-Cooperative Computing: Boolean Functions with Correctness and Exclusivity. *Theoretical Computer Science* 343(1–2): 97–113 (2005).
15. A. C.-C. Yao. How to Generate and Exchange Secrets. *27th Annual IEEE Symposium on Foundations of Computer Science (FOCS 1986)*.

On the Security of HMAC and NMAC Based on HAVAL, MD4, MD5, SHA-0 and SHA-1 (Extended Abstract)*

Jongsung Kim[1,**], Alex Biryukov[2], Bart Preneel[1], and Seokhie Hong[3]

[1] ESAT/SCD-COSIC, Katholieke Universiteit Leuven,
Kasteelpark Arenberg 10, B-3001 Leuven-Heverlee, Belgium
{Kim.Jongsung, Bart.Preneel}@esat.kuleuven.be
[2] FDEF, Campus Limpertsberg, University of Luxembourg,
162 A, Avenue de la Faiencerie L-1511 Luxembourg
alex.biryukov@uni.lu
[3] Center for Information Security Technologies(CIST),
Korea University, Seoul, Korea
hsh@cist.korea.ac.kr

Abstract. HMAC is a widely used message authentication code and a pseudorandom function generator based on cryptographic hash functions such as MD5 and SHA-1. It has been standardized by ANSI, IETF, ISO and NIST. HMAC is proved to be secure as long as the compression function of the underlying hash function is a pseudorandom function. In this paper we devise two new distinguishers of the structure of HMAC, called *differential* and *rectangle distinguishers*, and use them to discuss the security of HMAC based on HAVAL, MD4, MD5, SHA-0 and SHA-1. We show how to distinguish HMAC with reduced or full versions of these cryptographic hash functions from a random function or from HMAC with a random function. We also show how to use our differential distinguisher to devise a forgery attack on HMAC. Our distinguishing and forgery attacks can also be mounted on NMAC based on HAVAL, MD4, MD5, SHA-0 and SHA-1.

1 Introduction

HMAC, which was designed by Bellare, Canetti and Krawczyk, is a standardized hash-based MAC algorithm that is widely used as a MAC algorithm and as a pseudorandom function generator [2]. HMAC takes a message of an arbitrary

---

* This work was supported in part by the Concerted Research Action (GOA) Ambiorics 2005/11 of the Flemish Government and by the European Commission through the IST Programme under Contract IST2002507932 ECRYPT and in part by the MIC(Ministry of Information and Communication), Korea, under the ITRC(Information Technology Research Center) support program supervised by the IITA(Institute of Information Technology Assessment).
** The first author was financed by a Ph.D grant of the Katholieke Universiteit Leuven and by the Korea Research Foundation Grant funded by the Korean Government(MOEHRD) (KRF-2005-213-D00077).

R. De Prisco and M. Yung (Eds.): SCN 2006, LNCS 4116, pp. 242–256, 2006.
© Springer-Verlag Berlin Heidelberg 2006

bit-length and hashes it with one secret key. For the same length of the message it calls the compression function of the underlying hash function additionally three more times than the iterated hash construction, i.e., the MD construction. For long messages, its efficiency is thus almost the same as the MD construction. Furthermore, cryptographic hash functions such as MD5 and SHA-1 can be used in HMAC, which are more efficient in software than block ciphers, and thus HMAC is typically faster than block cipher based MACs. HMAC is proved to be a pseudorandom function under the assumption that the compression function of the underlying hash function is a pseudorandom function [1] (note that the security proof of pseudorandomness provides the MAC security [3]). However, this does not guarantee the security of HMAC if it is instantiated with a specific cryptographic hash function such as MD5 or SHA-1. The recent attacks of Wang et al. [14,15,16,17,18] and Biham et al. [5,6] have undermined the confidence in the most popular collision resistant hash functions such as MD5 and SHA-1. However, it is widely assumed that these attacks have no impact on the security of MAC algorithms based on these hash functions such as HMAC since they use a keyed initial value.

This paper is the first work which presents a detailed analysis of distinguishing and forgery attacks on HMAC based on MD5, SHA-1 and other MDx-type hash functions. Our results allow to quantify to which extent the vulnerabilities of these hash functions carry over to the HMAC construction. This is achieved by the introduction of two novel distinguishers of the general structure of HMAC. We use a message pair which induces a collision in its corresponding MAC pair for designing *a differential distinguisher* of HMAC and also use a message quartet which induces two collisions in its corresponding MAC quartet for designing *a rectangle distinguisher* of HMAC. With these two distinguishers we discuss the security of HMAC based on HAVAL [19], MD4 [12], MD5 [13], SHA-0 [20] and SHA-1 [21].

First, we construct new differentials of the full 3-pass HAVAL and reduced MD5 to form rectangle distinguishers of HMAC, and we use them to distinguish HMAC with the full 3-pass HAVAL and reduced MD5 from HMAC with a random function. Second, we investigate how effectively the differentials of MD4, SHA-0 and SHA-1 found by Wang et al. [14,15,16,17,18] and Biham et al. [5,6] are applied to our differential and rectangle distinguishers in HMAC. After converting their differentials into our differential and rectangle distinguishers, we devise distinguishing and forgery attacks on HMAC based on reduced or full versions of MD4, SHA-0 and SHA-1. In particular, we show how to distinguish HMAC with the full SHA-0 and MD4 from HMAC with a random function and present a forgery attack on HMAC with the full MD4. See for details of the results Table 2 in Sect. 6 (the function h_2 and the probabilities $\hat{p}$ and q in Table 2 will be defined in the following sections). Our distinguishing and forgery attacks can be mounted on NMAC based on HAVAL, MD4, MD5, SHA-0 and SHA-1 with the same complexity.

2   Description of HMAC

HMAC [2] applies in both its inner and outer parts the iterated MD construction of a hash function H given a compression function h, $H(IV, M) =$

$h(\cdots h(h(IV, M^1), M^2) \cdots, M^n)$, where IV is a l-bit fixed initial value and M is an arbitrary-length message which is padded to a multiple of b-bit and divided into n b-bit blocks $M^1 || M^2 || \cdots || M^n$ (note that the outputs of functions h and H are l-bit strings).

$$\textbf{HMAC}(K, M) = H(IV, (K \oplus opad) || H(IV, (K \oplus ipad) || M))$$
$$= h(h(IV, (K \oplus opad)), H(h(IV, (K \oplus ipad)), M)), \quad (1)$$

where K is the secret key, $opad$, $ipad$ are constants and $|K \oplus opad| = |K \oplus ipad| = b$. If HMAC takes a one-block message M, it can be expressed as

$$\textbf{HMAC}(K, M) = h(h(IV, (K \oplus opad)), h(h(IV, (K \oplus ipad)), M)). \quad (2)$$

In order to facilitate the description of our analysis of HMAC we denote the four compression functions h in (2) by h_1, h_2, h_3 and h_4, and the four functions in (1) by h_1, H_2, h_3 and h_4. See Fig. 1 for a schematic description of HMAC with this notation. Note that the outputs of H_2 and h_2 are padded to a b-bit string to be inserted into h_4.

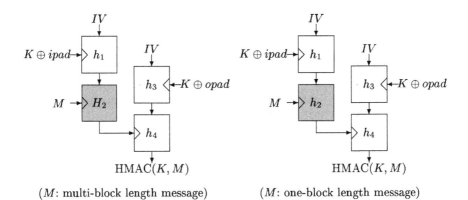

$(M$: multi-block length message) $(M$: one-block length message)

Fig. 1. A schematic description of HMAC

In practice the function h can be replaced by the compression function of cryptographic hash functions such as HAVAL [19], MD4 [12], MD5 [13], SHA-0 [20], SHA-1 [21] and so on.

3   Some General Attacks on HMAC

Using the birthday paradox we can induce a general distinguishing attack on HMAC as follows [11]:

1. Collect $2^{l/2}$ randomly chosen messages with a b-bit length, denoted M_i, and ask for their MAC values, denoted C_i.

2. Find message pairs M_j and M_k such that $C_j = C_k$.
3. For each of (M_j, M_k) pairs such that $C_j = C_k$, ask for a MAC pair of $M_j||P$ and $M_k||P$, where P is some non-empty string. If there is at least one MAC pair that collides in this step, output the MAC algorithm = HMAC.

This attack requires about $2^{l/2}$ messages and works with a probability of 0.63 by the birthday paradox when the MAC algorithm is HMAC (this is due to the fact that if there exists at least one message pair (M_j, M_k) such that their outputs of h_2 or H_2 are same, this attack always works). This attack can also easily be converted into a general forgery attack on HMAC. Once we get a MAC pair that collides in Step 3, we again ask for the corresponding MAC of $M_j||P||P'$, denoted C, where P' is some non-empty string. We can then construct a forgery, i.e., a new message $M_k||P||P'$ with a valid MAC, i.e., C with the same success rate.

These general attacks make distinguishing and forgery attacks on HMAC which require more than $2^{l/2}$ message queries have not much advantage. We thus consider attacks of distinguishing HMAC from a random function, and forgery attacks on HMAC which work with a data complexity of less than $2^{l/2}$ messages. In addition to these two kinds of attacks, we also consider attacks of distinguishing instantiated HMAC (by existing hash functions) from HMAC with a random function. In these attacks it does not matter whether or not they require more than $2^{l/2}$ message queries, since there does not exist a general attack based on the birthday paradox which can distinguish HMAC with existing hash functions from HMAC with a random function. For the clarification we denote the first and second distinguishing attacks by *distinguishing-R* and *distinguishing-H attacks*, respectively. The distinguishing-R attack is useful when the cryptanalyst wants to check whether output strings are produced from HMAC (in this case, the cryptanalyst does not know whether the output producing algorithm is HMAC), while the distinguishing-H attack is useful when the cryptanalyst wants to check which cryptographic hash function is embedded in HMAC (in this case, the cryptanalyst somehow already knew that the output producing algorithm is HMAC, for instance, by the distinguishing-R attack, but does not know the underlying hash function in HMAC).

4   Distinguishers of HMAC

In this section we present two distinguishers of the general structure of HMAC, which can lead to distinguishing or forgery attacks if HMAC is instantiated with some cryptographic hash function with a low difference propagation. These two distinguishers, called *differential* and *rectangle distinguishers*, are both built based on internal collisions. We focus on HMAC with one-block messages, which is the main target in our attacks.

4.1   Differential Distinguisher of HMAC

By using MAC collisions we construct a differential distinguisher of HMAC. It works as follows:

- Choose a message M_i at random and compute another message $M_i' = M_i \oplus \alpha$, where M_i has the same length as α ($\neq 0$).
- With a chosen message attack, obtain the MAC values $C_i = \text{HMAC}(K, M_i)$ and $C_i' = \text{HMAC}(K, M_i')$.
- Check if $C_i \oplus C_i' = 0$.

Assuming that the values $h_1(IV, K \oplus ipad)$ are uniformly distributed for a given key K, the last test holds with a probability[1] of approximately q, where $q = Pr_{X,I}[h_2(I, X) \oplus h_2(I, X \oplus \alpha) = 0]$. On the other hand, for a random function or HMAC with a random function[2], the last test holds with a probability of approximately 2^{-l}. Hence, we have the following differential distinguisher of HMAC.

Proposition 1. *[A Differential Distinguisher of HMAC] Assume that the output values of the function h_1 are distributed uniformly at random. Then HMAC can be distinguished from a random function and from HMAC with a random function if $q > 2^{-l}$, where $q = Pr_{X,I}[h_2(I, X) \oplus h_2(I, X \oplus \alpha) = 0]$.*

In order for this differential distinguisher to be used in distinguishing-R and forgery attacks, the probability q should be larger than $2^{-l/2}$, which makes possible for those attacks to work with less than $2^{l/2}$ message queries (details are described in Sect. 6).

4.2   Rectangle Distinguisher of HMAC

The rectangle distinguisher of HMAC can be built by the rectangle attack which is widely used in analyzing block ciphers [4]. In block ciphers the rectangle attack can be mounted based on their bijectivity. However, in MACs it can exploit the non-bijectivity, i.e., two different messages may correspond to a same MAC value or a same intermediate value (an internal collision). We use this non-bijective property to devise our rectangle distinguisher of HMAC. Our rectangle distinguisher of HMAC works as follows (refer to Fig. 2):

- Choose two messages M_i and M_j at random and compute two other messages $M_i' = M_i \oplus \alpha$ and $M_j' = M_j \oplus \alpha$, where M_i and M_j both have the same length as α ($\neq 0$).
- With a chosen message attack, obtain the MAC values $C_i = \text{HMAC}(K, M_i)$, $C_i' = \text{HMAC}(K, M_i')$, $C_j = \text{HMAC}(K, M_j)$ and $C_j' = \text{HMAC}(K, M_j')$.
- Check if $C_i \oplus C_j = C_i' \oplus C_j' = 0$ or $C_i \oplus C_j' = C_i' \oplus C_j = 0$.

We denote by X_i, X_i', X_j and X_j' the outputs of $h_2 \circ h_1$ for the messages M_i, M_i', M_j and M_j', respectively (see Fig. 2). Note that in Fig. 2 $K \oplus ipad$ and $K \oplus opad$ are inserted into the message parts of the functions h_1 and h_3,

---

[1] In fact, the last test holds with a probability of approximately $q + (1 - q) \cdot 2^{-l}$. Because even if the M_i and M_i' do not cause a collision after the function h_2, their MAC values can still have a same value. However, in the computation of a probability for our differential distinguisher we do not consider this case.

[2] From [1] we know that HMAC with a random function behaves like a random function.

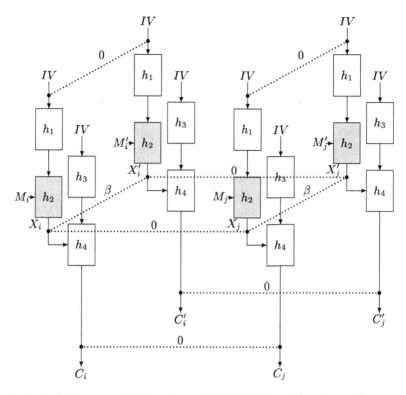

Fig. 2. A Rectangle Distinguisher of HMAC ($M_i \oplus M_i' = M_j \oplus M_j' = \alpha$)

respectively. In order to compute the probability to satisfy the last test we should consider the following probabilities: $p = Pr_{X,I}[h_2(I, X) \oplus h_2(I, X \oplus \alpha) = \beta]$ and $\hat{p} = \sqrt{\sum_{\beta}(p^2)}$.

Assuming that the values $h_1(IV, K \oplus ipad)$ are uniformly distributed for a given key K, we get $X_i \oplus X_i' = X_j \oplus X_j' = \beta$ with probability p^2. Since the function h_2 is not a permutation (here, the domain of h_2 is the message space and its co-domain is the space of hash values), we expect $X_i \oplus X_j = 0$ with probability 2^{-l} under the assumption that the output values of h_2 are distributed uniformly at random. Once we get $X_i \oplus X_i' = X_j \oplus X_j' = \beta$ and $X_i \oplus X_j = 0$, we have the following equation:

$$X_i' \oplus X_j' = (X_i \oplus \beta) \oplus (X_j \oplus \beta) = X_i \oplus X_j = 0$$

These equations allow us to get $C_i \oplus C_j = C_i' \oplus C_j' = 0$ and thus the probability[3] of satisfying $C_i \oplus C_j = C_i' \oplus C_j' = 0$ is approximately

---

[3] Note that the probability of satisfying $C_i \oplus C_j = C_i' \oplus C_j' = 0$ is slightly larger than $\hat{p}^2 \cdot 2^{-l}$. Because even if the X_i and X_j (or the X_i' and X_j') are not the same, still there is a chance to have $C_i \oplus C_j = C_i' \oplus C_j' = 0$. However, we believe that a simplified analysis is sufficient for the computation of the probability for our rectangle distinguisher.

$$\sum_{\beta} p^2 \cdot 2^{-l} = \hat{p}^2 \cdot 2^{-l}.$$

Similarly, we get $X_i \oplus X_j' = 0$ with a probability of 2^{-l} and thus $C_i \oplus C_j' = C_i' \oplus C_j = 0$ holds with the same probability $\hat{p}^2 \cdot 2^{-l}$.

On the other hand, for a random function or HMAC with a random function, $C_i \oplus C_j = C_i' \oplus C_j' = 0$ and $C_i \oplus C_j' = C_i' \oplus C_j = 0$ hold with a probability of approximately 2^{-2l}, respectively, since each requires a $2l$-bit restriction to be satisfied. Hence, we have the following rectangle distinguisher of HMAC.

Proposition 2. *[A Rectangle Distinguisher of HMAC] Assume that the output values of the functions h_1 and H_2 are distributed uniformly at random. Then HMAC can be distinguished from a random function and from HMAC with a random function if $\hat{p}^2 \cdot 2^{-l} > 2^{-2l}$, i.e., $\hat{p} > 2^{-l/2}$, where $\hat{p} = \sqrt{\sum_{\beta}(p^2)}$ and $p = Pr_{X,I}[h_2(I, X) \oplus h_2(I, X \oplus \alpha) = \beta]$.*

Our rectangle distinguisher cannot be used in distinguishing-R and forgery attacks, since its required data complexity is always larger than $2^{l/2}$ messages (details are described in Sect. 6). This is due to the fact that the rectangle probability is always less than or equal to 2^{-l}.

Unlike the differential distinguisher of HMAC, the rectangle distinguisher uses a number of differentials without any restriction for output differences, while its requirement to work is more expensive than that of the differential distinguisher, i.e., it uses probability $2^{-l/2}$ instead of 2^{-l} for its comparison. If it is easy to get some nonzero output difference from the compression function of the underlying hash function, but it is difficult to get a zero output difference, i.e., a collision, then this rectangle distinguisher would be useful.

The success of our two distinguishers for HMAC depends significantly on the strength of h_2, which means the distinguishers do not depend strongly on the properties of h_1, h_3 and h_4. Even if h_1, h_3 and h_4 employs cryptographically strong compression functions (even iterated hash functions), our distinguishers can still work if h_2 has a low difference propagation.

5   Differentials on HAVAL, MD4, MD5, SHA-0, SHA-1

First, we check how many rounds of the compression functions of HAVAL, MD4, MD5, SHA-0 and SHA-1 can be used for h_2 in our rectangle distinguisher, i.e., we investigate for how many rounds of each compression function $\hat{p} > 2^{-l/2}$ holds. Second, we present differential distinguishers of MD4, SHA-0 and SHA-1 with probabilities q such that $q > 2^{-l}$ or $q > 2^{-l/2}$. Here, we do not take into account multi-block differentials, for they are inferior to one-block differentials in HMAC. See the full version of this paper [9] for more details of multi-block differentials.

5.1 Differentials for Rectangle Distinguishers

In order to compute the number of rounds for each compression function such that $\hat{p} > 2^{-l/2}$, we investigate a differential with probability p from which the probability $\hat{p}$ can be estimated. We first consider the compression function of 3-pass HAVAL.

In the compression function of HAVAL we insert a one-bit difference to two message words to produce a collision after the first pass with a high probability. This enables us to get probability-one differentials through many rounds in the first and second passes. In more detail, if we denote by r_1, r_2, r_3, r_4, r_5 and r_6 the round numbers involved in two such message words in the three passes where $r_1 < r_2 < \cdots < r_6$, we can construct a 96-round differential with the following probability: for the rounds $0 \sim r_1$ probability 1, for each of the rounds $(r_1 + 1) \sim r_2$ probability 2^{-1}, for the rounds $(r_2 + 1) \sim (r_3 - 1)$ probability 1, for each of the rounds $r_3 \sim r_4$ probability 2^{-1}, for each of the rounds $(r_4 + 1) \sim (r_5 - 1)$ probability 2^{-2}, for each of the rounds $r_5 \sim r_6$ probability 2^{-3} and for each of the rounds $(r_6 + 1) \sim 95$ probability 2^{-4} (this can be done by the computation of differential probabilities derived from the differential distributions of Boolean functions and the use of both XOR and modular additions). These probabilities may be slightly different according to in which message word between the two a difference $0x80000000$ is given. But the total probability is the same: $2^{-(r_2 - r_1 + r_4 - r_3 + 1 + 2(r_5 - r_4 - 1) + 3(r_6 - r_5 + 1) + 4(95 - r_6))}$.

As a result of an exhaustive search[4], inserting a one-bit difference to the third and eleventh message words provides the best probability $p = 2^{-102}$. See Table 1 for more details. In Table 1 e_i represents a 32-bit word that has $0's$ in all bit positions except for bit i and $e_{i_1,\ldots,i_k}$ represents $e_{i_1} \oplus \cdots \oplus e_{i_k}$ (in our notation the leftmost bit is referred to as the 31-th bit, i.e., the most significant bit). Note that we use the XOR difference as the measure of difference and in the computation of the probability p in Table 1 the modular additions of the unknown initial value and the last output value are considered. In our analysis we take into account the probability that the last output difference is preserved through the final modular additions.

In order to calculate $\hat{p}$ we should sum the square of the probability of all differentials with message difference α. However, it is computationally infeasible and thus we have carried out experiments on the last three rounds (rounds $93 \sim 95$) to estimate a lower bound for $\hat{p}$ (our simulation is based on the assumption that chosen message pairs follow the first 93-round differential in Table 1). For this work, we have randomly chosen a number of IVs with 2^{28} message pairs M_i, M_i^* and 2^{28} input pairs of round 93 I_i, I_i^* each and computed $M_i' = M_i \oplus \alpha$, $M_i^{*'} = M_i^* \oplus \alpha$ and $I_i' = I_i \oplus \delta$ and $I_i^{*'} = I_i^* \oplus \delta$, where α is the message difference and δ is the input difference of round 93 in Table 1. We have then encrypted through rounds $93 \sim 95$ I_i, I_i', I_i^* and $I_i^{*'}$ with M_i, M_i', M_i^* and $M_i^{*'}$ to obtain outputs O_i, O_i', O_i^* and $O_i^{*'}$. Finally, we have checked if $(O_i + IV) \oplus (O_i' + IV) =$

---

[4] The exhaustive search has experimentally been done by considering all possible r_1, r_2, r_3, r_4, r_5 and r_6 which can produce a collision after the first pass.

Table 1. A Differential of HAVAL

Round (i)	ΔA^i	ΔB^i	ΔC^i	ΔD^i	ΔE^i	ΔF^i	ΔG^i	ΔH^i	Δm^i	Prob.
0	0	0	0	0	0	0	0	0	0	1
1	0	0	0	0	0	0	0	0	0	1
2	0	0	0	0	0	0	0	0	$e_{31}(=\Delta m^2)$	1
3	0	0	0	0	0	0	0	e_{31}	0	2^{-1}
4	0	0	0	0	0	0	e_{31}	0	0	2^{-1}
5	0	0	0	0	0	e_{31}	0	0	0	2^{-1}
6	0	0	0	0	e_{31}	0	0	0	0	2^{-1}
7	0	0	0	e_{31}	0	0	0	0	0	2^{-1}
8	0	0	e_{31}	0	0	0	0	0	0	2^{-1}
9	0	e_{31}	0	0	0	0	0	0	0	2^{-1}
10	e_{31}	0	0	0	0	0	0	0	$e_{20}(=\Delta m^{10})$	2^{-1}
11	0	0	0	0	0	0	0	0	0	1
⋮	⋮	⋮	⋮	⋮	⋮	⋮	⋮	⋮	⋮	⋮
44	0	0	0	0	0	0	0	0	0	1
45	0	0	0	0	0	0	0	0	$e_{20}(=\Delta m^{10})$	2^{-1}
46	0	0	0	0	0	0	0	e_{20}	0	2^{-1}
47	0	0	0	0	0	0	e_{20}	0	0	2^{-1}
48	0	0	0	0	0	e_{20}	0	0	0	2^{-1}
49	0	0	0	0	e_{20}	0	0	0	0	2^{-1}
50	0	0	0	e_{20}	0	0	0	0	0	2^{-1}
51	0	0	e_{20}	0	0	0	0	0	0	2^{-1}
52	0	e_{20}	0	0	0	0	0	0	0	2^{-1}
53	e_{20}	0	0	0	0	0	0	0	0	2^{-1}
54	0	0	0	0	0	0	0	e_9	0	2^{-1}
55	0	0	0	0	0	0	e_9	0	0	2^{-1}
56	0	0	0	0	0	e_9	0	0	0	2^{-1}
57	0	0	0	0	e_9	0	0	0	0	2^{-1}
58	0	0	0	e_9	0	0	0	0	0	2^{-1}
59	0	0	e_9	0	0	0	0	0	0	2^{-1}
60	0	e_9	0	0	0	0	0	0	$e_{31}(=\Delta m^2)$	2^{-1}
61	e_9	0	0	0	0	0	0	e_{31}	0	2^{-2}
62	0	0	0	0	0	0	e_{31}	e_{30}	0	2^{-2}
63	0	0	0	0	0	e_{31}	e_{30}	0	0	2^{-2}
64	0	0	0	0	e_{31}	e_{30}	0	0	0	2^{-2}
65	0	0	0	e_{31}	e_{30}	0	0	0	0	2^{-2}
66	0	0	e_{31}	e_{30}	0	0	0	0	0	2^{-2}
67	0	e_{31}	e_{30}	0	0	0	0	0	0	2^{-2}
68	e_{31}	e_{30}	0	0	0	0	0	0	0	2^{-2}
69	e_{30}	0	0	0	0	0	0	e_{20}	0	2^{-2}
70	0	0	0	0	0	0	e_{20}	e_{19}	0	2^{-2}
71	0	0	0	0	0	e_{20}	e_{19}	0	0	2^{-2}
72	0	0	0	0	e_{20}	e_{19}	0	0	0	2^{-2}
73	0	0	0	e_{20}	e_{19}	0	0	0	0	2^{-2}
74	0	0	e_{20}	e_{19}	0	0	0	0	0	2^{-2}
75	0	e_{20}	e_{19}	0	0	0	0	0	0	2^{-2}
76	e_{20}	e_{19}	0	0	0	0	0	0	0	2^{-2}
77	e_{19}	0	0	0	0	0	0	e_9	0	2^{-2}
78	0	0	0	0	0	0	e_9	e_8	0	2^{-2}
79	0	0	0	0	0	e_9	e_8	0	0	2^{-2}
80	0	0	0	0	e_9	e_8	0	0	0	2^{-2}
81	0	0	0	e_9	e_8	0	0	0	0	2^{-2}
82	0	0	e_9	e_8	0	0	0	0	0	2^{-2}
83	0	e_9	e_8	0	0	0	0	0	0	2^{-2}
84	e_9	e_8	0	0	0	0	0	0	0	2^{-2}
85	e_8	0	0	0	0	0	0	e_{30}	0	2^{-2}
86	0	0	0	0	0	0	e_{30}	e_{29}	0	2^{-2}
87	0	0	0	0	0	e_{30}	e_{29}	0	0	2^{-2}
88	0	0	0	0	e_{30}	e_{29}	0	0	0	2^{-2}
89	0	0	0	e_{30}	e_{29}	0	0	0	0	2^{-2}
90	0	0	e_{30}	e_{29}	0	0	0	0	0	2^{-2}
91	0	e_{30}	e_{29}	0	0	0	0	0	$e_{20}(=\Delta m^{10})$	2^{-3}
92	e_{30}	e_{29}	0	0	0	0	0	e_{20}	0	2^{-3}
93	e_{29}	0	0	0	0	0	e_{20}	e_{19}	0	2^{-3}
94	0	0	0	0	0	e_{20}	e_{19}	e_{18}	0	2^{-3}
95	0	0	0	0	e_{20}	e_{19}	e_{18}	0	$e_{31}(=\Delta m^2)$	2^{-3}
96	0	0	0	e_{20}	e_{19}	e_{18}	0	e_{31}	0	2^{-4}
$0 \sim 95$				$p = 2^{-102}$, $\hat{p} = 2^{-99.1}$					(3-pass HAVAL)	
97	0	0	e_{20}	e_{19}	e_{18}	0	e_{31}	0	0	2^{-4}
98	0	e_{20}	e_{19}	e_{18}	0	e_{31}	0	0	0	2^{-4}
99	e_{20}	e_{19}	e_{18}	0	e_{31}	0	0	0	0	2^{-4}
100	e_{19}	e_{18}	0	e_{31}	0	0	0	e_9	$e_{31}(=\Delta m^2)$	2^{-4}
101	e_{18}	0	e_{31}	0	0	0	e_9	$e_{8,31}$	0	2^{-5}
102	0	e_{31}	0	0	0	0	e_9	$e_{8,31}$	e_7	
$0 \sim 101$				$p = 2^{-127}$, $\hat{p} = 2^{-124.4}$					(reduced 4-pass HAVAL)	

$(O_i^* + IV) \oplus (O_i^{*'} + IV)$. In our experiments we have observed that the number of such quartets was ranging $320 \sim 2130$ for each IV. This simulation result suggests that the square of the probability $\hat{p}$ for rounds $93 \sim 95$ is approximately $2^{-18.2}$ and thus we can estimate the probability $\hat{p} \approx 2^{-9.1} \cdot 2^{-90} = 2^{-99.1}$ since the differential probability for rounds $0 \sim 92$ in Table 1 is 2^{-90}. Furthermore, we can extend this differential up to 101 rounds such that $\hat{p} > 2^{-128}$. See Table 1 for this extension. We have also performed a series of simulations on the last two rounds and from the simulation result we can estimate $\hat{p} \approx 2^{-124.4}$ for rounds $0 \sim 101$.

Similarly, we have investigated differentials on the compression function of MD5 with high probabilities by inserting a one-bit difference in two or three message words to produce a collision after the first pass. As a result, we can construct a 33-round differential on MD5 with probability 2^{-69}, which can be used to construct differentials with probability $\hat{p}$. See [9] for details of our reduced MD5 differential. Our investigations on HAVAL and MD5 have started from the assumption that low-weight differentials work out best when we can not use neutral bits and message modifications. However, still there is a possibility that HAVAL and MD5 have stronger differentials which can be derived by other methods.

For MD4, SHA-0 and SHA-1, we have used the previous differentials in our distinguishers, i.e., a 48-round differential on MD4 with probability 2^{-56} in [18], a 65-round differential on SHA-0 with probability 2^{-78} in [5,6] and a 43-round differential on SHA-1 with probability 2^{-80} in [6]. The 43-round differential on SHA-1 is an extended one for the 34-round differential described in [6], and the computations of differential probabilities on SHA-0 and SHA-1 are recomputed[5]. See [9] for the recomputed differentials of SHA-0 and SHA-1. We have also carried out the same experiments on the last few rounds to estimate each $\hat{p}$ and from our simulations we can estimate $\hat{p} \approx 2^{-56}$, $2^{-60.6}$, 2^{-78} and $2^{-73.4}$ for 48-round MD4, 33-round MD5, 65-round SHA-0 and 43-round SHA-1, respectively.

5.2   Differentials for Differential Distinguishers

As stated above, our differential distinguisher works based on a differential which causes a zero difference, i.e., a collision, after the function h_2. We use the foregoing differentials or the previously known differentials on MD4, SHA-0 and SHA-1 in our distinguishing and forgery attacks:

- For SHA-0, the 65-round differential with probability 2^{-78} of Table 5 in [9] can be extended into a 82-round differential with probability 2^{-98} ($\approx q$), which causes a collision (this extended differential has appeared in [5], but the differential probability is lower than that in [5] since we cannot use neutral bits.)

---

[5] The main difference of the computations of differential probabilities between [5,6] and this paper is the use of neutral bits. In the SHA-0 and SHA-1 initial values are known, which enables us to use neutral bits on message pairs to improve differential probabilities. However, in our analysis of HMAC initial values are determined by a secret key K, which implies they are unknown.

- For SHA-1, the first 34-round differential with probability 2^{-52} of Table 6 in [9] can be used as our differential distinguisher.
- For the full MD4, there exists a differential with probability 2^{-56} ($\approx q$), which causes a zero output difference from an unknown initial value [18].
- For the full SHA-0, there exists a differential with probability 2^{-107} ($\approx q$), which causes a zero output difference from an unknown initial value [15,17].

6 Distinguishing and Forgery Attacks on HMAC

We use the probabilities $\hat{p}$ and q to show two distinguishing and a forgery attacks on the HMAC construction, and apply these attacks to HMAC based on HAVAL, MD4, MD5, SHA-0 and SHA-1.

Our first distinguishing attack on HMAC using $\hat{p}$ and a rectangle distinguisher is described as follows:

1. Collect $2^{(l+1)/2} \cdot \hat{p}^{-1}$ message pairs (M_i, M_i') with difference α, where all the M_i and M_i' have the same bit-length t.
2. With a chosen message attack scenario, ask for MAC pairs of all the (M_i, M_i'). We denote the corresponding MAC pairs by (C_i, C_i'). (We assume that the MAC algorithm is either an instantiated HMAC or a random function (or HMAC with a random function) which maps from t bits to l bits.)
3. Check if $C_i \oplus C_j = C_i' \oplus C_j' = 0$ or $C_i \oplus C_j' = C_i' \oplus C_j = 0$ for all i, j such that $1 \leq i < j \leq 2^{(l+1)/2} \cdot \hat{p}^{-1}$. If there is at least one MAC quartet that satisfies this test, output the MAC algorithm = HMAC, otherwise, output the MAC algorithm = a random function (or HMAC with a random function).

The data complexity of this attack is $2^{1+((l+1)/2)} \cdot \hat{p}^{-1}$ chosen messages and this attack requires a memory of $2^{1+(l+1)/2} \cdot \hat{p}^{-1}$ l-bit blocks for storing all the MAC values. The time complexity of this attack is dominated by Step 1 (the data collection time) and Step 3, which seeks colliding MAC quartets. Since it can be done efficiently by sorting the MAC pairs (C_i, C_i')'s by C_i's, the time complexity of this attack is thus a fraction of the time required to compute the MAC values for the chosen messages (Step 1).

We now analyze the success rate of this attack. In Step 1 the $2^{(l+1)/2} \cdot \hat{p}^{-1}$ message pairs form $2^l \cdot \hat{p}^{-2}$ message quartets $((M_i, M_i'), (M_j, M_j'))$ corresponding to MAC quartets $((C_i, C_i'), (C_j, C_j'))$ for $1 \leq i < j \leq 2^{(l+1)/2} \cdot \hat{p}^{-1}$. Since for HMAC $C_i \oplus C_j = C_i' \oplus C_j' = 0$ holds with a probability of $2^{-l} \cdot \hat{p}^2$, and $C_i \oplus C_j' = C_i' \oplus C_j = 0$ also holds with the same probability (this probability has been computed in Sect. 4), the expected number of MAC quartets satisfying the last test is 2 ($= (2^l \cdot \hat{p}^{-2}) \cdot (2^{-l} \cdot \hat{p}^2) + (2^l \cdot \hat{p}^{-2}) \cdot (2^{-l} \cdot \hat{p}^2)$). On the other hand, for a random function (or HMAC with a random function), $C_i \oplus C_j = C_i' \oplus C_j' = 0$ holds with a probability of 2^{-2l}, and $C_i \oplus C_j' = C_i' \oplus C_j = 0$ also holds with the same probability and thus the expectation of satisfying the test is $2^{-l+1} \cdot (\hat{p}^{-2})(= 2^{-2l} \cdot (2^l \cdot \hat{p}^{-2}) + 2^{-2l} \cdot (2^l \cdot \hat{p}^{-2}))$. Hence, the success rate of this attack is

$$\frac{1 - (1 - 2^{-l} \cdot \hat{p}^2)^{2^{l+1} \cdot \hat{p}^{-2}}}{2} + \frac{(1 - 2^{-2l})^{2^{l+1} \cdot \hat{p}^{-2}}}{2} \approx \frac{1 - e^{-2}}{2} + \frac{e^{-2^{-l+1} \cdot \hat{p}^{-2}}}{2}.$$

Table 2. Distinguishing and forgery attacks on HMAC with HAVAL, MD4, MD5, SHA-0 and SHA-1

Hash Function	Type of Distinguisher	Type of Attack	h_2 #R	Probability of Distinguisher	Data Complexity	Success Rate
3-pass HAVAL (96 rounds)	$\mathbf{R}^{\dagger}$	**Distinguishing**	**96**	$\hat{p} = 2^{-99.1}$	$2^{228.6}$	0.93
4-pass HAVAL (128 rounds)	R	Distinguishing	102	$\hat{p} = 2^{-124.4}$	$2^{253.9}$	0.93
MD4 (48 rounds)	$\mathbf{R}^{\dagger}$	**Distinguishing**	**48**	$\hat{p} = 2^{-56}$	$2^{121.5}$	0.93
	$\mathbf{D}^{\dagger}$	**Forgery**	**48**	$q = 2^{-56}$	2^{58}	0.93
MD5 (64 rounds)	R	Distinguishing	33	$\hat{p} = 2^{-60.6}$	$2^{126.1}$	0.92
SHA-0	R	Distinguishing	65	$\hat{p} = 2^{-78}$	$2^{159.5}$	0.87
	$\mathbf{D}^{\dagger}$	**Distinguishing**	**82**	$q = 2^{-98}$	2^{100}	0.93
	$\mathbf{D}^{\dagger}$	**Distinguishing**	**80**	$q = 2^{-107}$	2^{109}	0.93
	D	Forgery	54	$q = 2^{-61}$	2^{63}	0.93
(80 rounds)	D	Forgery	65	$q = 2^{-78}$	2^{80}	0.93
SHA-1 (80 rounds)	R	Distinguishing	43	$\hat{p} = 2^{-73.4}$	$2^{154.9}$	0.93
	D	Forgery	34	$q = 2^{-51}$	2^{53}	0.93

$\dagger$: the attacks can work on HMAC based on full-round (or extended-round) hash functions.
R: Rectangle, D: Differential, #R: the number of rounds
Data complexity is the amount of chosen messages
In the rectangle attacks, memory complexity is the same as data complexity
Distinguishing attack is to distinguish instantiated HMAC from HMAC with a random function

Here, the first term is approximately 0.43. Our second distinguishing attack on HMAC using q and a differential distinguisher is described as follows:

1. Collect $2 \cdot q^{-1}$ message pairs (M_i, M_i') with difference α, where all the M_i and M_i' have the same bit-length t.
2. With a chosen message attack scenario, ask for MAC pairs of all the (M_i, M_i'). We denote the corresponding MAC pairs by (C_i, C_i'). We assume that the MAC algorithm is either an instantiated HMAC or a random function (or HMAC with a random function) which maps t bits to l bits.
3. Check if $C_i \oplus C_i' = 0$. If there is at least one MAC pair that satisfies this test, output the MAC algorithm = HMAC, otherwise, output the MAC algorithm = a random function (or HMAC with a random function).

The data complexity of this attack is $2^2 \cdot q^{-1}$ chosen messages and this attack does not require any storage, and the time complexity of this attack itself is a fraction of the time required to compute the MAC values for the chosen messages. Similarly, the success rate of this attack is computed as follows:

$$\frac{1 - (1-q)^{2 \cdot q^{-1}}}{2} + \frac{(1 - 2^{-l})^{2 \cdot q^{-1}}}{2} \approx \frac{1 - e^{-2}}{2} + \frac{e^{-2^{-l+1} \cdot q^{-1}}}{2}.$$

Finally, our forgery attack on HMAC using q and a differential distinguisher is described as follows:

1. Run Step 1 in the second distinguishing attack.
2. Run Step 2 in the second distinguishing attack, but we assume that the MAC algorithm is an instantiated HMAC.
3. Check if $C_i \oplus C_i' = 0$ and ask for the MAC pair of $M_i||P$ and $M_i'||P$, where M_i and M_i' have a same MAC value and P is some non-empty string. If the obtained MAC pair collides, again ask for the MAC value of $M_i||P||P'$, where P' is some non-empty string. We denote this obtained MAC value by C. Output C as the MAC value of $M_i'||P||P'$. Otherwise, restart this step until we check all MAC pairs (C_i, C_i').

It is easy to see that this forgery attack works with (almost) the same data complexity and the same success rate as our second distinguishing attack.

We can easily apply these three attacks to HMAC based on HAVAL, MD4, MD5, SHA-0 and SHA-1 by using their probabilities $\hat{p}$ and q. Table 2 shows the results of distinguishing and forgery attacks on those instantiations of HMAC[6]. In Table 2 forgery attacks also imply distinguishing-R and distinguishing-H attacks.

Note: Our distinguishing and forgery attacks are also applicable to HMAC in which the four components h_1, h_2, h_3, h_4 are instantiated with different compression functions (see for example the pseudorandom functions of SSL 3.0). For example, if HMAC employs full-round MD-5, full-round MD-4, full-round MD5 and full-round MD5 for h_1, h_2, h_3 and h_4, respectively, it can be forged with a data complexity of 2^{58} chosen messages. This is due to the fact that our distinguishing and forgery attacks depend only on the function h_2. Furthermore, the distinguishing and forgery attacks in Table 2 also work on NMAC based on HAVAL, MD4, MD5, SHA-0 and SHA-1.

7   Conclusions

We have presented differential and rectangle distinguishers on HMAC, which are derived from its structural property. They allow to present distinguishing and forgery attacks on HMAC that can be mounted when HMAC employs hash functions with slow difference propagations. With these distinguishing and forgery attacks we have shown that HMAC with the full versions of 3-pass HAVAL and SHA-0 can be distinguished from HMAC with a random function, and HMAC with the full version of MD4 can be forged. These distinguishing and forgery attacks have also been applied to HMAC based on reduced versions of MD5 and SHA-1. We have also shown that our distinguishing and forgery attacks can be mounted on NMAC (which is a generalized version of HMAC) with the same complexity. Furthermore, we have shown that our differential and rectangle distinguishers can lead to second-preimage attacks on HMAC and NMAC. All these attacks do not

---

[6] These attacks are mounted under the assumption that the output values of the functions h_1 and h_2 distribute uniformly over all possible values when K and M_i are chosen uniformly at random (differential distinguishers are independent of the distributions of the output values of the functions h_2 and H_2).

contradict the security proof of HMAC, but they improve our understanding of the security of HMAC based on existing cryptographic hash functions.

Our differential distinguisher on HMAC works only if the underlying hash function has a differential with a zero output difference with probability larger than $2^{-|\text{hash value}|}$. Our rectangle distinguisher on HMAC works only if the underlying hash function has differentials such that the sum of the square of their probabilities is larger than $2^{-|\text{hash value}|}$. Unlike the previous attacks on hash functions, our analysis on the hash function embedded in HMAC should be done under an unknown fixed initial value (which is determined by a secret key). This fact makes difficult to use the recently proposed message modification technique (Wang et al.'s attacks) and neutral-bit technique (Biham et al.'s attacks) in analyzing HMAC based on specific cryptographic hash functions. However, it is interesting to investigate if their methods can be applied to HMAC with some new other techniques when HMAC is instantiated with a specific cryptographic hash function. We expect that the method developed in this paper would be useful for the further analysis of HMAC.

References

1. M. Bellare, *New Proofs for NMAC and HMAC: Security without Collision-Resistance*, Advances in Cryptology – Proceedings of CRYPTO 2006, to appear, and Cryptology ePrint Archive, Report 2006/043, Available Online at *http://eprint.iacr.org/2006/043.pdf*
2. M. Bellare, R. Canetti and H. Krawczyk, *Keying Hash Functions for Message Authentication*, Advances in Cryptology – Proceedings of CRYPTO 1996, LNCS 1109, pp. 1-15, Springer-Verlag, 1996.
3. M. Bellare, J. Kilian and P. Rogaway, *The Security of the Cipher Block Chaining Message Authentication Code*, Journal of Computer and System Sciences, Vol. 61, No. 3, pp. 362-399, Dec 2000.
4. E. Biham, O. Dunkelman and N. Keller, *The Rectangle Attack – Rectangling the Serpent*, Advances in Cryptology – Proceedings of EUROCRYPT 2001, LNCS 2045, pp. 340-357, Springer-Verlag, 2001.
5. E. Biham and R. Chen, *Near-Collisions of SHA-0*, Advances in Cryptology – Proceedings of CRYPTO 2004, LNCS 3152, pp. 290-305, Springer-Verlag, 2004.
6. E. Biham, R. Chen, A. Joux, P. Carribault, C. Lemuet and W. Jalby, *Collisions of SHA-0 and Reduced SHA-1*, Advances in Cryptology – Proceedings of EURO-CRYPT 2005, LNCS 3494, pp. 22-35, Springer-Verlag, 2005.
7. F. Chabaud and A. Joux, *Differential Collisions in SHA-0*, Advances in Cryptology – Proceedings of CRYPTO 1998, LNCS 1462, pp. 56-71, Springer-Verlag, 1999.
8. ISO/IEC 9797, Data Cryptographic Techniques - Data Integrity Mechanism Using a Cryptographic Check Function Employing a Block Cipher Algorithm, 1989.
9. J. Kim, A. Biryukov, B. Preneel and S. Hong, *On the Security of HMAC and NMAC Based on HAVAL, MD4, MD5, SHA-0 and SHA-1*, Cryptology ePrint Archive, Report 2006/187, Available Online at *http://eprint.iacr.org/2006/187.pdf*
10. B. Preneel, A. Bosselaers, R. Govaerts and J. Vandewalle, *A chosen text attack on the modified cryptographic checksum algorithm of Cohen and Huang*, Advances in Cryptology – Proceedings of CRYPTO 1989, LNCS 435, pp. 154-163, Springer-Verlag, 1990.

11. B. Preneel, P.C. van Oorschot, *MDx-MAC and building fast MACs from hash functions*, Advances in Cryptology – Proceedings of CRYPTO 1995, LNCS 963, pp. 1-14, Springer-Verlag, 1995.

12. R.L. Rivest, *The MD4 Message Digest Algorithm*, Advances in Cryptology – Proceedings of CRYPTO 1990, LNCS 537, pp. 303-311, Springer-Verlag, 1991.

13. R.L. Rivest, *The MD5 Message Digest Algorithm*, Request for Comments (RFC 1320), Internet Activities Board, Internet Privacy Task Force, 1992.

14. X. Wang and H. Yu, *How to Break MD5 and Other Hash Functions*, Advances in Cryptology – Proceedings of EUROCRYPT 2005, LNCS 3494, pp. 19-35, Springer-Verlag, 2005.

15. X. Wang, X. Lai, D. Feng, H. Chen and X. Yu, *Cryptanalysis of the Hash Functions MD4 and RIPEMD*, Advances in Cryptology – Proceedings of EUROCRYPT 2005, LNCS 3494, pp. 1-18, Springer-Verlag, 2005.

16. X. Wang, Y.L. Yin and H. Yu, *Finding Collisions in the Full SHA-1*, Advances in Cryptology – Proceedings of CRYPTO 2005, LNCS 3621, pp. 17-36, Springer-Verlag, 2005.

17. X. Wang, H. Yu and Y.L. Yin, *Efficient Collision Search Attacks on SHA-0*, Advances in Cryptology – Proceedings of CRYPTO 2005, LNCS 3621, pp. 1-16, Springer-Verlag, 2005.

18. H. Yu, G. Wang, G. Zhang and X. Wang, *The Second-Preimage Attack on MD4*, Proceedings of CANS 2005, LNCS 3810, pp. 1-12, Springer-Verlag, 2005.

19. Y. Zheng, J. Pieprzyk and J. Seberry, *HAVAL-A One-way Hashing Algorithm with Variable Length of Output*, Advances in Cryptology – Proceedings of AUSCRYPT 1992, LNCS 718, pp. 83-104, Springer-Verlag, 1993.

20. U.S. Department of Commerce. *FIPS 180*: Secure Hash Standard, Federal Information Processing Standards Publication, N.I.S.T., May 1993.

21. U.S. Department of Commerce. *FIPS 180-1*: Secure Hash Standard, Federal Information Processing Standards Publication, N.I.S.T., April 1995.

Distinguishing Stream Ciphers with Convolutional Filters

Joan Daemen and Gilles Van Assche

STMicroelectronics – Smart Cards ICs Division
Excelsiorlaan 44–46, 1930 Zaventem, Belgium
joan.daemen@st.com, gilles.vanassche@st.com

Abstract. This paper presents a new type of distinguisher for the shrinking generator and the alternating-step generator with known feedback polynomial and for the multiplexor generator. For the former the distinguisher is more efficient than existing ones and for the latter it results in a complete breakdown of security. The distinguisher is conceptually very simple and lends itself to theoretical analysis leading to reliable predictions of its probability of success.

1 Introduction

In this paper we present efficient distinguishers for a class of stream ciphers. This class can be characterized as irregularly sampled linear feedback shift registers (LFSR). These stream ciphers have the following in common:

- A set of *source* registers, each of which generates a source sequence.
- The source sequences are sampled in an irregular fashion to form an *output* sequence. In most cases, the sampling is governed by an independent sequence generator, typically just another LFSR. The latter is called the *sampling* sequence or sampling LFSR.

Examples of this type of stream ciphers are the shrinking generator [2,17], the alternating-step generator [12,17] and some variants of the multiplexor generator [13,17]. The bits in an LFSR source sequence satisfy a linear recurrence that can be very easily detected. Clearly, as each bit in the output sequence corresponds to a bit in a source sequence, the bits in the output sequence may also satisfy a linear recurrence. The irregularity of the sampling process is supposed to make this hard to exploit. This paper now presents distinguishers for the shrinking and alternating-step generators exploiting all remainders of linear recurrence in the output sequence. To build such a distinguisher requires knowledge of the feedback polynomial of the source sequence, i.e., the generator has fixed connections. It also presents very powerful distinguishers for the multiplexor generator exploiting the weakness that a single bit in the source stream may appear multiple times in the output stream. We call the distinguishers presented in this paper *convolutional filters* as they make use of convolution as their main operation.

R. De Prisco and M. Yung (Eds.): SCN 2006, LNCS 4116, pp. 257–270, 2006.

Correlation attacks on the shrinking generator were already described in [4], analyzed in [18] and later improved in [14]. Detectable statistical weaknesses in the output stream were shown in [5] and [6] if the feedback polynomial has very low weight or moderate degree. More recent work includes another correlation analysis of the shrinking generator in [8] and of the alternating-step generator in [9] and [11]. A draft paper [10] saw the light describing a statistical distinguisher for the shrinking generator.

The work that lead to this paper was triggered by an efficient attack on the shrinking generator described in [3] and can be considered as an improvement and extension of the latter. It improves the attacks in [3] in that convolutional filters require less output stream for the same probability of success. As opposed to the distinguisher proposed in [3], convolutional filters are conceptually very simple: they return a real number and require no decision rules (hard or soft) in the computation thereof. As such, they require no parameter trade-offs or fine-tuning, their probability of success is easy to compute analytically and there is no discrepancy between the theory and the simulation results. Finally, while [3] describe attacks for the shrinking generator only, this paper presents distinguishers for the shrinking generator, the alternating-step generator and the multiplexor generator. In the rest of this paper we first provide a number of definitions, then the distinguishers for the shrinking and alternating-step generators, the distinguishers for multiplexor generators and finally a description of our simulation results.

2   Definitions

2.1   Sequences

We denote sequences by lowercase letters such as a and b and their individual components with notation a_t and b_t, where the indices start from 1. We define the product of two sequences $c = a \times b$ as the sequence with $c_t = a_t b_t$ and the convolution of a sequence a with a function f, $c = a \otimes f$ as the sequence with $c_t = \sum_i f(i) a_{t-i}$. sequences

2.2   Linear Feedback Shift Registers

Linear feedback shift registers (LFSR) come in two types. In the *Fibonacci configuration* the feedback is from a number of stages to the first stage while in a *Galois configuration*, the feedback is from the last stages to a number of stages. Both configurations are governed by a feedback polynomial that determines the positions of the stages involved in the feedback. The output bits of a linear feedback shift register (LFSR) satisfy a recurrence relation determined by its feedback polynomial:

$$a_i \oplus a_{i-G_1} \oplus a_{i-G_2} \oplus \cdots \oplus a_{i-G_{w-1}} = 0. \tag{1}$$

We call w the weight of the feedback polynomial and define the $w - 1$ *gaps* as $g_1 = G_1, g_2 = G_2 - G_1, \ldots, g_{w-1} = G_{w-1} - G_{w-2}$. The output bits of an

LFSR satisfy many recurrence relations, one for every multiple of the feedback polynomial. For some distinguishers, the efficiency tends to decrease with the weight of the polynomial and it is advantageous to find multiples of the feedback polynomial with low weight. Techniques for doing so are described in [1,7,15,20].

2.3   Index Maps

We define the index map $S(j)$ associated with a (sampling) sequence s as:

$$S(j) = \min\{k| \sum_{i=1}^{k} s_i = j\}, \tag{2}$$

where the bits s_i are interpreted as integers 0 and 1. Having $S(j) = k$ requires that $s_k = 1$ and that the interval $[s_1 \ldots s_{k-1}]$ contains $j - 1$ ones. Clearly, $S(j)$ is an increasing function. Given a random binary sequence s, $S(j)$ is a stochastic variable with probability distribution:

$$\Pr[S(j) = k] = 2^{-k} \binom{k-1}{j-1} \text{ if } k \geq j \text{ and } 0 \text{ otherwise.} \tag{3}$$

More generally, having $S(j+h) - S(j) = g$ requires the interval $[s_{S(j)} \ldots s_{S(j)+g-1}]$ to contain $h - 1$ ones and $s_{S(j+h)} = 1$:

$$\Pr[S(j+h) - S(j) = g] = 2^{-g} \binom{g-1}{h-1} \text{ if } g \geq h \text{ and } 0 \text{ otherwise.} \tag{4}$$

We denote $\Pr[S(j+h) - S(j) = g]$ by $\mathcal{S}(g, h)$ as it is independent of j. This function satisfies:

$$\sum_{g=h}^{\infty} \mathcal{S}(g, h) = 1 \text{ and } \sum_{h=1}^{g} \mathcal{S}(g, h) = 1/2. \tag{5}$$

For a given g, $\mathcal{S}(g, h)$ has a maximum in $h = (g + 1)/2$ for g odd and in $h = (g + 1 \pm 1)/2$ for g even. We denote the mean value of a stochastic variable x by $\langle x \rangle$ and its variance by σ^2. Unless g is very small or h is very far from $g/2$, $\mathcal{S}(g, h)$ is closely approximated by a (scaled) normal distribution:

$$\mathcal{S}(g, h) \approx \frac{1}{2} \frac{1}{\sigma\sqrt{2\pi}} e^{-\frac{(h - \langle h \rangle)^2}{2\sigma^2}}, \tag{6}$$

with $\langle h \rangle = (g + 1)/2$ and $\sigma^2 = (g - 1)/4$. For a given h, the shape of $\mathcal{S}(g, h)$ is slightly skewed with respect to a normal distribution. It reaches its maximum value in both $g = 2h - 2$ and $g = 2h - 1$ and has $\langle g \rangle = 2h$ and $\sigma^2 = 2h$.

2.4   The Shrinking Generator

A shrinking generator (SG) is a stream cipher with a single source LFSR and a sampling LFSR. During an iteration both registers are clocked. If the sampling bit is 1, the source bit is presented at the output of the generator. Otherwise, no output bit is generated. On the average the SG requires two iterations per bit generated. Its output bits satisfy:

$$z_i = a_{S(i)}, \tag{7}$$

with a the source sequence and $S(i)$ the index map of the sampling sequence.

2.5   The Alternating-Step Generator

An alternating-step generator (ASG) is a stream cipher with two source LFSRs generating sequences a and b and a sampling LFSR generating sequence s. During an iteration the sampling LFSR and only one of the two source LFSRs is clocked. Which one of the two source LFSRs is clocked depends on the output bit of the sampling LFSR. The output bit y of the ASG is the XOR of the two output bits of the source LFSR. The difference of two subsequent output bits $z_t = y_t \oplus y_{t-1}$ of an ASG is either the XOR of two output bits $a_i \oplus a_{i-1}$ of one source LFSR or $b_j \oplus b_{j-1}$ of the other source LFSR. Note that if a sequence a satisfies a recurrence relation, this is also the case for a sequence c with $c_i = a_i \oplus a_{i-1}$. In the following, we will deal with the sequences z, c and d and not the sequences y, a and b. The bits of c map to bits in z by

$$c_i = z_{S(i)}. \tag{8}$$

The bits of d with $d_i = b_i \oplus b_{i-1}$ map to bits in z in a similar way:

$$d_i = z_{S'(i)}, \text{ with } S'(i) = \min\{k | \sum_{j=1}^{k} (1 - s_j) = i\}. \tag{9}$$

2.6   Multiplexor Generators

We consider multiplexor generators with a single source LFSR and a single sampling LFSR. During an iteration both registers are clocked. A multiplexor taking as input a number n of stages in the sampling LFSR selects a stage in the source LFSR whose contents is presented as output bit. The input to the multiplexor can be modeled as a sampling sequence S of integers in the range $[0, 2^n - 1]$ and the stages selected as a function of S_t as an array M with 2^n stage positions. We call M the *selection position table*.

If the source LFSR has a Fibonacci configuration, the multiplexor generator can be modeled as a binary source sequence a sampled by a sampling sequence S in the following way:

$$z_t = a_{t+M[S_t]} . \tag{10}$$

If the source LFSR has a Galois configuration, this model does not apply.

3   A Basic Distinguisher for SG and ASG

If we select a number w output bits, they may correspond to w source bits that satisfy the recurrence relation. We denote the selected output bits by $z_t, z_{t-H_1}, z_{t-H_2}, \ldots, z_{t-H_{w-1}}$ and the *gaps* of this selection as $H = (h_1, h_2, \ldots, h_{w-1})$. Given H and the gaps $G = (g_1, g_2, \ldots, g_{w-1})$ of the recurrence relation, we can compute the probability that the selected output bits correspond to source bits that satisfy the recurrence relation. This probability is independent of t and only depends on G and H. We denote it by $P(G|H)$. Given a sequence z, we define x_t as:

$$x_t = (-1)^{z_t \oplus z_{t+H_1} \oplus \cdots \oplus z_{t+H_{w-1}}}. \tag{11}$$

Using the convention $\bar{z}_i = (-1)^{z_i}$, this becomes $x_t = \bar{z}_t \bar{z}_{t+H_1} \cdots \bar{z}_{t+H_{w-1}}$. We can model the probability distribution of x_t as the combination of two distributions:

- If the output bits correspond to source bits that satisfy the linear recurrence, the distribution of x_t has a peak equal to 1 at 1. For an SG or ASG, this happens with probability $P(G|H)$.
- Otherwise, the distribution of x_t has equal peaks of value $1/2$ both at positions 1 and -1. For an SG or ASG, this happens with probability $1 - P(G|H)$.

Hence, for an SG or ASG, x_t has a distribution with mean $\langle x_t \rangle = P(G|H)$ and variance is $1 - P(G|H)^2 \approx 1$. For a truly random sequence z, x_t has mean 0 and variance 1.

The basic distinguisher now consists of the following. Given a stream z, compute x_t for a large range of t values and take the average value X:

$$X = \frac{1}{L} \sum_{t=1}^{L} x_t. \tag{12}$$

If we consider the different x_t as independent, X is the average of a large number of independent stochastic variables all with variance 1 and so has a normal distribution with standard deviation $1/\sqrt{L}$. If z is the output of an SG or ASG, $\langle X \rangle = P(G|H)$ and if z is a random sequence $\langle X \rangle = 0$.

If $X > P(G|H)/2$ we decide z is the output of an SG (or ASG). If $L = P(G|H)^{-2}$, the probability of error is about 31%. To obtain a probability of error below 1%, we must take $L \approx 22 P(G|H)^{-2}$. For a given probability of success, the amount $P(G|H)^{-2}$ determines the length of the output sequence required with a given distinguisher. We denote $P(G|H)^{-2}$ by L_d.

3.1   The Shrinking Generator

The probability that a gap h in the output sequence maps to a gap g in the input sequence is given by $\Pr[S(j+h) - S(j) = g] = \mathcal{S}(g, h)$. The $w - 1$ gaps of H are mapped to $w - 1$ gaps in G in an independent way. Therefore it follows that:

$$P_s(G|H) = \prod_{i=1}^{w-1} \mathcal{S}(g_i, h_i). \tag{13}$$

Choosing the gaps $h_i = (g_i + 1)/2$ such that $P_s(G|H)$ is maximized and using the Gaussian approximation yields:

$$P_s(G|H) \approx \prod_{i=1}^{w-1} \frac{1}{\sqrt{2\pi(g_i - 1)}} \text{ and } L_d = (2\pi)^{w-1} \prod_{i=1}^{w-1} (g_i - 1). \tag{14}$$

3.2   The Alternating-Step Generator

The probability that a gap h in the output sequence maps to a gap g in the source sequences c is given by $\Pr[S(j + g) - S(j) = h] = \mathcal{S}(h, g)$. The $w - 1$ gaps of H are mapped to $w - 1$ gaps in G in an independent way. However, we require that the bits come from source sequence c and not d, which happens with probability $1/2$. Therefore it follows that:

$$P_a(G|H) = \frac{1}{2} \prod_{i=1}^{w-1} \mathcal{S}(h_i, g_i). \tag{15}$$

Choosing the gaps $h_i = 2g_i - 1$ such that $P_a(G|H)$ is maximized and using the Gaussian approximation yields:

$$P_a(G|H) \approx \frac{1}{2} \prod_{i=1}^{w-1} \frac{1}{2\sqrt{\pi(g_i - 1)}} \text{ and } L_d = 4(4\pi)^{w-1} \prod_{i=1}^{w-1} (g_i - 1). \tag{16}$$

4   A Convolutional Filter for SG and ASG

Instead of just considering combinations of bits of the output sequence for which $P(G|H)$ is optimum, we introduce a more sophisticated distinguisher that considers *all* combinations of w bits of z for which $P(G|H)$ is different from 0. We compute a function Y as:

$$Y = \frac{1}{L} \sum_t y_t \text{ with } y_t = \sum_H C_H \bar{z}_t \bar{z}_{t+H_1} \cdots \bar{z}_{t+H_{w-1}}. \tag{17}$$

Here the C_H are weighing factors as the optimum result is not necessarily obtained by just adding all combinations. Each y_t is the sum of a number of independent expressions $C_H \bar{z}_t \bar{z}_{t+H_1} \cdots \bar{z}_{t+H_{w-1}}$. Such an expression has variance C_H^2 and mean $C_H P(G|H)$. If we want y_t to have a variance equal to 1, we must choose the C_H values such that $\sum_H C_H^2 = 1$. In other words, the C_H values can be seen as the coordinates of a vector of length 1. The mean value of y_t is:

$$\langle y_t \rangle = \sum_H C_H P(G|H). \tag{18}$$

The latter can be seen as the inner product between two vectors, the C-vector and the $P(G|H)$-vector. The mean value $\langle y_t \rangle$ for a truly random sequence being zero, we wish to maximize this inner product so as to best distinguish SG or ASG from other generators. We must thus choose the vector C equal to the vector $P(G|H)$ divided by its norm, hence:

$$C_H = \frac{P(G|H)}{\sqrt{\sum_H P(G|H)^2}}. \tag{19}$$

For this choice of C_H, we obtain:

$$\langle y_t \rangle = \sqrt{\sum_H P(G|H)^2} \text{ and } L_d = \frac{1}{\sum_H P(G|H)^2}. \tag{20}$$

4.1   The Shrinking Generator

We can now compute the value of L_d for an SG given the feedback polynomial G of its source register:

$$L_d{}^{-1} = \sum_{h_1} \sum_{h_2} \cdots \sum_{h_{w-1}} \prod_{i=1}^{w-1} \mathcal{S}(g_i, h_i)^2 \tag{21}$$

$$= \sum_{h_1} \mathcal{S}(g_1, h_1)^2 \sum_{h_2} \mathcal{S}(g_2, h_2)^2 \cdots \sum_{h_{w-1}} \mathcal{S}(g_{w-1}, h_{w-1})^2. \tag{22}$$

Introducing following notation

$$\rho_g(h) = \frac{\mathcal{S}(g, h)}{\sqrt{\sum_h \mathcal{S}(g, h)^2}} \tag{23}$$

results in:

$$L_d{}^{-1} = \prod_{i=1}^{w-1} \sum_{h_i} \mathcal{S}(g_i, h_i)^2 \text{ and } C_H = \prod_{i=1}^{w-1} \rho_{g_i}(h_i) . \tag{24}$$

Using the Gaussian approximation yields $\sum_h \mathcal{S}(g, h)^2 \approx 1/4\sqrt{\pi(g-1)}$ and

$$L_d = (4\sqrt{\pi})^{w-1} \sqrt{\prod_i (g_i - 1)}. \tag{25}$$

In the following theorem we prove that the stream y can be computed iteratively by taking $w - 1$ convolutions and $w - 1$ stream multiplications.

Theorem 1. *The computation of $y_t = v_t^{(0)}$ for an SG is given as*

$$v^{(w-2)} = \bar{z} \times (\bar{z} \otimes \rho_{g_{w-1}}), \ldots$$

$$v^{(i)} = \bar{z} \times (v^{(i+1)} \otimes \rho_{g_{i+1}}), \ldots$$

$$v^{(0)} = \bar{z} \times (v^{(1)} \otimes \rho_{g_1}).$$

Proof. We have:

$$v_t^{(0)} = \sum_{h_1} \rho_{g_1}(h_1)\bar{z}_t v_{t-h_1}^{(1)}$$

$$= \sum_{h_1} \rho_{g_1}(h_1) \left(\sum_{h_2} \bar{z}_{t-h_1} \rho_{g_2}(h_2) v_{t-(h_1+h_2)}^{(2)} \right) \bar{z}_t$$

$$= \sum_{h_1} \rho_{g_1}(h_1) \sum_{h_2} \rho_{g_2}(h_2) v_{t-H_2}^{(2)} \bar{z}_{t-H_1} \bar{z}_t$$

$$= \sum_{h_1} \sum_{h_2} \rho_{g_1}(h_1) \rho_{g_2}(h_2) v_{t-H_2}^{(2)} \bar{z}_t \bar{z}_{t-H_1}$$

$$= \dots$$

$$= \sum_{h_1} \cdots \sum_{h_{w-1}} \prod_{i=1}^{w-1} \rho_{g_i}(h_i) \bar{z}_t \bar{z}_{t-H_1} \cdots \bar{z}_{t-H_{w-1}}$$

$$= \sum_{H} \left(\prod_{i=1}^{w-1} \rho_{g_i}(h_i) \right) \bar{z}_t \bar{z}_{t-H_1} \cdots \bar{z}_{t-H_{w-1}}.$$

We thus correctly obtain

$$y_t = v_t^{(0)} = \sum_{H} C_H \bar{z}_t \bar{z}_{t-H_1} \cdots \bar{z}_{t-H_{w-1}} \text{ with } C_H = \prod_{i=1}^{w-1} \rho_{g_i}(h_i). \qquad (26)$$

$\square$

4.2   The Alternating-Step Generator

We can now compute the values of L_d and C_H for an ASG given the gaps G of a feedback polynomial of one of its source registers:

$$L_d^{-1} = \sum_{h_1} \sum_{h_2} \cdots \sum_{h_{w-1}} \frac{1}{4} \prod_{i=1}^{w-1} \mathcal{S}(h_i, g_i)^2 \qquad (27)$$

$$= \frac{1}{4} \sum_{h_1} \mathcal{S}(h_1, g_1)^2 \sum_{h_2} \mathcal{S}(h_2, g_2)^2 \cdots \sum_{h_{w-1}} \mathcal{S}(h_{w-1}, g_{w-1})^2. \qquad (28)$$

Introducing following notation:

$$\mu_g(h) = \frac{\mathcal{S}(h, g)}{\sqrt{\sum_h \mathcal{S}(h, g)^2}} \qquad (29)$$

results in:

$$L_d = \frac{4}{\prod_{i=1}^{w-1} \sum_{h_i} \mathcal{S}(h_i, g_i)^2} \text{ and } C_H = \prod_{i=1}^{w-1} \mu_{g_i}(h_i). \qquad (30)$$

The expression $\sum_h \mathcal{S}(h,g)^2$ appears to be very closely approximated by $1/2\sqrt{2\pi(g-1)}$, yielding

$$L_d = 4(2\sqrt{2\pi})^{w-1}\sqrt{\prod_i(g_i-1)}. \tag{31}$$

Theorem 2. *The computation of $y_t = v_t^{(0)}$ for an ASG is given as*

$$v^{(w-2)} = \bar{z} \times (\bar{z} \otimes \mu_{g_{w-1}}), \dots$$
$$v^{(i)} = \bar{z} \times (v^{(i+1)} \otimes \mu_{g_{i+1}}), \dots$$
$$y = \bar{z} \times (v^{(1)} \otimes \mu_{g_1}).$$

The proof is very similar to that of Theorem 1.

4.3   Usage of Multiple Recursion Relations

In the ASG, we can conduct the same attack using the feedback polynomial of source sequence b. Moreover, we can conduct the attack for any polynomial that is a multiple of a feedback polynomial of (one of) the source registers. In general, given any number of independent distinguishers with mean $\langle y^{(i)} \rangle$, the optimum distinguisher is formed by

$$y_t = \frac{\sum_i \langle y^{(i)} \rangle y_t^{(i)}}{\sqrt{\sum_i \langle y^{(i)} \rangle^2}} \text{ yielding } L_d = \frac{1}{\sum_i \langle y^{(i)} \rangle^2} = \frac{1}{\sum_i \frac{1}{L_d(i)}}. \tag{32}$$

5   Distinguishers for Multiplexor Generators

We construct distinguishers exploiting the fact that source stream bits may appear multiple times in the output stream. Whereas the distinguishers for the SG and ASG reveal weaknesses in the source sequences, here the distinguishers work independently from the nature of the source stream and reveals weaknesses due to the sampling process itself.

5.1   Fibonacci Configuration

The probability that two bits in the output stream separated by a gap h originate from the same bit in the source stream is:

$$\Pr[t+h+M[S_{t-h}] = t+M[S_t]] = \Pr[M[s] - M[s'] = h], \tag{33}$$

for independent random variables s and s' following the same distribution as S. We define the distribution function of the selection position table, $P_M(i)$, as

$$P_M(i) = \Pr[M[a] = i] = 2^{-n}\sum_j \delta_{iM[j]}, \tag{34}$$

with δ the Kronecker delta. If we now define Q_M as the convolution of P_M with itself, $Q_M = P_M \otimes P_M$, we have:

$$\Pr(M[s] - M[s'] = h) = Q_M(h). \tag{35}$$

So $Q_M(h)$ gives the probability that two output bits separated by a gap h originate from the same bit in the source stream.

A basic distinguisher consists of the following. Find the gap h_m for which $Q_M(h)$ is maximum and compute $X = \sum_t x_t/\sqrt{L}$ with $x_t = \bar{z}_t \bar{z}_{t-h_m}$. Clearly $[x_t] = Q_M(h_m)$, yielding $L_d = Q_M(h_m)^{-2}$. We can build a convolutional filter that exploits the probabilities $Q_M(h)$ for all gaps h:

$$Y = \frac{1}{L} \sum_{t,h>0} C_h \bar{z}_t \bar{z}_{t-h} \text{ or } Y = \frac{1}{L} \sum_t y_t \text{ with } y_t = \bar{z}_t \sum_{h>0} C_h \bar{z}_{t-h} . \tag{36}$$

The restriction $h > 0$ is there to ensure that every expression of type $y_t y_{t+h}$ appears only once. With a similar argument as in Section 4, the optimum values for C_h are given by $C_h = q_{M(h)}$ with

$$q_{M(h)} = \frac{Q_M(h)}{\sqrt{\sum_{h>0} Q_M(h)^2}} \text{ if } h > 0 \text{ and } 0 \text{ otherwise.} \tag{37}$$

This yields:

$$L_d = \frac{1}{\sum_{h>0} Q_M(h)^2} \text{ and } C_h = q_M(h), \tag{38}$$

resulting in:

$$y = \bar{z} \times (\bar{z} \otimes q_M). \tag{39}$$

Hence the distinguisher takes one convolution and one stream multiplication. Both for the basic distinguisher and the convolutional filter L_d depends strongly on Q_M determined by the table M. In the worst case (for the attacker), M has been chosen such that for any gap h, $Q_M(h) = 2^{-2n}$ or zero. For example if $M = (0, 1, 3, 7)$, the resulting Q_M is 2^{-4} for $h \in \{1, 2, 3, 4, 6, 7\}$. For this kind of M, the simple distinguisher has $L_d = 2^{4n}$ and the convolutional filter has

$$L_d = 1/2^{n-1}(2^n - 1)2^{-4n} \approx 2^{2n+1} . \tag{40}$$

As there are $(2^n - 1)(2^n - 2)/2$ differences among 2^n entries, the choice of such an M is only possible if the length of the source register is in the order of 2^{2n-1}, so L_d is only a factor 4 longer than the source register. For example for a multiplexor choosing from 64 positions the source register must have a length in the order of 2000 bits and L_d is only 8000.

Another interesting case is when $M[i] = i$, i.e., the selection positions are subsequent. For $h \neq 0$ we have $Q_M(h) = (2^n - h)2^{-2n}$. The best simple distinguisher has $h_m = 1$ and yields $L_d = 2^{4n}/(2^n - 1)^2 \approx 2^{2n}$. For the convolutional filter this gives:

$$L_d{}^{-1} = \sum_{i=1}^{2^n-1} \frac{i^2}{2^{4n}} = 2^{-4n} \sum_{i=1}^{2^n-1} i^2, \tag{41}$$

resulting in

$$L_{\mathrm{d}} = 2^{4n} \frac{6}{(2^n - 1)(2(2^{2^n-1} + 1)(2^n)} \approx 3 \cdot 2^n. \tag{42}$$

Hence for a multiplexor selecting from 64 positions this yields $L_{\mathrm{d}} \approx 192$, again only a small factor larger than the minimum size of the source register. Both cases show that for a multiplexor generator with a Fibonacci source register we can construct distinguishers with L_{d} in the same order of magnitude as the source register.

5.2 Galois Configuration

If the source register has a Galois configuration the output sequence cannot be modeled as a simple sampling of the source sequence and the analysis above does not apply. The value of L_{d} depends on interaction between the selection position table and the feedback polynomial of the source LFSR. Given the weight of the feedback polynomial and characteristics of the selection position table upper bounds for L_{d} can be formulated. For example, for a 64-bit multiplexor and a source register with an LFSR of weight 17 a distinguisher similar to the one in Equation (39) can be built with L_{d} below $2^{15}/7 \approx 4700$.

6 Simulation Results

We have experimentally verified the correctness of the values L_{d} for all distinguishers presented in this paper. As $L_{\mathrm{d}} = \langle Y \rangle^{-2}$, it suffices to apply the distinguisher to sequences with length much larger than L_{d} and see whether Y converges to $\langle y_t \rangle$ in case it matches the generator and to 0 in case of a random sequence. All our experimentally obtained data confirmed the theoretical values.

The function $\rho_g(h)$ used for the simulation is based on the Gaussian approximation for $\mathcal{S}(g, h)$. To avoid the infinite domain of Gaussian variables, it is truncated beyond 5 times the standard deviation below and above the average $\langle h \rangle$. The same truncation is done for $\mathcal{S}(h, g)$, which is used to compute $\mu_g(h)$. With the roles of g and h reversed for $\mu_g(h)$, this results in a asymmetry in the truncation below and above $\langle h \rangle$ in order to preserve the actual shape of $\mu_g(h)$. For the multiplexor generators the exact expression of $Q_M(h)$ is used.

We illustrate our simulation results for a convolutional filter adapted to an SG with a source LFSR governed by the polynomial $p(x) = x^{300} + x^{219} + x^{131} + x^{73} + 1$ taken from [3]. For this polynomial, [3] gives a theoretical estimation of a parameter $N = 2^{30.3}$ where N plays the same role as L_{d} with $N = 4L_{\mathrm{d}}$. It reports an experiment with 48 successes out of 50 sequences each of length 2^{29}, i.e. a failure rate of 4 %. Our convolutional filter has $\langle Y \rangle \approx 0.000272$ resulting in $L_{\mathrm{d}} \approx 1.35 \times 10^7$. This is a factor 24 smaller than the equivalent in [3]. For sequences of length 2^{29} the expected failure rate of our convolutional filter is below 0.1 %.

For a sequence of L the standard deviation of Y is equal to $1/\sqrt{L}$. Relating that to $\langle Y \rangle$ of the convolutional filter yields $\sigma(Y) = \sqrt{L_d/L}\langle Y \rangle$. Figure 1 shows the convergence of Y to $\langle Y \rangle$ for an output sequence of the target SG and to 0 for the output of a pseudo-random generator based on SHA-1. Figure 2 compares the distribution of the value of Y over a set of 100 sequences of length L_d of the SG with the distributions predicted by the theory.

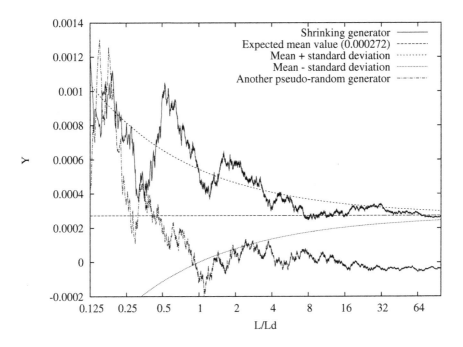

Fig. 1. Convergence of Y as a function of L

The experimental implementation uses explicit convolutions and component-wise multiplications. The complexity of the attack is dominated by the convolutions. For the SG and ASG, the convolution kernels have width of the order of $\sqrt{g_i}$. The complexity of the attack is thus $O(L_d \times \sum_i \sqrt{g_i})$. For the multiplexor generator with $M[i] = i$, the width of $Q_M(h)$ is of order 2^n. The complexity of this attack is thus $O(L_d^2)$. In this last case, we could make the convolution in the frequency domain using a fast Fourier transform (FFT), decreasing the complexity down to $O(L_d \log L_d)$.

Note that the convolution in our problem is very close to a convolution with a Gaussian, which in turn can be closely approximated by the iterated convolution with a rectangular kernel. The convolution with a rectangular kernel can be very efficiently implemented as a sliding window [3].

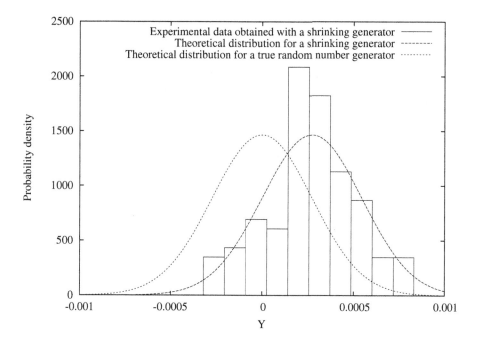

Fig. 2. Distribution of Y for 100 sequences of length L_d

7 Conclusions and Further Work

Convolutional filters are a new type of distinguisher applicable to shrinking generators, alternating-step generators and multiplexor generators. They are more powerful than existing distinguishers for those generators and their conceptual simplicity allows to predict their probability of success accurately.

The results of this paper can be extended by applying them to other stream cipher, such as the self-shrinking generator [16] and those of the LILI family [19].

References

1. A. Canteaut, M. Trabbia, "Improved Fast Correlation Attacks Using Parity-Check Equations of Weight 4 and 5", *Advances in Cryptology – Eurocrypt 2000*, LNCS 1807, Springer-Verlag, 2000, pp. 573-588.
2. D. Coppersmith, H. Krawczyk, Y. Mansour, "The Shrinking Generator", *Advances in Cryptology – Crypto '93*, LNCS 773, Springer-Verlag, 1994, pp. 22-39.
3. P. Ekdahl, W. Meier, T. Johansson, "Predicting the Shrinking Generator with Fixed Connections", *Advances in Cryptology – Eurocrypt 2003*, LNCS 2656, Springer-Verlag, 2003, pp. 330-344.
4. J. Dj. Golić, L. O'Connor, "Embedding and probabilistic correlation attacks on clock-controlled shift registers", *Advances in Cryptology – Eurocrypt '94*, LNCS 950, Springer-Verlag, 1995, pp. 230-243.

5. J. Dj. Golić, "Towards Fast Correlation Attacks on Irregularly Clocked Shift Registers", *Advances in Cryptology – Eurocrypt '95*, LNCS 921, Springer-Verlag, 1995, pp. 248-262.
6. J. Dj. Golić, "Linear Models for Keystream Generators", *IEEE Trans. on Computers*, Vol. 45, No 1 January, IEEE Press, 1996, pp. 41-49.
7. J. Dj. Golić, "Computation of low-weight parity-check polynomials", *Electronic Letters*, Vol. 32, No 21 October, 1996.
8. J. Dj. Golić, "Correlation analysis of the Shrinking Generator", *Advances in Cryptology – CRYPTO 2001*, LNCS 2139, Springer-Verlag, 2001, pp. 440-457.
9. J. Dj. Golić, "On the Success of the Embedding Attack on the Alternating Step Generator", *Selected Areas in Cryptography 2003*, 2003, pp. 262-274.
10. J. Dj. Golić, R. Menicocci, "A New Statistical Distinguisher for the Shrinking Generator", Cryptology ePrint Archive: Report 2003/041, `http://eprint.iacr.org/2003/041/`
11. J. Dj. Golić, R. Menicocci, "Correlation Analysis of the Alternating Step Generator", *Designs, Codes and Cryptography* 31(1), 2004, pp. 51-74.
12. C. G. Günther, "Alternating step generators controlled by de Bruijn sequences", *Advances in Cryptology – Eurocrypt '87*, LNCS 304, 1988, pp. 5-14
13. S. Jennings, "Multiplexed sequences: Some properties of the minimum polynomial", *Cryptography – Proceedings of the Workshop on Cryptography, Burg Feuerstein*, LNCS 149, Springer-Verlag, 1983, pp. 189-206.
14. T. Johansson, "Reduced complexity correlation attacks on two clock-controlled generators", *Advances in Cryptology – Asiacrypt '98*, LNCS 1514, Springer-Verlag, 1998, pp. 342-357.
15. T. Johansson, F. Jönsson, "Fast Correlation Attacks Through Reconstruction of Linear Polynomials", *Advances in Cryptology – CRYPTO 2000*, LNCS 1880, Springer-Verlag, 2000, pp. 300-315.
16. W. Meier and O. Staffelbach, "The Self-Shrinking Generator", *Advances in Cryptology – Eurocrypt '94*, LNCS 950, Springer-Verlag, 1994, pp. 205-214.
17. A. Menezes, P. van Oorschot, S. Vanstone, *Handbook of Applied Cryptography*, CRC Press, 1997.
18. L. Simpson, J. Dj. Golić, E. Dawson, "A probabilistic correlation attack on the shrinking generator", *Information Security and Privacy '98 - Brisbane*, LNCS 1438, Springer-Verlag, 1998, pp. 147-158.
19. L. Simpson, E. Dawson, J. Dj. Golić, W. Millan, "LILI Keystream Generator", *Selected Areas in Cryptography 2000*, LNCS 2012, Springer-Verlag, 2000, pp. 248-261.
20. D. Wagner, "A Generalized Birthday Problem", *Advances in Cryptology – CRYPTO 2002*, LNCS 2442, Springer-Verlag, 2002, pp. 288-303.

On Statistical Testing of Random Numbers Generators

F. El Haje[1,3], Y. Golubev[1], P.-Y. Liardet[2], and Y. Teglia[2]

[1] Université de Provence (Aix-Marseille 1)
CMI, 39 rue F. Joliot-Curie, 13453 Marseille, France
{Hussein, Youri.Golubev}@cmi.univ-mrs.fr
[2] STMicroelectronics,
ZI Rousset BP2 13106 Rousset, France
{Pierre-Yvan.Liardet, Yannick.Teglia}@st.com
[3] Centre Microélectronique de Provence
Georges Charpak
Avenue des Anémones - Quartier St. Pierre
13120 Gardanne - France

Abstract. Maurer's test is nowadays a basic statistical tool for testing physical random number generators in cryptographic applications. Based on a statistical analysis of this test we propose simple and effective methods for its improvement. These methods are related to the m - spacing technique common in goodness-of-fit problems and the L - leave out method used for a noise reduction in the final Maurer test statistic. We also show that the spacing distribution test represents a serious competitor for Maurer's test in the case when the random number generator is governed by a Markov chain with a long memory.

1 Introduction

1.1 Cryptographic Applications of Statistical Tests

Generating random numbers is not only a key issue in cryptographic applications, but also in counter measures against side-channel attacks on secure tokens like Smartcards (see [5] and [13] for some instances). The cornerstone character of these problems have brought institutional organizations, like the NIST in the USA and the BSI (Bundersamt für Sicherheit der Informationstechnik) in Germany, to develop standards to define Random Number Generators (RNGs), to classify them regarding their intended use and to analyze the confidence that one can have in claimed properties of RNGs.

The first approach developed in [9] and [10] was to qualify RNG using statistical tests. Canonical statistical tests include for instance the frequency test aimed to check uniformity of the outputs of the RNG and the long run test that verifies whether the RNG is not stuck at a given value during a defined period.

In the meantime, under the concern of completing security evaluation criteria of ITSEC or Common Criteria concerning random supply, RNG have been classified in two categories by the BSI:

R. De Prisco and M. Yung (Eds.): SCN 2006, LNCS 4116, pp. 271–287, 2006.

- Pseudo Random Number Generators (PRNG) that apply iterative numerical algorithms to an initial seed,
- True Random Number Generators (TRNG) that apply a numerical processing merged to a noise that come from the "real world", like thermal noise.

Typically, in testing of PRNGs, classical statistical tests are combined with thorough theoretical analysis of the cryptographic properties of the underlying algorithm [11]. On the other hand, TRNGs are more tricky to evaluate. So, the standard AIS 31 [12] has defined a way to qualify the expected quality of TRNG.

It classifies TRNG in two classes P1 and P2 regarding their intended use:

- P1 is the class of TRNG that will be used as nonce generators for authentication protocols,
- P2 embodies the class of "strong" TRNG that might be used as key generators

Notice that in contrast to testing of TRNG within the class P1, where statistical tests may be applied directly to the output of the generator, for strong TRNG, AIS 31 requires extra tests of the noise source. Testing the noise source aims at evaluating its intrinsic entropy, namely the degree of uncertainty that relies in the underlying physical phenomenon. The entropy of the noise source is a very delicate notion and nowadays there are still vast discussions regarding the best way to quantify and qualify it (see [16] for detail). In [8] Ueli Maurer has proposed the famous test based on a statistic asymptotically related to the source entropy. Roughly speaking, this test consists in counting the distances between patterns in the output data stream. In [2], J-S Coron and D. Naccache have proposed to modify this test in order to fit more precisely the source entropy (see also [3] for the latest version of this test which is now part of [12]). For industrial applications related to building new noise sources, failing the Maurer's test means failing AIS 31 certification. This means that applications and markets requiring AIS 31 certification are no longer accessible for suppliers whose devices did not succeed in this certification scheme.

In this paper, we will see how Maurer's test and its counterparts behave in the presence of specific statistical defects in the random source, how Maurer's test can be defeated and last but not least how it can be improved. We would like to stress in this context that essential applications of statistical tests are related to testing of physical random number generators.

1.2 Statistical Backgrounds of RNG Testing

From the mathematical viewpoint, the problem of testing of a random bit generator can be easily stated. Let $\mathbb{B}^n$ be the set of all n-bit vectors $\mathbf{b} = (b_1, \ldots, b_n)$. The distribution of a random vector $\mathbf{b} \in \mathbb{B}^n$ is described by a discrete distribution $p(\cdot)$ on $\mathbb{B}^n$

$$p(\mathbf{x}) = \mathbf{P}\Big(b_1 = x_1, \ldots, b_n = x_n\Big). \tag{1}$$

Recall that the random vector $\mathbf{b}$ is said uniformly distributed if $p(\cdot)$ equals the uniform distribution

$$p(\mathbf{x}) = \mu(\mathbf{x}) \stackrel{\text{def}}{=} \left(\frac{1}{2}\right)^n, \quad \mathbf{x} \in \mathbb{B}^n. \tag{2}$$

With these notations, the problem of testing of a random bit generator can be formulated as follows. Suppose we are given a random bit vector $\mathbf{b}$ distributed according an unknown law p. Then on the basis of $\mathbf{b}$ we want to test the null hypothesis

$$H_0: \quad p(\mathbf{x}) = \mu(\mathbf{x}) \quad \text{for all } \mathbf{x} \in \mathbb{B}^n$$

against the composite alternative

$$H_1: \quad p(\mathbf{x}) \neq \mu(\mathbf{x}) \quad \text{for some } \mathbf{x} \in \mathbb{B}^n.$$

In other words, we want to decide whether $\mathbf{b}$ is uniformly distributed on $\mathbb{B}^n$ or not. Our decision can be viewed as a measurable function $\varphi(\mathbf{b})$ (called *critical function*) taking two values $\{0, 1\}$. If $\varphi(\mathbf{b}) = 0$, then H_0 is accepted, otherwise H_1 is accepted. Usually the quality of testing is measured by two types of error probabilities: the probability of the first kind error

$$\alpha(\varphi) \stackrel{\text{def}}{=} \mathbf{P}_0(\varphi(\mathbf{b}) = 1),$$

where $\mathbf{P}_0(\cdot)$ is the probability measure corresponding to the uniform measure μ, and the probability of the second kind error

$$\beta(\varphi, \mathbf{P}) \stackrel{\text{def}}{=} \mathbf{P}(\varphi(\mathbf{b}) = 0).$$

Here $\mathbf{P}(\cdot)$ is any probability measure different from the uniform distribution. The value $1 - \beta(\varphi, \mathbf{P})$ is *called power of test*. Statistical sense of $\alpha(\varphi)$ is very transparent, since this is the probability to reject a good RNG. In contrast to classical statistical testing, where $\alpha(\varphi)$ varies typically from 0.01 to 0.05, in cryptographic applications, we deal with smaller probabilities of the first kind error residing in the range $(10^{-7}, 10^{-3})$. Usually this error probability is fixed regarding the losses which we shall have rejecting H_0. For instance, in nature, there exist chaotic processes such as thermal, Flicker or shot noises in a transistor, and it is a difficult engineering task to design an electronic circuit that exploits this randomness. So, rejection of a good generator might be very expensive. On the other hand, with very small $\alpha(\varphi)$ we can accept bad generators. Therefore a reasonable choice of the probability of the first kind error is a delicate issue (compare [9] and [10]).

From mathematics viewpoint, fixing α, we define the set of statistical tests

$$\Phi_\alpha = \{\varphi : \alpha(\varphi) \leq \alpha\}.$$

and the main goal of statistical testing is to find the most powerful test φ^* within the class Φ_α. In other words, we are looking for the test φ^* such that

$$\beta(\varphi^*, \mathbf{P}) \leq \beta(\varphi, \mathbf{P}) \quad \text{for all } \varphi \in \Phi_\alpha \text{ and for all } \mathbf{P} \neq \mathbf{P}_0.$$

It is easy to see that when the alternative contains all probability distributions, the most powerful test doesn't exist and any attempt to use directly maximum likelihood or Bayesian tests will immediately fail. This happens because we cannot recover the underlying probability distribution on the basis of the data at hand when the set of alternative is too rich. Therefore the basic idea to overcome this difficulty is to consider a smaller alternative family $\mathcal{P}$ satisfying the following properties

- the probability distributions within $\mathcal{P}$ can be recovered with a sufficiently high accuracy for large n
- the maximum likelihood test

$$\varphi_{ML}(\mathbf{b}, \mathcal{P}) = \mathbf{1}\left\{\max_{P \in \mathcal{P}} \frac{p(\mathbf{b})}{\mu(\mathbf{b})} > t_\alpha\right\} \tag{3}$$

is feasible from numerical complexity viewpoint.

Recall that the critical value t_α is defined by

$$t_\alpha = \inf\left\{t > 0 : \mathbf{P}_0\left(\max_{P \in \mathcal{P}} \frac{p(\mathbf{b})}{\mu(\mathbf{b})} > t\right) \le \alpha\right\}.$$

In order to shed some light on typical problems related to this approach, let us look at the classical frequency test. To construct this test, assume that a RNG generates independent identically distributed blocks $B_i = (b_{1i}, \ldots, b_{di})$ containing d bits. Our goal is to check whether B_i are uniformly distributed in $\mathbb{B}^d$ or not. If we associate with the block B_i the integer

$$x_i = \sum_{k=1}^{d} 2^{k-1} b_{ki},$$

our problem is reduced to the simplest goodness of fit testing: based on the sample $\mathbf{x} = (x_1, \ldots, x_N)$ of i.i.d. random variables to test the null hypothesis

$$H_0 : \quad \mathbf{P}(x_i = l) = 2^{-d} \quad \text{for all } l \in \{0, \ldots, 2^d - 1\}$$

against the alternative

$$H_1 : \quad \mathbf{P}(x_i = l) \ne 2^{-d} \quad \text{for some } l \in \{0, \ldots, 2^d - 1\}.$$

It is easy to check with a simple algebra, that the maximum likelihood test has the following form

$$\varphi_{ML}^d(\mathbf{x}) = \mathbf{1}\left\{N \sum_{s=0}^{2^d-1} \widehat{p}_s(\mathbf{x}) \log \frac{\widehat{p}_s(\mathbf{x})}{2^{-d}} > t_\alpha\right\}, \tag{4}$$

where

$$\widehat{p}_s = \frac{1}{N} \sum_{i=1}^{N} \mathbf{1}(x_i = s)$$

is the empirical distribution.

At the first glance everything goes smoothly with this test, but our approach has a serious drawback related to the fact that a priori it was assumed that the RNG generates independent blocks of length d. In fact, there is no reasonable argument justifying this hypothesis. For instance a RNG may work according to a Markov model. In this case, simple simulations reveal that the power of the test depends strongly on d and on the underlying Markov model, and fitting d, we can improve significantly the performance of the test. Since the statistical model of the RNG is hardly known in practice, we should choose the block length based on the data at hand.

In this paper, we are interested in the question "how could statistical tests be improved with the proper choice of the generating alternative family $\mathcal{P}$" (see (3)). In particular, we will discuss simple methods for improving Maurer's test and finally we will compare numerically this test with a test based on distribution of 1 - spacings in the data flow.

2   Maurer's Test

2.1   Uniformity Tests

Standard motivations of Maurer's test are related to the notion of entropy of ergodic bit flow (see [8]). In this paper, we present a slightly different viewpoint based on classical uniformity tests. This new interpretation will help us to understand why Maurer's test could be improved. Testing of uniformity means the following. Let $\mu(x) = 1$, $x \in [0,1]$ be the uniform probability density on the interval $[0,1]$. Suppose we observe n i.i.d. random variables $\mathbf{X}^n = (X_1, \ldots, X_n)$ with an unknown probability density $p(x)$, $x \in [0,1]$. The goal of the uniformity testing is to test on the basis of $\mathbf{X}^n$ the null hypothesis

$$H_0: \quad p(x) = \mu(x) \quad \text{for all } x \in [0,1]$$

against the composite alternative

$$H_1: \quad p(x) \neq \mu(x) \quad \text{for some } x \in [0,1].$$

In statistics, the most powerful tests are usually constructed with the help of the maximum likelihood principle which can be motivated by the famous Neyman-Pearson lemma. In order to explain how this principle works in our setting, let us assume for a moment that H_1 is a simple alternative, say $H_1: p(x) = p_1(x)$, where $p_1(x)$ is a known smooth probability density on $[0,1]$. In this case, in view of the Neyman-Pearson lemma the maximum likelihood test defined by

$$\varphi(\mathbf{X}^n) = 1\left\{L(\mathbf{X}^n) \geq h_\alpha\right\},$$

where

$$L(\mathbf{X}^n) = \sum_{i=1}^{n} \log p_1(X_i), \tag{5}$$

is the most powerful test. Recall also that the critical value of the test h_α is computed as a root of the equation $\mathbf{P}_0(\varphi(\mathbf{X}^n) = 1) = \alpha$.

Let's now return back to the composite alternative when the density p is unknown. A simple heuristic idea to overcome this difficulty is to construct a non parametric density estimator $\widehat{p}(x, \mathbf{X}^n)$ and then to plug-in it in (5). Thus we arrive at the following test statistics

$$S(\mathbf{X}^n) = \sum_{i=1}^{n} \log \widehat{p}(X_i, \mathbf{X}^n)$$

and the principal issue is to find a reasonable density estimator. Standard methods of nonparametric density estimation are motivated by the definition of probability density

$$p(x) = \lim_{h \to 0} \frac{\mathbf{P}\{X_1 \in [x, x+h]\}}{h}.$$

Roughly speaking, the above formula says that for all sufficiently small h

$$p(x) \approx \frac{\mathbf{P}\{X_1 \in [x, x+h]\}}{h}.$$

Estimating $\mathbf{P}\{X_1 \in [x, x+h]\}$ in the above display by the empirical probability $n^{-1} \sum_{i=1}^{n} \mathbf{1}\{X_i \in [x, x+h]\}$, we get the classical kernel density estimator

$$\widehat{p}_h(X_j, \mathbf{X}^n) = \frac{1}{nh} \sum_{i=1}^{n} \mathbf{1}\{X_i \in [X_j, X_j + h]\} = \frac{\#\{X_i \in [X_j, X_j + h]\}}{nh}.$$

Our final step is based on the fact that the bandwidth h in this formula might be data-dependent $h = h(X_j, \mathbf{X}^n)$. For instance, one can take

$$h = h(X_{(j)}, \mathbf{X}^n) = X_{(j+m)} - X_{(j)},$$

where $X_{(k)}$ stay for the order statistics $X_{(1)} \leq, \ldots, \leq X_{(n)}$. The increments $X_{(j+m)} - X_{(j)}$, $j = 1, \ldots, n-m$ are called m-spacings. Thus we get the following m-spacing density estimator

$$\widehat{p}_m(X_{(j)}, \mathbf{X}^n) = \frac{m}{n[X_{(j+m)} - X_{(j)}]}$$

or equivalently, the test statistic

$$S_m(\mathbf{X}^n) = \sum_{i=1}^{n} \log \frac{m}{n[X_{(j+m)} - X_{(j)}]}.$$

Certainly, the idea to use this statistics is well known and widely used in goodness of fit testing (see e. g. [15], [4], [17]). In order to shed some light on statistical properties of $S_m(\mathbf{X}^n)$, it is very instructive to look at its limit distribution under the alternative. The simplest way to do this is to apply the famous Pyke's theorem [14] about the distribution of order statistics.

Theorem 1. *Let* $U_1, \ldots, U_n$ *be i.i.d. uniformly distributed on* $[0, 1]$ *and* $e_1, \ldots, e_n$ *be i.i.d. standard exponentially distributed random variables. Then*

$$\left\{ U_{(k+1)} - U_{(k)}, \ 1 \le k \le n - 1 \right\} \overset{D}{=} \left\{ e_k \Big/ \sum_{s=1}^{n} e_s, \ 1 \le k \le n - 1 \right\}. \tag{6}$$

With this theorem, one can find the limit distribution of $S_m(\mathbf{X}^n)$. Unfortunately, the rigorous argument involve a lot of technical details, therefore we provide here only a simple heuristic motivation. Since $F(X_k) = U_k$, where F is the distribution function of X_1, we have by the Taylor formula

$$U_{(j+m)} - U_{(j)} = F[X_{(j+m)}] - F[X_{(j)}] \approx p(X_{(j)})[X_{(j+m)} - X_{(j)}].$$

This yields the following asymptotic $(n \to \infty)$ formula for the test statistics

$$\begin{aligned}
S_m(\mathbf{X}^n) &\approx \sum_{i=1}^{n} \log p(X_i) - \sum_{i=1}^{n} \log \frac{n[U_{(j+m)} - U_{(j)}]}{m} \\
&= -nH(p) + \sqrt{n} \frac{1}{\sqrt{n}} \sum_{i=1}^{n} [\log p(X_i) - \mathbf{E}_p \log p(X_i)] \\
&\quad + nC(m) + \sqrt{n} \frac{1}{\sqrt{n}} \sum_{i=1}^{n} \left[\log\left(\frac{1}{m} \sum_{l=0}^{m-1} e_{i+l} \right) - C(m) \right] \\
&\quad + n \log\left[1 + \frac{1}{n} \sum_{i=1}^{n} (e_i - 1) \right],
\end{aligned} \tag{7}$$

where $H(p)$ is the entropy

$$H(p) = -\int_0^1 p(x) \log p(x)\, dx \quad \text{and} \quad C(m) = \mathbf{E} \log\left(\frac{1}{m} \sum_{i=1}^{m} e_i \right).$$

Notice also that the last term at the right-hand side of (7) can be simplified by the Taylor formula

$$n \log\left[1 + \frac{1}{n} \sum_{i=1}^{n} (e_i - 1) \right] \approx \sqrt{n} \frac{1}{\sqrt{n}} \sum_{i=1}^{n} (e_i - 1).$$

Even a quick look at (7) shows that

$$\lim_{n \to \infty} \frac{S_m(\mathbf{X}^n)}{n} \overset{a.s.}{=} -H(p) + C(m).$$

Moreover, it is also well known (see e.g. [7]) that if $p(x)$ is strictly bounded for below on $[0, 1]$, then $S_m(\mathbf{X}^n)$ is asymptotically Gaussian

$$\lim_{n \to \infty} \frac{S_m(\mathbf{X}^n) - nH(p) - nC(m)}{\sqrt{n}} \overset{D}{=} \mathcal{N}\left(0, \sigma^2(p) + \sigma_m^2 \right),$$

where the asymptotic variance of this Gaussian law is defined by (see also [1])

$$\sigma_m^2(p) = \int_0^1 [\log p(x) + H(p)]^2 p(x)\, dx, \quad \sigma_m^2 = (2m^2 - 2m + 1)\psi'(m) - 2m + 1,$$

with

$$\psi'(m) = \frac{\pi^2}{6} - \sum_{j=1}^{m-1} \frac{1}{j^2}.$$

From the plot of σ_m^2 shown on Figure 1, we see that this function vanishes very rapidly. It means that with moderate m we could improve the performance of testing. In order to explain this phenomenon, notice that under the hypothesis, for large n

$$S_m(\mathbf{X}^n) \sim \mathcal{N}(nC(m), n\sigma_m^2).$$

Therefore, for a sufficiently small α, the critical value can be computed by

$$h_\alpha \approx nC(m) + \sqrt{2n\sigma_m^2 \log(1/\alpha)}$$

and if the entropy is large enough

$$H(p) \gg \sqrt{\frac{2\sigma_1^2 \log(1/\alpha)}{n}},$$

then the probability of the second kind error is given by

$$\log \mathbf{P}\Big(S_m(\mathbf{X}^n) \leq h_\alpha\Big) \approx -\frac{\Big[\sqrt{n}H(p) + \sqrt{2\sigma_m^2 \log(1/\alpha)}\Big]^2}{2[\sigma^2(p) + \sigma_m^2]}. \tag{8}$$

It is easy to check that the right-hand side in (8) is monotone in σ_m^2. Therefore the probability of the second kind error reaches its minimum when $m = \infty$. However, since σ_m^2 vanishes rapidly, we can get almost the minimal error probability with a relatively small m. In fact, the optimal choice of m should be data-driven.

2.2   Maurer's Test

This test has the standard form $\varphi^{ma}(\mathbf{b}) = \mathbf{1}\big(T(\mathbf{b}) \geq t_\alpha\big)$, where $T(\mathbf{b})$ is computed as follows:

1. Transform the input bit sequence $\mathbf{b} = (b_1, \ldots, b_n)$ into the sequence of integers $\mathbf{x} = (x_1, \ldots, x_s)$, $s = \lfloor n/d \rfloor$ taking values in $\mathbb{A}^d = \{0, \ldots, 2^d - 1\}$

$$x_k = \sum_{i=1}^{d} 2^{i-1} b_{(k-1)d+i}$$

2. For each motif $q \in \mathbb{A}^d$ compute its positions in $\mathbf{x}$:

$$N^q = \{k : x_k = q\}.$$

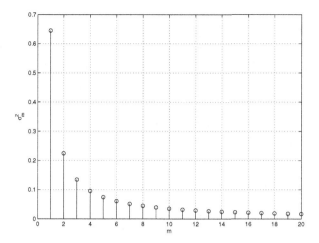

Fig. 1. The variance σ_m^2

3. For each motif $q \in \mathbb{A}^d$ compute the intermediate statistics

$$S^q(\mathbf{b}) = -\sum_i \log(N_{i+1}^q - N_i^q).$$

4. Compute the final test's statistic

$$T(\mathbf{b}) = \sum_{q \in \mathbb{A}^d} S^q(\mathbf{b}).$$

In order to describe completely the test, remember that the critical value t_α is defined as a root of the equation

$$\mathbf{P}_0\big(\varphi^{ma}(\mathbf{b}) = 1\big) = \alpha. \tag{9}$$

There are two standard ways to compute t_α

- compute the empirical distribution function of $T(\mathbf{b})$ by the Monte-Carlo method and solve the empirical counterpart of (9)
- use the fact that asymptotically ($n \to \infty$) the distribution of $T(\mathbf{b})$ is Gaussian.

We intentionally decomposed Maurer's test into 4 steps in order to stress its relations with the uniformity testing. From the viewpoint of the uniformity testing, the underlying ideas of Maurer's test are related to steps 3 and 4 that clearly show what does the test do: it checks whether the positions of patterns are uniformly distributed in the bit stream. Mathematically, this principal idea is based on the assumption that all x_k are independent (see [8], [3]). In other words, this means that d should be large. This hypothesis immediately entails that

- $N_{i+1}^q - N_i^q$ are almost independent and follow an exponential law under the null hypothesis and under the alternative (step 3)
- under the null hypothesis and under the alternative, the covariance matrix

$$r_{pq} = \mathbf{cov}(S^q(\mathbf{b}), S^p(\mathbf{b})), \ 0 \leq p, q \leq 2^d - 1$$

has always the form

$$r_{pq} \approx \begin{cases} 1, \ p = q \\ c, \ p \neq q, \end{cases}$$

where c is a constant (step 4).

Under the null hypothesis all these assumptions hold true, but unfortunately, they may fail for alternatives related to stationary ergodic processes. The reason is that we cannot take d very large, since there is a natural upper bound $d \leq \log_2(n/10)$ (see [8]). Therefore in practical applications, the cornerstone hypothesis that d is really large, is not well justified. It is surprising that this fact opens some perspectives for significant improvements of Maurer's test.

In order to illustrate numerically statistical phenomena in this paper, we shall use two statistical models for random bit generators. The first one called *Markov chain model* (see also [16]) works as follows. Let ξ_i be i.i.d. bits such that $\mathbf{P}(\xi = 0) = p$, then the random bits are generated as follows

$$b_i = \begin{cases} b_{i-m} & \text{if } \xi_i = 0 \\ 1 - b_{i-m} & \text{otherwise}, \end{cases}$$

where $m \geq 1$ is called memory of the chain and $p \in [0,1]$ is called transition probability. In all our numerical experiments, the length of the bit vector is $n = 20000$ and the probability of the first kind error is 0.001. We use these basic simulation parameters from now on.

Another statistical mechanism for random bit generation is called *season drift model*. In this case the bits b_i are independent but not identically distributed. Namely, it is assumed that

$$\mathbf{P}\left(b_i = 0\right) = (0.5 + A)\cos\left(\frac{2\pi i}{\tau}\right),$$

where $A \in [0.5, 1]$ is called the amplitude and τ is called *season period*.

First of all let us look at the covariance matrix of the intermediate test's statistic. Figure 2 illustrates the fact that this covariance matrix may substantially differ under the null hypothesis and the alternative. The left panel of this figure shows the covariance matrix under the null hypothesis whereas the right panel shows this matrix under an alternative. As an alternative we used the Markov chain with memory 5 and transition probability 0.7.

We start to analyze Maurer's test with the question whether the log-function in $\log(N_{i+1}^q - N_i^q)$ is good. At the first glance the answer is negative since log results from the hypothesis that $N_{i+1}^q - N_i^q$ are exponentially distributed. In fact, under the null hypothesis, these random variables follow a geometric law.

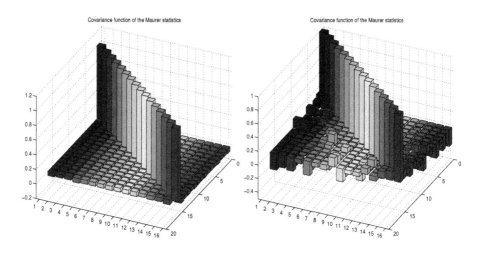

Fig. 2. The covariance matrix under the hypothesis and the alternative

It means that if the only one intermediate test's statistic, say S^0, was used, then $\log(x)$ should be replaced by $l(x) = x \log(x) - (x-1) \log(x-1)$. This fact doesn't mean that $l(x)$ is optimal in the case when we are dealing with the sum of S^q. This curious phenomenon can be explained by the correlation between statistics S^q, $q \in \mathcal{A}^d$. Moreover, $\log(x)$ is not optimal too and we illustrate this fact in the following statistical experiment. On Figure 3 we plotted the probability of the second kind error as function of the transition probability for standard Maurer's test (dotted line) and for Maurer's test with $\log(N_{i+1}^q - N_i^q + 10)$ (solid line) for 6-tuples ($d = 6$) partition. The bit vectors were generated by the Markov chain model with memory 1. As we see that there is a slight improvement of Maurer's test. In other numerical simulation the authors looked at, the function $\log(x + 10)$ always improves the power of the test but it seems to us that improvements are not very significant and therefore in practical applications $\log(x)$ may be considered as a reasonable choice. Another idea to use $\sum_{i=1}^{x-1} i^{-1}$ instead of $\log(x)$, was proposed in [3] and [2]. Unfortunately in our simulation study, this method doesn't result in visible improvements of the test's power. Typical behavior of Coron's test and Maurer's test are shown on Figure 4. Here we used the statistical model for the random bit source from the previous example.

Let us discuss another problem related to the step 3. Namely, the optimality of the first order spacings $N_{i+1}^q - N_i^q$. For the uniformity testing problem, we have seen that m-spacings may improve the test power. Similar effect takes place for Maurer's test, it turns out that using m-spacings $N_{i+m}^q - N_i^q$ with $m > 1$ it is possible to improve the power of this test.

The next natural question related to the final step 4 is: whether the sum of $S^q(\mathbf{b})$ is a good idea for testing or not? This statistics would be optimal if the covariance matrix of the vector $\left(S^1(\mathbf{b}), \ldots, S^{2^d}(\mathbf{b}) \right)$ doesn't change its form

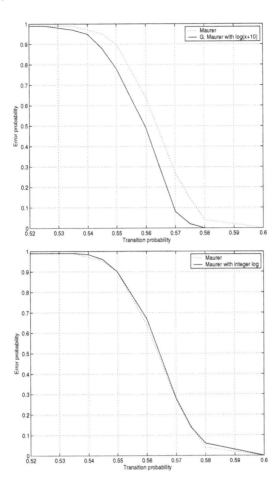

Fig. 3. Maurer's test with $\log(x + 10)$ **Fig. 4.** Coron's modification

under the alternative. Unfortunately, we have seen see that it isn't true. This phenomenon opens another way to improve Maurer's test.

3   Motif Uniformity Test

The term *Motif Uniformity* (MU) test is refereed to Maurer's test with the following modifications:

- in place of $S^q(\mathbf{b})$ computed at the step 3, we use m-spacing statistics

$$S^{q,m}(\mathbf{b}) = - \sum_i \log(N_{i+m}^q - N_i^q)$$

- the final test statistics $\sum_{q \in \mathbb{A}^d} S^q(\mathbf{b})$ computed at the step 4 is replaced by a special non-linear transform based on p-leave out method.

3.1   *m*-Spacing Method

In this section, we present two examples showing that $m - spacing$ technique improves the power of Maurer's test. Figure 5 shows the power of Maurer's test (dotted line) and the power of its modification based on 4-spacings (solid line) as function of the transition probability. We see that the improvement is clear. The

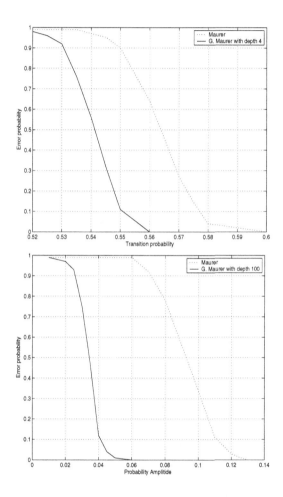

Fig. 5. The MU test with 4-spacings   **Fig. 6.** The MU test with 100-spacings

next example demonstrates a more significant improvement of Maurer's test. In this example, we deal with the season drift model with $T = 3000$ and plot the power of the tests as function of amplitude A. For this random bit model Maurer's test with $d = 1$ is, in some sense, optimal. Since p_k is a very smooth function of k, m-spacings with large m may improve substantially the test power. Figure 6 distinctly illustrates this fact.

3.2 *L*-Leave Out Method

We have seen that the covariance matrix of Maurer's test statistics $S^q(\mathbf{b})$, $q \in \mathcal{A}^d$ may change substantially under the alternative and now we use this phenomenon to improve the performance of this test. The underlying idea is very simple. We order the test statistics $\left(S^1(\mathbf{b}), \ldots, S^{2^d}(\mathbf{b})\right)$ such that

$$S^{(1)}(\mathbf{b}) \geq S^{(2)}(\mathbf{b}) \geq \ldots \geq S^{(2^d)}(\mathbf{b})$$

and compute the final test statistics

$$T^L(\mathbf{b}) = \sum_{i=1}^{2^d-L} S^{(i)}(\mathbf{b}).$$

Figure 7 illustrates improvements in the test power based on 4 - leave out technique. Here we plotted the probability of the second kind error as function of transition probability for 1-memory Markov chain.

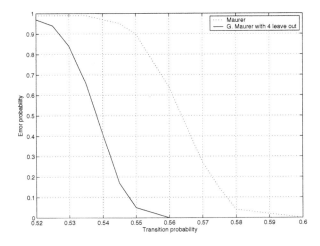

Fig. 7. Performance of Maurer's test with 4 leave out statistics

4 Spacings Distribution Test

In contrast to Maurer's test which checks whether the positions of motifs in the input vector are uniformly distributed or not, the goal in the Spacing Distribution (SD) test is to compare the empirical distribution of 1-spacings with a geometric distribution. For typical alternatives, the distribution of $N_{i+1}^q - N_i^q$ may be very far from geometric thus providing an additional and significant statistical information about RNG. From the statistical viewpoint, we can retrieve this information testing the hypothesis that the law of $N_{i+1}^q - N_i^q$ is geometric.

In this section, we propose to use the maximum likelihood method to test this hypothesis.

Remember that under the null hypothesis 1-spacing follows a geometric law

$$\mathbf{P}_0\left(N_{i+1}^q - N_i^q = k\right) = p_0(k) = \frac{1}{2^d - 1}\left(1 - 2^{-d}\right)^k.$$

We define the SD test as the maximum likelihood test assuming that for a given q the spacings $N_{i+1}^q - N_i^q$ are i.i.d. This test consists in the following steps

- For all motifs q compute the empirical distribution of $N_{i+1}^q - N_i^q$

$$\widehat{p}^q(k) = \frac{1}{\#N^q} \sum_{i=1}^{\#N^q} \mathbf{1}\left(N_{i+1}^q - N_i^q = k\right)$$

and compute the intermediate test statistics

$$S^q(\mathbf{b}) = \sum_{i=1}^{\#N^q} \log \frac{\widehat{p}^q(N_{i+1}^q - N_i^q)}{p_0(N_{i+1}^q - N_i^q)}.$$

- Compute the critical function

$$\varphi_{SD}(\mathbf{b}) = \mathbf{1}\left(\sum_{q=0}^{2^d-1} S^q(\mathbf{b}) \geq h_\alpha\right).$$

In some sense, the SD test can be viewed as a very good complementary of Maurer's test since this test is very stable and powerful for the Markov chains alternatives. Figure 8 illustrates this fact. In this numerical experiment we try to find out how the powers of Maurer's test and the SD test depend on the parameters of the Markov chain alternative. On left panel we plotted the power of Maurer's test with $d = 7$ as function of the memory of the chain varying from 1 to 20 and the transition probability belonging to $[0.5, 0.8]$. The left panel represents the power of SD test for the same alternatives.

This figure distinctly shows the principle differences Maurer's and SD test. First of all, Maurer's test detects very badly alternatives with memories greater than d. This is the principle drawback of the test since the block length d cannot be large. We have already mentioned that $d \leq \log_2(n/10)$, where n is the length of the bit flow at hand, otherwise the test statistics $S^q(\mathbf{b})$ may have no sense. On the other hand, Maurer's test with large d may detect badly the Markov alternatives with short memories. Therefore, it seems to us that Maurer's test with a priory fixed large d is not good for practical implementations. The only way to overcome this difficulty of Maurer's test is to use data driven methods for choosing this parameter.

Fortunately, these drawbacks are not inherent to SD test. Even with small d this test can detect the Markov chains with large memories. However, we would like to stress that the SD test should not be used as an universal test. It not surprising for instance that its power may be low for season drift models. In this case, the 1-spacing follows a geometric law and from the viewpoint of the SD test, there is no big difference between the hypothesis and the alternative.

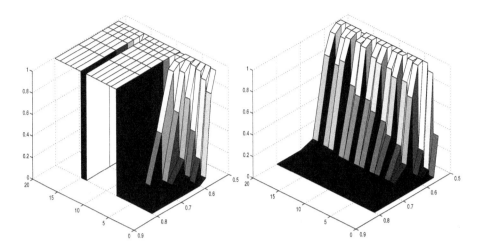

Fig. 8. Statistical performance of Maurer's and SD tests

5 Concluding Remarks

The motivation of Maurer's entropy test is based on the idea that the block length d should be large. Unfortunately, there are two natural limitations on d. The first one is related to the fact that it cannot exceed the log of the length of the bit vector at hand, since otherwise the test has no sense. The second one is that the numerical complexity of Maurer's test increases exponentially with d. So, in practice, we deal only with moderate block lengths, and the present paper is focused on possible improvements of the Maurer test in this situation. We propose a new interpretation of Maurer's test which is based on nonparametric maximum likelihood uniformity tests. This approach explains why and how Maurer's test can be improved. By the way, we provide three methods to improve it

- using m-spacing technique
- L-leave out correction of the test statistics
- spacing distribution test

In numerical examples, we demonstrate that all these methods improve significantly the test's power. On the other hand, from a numerical complexity viewpoint these modifications and Maurer's are equivalent.

Acknowledgments

We would like to thank Stefan Weggenkitl, Schindler Werner and two anonymous referee of this paper for interesting discussions and remarks.

References

1. Cressie, N. (1976) On the logarithms of high-order spacings. *Biometrika*, **63**, no. 2, 343-355.
2. Coron, J.-S. and Naccache, D. (1998). An Accurate Evaluation of Maurer's Universal Test, in *Proceedings of Selected Areas in Cryptography 98*. LNCS 1556 P57-71. Springer-Verlag.
3. Coron, J.S. (1999). On the security of Random sources, in *Public Key Cryptography: Second International Workshop on Practice and Theory in Public Key Cryptography, PKC'99, Kamakura, Japan, March 1999. Proceedings Editors: H. Imai, Y. Zheng (Eds.):* vol. 1560. Lecture Notes in Computer Science, http://www.gemplus.com/smart/rd/publications
4. Del Pino, G. (1979). On the asymptotic distribution of k-spacings with applications to goodness-of-fit tests. *Ann. Statist.* **8**, 1058–1065.
5. Goubin, L. and Patarin, J. (1999) DES and Differential Power Analysis the "Duplication" Method LNCS *Proceedings of CHESS'99*
6. Finner, H. Rotters, M. (2002). Multiple hypothesis testing and expected number of type 1 errors. *Ann. Statist.* **30**, no 1, 220–238.
7. Hall, P. limit theorems for sums of general functions of m-spacings. *Math. Proc. Cambridge Phil. Society,* **96**, 517-532.
8. Maurer, U. (1992). A universal statistical test for random bit generators. *J. Cryptology,* **5**, no. 2, 89–105.
9. National Institute of Standards and Technology, Security Requirements for Cryptographic Modules, FIPS 140-1, Jan. 1994 http://www.nist.gov/itl/div897/pubs/fip140-1.htm.
10. National Institute of Standards and Technology, Security Requirements for Cryptographic Modules, FIPS 140-2, May. 2001 http://csrc.nist.gov/publications/fips/fips140-2/fips1402.pdf
11. Functionality Classes and Evaluation Methodology for Deterministic Random Number Generators, Version 2.0 December 1999. www.bsi.de/zertifiz/zert/interpr/ais20e.pdf
12. Functionality Classes and Evaluation Methodology for True (physical) Random Number Generators, Version 3.1 September 2001. http://www.bsi.bund.de/zertifiz/zert/interpr/trngk31e.pdf
13. Oswald, E. and Preneel, B. A Survey on Passive Side Channel Attacks and their Counter Measures for the Nessie Public-Key Cryptosystems. https://www.cosic.esat.kuleuven.be/nessie/reports/phase2/kulwp5-027-1.pdf
14. Pyke, R. (1965) Spacings. *J.R. Statist. Soc. B* **27**, 395–436.
15. Shilling, M. (1983) Goodness of fit in $\mathbb{R}^n$ based on weighted empirical distributions of certain neighbor statistics *Ann. Statist.* **11**, 1–12.
16. Weggenkitl, S. (2001). Entropy estimators and Serial Tests for Ergodic Chains. *IEEE Trans. Inform. Theory.* **47**, no. 6, 2480-2489.
17. Weiss, L. (1957) Asymptotic of certain tests of fit based on sample spacings. *Ann. Math. Statist.,* **28**, 783-786.

Lightweight Email Signatures
(Extended Abstract)

Ben Adida[1], David Chau[1], Susan Hohenberger[2,*], and Ronald L. Rivest[1]

[1] CSAIL, Massachusetts Institute of Technology, Cambridge, MA 02139, USA
[2] IBM Research, Zurich Research Laboratory, CH-8803 Rüschlikon

Abstract. We present *Lightweight Email Signatures* (LES), a simple cryptographic architecture for authenticating email. LES is an extension of DKIM, the recent IETF effort to standardize domain-based email signatures. LES shares DKIM's ease of deployment: they both use the DNS to distribute a single public key for each domain. Importantly, LES supports common uses of email that DKIM jeopardizes: multiple email personalities, firewalled ISPs, incoming-only email forwarding services, and other common uses that often require sending email via a third-party SMTP server. In addition, LES does not require DKIM's implied intra-domain mechanism for authenticating users when they send email.

LES provides these features using identity-based signatures. Each domain authority generates a master keypair, publishes the public component in the DNS, and stores the private component securely. Using this private component, the authority delivers to each of its users, via email, an individual secret key whose identity string corresponds to the user's email address. A sender then signs messages using this individual secret key. A recipient verifies such a signature by querying the appropriate master public key from the DNS, computing the sender's public key, and verifying the signature accordingly. As an added bonus, the widespread availability of user-level public keys enables deniable authentication, such as ring signatures. Thus, LES provides email authentication with optional repudiability.

We built a LES prototype to determine its practicality. Basic user tests show that the system is relatively easy to use, and that cryptographic performance, even when using deniable authentication, is well within acceptable range.

1   Introduction

1.1   The State of Email and DKIM

Email has become a highly polluted medium. More than 75% of email volume is spam [27], and phishing attacks – spoofed emails that trick users into revealing private information – are on the rise, both in volume [3] and sophistication [20]. Email users are repeatedly warned that an email's `From:` field cannot be trusted [35], and that links distributed by email should not be followed [2,29]. Still, studies show that users remain highly vulnerable, even to low-tech phishing attempts [11].

---

[*] Research performed while at the Massachusetts Institute of Technology.

R. De Prisco and M. Yung (Eds.): SCN 2006, LNCS 4116, pp. 288–302, 2006.

Domain Keys & Identified Mail (DKIM) is a promising proposal for providing a foundation to solve the phishing problem: domains are made cryptographically responsible for the email they send. Roughly, bob@foo.com sends emails via outgoing.foo.com, which properly identifies Bob and signs the email content. The public key is distributed via a DNS TXT record for _domainkeys.foo.com. The details of how DKIM should handle mailing lists, message canonicalization, message forwarding, and other thorny issues, are being resolved in the context of a recently-formed IETF Working Group [18].

1.2   Lightweight Email Signatures

We propose *Lightweight Email Signatures*, abbreviated LES, as an extension to DKIM. We show how LES preserves all of the major architectural advantages of DKIM, while offering three significant improvements:

1. **Automatic Intra-Domain Authentication**: DKIM assumes that server outgoing.foo.com can tell its users bob@foo.com and carol@foo.com apart, which is not a safe assumption in a number of settings – e.g. university campuses or ISPs that authenticate only the sending IP address. By contrast, LES authenticates users without requiring additional authentication infrastructure within foo.com.

2. **Flexible Use of Email (Better End-to-End)**: LES allows Bob to send email via any outgoing mail server, not just the official outgoing.foo.com mandated by DKIM. This is particularly important when supporting existing use cases. Bob may want to alternate between using bob@foo.com and bob@bar.com, while his ISP might only allow SMTP connections to its outgoing mail server outgoing.isp.com. Bob may also use his university's alumni forwarding services to send email from bob@alum.univ.edu, though his university might not provide outgoing mail service.

3. **A Privacy Option**: LES enables the use of repudiable signatures to help protect users' privacy. Bellovin [6] and other security experts [32,7] warn that digitally signed emails entail serious privacy consequences. We believe the option for repudiable signatures can alleviate these concerns.

In a nutshell, LES provides more implementation flexibility for each participating domain – in particular flexibility that addresses *existing legitimate uses of email* –, without complicating the domain's public interface. A LES domain exposes a single public key in the DNS, just like DKIM. A LES domain can implement DKIM-style, server-based signatures and verifications, or user-based signatures and verifications where each user has her own signing key.

1.3   The LES Architecture

We now describe the LES architecture as diagrammed in figure 1.

The DKIM Baseline. A LES-signed email contains an extra SMTP header, X-LES-Signature, which encodes a signature of a canonicalized version of the

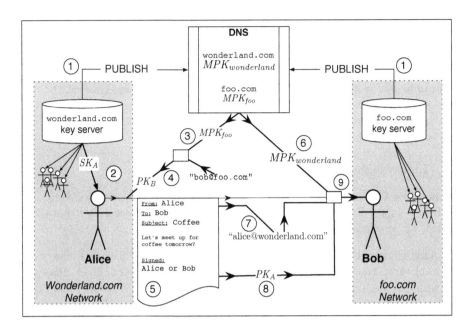

Fig. 1. LES: (1) The domain keyservers for Alice and Bob publish their *MPKs* in the DNS (2) Alice's domain sends Alice her secret key SK_A, via email (3) Alice obtains the MPK for Bob's domain, `foo.com` (4) Alice computes Bob's public key PK_B (5) Alice signs her email with a ring signature and sends it to Bob (6) Bob obtains the MPK for Alice's domain, from the DNS (7) Bob extracts the `From:` field value, `alice@wonderland.com`, from the email (8) Bob computes Alice's public key PK_A, using the claimed identity string "`alice@wonderland.com`" (9) Bob verifies the signature against the message and PK_A

message. We leave to the DKIM Working Group the details of this canonicalization – which includes the `From:` field, the subject and body of the message, and a timestamp –, as they do not impact the specifics of LES. Verification of a LES-signed email is also quite similar to the DKIM solution: the recipient retrieves the sender domain's public key from a specially crafted DNS record, and uses it to verify the claimed signature on the canonicalized message.

Limitations of DKIM. A DKIM domain uses a single key to sign all of its emails. This simple architecture is what makes DKIM so appealing and easy to deploy. Not surprisingly, it is also the source of DKIM's limitations: users must send email via their approved outgoing mail server, and this outgoing mail server must have some internal method of robustly distinguishing one user from another to prevent `bob@foo.com` from spoofing `carol@foo.com`. LES aims to overcome these limitations while retaining DKIM's deployment simplicity.

User Secret Keys with Identity-Based Signatures. LES assigns an individual secret key to each user, so that `bob@foo.com` can sign his own emails. This means Bob can use any outgoing server he chooses, and `outgoing.foo.com` does not need to authenticate individual users (though it may, of course, continue to use any mechanism it chooses to curb abusive mail relaying.)

To maintain a single domain-level key in the DNS, LES uses *identity-based signatures*, a type of scheme first conceptualized and implemented in 1984 by Shamir [36]. A LES domain publishes (in the DNS) a master public key MPK and retains the counterpart master secret key MSK. Bob's public key, PK_{Bob}, can be computed using MPK and an identification string for Bob, usually his email address "`bob@foo.com`". The corresponding secret key, SK_{Bob}, is computed by Bob's domain using MSK and the same identification string. Note that, contrary to certain widespread misconceptions, identity-based signatures are well tested and efficient. Shamir and Guillou-Quisquater signatures, for example, rely on the widely-used RSA assumption and are roughly as efficient as normal RSA signatures.

One might argue that a typical hierarchical certificate mechanism, where the domain certifies user-generated keypairs, would be just as appropriate here. There are some problems with this approach. First, a user's public-key certificate would need to be sent along with every signed message and would require verifying a chain of two signatures, where the identity-based solution requires only one signature and one verification operation. Second, with user-generated keypairs, it is much more difficult to use ring signatures (or any of the known deniable authentication methods) between a sender and a receiver who has not yet generated his public key. The identity-based solution ensures the availability of any user's public key.

Distributing User Secret Keys via Email. LES delivers the secret key SK_{Bob} by sending it via email to `bob@foo.com` [14], using SMTP/TLS [17] where available. Thus, quite naturally, only someone with the credentials to read Bob's email can send signed emails with `bob@foo.com` as `From` address. Most importantly, as every domain already has *some* mechanism for authenticating access to incoming email inboxes, this secret-key delivery mechanism requires no additional infrastructure or protocol.

Privacy with Deniable Signatures. Privacy advocates have long noted that digital signatures present a double-edged sword [6,32,7]: signatures may make a private conversation publicly-verifiable. The LES framework supports many forms of deniable authentication [8] through its use of identity-based keys: Alice can create a deniable signature using her secret key SK_{Alice} and Bob's public key PK_{Bob}. Only Bob can meaningfully verify such a signature. We note that this approach does not provide anonymity beyond that of a normal, unsigned email. However, unlike DKIM and other signature proposals, LES does not make the signature publicly-verifiable: only the email recipient will be convinced.

1.4   A Prototype Implementation

To determine the practical feasibility of deploying LES, we built a basic prototype, including a key server and a plugin to the Apple Mail client. We deployed a real MPK in the DNS for `csail.mit.edu`, using the Guillou-Quisquater identity-based scheme [15] for its simplicity, and ring signatures for deniability. We then conducted a small test with nine users. Though our test was too small to provide complete, statistically significant usability results, we note that most participants were able to quickly install and use the plugin with no user-noticeable effect on performance.

Detailed performance numbers, in section 6, show that basic ring signature and verification operations perform well within acceptable limits – under 40ms on an average desktop computer –, even before serious cryptographic optimizations. A small keyserver can easily compute and distribute keys for more than 50,000 users, even when configured to renew keys on a daily basis.

The complete prototype's source code is available for download at http://crypto.csail.mit.edu/projects/antiphishing/.

1.5   Previous and Related Work

The email authentication problem has motivated a large number of proposed solutions. End-to-end digital signatures for email have repeatedly been proposed [4,39] as a mechanism for making email more trustworthy and thereby preventing spoofing attacks such as phishing. One proposal suggests labeling email content and digitally signing the label [16]. Apart from DKIM, all of these past proposals require some form of Public-Key Infrastructure, e.g. X.509 [13], although the idea of using the DNS for identity-based master key distribution has appeared once before in the context of email encryption and IPSEC [37]. Alternatively, path-based verification has been proposed in a plethora of initiatives. Those which rely on DNS-based verification of host IP addresses were reviewed by the IETF MARID working group [19,24,23]. The latest proposal in this line of work is SIDF [30].

A number of spam-related solutions have been suggested to fight phishing. Blacklists of phishing mail servers are sometimes used [38,25], as is content filtering, where statistical machine learning methods are used to detect likely attacks [34,26,28]. Collaborative methods [12] that enable users to help one another have also been proposed. LES can help complement these approaches.

1.6   This Paper

In section 2, we review the necessary cryptographic and systems building blocks. In section 3, we detail the LES system based on these building blocks, specifically the identity-based key distribution infrastructure and the repudiability option. We then briefly explore the issue of technology adoption in section 4, discuss the threats model for LES in section 5, and describe our prototype and performance results in section 6. More detailed comments on these three issues appear in the appendix. Finally, we conclude in section 7.

2   Cryptographic and System Preliminaries

We now review and present new extensions to cryptographic and system building blocks involved in LES.

2.1   Identity-Based Signatures

In 1984, Shamir proposed the concept of identity-based signatures (IBS) [36]. Since then over a dozen schemes have been realized based on factoring, RSA, discrete logarithm, and pairings. (See [5] for an overview, plus a few more in [1].) Most IBS signatures can be computed roughly as fast as RSA signatures, and those based on pairings can be 200 bits long for the equivalent security of a 1024 bit RSA signature.

IBS schemes were introduced to help simplify the key management problem. Here, a single master authority publishes a master public key MPK and stores the corresponding master secret key MSK. Users are identified by a character string id_string, which is typically the user's email address. A user's public key PK can be publicly computed from MPK and id_string, while a user's secret key SK is computed by the master authority using MSK and the same id_string, then delivered to the user.

2.2   Ring Signatures from Any Keypairs

Ring signatures [9,33] allow an individual to sign on behalf of a group of individuals without requiring any prior group setup or coordination. Although rings can be of any size, consider the two party case. Suppose Alice and Bob have keypairs $(PK_{\mathtt{Alice}}, SK_{\mathtt{Alice}})$ and $(PK_{\mathtt{Bob}}, SK_{\mathtt{Bob}})$ respectively. Alice can sign on behalf of the group "Alice or Bob" using her secret key $SK_{\mathtt{Alice}}$ and Bob's public key $PK_{\mathtt{Bob}}$. Anyone can verify this signature using both of their public keys. We require the property of *signer-ambiguity* [1]; that is, *even if Alice and Bob reveal their secret keys*, no one can distinguish the actual signer.

In the full version of this paper, we describe a compiler for creating signer-ambiguous ring signatures using keypairs of almost any type. That is, Alice may have a PGP RSA-based keypair and Bob may have a pairing-based identity-based keypair, yet Alice can still create a ring signature from these keys! For our purposes here, it does not matter *how* this compiler works. It is enough to know that: (1) the security of the resulting ring signature is equivalent to the security of the weakest scheme involved, and (2) the time to sign (or verify) a ring signature produced by our compiler is roughly the sum of the time to sign (or verify) individually for each key involved, plus an additional hash. See [1] for the technical details.

Using ring signatures for deniable authentication is not a new concept [33,7]. The idea is that, if Bob receives an email signed by "Alice or Bob," he knows Alice must have created it. However, Bob cannot prove this fact to anyone, since he *could* have created the signature himself. In section 3.4, we describe how ring signatures are used to protect a user's privacy in LES.

2.3   Email Secret-Key Distribution

Web password reminders, mailing list subscription confirmations, and e-commerce notifications all use email as a semi-trusted messaging mechanism. This approach, called Email-Based Identity and Authentication [14], delivers semi-sensitive data to a user by simply sending the user an email. The user gains access to this data by authenticating to his incoming mail server in the usual way, via account login to an access-controlled filesystem, webmail, POP3 [31], or IMAP4 [10]. For added security, one can use SMTP/TLS [17] for the transmission.

3   Lightweight Email Signatures

We now present the complete design of LES, as previously illustrated in Figure 1.

3.1   Email Domain Setup

Each email domain is responsible for establishing the cryptographic keys to authenticate the email of its users. The setup procedure for that master authority run by wonderland.com is defined as follows:

1. select one of the identity-based signatures (IBS) discussed in section 2.1. (For our section 6 experiment, we chose the RSA-based Guillou-Quisquater IBS [15] because of its speed and simplicity.)
2. generate a master keypair ($MPK_{\text{wonderland}}, MSK_{\text{wonderland}}$) for this scheme.
3. define key issuance policy *Policy*, which defines if and how emails from this domain should be signed. (Details of this policy are defined in the full version of this paper.)
4. publish $MPK_{\text{wonderland}}$ and *Policy* in the DNS as defined by the DKIM specifications.

3.2   User Identities

Per the identity-based construction, a user's public key PK can be derived from any character string *id_string* that represents the user's identity. We propose a standard format for *id_string*.

Master Domain. In most cases, bob@foo.com obtains a secret key derived from a master keypair whose public component is found in the DNS record for the expected domain, foo.com. However, in cases related to bootstrapping (see section 4), Bob might obtain a secret key from a domain *other than* foo.com.

For this purpose, we build a *issuing_domain* parameter into the user identity character string. Note that foo.com should always refuse to issue secret keys for identity strings whose *issuing_domain* is not foo.com. However, foo.com may choose to issue a key for alice@wonderland.com, as long as the *issuing_domain* within the identity string is foo.com. We provide a clarifying example shortly.

Key Types. The LES infrastructure may be expanded to other applications in the future, such as encryption. To ensure that a key is used only for its intended purpose, we include type information in *id_string*. Consider *type*, a character string composed only of lowercase ASCII characters. This type becomes part of the overall identity string. For the purposes of our application, we define a single type: lightsig.

Key Expiration. In order to provide key revocation capabilities, the user iden-tity string includes expiration information. Specifically, *id_string* includes the last date on which the key is valid: *expiration_date*, a character string formatted according to ISO-8601, which include an indication for the timezone. For now, we default to UTC for timezone disambiguation.

Constructing Identity Character Strings. An *id_string* is thus constructed as: ⟨*issuing_domain*⟩, ⟨*email*⟩, ⟨*expiration_date*⟩, ⟨*type*⟩. For example, a 2006 LES identity string for email address `bob@foo.com` would be: `foo.com,bob@foo.com, 2006-12-31,lightsig`.

If Bob obtains his secret key from a master authority different than his do-main, e.g. `lightsig.org`, his public key would necessarily be derived from a different *id_string*: `lightsig.org,bob@foo.com,2006-12-31,lightsig`. Here `lightsig.org` happily issues a secret key for Bob, even though his email ad-dress is not within the `lightsig.org` domain. This is legitimate, as long as the *issuing_domain* in the *id_string* matches the issuing keyserver.

3.3   Delivering User Secret Keys

Each domain keyserver will choose its own interval for regular user secret key issuance, possibly daily, weekly or monthly. These secret keys are delivered by email, with a well-defined format – e.g. XML with base64-encoded key, including a special mail header – that the mail client will recognize. The most recent key-delivery email is kept in the user's inbox for all mail clients to access, in case the user checks his email from different computers. The mail client may check the correctness of the secret key it receives against its domain's master public key, either using an algorithm specific to the chosen IBS scheme (most schemes have such an algorithm), or by attempting to sign a few messages with the new key and then verifying those results. (For more details, see section 2.3.)

3.4   The Repudiability Option

The downside of signing email is that it makes a large portion of digital com-munication undeniable [6,32,7]. An off-the-record opinion confided over email to a once-trusted friend may turn into a publicly verifiable message on a blog! We believe that repudiable signatures should be the *default* to protect a user's privacy as much as possible, and that non-repudiable signatures should be an option for the user to choose.

Numerous approaches exist for realizing repudiable authentication: designated-verifier signatures [21], chameleon signatures [22], ring signatures [33], and more (see [8] for an overview of deniable authentication with RSA). In theory, any of these approaches can be used. We chose the ring signature approach for two rea-sons: (1) it fits seamlessly into our identity-based framework without creating new key management problems, and (2) our ring signature compiler can create ring signatures using keys from different schemes, as discussed in section 2.2. Thus, no domain is obligated to use a single (perhaps patented) IBS scheme.

Let us explore why ring signatures are an ideal choice for adding repudiability to LES. Most repudiation options require the sender to know something about the recipient; in ring signatures, the sender need only know the receiver's public key. In an identity-based setting, the sender Alice can easily derive Bob's public key using the $MPK_{\texttt{foo.com}}$ for $\texttt{foo.com}$ in the DNS and Bob's *id_string*. Setting the *issuing_domain* to $\texttt{foo.com}$, the *type* to $\texttt{lightsig}$, and the email field to $\texttt{bob@foo.com}$ for Bob's *id_string* is straight-forward. For *expiration_date*, Alice simply selects the current date. We then require that domains be willing to distribute back-dated secret keys (to match the incoming public key) on request to any of their members. Few users will take this opportunity, but the fact that they *could* yields repudiability. Such requests for back-dated keys can simply be handled by signed email to the keyserver.

This "Alice or Bob" authentication is valid: if Bob is confident that *he* did not create it, then Alice must have. However, this signature is also repudiable, because Bob cannot convince a third party that he did not, in fact, create it. In the full version of this paper, we discuss what Alice should do if $\texttt{foo.com}$ does not yet support LES, and in section 4, we discuss methods for achieving more repudiability.

3.5   Signing and Verifying Messages

Consider Alice, $\texttt{alice@wonderland.com}$, and Bob, $\texttt{bob@foo.com}$. On 2006-09-06, Alice wants to send an email to Bob with subject ⟨*subject*⟩ and body ⟨*body*⟩. When Alice clicks "send," her email client performs the following actions:

1. prepare a message $\mathcal{M}$ to sign, using the DKIM canonicalization (which includes the $\texttt{From:}$, $\texttt{To:}$, and $\texttt{Subject:}$ fields, as well as a timestamp and the message body).
2. if Alice desires repudiability, she needs to obtain Bob's public key:
   (a) obtain $MPK_{\texttt{foo.com}}$, the master public key for Bob's domain $\texttt{foo.com}$, using DNS lookup.
   (b) assemble $id\_string_{\texttt{Bob}}$, an identity string for Bob using 2006-09-06 as the *expiration_date*: $\texttt{foo.com,bob@foo.com,2006-09-06,lightsig}$
   (c) compute $PK_{\texttt{Bob}}$ from $MPK_{\texttt{foo.com}}$ and $id\_string_{\texttt{Bob}}$. (We assume that $PK_{\texttt{Bob}}$ contains a cryptosystem identifier, which determines which IBS algorithm is used here.)
3. sign the message $\mathcal{M}$ using $SK_{\texttt{Alice}}$, $MPK_{\texttt{wonderland.com}}$. Optionally, for repudiability, also use $PK_{\texttt{Bob}}$ and $MPK_{\texttt{foo.com}}$ with the section 2.2 compiler. The computed signature is σ.
4. using the DKIM format for SMTP header signatures, add $\texttt{X-LES-Signature}$ containing σ, $id\_string_{\texttt{Alice}}$, and $id\_string_{\texttt{Bob}}$.

Upon receipt, Bob needs to verify the signature:

1. obtain the sender's email address, $\texttt{alice@wonderland.com}$, and the corresponding domain name, $\texttt{wonderland.com}$, from the email's $\texttt{From}$ field.
2. obtain $MPK_{\texttt{wonderland.com}}$, using DNS lookup (as specified by DKIM).

3. ensure that $PK_{\mathtt{Alice}}$ is correctly computed from the claimed $id\_string_{\mathtt{Alice}}$ and corresponding issuing domain $MPK_{\mathtt{wonderland.com}}$, and that this id_string is properly formed (includes Alice's email address exactly as indicated in the From field, a valid expiration date, a valid type).

4. recreate the canonical message $\mathcal{M}$ that was signed, using the declared From, To, and Subject fields, the email body, and the timestamp.

5. If Alice applied an ordinary, non-repudiable signature, verify $\mathcal{M}$, σ, $PK_{\mathtt{Alice}}$, $MPK_{\mathtt{wonderland.com}}$ to check that Alice's signature is valid.

6. If Alice applied a repudiable signature, Bob **must** check that this signature verifies against both Alice's and his own public key following the proper ring verification algorithm [1]:

   (a) ensure that $PK_{\mathtt{Bob}}$ is correctly computed from the claimed $id\_string_{\mathtt{Bob}}$ and the DNS-advertised $MPK_{\mathtt{foo.com}}$, and that this id_string is properly formed (includes Bob's email address, a valid expiration date and type).

   (b) verify $\mathcal{M}$, σ, $PK_{\mathtt{Alice}}$, $MPK_{\mathtt{wonderland.com}}$, $PK_{\mathtt{Bob}}$, $MPK_{\mathtt{foo.com}}$ to check that this is a valid ring signature for "Alice or Bob."

If all verifications succeed, Bob can be certain that this message came from someone who is authorized to use the address alice@wonderland.com. If the wonderland.com keyserver is behaving correctly, that person is Alice.

3.6 LES vs. Other Approaches

The LES architecture provides a number of benefits over alternative approaches to email authentication. We consider three main competitors: SIDF [30] and similar path-based verification mechanisms, S/MIME [40] and similar certificate-based signature schemes, and DKIM, the system upon which LES improves. A comparison chart is provided in table 1, with detailed explanations as follows:

Table 1. LES compared to other approaches for authenticating email. [‡]: PGP and S/MIME can be adjusted to issue keys from the server, somewhat improving scalability.

Property	SIDF	S/MIME	DKIM	LES
Logistical Scalability	No	No[‡]	No	Yes
Deployable with Client Update Only	No	Yes	No	Yes
Deployable with Server Update Only	Yes	No[‡]	Yes	Yes
Support for Third-Party SMTP Servers	No	Yes	No	Yes
Easy Support for Privacy	Yes	No	No	Yes
Email Alias Forwarding	No	Yes	Yes	Yes
Support for Mailing Lists that Modify Content	Good	Poor	Fair	Fair

1. **Logistical Scalability:** When a large organization deploys and maintains an architecture for signing emails, it must consider the logistics of such a deployment, in particular how well the plan scales. With SIDF or DKIM, domain administrators must maintain an inventory of outgoing mail servers and ensure that each is properly configured. This includes having outgoing

mail servers properly authenticate individual users to prevent intra-domain spoofing. Meanwhile, with certificate-based signature schemes, domain administrators must provide a mechanism to issue user certificates. By contrast, LES does not require any management of outgoing mail servers or any additional authentication mechanism. LES only requires domains to keep track of which internal email addresses are legitimate, a task that each domain already performs when a user's inbox is created. Thus, LES imposes only a small logistical burden, while DKIM, SIDF, and S/MIME all require some new logistical tasks and potentially new authentication mechanisms. Note that it is technically possible to use PGP in a way similar to LES, with email-delivered certificates, though the PGP keyserver then needs to keep track of individual user keys where LES does not.

2. **Deployment Flexibility:** SIDF and DKIM can only be deployed via server-side upgrades, which means individual users must wait for their domain to adopt the technology before their emails become authentic. PGP can only be deployed via client-side upgrades, though one should note that many clients already have PGP or S/MIME support built in. LES can be implemented either at the server, like DKIM, or at the client, like PGP.

3. **Support for Third-Party SMTP Servers:** SIDF and DKIM mandate the use of pre-defined outgoing mail servers. A user connected via a strict ISP may not be able to use all of his email personalities. Incoming-mail forwarding services – e.g. alumni address forwarding – may not be usable if they do not also provide outgoing mail service. PGP and LES, on the other hand, provide true end-to-end functionality for the sender: each user has a signing key and can send email via any outgoing mail server it chooses, regardless of the `From` email address.

4. **Privacy:** LES takes special care to enable deniable authentication for privacy purposes. SIDF, since it does not provide a cryptographic signature, is also privacy-preserving. DKIM and S/MIME provide non-repudiable signatures which may adversely affect the nature of privacy in email conversations. (Note that is is *not* valid to claim that DKIM signatures are repudiable because the server signs messages instead of the user; either the server is trustworthy or it isn't.) Even a hypothetical LES-S/MIME hybrid, which might use certificates in the place of identity-based signatures, would not provide adequate privacy, as the recipient's current public key would often not be available to the sender without a PKI.

5. **Various Features of Email:** SIDF does not support simple email alias forwarding, while S/MIME, DKIM, and LES all support it easily. SIDF supports mailing lists and other mechanisms that modify the email body, as long as mailing list servers support SIDF, too. On the other hand, S/MIME, DKIM, and LES must specify precise behavior for mailing lists: if the content or `From` address changes, then the mailing list must re-sign the email, and the recipient must trust the mailing list authority to properly identify the original author of the message. This is particularly difficult for S/MIME, which must assume that the mailing list has an S/MIME identity, too, that recipients trust (this is related to the PKI requirement of S/MIME-like solutions).

LES provides a combination of advantages that is difficult to obtain from other approaches. Of course, these features come at a certain price: new security threats. We explore these LES-specific threats in section 5.

4   Technology Adoption

The most challenging aspect of cryptographic solutions is their path to adoption and deployment. The deployment features of LES resembles those of DKIM: each domain can adopt it independently, and those who have not yet implemented it will simply not notice the additional header information. Like DKIM, LES allows each domain to express a DNS-based policy about its use of signatures, letting certain high-risk organizations – e.g. financial institutions – simply declare that all emails should be LES-signed, while other organizations – e.g. small ISPs – may allow both signed and unsigned emails.

LES offers two distinct advantages over DKIM in technology adoption. LES can be deployed *either at the mail server or client* without altering the DNS LES record. LES can also be deployed using *alternate domain authorities* to let users adopt LES individually before their email domain has adopted it. Once again, this can be done without changes to the DNS records.

Details about these deployment extensions are in the full version of this paper, including mechanisms for deployment of the repudiability option when the recipient hasn't yet deployed LES or when the recipient is a mailing list.

5   Threats

LES shares enough in architectural design with DKIM that both systems face a number of common threats. For example, both solutions can be compromised by DNS spoofing, domain key compromise, zombie user machines, and user confusion. Fortunately, the unique properties of LES help to mitigate some DKIM-specific threats, such as the ability to keep the domain secret key offline and allowing for recovery from user key compromise without a DNS update.

Of course, the unique properties of LES also cause certain unique threats to emerge, such as potentially increasing user confusion and allowing for new denial of service attacks. We examine all these threats in detail in the full version.

6   Experimental Results

We implemented a complete LES environment using Guillou-Quisquater identity-based signatures [15] based on the RSA assumption. Ring signatures were formed using a CDS proof of partial knowledge construction [1]. Our implementation includes a web-based key distribution server and a plugin to the Apple Mail client that implements key storage, message signing with repudiability, and signature verification. We used Python for the server-side components, and Objective C with the GNU Multi-Precision Library for the client-side Apple Mail plugin.

Table 2. Performance estimates for an average of 1000 runs. Time is in milliseconds. The sizes are in bytes and do not include encoding overhead. The symbol * indicates the number includes an estimated 50 bytes for the identity string of the user.

Operation	Machine	1024-bit modulus		2048-bit modulus	
		Time	Size	Time	Size
Master Keypair Generation	server	143	200	1440	300
User Secret Key Computation	server	167	178*	1209	316*
User Public Key Computation	client	0.03	178*	0.03	316*
Ring Signature of 100K msg	client	37	575*	210	1134*
Ring Verification of 100K msg	client	37	N/A	211	N/A

For space reasons, the details of this implementation are provided in the full versionof this paper with a summary here. Briefly, our implementation shows that performance of the LES architecture is quite reasonable for transparent deployment. A small server can manage keys for tens of thousands of users, and the average desktop computer takes only 37ms to sign or verify a message. (Even with 2048-bit keys, signing/verification take only 210ms, before optimizations).

Experimental Setup. We ran server benchmarks on a single-processor, 3.2Ghz Intel Pentium 4 with 2 Gigs of RAM and 512MB of L2 cache, running Fedora Core Linux with kernel v2.6.9. We used Python v2.3.3. We instrumented the Python code using the standard, built-in `timeit` module, running each operation 1000 times to obtain an average performance rating. We did not make any overzealous attempts to cut down the number of standard background processes.

We ran client benchmarks on a 1.5Ghz Apple Powerbook G4 with 1.5Gigs of RAM, running Mac OS X 10.4.4. We instrumented the Objective C code using the built-in Cocoa call to `Microseconds()`, which returns the number of microseconds since CPU boot. We ran each operation 1000 times to obtain an average running time. Though we were not actively using other applications on the Powerbook during the test, we also made no attempt to reduce the typically running background processes and other applications running in a normal Mac OS X session.

7   Conclusion

We proposed Lightweight Email Signatures (LES), an extension to DKIM which conserves its deployment properties while addressing a number of its limitations. LES allows users to sign their own emails and, thus, to use any outgoing mail server they choose. This helps to preserve a number of current uses of email that DKIM would jeopardize: choosing from multiple email personalities with a single outgoing mail server because of ISP restrictions, or using special mail forwarding services, e.g. university alumni email forwarding, that do not provide an outgoing mail server.

LES also offers better privacy protection for users. Each individual email address is associated with a public key, which anyone can compute using only the domain's master public key available via DNS. With the recipient's public key available, any number of deniable authentication mechanisms can be used, in particular the ring signature scheme we propose.

Our prototype implementation shows that LES is practical. It can be quickly implemented using well-understood cryptographic algorithms that rely on the same hardness assumptions as typical RSA signatures.

We are hopeful that proposals like DKIM and LES can provide the basic authentication foundation for email that is so sorely lacking today. These cryptographic proposals are not complete solutions, however, much like viewing an SSL-enabled web site is not a reason to fully trust the site. Reputation systems and "smart" user interfaces will likely be built on the foundation that DKIM and LES provide. Without DKIM or LES, however, such reputation systems would be nearly impossible.

Acknowledgments

We wish to thank Rob Miller and Min Wu for their helpful pointers to and explanations of user-interface-related solutions to the phishing problem. We are also grateful to Seth Gilbert and Steve Weis for their comments. We thank our ten volunteer anonymous testers, as well as Greg Shomo and Matt McKinnon who provided the equipment and system administration for our pilot test. Susan Hohenberger was supported by an NDSEG Fellowship.

References

1. B. Adida, S. Hohenberger, and R. L. Rivest. Ad-hoc-group signatures from hijacked keypairs, 2005. http://theory.lcs.mit.edu/~rivest/publications.
2. American Banking Association. Beware of Internet Scrooges this Holiday. http://biz.yahoo.com/prnews/041209/dcth013_1.html.
3. Anti-Phishing Working Group. http://www.antiphishing.org/.
4. Anti-Phishing Working Group. Digital Signatures to Fight Phishing Attacks. http://www.antiphishing.org/smim-dig-sig.htm.
5. M. Bellare, C. Namprempre, and G. Neven. Security proofs for identity-based identification and signature schemes. In EUROCRYPT, pp. 268–286, 1999.
6. S. M. Bellovin. Spamming, phishing, authentication, and privacy. *Inside Risks, Communications of the ACM*, 47:12, December 2004.
7. N. Borisov, I. Goldberg, and E. Brewer. Off-the-record communication, or, why not to use PGP. In *WPES '04*, pp. 77–84. ACM Press, 2004.
8. D. R. Brown. Deniable authentication with rsa and multicasting. In *Cryptology ePrint Archive, Report 2005/056*, 2005.
9. R. Cramer, I. Damgård, and B. Schoenmakers. Proofs of partial knowledge and simplified design of witness hiding protocols. In CRYPTO, pp. 174–187, 1994.
10. M. Crispin. RFC 1730: Internet Mail Access Protocol - Version 4, Dec. 1994.
11. R. Dhamija and J. D. Tygar. Phish and hips: Human interactive proofs to detect phishing attacks. In *HIP*, vol. 3517 of *LNCS*, pp. 127–141, 2005.
12. E. D. et. al. Spam Attacks: P2P to the Rescue. In *WWW '04*, pp. 358–359, 2004.
13. M. C. et. al. Internet X.509 Public Key Infrastructure (latest draft). *IETF Internet Drafts*, Jan. 2005.

14. S. L. Garfinkel. Email-Based Identification and Authentication: An Alternative to PKI? *IEEE Security & Privacy*, 1(6):20–26, Nov. 2003.
15. L. C. Guillou and J.-J. Quisquater. A "paradoxical" identity-based signature scheme resulting from zero-knowledge. In *CRYPTO*, vol. 403, pp. 216–231, 1988.
16. A. Herzberg. Controlling spam by secure internet content selection. In *4th Security in Communication Networks (SCN)*, vol. 3352 of LNCS, pp. 337–350, 2004.
17. P. Hoffman. SMTP Service Exten. for Secure SMTP over Transport Layer Security. Internet Mail Consortium RFC. `http://www.faqs.org/rfcs/rfc3207.html`.
18. IETF. The DKIM Working Group. `http://mipassoc.org/dkim/`.
19. IETF. MTA Authorization Records in DNS (MARID), June 2004. `http://www.ietf.org/html.charters/OLD/marid-charter.html`.
20. M. Jakobsson. Modeling and Preventing Phishing Attacks. In A. Patrick and M. Yung, editors, *Financial Cryptography '05*, LNCS, 2005.
21. M. Jakobsson, K. Sako, and R. Impagliazzo. Designated verifier proofs and their applications. In *EUROCRYPT '96*, vol. 1233 of *LNCS*, 1996.
22. H. Krawczyk and T. Rabin. Chameleon signatures. In *Network and Distributed System Security (NDSS)*, 2000.
23. J. Levine, A. DeKok, and et al. Lightweight MTA Authentication Protocol (LMAP) Discussion and Comparison, Feb. 2004. `http://www.taugh.com/draft-irtf-asrg-lmap-discussion-01.txt`.
24. J. R. Levine. A Flexible Method to Validate SMTP Senders in DNS, 2004. `http://www1.ietf.org/proceedings_new/04nov/IDs/draft-levine-fsv-01.txt`.
25. MAPS. RBL - Realtime Blackhole List, 1996. `http://www.mail-abuse.com/services/mds_rbl.html`.
26. J. Mason. Filtering Spam with SpamAssassin. In *HEANet Conference*, 2002.
27. MessageLabs. Annual Email Security Report, Dec. 2004. `http://www.messagelabs.com/intelligence/2004report`.
28. T. Meyer and B. Whateley. SpamBayes: Effective open-source, Bayesian based, email classification system. In *Conference on Email and Anti-Spam*, July 2004.
29. Microsoft. Phishing Scams: 5 Ways to Help Protect Your Identity. `http://www.microsoft.com/athome/security/email/phishing.mspx`.
30. Microsoft. The Sender ID Framework. `http://www.microsoft.com/mscorp/safety/technologies/senderid/default.mspx`.
31. J. Myers. RFC 1939: Post Office Protocol - Version 3, May 1996.
32. Z. News. `http://news.zdnet.com/2100-9595_22-519795.html?legacy=zdnn`.
33. R. L. Rivest, A. Shamir, and Y. Tauman. How to leak a secret. In *ASIACRYPT '01*, vol. 2248 of *LNCS*, pp. 552–565, 2001.
34. M. Sahami, S. Dumais, D. Heckerman, and E. Horvitz. A Bayesian Approach to Filtering Junk E-Mail. In *Learning for Text Categorization*, May 1998.
35. B. Schneier. Safe Personal Computing. Schneier On Security Weblog, Dec. 2004. `http://www.schneier.com/blog/archives/2004/12/safe_personal_c.html`.
36. A. Shamir. Identity-based cryptosystems and signature schemes. In *CRYPTO '84*, vol. 196 of *LNCS*, pp. 47–53, 1985.
37. D. Smetters and G. Durfee. Domain-based administration of identity-based cryptosystems for secure email and IPSEC. In *USENIX Security Symposium*, 2003.
38. The Spamhaus Project. The Spamhaus Block List. `http://www.spamhaus.org/sbl/`.
39. Tumbleweed Communications. Digitally-Signed Emails to Protect Against Phishing Attacks. `http://www.tumbleweed.com/solutions/finance/antiphishing.html`.
40. P. Zimmerman. Pretty Good Privacy. `http://www.pgp.com`.

Shoehorning Security into the EPC Tag Standard

Daniel V. Bailey and Ari Juels

RSA Laboratories
Bedford, MA 01730, USA
{dbailey, ajuels}@rsasecurity.com

Abstract. The EPCglobal Class-1 Generation-2 UHF tag standard is certain to become the *de facto* worldwide specification for inexpensive RFID tags. Because of its sharp focus on simple "license plate" tags, it supports only the most rudimentary of security and privacy features, and essentially none of the cryptographic techniques that underpin authentication and privacy-protection in higher-powered computational devices. To support more-sophisticated applications, the drafters of this standard envisioned the re-use of the basic air interface and command set in higher-class standards. We propose ways to incorporate mainstream cryptographic functionality into the Class-1 Gen-2 standard. Our techniques circumvent the intended modes of operation of the standard, but adhere closely enough to preserve formal compliance. For this reason, we use the term *shoehorning* to describe our layering of new security functionality on the standard.

Keywords: authentication, cloning, counterfeiting, EPC, PIN, RFID.

1 Introduction

Radio Frequency IDentification (RFID) tags promise in the near future to become the most numerous computational devices in the world. Their impending pervasiveness owes much to the power and flexibility that they achieve through starkly minimalist design. In their most basic form, RFID tags are little more than wireless barcodes that facilitate the tracking of objects in supply chains – at present, generally bulk containers like crates.

Many industries are embracing a recently ratified standard for RFID tags called the EPCglobal Class-1 Generation-2 UHF tag standard [12]. *EPC tags*, as the tags compliant with this standard are called, seem certain to become the *de facto* standard for low-cost RFID. It is projected that Class-1 Gen-2 EPC tags will soon cost in the neighborhood of five cents apiece, and will number in the billions. Their basic purpose is to improve supply-chain visibility, meaning that they will furnish highly accurate real-time data on the whereabouts of objects. In contrast to barcodes, which are difficult to scan without precise object positioning and thus human intermediation, RFID tags transmit data automatically.

It seems natural to appeal to RFID to improve infrastructural security. Indeed, the United States Food and Drug Administration is promoting the use of EPC

R. De Prisco and M. Yung (Eds.): SCN 2006, LNCS 4116, pp. 303–320, 2006.

tags to facilitate the compilation of item pedigrees in the pharmaceutical supply chain in an effort to combat counterfeit and gray-market products. It is to be expected that other industries will likewise explicitly or implicitly draw on EPC tags as a security tool.

EPC tags *per se*, however, are poorly endowed as security devices. Apart from some rudimentary protocols that reduce over-the-air information leakage, they have only two basic security features:

1. **The "kill" command:** The EPC standard envisions that tags will eventually track individual consumer items in the supply chain. In order to protect consumer privacy, the standard provides for tags to be disabled at the point of sale in retail environments. When a reader transmits a special "kill" command to an EPC tag, along with a tag-specific, 32-bit PIN, the tag self-destructs; that is, it never again responds to reader interrogation. (Dead tags, of course, offer nearly impeccable RFID privacy.)
2. **Read/write access:** An optional feature in the EPC standard provides for access-controlled memory in EPC tags. In order to read and write to certain memory locations, an EPC reader must furnish a tag-specific PIN.

These two forms of PIN-based access control reduce the risk of certain types of attack, like malicious killing of tags, and unauthorized access to the contents of tag memory. EPC tags, however, are vulnerable to a range of other, elementary attacks. EPC tags emit static, unique identifiers, as well as data like that traditionally found in a printed barcode, namely a manufacturer name and product type. Thanks to their identifiers, EPC tags are subject to clandestine tracking; with a network of readers, an entity can correlate sightings of an individual tag – and thus potentially track its bearer. The product information on tags creates a risk of surreptitious inventorying; a reader can in principle determine what items a person is carrying with her. Such risks have been a flashpoint of concern for civil libertarians.[1]

The vulnerability of RFID tags to *cloning* has received somewhat less attention. EPC tags, in particular, release their identifiers and product information – known as EPC codes – in a promiscuous manner. Any reader may scan any EPC tag; no access control exists on EPC codes. Consequently, having scanned a target EPC tag once, a reader can harvest all of the information needed to duplicate that tag in its essentials. It is unclear whether field-programmable, i.e., blank EPC tags, will be a regular commercial offering, although it is not inconceivable. An attacker could easily imprint such a tag to create a counterfeit, i.e., duplicate EPC tag.[2] Even without blank tags, however, it is an elementary matter to create wireless devices that may not have the same physical appearance as EPC tags, but perfectly simulate their output.

---

[1] As noted above, EPC tags are unlikely to see widespread use on consumer products for some years. Consumers regularly carry other types of RFID tags on their persons, however, such as payment devices and proximity cards, i.e., RFID devices that unlock doors.

[2] It is even possible that the pre-programmed data in an EPC tag could be directly modified.

The drafters of the EPC standard were aware of these privacy and security concerns. They rejected potential countermeasures, like cryptographic functionality, in favor of low cost. Rather than incorporate security technologies into Class-1 tags, EPCglobal instead imagined a hierarchy of tags [12], each successive level adding functionality while incorporating all the features of lower-class tags. In this way, higher-class tags could build on the existing infrastructure without the need to develop a new air interface for each. By way of analogy, consider the long sequence of standards under the IEEE 802.11 banner. A common command set has been extended multiple times and adapted to different air interfaces, all while leveraging past investment and (when possible) maintaining backward compatibility and coexistence.

1. **Class-1: Identity Tags** Passive-backscatter tags offering only basic features like a fixed EPC identifier, a tag identifier, kill function, and optional password-protected access control
2. **Class-2: Higher-Functionality Tags** Passive tags with all of Class-1's features and extended tag identifier and user memory, as well as *authenticated access control*
3. **Class-3: Semi-Passive Tags** with all of Class-2's features as well as sensors and on-tag power sources like batteries
4. **Class-4: Active Tags** with all of Class-3's features as well as tag-to-tag communications and ad-hoc networking

In contrast to established HF RFID standards like ISO 14443 and ISO 15693, where security protocols have already been deployed, the Class-1 Gen-2 UHF air interface is designed to offer longer range, better handling of dense tag and reader environments, and lower cost. These factors will draw security applications to this standard just as they have driven its success in supply chains – as well as the tremendous expected economies of scale.

Our work. In this paper, we consider various ways in which it is possible to create RFID tags that perform cryptographic functionality *while remaining compliant with both the Class-1 Gen-2 standard and conformance specification [13]* and while extending the command set. Our techniques could serve as an alternative to the creation of a Class-2 EPC standard – or as the basis for such a standard.

Our key idea is to take an expansive view of EPC tag memory. Rather than treating this memory merely as a form of storage, we consider its use as an input/output medium capable of interfacing with a cryptographic module within the tag. Read and write commands to the tag, therefore, may be commandeered to carry cryptographic values. We focus on protocols for tag authentication, rather than privacy-enhancing protocols.[3]

---

[3] As an example of a privacy-enhancing protocol consonant with the principles we enunciate here, see [16], which proposes a system of cryptographically changing EPC codes.

Organization
We survey authentication in the appendix, and review related work on RFID
security in section 2. We explore the scope of the Class-1 Gen-2 EPC standard
in section 3, and in section 4, propose an example cryptographic command set
that may be fit into the standard. We conclude in section 5 with a brief summary.

2   Related Work

Privacy has been perhaps the major security focus in the RFID literature and
in press coverage as well. A number of approaches have been proposed, including simple RF shielding (e.g., aluminum foil), distance detection [8], interference
with RFID singulation [20] (i.e., the standard process by which readers establish one-to-one communication with tags), rotating pseudonyms [16], physical
disablement [23], proxying [28,21], trusted computing [24], and cryptographic
protocols, e.g., [3,9,25,26]. Cryptographic approaches to user privacy based on
symmetric-key primitives tend to be unsatisfactory from a practical standpoint.
They rely on readers performing intensive searches over databases of tag keys,
or else sharing of secrets across tags that can weaken their security guarantees.
Public-key-based protocols are expensive. (See [19] for an overview.) For these
reasons, we focus here on the more tractable problem of *authentication.*

Several researchers have proposed new, lightweight cryptographic primitives
aiming at RFID authentication [17,22,31]. A European project [1] aims to identify new stream ciphers; some of these are potentially lightweight enough for
inclusion in low-cost devices. It is as yet unclear whether any of these recently
proposed primitives are both strong enough and agile enough for use in low-cost
RFID tags, but they represent an important continuing area of inquiry. Feldhofer et al. [7] have described an AES implementation designed specifically for
RFID devices. This implementation requires security resources exceeding those
presently possible in EPC tags, but perhaps suitable for some of the enhancements we describe here.

Some current RFID tags do employ cryptographic primitives for authentication. Today, these tags tend to be more expensive than EPC tags, and therefore
address niche applications like defense logistics. They also demonstrate that design of good cryptographic protocols for RFID requires careful attention [4].

The Auto-ID Lab, the research arm of EPCglobal, operates a special interest
group devoted to use of RFID to combat counterfeiting. Researchers there have
proposed uses of EPC to combat counterfeiting of consumer items [29]. They
suggest that track-and-trace technologies, i.e., supply-chain monitoring based
on current EPC tags, can yield good improvements over existing security. They
also discuss the benefits of challenge-response protocols for tag authentication,
and review extensions to existing EPC architecture for this purpose. They do not
investigate incorporation of cryptography into Class-1 Gen-2 EPC tags. Instead,
they propose support in future, higher-class EPC standards.

Juels proposes ways to leverage the PIN-controls for killing and read/write
access to achieve *ad hoc* authentication in Class-1 Gen-2 EPC tags [18]. The re-

sulting protocols are cryptographically weak, e.g., they are vulnerable to eaves-dropping attacks, but they permit authentication of EPC tags that would otherwise not be possible. That work is similar to our proposals here in that it aims to leverage the existing standard to achieve stronger security functionality.

Of course, it is common practice to repurpose or co-opt communication-protocol standards as we propose here. As seen in the past, the broad deployment of a communications standard yields many uses beyond the imagination of its original designers. Perhaps the most notable example in recent times is the TCP/IP suite of networking protocols. Originally designed for communication among mainframe and minicomputers housed in government labs, it is now supporting transmission of video clips to cell phones and replacing the traditional public switched telephone and cable-television networks.

What is unusual about our work here is the very constrained nature of the protocol set that we propose to co-opt. The EPC standard specifies an *artifact*, i.e., a device with a fixed command set specified down to the bit level, and virtually no margin for extensions and no underlying intention to support them. Yet our goal is to achieve *general, extensible security services* within the EPC standard. We require a large shoehorn indeed – but thankfully one of essentially simple design.

3   Shoehorning

The huge economies of scale will drive down the cost of tags, readers, and their components. The low cost of components will lead to their inclusion in many devices beyond the simple "license plate" item-identification application. The extension of the Class-1 Gen-2 standard to meet these needs, including anti-counterfeiting, requires a slightly different view of the specification. Instead of implying the characteristics of an artifact that implements the protocol, we can view it simply as a communication protocol. With this approach, Class-1 Gen-2 offers a logical and physical layer protocol which can be used to carry bulk data, including that of higher-layer protocols.

To implement the security services needed especially in pharmaceutical applications, we could develop new customized extensions to the logical layer, similar to the 802.11i [11] effort. But as experience has shown, this is not a trivial task. Simply taking an otherwise secure cipher and using it to encrypt data can lead to an insecure protocol [2]. Moreover, doing so presents a difficult choice: either select a single set of algorithms all implementors must use, or provide a negotiation scheme. Fortunately, several standard interfaces have been devised for secure communications with simple devices. Given their broad deployment, they have been thoroughly implemented and analyzed, and can be applied here.

3.1   A Simple Protocol for Entity Authentication

The Class-1 Gen-2 protocol already has a limited protocol for entity authentication: in order to access protected memory or privileged commands like kill, the reader must present a static password. In principle, to authenticate itself to the reader, the tag could do the same: we could imagine a new command that would request a password from a tag. But we observe that having the tag present static data like a password provides no additional security services than providing the EPC. Presumably, an attacker who is able to clone an EPC could just clone the password as well.

With this observation in hand, we provide a motivating example of the flexibility of our approach. Challenge-response protocols prevent an eavesdropping attacker from obtaining a static password and simply reusing it. In such a protocol depicted below, the tag computes a 32- or 64-bit response $R_T = H(K_{TS}, C_R)$ where $H()$ is a cryptographic function like a block cipher, K_{TS} is some secret key known to the tag and the reader (or server), and C_R, is a unique challenge. Of course, R_T could be chosen to have a length longer than 64 bits if conditions warrant. In an application where an attacker could feasibly try such a large number of interactive queries with the reader, a longer R_T value would be a good choice, but 64 bits is appropriate for many applications given the relatively short range of Class-1 Gen-2. To address off-line attacks, one can choose K_{TS} to be much longer – such as 128 bits – without increasing the number of bits sent over the air. We have seen several implementation reports of block ciphers like AES adapted to the severe constraints of passive RFID [7] which could serve as our function $H()$.

An extraordinary number of challenge-response protocols have been developed to suit various needs and resist various attackers. This one is presented as an example because of simplicity and a particular quirk of the Class-1 Gen-2 standard: tags do not have a method to obtain the identity of a reader. For its part, the Electronic Product Code carried by the tag is denoted ID_T.

1. $Reader \rightarrow Tag : C_R$
2. $Tag \rightarrow Reader : ID_T, R_T$

There are several types of challenge-response protocols classified by how the value C_R is chosen. Perhaps the most familiar method is for the value C_R to be chosen by the reader and explicitly sent to the tag, which we'll explore in much more detail below. In a special case called a time-synchronous one-time password, however, if the tag has a real-time clock, then it can use the time of day as an implicit challenge. This approach eliminates the need for a special message from the reader carrying C_R. To ensure a password is not being replayed, one can choose a time interval for C_R short enough to preclude replay attacks and the reader can store the last correct password value received from the tag.

Given this capability, our two-message protocol above can be collapsed into a single message: when asked for its EPC in Read, ACK, or any other command, the tag responds with its EPC concatenated with its one-time password.

1. $Tag \rightarrow Reader : ID_T, R_T$

Since according to Section 6.3.2.10.2.4, the transmitted EPC data field may be up to 512 bits, using 32 or 64 of these for a one-time password still leaves a tremendous number of available identifiers. No modifications to the spec are required, save perhaps a general agreement on the placement of the one-time password R_T within a transmitted EPC field. In this way, the tag provides additional evidence of its identity which the reader may check or not. For high throughput applications, the reader can simply ignore the one-time password value, only checking the password when it wants to gain assurance that the tag has not been cloned.

If our application requires more robust reader authentication, we could additionally require the reader to respond to a challenge. The Class-1 Gen-2 standard already provides data fields for the reader to transmit 16-bit passwords. Nothing prevents us from using a one-time password instead, verifying the provided value on the tag. In practice, the tag needs either a real-time clock or a way to deliver a challenge to the reader. In addition, given the fact that different applications need different security services and/or algorithms, we need a way for the tag and reader to negotiate a common set of features as in an SSL cipher suite [6]. Fixing a single algorithm for all applications for all time seems short-sighted since we know algorithms - even those trusted by governments and large financial institutions - get broken from time to time. We can of course define frame formats for all these things, but we quickly find that we are creating a complete customized security layer, when there are robust tools already in existence that can help.

3.2   Protocol Convergence

In contrast to typical communication protocols, Class-1 Gen-2 lacks a command to simply send bulk data over the air. In fact, most data payload fields in the protocol are limited to sixteen bits in length. This design choice is guided by the challenging environment faced by tags applied to fast-moving consumer goods. Many use cases involve hundreds or thousands of tags arranged on pallets and speeding toward a dock door. The uncertainties of antenna orientation together with the sheer number of tags make the short data frames a wise choice for this application. But in other settings, such as checking the authenticity of high-value goods like pharmaceuticals, we can have the luxury of communicating with fewer tags at a time, for longer durations. This fact means we can appeal to the commands in Class-1 Gen-2 with variable-length data payload. To implement a security protocol, we will have to reuse commands designed for another purpose, or define custom or new commands.

This task of defining the use of one protocol to carry the protocol data units of another is often called *protocol convergence*. See [10], for instance, which explicitly defines a physical-layer convergence protocol. To refer to data units consumed by a protocol entity not contained in the Class-1 Gen-2 spec, we will use the phrase *application protocol data units*, or APDUs.

Section 6.3.2.1 of the standard specifies four banks of memory which may be read or written by a reader: reserved, EPC, TID, and User. The User bank offers the most flexibility, allowing user-defined organization of arbitrary amounts of memory arranged in 16-bit words. Subject to some conditions possibly involving the presentation of a fixed password, the tag is obliged to obey Read or BlockWrite commands. But the contents of memory need not be fixed: neither the standard nor the conformance document [13] prohibit the manipulation of memory by logic in the tag. In fact, we could view the situation as interprocess communication implemented by shared memory. The reader writes data to a particular memory location in the tag. Logic in the tag reads from this location, processes the data frame, and writes its response to that (or a different but commonly agreed-upon) memory location. The reader obtains its result by reading from this memory location.

As a concrete example, consider a tag that has been singulated by a reader so that they may engage in a one-to-one communication. This task is accomplished by the tag successfully responding to a sequence of Query, ACK, and Req_RN commands to arrive in the Access state [12]. Now the reader and tag can participate in a security protocol. We use a special block of shared memory in the User memory bank, starting with word zero to transfer the security protocol's APDUs between the reader and logic in the tag. Since the Class-1 Gen-2 protocol follows a reader-talks-first paradigm, the exchange begins with a BlockWrite command which writes the contents of the APDU to the shared memory, as shown in Table 9, found in the appendix along with all other frame formats referenced in this paper.

The tag's Class-1 Gen-2 interface writes the data to the appropriate location, and then transmits its normal reply to indicate success. We observe at this point that because protocol APDUs are meant for immediate consumption, rather than long-term storage, the contents of the shared memory can be stored in RAM instead of EEPROM. This allows the tag to use the time and power ordinarily used for writing nonvolatile storage for interpretation of, and response to, the APDU. As usual following command transmission, the reader broadcasts a continuous wave (CW) for up to 20 msec to power the tag and allow it to complete its operation. Additional logic in the tag uses this power and time to interpret the APDU, compute a response if necessary, and write its response to the same - or another previously agreed-upon - memory location. Once this is done, the tag sends its usual reply frame, which in this case indicates the tag has interpreted the APDU and a response is available. If processing a command takes longer than 20 msec, the response APDU prepared by the tag can indicate that processing has not yet completed.

The reader can now obtain its response by issuing a Read command. As before, we will assume that the special block of shared memory is located in the User memory bank and starts at word zero. This command frame is illustrated in Table 10.

Using this message sequence in principle allows us to implement virtually any protocol. Rather than overloading the Read and BlockWrite commands, we could define new commands with the same intent: a WriteGenericAPDU and ReadGenericAPDU could be assigned their own command identifiers without changing the basic approach. Of course, since the underlying logical layer follows a reader-talks-first paradigm, some protocols will work better than others. In order to handle APDUs originated by the tag, one could have the reader periodically use a read command to check if the contents of shared memory have changed. But this polling-based approach is unwieldy, so we instead look for existing protocols that fit nicely with the tools at hand.

4   A Natural Command Set: ISO 7816-4

This problem of authenticating a severely constrained device is not unique to supply chain applications: smart cards have long been used for authentication. Given the protocol convergence ideas articulated above, our enhanced tag looks more like a contactless smartcard and less like a traditional "license plate" RFID tag. So we aim to draw on the collective design and widespread implementation experience available in the smartcard arena to address our need for authentication and security feature negotiation. An ideal protocol would allow for extreme optimization of the most commonly used security features while also allowing other security operations possibly involving long APDUs fragmented into several data frames, and feature negotiation among cards and readers from different vendors.

We find such a protocol in part of ISO 7816 [15], a series of international standards that forms the basis for millions of smart cards worldwide including pay-TV and GSM SIM cards. As with many standards for communicating systems, the several documents in the ISO 7816 series are each devoted to a particular layer in a stack of protocols. This layered approach allows particular standards in the series to be applied to different environments. For instance, the ISO 14443 [14] series of standards for contactless proximity cards explicitly allows for the use of ISO 7816-4 APDUs to be carried over its logical and physical layers. From the perspective of a lower layer protocol, an ISO 7816-4 APDU would simply be seen as a data payload.

ISO 7816-4 offers a set of APDUs arranged in command-response pairs to authenticate and securely access data stored on a card. The specification declines to specify algorithms, physical interface technology, or the internal implementation within the card. Fortunately, most of its features are designed for systems where the reader talks first, nicely complementing the logical layer features in Class-1 Gen-2.

ISO 7816-4 defines general command and response frames, depicted in Table 1 and Table 2, respectively. It further specifies instantiations of these to perform tasks like entity authentication of tag, reader, or both as well as transfer of encrypted or integrity-protected data. To make things concrete, we'll focus on one command called Internal Authenticate, while our techniques extend to other commands as well.

With this set of headers, data lengths, and trailers, the reader can unambiguously specify precisely which command is desired along with details on algorithms, protocols, parameters, key identifiers, and of course, command data. The tag can reply with status bytes indicating success, reasons for failure, or the fact that processing has not yet completed.

Given the rich feature set of ISO 7816-4, one can address a great number of applications. But we observe that in this environment, tags may specialize on

Table 1. ISO 7816-4 Command

Field	Description	Number of bytes
Command header	Class byte denoted CLA	1
Command header	Instruction byte denoted INS	1
Command header	Parameter bytes denoted P1-P2	2
Command data-length L_c	Absent if $N_c = 0$, otherwise equal to N_c	0, 1, or 3
Command data	Absent if $N_c = 0$, otherwise a string of N_c bytes	N_c
Maximum response length	Absent if $N_e = 0$, otherwise equal to N_e	0, 1, or 3

Table 2. ISO 7816-4 Response

Field	Description	Number of bytes
Response data	Absent if $N_r = 0$, otherwise a string of N_r bytes	N_r
Response trailer	Status bytes SW1 and SW2	2

one or two security services such as authentication of a tag to a reader to prevent counterfeiting. In the rest of this paper, we focus on heavily optimizing a tag's most-used feature while still allowing the richness of the 7816-4 command set.

From the tables one can see there is some overhead associated with this command set: a typical command would see six bytes overhead, while a response would see two. Since communication bandwidth is at a premium in this environment, we must explore some examples to determine if the cost is acceptable and consider ways to reduce it.

4.1 Tag Authentication

In Section 3.1, we outlined a simple tag authentication protocol using challenge-response and one-time passwords. Using the techniques outlined in Section 3.2, we can go beyond this approach to support virtually any entity authentication protocol from simple passwords to robust cryptography. Let us consider the use of the ISO 7816 command set to achieve entity authentication of the tag.

Of course, we must choose some algorithm to achieve this goal. When it comes to cryptographic functions, we face an embarrassment of riches. Such a broad set of protocols, algorithms, and associated modes of operation has been devised that it seems shortsighted to attempt to fix one choice for all secure applications. Like the various options offered in the Class-1 Gen-2 physical layer, each of these cryptographic primitives conducts a careful trade off among attributes. In this case, the attributes are computational complexity, communication complexity, security services offered, and resistance to various types of attackers. We are forced then to choose one algorithm or devise some sort of negotiation scheme for a tag and reader to agree on a protocol, algorithms, and modes.

This service is precisely what ISO 7816 provides: security protocol messages tagged to reference an algorithm and any associated reference data such as a key identifier. By way of example, in Table 3, let us consider the Internal Authenticate command to implement our protocol. The value C_R will be provided by the reader in the protocol. Values postfixed by "h" indicate hexadecimal notation.

Table 3 shows the reader providing an eight-byte challenge value to the tag. Note that the class and command parameter bytes are set to zero. Tables 2 and 3 in [15] define the semantics of the class byte. A reader can indicate if this

Table 3. Internal Authenticate Command from Reader

Field	Description	Number of bytes
Command Class Byte	0h	1
Command Instruction Byte	88h	1
Command Parameters	0h	2
Command data-length	8h	1
Command data	C_R	8
Maximum response length	8h	1

Table 4. ISO 7816-4 Response

Field	Description	Number of bytes
Response data	R_T	8
Status bytes	6100h	2

command frame is a fragment of a longer command and if any encryption or integrity protection has been applied. In our case, neither of these conditions is true and therefore these bytes are set to zero. The command parameter identifies the algorithm, protocol, and modes, but ISO 7816 allows these bytes to be set to zero if their values are implicitly known. For reasons of cost and efficiency, many tags may support only one set of these values.

When these APDUs are carried by Read or BlockWrite commands, we can calculate the total number of bytes sent over the air before our compression techniques in Section 4.2. By way of comparison, we also consider the case when the challenge, C_R, is implicitly known by the tag such as in time-synchronous onetime passwords.

Table 5. Frame sizes for shoehorned Internal Authenticate

Frame Type	Bytes	Bits
BlockWrite Carrying Internal Authenticate with Challenge	22	169
BlockWrite Carrying Internal Authenticate with Implicit Challenge	13	97
Read Carrying Response	18	137

4.2   Compressing ISO 7816-4

Clearly, these commands are larger than we would like. Our goal is to optimize the most common usage while allowing flexibility. Our working assumption is that most tags will support a small number of security methods and generally their usage will be implicit. This means in general that the class and parameter bytes - and sometimes the instruction byte - will be redundant. So we can eliminate these, but we need some way to signal to the tag which fields are present in a received data frame.

As above, we have two options: we can carry on using the Read and BlockWrite commands and specify a wrapper with a bit field to indicate which ISO 7816 fields are present. In essence, this wrapper becomes our security sublayer and allows the tag unambiguously reconstruct the original ISO 7816 APDU, if desired. As an alternative to Read and BlockWrite,we can define custom commands for this purpose. Both new and custom commands are considered below.

Security Sublayer. Continuing our use of the Read and BlockWrite commands, we can prepend all ISO 7816-4 APDUs with a header to indicate which fields are present as shown in Table 6.

Table 6. Security Sublayer Header

	Command Class Byte	Command Instruction Byte	Command Parameters
Number of bits	1	1	1

Then in Table 11, we specify a complete BlockWrite data frame to send an ISO 7816-4 APDU for an entity authentication protocol as above; here we compute the 64-bit value R_T given the 64-bit value C_R provided by the reader; we obtain a savings of 29 bits compared with Table 5. As noted above, these parameters are provided as an example and many other combinations are possible, including an implied C_R value and a 32-bit password returned as in Table 12. Observe that ISO 7816-4 already allows the DataLen and Data fields to be omitted entirely if their values are implied, relieving us of the need to explicitly signal their presence. This result leaves us with a data frame of only 68 bits, 32 of which are the handle and CRC. Response frames are unchanged and remain as above. A summary of over-the-air complexity is in Table 7. But further reductions are possible if we turn to specialized commands.

Table 7. Frame sizes for Compressed Internal Authenticate using BlockWrite

Frame Type	Bytes	Bits
Compressed BlockWrite Carrying Internal Authenticate with Challenge	18	140
Compressed BlockWrite Carrying Internal Authenticate with Implicit Challenge	9	68
Read Carrying Response	18	137

New Commands. To save even more bits over the air, we can turn to new commands. The standard defines command identifiers using up to 8 bits each for base commands, and 16 bits each for custom or proprietary commands. We observe that in our use of the Read and BlockWrite commands, quite a few bits are devoted to specifying a memory location and data length. A new or custom command's identifier would directly imply the memory location, saving some bits. In addition, the ISO 7816 APDU either specifies its own length explicitly in the DataLen field, or – like other parameters – it is previously known by both parties, allowing us to optionally dispense with the WordCount field. By defining a new command we can save a total of 17 bits by using an unreserved 8-bit identifier, of which there are 22 currently available. Of course, we could define a custom command instead, but then we would only save 9 bits since an additional 8 bits are required to specify a custom command. The command and response versions are illustrated in Tables 13-16.

Using this approach, we can compare the size of the data frames in each of these scenarios when used with our example cryptographic protocol in Table 8.

Table 8. Sizes of New or Custom Commands

Frame Type	Bytes	Bits
New EPC-layer Command for ISO 7816 APDU Command with Challenge	15	123
New EPC-layer Command for ISO 7816 APDU Command with Implicit Challenge	6	51
Custom EPC-layer Command for ISO 7816 APDU Command with Challenge	16	131
Custom EPC-layer Command for ISO 7816 APDU Command with Implicit Challenge	8	59
EPC-layer Tag Reply to Response APDU	15	113

Authentication of a Group of Tags. We have focused on commands that require a tag to be fully singulated before a cryptographic protocol takes place. Recalling our example security function $R_T = H(K_{TS}, C_R)$, we observe that if each tag has a unique key K_{TS}, then the value C_R need not be unique to each tag. This is common practice in the application of one-time passwords for user login, as C_R will often be either the time of day or a counter. Performing entity authentication of a group of tags can be greatly optimized by delivering C_R to all tags and allowing them to respond individually. Toward this end, we propose QuerySecure and ACKSecure commands which perform these functions using the protocol convergence ideas outlined above. Essentially, QuerySecure extends Query by appending the Header, DataLen, Data, RespLen, and 7816 APDU fields and replacing the CRC-5 with a CRC-16. The resulting data frame weighs in at 101 bits, but in contrast to the commands listed above, only needs to be sent once to a population of tags. The ACKSecure command likewise simply appends the Response Data and Status Bytes fields to the existing ACK command, which then scrolls back its EPC followed by the R_T value it computed.

5   Conclusion

The optimizations we have presented here are driven by the desire to optimize one commonly used cryptographic operation for each tag, while allowing the flexibility of a fully extensible, broadly supported, and internationally recognized protocol to handle issues of feature negotiation.

This is the motivation behind our fusing the EPC standard with ISO 7816-4. In the case of tag authentication using a block cipher, the resulting optimized data frames are shorter than many Electronic Product Codes. An implementor is not restricted to our example cryptographic protocol, or even to the ISO 7816-4 Internal Authenticate command. By either inspecting or knowing the tag's TID, the reader can use whichever 7816-4 command and associated parameters for which the tag is optimized. To access other commands, the reader can explicitly specify the desired command and parameters. We have shown three different ways to add this functionality to the Class-1 Gen-2 standard while maintaining backward compatibility: by using the BlockWrite and Read commands, by defining custom commands, and by defining new commands. An implementor could choose whichever of these methods is most suited to a particular deployment.

In summary, our proposed techniques permit the creation of RFID tags that are compliant with the Class-1 Gen-2 EPC standard, but offer the broad and widely supported cryptographic functionality of standards like ISO 7816-4. We hope that the simplicity and ready extensibility of our techniques will pave the way for the penetration of EPC into a broader array of security applications. EPCglobal has expressed the intention to create a Class-2 standard that specifies higher-functionality, higher-security, next generation EPC tags. Our approach could make this a much easier job, and allow also a broad spectrum of new devices to benefit from the infrastructure of today's EPC standard.

References

1. ECRYPT (European network for excellence in cryptology), stream cipher project Web page, 2006. Referenced 2006 at http://www.ecrypt.eu.org/stream/.
2. William A. Arbaugh, Narendar Shankar, and Y.C. Justin Wan. Your 802.11 wireless network has no clothes.
   Referenced 2006 at http://citeseer.ist.psu.edu/arbaugh01your.html.
3. G. Avoine, E. Dysli, and P. Oechslin. Reducing time complexity in RFID systems. In B. Preneel and S. Tavares, editors, *Selected Areas in Cryptography – SAC 2005*, Lecture Notes in Computer Science. Springer-Verlag, 2005.
4. S. Bono, M. Green, A. Stubblefield, A. Juels, A. Rubin, and M. Szydlo. Security analysis of a cryptographically-enabled RFID device. In P. McDaniel, editor, *14th USENIX Security Symposium*, pages 1–16. USENIX, 2005. Dedicated Web site at www.rfidanalysis.org.
5. J. Collins. Ge uses RFID to secure cargo. *RFID Journal*, 12 January 2005. Referenced 2006 at http://www.rfidjournal.com/article/articleview/1317/1/1/.
6. T. Dierks and C. Allen. The TLS protocol version 1.0. Referenced 2006 at http://www.ietf.org/rfc/rfc2246.txt.
7. M. Feldhofer, S. Dominikus, and J. Wolkerstorfer. Strong authentication for RFID systems using the AES algorithm. In M. Joye and J.-J. Quisquater, editors, *Workshop on Cryptographic Hardware and Embedded Systems – CHES '04*, volume 3156 of *Lecture Notes in Computer Science*, pages 357–370. Springer-Verlag, 2004.
8. K. P. Fishkin, S. Roy, and B. Jiang. Some methods for privacy in RFID communication. In *1st European Workshop on Security in Ad-Hoc and Sensor Networks (ESAS 2004)*, 2004.
9. P. Golle, M. Jakobsson, A. Juels, and P. Syverson. Universal re-encryption for mixnets. In T. Okamoto, editor, *RSA Conference - Cryptographers' Track (CT-RSA)*, volume 2964 of *Lecture Notes in Computer Science*, pages 163–178, 2004.
10. IEEE. IEEE 802.11-1999. IEEE standard for information technology–telecommunications and information exchange between system–local and metropolitan area networks specific requirements–part 11: Wireless LAN medium access control (MAC) and physical layer (PHY) specifications.
11. IEEE. IEEE 802.11i-2004 amendment to IEEE std 802.11, 1999 edition (reaff 2003). IEEE standard for information technology–telecommunications and information exchange between system–local and metropolitan area networks specific requirements–part 11: Wireless LAN medium access control (MAC) and physical layer (PHY) specifications–amendment 6: Medium access control (MAC) security enhancements. Referenced 2006 at http://standards.ieee.org/getieee802/download/802.11i-2004.pdf.
12. EPCglobal Inc. Class 1 generation 2 UHF air interface protocol standard version 1.0.9. Referenced 2006 at http://www.epcglobalinc.com/standards_technology/EPCglobalClass-1Generation-2UHFRFIDProtocolV109.pdf.

13. EPCglobal Inc. Class 1 generation 2 UHF RFID conformance requirements version 1.0.2. Referenced 2006 at http://www.epcglobalinc.com/standards_technology/EPCglobalClass-1Generation-2UHFRFIDConformanceV102.pdf.

14. ISO. Identification cards – contactless integrated circuit(s) cards – proximity cards – part 4: Transmission protocol. Referenced 2006 at http://www.iso.org/iso/en/CatalogueDetailPage.CatalogueDetail?CSNUMBER=31425.

15. ISO. Identification cards – integrated circuit cards – part 4: Organization, security and commands for interchange. Referenced 2006 at http://www.iso.org/iso/en/CatalogueDetailPage.CatalogueDetail?CSNUMBER=36134.

16. A. Juels. Minimalist cryptography for low-cost RFID tags. In C. Blundo and S. Cimato, editors, *The Fourth International Conference on Security in Communication Networks – SCN 2004*, volume 3352 of *Lecture Notes in Computer Science*, pages 149–164. Springer-Verlag, 2004.

17. A. Juels. 'Yoking-proofs' for RFID tags. In R. Sandhu and R. Thomas, editors, *Workshop on Pervasive Computing and Communications Security – PerSec 2004*, pages 138–143. IEEE Computer Society, 2004.

18. A. Juels. Strengthing EPC tags against cloning. In *ACM Workshop on Wireless Security (WiSe)*, pages 67–76. ACM Press, 2005.

19. A. Juels. RFID security and privacy: A research survey. *J-SAC*, 2006. To appear. Online version referenced 2005 at
http://www.rsasecurity.com/rsalabs/node.asp?id=2937.

20. A. Juels, R.L. Rivest, and M. Szydlo. The blocker tag: Selective blocking of RFID tags for consumer privacy. In V. Atluri, editor, *8th ACM Conference on Computer and Communications Security*, pages 103–111. ACM Press, 2003.

21. A. Juels, P. Syverson, and D. Bailey. High-power proxies for enhancing RFID privacy and utility. In G. Danezis and D. Martin, editors, *Privacy Enhancing Technologies (PET)*, 2005.

22. A. Juels and S. Weis. Authenticating pervasive devices with human protocols. In *Advances in Cryptology – CRYPTO 2005*, pages 293–308. Springer-Verlag, 2005. Lecture Notes in Computer Science, Volume 3621.

23. G. Karjoth and P. Moskowitz. Disabling RFID tags with visible confirmation: Clipped tags are silenced (short paper). In S. De Capitani di Vimercati and R. Dingledine, editors, *Workshop on Privacy in the Electronic Society (WPES)*, 2005.

24. D. Molnar, A. Soppera, and D. Wagner. Privacy for RFID through trusted computing (short paper). In S. De Capitani di Vimercati and R. Dingledine, editors, *Workshop on Privacy in the Electronic Society (WPES)*, 2005.

25. D. Molnar and D. Wagner. Privacy and security in library RFID : Issues, practices, and architectures. In B. Pfitzmann and P. McDaniel, editors, *ACM Conference on Communications and Computer Security*, pages 210 – 219. ACM Press, 2004.

26. M. Ohkubo, K. Suzuki, and S. Kinoshita. Efficient hash-chain based RFID privacy protection scheme. In *International Conference on Ubiquitous Computing – Ubicomp, Workshop Privacy: Current Status and Future Directions*, 2004.

27. R. Pappu, B. Recht, J. Taylor, and N. Gershenfeld. Physical one-way functions. *Science*, 297:2026–2030, September 2002.

28. M. Rieback, B. Crispo, and A. Tanenbaum. RFID Guardian: A battery-powered mobile device for RFID privacy management. In Colin Boyd and Juan Manuel González Nieto, editors, *Australasian Conference on Information Security and Privacy – ACISP 2005*, volume 3574 of *Lecture Notes in Computer Science*, pages 184–194. Springer-Verlag, 2005.

29. T. Staake, F. Thiesse, and E. Fleisch. Extending the EPC network – the potential of RFID in anti-counterfeiting. In *ACM Symposium on Applied Computing*, pages 1607–1612. ACM Press, 2005.
30. P. Tuyls and L. Batina. Rfid-tags for anti-counterfeiting. In *CT-RSA 06*. Springer-Verlag, 2006. To appear.
31. I. Vajda and L. Buttyán. Lightweight authentication protocols for low-cost RFID tags. In *Workshop on Security in Ubiquitous Computing – Ubicomp 2003*, 2003.

A   Security Services

A.1   Device Authentication

EPC tags and other low-cost RFID devices are often referred to as "license plates:" They carry and broadcast fixed identifiers. In consequence, such devices are easy to *clone*. An attacker can read an identifier and write it to a new, programmable RFID tag or simulate it in a different type of RF device. Mitigating the risk of tag cloning is an essential security goal in an RFID system. Tags that possess secret keys and execute well-designed cryptographic protocols to authenticate themselves to readers can resist cloning in the face of over-the-air attack. Conversely, it may also be desirable for tags to be able to authenticate readers to prevent the release of sensitive tag data to unauthorized readers.

Of course, cryptographic protocols are effective only in logical-layer defense. An attacker that physically probes an RFID tag and extracts keys can clone it. While the cryptographic services that we propose here cannot directly forestall such attacks, they can support tamper-resistance mechanisms, like PUFs and POWFs [30,27], that rely on a blend of logical and physical countermeasures.

A.2   Device-Binding Authentication

A valid, un-cloned tag applied to the wrong item will furnish erroneous information. So it is important to establish the correctness of the physical context for an RFID tag. Toward this end, for example, shipping containers have been designed that contain internal RFID devices whose state changes in response to the opening of the container [5]. PUFs [30] and POWFs [27] are physical objects – silicon and glass-and-plastic respectively – whose state changes in response to physical stresses, and can help in the detection of RFID-tag removal. (Of course, good adhesives can also help.) Various chemical fingerprinting and watermarking techniques combat counterfeiting, and complement RFID devices.

A.3   Data-Origin Authentication

An RFID tag can also as a carrier of ancillary data, e.g., information about goods in a pallet. Data-origin authentication can support the physical integrity of the tag itself, as when an RFID tag stores information about the state of physical tamper-detection objects like PUFs or POWFs or chemical markers.

As a cryptographic service, data-origin authentication binds the production of a block of data to a particular entity by means of a digital signature (or message-authentication code (MAC)). It also attests that the data have not been modified since their original encoding. An RFID tag can carry data digitally signed by an external entity or dynamically produce its own signature. In the former case, the tag serves as a data carrier, and need not itself perform the cryptographic operation of signing.

B Frame Formats

Table 9. Using BlockWrite command to carry an APDU

	Command	MemBank	WordPtr	WordCount	Data	Handle	CRC-16
Number of bits	8	2	EBV	8	Variable	16	16
Description	11000111	11	0000000	Number of words to write	APDU	handle	

Table 10. Using Read command to carry an APDU

	Command	MemBank	WordPtr	WordCount	Handle	CRC-16
Number of bits	8	2	EBV	8	16	16
Description	11000010	11	0000000	Number of words to read	handle	

Table 11. Using BlockWrite command with explicit challenge value

EPC Layer	Cmd	Bank	Ptr	Count	Data				Handle	CRC
Security Layer					Header	DataLen	Data	RespLen		
Number of bits	8	2	EBV	8	3	8	64	8	16	16
Description	11000111	11	0000000	00000110	000	00001000	C_R	00001000	handle	

Table 12. Using BlockWrite command with implicit challenge value

EPC Layer	Cmd	Bank	Ptr	Count	Data				Handle	CRC
Security Layer					Header	DataLen	Data	RespLen		
Number of bits	8	2	EBV	8	3	0	0	8	16	16
Description	11000111	11	0000000	00000110	000			00000100	handle	

Table 13. New EPC-layer Command for ISO 7816 Command APDU

	Command	Header	Compressed 7816 APDU	Handle	CRC-16
Number of bits	8	3	Variable	16	16
Description	11001001		C_R	handle	

Table 14. EPC-layer Tag Reply to ISO 7816 Command APDU

	Header	Handle	CRC-16
Number of bits	1	16	16
Description	0	handle	

Table 15. New EPC-layer Command for ISO 7816 Response APDU

	Command	Handle	CRC-16
Number of bits	8	16	16
Description	11001010	handle	

Table 16. EPC-layer Tag Reply for ISO 7816 Response APDU

	Header	Response Data	Status Bytes	Handle	CRC-16
Number of bits	1	Variable	16	16	16
Description	0	R_T			

Proof-Carrying Proxy Certificates

Walid Bagga, Stefano Crosta, and Refik Molva

Institut Eurécom
Corporate Communications
2229, route des Crêtes B.P. 193
06904 Sophia Antipolis, France
{bagga, crosta, molva}@eurecom.fr

Abstract. The term proxy certificate is used to describe a certificate that is is-sued by an end user for the purpose of delegating responsibility to another user so that the latter can perform certain actions on behalf of the former. Such cer-tificates have been suggested for use in a number of applications, particularly in distributed computing environments where delegation of rights is common. In this paper, we present a new concept called *proof-carrying proxy certificates*. Our approach allows to combine the verification of the validity of the proxy certifi-cate and the authorization decision making in an elegant way that enhances the privacy of the end user. In contrast with standard proxy certificates that are gener-ated using standard (public-key) signature schemes, the proposed certificates are generated using a signature scheme for which the validity of a generated signature proves the compliance of the signer with a credential-based policy. We present a concrete realization of our approach using bilinear pairings over elliptic curves and we prove its security under adapted attack models.

Keywords: Proxy Certificates, Credentials, Authorization, Bilinear Pairings, Data Minimization.

1 Introduction

The concept of proxy certificates, first formalized in [16], allows an end user to delegate some responsibility to another user, called agent, so that the latter can perform certain actions on behalf of the former. A proxy certificate is a certificate that, in contrast with the public-key certificates issued by trusted certification authorities (such as X.509 cer-tificates), is generated by an end user. It represents the signature of the end user on a message that typically contains the identity of the end user himself, the public key of the agent and a set of statements defining the terms of the delegation. It allows the agent to authenticate with other users as if he was the end user when performing the dele-gated actions. Proxy certification has been suggested for use in a number of applications particularly in distributed computing environments where delegation of rights is quite common. Examples include grid computing [6], mobile agents for e-commerce [8], and mobile communication [7]. More recently, an X.509 certificate profile for proxy certifi-cates was proposed in [19].

Whenever an agent wants to perform an action on behalf of an end user, he must prove that he is authorized by the end user to perform the action on his behalf. This is achieved by providing a valid proxy certificate and proving the possession of the private

R. De Prisco and M. Yung (Eds.): SCN 2006, LNCS 4116, pp. 321–335, 2006.

key corresponding to the agent's public key specified by the certificate. Furthermore, the agent has to prove that the end user is compliant with the authorization policy associated to the action he wants to perform. An increasingly popular approach for authorization in large-scale open environments like the Internet consists in using policies fulfilled by digital credentials. Basically, a digital credential is composed of a set of statements about certain user and the signature of this set by a trusted entity (called credential issuer). In this context, a commonly taken approach consists in that the agent provides a set of end user's credentials fulfilling the authorization policy (called a qualified set of credentials for the policy). The entity that is in charge of making the authorization decision is called the verifier. On one hand, the verifier has to check the validity of each of the received credentials. On the other hand, he has to check that the received set of credentials fulfills the authorization policy associated to the requested action.

The standard approach is not satisfactory for three reasons: first, verifying the validity of the proxy certificate and the validity of the different credentials separately is a burden for the verifier. Second, we believe that managing the end user's credentials and proving his compliance with an authorization policy should not be the role of the agent. Third, proving the compliance with a credential-based policy through the disclosure of a qualified set of credentials is not optimal from a privacy point of view. More precisely, it is not compliant with the privacy principle of data minimization (called the data quality principle in OECD guidelines [10]) that states that only strictly necessary information should be collected for a given purpose. For instance, assume that the authorization policy requires the possession of at least one credential belonging to a set of multiple credentials. Then, according to the data minimization principle, the verifier should not know more than the fact that the end user is compliant with the policy. In other words, the verifier should not know which specific credential fulfilling the authorization policy is held by the end user.

In this paper, we introduce a novel form of proxy certificates called *proof-carrying proxy certificates*. In contrast with standard proxy certificates that are generated using standard (public-key) signature schemes, the proposed certificates are generated using a signature scheme for which the validity of a generated signature proves the compliance of the signer with a credential-based policy. Using this special form of proxy certificates, the end user does not disclose any of his credentials. He uses them to generate a proof of compliance with the verifier's authorization policy. Besides, the agent does not have to deal with the end user's credentials. He just provides his proof-carrying proxy certificate (in addition to proving the possession of the private key corresponding to the agent's public key specified by the certificate). Finally, the verifier will just need to verify the validity of the received proxy certificate with respect to his policy i.e. the verification of the validity of the proxy certificate and the authorization decision making are performed in a logically single step.

The signature scheme used for the generation of proof-carrying proxy certificates should be unforgeable as for standard signature schemes. Furthermore, the scheme has to fulfill a privacy property called credential ambiguity in order to fulfill the data minimization principle i.e. the validity of a the signature on the proof-carrying proxy certificate proves that the end user is compliant with the authorization policy. However, if multiple qualified sets of credentials can fulfill the policy, the verifier should not know which specific one is held by the end user. In the following, an application scenario is described as an illustration of our approach.

Application Scenario. Consider the following scenario: a researcher (end user) wants to perform some operations on various hosts on a scientific computation oriented grid environment. The operations can be executed independently, can depend on each other, or can be executed only at specific periods of time. From his laptop the researcher wants to submit a number of requests to the destination hosts and have the operations executed while he is doing other things including being offline. For each request, an authenticated connection needs to be established with the corresponding destination host. An authorization policy is associated to the operations and the researcher has to prove his compliance with the policy in order for the operations to be authorized to be executed. The researcher delegates the management of the different operations to one or more agents.

Currently, authorization in grid environments is identity-based. The researcher whose public/private key pair is denoted (pk_u, sk_u) holds an X.509 certificate binding his global identity to his public key. In order to make the agent act on his behalf, he generates for the agent a random pair of keys denoted (pk_a, sk_a). Then, he issues an X.509 proxy certificate [19] associated to the generated key pair. The certificate contains in addition to the agent's public key pk_a, a set of statements indicating the valid operations that the agent is allowed to perform on behalf of the researcher, as well as a restricted validity period. The authentication of the agent is therefore based on its key pair, the proxy certificate generated by the researcher and the public-key certificate of the researcher. Authorization to perform a specific task is based on the identity of the researcher (taken from his X.509 certificate) as well as on the statements within the proxy certificate.

As explained in [6], an identity-based approach to authorization and authentication for large grids "will not provide the scalability, flexibility, and ease of management that a large grid needs to control access to its sensitive resources", while a property-based approach where properties are carried by digital credentials is more appropriate. In scientific grids for instance, properties may include whether the requesting agent is acting on behalf of a professor, a student or an administrator; whether the agent is acting on behalf of a member of a particular research project whose membership list is not maintained locally; whether the agent is acting on behalf of a researcher from academy or industry; etc.

In the credential-based approach, the agent needs to prove that its owner (the researcher) is compliant with a specific credential-based authorization policy in order for the operations to be executed. Using standard credential systems such as X.509 attribute certificates, the agent needs to have access to the credentials of its owner to provide the necessary authorization arguments. For example, assume that a policy requires the researcher to be either a research staff member of company X or company Y. Suppose that the researcher is employed by company X, therefore he has been issued a credential $cred_X^u$ (associated to his public key pk_u). In addition to the proxy certificate, the researcher gives to the agent the credential $cred_X^u$. During authentication and authorization phase, the agent submits in addition to its proxy certificate, the researcher's credential $cred_X^u$. The remote host where the operation needs to be executed does the following: (1) check the validity of the proxy certificate using the public key pk_u, (2) check the validity of $cred_X^u$ using the public key of the 'trusted' credential issuer, (3) check whether the provided credential fulfills the authorization policy for the requested operations. If all the validity checks are successful, the task is executed. Otherwise, an error message is returned.

Using proof-carrying proxy certificates allows to combine the verification of the validity of the proxy certificate and the authorization decision making in a way that improves the privacy of the researcher. In fact, instead of using a standard signature scheme, the researcher generates the agent's proxy certificate by running an advanced signature algorithm on input of his private key sk_u, his credential $cred_X^u$ and the credential-based policy '$cred_X^u$ or $cred_Y^u$'. The new proxy certificate carries in addition to delegation rights, the authorization arguments necessary for the execution of the operations. Hence, instead of performing three validity checks, the remote host needs just to verify the validity of the proxy certificate with respect to the policy '$cred_X^u$ or $cred_Y^u$' using the researcher's public key pk_u. Furthermore, thanks to the credential ambiguity property, the remote host will not know whether the agent is acting on behalf of a company X or company Y.

Contributions and Organization of the Paper. In this paper, we present the concept of proof-carrying proxy certificates that allows to combine the verification of the validity of the proxy certificate and the authorization decision making in a way that enhances the privacy of the end user. After discussing the related work in Section 2, we provide a comprehensive overview of the proof-carrying proxy certification mechanism in Section 3. In Section 4, we provide precise definitions for the algorithms specifying a proof-carrying proxy certification scheme. Then, we define the related security models, namely unforgeability and credential ambiguity. In Section 5, we describe a provably secure construction of proof-carrying proxy certification scheme based on bilinear pairings over elliptic curves. In Section 6, we summarize the paper and discuss current and future research work.

2   Related Work

The intuition behind the concept of proof-carrying proxy certificates comes originally from proof-carrying codes [15]. The latter is a technique that can be used for safe execution of untrusted code. In a typical scenario, a code receiver establishes a set of safety rules that guarantee safe behavior of programs, and the code producer creates a formal safety proof that proves, for the untrusted code, adherence to the safety rules. Then, the receiver is able to use a proof validator to check that the proof is valid and hence the untrusted code is safe to execute. By analogy with proof-carrying codes, a proof-carrying authentication mechanism based on higher-order logic was presented in [1]: the client desiring access must construct a proof using his attribute certificates, and the server will simply check the validity of the proof. The logic-based approach leads to a simple and efficient solution that integrates different authentication frameworks including X.509 and SPKI/SDSI. However, it cannot be used in the context of proof-carrying proxy certification because it does not provide a signature scheme fulfilling the required properties.

Providing a privacy preserving proof of compliance with a credential-based policy is a problem that has been studied in recent literature. In [2], the authors exploit cryptographic zero-knowledge proofs to allow requesting users to prove their adherence with a credential-based policy. The proposed solution provides better privacy guarantees than our concrete implementation of proof-carrying proxy certificates as the users may prove their compliance while preserving their anonymity. However, as the described protocol requires interaction between the credentials holder (end user) and the verifier, it can not be directly used to implement proof-carrying proxy certificates. An interesting line for future research would be to exploit the Fiat-Shamir heuristic [9] to transform their interactive protocols into a signature scheme that could be used to implement proof-carrying proxy certificates.

The concept of self-certified signatures presented in [13] shares with proof-carrying proxy certificates the idea of combining signature's validity verification with certification information verification: the signer (end user) first generates a temporary signing key (analog to the agent's private key) using his long-term signing key and his public-key certification information together. Then, he signs a message and certification information using this temporary signing key. In the verification stage both the signature on the message and certification are checked together. Self-certified signature was extended to multi-certification signature in which multiple certificates are verified together with the signature. The multi-certification signature scheme described in [13] could be used to construct proof-carrying proxy certificates for which policies are restricted to conjunctions of credentials. However, they cannot support disjunctions of credentials while respecting the credential ambiguity property. Thus, the signature scheme used in proof-carrying proxy certification could be seen as a generalization of self-certified signatures that supports both disjunctive and conjunctive authorization structures.

Our pairing-based signature scheme for proof-carrying proxy certificates is based on the policy-based signature scheme proposed in [4]. The latter allows to generate a signature on a message so that the signature is valid if and only if the signer is compliant with a credential-based policy written in standard normal form. However, it cannot be used to implement proof-carrying proxy certificates as it suffers from collusion attacks. In fact, in addition to the legitimate signer, any collusion of credential issuers or end users who are able to collect a qualified set of credentials for the policy according to which the message is signed can generate a valid signature. Besides, the scheme is not satisfactory as it is not supported by formal security arguments. In this paper, we propose a scheme that solves the collusion problem and provides a formal security analysis based on reductionist proofs, thus fulfilling the security requirements of proof-carrying proxy certificates.

3   Proof-Carrying Proxy Certification

In this section, we provide a general description of our approach as well as the notations used along the paper. We define the different components of a proof-carrying proxy certification scheme, including our policy model. Then, we describe how the proof-carrying proxy certificates are created and used.

3.1 Setting the Context

The setting for proof-carrying proxy certification comprises four types of players: end users, credential issuers, agents and verifiers (service providers). We consider a public key infrastructure where each end user holds a pair of keys (pk_u, sk_u). An end user is identified by his public key pk_u. The public key does not has to be bound to the end user's name/identity (through public-key certification) as for standard PKI systems such as X.509. In fact, in large-scale open environments, the identity of an end user is rarely of interest to determining whether the end user could be trusted or authorized to conduct some sensitive transactions. Instead statements about the end user such as attributes, properties, capabilities and/or privileges are more relevant. The validity of such statements is checked and certified by trusted entities called credential issuers.

We consider a set of credential issuers $I = \{I_1, \dots, I_N\}$, where the public key of I_κ, for $\kappa \in \{1, \dots, N\}$, is denoted R_κ while the corresponding master key is denoted s_κ. We assume that a trustworthy value of the public key of each of the credential issuers is known by the end users. Any credential issuer $I_\kappa \in I$ may be asked by an end user to issue a credential corresponding to a set of statements. The requested credential is basically the digital signature of the credential issuer on an assertion denoted A^{pk_u}. The assertion contains, in addition to the set of statements, the end user's public key pk_u as well as a set of additional information such as the validity period of the credential. As the representation of assertions is out of the scope of this paper, they will simply be encoded as binary strings. Upon receiving a request for generating a credential on assertion A^{pk_u}, a credential issuer I_κ first checks the validity of the assertion. If it is valid, then I_κ executes a credential generation algorithm and returns a credential denoted $\varsigma(R_\kappa, A^{pk_u})$. Otherwise, I_κ returns an error message. Upon receiving the credential $\varsigma(R_\kappa, A^{pk_u})$, the end user may check its integrity using I_κ's public key R_κ. The process of checking the validity of a set of statements about a certain entity is out of the scope of this paper.

Each service provider defines an authorization policy for each action on a sensitive resource he controls. We consider credential-based policies formalized as monotone boolean expressions involving conjunctions (AND/$\wedge$) and disjunctions (OR/$\vee$) of credential-based conditions. A credential-based condition is defined through a pair $\langle I_\kappa, A^{pk_u} \rangle$ specifying an assertion $A^{pk_u} \in \{0,1\}^*$ (about an end user whose public key is pk_u) and a credential issuer $I_\kappa \in I$ that is trusted to check and certify the validity of A^{pk_u}. An end user whose public key is pk_u fulfills the condition $\langle I_\kappa, A^{pk_u} \rangle$ if and only if the end user has been issued the credential $\varsigma(R_\kappa, A^{pk_u})$. We consider policies written in standard normal forms, i.e. written either in conjunctive normal form (CNF) or in disjunctive normal form (DNF). In order to address the two standard normal forms, we use the conjunctive-disjunctive normal form (CDNF) introduced in [18]. Thus, a policy denoted Pol^{pk_u} is written as follows:

$$Pol^{pk_u} = \wedge_{i=1}^{m}[\vee_{j=1}^{m_i}[\wedge_{k=1}^{m_{i,j}} \langle I_{\kappa_{i,j,k}}, A_{i,j,k}^{pk_u} \rangle]], \text{ where } I_{\kappa_{i,j,k}} \in I \text{ and } A_{i,j,k}^{pk_u} \in \{0,1\}^*$$

Under the CDNF notation, policies written in CNF correspond to the case where $m_{i,j} = 1$, for all i, j, while policies written in DNF correspond to the case where $m = 1$. Let $\varsigma_{j_1, \dots, j_m}(Pol^{pk_u})$ denote the set of credentials $\{\{\varsigma(R_{\kappa_{i,j_i,k}}, A_{i,j_i,k}^{pk_u})\}_{k=1}^{m_{i,j_i}}\}_{i=1}^{m}$, for some $\{j_i \in \{1, \dots, m_i\}\}_{i=1}^{m}$. Then, $\varsigma_{j_1, \dots, j_m}(Pol^{pk_u})$ is a qualified set of credentials for Pol^{pk_u}.

3.2 Creating and Using Proof-Carrying Proxy Certificates

When an end user wants to interact with a service provider (verifier) through an agent, he first generates a pair of keys (pk_a, sk_a) for the agent. Then, he specifies the content of the proxy certificate - a message, denoted M, containing the end user's public key pk_u, the public key of the agent pk_a and the delegation constraints. Finally, the end user generates a signature on the content of the proxy certificate using a dedicated signature algorithm. The latter takes as input the message to be signed, the private key of the end user sk_u, the policy of the service provider Pol^{pk_u} with respect to the end user's public key pk_u, and a qualified set of credentials for the policy $\varsigma_{j_1,...,j_m}(Pol^{pk_u})$.

When the agent decides to interact with the verifier, he provides his proof-carrying proxy certificate along with a proof of possession of the private key sk_a corresponding to the public key pk_u contained in the proxy certificate. The verifier first checks the delegation constraints specified by the proxy certificate to be sure that the agent is allowed by the end user to perform the requested action on his behalf. Then, he checks the validity of the signature on the content of the proxy certificate using the adequate verification algorithm. This algorithm takes as input the proof-carrying proxy certificate, the end user's public key pk_u, and the authorization policy Pol^{pk_u}. At the end, the verifier obtains a proof that the agent whose public key is pk_a is allowed by an end user whose public key is pk_u to perform the action on his behalf and that the end user is compliant with the authorization policy specified by the verifier.

The signature and verification algorithms used for the creation and verification of proof-carrying proxy certificates must fulfill two security requirements:

- Unforgeability: the signature on a proof-carrying proxy certificate must not be valid with respect to policy Pol^{pk_u} if the signer does not use the private key sk_u or a qualified set of credentials for policy Pol^{pk_u}. In other words, the agent cannot obtain a valid proof-carrying proxy certificate with respect to policy Pol^{pk_u} from a user that does not have access to the private key sk_u, and the end user cannot generate a valid proof-carrying proxy certificate with respect to policy Pol^{pk_u} if he does not have access to a qualified set of credentials for the policy.
- Credential ambiguity: in the case where there exists multiple qualified sets of credentials for policy Pol^{pk_u}, a valid proxy-carrying proxy certificate must not reveal which specific set of credentials has been used to generate the certificate.

4   Definitions

Following the functional description provided in Section 3, we give in this section precise definitions for the algorithms used during the proof-carrying proxy certification process. In addition, we formally define the corresponding security models.

4.1 Algorithms

A proof-carrying proxy certification scheme (in short PCPC) is specified by six algorithms: *System-Setup, Issuer-Setup, User-Setup, CredGen, Sign* and *Verify*.

System-Setup. On input of a security parameter k, this algorithm generates the system public parameters $\mathcal{P}$ including the different spaces, groups and public functions that will be referenced by subsequent algorithms.

Issuer-Setup. This algorithm generates a random master key s_{K} and the corresponding public key R_{K} for credential issuer $I_{\mathsf{K}} \in I$.

User-Setup. This algorithm generates a random private key sk_u and the corresponding public key pk_u.

CredGen. On input of the public key R_{K} of a credential issuer $I_{\mathsf{K}} \in I$ and an assertion $A^{pk_u} \in \{0,1\}^*$, this algorithm generates the credential $\varsigma(R_{\mathsf{K}}, A^{pk_u})$ using the master key s_{K} associated to R_{K}.

Sign. On input of a message M, a pair of keys (pk_u, sk_u), a policy Pol^{pk_u} and a qualified set of credentials $\varsigma_{j_1,\ldots,j_m}(Pol^{pk_u})$, this algorithm returns a signature σ.

Verify. On input of a message M, a signature σ, a public key pk_u and a policy Pol^{pk_u}, this algorithm returns $\top$ (for *true*) if σ is a valid signature on M according to policy Pol^{pk_u}. Otherwise, it returns $\bot$ (for *false*).

The algorithms described above have to satisfy the standard consistency constraint i.e.

$$\sigma = Sign(M, pk_u, sk_u, Pol^{pk_u}, \varsigma_{j_1,\ldots,j_m}(Pol^{pk_u})) \;\Rightarrow\; Verify(M, \sigma, pk_u, Pol^{pk_u}) = \top$$

4.2 Security Models

A PCPC scheme has to fulfill the security requirement of unforgeability and the privacy requirement of credential ambiguity.

Unforgeability. The standard acceptable notion of security for standard signature schemes is existential unforgeability against chosen message attacks [11]. Therefore, we require the same security notion for proof-carrying proxy certification schemes. The definition of existential unforgeability should naturally be adapted to the advanced form of signature used by proof-carrying proxy certificates.

Existential unforgeability for PCPC schemes is defined in terms of an interactive game, played between a challenger and an adversary. The game consists of three stages: *Setup*, *Queries* and *Forge* which we describe below.

- **Setup.** On input of a security parameter k, the challenger does the following: (1) Run algorithm *System-Setup* to obtain the system public parameters $\mathcal{P}$, (2) Run algorithm *Issuer-Setup* once or multiple times to obtain a set of credential issuers $I = \{I_1, \ldots, I_N\}$, (3) Run algorithm *User-Setup* to obtain a public/private key pair (pk_f, sk_f), (4) Give to the adversary the parameters $\mathcal{P}$, the public key pk_f and the public keys of the different credential issuers included in I.
- **Queries.** The adversary performs adaptively a polynomial number of oracle queries which we define below. By "adaptively", we mean that each query may depend on the challenger's replies to the previously performed queries.
- **Forge.** Once the adversary decides that *Queries* is over, it outputs a message M_f, a policy $Pol_f^{pk_f}$, a signature σ_f, and wins the game if $\mathsf{Verify}(M_f, \sigma_f, pk_f, Pol_f^{pk_f}) = \top$.

During the *Queries* stage, the adversary may perform queries to two oracles controlled by the challenger. On one hand, a credential generation oracle denoted **CredGen-O**. On the other hand, a signature oracle denoted **Sign-O**. While the oracles are executed by the challenger, their input is specified by the adversary. The oracles are defined below:

- **CredGen-O.** On input of a credential issuer $I_\kappa \in I$ and an assertion $A^{pk_u} \in \{0,1\}^*$ (associated to a key pair (pk_u, sk_u) chosen by the adversary), run algorithm *CredGen* on input of the tuple (I_κ, A^{pk_u}) and return the resulting credential $\varsigma(R_\kappa, A^{pk_u})$.
- **Sign-O.** On input of a message M and a policy Pol^{pk_f}, first run algorithm *CredGen* once or multiple times to obtain a qualified set of credentials $\varsigma_{j_1,...,j_m}(Pol^{pk_f})$ for Pol^{pk_f}, then run algorithm *Sign* on input of $(M, pk_f, sk_f, Pol^{pk_f}, \varsigma_{j_1,...,j_m}(Pol^{pk_f}))$ (for some $j_i \in \{1,...,m_i\}$ for $i = 1,...,m_i$) and return the resulting output.

The oracle queries made by the adversary during *Queries* are subject to some restrictions depending on the type of adversary. In fact, we distinguish two types of attackers:

- Insider: the adversary is given, in addition to the parameters provided by the challenger during *Setup*, the private key sk_f. An adversary of this type is not allowed to obtain (through queries to oracle *CredGen-O*) a qualified set of credentials for the forgery policy $Pol_f^{pk_f}$. This type of attackers corresponds to entities that are not compliant with a policy and that try to generate a valid signature w.r.t the policy.
- Outsider: the adversary is given, in addition to the parameters provided by the challenger during *Setup*, the master keys of the different credential issuers included in I. An adversary of this type does not have access to the private key sk_f and do not need to perform queries to oracle *CredGen-O*. This type of attackers corresponds to entities that might have access to a qualified set of credentials for the policy but do not have access to the corresponding public key.

Obviously, an adversary, be it insider or outsider, is not allowed to perform a query to oracle *Sign-O* on the tuple $(M_f, Pol_f^{pk_f})$.

The game described above is denoted EUF-PCPC-CMA^X, where $X = I$ for insider adversaries and $X = O$ for outsider adversaries. A formal definition of existential unforgeability against chosen message attacks for PCPC schemes is given below. As usual, a real function g is said to be negligible if $g(k) \leq \frac{1}{f(k)}$ for any polynomial f.

Definition 1. *The advantage of an adversary $\mathcal{A}^X$ in the* EUF-PCPC-CMA^X *game is defined to be the quantity* $Adv_{\mathcal{A}^X} = Pr[\mathcal{A}^X \text{ wins}]$. *A* PCPC *scheme is* EUF-PCPC-CMA^X *secure if no probabilistic polynomial time adversary has a non-negligible advantage in the* EUF-PCPC-CMA^X *game.*

Credential Ambiguity. We define credential ambiguity against chosen message attacks for PCPC schemes in terms of an interactive game (denoted CrA-PCPC-CMA), played between a challenger and an adversary. The game consists of three stages: *Setup*, *Challenge* and *Guess* which we describe below.

- **Setup.** On input of a security parameter k, the challenger does the following: (1) Run algorithm *Setup* to obtain the system public parameters $\mathcal{P}$, (2) Run algorithm *Issuer-Setup* once or multiple times to obtain a set of credential issuers

$I = \{I_1, \ldots, I_N\}$, (3) Give to the adversary the parameters $\mathcal{P}$ as well as the public and master keys of the different credential issuers included in I.

- **Challenge.** The adversary chooses a message M_{ch}, a pair of keys (pk_{ch}, sk_{ch}) and a policy $Pol_{ch}^{pk_{ch}}$ on which he wishes to be challenged. The challenger does the following: (1) For $i = 1, \ldots, m$, pick at random $j_i^{ch} \in \{1, \ldots, m_i\}$, (2) Run algorithm *Cred-Gen* m times to obtain the qualified set of credentials $\varsigma_{j_1^{ch}, \ldots, j_m^{ch}}(Pol_{ch}^{pk_{ch}})$, (3) Run algorithm *Sign* on input the tuple $(M_{ch}, pk_{ch}, sk_{ch}, Pol_{ch}, \varsigma_{j_1^{ch}, \ldots, j_m^{ch}}(Pol_{ch}^{pk_{ch}}))$ and return the resulting output to the adversary.
- **Guess.** The adversary outputs a tuple $(j_1, \ldots, j_m)$, and wins the game if the equality $(j_1^{ch}, \ldots, j_m^{ch}) = (j_1, \ldots, j_m)$ holds.

Definition 2. *The advantage of an adversary $\mathcal{A}$ in the* CrA-PCPC-CMA *game is defined to be the quantity* $Adv_{\mathcal{A}} = \mathsf{Max}_i\{|Pr[j_i = j_i^{ch}] - \frac{1}{m_i}|\}$, *where the parameters m_i are those defined by the challenge policy* $Pol_{ch}^{pk_{ch}}$. *A PCPC scheme is* CrA-PCPC-CMA *secure if no probabilistic polynomial time adversary has a non-negligible advantage in the* CrA-PCPC-CMA *game.*

5   Concrete Implementation

In this section, we describe a concrete implementation of proof-based proxy certificates. Our implementation is based on bilinear pairings over elliptic curves. Our scheme owes much to the work on pairing-based signature and ring signatures presented in [14,20,21]. After describing our concrete algorithms, we analyze their consistency and efficiency. Then, we prove their security in the random oracle model.

5.1   Description

Before describing the algorithms defining our PCPC scheme, we define algorithm *BDH-Setup* as follows:

BDH-Setup. Given a security parameter k, generate a tuple $(q, \mathbb{G}_1, \mathbb{G}_2, e, P)$ where the map $e : \mathbb{G}_1 \times \mathbb{G}_1 \to \mathbb{G}_2$ is a bilinear pairing, $(\mathbb{G}_1, +)$ and $(\mathbb{G}_2, *)$ are two groups of the same order q, and P is a random generator of $\mathbb{G}_1$. The generated parameters are such that the following mathematical problem are hard to solve:

- Computational Diffie-Hellman Problem (CDHP): given a tuple $(P, a \cdot P, b \cdot P)$ for randomly chosen $a, b \in \mathbb{Z}_q^*$, compute the value $ab \cdot P$.
- $(k+1)$-Exponent Problem $(k+1\mathrm{EP})$: given the tuple $(P, a \cdot P, a^2 \cdot P, \ldots, a^k \cdot P)$ for $a \in \mathbb{Z}_q^*$, compute $a^{k+1} \cdot P$.

Note. We recall that a bilinear pairing satisfies the following three properties: (1) Bilinear: for $Q, Q' \in \mathbb{G}_1$ and for $a, b \in \mathbb{Z}_q^*$, $e(a \cdot Q, b \cdot Q') = e(Q, Q')^{ab}$, (2) Non-degenerate: $e(P, P) \neq 1$ and therefore it is a generator of $\mathbb{G}_2$, (3) Computable: there exists an efficient algorithm to compute $e(Q, Q')$ for all $Q, Q' \in \mathbb{G}_1$.   ◇

Our PCPC scheme consists of the algorithms described below.

System-Setup. On input of a security parameter k, do the following:

1. Run algorithm *BDH-Setup* on input k to generate output $(q, \mathbb{G}_1, \mathbb{G}_2, e, P)$
2. Define three hash functions: $H_0 : \{0,1\}^* \to \mathbb{G}_1$, $H_1 : \{0,1\}^* \to \mathbb{Z}_q^*$ and $H_2 : \mathbb{G}_1 \to \mathbb{Z}_q^*$
3. Let $\mathcal{P} = (q, \mathbb{G}_1, \mathbb{G}_2, e, P, H_0, H_1, H_2)$.

Issuer-Setup. Let $I = \{I_1, \ldots, I_N\}$ be a set of credential issuers. Each credential issuer $I_\kappa \in I$ picks at random a secret master key $s_\kappa \in \mathbb{Z}_q^*$ and publishes the corresponding public key $R_\kappa = s_\kappa \cdot P$.

User-Setup. This algorithm picks at random a private key $sk_u \in \mathbb{Z}_q^*$ and computes the corresponding public key $pk_u = sk_u \cdot P$.

CredGen. On input of the public key R_κ of issuer $I_\kappa \in I$ and assertion $A^{pk_u} \in \{0,1\}^*$, this algorithm outputs $\varsigma(R_\kappa, A^{pk_u}) = s_\kappa \cdot H_0(A^{pk_u})$.

Sign. On input of a message M, a pair of keys (pk_u, sk_u), a policy Pol^{pk_u} and a qualified set of credentials $\varsigma_{j_1, \ldots, j_m}(Pol^{pk_u})$, do the following:

1. For $i = 1, \ldots, m$, do the following:
   (a) Pick at random $Y_i \in \mathbb{G}_1$, then compute $x_{i, j_i+1} = e(P, Y_i)$
   (b) For $l = j_i + 1, \ldots, m_i, 1, \ldots, j_i - 1 \bmod (m_i + 1)$, do the following:
      i. Compute $\tau_{i,l} = \prod_{k=1}^{m_{i,l}} e(R_{\kappa_{i,l,k}}, H_0(A_{i,l,k}^{pk_u}))$
      ii. Pick at random $Y_{i,l} \in \mathbb{G}_1$, then compute $x_{i,l+1} = e(P, Y_{i,l}) * \tau_{i,l}^{H_1(M\|x_{i,l}\|m\|i\|l)}$
   (c) Compute $Y_{i,j_i} = Y_i - H_1(M\|x_{i,j_i}\|m\|i\|j_i) \cdot (\sum_{k=1}^{m_{i,j_i}} \varsigma(R_{\kappa_{i,j_i,k}}, A_{i,j_i,k}^{pk_u}))$
2. Compute $Y = \sum_{i=1}^{m} \sum_{j=1}^{m_i} Y_{i,j}$, then compute $Z = (sk_u + H_2(Y))^{-1} \cdot P$
3. Return $\sigma = ([[x_{i,j}]_{j=1}^{m_i}]_{i=1}^{m}, Y, Z)$

Verify. Let $\sigma = ([[x_{i,j}]_{j=1}^{m_i}]_{i=1}^{m}, Y, Z)$ be a signature on message M according to policy Pol^{pk_u} and public key pk_u. To check the validity of σ, do the following:

1. Compute $\tau_{i,j} = \prod_{k=1}^{m_{i,j}} e(R_{\kappa_{i,j,k}}, H_0(A_{i,j,k}^{pk_u}))$ (for $j = 1, \ldots, m_i$ and $i = 1, \ldots, m$)
2. Compute $\alpha_0 = e(pk_u + H_2(Y) \cdot P, Z)$
3. Compute $\alpha_1 = \prod_{i=1}^{m} [\prod_{j=1}^{m_i} x_{i,j}]$ and $\alpha_2 = e(P, Y) * \prod_{i=1}^{m} \prod_{j=1}^{m_i} \tau_{i,j}^{H_1(M\|x_{i,j}\|m\|j\|i)}$
4. If $\alpha_0 = e(P, P)$ and $\alpha_1 = \alpha_2$, then return $\top$, otherwise return $\perp$

The intuition behind our signature algorithm is as follows: each conjunction of conditions $\wedge_{k=1}^{m_{i,j}} \langle I_{\kappa_{i,j,k}}, A_{i,j,k}^{pk_u} \rangle$ is associated to a tag $\tau_{i,j}$. For each index i, the set of tags $\{\tau_{i,j}\}_{j=1}^{m_i}$ is equivalent to a set of ring members. The signature key of the ring member corresponding to the tag $\tau_{i,j}$ consists of the credentials $\{\varsigma(R_{\kappa_{i,j,k}}, A_{i,j,k}^{pk_u})\}_{k=1}^{m_{i,j}}$. Thus, the generated signature corresponds to a set of ring signatures which validity can be checked using the global 'glue' value Y. The latter can be computed only by a user having access to a qualified set of credentials for policy Pol^{pk_u}. The element Z represents the [21] short signature on Y using the private key sk_u. Therefore, σ proves that the entity whose public key is pk_u is compliant with policy Pol^{pk_u}. Note that we can use any standard signature scheme to generate the value Z.

5.2   Consistency and Efficiency

Our *PCPC* scheme satisfies the standard consistency constraint thanks to the following statements:

$$\alpha_0 = e(pk_u + H_2(Y) \cdot P, Z) = e((sk_u + H_2(Y)) \cdot P, (sk_u + H_2(Y))^{-1} \cdot P) = e(P, P) \quad (1)$$

$$\tau_{i,j}^{H_1(M\|x_{i,j}\|m\|i\|j)} = x_{i,j+1} * e(P, Y_{i,j})^{-1} (\text{where} x_{i,m_i+1} = x_{i,1}) \quad (2)$$

$$\alpha_2 = \lambda * \prod_{i=1}^{m}[\prod_{j=1}^{m_i} \tau_{i,j}^{H_1(M\|x_{i,j}\|m\|i\|j)}] \quad (\text{where } \lambda = e(P, Y))$$

$$= \lambda * \prod_{i=1}^{m}[\prod_{j=1}^{m_i-1} x_{i,j+1} * e(P, Y_{i,j})^{-1} * x_{i,1} * e(P, Y_{i,m_i})^{-1}]$$

$$= \lambda * \prod_{i=1}^{m}[\prod_{j=1}^{m_i} x_{i,j} * \prod_{j=1}^{m_i} e(P, Y_{i,j})^{-1}]$$

$$= \lambda * [\prod_{i=1}^{m}\prod_{j=1}^{m_i} x_{i,j}] * [e(P, \sum_{i=1}^{m}\sum_{j=1}^{m_i} Y_{i,j})]^{-1} = \lambda * \alpha_1 * \lambda^{-1} \quad (3)$$

The essential operation in pairing-based cryptography is pairing computations. Our signature algorithm requires a total of $\sum_{i=1}^{m} m_i + \sum_{i=1}^{m}\sum_{j \neq j_i} m_{i,j}$ pairing computations. Note that the values $\tau_{i,l}$ does not depend on the signed message M. Thus, they can be pre-computed by the end user, cached and used in subsequent signatures involving the corresponding credential-based conditions i.e. $\langle R_{\kappa_{i,l,k}}, A_{i,l,k}^{pk_u}\rangle$. On the other hand, our verification algorithm requires a total of $3 + \sum_{i=1}^{m}\sum_{j=1}^{m_i} m_{i,j}$ pairing computations. Although pairing computations could be optimized as explained in [5], the performance of our signature and verification algorithms still need to be improved. This is the main focus of our current research work.

Let l_i denote the bit-length of the bilinear representation of an element of group $\mathbb{G}_i$ $(i = 1, 2)$. Then, the bit-length of a signature produced by our PCPC scheme is equal to $(\sum_{i=1}^{m} m_i).l_2 + 2.l_1$. Note that the signature's length does not depend on the values $m_{i,j}$.

5.3   Security

In the following, we provide the security results related to our PCPC scheme.

Notation. Given the notation used in Section 3, the maximum values that the quantities m, m_i and $m_{i,j}$ can take are denoted, respectively, $m_{\vee\wedge} \geq 1, m_{\vee} \geq 1$ and $m_{\wedge} \geq 1$. We assume that these upper-bounds are specified during system setup.   ◇

Theorem 1. *Our PCPC scheme is* EUF-PCPC-CMA^l *secure in the random oracle model under the assumption that CDHP is hard. In fact, let* $\mathcal{A}^{\circ}$ *be an* EUF-PCPC-CMA^l *adversary with advantage* $Adv_{\mathcal{A}^{\circ}} \geq \varepsilon$ *when attacking our* PCPC *scheme. Assume that adversary* $\mathcal{A}^{\circ}$ *has running time* $t_{\mathcal{A}^{\circ}}$ *and makes at most* q_c *queries to oracle CredGen-O,*

q_s queries to oracle Sign-O, q_0 queries to oracle H_0 and q_1 queries to oracle H_1. Then, there exists an adversary $\mathcal{A}^\bullet$ the advantage of which, when attacking CDHP, is such that

$$Adv_{\mathcal{A}^\bullet} \geq 9/(100 q_0^{m_{\vee\wedge} m_{\vee}} \textstyle\sum_{l=1}^{m_{\vee}} l!\binom{m_{\vee}}{l}))$$

For $q \geq Max\{2m_{\vee\wedge} m_{\vee}, 2m_{\vee\wedge} q_s q_1\}$ and $\varepsilon \leq 32(q_1 + 1 - m_{\vee\wedge} m_{\vee})/q$, its running time is $t_{\mathcal{A}^\bullet} \leq (32 q_1 + 4) t_{\mathcal{A}^\circ}/\varepsilon$.

Proof. Proof of Theorem 1 follows the method described in [12], which is based on the oracle replay technique [17]. Informally, by a polynomial replay of the attack with different random oracles, we allow the attacker to forge two signatures that are related so that the attacker is able to solve the underlying hard problem (*CDHP*). The details of our proof are given in [3]. Note that our security reduction does not depend on the parameter $m_\wedge$. On the other hand, it depends exponentially on the parameters $m_{\vee\wedge}$ and $m_\vee$ which needs further improvement. Finally, note that the ID-based ring signature presented in [21] is not supported by any security arguments. Our proof could be easily adapted to realize the missing proofs. In fact, the ID-based ring signature of [21] is almost similar to our signature algorithm applied in the particular case where the policies are such that $m_{\vee\wedge} = m_\wedge = 1$. □

Theorem 2. *Our PCPC scheme is EUF-PCPC-CMA^O secure in the random oracle model under the assumption that $k + 1 EP$ is hard.*

Proof. The security of our scheme PCPC in the EUF-PCPC-CMA^O game is equivalent to the security of the short signature scheme presented in [21]. In fact, the outsider adversary succeeds in forging a proof-carrying proxy certification if and only if it succeeds in generating a valid Z corresponding to a valid $([[x_{i,j}]_{j=1}^{m_i}]_{i=1}^{m}, Y)$ associated to the pair of keys (pk_f, sk_f). As the adversary has access to the master keys of the different credential issuers, its is able to generate a valid tuple $([[x_{i,j}]_{j=1}^{m_i}]_{i=1}^{m}, Y)$ corresponding to any policy associated to pk_f. Therefore, the adversary needs to be able to generate a [21] short signature on Y using the protected private key sk_f. The short signature of [21] is proved to be secure in the random oracle model under the assumption that the $k+1EP$ problem is hard. □

Theorem 3. *Our PCPC scheme is CrA-PCPC-CMA secure in the random oracle model.*

Proof. Let M_{ch} be the message and $\sigma_{ch} = ([x_{i,j}^{ch}]_{j=1}^{m_i}]_{i=1}^{m}, Y^{ch}, Z^{ch})$ be the signature which the adversary is challenged on in the CrA-PCPC-CMA game. Our PCPC scheme is such that the following holds

1. $x_{i,j}^{ch} = e(P, Y_{i,j-1}) * \tau_{i,j-1}^{H_1(M_{ch}||x_{i,j-1}^{ch}||m||i||j-1)}$ for $j \neq j_i^{ch} + 1$ and $x_{i,j_i^{ch}+1}^{ch} = e(P, Y_i)$

2. $Y^{ch} = \sum_{i=1}^{m} [\sum_{j \neq j^{ch}} Y_{i,j} + Y_i - H_1(M_{ch}||x_{i,j_i^{ch}}^{ch}||m||i||j_i^{ch}) \cdot (\sum_{k=1}^{m_{i,j_i^{ch}}} \varsigma(R_{\kappa_{i,j_i^{ch},k}}, A_{i,j_i^{ch},k}))]$

Since Y_i and $Y_{i,j-1}$ are chosen at random from $\mathbb{G}_1$, and H_1 is assumed to be a random oracle, we have that $x_{i,j}^{ch}$ and Y^{ch} are uniformly distributed in $\mathbb{G}_2$ and $\mathbb{G}_1$ respectively. If $(j_1, \ldots, j_m)$ is the tuple output by the adversary in the CrA-PCPC-CMA game, then we have $Pr[j_i = j_i^{ch}]$, for $i = 1, \ldots, m$. □

6   Conclusion

In this paper, we presented the concept of proof-carrying proxy certificates. The idea is to generate the proxy certificate using a special signature scheme for which the validity of the generated signature proves the compliance of the signer with a credential-based policy. The proof adheres to the privacy principle of data minimization i.e. in the case where there exists multiple qualified sets of credentials for a policy, the proof does not reveal which specific set has been used to generate the signature. To implement our approach, we developed a concrete proof-carrying proxy certification scheme using bilinear pairings over elliptic curves. We defined formal security models for proof-carrying proxy certification schemes and proved the security of our construction under the defined models in the random oracle model. We are currently developing an experimental implementation framework for proof-carrying proxy certificates in the context of grid computing. The integration of well established credential standards (e.g. SPKI, SAML) is one of our goals. We are also working on improving the performance of our construction in terms of both computational and bandwidth consumption costs, and preparing and in-depth analysis of such costs. As discussed in the related work, an interesting line for future would be the construction of a proof-carrying proxy certification scheme based on the well known zero-knowledge proof of knowledge protocols.

References

1. A. Appel and E. Felten. Proof-carrying authentication. In *ACM Conference on Computer and Communications Security*, pages 52–62, 1999.
2. M. Backes, J. Camenisch, and D. Sommer. Anonymous yet accountable access control. In *WPES '05: Proceedings of the 2005 ACM workshop on Privacy in the electronic society*, pages 40–46, New York, NY, USA, 2005. ACM Press.
3. W. Bagga, S. Crosta, , and R. Molva. An application of policy-based signature: Proof-carrying proxy certificates. Institut Eurecom, Research Report RR-06-169, April 2006.
4. W. Bagga and R. Molva. Policy-based cryptography and applications. In *Proceedings of Financial Cryptography and Data Security (FC'05)*, volume 3570 of *LNCS*, pages 72–87. Springer-Verlag, 2005.
5. P. Barreto, H. Kim, B. Lynn, and M. Scott. Efficient algorithms for pairing-based cryptosystems. In *Proceedings of the 22nd Annual International Cryptology Conference on Advances in Cryptology*, pages 354–368. Springer-Verlag, 2002.
6. J. Basney, W. Nejdl, D. Olmedilla, V. Welch, and M. Winslett. Negotiating trust on the grid. In *2nd WWW Workshop on Semantics in P2P and Grid Computing*, New York, USA, May 2004.
7. J. Choi, K. Sakurai, and J. Park. Proxy certificates-based digital fingerprinting scheme for mobile communication. In *IEEE 37th Annual 2003 International Carnahan Conference on Security*, pages 587 – 594. IEEE Computer Society, 2003.
8. J. Claessens, B. Preneel, and J. Vandewalle. (how) can mobile agents do secure electronic transactions on untrusted hosts? a survey of the security issues and the current solutions. *ACM Trans. Inter. Tech.*, 3(1):28–48, 2003.
9. A. Fiat and A. Shamir. How to prove yourself: Practical solutions to identification and signature problems. In *Advances in Cryptology — Crypto '86*, pages 186–194, New York, 1987. Springer-Verlag.

10. Organization for Economic Cooperation and Development (OECD). Recommendation of the council concerning guidelines governing the protection of privacy and transborder flows of personal data, 1980. http://www.oecd.org/home/.

11. S. Goldwasser, S. Micali, and R. L. Rivest. A digital signature scheme secure against adaptive chosen-message attacks. *SIAM J. Comput.*, 17(2):281–308, 1988.

12. J. Herranz. A formal proof of security of Zhang and Kim's ID-based ring signature scheme. In *WOSIS'04*, pages 63–72. INSTICC Press, 2004. ISBN 972-8865-07-4.

13. B. Lee and K. Kim. Self-certified signatures. In *INDOCRYPT '02: Proceedings of the Third International Conference on Cryptology*, pages 199–214, London, UK, 2002. Springer-Verlag.

14. C. Lin and T. Wu. An identity-based ring signature scheme from bilinear pairings. Cryptology ePrint Archive, Report 2003/117, 2003. http://eprint.iacr.org/.

15. G. Necula. Proof-carrying code. In *POPL '97: Proceedings of the 24th ACM SIGPLAN-SIGACT symposium on Principles of programming languages*, pages 106–119, New York, NY, USA, 1997. ACM Press.

16. B. Clifford Neuman. Proxy-based authorization and accounting for distributed systems. In *International Conference on Distributed Computing Systems*, pages 283–291, 1993.

17. D. Pointcheval and J. Stern. Security arguments for digital signatures and blind signatures. *Journal of Cryptology: the journal of the International Association for Cryptologic Research*, 13(3):361–396, 2000.

18. N. Smart. Access control using pairing based cryptography. In *Proceedings CT-RSA 2003*, pages 111–121. Springer-Verlag LNCS 2612, April 2003.

19. S. Tuecke, V. Welch, D. Engert, L. Pearlman, and M. Thompson. Internet X.509 Public Key Infrastructure (PKI) Proxy Certificate Profile. *RFC 3820*, June 2004.

20. F. Zhang and K. Kim. ID-based blind signature and ring signature from pairings. In *ASIACRYPT*, pages 533–547. Springer-Verlag LNCS 2501, 2002.

21. F. Zhang, R. Safavi-Naini, and W. Susilo. An efficient signature scheme from bilinear pairings and its applications. In *Public Key Cryptography*, pages 277–290, 2004.

Cryptanalysis of Rainbow[*]

Olivier Billet and Henri Gilbert

France Télécom R&D
38–40, rue du Général Leclerc
92794 Issy les Moulineaux Cedex 9 — France
forname.lastname@orange-ft.com

Abstract. Rainbow is a fast asymmetric multivariate signature algorithm proposed by J. Ding and D. Schmidt in [5]. This paper presents a cryptanalysis of Rainbow which enables an attacker provided with the public key to recover an equivalent representation of the secret key, thus allowing her to efficiently forge a signature of any message. For the set of parameter values recommended by the authors of Rainbow in order to achieve a security level strictly higher than 2^{80}, the complexity of our attack is less than 2^{71} operations. This is 2^{40} times less than the complexity of the best known attack used by the authors to dimension their system.

Keywords: Public Key Cryptography, Multivariate Cryptography, Rainbow, UOV (Unbalanced Oil and Vinegar), Signature Schemes.

1 Introduction

Rainbow [5] is an asymmetric signature scheme proposed by Jintai Ding and Dieter Schmidt in 2005. It belongs to the family of multivariate asymmetric schemes, a promising sub-area of public key cryptography which development was motivated by the search to alternatives to RSA and initiated by the seminal work of T. Matsumoto and H. Imai [6,9] and J. Patarin [10]. Instead of using the difficulty of solving a single variable equation over a large finite ring as is the case for RSA and discrete logarithm based systems such as DSA, multivariate schemes exploit the difficulty of solving a multivariate system of equations over a small finite field.

Numerous multivariate encryption, signature, or public key authentication schemes have been proposed over the past years. Though many of them (C^* [6], the balanced Oil and Vinegar [12], and HFE [11]) turned out to be weak, several multivariate signature schemes have successfully resisted cryptanalysis so far and allow for efficient implementations. Two of these unbkroken signature schemes seem particularly attractive since they are better suited than RSA for implementation in low cost smart cards: UOV (Unbalanced Oil and Vinegar) [7] and SFLASH v2 [1] which is one of the three digital signature algorithms selected in 2002 by the European project NESSIE.

---

[*] This work is supported in part by the European Commission through ECRYPT.

R. De Prisco and M. Yung (Eds.): SCN 2006, LNCS 4116, pp. 336–347, 2006.
© Springer-Verlag Berlin Heidelberg 2006

Rainbow is built upon the UOV scheme and uses several instances of the Oil and Vinegar construction organized in a set of embedded layers. This allows Rainbow to improve on the efficiency of the original UOV scheme. The authors of Rainbow propose in [5] a fully instantiated version of their scheme, which is shown to outperform SFLASH v2 in terms of running time–it is claimed to be twice as fast, and in terms of public key length–it is about 16 KB instead of 112 kB for SFLASH v2. It is conjectured by the authors of [5] that no attack of complexity less than 2^{80} can be found against Rainbow.

In this paper we present a cryptanalysis of Rainbow which complexity is substantially lower than the one of the best attack considered in the security analysis of [5]. The attack provides the adversary with an equivalent representation of the private (signature) function, thus allowing an attacker to forge a signature of any message. For the set of parameter values recommended by the authors of Rainbow [5], the complexity of our attack is about $q^7 \cdot 27^3 < 2^{71}$ operations (where $q = 256$ is the field size) instead of $q^{12} \cdot 27^3 > 2^{110}$ for the best attack described in [5].

2   UOV and Rainbow Multivariate Signature Schemes

In this section, we first outline those features of UOV which are useful to the understanding of Rainbow and then provide a general description of the Rainbow signature scheme together with the parameters choice recommended by its authors.

2.1   Outline of UOV

UOV is a digital signature scheme proposed by A. Kipnis, J. Patarin, and L. Goubin in [7]. It uses the same trapdoor technique as the previously proposed oil and vinegar system cryptanalyzed in 1997 by A. Shamir and A. Kipnis in [13], but other parameters preventing this cryptanalysis as well as all known attack techniques.

The public key consists of a system $\bar{\mathcal{F}}$ of m multivariate quadratic equations in n unknowns over a finite field $GF(q)$, with $n > m$. To ease the exposition, we hereafter assume $q > 2$. Signing a message M of $GF(q)^m$ consists in finding a preimage of M by $\bar{\mathcal{F}}$ in $GF(q)^n$. The secret key lies in the knowledge of a bijective $GF(q)$-linear change of variable L_1 and a set $\mathcal{F}$ of m multivariate quadratic equations in n unknowns of a special type so that the composition $\mathcal{F} \circ L_1$ is the public key: $\bar{\mathcal{F}} = \mathcal{F} \circ L_1$. Equations of the quadratic system $\mathcal{F}$ in n unknowns $x_1, \ldots, x_n$ have the following property. The set of variables being partitioned in two sets $\{x_i\}_{i \in V}$ and $\{x_i\}_{i \in O}$ where $V = \{1, \ldots, n-m\}$ is the set of vinegar indices and $O = \{n-m+1, \ldots, n\}$ the set of oil indices, the quadratic part Q_k of the kth-polynomial of $\mathcal{F}$ has the specific form:

$$Q_k(x_1, \ldots, x_n) = \sum_{(i,j) \in V \times V | i \leq j} \alpha_{i,j}^{(k)} x_i x_j + \sum_{(i,j) \in V \times O} \beta_{i,j}^{(k)} x_i x_j. \tag{1}$$

After the secret change of variables $(x_1, \ldots, x_n) = L_1(z_1, \ldots, z_n)$ this specific form disappears as the expression of the quadratic part of the public key's polynomials now have the general form:

$$\bar{Q}_k(z_1, \ldots, z_n) = \sum_{1 \leq i \leq j \leq n} \gamma_{i,j}^{(k)} z_i z_j.$$

We further note that there is no need for a secret linear output mixing layer in this scheme as it would not change the look of the public key.

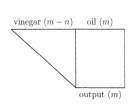

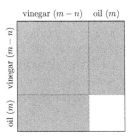

Fig. 1. The figure on the left is a visual representation of the mapping $\mathcal{F}$ of UOV while the figure on the right shows the special structure of the symmetric matrix associated to the quadratic part Q_k of any polynomial of the hidden transformation $\mathcal{F}$ of UOV

As a consequence of this very special structure, the equations of induced by Eqs. 1 when fixing the vinegar variables to constant values are linear in the remaining (oil) variables. This provides an efficient method for inverting system $\mathcal{F}$ with a high probability–the linear system in the oil variables we obtain is invertible with high probability. In order to find a preimage through $\bar{\mathcal{F}}$ of a tuple $(y_1, \cdots, y_m)$ of $GF(q)^m$, the signer just has to randomly draw values for the vinegar variables and solve the induced linear system in m remaining oil variables. (This procedure has to be repeated until a solvable system (e.g. a full rank system) is obtained.) Thus in order to sign a message M, the owner of the secret key can use her secret representation of $\bar{\mathcal{F}}$ to consecutively invert $\mathcal{F}$ and L_1 and thus find a preimage of M by $\bar{\mathcal{F}}$. On the opposite, it appears to be difficult for an adversary who only knows $\bar{\mathcal{F}}$ to derive a similar representation from the public key, and more generally to invert $\bar{\mathcal{F}}$.

The authors of UOV recommend in [7] to choose parameter values such that $n > 3m$ in order to thwart generalizations of A. Kipnis and A. Shamir's attack [13], where $v = n - m$ is the number of vinegar variables and $o = m$ is the number of oil variables. (This generalization of A. Kipnis and A. Shamir's attack presented in [7] has a complexity of $q^{v-o-1} o^4$.)

2.2   General Description of Rainbow

The public key of Rainbow consists of a set of m multivariate quadratic polynomials $\bar{F}_1, \ldots, \bar{F}_m$ in n unknowns over a finite field $GF(q)$. The general problem of solving such a set of multivariate polynomials being hard, those polynomials are constructed in a special way using the UOV contruction several times in an embedded manner to insert a trapdoor.

To construct a Rainbow signature scheme with l layers, let us consider a set of $l + 1$ integers v_i verifying $0 < v_1 < v_2 < \cdots < v_{l+1} = n$ as well as the set $\mathcal{P}_k$ of polynomials of the special form:

$$\sum_{\substack{v_k < i \leq v_{k+1} \\ 1 \leq j \leq v_k}} \alpha_{i,j}\, x_i x_j + \sum_{1 \leq i,j \leq v_k} \beta_{i,j}\, x_i x_j + \sum_{1 \leq i \leq v_{k+1}} \gamma_i\, x_i + \eta.$$

Such polynomials are Oil and Vinegar polynomials since no monomial of degree two have both variables coming from the set $O_k = \{x_{v_k+1}, x_{v_k+2}, \ldots, x_{v_{k+1}}\}$, whereas there are monomials of degree two where both variables come from the set $V_k = \{x_1, \ldots, x_{v_k}\}$. Hence, variables from the set O_k are called oil variables of layer k, and variables from the set V_k are called vinegar variables of layer k.

Now, for every $1 \leq k \leq l$, the kth layer of Rainbow is built as a list $(F_{v_k-v_1+1}, \ldots, F_{v_{k+1}-v_1})$ of $o_k = (v_{k+1} - v_k)$ polynomials randomly drawn from the set $\mathcal{P}_k$.

Therefore, the l layers of Rainbow are made of a total of $m = n - v_1$ polynomials which results in the following map:

$$\mathcal{F} : \quad \begin{aligned} \text{GF}(q)^n &\longrightarrow \text{GF}(q)^m, \\ (x_1, \ldots, x_n) &\longmapsto (F_1(x_1, \ldots, x_n), \ldots, F_m(x_1, \ldots, x_n)). \end{aligned}$$

Then, in order to hide the very specific structure of each layer, the key generation process randomly choses a bijective linear input transformation L_1 of $\text{GF}(q)^n$ as well as a bijective linear output transformation L_2 of $\text{GF}(q)^m$ which are applied to $\mathcal{F}$ so as to produce the public key $\bar{\mathcal{F}}$ as follows:

$$\bar{\mathcal{F}}(z_1, \ldots, z_n) = L_2 \circ \mathcal{F} \circ L_1(z_1, \ldots, z_n).$$

2.3   Recommended Values for Rainbow

The authors of Rainbow proposed the following typical set of parameters. The number of layers is set to four, and $v_1 = 6$, $o_1 = 6$, $v_2 = 12$, $o_2 = 5$, $v_3 = 17$, $o_3 = 5$, $v_4 = 22$, $o_4 = 11$, and $v_5 = 33$. Thus, the public key $\bar{\mathcal{F}}$ consists of $m = 27$ polynomials $\bar{F}_1$, ..., $\bar{F}_{27}$. Figure 2 further describes each of the internal polynomial F_i depending of the layer it belongs to by displaying the structure of its corresponding symmetric matrix.

3   Cryptanalysis of Rainbow

We now describe our cryptanalysis of the Rainbow signature scheme. The description of the cryptanalysis is done in three steps. First of all, we describe the well known rank attack suggested by N. Courtois and L. Goubin in [4], since it is an essential tool in our attack. Then we show how to extract the first layer of Oil

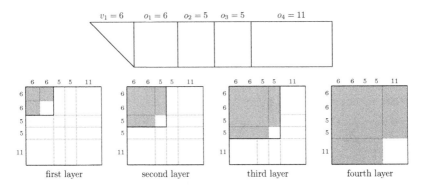

Fig. 2. On top, the four layers of Rainbow together with the recommended parameters values. Below, the pictures show the four different types of quadratic forms used in the internal transformation $\mathcal{F}$. The greyed areas represent the entries which are possibly non-zero, while blank areas denote the null entries. The small numbers show the size of the vector spaces involved.

and Vinegar out of the whole Rainbow description which allows to peal off every layer one by one. Finally, we show how to recover an isomorphic representation of each of the set of layered vinegar variables which obviously allows an attacker to sign in place of the legitimate user.

3.1 The Classical Rank Attack

One way of attacking an Oil and Vinegar style cryptosystem is to look for a combination of the m public multivariate polynomials that exhibits a very low rank. In the special case of the Rainbow cryptosystem, this would amount to searching for a linear combination of the public quadratic polynomials having a rank of at most 12. Such a polynomial would actually be a linear combination of the six polynomials belonging to the first layer of Oil and Vinegar. One standard way of representing a quadratic multivariate polynomial is by its associated symmetric matrix. (Over fields of even characteristic, one has to consider the symmetric matrix Q associated to the multivariate quadratic polynomial g in the n unknowns $x_1, \ldots, x_n$ over a finite field $\mathrm{GF}(q)$ where the entries $Q_{i,j} = Q_{i,j}$ for $1 \leq i < j \leq n$ are defined as the coefficients of the monomial $x_i x_j$ in the expression of $g(x)$; we recall that the diagonal entries are set to zero as they correspond to terms that are essentially linear.) This problem, which is a special instance of the so-called MinRank problem [3], can thus be stated as follows: Given a set of $n \times n$ matrices $Q_1, \ldots, Q_m$, find a linear combination $M = \sum_{k=1}^{m} \lambda_k Q_k$ of these matrices which has rank r.

In the paper [4], a powerful algorithm was suggested to solve this problem when a solution exists and the rank r is low enough. The idea underlying this algorithm is to search for a vector lying in the kernel of the desired linear combination M. Since M has rank r, there are exactly $\frac{1}{q^r}$ chances that a randomly drawn vector lies in the kernel of M. Moreover, any vector w lying in the kernel of M verifies equation:

$$\left(\sum_{k=1}^{m} \lambda_k Q_k\right) w = 0,$$

which is linear in the m unknowns $\lambda_1, \ldots, \lambda_m$. This vectorial equation is nothing but a system of $n = |w|$ linear equations. Thus, as $m < n$, if the randomly chosen vector w lies in the kernel of M, linear algebra allows to recover a solution $(\lambda_1, \ldots, \lambda_m)$ and the average cost of finding a solution is $q^r m^3$.

Refering to this state of the art attack, the designers of Rainbow claimed that: "From the MinRank method [3] we know that the complexity to find such a matrix is $q^{12} \times 27^3$, which is much larger than 2^{100}." We show in the following, that this security level was highly overestimated, since we demonstrate an attack against Rainbow with time complexity $q^7 27^3$. In particular, we show that the set of parameters recommended in [5] are insecure.

3.2   Extracting the First Layer of Rainbow

In this section, we show that the first layer of Rainbow can be extracted from the public key. This is the starting point of our cryptanalysis and this initial step allows an attacker to peal off each Oil and Vinegar layer of Rainbow one by one and inside out.

Recall that the first layer of Rainbow is a balanced Oil and Vinegar with 6 oil variables and 6 vinegar variables. Thus, there exist six linearly independent linear combinations defined by $M^{(i)} = \sum_{k=1}^{27} \lambda_k^{(i)} Q_k$ where $1 \leq i \leq 6$ of the 27 matrices $Q_1, \ldots, Q_{27}$ corresponding to the public quadratic polynomials of Rainbow which are of small rank 12 and any linear combination of the $M^{(i)}$ has rank at most 12. We make use of this additional property exhibited by Rainbow to improve the complexity of the MinRank resolution algorithm presented in Section 3.1. Based on a heuristic assumption, we make the following:

Proposition 1. *Given the six matrices $F_1, \ldots, F_6$ of the first type*

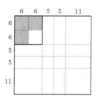

and a vector w randomly chosen of the form ⊏▭▭▭▭▭ *(that is, such that every entry takes a value randomly chosen in* GF(q) *except for the six first entries which are requested to be zero), with probability greater than $\frac{1}{q}$, there exists a (non trivial) linear combination M of matrices $F_1, \ldots, F_6$ such that the vector w lies in the kernel of M.*

Proof. Because of the very specific form of matrices $F_1, \ldots, F_6$, all the vectors defined by $w_1 = F_1 w, \ldots, w_6 = F_6 w$ have at most six non-zero entries, which are located at position $1, \ldots, 6$. Assuming that these vectors $w_1, \ldots, w_6$ are uniformly distributed, the probability that they are linearly independent is equal to:

$$\prod_{i=0}^{5}\left(1 - \frac{q^i}{q^6}\right) < \left(1 - \frac{1}{q}\right).$$

Hence, given a vector w randomly chosen among those having their six first entries equal to zero, there is a probability greater than $\frac{1}{q}$ that it lies in the kernel of a non-trivial linear combination of the matrices $F_1, \ldots, F_6$.   □

Corollary 1. *An attacker is able to extract a representation of the first layer of Rainbow with a time complexity less than* $6 \cdot q^7 \cdot 27^3 \simeq 2^{72}$.

Proof. The attacker does not have access to the secret change of base L_2 operated before applying matrices $F_1, \ldots, F_6$. However, this does not change the fact that a randomly chosen vector v has probability $\frac{1}{q^6}$ that its image through L_2 has the form required by Assumption 1. Hence, applying Assumption 1 together with an exhaustive search on v, one sees that an attacker has more than $\frac{1}{q^7}$ chances to find a vector v_0 lying in the kernel of an unknown linear combination

$$M = \sum_{k=1}^{27} \lambda_k Q_k$$

of the 27 matrices Q_k corresponding to the public quadratic polynomials. The attacker is then in the situation of applying the strategy described in the previous section: The matricial equation

$$\sum_{k=1}^{27} \lambda_k (Q_k v_0)$$

indeed gives 33 linear equations in the 27 unknowns $\lambda_1, \ldots, \lambda_{27}$. Solving this system then gives a linear combination of the 27 public quadratic polynomials that has rank 12. Since solving the linear system has a complexity of 27^3, the overall complexity to recover the linear combination is upper bounded by $q^7 \cdot 27^3$.

However, this step has to be repeated about six times to recover a total of six linearly independent linear combinations of the polynomials of the first layer of Rainbow.   □

Appendix A contains a very simple MAGMA source file implementing this step, which was run for several different parameters. The program indeed took less than q^7 in average trials in order to find a linear combination of the public polynomials having rank 12.

3.3   Recovering the Other Layers

The previous section showed how to recover the first layer of Rainbow. There are now various ways to end the cryptanalysis. The interested reader may find further information about this in [14,15]. We sketch here a strategy which additional complexity is negligible compared to the complexity of the previous step. It enables us to peal off every layer of Rainbow one by one. First of all, let us recall a fundamental result in the theory of quadratic forms over a finite field:

Theorem 1 (See [8], p.287). *Let* $\mathrm{GF}(q)$ *be a finite field of even characteristic. For any quadratic form* $f \in \mathrm{GF}(q)[x_1, \ldots, x_n]$ *of rank* r, *there exists a matrix* B *of rank* r *that maps* $x_1, \ldots, x_n$ *to* $z_1, \ldots, z_r$ *such that*

$$f(x_1, \ldots, x_n) = g \circ B(x_1, \ldots, x_n),$$

where $g(z_1, \ldots, z_r)$ *is defined by one of the canonical forms*

$$z_1 z_2 + \cdots + z_{r-2} z_{r-1} + z_r^2, \qquad\qquad\qquad \text{if } r \text{ is odd,}$$

$$z_1 z_2 + \cdots + z_{r-1} z_r + b\big(z_{r-1}^2 + a z_r^2\big), \ b \in \{0, 1\} \qquad \text{if } r \text{ is even.}$$

The matrix B *can be computed by a deterministic algorithm of complexity lower than* n^3.

This result can be combined with the result of the previous Section as follows. We are given a set of six quadratic polynomials which are known to have rank 12 and the set of independent variables involved in those six polynomials are the same. Hence, the process of putting any of the quadratic polynomials into its canonical form uncovers part of the change of base L_1 and gives the value of the preimage through L_1 of the vector space spanned by the twelve first elements of the canonical base of $\mathrm{GF}(q)^n$. This gives an attacker an isomorphic knowledge of the set of inner variables $x_1, \ldots, x_{12}$, that is an equivalent representation of the first twelve rows of the secret change of variables.

The attacker is now left with 21 matrices to which she can once again apply the strategy presented in the previous Section to discover the second layer. However, she does not have to perform the exhaustive search step this time. Indeed, using its knowledge of the preimage $L_1^{-1}(V_2)$ through L_1 of the vector space V_2 spanned by the first twelve inner variables, she can make the input vector v_0 directly lie into the kernel of the seeked linear combination. The cost of pealing the second layer thus boils down to the cost of solving a linear system of 33 equations in 21 unknowns, repeated five times, once for each polynomial of the layer. Since, this second layer contains five polynomials having rank 17, putting one of these polynomials into its into its canonical form allows the attacker to recovers the preimage through L_1 of the vector space spanned by the next set of variables V_3.

The same process goes for extracting the third layer and for recovering the preimage through L_4 of the vector space V_4.

Note that the complexity of each of these steps is bounded above by $11 \cdot 33^3$ and thus negligible compared to the complexity of attacking the first layer. The overall complexity of our attack is thus $6 \cdot q^7 \cdot 27^3$.

3.4   Spoofing a Signature

The attacker now have separated all four layers of Rainbow. It remains for her to show that she is now able to sign in place of the legitimate user. Since the attacker was able to separate all four layers of Rainbow, the process is identical to the signature process followed by the legitimate user except for the first layer.

However, the first layer is just a very small balanced oil and vinegar scheme which can be easily broken as shown in [13] with a polynomial time complexity in the number of variables–twelve in the case of Rainbow. More precisely, this allows an attacker to find a set of $v_2 = v_1 + o_1$ variables that evaluates through the set of the six polynomials of the first layer to the requested value, which is exactly what a legitimate user was requested to do.

The end of the signature process goes exactly the same as for the legitme user as every additional layer is linear in the new set of variables and hence just requires to incrementally solve three square linear systems of size 5, 5, and 11 respectively over $\mathrm{GF}(q)$.

4   Discussion and Conclusion

The complexity of the attack presented in this paper is $q^{v_1+1} \times m^3$ instead of the expected complexity of $q^{v_1+o_1} \times m^3$ resulting from the direct application of the Minrank solving method exposed in [3], which was taken as a reference by the authors of Rainbow to dimension their system.

In order to prevent our attack, the number v_1 of vinegar variables involved in the first layer of Rainbow must be increased as to ensure $q^{v_1+1} \times m^3 > 2^{80}$, or even better $q^{v_1} > 2^{80}$. Preventing our attack thus has some negative impact upon the scheme's bit efficiency and overall performance. We do not preclude that it might be possible to produce a patched variant of Rainbow (say Rainbow v2) which would still outperform SFLASH v2 in terms of performance and public key length. However, our attack illustrates the fact that the embedded trapdoor structure of Rainbow results in so numerous potential lines of attack that it is quite difficult to get a reasonable confidence that Rainbow is as secure as the UOV signature scheme it is based upon.

References

1. Mehdi-Laurent Akkar, Nicolas Tadeusz Courtois, Louis Goubin, and Romain Du-teuil. A fast and secure implementation of sflash. In Yvo G. Desmedt, editor, *Public Key Cryptography – PKC 2003*, volume 2567 of *Lecture Notes in Computer Science*, pages 267–278. Springer-Verlag, 2003.
2. An Braeken, Bart Preneel, and Christopher Wolf. A Study of the Security of Unbalanced Oil and Vinegar Signature Schemes. In Alfred Menezes, editor, *Topics in Cryptology – CT-RSA 2005*, volume 3376 of *Lecture Notes in Computer Science*, page 29. Springer-Verlag, 2005.

3. Nicolas Tadeusz Courtois. Efficient Zero-Knowledge Authentication Based on a Linear Algebra Problem MinRank. In Colin Boyd, editor, *Advances in Cryptology – ASIACRYPT 2001*, volume 2248 of *Lecture Notes in Computer Science*, pages 402–421. Springer-Verlag, 2001.

4. Nicolas Tadeusz Courtois and Louis Goubin. Cryptanalysis of the TTM Cryptosystem. In Tatsuaki Okamoto, editor, *Advances in Cryptology – ASIACRYPT 2000*, volume 1976 of *Lecture Notes in Computer Science*, pages 44–57. Springer-Verlag, 2000.

5. Jintai Ding and Dieter Schmidt. Rainbow, a New Multivariable Polynomial Signature Scheme. In John Ioannidis, Angelos D. Keromytis, and Moti Yung, editors, *Applied Cryptography and Network Security – ACNS 2005*, volume 3531 of *Lecture Notes in Computer Science*, pages 164–175, 2005.

6. Hideki Imai and Tsutomu Matsumoto. Algebraic Methods for Constructing Asymmetric Cryptosystems. In Jacques Calmet, editor, *Applied Algebra, Algebraic Algorithms and Error-Correcting Codes – AAECC 3*, volume 229 of *Lecture Notes in Computer Science*, pages 108–119. Springer-Verlag, 1985.

7. Aviad Kipnis, Jacques Patarin, and Louis Goubin. Unbalanced Oil and Vinegar Signature Schemes. In Jacques Stern, editor, *Advances in Cryptology – EUROCRYPT '99*, volume 1592 of *Lecture Notes in Computer Science*, pages 206–222. Springer-Verlag, 1999.

8. Rudolf Lidl and Harald Niederreiter. *Finite fields*, volume 20 of *Encyclopedia of Mathematics and its Applications*. Cambridge University Press, second edition, 1997.

9. Tsutomu Matsumoto and Hideki Imai. Public Quadratic Polynominal-Tuples for Efficient Signature-Verification and Message-Encryption. In C. G. Günther, editor, *Advances in Cryptology – EUROCRYPT '88*, volume 330 of *Lecture Notes in Computer Science*, pages 419–453. Springer-Verlag, 1988.

10. Jacques Patarin. Cryptoanalysis of the Matsumoto and Imai Public Key Scheme of Eurocrypt '88. In Don Coppersmith, editor, *Advances in Cryptology – CRYPTO '95*, volume 963 of *Lecture Notes in Computer Science*, pages 248–261. Springer-Verlag, 1995.

11. Jacques Patarin. Hidden fields equations (hfe) and isomorphisms of polynomials (ip): Two new families of asymmetric algorithms. In Ueli M. Maurer, editor, *Advances in Cryptology – EUROCRYPT '96*, volume 1070 of *Lecture Notes in Computer Science*, pages 33–48. Springer-Verlag, 1996.

12. Jacques Patarin. The Oil and Vinegar Algorithm for Signatures. presented at the Dagsthul Workshop on Cryptography, September 1997.

13. Adi Shamir and Aviad Kipnis. Cryptanalysis of the Oil & Vinegar Signature Scheme. In Hugo Krawczyk, editor, *Advances in Cryptology – CRYPTO '98*, volume 1462 of *Lecture Notes in Computer Science*, pages 257–266. Springer-Verlag, 1998.

14. Christopher Wolf, An Braeken, and Bart Preneel. Efficient cryptanalysis of rse(2)pkc and rsse(2)pkc. In Carlo Blundo and Stelvio Cimato, editors, *Security in Communication Networks – SCN 2004*, volume 3352 of *Lecture Notes in Computer Science*, pages 294–309. Springer, 2004.

15. Bo-Yin Yang and Jiun-Ming Chen. Tts: Rank attacks in tame-like multivariate pkcs. Cryptology ePrint Archive, Report 2004/061, 2004. `http://eprint.iacr.org/`.

A   Magma Program for Corollary 1

We first define the number of variables n, the number of public polynomials m, as well as the ground field FF= $\mathrm{GF}(q)$.

```
1       n := 33;
2       m := 27;
3       q := 8;
4       FF:= GF(q);
```

The following is an auxiliary function generating a random invertible $N \times N$ matrix B over $\mathrm{GF}(q)$.

```
5       genRandInvMat := function(N)
6           repeat B := MATRIX(N, N, [ RANDOM(FF) : i in [1..N²] ]);
7           until (RANK(B) eq N);
8           return B;
9       end function;
```

Now the procedure *genMatrix* generates m matrices corresponding to the m quadratic polynomials of the internal transformation $\mathcal{F}$.

```
10      procedure genMatrix(r, k, ~M)
11          for j:= 1 to k do
12              L := [ RANDOM(FF) : i in [1..FLOOR(r*(r+1)/2)] ];
13              Z := ZEROMATRIX(FF, n, n);
14              MJ:= INSERTBLOCK(Z, SYMMETRICMATRIX(L), 1, 1);
15              Z := ZEROMATRIX(FF, k, k);
16              MJ := INSERTBLOCK(MJ, Z, r−k+1, r−k+1);
17              M := M cat [MJ];
18          end for;
19      end procedure;
```

We generate the first layer of Rainbow and store it into SYS:

```
20      SYS:= [];
21      genMatrix(12, 6, ~SYS);
```

and then the second, third, and fourth layer of Rainbow:

```
22      genMatrix(17, 5, ~SYS);
23      genMatrix(22, 5, ~SYS);
24      genMatrix(33, 11, ~SYS);
```

We apply a randomly chosen change of base L_1 to each matrix SYS$[j]$ corresponding to a polynomial F_j of the internal transformation and store the resulting matrix into SYSL1$[j]$ which corresponds to the polynomial $F_j \circ L_1$.

```
25      L₁ := genRandInvMat(33);
26      SYSL1:= [];
27      for j:=1 to m do
28          SYSL1[j] := L₁ * SYS[j] * TRANSPOSE(L₁);
29      end for;
```

Finally, we apply the output mixing layer L_2 to obtain the m public polynomials. Thus, $L2SysL_1[j]$ stores the matrix corresponding to the public polynomial $\bar{F}_j$ where $\bar{\mathcal{F}} = L_2 \circ \mathcal{F} \circ L_1$.

```
30      L₂ := genRandInvMat(27);
31      L2SysL₁:= [];
32      Z := ZEROMATRIX(FF, n, n);
33      for j:=1 to m do
34          L2SysL₁[j] := Z;
35          for i:=1 to m do
36              L2SysL₁[j] := L2SysL₁[j] + L₂[j,i] * SYSL1[i];
37          end for;
38      end for;
```

The following loop draws a randomly chosen vector v and check if it lies in the kernel of a non-trivial linear combination of the matrices $L2SysL_1$. (Variable k keeps track of the number of trials in order to verify the complexity.)

```
39      l := 0; k := 0;
40      repeat
41          ok:= false;
42          v := VECTOR([ RANDOM(FF) : i in [1..n] ]);
43          Qv:= MATRIX([ v * L2SysL₁[j] : j in [1..m] ]);
44          k := k+1; if k ge qˡ then l := l+1; end if;
45          r := RANK(Qv);
46          if ((r lt m) and (r gt 1)) then
47              KER := KERNEL(Qv);
48              CL := ZEROMATRIX(FF, n, n);
49              for i in [1..m] do CL := CL+(KER.1)[i]*L2SysL₁[i]; end for;
50              ok := RANK(CL) lt 13;
51          end if;
52      until ( ok );
```

We output the complexity of our algoritm:

```
53      "complexity is q ^", l;
```

The corresponding linear combination of the public polynomials having rank at most 12 is represented by the matrix CL. Thus we can make sure it actually lies in the vector space spanned by the first layer of Rainbow:

```
54      L₁⁻¹ * CL * TRANSPOSE(L₁⁻¹);
```

An Improved LPN Algorithm

Éric Levieil and Pierre-Alain Fouque

École normale supérieure, 45 rue d'Ulm, 75230 Paris Cedex 05, France
{Eric.Levieil, Pierre-Alain.Fouque}@ens.fr

Abstract. HB$^+$ is a shared-key authentication protocol, proposed by Juels and Weis at Crypto 2005, using prior work of Hopper and Blum. Its very low computational cost makes it attractive for low-cost devices such as radio-frequency identification(RFID) tags. Juels and Weis gave a security proof, relying on the hardness of the "learning parity with noise" (LPN) problem. Here, we improve the previous best known algorithm proposed by Blum, Kalai, and Wasserman for solving the LPN problem. This new algorithm yields an attack for HB$^+$ in the detection-based model with work factor 2^{52}.

1 Introduction

Providing lightweight and secure cryptographic protocols for radio-frequency identification (RFID) tags is an area under quick development. The HB protocol family is one of the most promising in this field and uses very few operations and gates on the chip. The original protocol has been proposed by Hopper and Blum [8].

All protocols in the HB family rely on the computational hardness of the LPN problem.

The LPN Problem. In machine learning theory, this problem is described in the *uniform distribution model* where the algorithm only has access to a source of random samples. The LPN problem is the following:

Definition 1. (LPN PROBLEM)
Let $\langle \cdot | \cdot \rangle$ denote the binary inner product. Let $\mathbf{s}$ be a random k-bit vector, let $\varepsilon \in]0, 1/2[$ be a constant noise parameter, let Ber_ε be the Bernoulli distribution with parameter ε (so if $\nu \leftarrow Ber_\varepsilon$ then $Pr[\nu = 1] = \varepsilon$ and $Pr[\nu = 0] = 1 - \varepsilon$), and let $A_{\mathbf{s},\varepsilon}$ be the distribution defined as

$$\left\{ \mathbf{a} \leftarrow \{0,1\}^k; \nu \leftarrow Ber_\varepsilon : (\mathbf{a}, \langle \mathbf{s} | \mathbf{a} \rangle \oplus \nu) \right\}$$

Let $A_{\mathbf{s},\varepsilon}$ denote an oracle which outputs independent samples according to this distribution. Algorithm M is said to (q, t, m, θ)-solve the $LPN_{k,\varepsilon}$ problem if

$$Pr[\mathbf{s} \leftarrow \{0,1\}^k : M^{A_{\mathbf{s},\varepsilon}}(1^k) = \mathbf{s}] \geq \theta$$

and furthermore M runs in time at most t, memory at most m, and makes at most q queries to its oracle.

R. De Prisco and M. Yung (Eds.): SCN 2006, LNCS 4116, pp. 348–359, 2006.
© Springer-Verlag Berlin Heidelberg 2006

This is the definition of Regev [13], and Katz *et al.* [10]. An alternative (and equivalent) definition can be found for example in [9].

In the following, we define δ as $\delta = 1 - 2\varepsilon$. This notation will be better to analyze the complexity of the algorithms. For the classical parameters $\varepsilon = 1/4$ and $1/8$, δ is equal to $1/2$ and $3/4$.

The LPN problem is an average-case version of the following problem: given a set of equations over $GF(2)$, find a vector **s** that maximally satisfies the equations. The latter problem has been first studied as the decoding of a random linear code and has been proved to be NP-hard by Berlekamp *et al.* in [1]. It has also be shown to be hard to approximate even within a factor of two by Hastad in [7]: it is hard to find a **s** that satisfies more than half of the optimum number of equations. In the LPN problem, the instances (set of equations and values) maybe do not represent the worst case of the problem, but studies of the average-case hardness of this problem have been proposed in [8,11,2,3,13].

The HB Protocol. The Reader and the Tag share public values k, ϵ, u and r, and a k-bit secret value **s**. To be authenticated by a Reader, the Tag and the Reader repeat the following round many times:

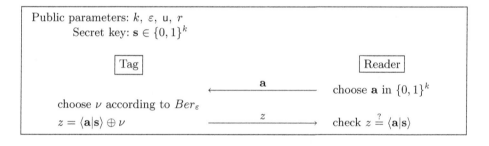

Fig. 1. Round identification of HB scheme

The round is repeated r times so that the Reader has good confidence in the answers of the Tag. To this end, the protocol has a parameter u so that if the number of errors is less than $r \cdot u$, then the authentication is successful. Typical values of ε are $1/4$ or $1/8$. This value cannot be chosen too close to $1/2$, otherwise the probability of rejecting an honest Tag increases too much. If it is too close to 0, then you can find k independent equations without errors easily.

A completeness error occurs when an honest Tag is rejected. We want the probability of a completeness error, P_c to be less than 2^{-40}.

A soundness error occurs when a Tag making random answers succeeds in authenticating itself. We want the probability of a soundness error, P_s to be less than 2^{-80}.

Given ε, u, and r, we can compute the value of P_c and P_s. Let

$$g(x,y) = \left(\frac{x}{y}\right)^x \left(\frac{1-x}{1-y}\right)^{1-x}.$$

The probabilities P_c and P_s can be expressed as sums of the tail of a binomial distribution, and using Stirling's formula, we obtain:

$$P_c \sim g(\mathsf{u}, \varepsilon)^{-r} \text{ and } P_s \sim g(\mathsf{u}, 1/2)^{-r}.$$

For each ε, we compute the values of u and r such that r is as small as possible, and the above conditions on P_c and P_s are true.

We gather the result in the following table:

ε	0.01	0.05	0.125	0.25	0.4	0.49
u	0.112	0.181	0.256	0.348	0.442	0.495
r	159	249	441	1164	7622	554360

Fig. 2. Values for $r(\varepsilon)$

In this protocol, secure only against passive attackers, an adversary gets pairs of the form $(\mathbf{a}, \langle \mathbf{a}|\mathbf{s} \rangle \oplus \nu)$ and must compute $\mathbf{s}$.

There is a simple active attack against HB. Indeed, if an adversary can change the challenge, it can send several times the same value $\mathbf{a}$. Since the answer is incorrect with probability $\varepsilon \ll 1/2$, majority votes enable to recover $\langle \mathbf{a}|\mathbf{s} \rangle$. Then, k scalar products with independent $\mathbf{a}$, allow to entirely recover $\mathbf{s}$.

The HB$^+$ Protocol. Consequently, Juels and Weis in [9] have proposed HB$^+$, a protocol robust against active attacks in the detection-based model. The idea is to use a blinding factor. The Tag and the Reader now share two k-bit secret values $\mathbf{s}_1$ and $\mathbf{s}_2$. The protocol round is the following:

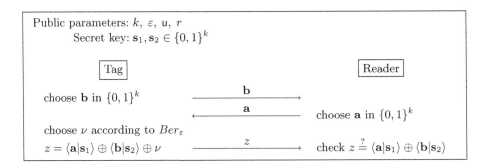

Fig. 3. Round identification of HB$^+$ scheme

The security of this protocol relies on the LPN problem for $\mathbf{s}_2$. Indeed, an active attacker can interact with the Tag in the first stage of his attack and then tries to impersonate the Tag against a Reader. The attacker can choose $\mathbf{a} = 0^k$, obtaining values of $\langle \mathbf{b}|\mathbf{s}_2 \rangle \oplus \nu$. If he can solve a $LPN_{k,\varepsilon}$ problem, he can recover $\mathbf{s}_2$. Then, once $\mathbf{s}_2$ is recovered, he must recover $\mathbf{s}_1$. This can be easily done since the attacker is now faced to a HB protocol that can be defeated by choosing the same **a** many times to know $\langle \mathbf{a}|\mathbf{s}_1 \rangle$ with high confidence.

Remark 1. The length of $\mathbf{s}_1$ is used in HB^+ proofs only to guarantee that the attack that consists to guess $\mathbf{s}_1$ is not efficient. But $|\mathbf{s}_1| = 80$ is sufficient to guarantee 80 bits security.

Related Works. Gilbert, Robshaw, and Sibert [5] found a man-in-the-middle attack against HB^+ when the adversary can interact with the Reader and the Tag during the same round. Consequently, Bringer, Chabanne and Dottax [4] proposed a new derived protocol, HB^{++}, that is resistant to a generalization of Gilbert *et al.* attack.

The security proof of HB^+ of Juels and Weis has also been simplified and improved by Katz and Sun Shin [10], using a recent result of Regev [13].

Our Work. The best algorithm to solve the LPN problem had been proposed by Blum, Kalai and Wasserman in [3], hereafter denoted as the BKW algorithm. The parameter security k of the HB protocols has therefore been estimated using the complexity of this algorithm. But, Blum, *et al.* only give a high-level description of the BKW algorithm and estimate the overall subexponential complexity of order $2^{O(k/\log k)}$. Juels and Weis in [9] propose practical parameters by giving an effective estimate of the query and time complexity.

However, they have not seen that the BKW algorithm could be improved. In this paper, we present in detail the BKW algorithm, analyze it precisely and give its complexity. Then, we propose an improvement for the final stage of the algorithm. Instead of throwing away almost all equations, we manage to use every one. Therefore, we need much less queries. We also use a Walsh-Hadamard transform to speed up this phase. Then, we give an heuristic improvement using Wagner's method to solve the Generalized Birthday Paradox of [14]. Finally, we compare the performance of the BKW and our algorithm. Our algorithm yields an attack in 2^{52} for the actual key-length of HB^+ as proposed by Juels and Weis in Crypto '05, instead of the conjectured 2^{80}.

The next section is a full analysis of BKW. In the third one, we describe and prove an improved algoritm (LF1). In the fourth, we propose an heuristic algorithm (LF2) that is more efficient in practice than LF1, as will be shown in the last section, that is focused on implementation techniques and complexity results.

2   The BKW Algorithm

The aim of this section is to describe the algorithm and the ideas behind. We also make a detailed and precise analysis of the success probability, using explicit Chernoff's bounds that are recalled in appendix A. This part is not contained in the previous papers.

2.1   Description

In the following, we denote by a and b two different parameters from **a** and **b**. We use those very close notations since the first come from Blum *et al.* in [3] and the second come from [10,9].

To solve the learning parity with noise problem Blum, Kalai and Wasserman in [3] use the following idea: by picking carefully a few well-chosen vectors in a quite large set of samples and computing the xor of these vectors, we can find basis vectors, *i.e.* e_j where the jth bit is a one and all other coordinates are null. First, we have to choose a parameter a. Typical values run from 4 to 6. The main point is that we are able to find $2^a = O(k/\log k)$ vectors such that

$$\mathbf{a}_{i_1} \oplus \cdots \oplus \mathbf{a}_{i_{2^a}} = e_j. \tag{1}$$

Then, since the number (2^a) of vectors is small, the bias of the equations obtained is not too small. Consequently, if we have enough independent combinations of vectors equals to e_j, then a majority vote enables us to recover the correct value of $\mathbf{s}_j$ since $\langle \mathbf{s} | \mathbf{a}_{i_1} \oplus \cdots \oplus \mathbf{a}_{i_{2^a}} \rangle = \langle \mathbf{s} | e_j \rangle = \mathbf{s}_j$.

We set b to be $\lceil \frac{k}{a} \rceil$. From now on, we will assume for simplicity that $k = a \cdot b$. The algorithm has to search enough such independent combinations of the $\mathbf{a}_i$'s. To this end, it splits the k bits of $\mathbf{a}_i$ into a blocks of b bits. Then, according to the last b bits, the algorithm computes 2^b equivalent classes and classifies the $\mathbf{a}_i$ according to these bits. In each class, it chooses a vector at random, performs the xor with all other vectors of the same class and finally throws away this vector. Therefore, at the end of this step, in each equivalent class, the last b bits are zeroes. This procedure is called recursively beginning at the last block until the second block. Then, we keep only the equations that are of the form $\langle \mathbf{s} | e_j \rangle = \nu$. If there are enough of such equations, the majority vote says something meaningful about the value of $\mathbf{s}_j$ with high probability. By applying this algorithm for different j, we can recover all the bits of **s**.

2.2   Analysis

Now, we will analyse this algorithm. To this end, we present two lemmas that will be helpful. The first lemma analyses the bias at the end of the recursion steps, while the second lemma estimates the number of elements and is useful to show an invariant of the algorithm.

Lemma 1. *If* $(\mathbf{a}_1, \nu_1), \ldots, (\mathbf{a}_n, \nu_n)$ *are the result of n queries to $A_{\mathbf{s}, \varepsilon}$, then the probability that:*

$$\langle \mathbf{a}_{i_1} \oplus \ldots \oplus \mathbf{a}_{i_n} | s \rangle = \nu_{i_1} \oplus \ldots \oplus \nu_{i_n}$$

is equal to $\frac{1+\delta^n}{2}$.

This lemma is equivalent to lemma 3 of [3].

Proof. For $n = 1$, the lemma is trivially true. By induction, and using the $\mathbf{a}_i$'s independence, we have:

$$Pr[\langle \mathbf{a}_{i_1} \oplus \ldots \oplus \mathbf{a}_{i_n} | \mathbf{s} \rangle = \nu_{i_1} \oplus \ldots \oplus \nu_{i_n}] =$$
$$Pr[\langle \mathbf{a}_{i_1} \oplus \ldots \oplus \mathbf{a}_{i_{n-1}} | \mathbf{s} \rangle = \nu_{i_1} \oplus \ldots \oplus \nu_{i_{n-1}}] Pr[\langle \mathbf{a}_{i_n} | \mathbf{s} \rangle = \nu_{i_n}]$$
$$+ Pr[\langle \mathbf{a}_{i_1} \oplus \ldots \oplus \mathbf{a}_{i_{n-1}} | \mathbf{s} \rangle \neq \nu_{i_1} \oplus \ldots \oplus \nu_{i_{n-1}}] Pr[\langle \mathbf{a}_{i_n} | \mathbf{s} \rangle \neq \nu_{i_n}]$$
$$= \frac{1}{2}(1 + \delta^{n-1})\frac{1}{2}(1 + \delta) + \frac{1}{2}(1 - \delta^{n-1})\frac{1}{2}(1 - \delta) = \frac{1}{2}(1 + \delta^n).$$

$\square$

The following definition and lemma are equivalent to definition 2 and lemma 4 in [3].

Definition 2. *Let $A_{\mathbf{s},\delta,i}$ be the distribution defined as*

$$\left\{ \mathbf{a} \leftarrow \{0,1\}^{(a-i)b} \times \{0\}^{ib}; \nu \leftarrow Ber_{(1+\delta)/2} : (\mathbf{a}, \langle \mathbf{s}|\mathbf{a}\rangle \oplus \nu) \right\}$$

Also, let $A_{\mathbf{s},\delta,i}$ denote an oracle which outputs independent samples according to this distribution. We define an $(\mathbf{s},\delta,i)$-set of size n as the result of n queries to oracle $A_{\mathbf{s},\delta,i}$.

Lemma 2. *Assume we are given an $(\mathbf{s},\delta,i)$-set of size n. We can in time $O(n)$ construct an $(\mathbf{s},\delta^2, i+1)$-set of size $n - 2^b$.*

Proof. Let us call $(\mathbf{a}_1, \nu_1), \ldots (\mathbf{a}_n, \nu_n)$ the elements of the $(\mathbf{s},\delta,i)$-set. Vectors $\mathbf{a}_j$ have their last ib coordinates equal to 0. We partition them with regard to their value on the precedent b coordinates, obtaining a partition with at most 2^b classes. In each class, we pick a vector at random and add it (modulo 2) to all the others vectors in that class, and then discard it. Compiling the results for each class, and using lemma 1, we obtain a $(\mathbf{s},\delta^2, i+1)$-set of size (at least) $n - 2^b$. $\square$

Consequently, according to lemma 1, at the end of the algorithm, the bias of the equation 1 is $\delta^{-2^{a-1}}$ where $\delta = (1 - 2\varepsilon)$.

The next lemma give the number of combinations of equations that must xored to the vector e_j in order to have a high probability of success.

Lemma 3. *Let $A_{\mathbf{s}_i,\delta,a}$ be the distribution defined as*

$$\left\{ \nu \leftarrow Ber_{(1+\delta^{2^{a-1}})/2} : \mathbf{s}_i \oplus \nu) \right\}$$

Also, let $A_{\mathbf{s}_i,\delta,a}$ denote an oracle which outputs independent samples according to this distribution.

Then it is possible to guess the value of $\mathbf{s}_i$ with $c\delta^{-2^a}$ calls to the oracle with error probability bound by $2e^{-c/20}$.

Proof. We define that a sample $\mathbf{a}_i, \nu$ is *compatible* with the i-th bit of $\mathbf{s}$ if $\mathbf{s}_i \cdot \mathbf{a}_i = \nu$.

The idea for guessing the ith bit is to compute for $\mathbf{s}_i = 0$ and $\mathbf{s}_i = 1$, the number of compatible samples and predict that $\mathbf{s}_i = b$ according to the majority number of compatible samples.

Therefore, in order to upper bound the probability of failure of the BKW algorithm, we have to upper bound the following probability where $\mathbf{x}_i = 1 - \mathbf{s}_i$: $\Pr[\mathbf{x}_i$ has more compatible samples than $\mathbf{s}_i]$.

To this end, we upper bound the previous probability by the sum of two more easily computable probabilities.

$$\mathsf{pr}_1 = \Pr[\mathbf{x}_i \text{ is compatible with at least } \frac{1 + \alpha \delta^{2^{a-1}}}{2} \cdot N \text{ samples}]$$

$$\mathsf{pr}_2 = \Pr[\mathbf{s}_i \text{ is compatible with at most } \frac{1 + \alpha \delta^{2^{a-1}}}{2} \cdot N \text{ samples}]$$

If $\mathbf{s}_i$ is correct, then it is compatible with $\mathbf{a}_i, \nu$ with probability $\frac{1 + \delta^{2^{a-1}}}{2}$ and otherwise with probability $1/2$. We will justify the last assertion later. Let us denote by N the number of equations $c\delta^{-2^a}$. The random variable X_j for $j = 1$ to N, is equal to 1 if $\mathbf{s}_i$ is compatible with the jth sample, and 0 otherwise.

Bounding pr_2. The expectation of X_j, $\mathbf{E}[X_j] = \Pr[X_j = 1] = \frac{1 + \delta^{2^{a-1}}}{2}$ We sum these random variables and denote by X their sum, $X = \sum_{j=1}^{N} X_j$, and so $\mathbf{E}[X] = N \cdot \mathbf{E}[X_j] = N \cdot \frac{1 + \delta^{2^{a-1}}}{2}$.

pr_2 is equal to $\Pr[X \leq (1 + \alpha \delta^{2^{a-1}})(N/2)]$ which can be bounded using Chernoff bounds (cf. appendix A). To this end, we have $(1 - \Delta)\mathbf{E}[X] = (1 + \alpha \cdot \delta^{2^{a-1}}) \cdot (N/2)$.

To determine Δ, we divide the right-hand side by $\mathbf{E}[X]$, and we get

$$1 - \Delta = \frac{1 + \alpha \cdot \delta^{2^{a-1}}}{1 + \delta^{2^{a-1}}} \approx 1 - (1 - \alpha) \cdot \delta^{2^{a-1}}$$

and so $\Delta = (1 - \alpha) \cdot \delta^{2^{a-1}}$.

$$\mathsf{pr}_2 \leq e^{-(c\delta^{-2^a}/4) \cdot (1 + \delta^{2^{a-1}}) \cdot (1-\alpha)^2 \delta^{2^{a-1} \cdot 2}} \leq e^{-(c/4)(1-\alpha)^2(1+\delta^{2^{a-1}})}$$
$$\leq e^{-(c/4)(1-\alpha)^2}$$

Bounding pr_1. In order to upper bound pr_1, we use the fact that for a bad guess, the expectation $\mathbf{E}[X]$ is equal to $\frac{N}{2}$, and the theorem 3 in appendix A. We have

$$\mathsf{pr}_1 \leq \Pr[X > (1 + \Delta)\mu] \leq e^{-N\Delta^2/(3 \cdot 2)}$$

Here, $\Delta = \alpha \cdot \delta^{2^{a-1}}$ and as $N = c\delta^{-2^a}$, then $N\Delta^2 = c\alpha^2$ and

$$\mathsf{pr}_1 \leq e^{-c\alpha^2/6}$$

$\mathbf{Pr}[\mathbf{x}_i \cdot \mathbf{a}_i = \nu | \mathbf{x}_i = 1 - \mathbf{s}_i] = 1/2$. It remains to justify that when $\mathbf{s}_i$ is not correct, then $\mathbf{s}_i \cdot \mathbf{a}_i = \nu$ with probability $1/2$. Let $(\mathbf{a}, \nu) \leftarrow A_{\mathbf{s},\varepsilon}$ and $\mathbf{x}_i = 1 - \mathbf{s}_i$. We want to show that $\Pr[\mathbf{x}_i \cdot \mathbf{a}_i = \nu] = 1/2$. To this end, we split the event into two incompatible events:

$$
\begin{aligned}
\Pr[\mathbf{x}_i \cdot \mathbf{a}_i &= \mathbf{s}_i \cdot \mathbf{a}_i] \Pr[\mathbf{s}_i \cdot \mathbf{a}_i = \nu] + \Pr[\mathbf{x}_i \cdot \mathbf{a}_i \neq \mathbf{s}_i \cdot \mathbf{a}_i] \Pr[\mathbf{s}_i \cdot \mathbf{a}_i \neq \nu] \\
&= \Pr[(\mathbf{x}_i \oplus \mathbf{s}_i) \cdot \mathbf{a}_i = 0] \Pr[\mathbf{s}_i \cdot \mathbf{a}_i = \nu] \\
&\quad + \Pr[(\mathbf{x}_i \oplus \mathbf{s}_i) \cdot \mathbf{a}_i \neq 0] \Pr[\mathbf{s}_i \cdot \mathbf{a}_i \neq \nu] \\
&= (1/2) \cdot (\Pr[\mathbf{s}_i \cdot \mathbf{a}_i = \nu] + \Pr[\mathbf{s}_i \cdot \mathbf{a}_i \neq \nu]) \\
&= 1/2
\end{aligned}
$$

since the first equation comes from the fact that $\mathbf{a}_i$ and ν are independent and second equation as since $\mathbf{x}_i \neq \mathbf{s}_i$ and $\mathbf{a}_i$ is taken uniformly, the probability that $\mathbf{a}_i = 0$ is exactly $1/2$.

Choosing $\alpha = 3 - \sqrt{6}$ finishes the proof.   □

The main ingredient of the algorithm is that with a small number of vectors, a combination of such vectors yields a basis vector. If the number required is too high, then the bias of equation (1) is too small and the number of queries becomes very large.

We are now ready to prove the theorem that gives the complexity of the BKW algorithm.

Theorem 1. For $k = a \cdot b$, the BKW algorithm ($q = 20 \cdot \ln(4k) \cdot 2^b \cdot \delta^{-2^a}, t = O(kaq), m = kq, \theta = 1/2$)-solves the $LPN_{k,\varepsilon}$ problem .

Proof. The original queries form a $(\mathbf{s}, \delta, 0)$-set of size q. Using lemma 2 $(a - 1)$ times, we obtain a $(\mathbf{s}, \delta^{2^{a-1}}, 0)$-set of size $q - (a-1)2^b$. Keeping only the equations with one non-zero coordinate, then using lemma 3, we obtain one bit of $\mathbf{s}$ with error probability at most $1/(2k)$. Repeating this for different bits of $\mathbf{s}$, we find $\mathbf{s}$ with probability at least $1/2$.   □

3   An Improved Algorithm: LF1

This algorithm is a variation of the BKW algorithm. In the BKW algorithm, the last step wastes a lot of time and queries. The idea is to deal in the last step with equations over b bits instead of one. Moreover, we will use the Walsh-Hadamard transform to quickly find the best possibility over b bits.

This algorithm does not use any heuristics. This section is devoted to prove the correctness and the performances of this algorithm. It needs lots of queries (less than BKW, though).

We now state our main theorem:

Theorem 2. For $k = a \cdot b$, there is an algorithm that
$q = (8b + 200) \cdot \delta^{-2^a} + (a - 1)2^b, t = O(kaq), m = kq + b2^b, \theta = 1/2$
solves the $LPN_{k,\varepsilon}$ problem.

Proof. For any b-bit vector $\mathbf{x}$, we say that a sample $\mathbf{a}_i, \nu$ is $\mathbf{x}$-compatible if $\langle \mathbf{a}_i | \mathbf{x} \rangle = \nu$. The q inital queries constitues a $(\mathbf{s}, \delta, 0)$-set of size q. By iterating lemma 2, we obtain an $(\mathbf{s}, \delta^{2^{a-1}}, a)$-set S of size $q - (a-1) \cdot 2^b = N = (8b + 200)\delta^{-2^a}$.

We now try every possibility for the first b bits and choose the one that is compatible with the greatest number of examples. The naive time complexity is 2^{2b}, but using a fast Walsh-Hadamard transform reduces it to $b2^b$.

Using the same analysis as for the BKW algorithm, except that we choose $\alpha = 3/4$, we get that the probability of failure is less than

$$e^{-200/64} + 2^b e^{-(8b+200)9/96} \leq 1/(2a).$$

Repeating this a times allows us to recover all the bits of $\mathbf{s}$ with probability at least $1/2$. $\qquad\square$

In this section, we have shown that we can lower the query complexity to $q = (a-1)2^b + (8b+200)\delta^{-2^a}$. Time and memory complexity remains comparatively small.

4   A Heuristic Algorithm: Computing All Sums: LF2

Following [14], instead of picking a vector in each class (cf. proof of 2), we could compute the sum of any couple of class elements. Unfortunately, we lose the independence that is necessary to use Chernoff bounds. However, linear relations between equations are not numerous and our implementation confirms this phenomenon has no visible effect on the success of the algorithm.

This also allows us to overcome a lack of queries: if there are only $2^{b'} (b' > b/2)$ queries available, the first partitioning is made according to the last b_1 bits where $b_1 = 2b' - b - 1.5$. And for all the subsequent phases, we will have 2^b equations. Bounding the number of requests was an easy and effective defence against BKW and LF1, but it does not work against this new version.

For example, we succeed in breaking a LPN problem with $k = 66, \varepsilon = 1/4$ with 10000 queries (10 authentications) with 1 GB memory in 30 seconds.

5   Implementation

We want to do the partitioning, using only small additional memory and (almost) linear time. First, we divide our memory in $2^{b/2}$ packs of size $3.2^{b/2}$. We begin at the first equation in the first pack. Its last $b/2$ bits give the address of the pack where we send it. Here, it takes the place of an other equation, which is sent to the pack corresponding to its last $b/2$ bits, and so on. It could happen that a pack is full. In this case, the equation is lost. But few equations are lost in the process, and very few if the packs are a little bigger.

We now use an array of size $2^{b/2}$, each case being able to contain 10 equations. We put the equations of the first pack in this array, according to the values of bits $2^{b/2}+1$ to 2^b (in reverse order). We could afford ten equations that have the same value (the average being 3).

Then we compute the xor between the first and the others for LF1, or the xor of all couples of equations in the same case for LF2, and put our new equations back to the pack.

We make an implementation in C, and make it run on a Pentium 4, with a CPU frequency of 3 GHz, and a little less than 1 GB of memory.

For $\varepsilon = 1/4$, using 1 GB of memory, our implementation breaks a LPN problem with $k = 99$ (we split the equations in four parts of sizes 24,24,27,24) with LF2, instead of a theoretic $k = 96$ with LF1. But we were able to break only a $k = 92$ with our implementation of LF1 because we need additional memory for pointers to equations. In both cases, the computing time was around 30 seconds.

5.1   Accurate Complexity

The factor $8b + 200$ in the complexity is a rough upper bound. It can often be replaced by 25. On the other hand, reading and writing in a large memory (1 GB for example) could take tens of cycle per 32-bit int. If one uses a hard drive's memory, it will be a lot worse, even if one programs very carefully to make almost only sequential access to the drive.

5.2   Performances of Our Algorithm

First, we give a comparison between BKW and LF1.

For $\varepsilon = 1/4$, we have the following results:

The value given is the maximum value for k you could hope to break with the given memory. The needed time is roughly the time for sorting the memory a times.

Memory available	BKW	LF1
1 GB	39	96
2^{52} bytes	104	225
2^{80} bytes	180	426

The following tables contains a more exhaustive study of LF1. It should be read in the following way: It takes 2^{46} bytes of memory to solve a LPN problem with $k = 256$ and $\varepsilon = 1/8$.

$\varepsilon\backslash k$	64	128	256	512	768	1024
0.01	13	19	33	56	74	98
0.05	16	25	40	67	90	118
0.125	18	29	46	77	113	131
0.25	24	34	55	89	131	150
0.4	28	45	66	106	157	174
0.49	33	55	88	130	192	208

We suggest to take a safety margin, in order to be able to resist to small improvements like LF2. We have explored a variety of other improvements, but none of them gave substantial results.

We recommend to use $k = 512$ to achieve 80 bits security for $\varepsilon = 1/4$. Choosing the value of ε depends upon a compromise between the key size and the computing time for an authentication. Using tables 2 and the above one should help. The couple $k = 768, \varepsilon = 0.05$ with $r = 249$ seems quite good.

6   Conclusion

In this article, we give a better algorithm to solve the LPN problem, thus breaking the HB^+ protocol with suggested size parameters. However, with a moderate increase of the key length, our attack becomes infeasible. Our algorithm gives a more precise idea of the complexity of the LPN problem.

On the other side, remark 1 allows to decrease the length of one of the secret parameters.

So, summing everything, we have shown that to achieve 80 bits security, HB^+ should be used with $|\mathbf{s}_1| = 80$ and $|\mathbf{s}_2| = 512$ instead of $|\mathbf{s}_1| = |\mathbf{s}_2| = 224$. The overall complexity of this protocol remains almost unchanged.

Proving algorithm LF2 is in our opinion quite difficult although feasible.

Acknowledgment. We would like to thank Louis Granboulan for various discussions and suggestions about this work.

References

1. E. R. Berlekamp, R. J. McEliece, V. Tilborg. On the Inherent Intractability of Certain Coding Problem. *IEEE Transactions on Information Theory 24*, 1978, pp. 384-386.
2. A. Blum, M. Furst, M. Kearns, and R. J. Lipton. Cryptographic Primitives Based on Hard Learning Problems. *Crypto '93*, pp. 278-291, LNCS 773, Springer-Verlag, 1994.
3. A. Blum, A. Kalai, and H. Wasserman. Noise-tolerant Learning, the Parity Problem, and the Statistical Query Problem *Journal of the ACM 50,4*, July 2003, pp. 506-519.
4. J. Bringer, H. Chabanne, and E. Dottax. HB++: A Lightweight Authentication Protocol Secure againt Some Attacks. IEEE International Conference on Pervasive Services, Workshop on Security, Privacy and Trust in Pervasive and Ubiquitous Computing, SecPerU, 2006 Available at `http://eprint.iacr.org/2005/440`.
5. H. Gilbert, M. Robshaw, and H. Sibert. An Active Attack Against HB+ - A Provably Secure Lightweight Authentication Protocol. Available at `http://eprint.iacr.org/2005/237`.
6. O. Goldreich and L. Levin. A Hard Predicate for all one-way functions, *STOC '89*, pp. 25-32, ACM 1998.
7. J. Hastad. Some Optimal Inapproximability Results, *STOC '97*, pp. 1-10, ACM 1997.

8. N. Hopper and M. Blum. Secure Human Identification Protocols *ASIACRYPT '01*, pp. 52-66, LNCS 2248, Springer-Verlag, 2001.
9. A. Juels and S. Weis. Authenticating Pervasive Devices with Human Protocols *Crypto 2005*, pp. 293-308, LNCS 3621, Springer-Verlag, 2005. Updated version available at: `http://www.rsasecurity.com/rsalabs/staff/bios/ajuels/publications/pdfs/lpn.pdf`.
10. J. Katz and J. Sun Shin. Parallel and Concurrent Security of the HB and HB+ Protocols. *Eurocrypt '06*, pp., LNCS 4004, Springer-Verlag, 2006.
11. M. Kearns. Efficient Noise-Tolerant Learning from Statistical Queries. *J. ACM*, 45(6): 983-1006, 1998.
12. M. Mitzenmacher and E. Upfal. Probability and computing, Cambridge University Press, 2005
13. O. Regev. On Lattices, Learning with Errors, Random Linear Codes, and Cryptography *STOC 2005*, pp. 84-93, ACM 2005.
14. D. Wagner. A Generalized Birthday Problem *Crypto 2002*, pp. 288-303, LNCS 2442, Springer-Verlag, 2002.

A   Chernoff's Bounds

We need the following Chernoff's bounds that have been proved in [12].

Theorem 3. *Let $X_1, \ldots, X_n$ be n independent Bernoulli trials such that $\Pr(X_i) = p$. Let $X = \sum_{i=1}^{n} X_i$ and $\mu = \mathbf{E}[X] = n \cdot p$. Then, the following Chernoff bounds hold:*

1. *for $0 < \Delta \leq 1$, $\Pr(X \geq (1 + \Delta)\mu) \leq e^{-\mu\Delta^2/3}$*
2. *for $0 < \Delta < 1$, $\Pr(X \leq (1 - \Delta)\mu) \leq e^{-\mu\Delta^2/2}$*

Theory and Practice of Multiparty Computation

Ivan Damgård

Dept. of Computer Science, University of Aarhus

Abstract. This is a short summary of the invited talk given by the author at the SCN conference.

1 Introduction

Multiparty computation (MPC) is an extremely general subject, and a protocol enabling general secure multiparty computation is a very strong tool that can – in principle – solve almost any cryptographic protocol problem.

In multiparty computation, we usually consider a number of players $P_1, ..., P_n$, who initially each possess some inputs $x_1, ..., x_n$, and we then want to securely compute some function f on these inputs where $f(x_1, ..., x_n) = (y_1, ..., y_n)$ such that P_i learns y_i but no other information.

This should be accomplished by some interactive protocol π that the players execute. Intuitively, we want that executing π is equivalent to having a trusted party T that receives privately x_i from P_i, computes the function, and returns y_i to each P_i. We note that this "equivalence" is not only intuition – it can be formalized using, for instance, Canetti's Universal Composability framework[4].

What we have described here is actually *secure function evaluation*, and not general secure MPC. The latter would correspond to the case where T has memory and can be called several times, perhaps computing a new function every time it is invoked. In this case, T is in essence a secure general purpose computer.

Of course, we do not assume that all parties are honest, usually an *adversary* is assumed who may corrupt some of the players. An adversary can be active or passive, depending on whether he takes full control over corrupted players or just observes their internal data and messages.

The protocol π is usually only required to be secure assuming the adversary is limited in some way. For instance, a limitation is usually be put on the number of players that can be corrupt, or in general we can specify an adversary structure, which is a list of the sets that may be corrupted. We may also want to assume that the adversary is limited to polynomial time computation.

2 The Classical Theory

The general theory of MPC was founded in the late 80-ties [12,2,6]. The theory was later developed in several ways in many papers by different authors – see for instance [15,14,7]. An overview of the theoretical results known can be found in [5].

R. De Prisco and M. Yung (Eds.): SCN 2006, LNCS 4116, pp. 360–364, 2006.

We will not give a complete account of the results proved here, since this is not important for our main objective here. The essence is that if not too much corruption is around, fully general and secure MPC is possible. Typically, if less than $n/2$ (or in some cases $n/3$) of the players are corrupt, we are in business. If we are willing to accept that the protocol may not terminate with an output to all honest players (and if the adversary is polynomial time bounded) then up to $n-1$ players can be corrupt. On the other hand, if these bounds are violated, then some functions cannot be computed securely.

This line of research was clearly oriented towards basic research - the objective was to answer fundamental questions about what is possible and what is not. There was not much interest in the efficiency of the protocols, beyond the fact that they were polynomial time. Indeed, if one would implement the protocols from the first papers mentioned, the result would not be practical at all. A main reason for this is that to use these so called generic methods, the desired computation must be written as a Boolean circuit, or as an arithmetic circuit over some finite field. For most non-trivial computations, this will result in a very large circuit and a correspondingly inefficient protocol.

3   Efficiency Improvements

It is only natural that many researchers have tried to improve the efficiency of the first protocols. Examples can be found in [9,13,8]. What these works do, is usually to set generic MPC as the goal, more specially, we assume we are given a circuit (Boolean or arithmetic), and the goal is to compute this circuit securely as efficiently as possible. This means that we do not address the loss of efficiency that results from expressing the computation as a circuit in the first place. Of course, the advantage, on the other hand, is that we get a fully general solution.

Other lines of research have followed a different path, namely to look for efficient solutions to special cases of the MPC problem, hoping that special properties of the particular kind of computation we are after can be exploited to get better efficiency. Electronic voting is one example where this approach has been successful to the extent that genuinely practical solutions are known today, see for instance [3,10]. Of course, the downside of the "special-case" approach, is that generality is lost.

4   Applications as the Driver

Recently, a different trend can be seen in various works, which is a sort of hybrid between the generic and the special-case approaches. Examples of this are the research projects SCET (Secure Computing, Economy and Trust) and SIMAP (Secure Information Managing and Processing) that the author has been involved in. The idea here is to look at a range of applications, identify the essential operations one needs to do securely in all of the applications, and finally design special-purpose implementations for precisely those operations. In this way we can hope to have the best of both worlds: generality, because we consider a whole range of applications simultaneously, as well as efficiency, because we make special purpose protocols for the most common elementary operations, rather than reducing everything to, say, binary operations.

More concretely, SCET has considered the following types of problems

- Various types of auctions. This is not limited to only standard highest bid auctions with sealed bids but also includes, for instance, variants with many sellers and buyers, so called double auctions - essentially scenarios where one wants to find a fair market price for a commodity given the existing supply and demand in the market.
- Benchmarking, where several companies want to combine information on how their businesses are running, in order to compare themselves to best practice in the area. This of course has to be done while preserving confidentiality of companies' private data.

When looking at such applications, we found that the computation needed is basically elementary arithmetic on integers. More concretely, quite a wide range of the cases require only addition, multiplication and comparison of integers. The known generic MPC protocols can usually handle addition and multiplication very efficiently. What they really do is actually operations modulo some prime p, because the protocols are based on secret sharing over Z_p. So by choosing p large enough compared to the input numbers, we can avoid modular reductions and get integer addition and multiplication.

This is efficient because each number is shared "in one piece" using a linear secret sharing scheme, so that secure addition, for instance, requires only one local addition by each player. Unfortunately, this also implies that comparison is much harder. A generic solution would express the comparison operation as an arithmetic circuit over Z_p, but this would be far too large to give a practical solution, because the circuit would not have access to the binary representation of the inputs. So instead we developed special purpose techniques for comparison. This enables comparison in constant-round with unconditional security [11] and also a logarithmic round solution that is more practical for the size of numbers we are interested in. For more details on the applications and protocols, see [1]. These techniques enable, for instance, truly practical double auctions with several thousand participants.

The SIMAP project goes a step further and has as an additional goal to develop a domain specific programming language smcl. This language allows you to express the desired computation, and specify which information should be available to which players at any given time. Such a program can then be compiled to code that will run on the players' machines and execute the appropriate protocols. We use a client/server model where clients supply inputs and receive outputs, while servers are responsible for doing the computation. A single player can play all roles, so this is just a generalization of the standard model. But it also allows us to have cases where a large number of clients supply input to a small committee of servers, which would be natural for a large auction. As an example, we show the source code in the first version of our language for a multiparty version of Yao's millionaire's problem: A set of billionaires want to know which among them is the richest. Each participant only relies on him self. A server is co-located with an output client and an input client. The role of an input client is to deliver the player's personal net worth as a secret integer. The role of an output client is to receive the answer. The servers must decide which billionaire is the richest and send a boolean value of true to him and only him. The rest should get a false. We show here only the code specifying the computation for the servers. Types with an "s" in front of their names are secret types, where values should be secret shared or encrypted. The names BillionaireIn and BillionaireOut refer to code written for the clients which we do not show here.

```
function void main(int[] args) {
  Group of BillionaireIn billIn;
  Group of BillionaireOut billOut;

  sClient richest;  //pointer to richest client
  sint max = 0; //eventually holds networth of richest client

  foreach (Client c in billIn) {
    sint netWorth = c.netWorth.get(); //get input from client
    sbool b = netWorth > max;  //richer than current record?
    max = b ? netWorth : max;  //set max accordingly
    richest = b ? c : richest; //set pointer to richest client
  }

  foreach (sClient c in billOut) {
    c.tell(c == richest);  //send output
  }
}
```

For further information, see the home pages of the projects http://sikkerhed.alexandra.dk/uk/projects/scet.htm and http://sikkerhed.alexandra.dk/uk/projects/simap.htm.

We hope and believe that these new trends will lead to new practical uses of MPC, as well further theoretical development.

References

1. Peter Bogetoft, Ivan Damgård, Thomas Jakobsen, Kurt Nielsen, Jakob Pagter and Tomas Toft: *A Practical Implementation of Secure Auctions based on Multiparty Integer Computation.* Proc. of Financial Cryptography 2006, Springer Verlag LNCS.
2. M. Ben-Or, S. Goldwasser, A. Wigderson: *Completeness theorems for Non-Cryptographic Fault-Tolerant Distributed Computation,* Proc. ACM STOC '88, pp. 1–10.
3. Cramer, Gennaro and Schoenmakers: *A Secure and Optimally Efficient Multi-Authority Election Scheme,* Proc. of EuroCrypt 1997
4. R.Canetti: *Universally Composable Security,* The Eprint archive, www.iacr.org.

5. Cramer and Damgård: *Multiparty Computation, an Introduction*, in Contemporary Cryptology, Advanced courses in Mathematics CRM Barcelona, Birkhäuser.
6. D. Chaum, C. Crépeau, I. Damgård: *Multi-Party Unconditionally Secure Protocols*, Proc. of ACM STOC '88, pp. 11–19.
7. R. Cramer, I. Damgård and U. Maurer: *Multiparty Computations from Any Linear Secret Sharing Scheme*. In: Proc. EUROCRYPT '00.
8. R. Cramer, I. Damgård, S. Dziembowski, M: Hirt and T. Rabin: *Efficient Multiparty Computations With Dishonest Minority*, Proceedings of EuroCrypt 99, Springer Verlag LNCS series.
9. I. Damgård and J. Nielsen: *Universally Composable Efficient Multiparty Computation from Threshold Homomorphic Encryption*, Proc. of Crypto 2003, Springer Verlag LNCS.
10. Ivan Damgård, Mads Jurik: *A Generalisation, a Simplification and Some Applications of Paillier's Probabilistic Public-Key System*. Public Key Cryptography 2001: 119-136
11. Ivan Damgård, Matthias Fitzi, Eike Kiltz, Jesper Buus Nielsen, Tomas Toft: *Unconditionally Secure Constant-Rounds Multi-party Computation for Equality, Comparison, Bits and Exponentiation*. Proc. of TCC 2006, pp. 285-304, Springer Verlag LNCS.
12. O. Goldreich, S. Micali and A. Wigderson: *How to Play Any Mental Game or a Completeness Theorem for Protocols with Honest Majority*, Proc. of ACM STOC '87, pp. 218–229.
13. R. Gennaro, M. Rabin, T. Rabin, *Simplified VSS and Fast-Track Multiparty Computations with Applications to Threshold Cryptography*, Proc of ACM PODC'98.
14. M. Hirt, U. Maurer: *Complete Characterization of Adversaries Tolerable in General Multiparty Computations*, Proc. ACM PODC'97, pp. 25–34.
15. T. Rabin, M. Ben-Or: *Verifiable Secret Sharing and Multiparty Protocols with Honest majority*, Proc. ACM STOC '89, pp. 73–85.

Author Index

Lecture Notes in Computer Science

For information about Vols. 1–4037

please contact your bookseller or Springer